THE ELEVENTH DAY

www.transworldbooks.co.uk

THE ELEVENTH DAY

THE ULTIMATE ACCOUNT OF 9/11

ANTHONY SUMMERS
and ROBBYN SWAN

Doubleday

LONDON · TORONTO · SYDNEY · AUCKLAND · JOHANNESBURG

TRANSWORLD PUBLISHERS
61–63 Uxbridge Road, London W5 5SA
A Random House Group Company
www.rbooks.co.uk

First published in Great Britain
in 2011 by Doubleday
an imprint of Transworld Publishers

A CIP catalogue record for this book
is available from the British Library.

ISBNs 9780385612814 (hb)
9780385612821 (tpb)

Addresses for Random House Group Ltd companies outside the UK
can be found at: www.randomhouse.co.uk
The Random House Group Ltd Reg. No. 954009

The Random House Group Ltd supports the Forest Stewardship Council® (FSC®),
the leading international forest-certification organization. All our titles that are
printed on Greenpeace-approved FSC®-certified paper carry the FSC® logo.
Our paper procurement policy can be found at
www.rbooks.co.uk/environment

Printed and bound by
CPI Group (UK) Ltd, Croydon, CR0 4YY

4 6 8 10 9 7 5 3

For Angela Santore Amicone

and

Chris and Gaye Humphreys

"I don't believe for a minute that we got everything right. We wrote a first draft of history."

—LEE HAMILTON,
vice chairman, 9/11 Commission

CONTENTS

AUTHORS' NOTE

OVER THE YEARS, THE EVENT TO WHICH THE WORLD GAVE THE BRIEF name "9/11" has burgeoned into a universe of facts and factoids. Our approach to the writing of this book was to build a chronology, which eventually ran to well over a thousand pages, to gather information from a multitude of sources, including published material in both paper and electronic form, and to conduct interviews of our own. We read as deeply as possible the many thousands of pages of staff reports, original memoranda, and other 9/11 Commission records that began to be released as of 2009.

Additional information on numerous points can be found in the Notes and Sources section at the back of the book. These are linked to the text by page number.

For ease of reading, we have adopted a single standard for Arabic names that are rendered differently in different texts. The name "bin Laden," for example, can be found elsewhere as "bin Ladin" or even "ben Ladin," and the organization associated with him as "al-Qaeda," or "al Qida"—and more. We have stuck to "bin Laden" and "al Qaeda."

The full rendering of many Arab persons' names is lengthy, and we have in many cases shortened them. After a full first mention, for example, "Khalid al Mihdhar" becomes just "Mihdhar." We render "Ramzi bin al-Shibh," as have many other texts, simply as "Binalshibh." Though perhaps not strictly correct, or satisfactory to the purist, this makes for smoother reading.

Our aim has been to make readable sense out of a kaleidoscopic story, to offer rational explanation where there has been confusion or unnecessary controversy, and to serve history as well as possible.

A.S.   R.S.
May 2011

THE ELEVENTH DAY

PREFACE

TEN YEARS ON, MEMORY AND LOSS. WHERE TWO WONDERS OF THE modern world once soared high over the city, two great cascades feed reflecting pools of shimmering water. The abyss into which it flows is now a hallowed place of remembrance. Pilgrims about to descend to the underworld, the underworld of what once was the World Trade Center, will pass a ribbon of names etched into parapets of bronze.

They identify those killed in New York City on September 11, 2001: the 206 passengers and crew aboard the three planes that were used as missiles that day; the forty who died when a fourth airliner fell from the sky in Pennsylvania; the 2,605 office workers and visitors and would-be rescuers known to have died in and around the Trade Center; and the 125 men and women who died at the Pentagon in Washington. Included, too, are the names of the six people killed eight years earlier, in 1993, in the first attempt to bring down the towers with a truck bomb.

The memorial names 2,982 men, women, and children as of the

spring of 2011. The true tally of 9/11 fatalities, however, is incomplete. Some of those who labored in the rubble of the fallen towers have died since, agonizingly slowly, from respiratory disease contracted in the fire and poisoned dust of the place they called Ground Zero. Some nineteen thousand others are reported to be sick and receiving treatment. By one prediction, disease will eventually cripple and kill as many again—more perhaps—as died on the day of the attacks.

We do not know, shall never know, how many have died in the far-off wars that followed the onslaught launched that September day. Fighting men aside, the vast majority of the dead have been civilians: unknown thousands—conservatively, many tens of thousands—of men, women, and children killed in Afghanistan and in Iraq.

Of the three thousand who died on 9/11 itself, fewer than half have graves. Some bodies were consumed by fire, others reduced to minute fragments of mortality, morsels of burned bone, decaying flesh, a single tooth with a silver filling. To this day, forensic pathologists are confronted by a monstrous human jigsaw, one they know they will never complete.

Consider five of the names that are etched, lettered in bronze, above the curtain of water at the 9/11 memorial.

Jimmy Riches, a New York firefighter, died in the lobby of the North Tower. His father, James, himself a Fire Department battalion chief, recovered his son's mangled body months later.

Donald McIntyre, a Port Authority police officer, also died at the Trade Center. His handcuffs, recovered at the scene, were given by his widow to a colleague assigned to hunt down terrorists in Afghanistan.

No identifiable remains were ever found for Eddie Dillard, an American Airlines passenger who died at the Pentagon. His widow, by odd happenstance, had been American's base manager in Washington, D.C., when his plane took off that day.

Ronald Breitweiser, a money manager, died in the South Tower of the Trade Center. Only his arms and hands were recovered, identified by fingerprints—and by his wedding ring, which his widow now wears.

Only part of a leg and one foot were found—six years later—to account for Karen Martin, chief flight attendant on the plane that plunged into the North Tower. Attendant Martin was probably the first person harmed by the hijackers on 9/11.

• • •

SOMETHING ELSE WAS LOST that day, something precious that touches on the stories of all the thousands who have died. The Greek tragic dramatist Aeschylus, twenty-five centuries earlier, understood well what it was. "In war," he wrote, "the first casualty is truth."

James Riches worked in the rubble for months, motivated in part by the hope of recovering his own son's dead body. He labored, like thousands of others, buoyed by the assurance of the Environmental Protection Agency, that the air in Lower Manhattan was safe to breathe. Today, no longer a fire chief, Riches Sr.'s health is irreparably damaged, his lung capacity reduced by 30 percent.

Like so many others, meanwhile, Riches wants vengeance against those who killed his son. The Saudi exile Osama bin Laden, said to have ordered the 9/11 attacks, became—in the West—a constant demon, a symbol of the dark forces of terror. President George W. Bush at first promised to get him "dead or alive," only to backtrack months later and say, "I don't know where bin Laden is . . . and really don't care. It's not that important."

In 2009, at the White House, Riches and others met Bush's successor, Barack Obama. "I pulled out Jimmy's bracelet and funeral mass card and gave them to him," the former fire chief said later. "I told him that I'm frustrated that I haven't seen justice for my son Jimmy. . . . Please capture Osama bin Laden." Obama promised "swift and certain justice."

Police officer McIntyre's handcuffs, engraved "Mac," were later snapped on to the wrists of a fugitive named Abu Zubaydah—a native of Saudi Arabia like bin Laden. Imprisoned ever since, Zubaydah remains today the subject of serious controversy. For U.S. interrogators treated him with extreme brutality, using duress that has been defined by the International Committee of the Red Cross, and many others, as torture.

Eddie Dillard's widow, Rosemary, for all her grief, was one of a number of bereaved family members incensed by the ill treatment of prisoners and by plans to try them before military tribunals. "The secret and unconstitutional nature of these proceedings," they said, "deprives us of the right to know the full truth about what happened on 9/11."

Ronald Breitweiser's widow, Kristen, for her part, has been one of the most articulate of those whose lives were devastated. She testified to a joint House-Senate inquiry and fought for a further, full, independent investigation. When that aspiration was realized—in the shape of the National Commission on Terrorist Attacks Upon the United States—Breitweiser excoriated its failings. She believes that much is still hidden, and wants convincing explanations. The CIA, she points out, identified two of the hijackers as terrorists more than eighteen months before 9/11, learned they had visas to enter the United States, yet kept the information from U.S. law enforcement. Why?

Though the final chapter of the congressional report into 9/11 is said to discuss Saudi financial links to the hijackers, all but one page of the chapter was kept secret on the orders of President Bush. Why? At a 2009 meeting with bereaved families, Breitweiser says, President Obama said he was willing to declassify the suppressed material. As of this writing, two years later, the chapter remains classified. Why?

Though less than complete, and though it left some questions open, the Final Report of the National Commission—known as the 9/11 Commission Report—was overwhelmingly well received by an uncritical media. It went to the top of *The New York Times* best-seller list, and was nominated for a National Book Award. The CIA obstructed the Commission's work, as its chairmen—former New Jersey governor Thomas Kean and former congressman Lee Hamilton—later acknowledged. Senator Bob Kerrey, who served on the Commission, shared their concerns. Alleging a Bush White House cover-up, Senator Max Cleland had resigned from the Commission early on. It was, he said, a "national scandal." The final Report was in fact not final, Hamilton said, merely "a first draft of history."

A 2006 *New York Times*/CBS poll found that only 16 percent of those responding thought Bush administration members had told the truth about 9/11. Fifty-three percent of responders thought they were "mostly telling the truth but hiding something." Twenty-eight percent thought Bush's people were "mostly lying." A year later, a Scripps Howard poll found that 32 percent thought it "very likely" that the government had chosen to ignore specific warnings of the 9/11 attacks. A further 30 percent thought that "somewhat likely." A Zogby poll found that 51 percent of Americans wanted a congressional investigation of President Bush's and Vice President Dick Cheney's performance in the context of the attacks.

In 2008, a poll conducted by the Program on International Policy Attitudes—at the University of Maryland—asked questions of sixteen thousand people in seventeen countries. Only 46 percent of those responding thought al Qaeda had been responsible for the attacks. Fifteen percent thought the U.S. government was itself responsible for the attacks, as a ploy to justify an invasion of Iraq. A large number of Americans, meanwhile, have thought Iraq was behind the attacks—a notion encouraged by the Bush administration but unsupported by the evidence. As late as 2010, though, an Angus Reid poll indicated that one in four Americans still thought 9/11 was "a fabrication designed to facilitate the campaign against terrorism." This all reflects an epidemic of doubt and disbelief. It has been spread in part, to be sure, by conspiracy theorists—the "9/11 truth" movement, as it has become known—preaching to the gullible through the phenomenal influence and reach of the Internet. Less well known is the prevalence of doubt in people one would expect less likely to challenge official orthodoxy.

Those who have expressed grave doubt or called for a new investigation have included five past or present U.S. senators, four members of the U.S. House of Representatives, a former governor, three state deputy or assistant attorneys general, members of state legislatures, numerous public officials and civil servants, diplomats, engineers, and twenty-six former Army, Navy, or Air Force officers. In 2010, two gubernatorial candidates in Texas, a Republican and a Democrat, both said they had questions as to whether the U.S. government had been involved in the 9/11 attacks.

Former CIA officers, FBI agents, and intelligence officials from other agencies have also spoken out. Twenty-five of them expressed their views in a letter to the Congress. Louis Freeh, who was FBI director until the summer of 2001, raised specific issues on television and in a 2005 *Wall Street Journal* article.

Three sometime presidential contenders have expressed concerns. Former Vice President Walter Mondale said he favored a new investigation. "We've never completed the investigation of 9/11," said General Wesley Clark, former Supreme Allied Commander Europe, "and whether the administration actually misused the intelligence information it had." Former U.S. senator Bob Graham, who had been cochair of Congress's Joint Inquiry into 9/11, pointed the finger at Saudi Arabia. The investigation, he said, found grounds for "suspicion that the Saudi government and various representatives of Saudi interests supported some of the hijackers and might have supported all of them." President Bush, he said, "engaged in a cover-up."

TEN YEARS ON, there is a lingering sense that the nation and the world have been let down, deprived of the right to know—deceived, even—on a matter of greater universal concern than any event in living memory. It need not have been that way.

The release in the past two years of some 300,000 pages of 9/11 Commission documents, a plethora of other material, and new interviews make it possible to lay some of the perceived mysteries to rest.

With access to the new information, we strive in this book to blow away unnecessary controversy, to make up for omissions in the record, and to throw light into the shadows of deception. In a time of anxiety, to tell the story as honestly as it can be told.

ONE

DID THE STORY BEGIN TWENTY YEARS AGO DURING THE GULF WAR, when a great American army was installed in Saudi Arabia, a land sacred to Muslims? Did it begin in 1948, when the United States recognized the declaration of a Jewish state to be known as Israel? Or on the day in 1938 when Americans discovered in Saudi Arabia one of the largest reserves of oil on the planet? From then on, certainly, the West began an addictive dance with danger, one that it dances to this day.

This is a story, moreover, rooted in a world and a culture that few Westerners really know or can begin to understand, yet played out in the heart of the United States. Mystery and terror, a frightening mix. Yet there is a simple point of entry, a routine event on an ordinary American morning.

IN THE DAWN of September 11, 2001, in Massachusetts, ninety-two people were getting up, breakfasting, heading for Boston's Logan Airport. They were the passengers and crew of American Airlines Flight

11, one of some forty thousand planes scheduled to crisscross the country that day.

To glance at some of the names on the passenger manifest, to learn a little about them, is to glimpse the melting pot nature of the country. Philip Rosenzweig, an executive for Sun Microsystems; Thelma Cuccinello, a grandmother on her way to see a sister in California; Peter Gay, a vice president for Raytheon Electronic Systems, traveling with two colleagues; Laura Lee Morabito, U.S. sales manager for the Australian airline Qantas; photographer Berinthia Berenson, widow of the actor Anthony Perkins; David Angell, executive producer of the television series *Frasier,* accompanied by his wife, Lynn; Jeffrey Mladenik, an ordained minister and acting CEO of a trade publishing company; Lisa Gordenstein, an executive with a discount clothing company; Michael Theodoridis, on his way to a wedding with his wife, Rahma, who was six months pregnant; Walid Iskandar, a business strategy consultant for a British company, setting off to visit his parents; Alexander Filipov, a retired electrical engineer; Daniel Lewin, chief technology officer for Akamai Technologies in Cambridge, Massachusetts. Also on their way to the flight were five young men from the Middle East, an Egyptian and four Saudis.

The pilot who was to fly these people to California, John Ogonowski, flew twelve days a month and worked the rest of the time on his 150-acre farm. At fifty, he was a veteran of twenty-three years with American, married to a flight attendant. He had hoped to attend a farming event on the 11th, but the schedule proved unchangeable. At 5:00 that morning Ogonowski awoke, kissed his wife, peeked in at their three sleeping teenage daughters, and climbed into his pickup to drive to the airport. His copilot that day would be Tom McGuinness, a former Navy fighter pilot.

Flight 11, a "turn-around"—an airplane that had flown through the night from San Francisco—was parked at Logan's Gate 32. Captain Ogonowski arrived to a scene of busy activity. The cleaners were working their way through the plane, the fuelers delivering 76,000 pounds of jet fuel. The nine flight attendants in their blue uniforms were gathering.

Karen Martin, in First Class, was in charge. At forty, she was renowned for her efficiency—"organized . . . on the stick to a fault." Her backup, Barbara "Bobbi" Arestegui, was diminutive—small enough, crews joked, to fit on the luggage rack. Several colleagues who had been scheduled to fly were not on board. One had called in sick, another had switched to a different flight—she wanted to accompany her father to a doctor's appointment. Two others, waiting on standby, were told they were not required.

The check-in process went normally. No one knew until later that, even before they reached the terminal, three of the Arab passengers had been involved in an odd incident. A driver next to them in the parking lot would remember how they had dawdled, leaving the door of their rental car open, "fiddling with their things." Irritated, he pushed at the offending door, shoved it against one of the Arabs, half expecting a shouting match. Instead, studiously avoiding a scene, the three Middle Easterners said not a word.

In the terminal, though, the check-in attendant found only passenger Filipov, the electrical engineer, to be acting out of the ordinary. He seemed nervous, paced up and down, seemed to know nothing of airport procedure. The attendant found it a little "suspicious." Otherwise, no one else's behavior caught her attention.

The copilot of the incoming flight, however, deplaning as the fresh crew took over, would remember a strange encounter. As first officer Lynn Howland left the airplane an Arab man stopped her to ask if she would be piloting the soon to depart Flight 11. When she said she would not, he turned away in an "extremely rude" way. Later, shown a picture of the Egyptian passenger on Flight 11, she at once identified him as the man who had approached her.

At check-in, a computer profiling system had selected three of the five young Arab passengers as potentially suspect. Their checked baggage was screened for explosives, the men themselves given special scrutiny by security. Like the carry-on bags of all passengers, theirs were X-rayed. Nothing was spotted.

All five young Arabs, one reportedly carrying a wooden crutch, then proceeded to the gate. One of them—the Egyptian, the agent thought—arrived "sweating bullets . . . his forehead was drenched." With no good reason to stop him, she handed the man his boarding card. He and a companion were the last to board, there to be greeted by senior attendant Karen Martin.

The Egyptian settled down in First Class in aisle Seat 8D, next to passengers David and Lynn Angell. One of the Saudis sat next to him. Two of the others sat further forward, near the cockpit, next to Laura Lee Morabito. Another sat directly behind Daniel Lewin.

The food was on board by now, the in-flight movies loaded. Her final checks completed, Karen Martin prepared to recite the airplane's safety features. Her colleague Madeline Sweeney, whom everyone knew as "Amy," had grabbed a few moments to call her husband. She wanted to say she was sorry not to have been able to see her five-year-old daughter off to kindergarten. Now, though, it was time to switch off all cell phones.

Flight 11 pushed back from the gate at 7:40 and by 8:00 it was soaring skyward. September 11 was a glorious morning for flying, with virtually no cloud or wind—"severe clear" in pilots' parlance.

The Air Traffic Control transcript of air-to-ground exchanges shows that Flight 11 flew routinely for thirteen minutes. "Departure. Good morning. American 11 heavy with you," Captain Ogonowski told Boston control. "Passing through, ah, 2,000 [feet] for 3,000." Boston alerted him to a small Cessna nearby, asking him to climb and turn right. Then, with a "So long," management of Flight 11 passed to other controllers.

The laconic back-and-forth continuing, Ogonowski climbed his plane toward its assigned altitude of 29,000 feet. Then, just after 8:13, Federal Aviation Administration controller Pete Zalewski, at Boston Center—one of the FAA's twenty-one Air Route Traffic Control Centers—told the pilots to turn twenty degrees to the right. "20 right. American 11," a pilot acknowledged, and the plane turned.

Sixteen seconds later, when Zalewski told them to climb, Flight 11 did not reply. The controller would try again and again for the next eleven minutes. "American one one . . . do you hear me? . . . American eleven, if you hear Boston Center, ident please . . ." Only static came back across the ether, with one exception—later to be logged as "a brief unknown sound (possibly a scream)."

At 8:18, unbeknownst at the time to the controllers, a telephone rang at an American Airlines office almost a thousand miles away, in the town of Cary, North Carolina. Vanessa Minter, an employee accustomed to dealing with calls about reservations, heard a woman's voice say, "I think we're being hijacked."

Flummoxed, failing to find the emergency button on her phone, Minter transferred the call to a colleague. He did press the button, automatically starting a recording, and brought in a supervisor named Nydia Gonzalez. Soon Gonzalez was passing on what she heard to American's security office in Texas.

The woman calling was a senior Flight 11 attendant, forty-five-year-old Betty "Bee" Ong. Using a seatback Airfone, Ong had dialed a number that crews knew well—they used it to help passengers with onward travel plans. She sounded "calm, professional, and poised," and we know exactly what she said for four and a half minutes, the standard duration of the recording system. The rest of the conversation—Ong talked for about twenty-eight minutes—is as remembered by the employees who dealt with the call:

> ONG: [I'm] number 3, in the back. The cockpit's not answering. Somebody's stabbed in business class and, ah, I think there's Mace that we can't breathe. I don't know. I think we're getting hijacked.

The seconds ticked by. Time was lost as the staff on the ground asked repetitive questions, mostly to confirm Ong's identity. Then:

> ONG: . . . Somebody is coming back from business . . . hold on for one second . . . Karen and Bobbi got stabbed. [This last sentence, the tape shows, was spoken by a fellow attendant close by.] . . . Our number 1 got stabbed . . . our galley flight attendant and our purser has been stabbed. And we can't get into the cockpit. The door won't open.

An airline employee on the ground made an unhelpful interjection. "Well, if they were shrewd they would keep the door closed . . . Would they not maintain a sterile cockpit?"

"Karen" was lead flight attendant Karen Martin, "Bobbi" her backup Barbara Arestegui. Martin, Ong said, lost consciousness, then came around and was being given oxygen. Arestegui appeared not to be seriously injured. The passenger in First Class Seat 9B, however, appeared to be dead.

The man in Seat 9B had perhaps tried to intervene and fight the hijackers. He was Daniel Lewin, an American-Israeli who had served in a crack Israeli commando unit. Lewin spoke Arabic, and may have understood before anyone else what the hijackers intended. Ong said the passenger in Seat 10B, directly to his rear, had stabbed Lewin to death. The man in 10B was one of the five young Arabs who had boarded that morning. The killer and another hijacker, Ong said, had gotten into the cockpit. The sound of "loud arguing" had been heard.

Four minutes into the call, Ong's colleague Amy Sweeney began trying to phone American Airlines back at the airport in Boston. At 8:32, using a borrowed calling card, she began speaking with duty manager Michael Woodward.

Sweeney, who also reported the stabbings, said the hijackers had "boxes connected with red and yellow wire"—a bomb, she thought. One, she said, spoke good English. So far, passengers in Coach seemed unaware of what was going on.

If the cockpit door had been locked, as required by FAA rules, how had the hijackers gotten in? All American flight attendants held keys, and that was almost certainly why the attendants in First Class— Martin and Arestegui—had been attacked.

There is no knowing exactly what happened when the hijackers erupted into the cockpit. "There was no warning to be more vigilant," Captain Ogonowski's wife, Peg, would later say. "These people come in behind him. He's sitting low, forward, strapped in—the same with his copilot. No warning . . ."

Ogonowski and copilot Tom McGuinness had been trained not to respond to force with force. FAA policy was still geared to hijackings designed to take over airliners, not destroy them. It called for pilots to "refrain from trying to overpower or negotiate with hijackers, to land the aircraft as soon as possible, to communicate with authorities, and to try delaying tactics." According to an FAA security report, the agency did know that "suicide was an increasingly common tactic among terrorists in the Middle East." Its brief to its pilots, however, offered no guidance on how to deal with hijackers bent on suicide.

Attendant Ong had not sounded panicky as she reported from Flight 11. From time to time, though, she asked staff on the ground to "Please pray for us." There were moments, she said, when the plane was being flown erratically, "sideways." It was descending. The phone line had started to fade in and out. Her colleague Amy Sweeney said she could see they were now "over New York City."

Then Ong exclaimed, "Oh, God! . . . Oh, God! . . ." and began to cry. Sweeney screamed and said, "Something is wrong. I don't think the captain is in control. We are in a rapid descent . . . We are all over the place . . . I see water! I see buildings! . . ." Next, a deep breath and, slowly, calmly, "Oh, my God! . . . We are flying low. We are flying very, very low. We are flying way too low." Seconds later, again, "Oh, my God, we are way too low . . ."

American Airlines' people on the ground could no longer hear either flight attendant. In Boston, duty manager Woodward got only "very, very loud static." In North Carolina, Gonzalez was saying, "Betty, talk to me. Betty, are you there, Betty? . . ."

And finally, "I think we may have lost her."

TWO

IT WAS JUST OVER HALF AN HOUR SINCE THE HIJACKERS HAD STRUCK.
In an office in Lower Manhattan, high in the North Tower of the World Trade Center, a data processor glanced up from his computer. On the horizon to the north, a dot in the sky got his attention. Unusual to see a plane over there, he thought, and turned back to his work.

Moments later, from his perch on a structure on East 77th Street, a steelworker was startled by the sight and the roar of an airliner flying so low that—it seemed to him—it almost hit the antenna atop the Empire State Building. At Madison Avenue and 45th Street, construction workers stared in astonishment. In SoHo, twenty blocks north of the Trade Center, a composer seated in a restaurant window heard a jet thunder overhead. Pigeons, normally blasé, rose in alarm. A window-gazing student at Stuyvesant High—on the banks of the Hudson River—glimpsed the plane for a second and blurted a stunned, "Did you see that?"

A "freakish noise" sent author-photographer Lew Rubenfien rushing onto the roof of his apartment building.

It was the sound jet engines make on a runway when they have been powered all the way up for takeoff—though much more violent, somehow enraged. . . . The plane was moving far faster than you ever saw one go so low in the sky. . . . I began to shout telepathically, "Get away from the building, get away from the building." . . . The plane made a perfect bull's-eye, leaving a jagged tear . . . and then, just as it happens in dreams, everything stretched a long way out. . . . There could only have been a fraction of a second. . . . Then, at last, the building exploded. Hot and orange, the great gassy flower blew out.

It was 8:46 A.M.

The impact had been caught on film thanks to the snap reaction of French documentary maker Jules Naudet, filming nearby with a unit of the New York Fire Department. "I look up, and it's clearly an American Airlines jet," the Frenchman said later. "I turned the camera toward where it was going to go . . . I see it go in. I'm filming it." The image he shot, destined to become iconic, precisely matches Rubenfien's verbal description—orange burst at the core, great bloom of gray smoke or vapor to the left.

In the North Tower, the man who had seen the plane as a distant dot had not been looking when it came right at him. To Chuck Allen of Lava Trading, busy in his 83rd floor office, the memory instead would be of a "muffled, sucking, unbearably loud noise. Like the sound of two high-speed trains crossing in high proximity to each other."

Through the windows, still unbroken, he saw debris falling, paper floating. Liquid was running down the windowpanes. There was a grinding and squeaking in the walls and—Allen was vividly conscious of it—the entire building leaned to one side. Then, gradually, it righted itself.

On the 86th floor, the windows had shattered. James Gartenberg, a broker with Julian Studley real estate, reported by phone that the glass had blown "from the inside of the building out." And that: "The core of the building, the interior core part of the building, collapsed."

American Flight 11 had sliced into the tower between the 93rd and 99th floors. The liquid Allen saw on the windows was almost certainly jet fuel from the plane's wing tanks, a dribble of the ten thousand gallons said to have been on board.

Filmmaker Naudet, far below, stayed with the crew of firefighters as it switched from exercise mode to rapid response and rushed to the tower. Minutes later, in the downstairs lobby, he saw what exploding aviation fuel can do. Fireballs had shot down some of the many elevator shafts, detonating on several floors and then in the lobby. "The windows had all been blown out," Naudet said. "The marble had come off the walls. I saw two bodies burning on the floor. One was screaming, a woman's scream . . . I just didn't want to film that."

Some fourteen thousand people worked each day in the Trade Center towers. Its Twin Towers—North and South, each 110 stories high—loomed more than a fifth of a mile over Manhattan. They were the tallest buildings in the city of skyscrapers, symbols of America's financial power, the heart of a great complex that housed offices, a shopping mall, a hotel, and two subway stations. Vast numbers of workers had not yet been at work when Flight 11 hit. They had been milling around on the lower levels, buying newspapers, grabbing a coffee or a snack. It was primary election day in the city, moreover, and many had stopped to vote before going to the office. Some commuters had been delayed, too, by especially heavy traffic through the tunnels in Manhattan. Innumerable lives were saved that morning by being late.

As filmmaker Naudet had seen, some were killed or terribly injured in the North Tower lobby. It was the 91st floor far above, though, just below the impact point, that became the frontier between certain death and possible, even probable, survival. Above, on levels 92 to 105, were the hundreds of international bankers, the bond traders, investment and insurance managers and their staffs, who regularly came in early to get a jump on the markets. Higher still, near the tower's summit, were the customers and staff of Windows on the World, the celebrated restaurant atop the Trade Center—and engineers who manned television and radio transmitters.

Of the 1,344 souls on those upper floors, none would survive. Some had died instantly, and hundreds had no way of escaping.

On the 92nd floor, which was intact for a while, debris blocked the stairways. At Carr Futures, John San Pio Resta; his wife, Silvia, seven months pregnant; and trader Damian Meehan were trapped. So, too, was Michael Richards, a sculptor who used studio space on the same floor—an anomaly in a building dedicated to commerce—provided by the Lower Manhattan Cultural Council.

Meehan had time to phone one of his brothers, to tell him the elevators were gone and that there was smoke. His last words were "We've got to go," as he headed for one of the blocked stairways. We know nothing of the last moments of the San Pio Restas and Michael Richards. Richards had last been seen at midnight, saying he planned to work till morning. Long preoccupied with the theme of aviation, his final work had been a bronze of himself amidst flames and meteors, pierced by airplanes.

The area immediately above the 92nd floor was a tomb. Fred Alger Management lost thirty-five people, Marsh and McLennan, spread over several floors, 295. For Marsh analyst Patricia Massari, on the phone to her husband when the plane hit, there had been time only for "Oh, my God!" Then the phone went dead. The remains of one of her colleagues would be found five blocks away.

Cantor Fitzgerald, the bond trading company, had occupied floors 100 to 105. Six hundred fifty-eight people had been in their offices at the moment of impact. Michael Wittenstein had hung up in the middle of a call to a customer, then—courteous to a fault—phoned back to apologize. "I believe," he had time to say, "there was an explosion in the boiler room."

Andrew Rosenblum broke into a conversation with his wife to say there had been "a really loud bang," that he would call right back. When he did, on a cell phone, he said he and colleagues needed air. They had used a computer to smash a window, and his wife heard coughing, gasping for breath. Kenneth van Auken tried to call his wife but got the answering machine. "I love you," he said. Then again, "I love you very much. I hope I'll see you later."

All 658 people at Cantor Fitzgerald would soon be dead. One staffer's body would be found months later, intact, in his suit and tie, seated upright in the rubble.

From Windows on the World, they used to say, you could see for fifty miles on a clear day. That morning, a very clear one, the seventy-nine greeters, waiters, chefs, and kitchen staff had been busy. Regulars had been at breakfast meetings. In the ballroom, a conference sponsored by the British firm Risk Waters had been about to begin. Guests had been greeted, an audiovisual presentation prepared. Manager Howard Kane, on the phone to his wife, had—inexplicably to her—dropped the receiver at exactly 8:46. She wondered for a moment if her husband had had a heart attack. Then she heard a woman scream, "We're trapped." Another man picked up the phone to say there was a fire, that they needed the phone to call 911.

Death came slowly at Windows on the World. The story told by the cell phones showed that customers and staff hurried down a floor, to the 106th, to wait for help. Assistant general manager Christine Olender, who phoned downstairs for advice, was told to phone back in a couple of minutes. To help with the smoke, it was suggested, those trapped should hold wet towels to their faces—difficult, for the water supply had been severed. They got some water from the flower vases, a waiter told his wife.

"The situation is rapidly getting worse," Olender reported. "What are we going to do for air?" Stuart Lee, vice president of a software company, got off an email to his home office. "A debate is going on," he wrote, "as to whether we should break a window. Consensus is no for the time being." Then they did break the glass, and people flocked to the window openings.

Every person still alive on those upper floors, some thirteen hundred feet above the ground, was facing either intense heat or dense smoke rising from below. Some pinned their hopes of survival on the one way out they imagined open to them—the roof.

"Get everybody to the roof," former firefighter Bernie Heeran had told his son Charles, a trader for Cantor Fitzgerald, when he phoned for advice. "Go up. Don't try to go down." A colleague, Martin Wortley, told his brother he hoped to escape by helicopter. People had been taken to safety from the roof in the past. On September 11, two police helicopter pilots arrived over the North Tower within minutes—only to realize that any rescue attempt would be jeopardized by the billowing, impenetrable smoke.

Regulations in force at the Trade Center in 2001, moreover, made it impossible even to reach the roof. The way was blocked by three sets of doors, two that could be opened only by authorized personnel with a swipe card, a third operable at normal times only by remote control by security officers far below. The system did not work on 9/11, for vital wires had been cut when the plane hit the tower. Those hoping to escape knew nothing of this.

Early on, one of the helicopter pilots sent a brief message. "Be advised," he radioed, "that we do have people confirmed falling out of the building at this time." In the lobby, a firefighter told filmmaker Naudet simply, "We got jumpers."

VIEWERS AROUND THE WORLD were by now watching events live on television. At the time, however, few in the United States saw the men and women of the Trade Center as they jumped to certain death. Most American editors ruled the pictures too shocking to be shown.

The jumping had begun almost at once. Alan Reiss, of the Port Authority, would remember seeing people falling from high windows within two minutes. Naudet thought "five, ten minutes" passed before he and those around him heard what sounded like explosions—the sound the bodies made as they struck the ground. "They disintegrated. Right in front of us, outside the lobby windows. There was completely nothing left of them. With each loud boom, every firefighter would shudder."

In the heat of an inferno, driven by unthinkable pain, jumping may for many have been more reflexive action than choice. For those with time to think, the choice between incineration and a leap into thin air may not have been difficult.

Firefighters had never seen anything on this scale, the sheer number of human beings falling, a man clutching a briefcase, another ripping off his burning shirt as he jumped, a woman holding down her skirt in a last attempt at modesty. Some fell in pairs holding hands, others in groups, three or four at a time. Some appeared to line up to jump, like paratroopers.

At least one jump seemed involuntary. Gazing through a long lens, photographer Richard Smiouskas was watching five or six people huddled together in a narrow window when one figure suddenly fell forward and away. It looked as though he had been shoved.

"As the debris got closer to the ground," firefighter Kevin McCabe said, "you started seeing arms and legs. You couldn't believe what you were watching . . . [then] it was like cannon balls hitting the ground. Boom. I remember one person actually hitting a piece of structural steel over a glass canopy . . . I remember turning my face away . . . you'd just hear the pounding . . . tremendously loud, like taking a bag of concrete and throwing it into a closed courtyard. A loud echo . . . Boom. Boom . . ."

To Derek Brogan, McCabe's companion, it "looked like it was raining bodies." The bodies spelled danger. "We started to get hit," said Lieutenant Steve Turilli. "You would get hit by an arm or a leg and it felt like a metal pole was hitting you. It was like a war zone."

Cascading humanity.

JUST FORTY-NINE MINUTES had passed since the hijacking aboard Flight 11 had begun, seventeen since the great airplane roared over Manhattan to bring mayhem and murder to the North Tower. Now, in the sky high above the carnage, a police helicopter pilot spotted something astounding. "Christ!" he shouted into the microphone. "There's a *second* plane crashing . . ."

THREE

"**W**E HAVE *SOME PLANES.*"

More than three quarters of an hour earlier, as air traffic controller Pete Zalewski tried to get a response from the hijacked Flight 11, he had suddenly heard an unfamiliar voice on the frequency—a man's voice, with an Arabic accent. Zalewski had trouble making out the words, but moments later a second, clearer transmission persuaded him and colleagues that a hijack was under way. The hijacker, they would conclude, had been trying to address the passengers and—unfamiliar with the equipment—inadvertently transmitted to ground control instead.

A quality assurance specialist then pulled the tape, listened very carefully, and figured out what the Arabic voice had said on the initial, indistinct transmission. "We have some planes. Just stay quiet and you'll be okay. We are returning to the airport."

This was a giveaway that—had the U.S. military been able to intervene in time—could have wrecked the operation. The hijackers

NATIONAL TRANSPORTATION SAFETY BOARD
Vehicle Recorders Division
Washington, D.C. 20594

December 21, 2001

Air Traffic Control Recording

```
1224:38   AAL-11   we have some planes. just stay quiet and you'll be okay we are
                   returning to the airport. [BOS 1204-1233 Sector 46R]
1224:46   46R      and uh who's trying to call me here? [BOS 1204-1233 Sector 46R]
1224:53   46R      American eleven are you trying to call? [BOS 1204-1233 Sector
                   46R]
1224:56   AAL-11   nobody move. everything will be okay. if you try to make any
                   moves, you'll endanger yourself and the airplane. just stay
                   quiet. [BOS 1204-1233 Sector 46R]
1233:59   AAL-11   nobody move please we are going back to the airport don't try
                   to make any stupid moves. [BOS 1204-1233 Sector 46R]
```

had seized not two but *four* airplanes. What remained unknown, until even later, was that there may have been plans to seize even more.

As AMERICA's FLIGHT 11 had been boarding, United Airlines Flight 175—also departing from Boston—had been readying for takeoff. Copilot Michael Horrocks, a former Marine, called his wife about then, joking that he was flying that day with "some guy with a funny Italian name." Flight 175's captain was Victor Saracini, a veteran like Flight 11's Ogonowski. The team of flight attendants included Kathryn Laborie and Alfred Marchand—a former police officer—in First Class; Robert Fangman in Business; and Amy King and Michael Tarrou—a couple thinking of getting married—in Coach.

Their fifty-six passengers were the usual mix: a computer expert, a scout for the Los Angeles Kings hockey team, a commercials producer, a senior marketer for a software company, a systems consultant for the Defense Department. There were also foreigners: three Germans, an Israeli, a British man, and an Irish woman—and five young Arabs, three Saudis and two Emiratis. All the Arabs had booked seats in First or Business Class.

As they had in the case of Flight 11, ground staff were to recall odd details about the passengers from the Middle East. Two Arabs bungled the boarding process—one of them boarded using his companion's boarding card, and a new one had to be printed. One man asked twice in poor English if he could purchase a ticket, when he already had one. Two waiting passengers, possibly the same man and a companion, behaved strangely at the gate ticket counter. They stood in line, only to walk away on reaching the counter, line up again, and walk away again. In all, they went through the process three times. They seemed nervous, "looked down at the ground as if they were attempting to avoid eye contact." Nevertheless, they both eventually boarded successfully.

Captain Saracini took United Flight 175 into the air before 8:15 and climbed steadily to 31,000 feet. Twenty-three minutes into the flight, a controller looking for the missing Flight 11 asked him and his copilot to see if they could spot it. They did, and were told to stay out of its way. Three minutes later, as 175 entered New York airspace, Saracini came on the air to report to controller Dave Bottiglia:

> SARACINI: We figured we'd wait to go to you[r] Center. Ah, we heard a suspicious transmission on our departure out of Boston, ah . . . sound[ed] like someone keyed the mike and, ah, said, ah, "Everyone, stay in your seats."
> BOTTIGLIA: Oh, okay. I'll pass that along . . .

Saracini had probably decided to wait a while before reporting the suspect transmission from Flight 11 because—surmising that it indicated a hijack—he wanted to avoid being overheard. United passengers using headsets could listen in on the cockpit chatter simply by listening to Channel 9—it was a form of entertainment. It is possible that on Saracini's plane, unbeknownst to him, some of those listening in were the men planning to hijack the aircraft.

Whether or not they overheard the cockpit chatter, hijackers struck Flight 175 within five minutes of the captain's report about the sinister transmission. At 8:47 the transponder code—the signal that identifies an aircraft—changed twice in the space of a minute. Four minutes later, when ground control asked the pilots to readjust the transponder, there was no response. In the same minute, the airplane deviated from its assigned altitude, climbed, and then—near Allentown, Pennsylvania—began a turn to the southeast. Pilots Saracini and Horrocks were silent now.

Others on board found a way to communicate. Five minutes after the change of course, the phone rang at Starfix, a United facility in California assigned to handle crew calls about minor maintenance problems. The mechanic who took the call, Marc Policastro, found himself talking to a male flight attendant aboard Flight 175, probably Robert Fangman. He said the flight had been hijacked, the pilots killed.

On another phone, a passenger named Peter Hanson got through to his parents' home in Connecticut. He described the hijack, speaking in low tones as his father made notes. "I think they've taken over the cockpit," Hanson said. "An attendant has been stabbed. Someone else up front may have been killed. The plane is making strange moves."

On the ground at New York Center, the silence from 175 by now had controller Dave Bottiglia thoroughly alarmed. He alerted an air traffic manager, Mike McCormick. The turn Flight 175 had been making became a U-turn, until the plane was pointed directly at New York City. "We might," Bottiglia heard McCormick say, "have multiple hijacks."

At 8:58, another phone began ringing. Passenger Brian Sweeney, the Defense Department consultant on the plane, was trying to reach his wife, Julie, in Massachusetts. She was a teacher, already at school, so he left a voice message. "Hey Jules, it's Brian. I'm on a plane and it's hijacked, and it doesn't look good. I just wanted to let you know that I love you, and I hope to see you again. If I don't, please have fun in life. Please be happy. Please live your life. That's an order."

Sweeney, a former Navy lieutenant who had taught at the Top Gun Fighter Weapons School, did get through to his mother, Louise—with a very different sort of message. He and other passengers, he said, were thinking of storming the cockpit. "I might have to hang up quickly, we're going to try to do something about this."

Peter Hanson, meanwhile, managed another call to tell his father, who again made notes: "It's getting bad, Dad . . . They seem to have knives and Mace. They said they have a bomb. It's getting very bad on the plane. Passengers are throwing up . . . The plane is making jerky movements . . . I think we are going down . . . Don't worry, Dad. If it happens, it'll be very fast."

Hanson Sr. had heard a woman's scream in the background. His son said, "My God! My God! . . ." Then the call ended.

It was 9:02. Ground controllers north of New York were gradually catching up with the reality. Boston Center told New England Region that the tape of the Flight 11 hijacker showed that he had spoken of "planes, as in plural." Also: "It sounds like—we're talking to New York—that there's another one aimed at the World Trade Center."

Even as they talked, controllers at New York Center were watching the radar blip that was Flight 175. "He's not going to land," one man exclaimed, leaping to his feet. "He's going in . . ."

THE BOEING 767 roared in from New Jersey, looking for a moment as though it might collide with the Statue of Liberty. It rocked from side to side, then the nose pointed down. Fire marshal Steven Mosiello, already at the Trade Center, heard rather than saw it as it came ever "closer . . . louder and louder." The *Irish Times*'s America correspondent, Conor O'Clery, watching the scene at the Trade Center through binoculars, saw the plane "skim" across the Hudson River.

On the 81st floor of the South Tower, Fuji Bank official Stanley Praimnath was at his desk, talking on the phone. Praimnath would recall how, in mid-sentence, for no apparent reason, "I just raised my head and looked to the Statue of Liberty. And what I see is a big plane coming towards me . . . I am looking at an airplane coming, eye level, eye contact, toward me—giant gray airplane . . . with a red stripe . . . I am still seeing the letter U on its tail, and the plane is bearing down on me. I dropped the phone and I screamed and I dove under my desk."

Three floors up, on the 84th, Brian Clark of Euro Brokers had been consoling a woman colleague distraught at the sight of people jumping from the North Tower. He escorted her to the door of the ladies' room, on the far side of the building, when: "*Whomf!* It wasn't a huge explosion. It was something muffled, no flames, no smoke, but the room fell apart . . . For seven to ten seconds there was this enormous sway in the building . . . I thought it was over."

It was 9:03. United Flight 175 had struck the South Tower between the 77th and 85th floors, at an angle. Clark's chivalrous action in helping a distressed colleague had saved his own life. It had taken him to the side of the building furthest from the point of impact. Praimnath found himself, still under his desk, covered in debris, peering out at what looked like part of the airplane's wing. He began shouting for help and was soon extricated by Clark, who had headed down a passable stairwell. The two were to make the long descent to the ground and safety.

Many others who had been working in their part of the tower had died instantly. Those who survived the initial impact and headed up, rather than down, would not survive.

Fifty minutes had elapsed since the terror began.

For those fighting for their lives in the towers, those rushing to the rescue, those charged with orchestrating the air traffic still in the sky, and those responsible for the defense of the United States, all was now confusion and chaos—against a drumbeat of breaking news, the biggest, most stunning news in the lifetimes of almost everyone it reached.

FOUR

CNN HAD THE BREAK. ON THE HEELS OF A REPORT ABOUT MATERNITY wear, Carol Lin cut into a commercial within two minutes of the first strike.

"This just in. You are looking at obviously a very disturbing live shot . . . We have unconfirmed reports this morning that a plane has crashed into one of the towers of the World Trade Center . . . Clearly something relatively devastating happening this morning there on the south end of the island of Manhattan."

On *Good Morning America*, ABC's Diane Sawyer and Charles Gibson had been smiling through a serving of breakfast-time fluff. Then, four minutes after CNN, they launched into nonstop blanket coverage. Like all the other networks, ABC was confronting a major national story armed with a minimum of facts.

"Was it in any sense deliberate?" asked Sawyer, now serious-faced. "Was it an accident? . . . We simply don't know." Behind the cameras, assuming pilot error, one ABC staffer made a reference he was to regret—to "stupidity." On the radio, someone said the pilot must have been drunk.

The early news flashes triggered differing reactions at the highest levels of government. At the National Security Agency outside Washington, where America spies on worldwide phone and email communications, director Michael Hayden glanced at CNN's live shots of the burning North Tower. He thought, "Big fire for a small plane," and went back to his meeting.

Breakfasting with a friend at the St. Regis Hotel, CIA director George Tenet responded very differently. His instant reaction, he would recall, was that this was a terrorist attack. "It was obvious that I had to leave immediately. . . . I climbed back into my car and, with lights flashing, began racing back to headquarters."

Earlier that morning, at a meeting at the Pentagon, Defense Secretary Donald Rumsfeld had made a prediction. In the coming months, he said, there would be an event "sufficiently shocking that it would remind people again how important it is to have a strong, healthy Defense Department." He has not said what he thought when passed a note with news of the crash at the Trade Center, but he left for his office.

Richard Clarke, the long-serving national coordinator for security and counterterrorism, assumed the worst, summoned senior security officials to a videoconference, and headed for the White House.

Vice President Dick Cheney and National Security Adviser Condoleezza Rice were already at the White House. Rice merely thought, "What an odd accident!" Cheney, told of the crash while going over speeches with an aide, began watching the TV coverage.

The President, George W. Bush, was absent from the capital and would be all day, a circumstance that was to do his image no good in the hours that followed. When the first plane hit, he was in Sarasota, Florida, on his way to visit an elementary school—part of a drive for child literacy. White House photographer Eric Draper was in a limousine with press secretary Ari Fleischer and Mike Morell, a senior CIA official, when Fleischer's cell phone rang.

"I heard him say, 'Oh, my God! I don't believe it,' " Draper recalled. " 'A plane just hit the World Trade Center.' " Fleischer then turned to Morell to ask if he knew anything about a "small plane" hitting one of the towers. Morell, who phoned CIA Operations, was told that the plane was in fact a large one.

Most likely, the President first learned of the crash as the motorcade arrived at Emma E. Booker Elementary. Navy captain Deborah Loewer, director of the White House Situation Room, ran over with the news as, at about the same moment, chief of staff Andy Card asked Bush to take a call from Condoleezza Rice in Washington. Rice knew less, apparently, than the CIA.

"The first report I heard," Bush would recall, "was a light airplane, twin-engine airplane. . . . And my first reaction was, as an old pilot, 'How could the guy have gotten so off course to hit the towers?' . . . I thought it was pilot error . . . that some foolish soul had gotten lost and made a terrible mistake." He told school principal Gwendolyn Tose-Rigell, "We're going to go on and do the reading thing," and they went off to meet a class of second graders.

A THOUSAND MILES to the north, the first fire chief to reach the North Tower had called in three alarms in quick succession. Even before the second plane hit, a thousand first responders had been deployed. They included men who were off duty, who dropped everything on hearing of the crash and rushed to the scene. One man thought idly that the job would last "twenty-four hours easy—that's a few hundred dollars, no problem." In fact, he was joining what was to be the largest rescue operation in the history of New York City—focused principally on saving lives. Senior firemen rapidly concluded that it would not be possible to put out the fire in the North Tower.

Instructions to evacuate the North Tower had been announced over the public address system within a minute of the crash. The system had been knocked out of action, though, so no one heard the announcement. In the South Tower, where the system did still work, the disembodied voice at first advised, "There is no need to evacuate . . . If you are in the midst of evacuation, return to your office." The instruction changed at 9:02, when occupants were told they could leave after all. Some four thousand people, two thirds of those reckoned to have been in the South Tower, had by that time chosen to leave anyway.

Then at 9:03, Flight 175 hit the South Tower. For the networks, broadcasting live, the task of reporting became incalculably complex—and totally impromptu. This from the ABC *Good Morning America* transcript:

SAWYER: Oh, my God! Oh, my God!
GIBSON: That looks like a second plane has just hit . . .
SAWYER: Terrible! . . . We will see that scene again, just to make
sure we saw what we thought we saw.
GIBSON: We're going to give you a replay . . . That looks like a
good-sized plane, came in and hit the World Trade Center from
the other side . . . it would seem like there is a concerted attack . . .
SAWYER: We watch powerless . . .

On Channel 5's *Good Day New York*, the anchorman Jim Ryan took
a flyer and got it right. "I think," he said, "we have a terrorist act of
proportions we cannot begin to imagine at this point."

At the NSA, director Hayden said, "One plane's an accident. Two
planes is an attack," and ordered that top priority be given to intercepts originating in the Middle East.

At the Defense Department, assistant secretary for public affairs
Torie Clarke, accompanied by colleague Larry Di Rita, hurried to
Secretary Rumsfeld's office with the news. He said he would take his
daily intelligence briefing, then meet them at the Executive Support
Center where military operations are coordinated during emergen-
cies. They left Rumsfeld standing at the lectern in his office—he liked
to work standing up—one eye on the television.

Word of the second strike was slow to reach CIA director Tenet,
still in his car racing back to headquarters. "With all hell breaking
loose," he remembered, "it was hard to get calls through on the secure
phone. . . . I was in a communications blackout between the St. Regis
and Langley, the longest twelve minutes of my life. It wasn't until I
arrived at headquarters that I learned that, as we were tearing up the
George Washington Parkway at something like eighty miles an hour,
a second plane had hit."

Counterterrorism coordinator Richard Clarke learned of the second attack as he drove up to the White House. He was told Condoleezza Rice wanted him "fast," and found her with the Vice President.
"The Secret Service," Rice said, "wants us to go to the bomb shelter."
Cheney, famous for his imperturbability, was looking a little shaken.
He "began to gather up his papers," Clarke recalled. "In his outer
office the normal Secret Service presence was two agents. As I left, I
counted eight, ready to move [Cheney] to the PEOC, the Presidential
Emergency Operations Center, a bunker in the East Wing."

Clarke, for his part, headed for the West Wing, to prepare for the videoconference of counterterrorism and other senior officials he would soon chair. He asked, "Where's POTUS?"—White House shorthand for the President—and learned Bush was at the school in Florida.

"GET READY TO READ all the words on this page without making a mistake. Look at the letter at the end everyone, with the sound it makes. Get ready!"

As the second plane hit the Trade Center, George Bush had been listening intently to teacher Kay Daniels and her class of second graders. The teacher was going into a routine the children knew well, using a phonics-based system designed to promote reading skills. She intoned, "Boys and girls! Sound this word out, get ready!" "Kite!" chorused the children, then "kit!" then "seal" and "steal," and so on, as Ms. Daniels beat time. Then, "Boys and girls, pick your reader up from under your seat. Open your book up to Lesson 60, on page 153." The children and the President picked up the readers.

In a nearby room, members of Bush's staff had been watching the news coverage from New York—the Marine assigned to carry the President's phone had asked for the television to be turned on. One of those watching as Flight 175 hit was Captain Deborah Loewer, the woman who had run to tell the President about the initial crash. "It took me about thirty seconds," she recalled, "to realize this was terrorism."

Loewer spoke rapidly to chief of staff Andy Card, and—we calculate within about ninety seconds—Card was in the classroom and whispering in the President's ear. By one account he said, "A second plane hit the second tower. America is under attack." As likely, given Loewer's role as Situation Room director, is a version that had Card telling Bush, "Captain Loewer says it's terrorism."

IN NEW YORK at about that time, high in the South Tower, Brian Clark of Euro Brokers was pausing to pull Stanley Praimnath out of a wrecked wall, glimpsing fires raging through cracks in walls.

Operators at the Fire Department were logging a stream of emergency calls:

> 9:04 MC [male caller] CAGGIANO . . . STS [states] PEOPLE
> TRAPPED ON THE 104 FLR . . . IN BACK ROOM . . . STS 35–40
> PEOPLE
>
> 9:04 MC—STS 103 FLR—CAN'T GET OUT—FIRE ON FLR—
> PEOPLE GETTING SICK

IN THE CLASSROOM in Florida, Bush's expression changed. Told of the second strike, the President pursed his lips, gazing back at his chief of staff as he moved away. ABC's Ann Compton, watching him, thought "his eyes got wide." Teacher Daniels thought he seemed distracted. Natalia Jones-Pinkney, one of the pupils, thought he "looked like he was going to cry." "His face just started to turn red," said Tyler Radkey, another student. "I thought, personally, he had to go to the bathroom."

In the adjacent room, the Marine carrying Bush's phone turned to the local sheriff and said, "Can you get everybody ready? We're out of here." Not so—not yet, for the President did not move.

"On the count of three," teacher Daniels said, "everyone should be on page 153 . . ." The children obeyed, and so did Bush. "Fingers under the title," came the order. "Get ready!" The children chorused the title of a story: "The Pet Goat . . ."

For long and unforgettable minutes, the President of the United States sat dutifully as the second graders read:

> The girl had a pet goat. She liked to go running with her pet
> goat. She played with her goat in her house. She played with
> her goat in her yard. But the goat did something that made
> the girl's dad mad. The goat ate things. He ate cans and he
> ate cakes. He ate cakes and he ate cats. One day her dad said,
> "That goat must go. He ate too many things."

On the other side of the room, press secretary Ari Fleischer had held up a handwritten sign for Bush's attention. It read, in large black letters, "DON'T SAY ANYTHING YET."

IN THE NORTH TOWER, realtor James Gartenberg and secretary Patricia Puma had by now realized they were stuck in their office. "A fire door has trapped us," Gartenberg told a WABC reporter who reached him on the phone. "Debris has fallen around us. I'm with one other person . . . on the 86th floor, facing the East River . . . I want to tell anybody that has a family member that may be in the building that the situation is under control at the moment . . . So please, all family members take it easy."

It was a brave statement, but neither Gartenberg nor Puma would survive.

The flood of calls to the Fire Department continued:

09:07 CALL FLR 103—ROOM 130—APPROX 30 PEOPLE—LOTS OF SMOKE—FC [female caller] IS PREGNANT

09:08: FC SCREAMING

09:08: FC STS FIRE DEPARTMENT NEEDED TO PUT OUT FIRE

09:09: MC STS 2WTC—PEOPLE ARE JUMPING OUT THE SIDE OF A LARGE HOLE—POSS NO ONE CATCHING THEM

09:09: ON FLR 104—MC STS HIS WIFE IS ON THE 91 FL—STS STAIRS ARE ALL BLOCKED—STS WORRIED ABOUT HIS WIFE

In Florida, the children chorused on:

The goat stayed . . . the girl made him stop eating cans and cakes and cats and cakes. But one day a car robber went into the girl's house. He saw a big red car in the house and said, "I will steal that car." He ran to the car and started to open the door. The girl and the goat were playing in the back yard. They did not see the car robber. More to come.

The President, seemingly all attention, asked, "What does that mean—'More to come'?" It meant, a child told him brightly, that there would be "More later on."

• • •

MORE WAS IN FACT already happening. Since 8:56, well before Bush began listening to the second graders, FAA ground controllers had begun worrying about a third airliner. American Flight 77, bound for Los Angeles out of Washington's Dulles Airport, had failed to respond to routine messages, and deviated from its assigned course. Its transponder was turned off and it could not be seen on radar. The controller of the moment, in Indianapolis, knew nothing of the events in New York. He thought the plane had experienced serious technical failure and was "gone."

Soon after 9:00, as the second hijacked airplane crashed into the South Tower, controllers began circulating information that Flight 175 was missing, perhaps crashed. Air Force Search and Rescue and the police were alerted, American Airlines notified. Some at American, meanwhile, thought for a while that it was Flight 77—not United's 175—that had crashed into the Trade Center's South Tower. "Whose plane is whose?": the gist of one conversation between an American manager and his counterpart at United summarizes the general confusion.

United dispatcher Ed Ballinger, responsible for sixteen of the airline's transcontinental flights, had learned that a Flight 175 attendant had called reporting a hijacking. He composed a cautious message to 175 that read, "How's the ride? Anything Dispatch can do for you?" It was too late. By the time the message went out, at 9:03, the crew and passengers on board the plane were beyond help. In the same minute, Flight 175 struck the South Tower.

Four minutes after that, Boston area Air Traffic Control advised all commercial airplane pilots in its sector to secure their cockpits. Boston also recommended that the FAA's Command Center issue a nationwide warning, but the Command Center failed to do so. At 9:19 at United, however, dispatcher Ballinger acted on his own initiative and began sending messages to all "his" flights. They read: "Beware any cockpit intrusion. Two a/c [aircraft] hit World Trade Center."

By 9:05, aware now of the Flight 11 hijacker's transmission about having "planes," FAA's New York Center issued orders forbidding any aircraft to leave, arrive at, or travel through, their airspace until further notice. "We have several situations going on here," a New York Center manager told the Command Center. "We have other aircraft that may have a similar situation going on here." With 4,546 airplanes under their control in the United States that morning, the managers were facing into a situation covered by no training manual.

CONTROLLERS REMAINED totally ignorant of the true status of American 77, the third plane in trouble—though not for want of trying on the part of one of its crew. At 9:12, flight attendant Renee May—assigned to First Class on this latest missing aircraft—got through by phone to her mother in Las Vegas. She spoke just long enough to say six hijackers had taken control, and that passengers and crew were being moved to the back of the plane. She asked her mother to call American Airlines and raise the alarm. Then she got out, "I love you, Mom," before the call was disconnected.

May's mother got through to American in Washington, waited while she was put on hold, then relayed her daughter's message. With staff already distracted by news of events in New York, some wondered whether Flight 77 had hit the World Trade Center. The import of May's call became lost in the general confusion.

In the West Wing of the White House, the videoconference of senior officials was yet to get under way. After the second strike, meanwhile, Vice President Cheney had picked up a phone and said, "I need to talk to the President . . . The Cabinet is going to need direction."

AT THE SCHOOL in Florida, the President's reading session with the children finally came to an end. "Hoo!" he exclaimed. "These are great readers . . . *Very* impressive! Thank you all so very much for showing me your reading skills . . . Thanks for having us."

Why had Bush continued to sit in the classroom—for more than five minutes—*after* being told of the second strike on the Trade Center? Why, many were to wonder, had he not responded instantly—even with a single terse presidential instruction—when Card told him the second crash indicated a terrorist attack?

Two months later, the President would offer a sort of explanation. He had gone on listening to the schoolchildren, he said, because he was "very aware of the cameras. I'm trying to absorb that knowledge. I have nobody to talk to . . . and I realize I'm the commander-in-chief and the country has just come under attack."

Once out of the classroom, Bush joined aides watching the TV news, saw the Trade Center burning, and talked on the phone with Cheney and Rice. He decided to make a brief statement, then fly back to Washington.

Unknown to the President, though, as he mulled what to tell the national audience, crisis was spiraling into calamity.

FIVE

SIX TIMES, MAYBE MORE, THE PHONE HAD RUNG THAT MORNING IN THE office at the Justice Department of Theodore Olson, the solicitor general. The caller was his wife, Barbara, and she finally got through some time after 9:15. Mrs. Olson, a prominent attorney who often made television appearances, was no shrinking violet. Now, though, she sounded hysterical.

Olson knew his wife was flying to California that day. He had seen the television coverage of the Trade Center attacks, had thanked God there had not been time for his wife's flight to get to New York. Now Barbara was on the line—from American 77.

Her flight had been seized, she said, by men "with knives and box cutters." After an interruption—Mrs. Olson was cut off—she came back on the line and spoke with her husband for about ten minutes.

The pilot, she told him, had announced that the flight had been hijacked. Had Flight 77's legitimate pilot, Charles Burlingame, remained alive and told his passengers what was happening? Today, there is no way of knowing. Mrs. Olson, who by now sounded calmer, consulted with someone nearby and said she thought the plane was headed northeast. She could see houses below, so the plane must—she realized—have been flying fairly low. She and her husband talked of their feelings for each other, and Olson assured her that things were "going to come out okay." In his heart, he thought otherwise.

Nothing more would be heard from anyone aboard Flight 77. Ted Olson tried to reach the attorney general, John Ashcroft, only to find that he, too, was out of Washington and in the air. Olson spoke with the Department of Justice Command Center and provided his wife's flight number, but the effort went nowhere. With the minutes rushing by, the solicitor general of the United States proved no more effective than had flight attendant Renee May's mother, calling American Airlines to report her daughter's desperate call.

Flight 77 had been flying on undetected, for ground controllers worked on the assumption that it was still flying not east but west. Then at 9:32, controllers monitoring radar at Dulles Airport, outside Washington, spotted an unidentified airplane speeding toward the capital. Reagan National, the airport situated alongside the Potomac River in Washington itself, was notified. So were Secret Service agents, who were by now fretting both about the safety of the Vice President—still in his White House office—and of the President, still at that school in Florida.

ISOLATED FROM THE ONRUSH of events, but very aware of the catastrophe in New York, the President was launching into his thank-you remarks to the teachers and fifth-grade students—remarks rapidly reshaped to take account of the attacks and suggest that the nation's leader was at the helm:

> Ladies and gentlemen, this is a difficult moment for America. I unfortunately will be going back to Washington. . . . Today we have had a national tragedy. Two airplanes have crashed into the World Trade Center in an apparent terrorist attack on our country. . . . I have ordered the full resources of the federal government to go to help the victims and their families and to conduct a full-scale investigation to hunt down and find those folks who've committed this act. Terrorism against our nation will not stand. Now, if you'll join me in a moment

of silence. . . . May God bless the victims and their families and America.

Bush was gone from the school moments later. A Secret Service agent emerged at a run to tell local police officers, "We're under terrorist attack. We have to go now." The presidential motorcade sped off, heading for the Sarasota airport. Before it got there, however, events would torpedo the plan to return to Washington.

FROM THE TOWER at Reagan Airport in Washington, a supervisor had been talking urgently with the Secret Service's Operations Center at the White House. "We've got an aircraft coming at you," he said, "and not talking with us." It is less than four miles from the airport to the White House. Within three minutes, by 9:36, according to the Secret Service record, the agents who had been waiting in Cheney's outer office—submachine guns in hand—acted. "They came in," the Vice President remembered, "grabbed me and . . . you know, your feet touch the floor periodically. But they're bigger than I am, and they hoisted me up and moved me very rapidly down the hallway, down some stairs, through some doors, and down some more stairs into an underground facility under the White House." He was on his way to the Presidential Emergency Operations Center, a fortified bunker originally built for President Roosevelt in World War II, where he was to remain for many hours.

DULLES CONTROLLERS had reported that the suspect airplane was headed toward the restricted airspace around the White House, known as P-56. It was ten miles out, still pointed that way, when radar at Reagan National picked it up. Then it turned south. A National Guard cargo aircraft pilot, asked if he had it in sight, could see it clearly. It looked "like a 757 with a silver fuselage" descending, Colonel Steve O'Brien would recall.

Then, squinting through the haze, O'Brien saw the plane begin to turn back again toward the city. Suddenly, horrified controllers in the Reagan control tower no longer needed the reports of the National Guard pilot. There the airliner was, in plain sight and less than a mile away.

A fire engine captain and his crew on Interstate 395, en route to a training session, saw the plane in steep descent, banking right. A policeman on a motorcycle on Columbia Pike saw it, flying so low that its fuselage reflected the shapes of the buildings beneath. A Catholic priest, on his way to a graveside service at Arlington Cemetery, saw it—flying no more than twenty feet above the road, he said. Steve Anderson, an executive for *USA Today*, who saw it from his 19th floor office, couldn't believe his eyes.

"I heard an airplane, a very loud airplane, come from behind me," said Richard Benedetto, a reporter for the paper, "an American Airlines airplane. I could see it very clearly."

"I was close enough—about a hundred feet or so—that I could see the American Airlines logo on the tail," said Steve Riskus. "It was not completely level but . . . kind of like it was landing with no gear down . . . It knocked over a few light poles on its way."

"I looked out my driver's side window," said insurance company employee Penny Elgas, "and realized I was looking at the nose of an airplane . . . I saw the end of the wing closest to me and the underside closest to me . . . I remember recognizing it as an American Airlines plane . . . The plane seemed to be floating as if it were a paper glider."

AT THE PENTAGON, on the south bank of the Potomac, the news from New York had set some people thinking. "What do we have in place to protect from an airplane?" someone had asked Pentagon police chief John Jester. "Nothing," he replied. There were measures in place to counter a terrorist attack on the ground, but there was no antiaircraft system. Jester raised the "Protection Condition" to "Alpha," all he could do in the circumstances.

Controller Sean Boger, in the little tower beside the Pentagon heliport, wondered aloud why it was that no airplane had ever hit the Pentagon—even by accident. The vast complex was, after all, only a mile from Reagan National. Then, out of nowhere, Boger saw "the nose and the wing of an aircraft just like, coming right at us."

The plane hit just as Jester's deputy was passing on the "Alpha" alert order. Six hundred feet from the point of impact, Jester heard the noise, felt a shaking, but—so huge and so solidly built is the Pentagon—thought it was caused by "furniture on a pallet rolling over an expansion joint." Others heard the sound as a muffled "thwoom."

Flight 77, still with some 5,300 gallons of fuel in its tanks, had hurtled into the military nerve center of the United States at a speed later calculated to have been about 530 miles per hour. The plane struck the west side of the Pentagon just above ground level, going on in diagonally at an angle of about forty-two degrees.

To Penny Elgas, watching petrified in her car, the airliner seemed to "simply melt into the building. I saw a smoke ring surround the fuselage as it made contact with the wall."

"I saw the plane," another driver, Rebecca Gordon, said. "It was there . . . Then it was gone . . . it just vanished."

"I expected to see the tail sticking out," recalled Sheryl Alleger, a naval officer who saw the crash site afterward. "But—nothing. It was like the building swallowed the plane."

As the airplane pierced the structure, a great mass of flame blossomed above the Pentagon's roof. There were explosions. The carnage and destruction covered a ragged area of more than an acre of the vast complex.

A total of 189 people, 64 on the airliner and 125 military and civilian staff of the Defense Department, were killed—many instantaneously, more within minutes. Some of the Pentagon's dead would be found still seated at their desks and conference tables. Forty-nine people suffered injuries sufficient to warrant admission to hospitals.

Christine Morrison, a survivor, described vividly what happened to her. "From the back of the room there was a heatwave-like haze . . . moving. Before I could register or complete that thought, this force hit the room, instantly turning the office into an inferno hell. Everything was falling, flying, and on fire, and there was no escaping it . . . I felt the heat and I heard the sizzling of me . . . Oxygen disappeared; my lungs felt like they were burning or collapsing. My mind was like sludge and thoughts took forever to form and longer to reach the brain, and even longer to make use of them . . . Everyone lost his or her sense of direction."

Morrison would emerge into the daylight relatively unharmed. Juan Cruz Santiago was terribly injured. In the words of the official Defense Department history, he was "engulfed by fire. Most of his body was scorched with second, third, and fourth-degree burns. . . . Hospitalized for three months, Cruz underwent some thirty surgeries, including skin grafts to his face, right arm, hands, and legs. He was left with cruel damage to his face, eyes, and hands."

Louise Kurtz, who had been standing at a fax machine, was—in her words—"baked, totally . . . I was like meat when you take it off the grill." She lost her ears and fingers, underwent multiple skin grafts, and spent three months in the hospital.

Astonishing escapes included Sheila Moody, in the accounts department, who had been seated near the outer wall of the building. Instead of calling out when she heard a rescuer close by—she was stifled by smoke and flames and unable to make a sound—she had been able only to clap her hands. A staff sergeant heard her and got her to safety. Thirty-four others in the department died.

April Gallop, in information management, had brought her two-month-old son to work with her because the babysitter was sick. After the plane hit, and waist-deep in debris, she was horrified to see that the infant's stroller was on fire—and empty. She found the baby, however, curled up in the wreckage and virtually unscathed, and both were rescued.

The crash site being the Pentagon, trained military men were on hand at once. Marines—doing "what we're supposed to do," as one of them put it—went into the wreckage time and again. They and the hundreds of firefighters who arrived would more than once have to retreat—once when it became clear that part of the building was going to collapse, again when it was feared that another hijacked plane was approaching. The firefighting operation lasted thirty-six hours.

WHEN THE PLANE HIT, Defense Secretary Rumsfeld was still in his office with his CIA briefer. The room shook, even though his quarters were at the furthest point from the impact—in a building each side of which is longer than three football fields. Told that an airplane had crashed, Rumsfeld set off fast to investigate, bodyguards in his wake. They came eventually, a member of the escort recalled, to a place where "it was dark and there was a lot of smoke. Then we saw daylight through a door that was hanging open."

The defense secretary would remember emerging to see the building ablaze, "hundreds of pieces of metal all over the lawn," "people lying on the grass with clothes blown off and burns all over them." He examined a piece of wreckage, saw writing on it, and muttered: "American Airlines . . ." He helped push a gurney, was photographed doing so, then headed back inside.

Assistant secretary Torie Clarke, waiting in the Executive Support Center as instructed, remembered seeing Rumsfeld arrive at about 10:15, "suit jacket over his shoulders and his face and clothes smeared with ashes, dirt, and sweat." He was "quiet, deadly serious, completely cool."

WHILE DONALD RUMSFELD was on the move around the Pentagon, President Bush had been on the short limousine ride from Booker Elementary to the Sarasota airport. News of the Pentagon attack reached the party as they were en route, leading the President's Secret Service escort to advise against the planned return to Washington. Chief of staff Card agreed.

From the airport, on board Air Force One, Bush spoke with Cheney at the White House. "Sounds like we have a minor war going on here," he told the Vice President, according to an aide's notes. "I heard about the Pentagon. We're at war . . . somebody's going to pay."

The Secret Service wanted Air Force One off the ground fast. "They were taxiing before the door was closed," an officer recalled, "and the pilot shot off using only half the runway. There was so much torque that they actually tore the concrete."

Air Force colonel Mark Tillman, at the controls, took the plane up "like a rocket," a passenger remembered, "almost straight up." After flying northeast for a while, it turned west. Those recommending caution had won out. Instead of returning to Washington the President would simply fly on—destination, for the time being, undecided.

In the skies to the north, and even before the Pentagon was hit, the crisis had become yet more serious. Unknown to the President, unknown to anyone at the White House, and once again as predicted in the children's story at the Sarasota school, there was more to come.

SIX

A T HOME IN NEW JERSEY, A WOMAN NAMED MELODIE HOMER HAD been worried by the television pictures from the World Trade Center. Her concern was for her husband, Leroy, copilot that morning on United 93, a Boeing 757 flying from Newark to San Francisco. Through a contact at the airline, Mrs. Homer sent him a text message asking if all was well.

That message was quickly followed by another. As Flight 93 cruised 35,000 feet over eastern Ohio, it received the warning dispatcher Ballinger was by now sending to all United aircraft: "Beware any cockpit intrusion—two a/c [aircraft] hit World Trade Center."

Captain Jason Dahl was evidently nonplussed. "Ed," he messaged back, "confirm latest mssg plz." It was 9:26, and clarification came swift and savage.

At 9:28, the sound of mayhem crackled over the radio from Flight 93. Cleveland control heard a shout of "Mayday!"; then, "Hey! Get out of here!"; and finally, sounds of physical struggle. Thirty-two seconds later, more fighting. Again, three times: "Get out of here! . . . Get out of here! . . . Get out of here!" And screaming.

Melodie Homer never would receive the reassuring reply for which she had hoped. Ballinger's warning had been in vain, and there would be no more legitimate transmissions from Flight 93.

Instead, at 9:32, came a stranger's voice, panting as though out of breath. It intoned: "Ladies and gentlemen. Here the captain. Please sit down. Keep remaining sitting. We have a bomb on board. So sit." Some investigators would surmise that lack of familiarity with the communications system led this hijack pilot—and, earlier, his accomplice on Flight 11—to transmit not to the passengers as intended, but to ground control.

Though the United pilots could no longer transmit, we know a good deal of what went on in the cockpit. Unlike voice recorders on board the three other hijacked flights, all either never found or irreparably damaged, Flight 93's Cockpit Voice Recorder survived. So did the Flight Data Recorder. Though often difficult to interpret, the voice recorder made for a unique partial record of the final thirty-one minutes aboard the plane.

The cockpit recording began four minutes into the hijack, as the hijacker "captain" tried to tell passengers to remain seated. The microphones picked up a clattering sound, followed by the voice of someone giving orders: "Don't move . . . Come on. Come . . . Shut up! . . . Don't move! . . . Stop!"

Then the sound of an airline seat moving, and more commands: "Sit, sit, sit down! . . . Sit down!" More of the same, and a voice repeating in Arabic, "That's it, that's it . . ." Then in English, loudly, "SHUT UP!" Someone other than the terrorists was alive in the cockpit, and evidently captive.

Though one cannot know for sure, the person being told to sit down and shut up was almost certainly one of the female flight attendants. Perhaps she was senior attendant Deborah Welsh, who spent much of her time in First Class. Or perhaps she was Wanda Green, who was also assigned to the front of the airplane. Some United attendants carried a key to the cockpit, and one key was usually kept in the forward galley. By arrangement with Captain Dahl, reportedly, his attendants could also gain access to the cockpit by means of a coded knock. Welsh, aged forty-nine, was a veteran with a reputation for being tough. She had once managed to shove a drunken male passenger back into his seat. Green, the same age as Welsh, doubled as a real estate agent and had two grown children. One of these two attendants was likely used to gain access to the cockpit.

The woman in the hijackers' hands did not keep quiet or sit down. A minute into the series of orders to the captive, a terrorist's voice is heard to intone in Arabic the Basmala: "In the name of Allah, the Most Merciful, the Most Compassionate." This is an invocation used frequently by observant Muslims, often before embarking on some action.

Next on the recording, the man exclaims: "Finish, no more. NO MORE!" and "Stop, stop, stop, STOP!" Repeatedly: "No! No, no, no, NO!" Time and time again, frantically: "Lie down! . . . DOWN! . . . Down, down, down . . . Come on, sit down, sit!"

For two minutes of this, the captive has not spoken. Now, however, a female American voice is heard for the first time. She begs, "Please, please, please . . ." Then, again ordered to get down, she pleads, "Please, please, don't hurt me . . . Oh, God!"

According to Deborah Welsh's husband, the attendant had spoken of Muslim terrorists with scorn, thought them cowards. If the captive in the cockpit was Welsh, perhaps she now tried an acid response. After another minute of being told to stay down, the female voice on the recording asks, "Are you talking to me?" Her reward, within moments, is violence.

Barely has the hijacker started in again on his mantra of "Down, down!" than the woman is heard pleading, "I don't want to die." She says it three times, her cries accompanied by words—or sounds—that are blanked out in the transcript as released. Then, the transcript notes, there is the "sound of a snap . . . a struggle that lasted for few seconds." Moments later, a voice in Arabic says, "Everything is fine. I finished." The woman's voice is not heard again.

Two minutes after the silencing of the attendant, the terrorist pilot tried again to make an announcement to the passengers. He asked that passengers remain seated, adding this time: "We are going back to the airport . . . we have our demands. So, please remain quiet."

About a minute later, at 9:40, a surviving flight attendant on board got through to Starfix, United's maintenance facility in California. This was Sandra Bradshaw, probably seated toward the rear of the plane in Coach. Those who handled the call thought she sounded "shockingly calm" as she told of hijackers, armed with knives, on the flight deck and in the cabin. Bradshaw said that a fellow flight attendant had been "attacked" and—as relayed to United Airlines Operations by a Starfix operator—that "knives were being held to the crew's throats."

It may be that Captain Dahl and copilot Homer were not killed at once. Well into the hijack, the voice recorder transcript shows that a "native English-speaking male" in the cockpit says—or perhaps groans—"Oh, man! . . ." A few minutes later a hijacker is heard saying in Arabic, " . . . talk to the pilot. Bring the pilot back."

A flight attendant—perhaps CeeCee Lyles, who also worked in Coach—at one point passed word that the hijackers had "taken the pilot and the copilot out" of the cockpit. They were "lying on the floor bleeding" in First Class. It was not clear whether the pilots were dead or alive.

Did the hijackers try to get the pilots, already wounded, to help with the controls? Did they then move them to the forward passenger area and leave them lying there? There is no way to know.

FAR BELOW, ALL WAS CHAOS. At the very moment that the attendant in 93's cockpit had fallen ominously silent—all unknown to those wrestling with the crisis on the ground—Flight 77 had slammed into the Pentagon. On his first day of duty in the post, FAA national operations manager Ben Sliney and his senior colleagues had no way of knowing what new calamity might be imminent.

A Delta flight on its way from Boston to Las Vegas missed a radio call, triggering suspicion. Was this another hijack? Boston had been the point of departure for two of the planes already attacked. Then word reached the FAA Command Center that Flight 93 might have a bomb on board.

At 9:25, Sliney had ordered a nationwide "ground stop," prohibiting any further takeoffs by civilian aircraft. At 9:42, when the Command Center learned of the crash into the Pentagon, FAA officials together decided to issue a command unprecedented in U.S. aviation history. Sliney reportedly boomed, "Order everyone to land! . . . Regardless of destination. Let's get them on the ground."

There were at that moment some 4,540 commercial and civilian planes in the air or under American control. For the more than two hours that followed, controllers and pilots would work to empty the sky of aircraft. It was the one drastic action that might avert fresh disaster.

By 12:16, the FAA was able to inform government agencies that all commercial flights had landed or been diverted away from U.S. airspace.

BACK IN WASHINGTON, Clarke's videoconference had finally gotten under way at about 9:37. Extraordinarily, though, it would be an hour before the Defense Department fielded anyone involved in handling the situation. Secretary Rumsfeld himself was out of touch, as noted, having headed outside to view the carnage at the Pentagon.

Absent anyone with a real grasp of what was going on—let alone expertise in how to deal with it—the first matter discussed in the videoconference had been not the crisis itself but the safety of the President and Vice President. In case they were killed or incapacitated, contingency plans were in place for those next in line to the presidency to be taken to a secret underground shelter outside Washington. Speaker of the House Dennis Hastert and Senator Robert Byrd, president pro tempore of the Senate, third and fourth in line, would soon be rushed to the shelter.

All over the capital, people were now pouring out of office buildings. Thousands rushed to get out of the downtown area. The Secret Service ordered an evacuation of nonessential personnel from the White House, and departure—already under way—became headlong flight. Agents yelled at women to take off their high heels and run, and the sidewalks were soon littered with shoes.

Rumor took hold. "CNN says car bomb at the State Department. Fire on the Mall near the Capitol," read a note passed to Clarke. There was no fire on the Mall. Vietnam veteran Richard Armitage, the deputy secretary representing the Department of State on the videoconference, had a blunt response when asked about the "car bomb." "Does it fucking look," he asked, looming large on the monitor, "as if I've been bombed?"

TO THE NORTH, in New York City, humor survived in the midst of suffering. A firefighter in the North Tower—on the way up—noticed a fellow coming down toting an odd piece of salvage, a golf club. "Hey!" exclaimed the fireman, "I saw your ball a few flights down." There were bizarre sights, too. Officers moving from floor to floor found a few people still hard at work at their computers—blind to the peril.

As in Washington, rumors flew. "There's another plane in the air," a senior fireman hollered into his radio. "Everybody stay put . . . We don't know what's going on." A police sergeant told a firefighter, "They hit the White House. And we have another inbound coming at us now." "Yeah," a radio dispatcher confirmed, "another one inbound. Watch your back."

There was no third hijacked airplane heading to New York. Some in the North Tower, meanwhile, were still unaware that even one airplane had hit the building. "What happened?" enquired Keith Meerholz, who had escaped with minor burns. "A plane hit each tower," a fireman confided, "but don't tell anyone." He did not want evacuation to become panic.

For those still alive on the higher floors of the tower, the grim ordeal continued. They were stranded, unable to go down—because of blocked stairways and jammed elevators—or up, with the faint prospect of rescue by helicopter, because of the locked doors.

Down on the 27th floor, from which most workers would escape, a man in a wheelchair named Ed Beyea waited patiently with Abe Zemanowitz, a colleague who had stayed protectively at his side. So far below the point of impact, with emergency services on the scene, real danger perhaps seemed remote. Yet neither man would survive.

Outside, paramedic Carlos Lillo was crying as he worked. His wife, Cecilia, worked on the tower's 64th floor, and he was frantically worried about her. Cecilia would get safely down and out of the building. Carlos, who lost touch with his comrades, died.

The dying had begun in a horrific way for the firefighters. "The Chief said, 'You're going into the lobby command post,'" Paul Conlon remembered. "He pointed to the entrance of Two World Trade Center [the South Tower] . . . It was probably two hundred yards . . . There were people jumping . . . Dan Suhr said something like, 'Let's make this quick . . . ' We got about halfway there, and Dan gets hit by a jumper."

Daniel Suhr, aged thirty-seven, had been with an engine company from Brooklyn. "It was as if he exploded. It wasn't like you heard something falling and you could jump out of the way . . . We go to pick him up. He's a big guy . . . Someone picked up his helmet . . . One of the guys says, 'He still has a pulse.' . . . I called the Mayday . . . The guys were doing CPR. The ambulance came up pretty quickly."

Suhr, dead on arrival at St. Vincent's Hospital, was the first firefighter to die, first on a list that, it would soon become clear, was to be numbingly long.

Communications, crucial to any firefighting operation, failed dismally that day. "We didn't have a lot of information coming in," Chief Joe Pfeifer recalled of the Command Center in the North Tower lobby. According to the Fire Department's own investigation, the portable radios in use on 9/11 did not "work reliably in high-rise buildings without having their signals amplified or rebroadcast by a repeater system."

"We didn't receive any reports of what was seen from the helicopters," Pfeifer said. "It was impossible to know what was done on the upper floors, whether the stairwells were intact or not." "People watching on TV," Deputy Chief Peter Hayden said, "had more knowledge of what was happening a hundred floors above us than we did in the lobby."

As their chiefs worked blind, men struggled up the North Tower weighed down by equipment. Company followed company on the strenuous ascent into the unknowable. Of those they had come to rescue, some 1,500 souls had already died or were going to die, those trapped above the impact zone and the injured, handicapped, severely obese, or the elderly, for whom movement was difficult. Of the roughly 7,500 civilians who had been in the North Tower before the attack, however, 6,000 would manage to leave the building by 10:00 A.M.

Of perhaps 7,000 people in the South Tower, some 6,000 are thought to have made their way to safety by 9:30. Of about a thousand who remained, 600 would die.

Brian Clark and Stanley Praimnath, the man Clark had pulled from the wreckage on the 81st floor of the South Tower, had continued to make their painful way down. Slithering at first over ceiling tiles and sheet rock, they sloshed through water, groped through smoke, hurried past fingers of flame. Then the way seemed clear for the long trudge down to safety. "Let's slow down," Clark said as they reached the mid-20s. "We've come this far. There's no point in breaking an ankle." There no longer seemed any need to rush.

High above, hope of escape had withered. Sean Rooney, an Aon insurance executive, had tried to reach the roof and been defeated by the locked doors. From the 105th floor, on the phone to his wife, Beverly, he said, "The smoke is very thick . . . the windows are getting hot." Some two hundred other people were trapped in a nearby conference room.

Below, too far below, firefighters were still climbing, climbing. One group, that reached the 70th floor, found numerous victims with serious injuries. Chief Orio Palmer, who got to the 78th floor, reported that there were many "Code Ones"—firefighterspeak for dead. Palmer could see pockets of fire but, speaking as though there would be time to do the job, said he thought it should be possible to put them out.

Emergency operators had continued to log piteous calls:

09:32 105 FLR—PEOPLE TRAPPED—OPEN ROOF TO GAIN ACCESS

09:36 FC STS THEY ARE STUCK IN THE ELEVATORS . . . STS THEY ARE DYING

09:40 MC STS PEOPLE PASSING OUT

09:42 PEOPLE STILL JUMPING OFF THE TOWER

09:39 FC MELISSA STS FLOOR VERY HOT NO DOOR STS SHE'S GOING TO DIE . . . STILL ON PHONE . . . WANT TO CALL MOTHER

Emergency workers in the South Tower lobby were overwhelmed by the number of injured people who could go no further.

Outside, butchered corpses. "Some of them had no legs," said Roberto Abril, a paramedic, "some of them had no arms. There was a torso with one leg, with an EMS jacket on top. I guess somebody just wanted to cover it. We kept going back, but at one point it was useless because most of the people that could get out were already walking."

EARLY THAT MORNING, a handful of high-ranking firemen had pondered the unthinkable. How long would the fires burn on the upper floors, chief of safety Al Turi wondered, before there were partial collapses? Three hours, perhaps? He shared his concern with chief of department Peter Ganci and other colleagues. "The potential and the reality of a collapse," deputy division chief Peter Hayden said, was discussed early on. "I think we envisioned a gradual burning of the fire for a couple of hours and then a very limited type of collapse—the top fifteen or twenty floors all folding in."

Rick Rescorla, security chief for Morgan Stanley, saw it coming from the start. "Everything above where that plane hit is going to collapse," he forecast right after the strike on the North Tower, "and it's going to take the whole building with it." He ordered his staff to evacuate at once, even though they were based in the South Tower— at the time still undamaged.

When the top of the South Tower in turn became an inferno, the same thought occurred to firefighter Richard Carletti. "Tommy," he told a colleague as they stood staring upward, "this building is in danger of collapse."

Only months earlier, Frank De Martini, construction manager for the New York Port Authority, had dismissed the notion of one of the towers collapsing. "I believe the building probably could sustain multiple impacts of jetliners because this structure is like the mosquito netting on your screen door," he said in an interview. "And the jet plane is just a pencil puncturing the screen netting. It really does nothing to the screen netting . . . The building was designed to have a fully loaded 707 crash into it."

An early design study had indeed suggested that the Trade Center would survive were a Boeing 707, the largest airliner of the day—"low on fuel and at landing speeds"—to strike one of the towers. Now, the buildings had been hit by far larger, far more powerful, 767s heavily laden with fuel. On 9/11, De Martini became concerned early on, and asked that structural inspectors be summoned. He was himself to die that day.

By about 9:50, photographs analyzed much later would show, the South Tower's 83rd floor gave the appearance of drooping down over the floor below. Video footage showed a stream of molten metal cascading from a window opening near one corner. A minute later, a police helicopter pilot warned that there were "large pieces of debris hanging" from the South Tower. They looked as though they were about to fall.

Even earlier, at 9:37, a man on the 105th floor of the South Tower had called 911 with a frantic message. As regurgitated ten minutes later by a computer, it read in part:

STS FLOOR UNDERNEATH—COLLAPSE

In the welter of calls pouring in, that message went unread—or misread. The 911 caller had in fact been referring to floors beneath him, and he had used the past tense. The floors beneath him, "in the 90-something," had *already* collapsed.

That word, from many mouths, and from early on.

Collapse.

SEVEN

FOUR HUNDRED MILES AWAY, OVER OHIO, THREE DOZEN OTHER civilians remained in their airborne purgatory. From about 9:30, for some thirty minutes, fourteen passengers and crew members of United Flight 93 managed to telephone either loved ones or operators on the ground.

The first to do so long enough to have a significant conversation, public relations man Mark Bingham, got through to his aunt's home in California. "This is Mark," he began. "I want to let you guys know that I love you, in case I don't see you again." Then: "I'm on United Airlines, Flight 93. It's being hijacked."

Two other callers from the plane not only provided information but gleaned vital news from those they phoned—news that may have influenced their actions in the minutes that followed. Tom Burnett, chief operating officer for a medical devices firm, made a number of brief calls to his wife, Deena. Speaking quietly, he asked her to contact the authorities, and told her that a male passenger had been stabbed—

later that he had died. A woman, perhaps a flight attendant, was being held at knife point, and the hijackers claimed they had a bomb.

Jeremy Glick, a salesman for an Internet services company, also managed to phone. In a long conversation with his wife, Lyz, Glick said the hijackers had "put on these red headbands. They said they had a bomb . . . they looked Iranian." The "bomb" was in a red box, he said. The couple told each other how much they loved each other. Glick said, "I don't want to die," and his wife assured him that he would not. She urged him to keep a picture of her and their eleven-week-old daughter in his head, to think good thoughts.

Burnett's wife, who had been watching the breaking news on television, told him that two planes had crashed into the World Trade Center. "My God," he responded, "it's a suicide mission." By the time he phoned a third time, after news of the crash into the Pentagon, she told him about that, too. Burnett seems to have been seated beside Glick, and apparently relayed all this information to him.

Were they to do nothing, the two men must have agreed, they were sure to die anyway when the hijackers crashed the plane. They resolved to fight for their lives. "A group of us," Burnett told his wife, "are getting ready to do something." "I'm going to take a vote," Glick said on his call. "There's three other guys as big as me and we're thinking of attacking the guy with the bomb."

So began the minutes of brave resistance, the clearly defined act of courage that has lived on in the national memory. Glick and others were equipped in more ways than one to confront the hijackers. He was six foot one and a former college judo champion. Burnett, at six foot two, had played quarterback for his high school football team. He admired strong leaders, had busts of Lincoln, Theodore Roosevelt, and Churchill in his office, liked Hemingway's books and Kipling's poetry. Mark Bingham was a huge man, six foot four and at thirty-one still playing rugby. A few years earlier, he had fended off a mugger who had a gun. His mother got the impression, as he talked from Flight 93, that her son was talking "confidentially" with a fellow passenger. She felt that "maybe someone had organized a plan."

At 9:42, a GTE-Verizon supervisor based near Chicago began handling a call from yet another powerfully built Flight 93 passenger. Todd Beamer, a star Oracle software salesman, was married with two sons, and his wife was expecting again. He first dialed his home number, but either failed to get through or thought better of it. Instead, explaining that he did not want to upset his pregnant wife, he asked phone supervisor Lisa Jefferson to pass on a loving message.

As they talked, Beamer suddenly exclaimed, "Shit! . . . Oh, my God, we're going down . . . Jesus help us." From the passengers around Beamer came prolonged shrieks of terror. Then he said, "No, wait. We're coming back up. I think we're okay now."

Today we have an explanation for those moments of panic. The Flight Data Recorder shows that, as Beamer and operator Jefferson talked on, the plane had gone into a rapid descent.

Shaken, Beamer asked Jefferson to say the Lord's Prayer with him. "Our Father, who art in heaven . . ." Across the airwaves, they prayed together. Then Beamer began to recite the Twenty-third Psalm. "The Lord is my shepherd; I shall not want . . . Yea, though I walk through the valley of the shadow of death . . ."

Just before Beamer and the operator had begun talking, Cleveland control lost Flight 93's transponder, the signal that indicates an airplane's location and altitude. "We just lost the target on that aircraft," controller John Werth exclaimed, and began struggling to find it on radar. He was in contact, too, with an executive jet still in flight in the area, which reported sighting 93. At 9:55, the recovered flight recorder shows, the hijacker pilot dialed in a navigational aid relating to the plane's direction. He was heading, it indicated, for Washington, D.C.

For some six minutes, a female passenger named Marion Britton had been talking to a friend on one of the seatback phones. She said she thought the plane was turning and going to crash. There were sounds of screaming again, and the plane did turn. But there was no crash, not yet.

Jeremy Glick, still on the phone to his wife, Lyz, said, "I know I could take the guy with the bomb." Then, joking—he had mentioned that the hijackers had knives—"I still have my butter knife from breakfast."

Todd Beamer, continuing his conversation with GTE supervisor Jefferson, told her that he and a few others were getting together "to jump the guy with the bomb." Was he sure that was what he wanted to do? "Yes," came the response. "I'm going to have to go out on faith . . . I don't have much of a choice."

There was, it seems, more to the passengers' plan than merely overpowering the hijackers. If the legitimate pilots were out of action, that alone would have been pointless. Beamer, however, talked as if there was someone on the plane who could act as pilot if they overpowered the hijackers. He gave Jefferson "the impression their plan would be to try to land it safely."

There was indeed a pilot among the passengers. Donald Greene, a senior executive of Safe Flight Instrument Corporation, was licensed to fly single-engine four-seaters or copilot a King Air twin-engine turboprop, and flew regularly. To fly and land a Boeing 757 like Flight 93, though, with its complex systems and massive power—40,200 pounds of thrust—would have been another matter. Could Greene have pulled off such a feat? The weather, a key factor for any pilot flying visually rather than on instruments, was perfect, with excellent visibility. It was possible, given time and painstaking instructions radioed from the ground, that a pilot with Greene's experience could do it. Those hoping to overpower the hijackers well knew, after all, that they had nothing to lose.

The plane was flying erratically again. Operator Jefferson heard the sounds of an "awful commotion": raised voices, more screams. Then: "Are you guys ready?" and Todd Beamer's voice saying, "Let's roll!"—a phrase that, in family life, he liked to use to get his children moving.

"OK," Jeremy Glick told Lyz, "I'm going to do it." His wife told him he was strong and brave, that she loved him. "OK," he said again. "I'm going to put the phone down. I'm going to leave it here and I'm going to come right back to it." Lyz handed the phone to her father, ran to the bathroom, and gagged.

For some minutes, passenger Elizabeth Wainio, a Discovery Channel store manager, had been on the line to her mother. She had been quiet, her breathing shallow—as if she were already letting go, her mother thought. Her deceased grandmothers were waiting for her, Wainio said. Then: "They're getting ready to break into the cockpit. I have to go. I love you. Goodbye."

Sandra Bradshaw, the flight attendant who had earlier phoned to alert the airline, now got through to her husband. She was in the galley, she said, boiling water for the passengers to throw on the hijackers. Then, "Everyone's running up to first class. I've got to go. Bye . . ."

CeeCee Lyles, Bradshaw's fellow crew member, also got through to her husband, told him rapidly about the hijacking, that she loved him. Then, "I think they're going to do it. Babe, they're forcing their way into the cockpit . . ."

The Cockpit Voice Recorder registered the moment the hijackers realized what was happening. At just before 9:58, a hijacker asks, "Is there something? . . . A fight?" There is a knock on the door, followed by sounds of fighting. Then, in Arabic, "Let's go, guys! Allah is Greatest. Allah is Greatest. Oh guys! Allah is Greatest . . . Oh Allah! Oh Allah! Oh the most Gracious!" Then, loudly, "Stay back!"

A male voice, a native-English-speaking voice that Tom Burnett's wife has recognized as that of her husband, is heard saying, "In the cockpit. In the cockpit."

Followed by a voice exclaiming, in Arabic, "They want to get in there. Hold, hold from the inside . . . Hold."

Then, from several English speakers in unison, "Hold the door . . ." And from a single English speaker, "Stop him," followed repeatedly by "Sit down! Sit down!" Then, again from an English speaker, "Let's get them . . ."

Flight 93, now down to five thousand feet, had begun rolling left and right. The pilot of a light aircraft, on a mapping assignment for the Pennsylvania Department of Agriculture, saw the airliner at about this moment. "The wings started to rock," he recalled. "The rocking stopped and started again. A violent rocking back and forth."

Jeremy Glick's father-in-law, listening intently on the phone his daughter had handed him, now heard screams in the background. On the Cockpit Voice Recorder, there is the sound of combat continuing. Then, in Arabic:

"There is nothing . . . Shall we finish it off?"

"No. Not yet."

"When they all come, we finish it off."

Then, from Tom Burnett: "I am injured."

The Flight Data Recorder indicates that the plane pitched up and down, climbed to ten thousand feet, turned. Glick's father-in-law, phone clapped to his ear, heard more shrieks, muffled now, like those of people "riding on a roller coaster."

In Arabic, on the voice recorder, "Oh Allah! Oh Allah! Oh Gracious!"

In English, "In the cockpit. If we don't, we'll die!"

In Arabic, "Up down. Up down . . . Up down!"

From a distance, perhaps from Todd Beamer, "Roll it!"

Crashing sounds, then, in Arabic, "Allah is the greatest! Allah is the greatest! . . . Is that it? I mean, shall we pull it down?"

"Yes, put it in it, and pull it down."

"Cut off the oxygen! Cut off the oxygen! Cut off the oxygen! . . . Up down. Up, down . . . Up down."

More violent noises, for as long as a minute, then—apparently by a native English speaker: "Shut them off! . . . Go! . . . Go! . . . Move! . . . Move! . . . Turn it up."

In Arabic, "Down, down . . . Pull it down! Pull it down! DOWN!"

Apparently from an English speaker, "Down. Push, push, push, push, push . . . push."

In Arabic, "Hey! Hey! Give it to me. Give it to me . . . Give it to me. Give it to me . . . Give it to me . . . Give it to me . . . Give it to me . . . Give it to me."

Intermittent loud "air noise" on the cockpit recorder.

Moments later, in Arabic, "Allah is the greatest! Allah is the greatest! Allah is the greatest! Allah is the greatest! Allah is the greatest!"

Sounds of further struggle, and a loud shout by a native English speaker, "No!!!"

Two seconds later, in Arabic, in a whisper now, "Allah is the greatest! Allah is the greatest! Allah is the greatest! Allah is the greatest!"

Jeremy Glick's father-in-law, still listening on the ground, heard high-pitched screams coming over the line Glick had left open when he left to join the rush to the cockpit. Then "wind sounds" followed by banging noises, as though the phone aboard the plane was repeatedly banging on a hard surface.

After that, silence on the phone. Silence on the Cockpit Voice Recorder. Then, in less than a second, the recording ended.

NEAR THE LITTLE TOWN of Shanksville, Pennsylvania, a man working in a scrapyard had seen an airliner, flying low but seemingly trying to climb, just clear a nearby ridge. The assistant chief of Shanksville's volunteer fire department had been talking on the phone with his sister, who said she could see a large airplane "nosediving, falling like a stone." A witness who saw it from his porch said it made a "sort of whistling" noise.

Half a mile away, another man saw the final plunge. It was "barely

United Airlines Flight #93 Cockpit Voice Recorder Transcript

Key:
Bolded text = English translation from Arabic

10:00:06	**There is nothing.**
10:00:07	**Is that it? Shall we finish it off?**
10:00:08	**No. Not yet.**
10:00:09	**When they all come, we finish it off.**
10:00:11	**There is nothing.**
10:00:13	Unintelligible.
10:00:14	*Ahh.*
10:00:15	*I'm injured.*
10:00:16	Unintelligible.
10:00:21	*Ahh.*
10:00:22	**Oh Allah. Oh Allah. Oh Gracious.**
10:00:25	*In the cockpit. If we don't, we'll die.*
10:00:29	**Up, down. Up, down, in the** *cockpit.*
10:00:33	**The** *cockpit.*
10:00:37	**Up, down. Saeed, up, down.**
10:00:42	*Roll it.*
10:00:55	Unintelligible.
10:00:59	**Allah is the Greatest. Allah is the Greatest.**
10:01:01	Unintelligible.
10:01:08	**Is that it? I mean, shall we pull it down?**
10:01:09	**Yes, put it in it, and pull it down.**
10:01:10	Unintelligible.
10:01:11	**Saeed.**
10:01:12	*. . . engine . . .*
10:01:13	Unintelligible.
10:01:16	**Cut off the oxygen.**

fifty feet above me," he said, "rocking from side to side. Then the nose suddenly dipped and it just crashed . . . There was this big fireball and then a huge cloud of smoke."

It was 10:03. Thirty-five minutes had passed since the hijackers struck, four minutes since the passengers counterattacked.

The grave of Flight 93 and the men and women it had carried was an open field bounded by woods on the site of a former strip mine.

"Where's the plane crash?" thought a state police lieutenant, one of the first to reach the scene. "All there was was a hole in the ground and a smoking debris pile." The crater was on fire, and the plane itself had seemingly vanished. On first inspection, there seemed to be few items on the surface more than a couple of feet long. The voice recorder, recovered days later, would be found buried twelve feet under the ground. There were no bodies, it appeared, only shreds of clothing hanging from the trees. For a while, a white cloud of "sparkly, shiny stuff like confetti" floated in the sky.

Three hundred miles away in the little town of Cranbury, New Jersey, Todd Beamer's wife, Lisa, saw the first pictures of the crash site on television and knew her husband was dead.

In Windham, New York, someone told Jeremy Glick's wife, Lyz, that there might be survivors. Then her father returned from the garden, where—at the request of the FBI—he had kept open the line on which Jeremy had called. He had waited, waited, for an hour and a half. Now, as he came back in, Lyz saw that her father was weeping.

Hundreds of miles apart, the two wives, now widows, sank to their knees in grief. Sudden, unforeseeable grief was invading homes across the country, across the world.

EIGHT

At the Trade Center in New York, unseen by the cameras, a lone fire chief was grappling with the possibility for which no one had planned. John Peruggia, of Medical Services, was at the mayor's Office of Emergency Management—in normal times, the city's crisis headquarters.

By an irony of history, though, the office was located in the Trade Center's Building 7. That was too close to the North Tower, and Building 7 had been evacuated within an hour of the initial strike. Peruggia was one of a handful of officials who remained. He was still there, standing in front of the building and giving instructions to a group of firefighters, when an engineer—he thought from the Building Department—made a stunning prediction.

Structural damage to the towers, the official told him, was "quite significant . . . the building's stability was compromised . . . the North Tower was in danger of a near imminent collapse."

This was a warning Peruggia knew he had to pass urgently to the very top, to chief of department Ganci, now at his command post opposite the North Tower. With the usual command and control system out of action, the only way to get word to him was the old-fashioned way—by runner. Peruggia's aide that day, EMT Richard Zarrillo, set off on a hazardous five-hundred-yard journey.

AROUND THAT TIME, Brian Clark and Stanley Praimnath, on the final lap of their escape from the South Tower, reached the concourse at plaza level. "We stared, awestruck," Clark remembered. "What we looked at was, normally, a flowing fountain, vendors with their wagons . . . tourists . . . a beautiful 'people place.' Yet this area, several acres, was dead . . . a moonscape . . . it looked like it had been deserted for a hundred years."

No one was running or obviously panicking. Clark and his companion were told to proceed "down to the Victoria's Secret shop, turn right, and exit by the Sam Goody store." Then a policeman urged them to get moving and not look up. They ran a block or so, and turned to look back. "You know," Praimnath said, "I think those buildings could go down."

"No way," Clark replied. "Those are steel structures."

HIGH IN THE TOWER the two men had just escaped, an Aon Insurance vice president named Kevin Cosgrove was on the phone to a 911 operator.

> COSGROVE: Lady, there's two of us in this office . . . 105. Two Tower. We're not ready to die, but it's getting bad . . . Smoke really bad . . .
> FIRE DEPARTMENT OPERATOR (joining the call): We're getting there. We're getting there.
> COSGROVE: Doesn't feel like it, man. I got young kids . . . I can barely breathe now. I can't see . . . We're young men. We're not ready to die.
> 911 OPERATOR: Okay, just try to hang in there.

On the same floor, Cosgrove's colleague Sean Rooncy was still on the line to his wife, Beverly. Neither of them now hoped for rescue. "I think," Beverly said, "that we need to say goodbye."

• • •

FAR BELOW, on the ground near the towers, EMT Zarrillo completed his dangerous run to get to Chief Ganci and began blurting out the warning from Chief Peruggia. "Listen . . . the message I was given was that the buildings are going to collapse. We need to get our people out."

"Who the fuck," Ganci had time to say, "told you that?"

At that moment, Zarrillo would recall, there was "this thunderous, rolling roar."

FIREFIGHTER RICHARD CARLETTI, peering up at the South Tower, had noted a sudden change. It "started to lean. The top thirty floors leaned over . . . I saw the western wall start to belly out." The columnist Pete Hamill saw the walls "bulge out," and heard "snapping sounds, pops, little explosions." The explosive noises—to some they seemed "real loud"—were followed by a sort of "groaning and grinding."

High in the tower itself, Aon's Kevin Cosgrove finally lost patience with the 911 operator. "Name's Cosgrove," he said. "I must have told you a dozen times already. C.O.S.G.R.O.V.E. My wife thinks I'm all right. I called and said I was leaving the building and that I was fine . . . There are three of us in here . . . Three of us . . . Two broken windows. Oh, God . . . OH . . . !" Against a background of huge noise, Cosgrove screamed. Then the line went dead.

Beverly Rooney, still on the phone to her husband, heard sounds she, too, recalled as sounding like an explosion, followed by a crack, followed by a roaring sound. "The floor fell out from under him," she thought. "It sounded like Niagara Falls. I knew without seeing that he was gone."

Rooney and Cosgrove and so many others were gone. Then, and in little more than the time it takes to read these words, the South Tower itself was gone.

"The entire structure just sank down on to itself with a colossal whoosh," reported the British journalist David Usborne, who had watched from the park in front of City Hall. "For a second, the smoke and dust cleared enough to reveal a stump of the core of the building . . . But the clouds closed in again and nothing more could be seen. All of us simply stood and gaped, hands to our faces."

• • •

IN THE STUDIO AT ABC, Peter Jennings had been juggling the cascade of brutal news, his eye on one live monitor, then another. "It may be," he said, puzzled by the vast new plume of smoke that had appeared where the South Tower had been, "that something fell off the building." Jennings asked a colleague closer to the scene what had happened.

"The second building that was hit by the plane," Don Dahler told him, "has just completely collapsed. The entire building has just collapsed . . . It folded down on itself, and it's not there anymore." The famously unflappable Jennings allowed himself an on-air "My God! My God!" Then, as if in the hope that he had misheard, "The whole side has collapsed?"

Dahler said it again. "The whole building has collapsed . . . There is panic on the streets. Thousands of people running . . . trying to get away."

It was 9:59 A.M. One of the tallest buildings in the world had collapsed in no more than twenty seconds. "From a structure," in the words of a witness, "to a wafer."

IN THE WAKE of the roar there was darkness—an all-enveloping, suffocating, blinding dust cloud—and cloaked in the cloud a mass of humanity, rushing pell-mell for refuge.

Fire chief Ganci and his senior aides, and Zarrillo, the EMT who had brought word of a possible collapse, rushed into the garages of adjacent buildings. "I took ten or fifteen rolling steps into the garage," Zarrillo recalled, "and hugged into a corner, an indentation, and I felt two or three guys get in behind me . . . The dust, the cloud, came rolling in."

Chief Peruggia, still outside Building 7, became aware of the cloud as he answered a woman reporter's question. "I grabbed the female, threw her through the revolving doors of Number 7 . . . Everything came crashing through the front . . . Next thing I remember I was covered in glass and some debris . . . I had shards of glass impaled in my head . . . I was able to get all this debris and rubble off me and cover my face with my coat so that I could breathe. It was very thick dust. You couldn't see."

When the building began to fall, EMT Jody Bell had been strapping a hysterical patient into a stair chair. "Everybody's like, 'Run for your lives!' " he remembered. "She's hyperventilating . . . It's like, a tidal wave of soot and ash coming in my direction. My life flashed before my eyes . . . I started to run—took about ten steps, and the lady started screaming, 'Don't leave me!' . . . I got ahold of myself. 'Wait, what the hell am I doing?' I turned back, got her out of the chair. I said, 'Ma'am, can you run?' She said, 'Yes.' She took off. I've never moved so fast . . . The dust was like snowfall. The cars are covered . . . I'm breathing in mouthfuls . . . The scene was totally blacked out."

Firefighter Timothy Brown had just left the South Tower, where he had seen people—only their legs and feet visible through the door of a stranded elevator—being "smoked and cooked." On his way to fetch medics when the tower fell, he had ducked into the lobby of the Marriott, the eight-hundred-room hotel adjoining the Trade Center.

"Everything started blowing towards us that wasn't nailed down . . . I'm guessing that the wind at its height was around 70, 75 miles an hour . . . You couldn't see anybody . . . You couldn't hear anything. It was becoming our grave . . . I thought it lasted four minutes . . . You could hear an eerie silence at first, and then you could start to hear people starting to move around a little bit, people that were still alive."

Sixteen of some twenty firefighters who had been on a stairwell in the hotel were not alive. The collapsing tower had sliced the Marriott in two.

Spared thanks to their final dash, Brian Clark and Stanley Praimnath had sheltered outside a church. They "stared in awe, not realizing what was happening completely . . . You at least thought people had a chance—until that moment. Then this great tsunami of dust came over . . . I suppose it was a quarter of an inch of dust and ash, everywhere."

To Usborne, the British reporter, the dust was a "huge tidal wave, barrelling down the canyons of the financial district . . . The police went berserk, we went berserk, just running, running for our lives . . . we were in a scene from a Schwarzenegger film . . . thousands of Hollywood extras, mostly in suits for the office, with handbags and briefcases, just tearing through the streets of the city. Every few seconds we would snatch a look behind us."

Columnist Hamill remembered dust blossoming perhaps twenty-five stories high, leaving the street a pale gray wilderness peopled by "all the walking human beings, the police and the civilians, white people and black, men and women . . . an assembly of ghosts. . . . Sheets of paper scattered everywhere, orders for stocks, waybills, purchase orders, the pulverized confetti of capitalism."

INSIDE THE NORTH TOWER, few were even aware of the collapse. "We felt it," one said. "Our tower went six feet to the right, six feet to the left . . . it felt like an earthquake." "You just heard this noise that sounded like the subway train going by," said another, "multiplied by a thousand."

"It didn't register," recalled James Canham, a firefighter who was on the 11th floor. "There was the sound of the wind blowing through the elevator shafts . . . air pressure coming in . . . the entire floor enveloped in dust, smoke . . . Then I had gone right into the stairwell. There had to be twenty people piled up—I mean actually in a pile . . . I told them to grab the railing . . . to grab the belt loop of the person in front of them . . . If it was a woman . . . the bra strap. I told them, 'Hold the bra, with the other hand hold the railing, and make your way down.' Panicking and crying as they were, they were listening . . . on their way . . . coughing . . . disoriented."

On hearing by radio of the South Tower's collapse, police officer David Norman—on the 31st floor—could not comprehend what the operator told him. "To think that a building of one hundred and some stories had fallen was like, you know, not believable . . . He then explained that there was no South Tower, that it was absolutely gone."

A great burst of energy, generated by the fall of the South Tower, had translated into a blast of air and dust shooting into the North lobby and on up into the building. For a while it was pitch black. Debris rained down, fatally for some—including the Fire Department chaplain, Mychal Judge. He died in the lobby, hit on the head by flying debris, as he returned from giving last rites to the dead and dying outside.

Fire chief Pfeifer, still running operations in the lobby, knew nothing at first of the collapse on the other side of the plaza. Thinking that something catastrophic was going on *above* him, though, he decided to pull his men out. Police commanders made the same decision, and an evacuation began.

The order did not reach battalion chief Richard Picciotto, on the

35th floor, but he took the decision on his own initiative. "All FDNY, get the fuck out!" he hollered on his bullhorn. And, over the radio, "We're evacuating, we're getting out, drop your tools, drop your masks, drop everything, get out, get out!"

Outside, meanwhile, Fire Department chief Ganci had sent his command group off in one direction while—with just one colleague— he headed back toward the North Tower. He went back, an aide explained simply, because he "knew that he had men in that building." Some of those men, on the 54th floor, defied the order to evacuate. Intent on continuing to help civilians, they radioed, "We're not fucking coming out."

On the higher floors, civilians and firemen alike now had no chance of survival. For those really high up, it had long been so. Tom McGinnis, a trader with Carr Futures on the 92nd floor, had been trapped behind jammed doors since Flight 11 hit. He and colleagues had long been ankle-deep in water from either burst pipes or the sprinkler system. Now they were forced to the windows to get air. The phones were still working, and McGinnis told his wife he was going to crouch down on the floor. Then the connection was broken.

"What we didn't know," Chief Pfeifer said later, "was that we were running out of time." In the dark and confusion of the lobby, he and other chiefs were for all intents and purposes operating blind. Firefighter Derek Brogan recalled the chaos that greeted him when he got there from above. "There was gas leaking all over the place. The marble was falling on top of us . . . You couldn't see anything."

Brogan stepped outside, to realize it was suddenly "raining" bodies. Fireman Robert Byrne found himself dodging jumpers and falling debris, weaving between corpses "littering the courtyard." "Everything was on fire . . . I took a peek up . . . aluminum was coming down . . . going through thick plate glass like a hot knife through butter."

Pilots in the helicopters, circling above, could see what was coming. As early as five minutes after the South Tower's collapse, a Police Department pilot reported thinking that the North Tower's top floors might collapse. Nine minutes on, another pilot said he thought the tower might not last long. Twenty minutes on, the pilot who had made the first report radioed that the tower was now "buckling and leaning."

In the absence of an effective liaison arrangement between the Police and Fire Departments, this crucial information was not passed on to the firefighters.

AT 10:28, not quite half an hour after the South Tower's slide to ruin, time did run out.

Fireman Carletti, now watching from the safety of a fire truck, saw the antenna atop the North Tower "do a little rock back and forth, and I could just hear the floors pancaking. I heard it for about thirty pancakes . . . boom, boom, boom, boom." As when the first tower had fallen, others spoke of "explosions," "pop, pop, pop" noises, a "thunderous, rumble sound."

Firefighter Dean Beltrami saw "the entire facade starting to buckle . . . Nobody said anything. We just turned and ran." EMT Jody Bell saw the tower "looking like it was going to tip, and there was a piece of the building coming down right on top of me . . . The building was hitting other buildings . . . This time it was worse . . . We were just running . . . I was damn near ready to jump in the river . . . The debris went well into the Hudson. It almost went to Jersey."

"I opened up my eyes," said EMS chief James Basile, "dust and dirt, debris . . . total darkness, I guess for about two, three minutes. I thought, 'I guess this is what it's like to be dead.' Then I heard a woman screaming."

"This beautiful sunny day now turned completely black," said Chief Pfeifer, who survived the fall of the tower. "We were unable to see a hand in front of our faces. And there was an eerie silence."

The 110-story North Tower had become a pile of flaming, noxious rubble—like its twin before it, in about twenty seconds.

THE SILENCE WAS BROKEN by the high-pitched tones of locator alarms, the devices that are triggered when a firefighter goes down and does not move. Three hundred forty-three men of the New York Fire Department would never move again.

The number of firefighters killed on 9/11 was almost a third of the total killed since the department's inception in 1865.

Chief Ganci had been killed near the North Tower, and his body was one of the first to be found. Chief Pfeifer's brother Kevin would be found dead in the rubble, his fireman's pick at his side. Firefighting runs in families in New York, and fathers and sons, brothers and in-laws, would search for fallen comrades and kin for months to come.

Thirty-seven Port Authority police officers, including their superintendent, Fred Morrone, had died. Five of their bodies were found grouped around that of a woman in a steel chair, a device used to carry the disabled. They had died, it seemed, trying to carry her to safety.

The New York Police Department lost twenty-two men—and one female officer. She had brought an injured person out of the South Tower, only to be killed when she went back in to help another.

"THE NUMBER OF CASUALTIES," New York mayor Rudolph Giuliani said, "will be more than any of us can bear." Government officials would at first suggest, in a serious overestimate, that as many as seven thousand people had been killed in the city. The death toll was nevertheless stunningly high.

The number of fatalities in New York was eventually to stand at 2,763. That figure included the people in or near the Twin Towers, the passengers, crew, and hijackers aboard the two flights that crashed into the complex, and firefighters, police, paramedics, and other emergency workers. The highest number of casualties was in the North Tower—1,466, the majority of them above the point of impact—followed by 624 in the South Tower, all but 6 of them above the point of impact. One hundred and fifty-seven people died aboard the two planes.

Rarely mentioned, if at all, is the fact that this was not exclusively an American catastrophe. Five hundred and eleven nationals, perhaps more, from more than two dozen other countries, died in New York. They included dozens of Hispanic immigrants, delivery men, cooks, and dishwashers, with no work permits. They are almost all nameless now, remembered on no memorial.

THE TRADE CENTER COMPLEX rapidly became known as Ground Zero, for good reason. Assault by airplane had transformed it in an hour and forty-two minutes from iconic landmark to sixteen-acre wilderness. "All that remained standing," wrote *Atlantic Monthly* correspondent William Langewiesche, "were a few skeletal fragments . . . vaguely gothic structures that reached like supplicating hands toward the sky. After the dust storms settled, people on the streets of Lower Manhattan were calm. They walked instead of running, talked without shouting, and tried to regain their sense of place and time. Hiroshima is said to have been similar in that detail."

The towers had thrown mighty shards of steel and rubble to the ground and—such was the force involved—beneath it to a depth of thirty feet. Vehicles on the surface were flattened, power and telephone systems crippled, subways and watercourses severely damaged. Even before the collapse, plummeting rubble devastated nearby buildings.

The lesser giants of the complex had been known by numbers. Trade Center 3—the Marriott Hotel—was now wreckage. Great chunks of debris had fallen on Trade Center 7, which collapsed into its own footprint in the late afternoon. Trade Center Buildings 4, 5, and 6 suffered serious damage and were later demolished. Eight more structures, including World Financial Center 2 and 3—American Express—the Winter Garden pavilion, Bankers Trust, a City University of New York building, and Verizon Communications, were damaged but not beyond repair. Tiny St. Nicholas Greek Orthodox Church, in the shadow of the South Tower, had been flattened.

The attackers had succeeded in stopping the engine room of America's economy, if only briefly. Damage to Verizon Communications, gored by Building 7's fall, crippled the electronics that connect the financial markets to the New York Stock Exchange. Exchange chairman Dick Grasso delayed opening the market, then closed it as the strikes escalated. It would not open again until the start of the following week.

Unlike the New York Stock Exchange, located at a relatively safe distance from the Trade Center, its cousin the American Stock Exchange was jolted by the second strike. The towers' collapse left its offices filled with debris and remaining staff—the chairman and the president included—trapped for hours, covered in soot and dust. Seeing the exchange afterward, a leader of commerce would recall loftily, was like "visiting a third world country."

Its communications cut, NASDAQ's corporate offices closed. The New York branch of the Federal Reserve Bank was evacuated, not without a moment of comedy. The building had never before been left unmanned, and no one present knew how to lock up.

Many key financial figures were far from the decision making on the morning of 9/11. The chairman of the Federal Reserve, Alan Greenspan, was in the air halfway across the Atlantic, returning with colleagues from a meeting in Switzerland, when U.S. airspace closed down. His airplane, like others in mid-flight, had to turn back. Frantic calls to the White House eventually got Greenspan back to Washington courtesy of the military, part of the way aboard a U.S. Air Force tanker.

The minders of the American economy wrestled for days with problems ranging from sustaining liquidity to averting the nightmare scenario—potential public panic if the cash at ATM machines ran out, which in turn might spark a run on the banks. New York City, meanwhile, faced the daunting costs that had been inflicted in less than two hours. Reporting a year later, New York's comptroller would calculate the economic cost to the city at between $83 and $95 billion.

ON 9/11, after the second collapse, there was at first a long, empty moment, a vacuum in time. Then the start of an epic, heartrending, recovery operation.

NINE

"AMBULANCES GOING THIS WAY, ESU TRUCKS FLYING DOWN THE street . . . Nobody had any idea what was going on. Where is the command post? Where is staging? We had no radio . . . You looked where you thought the buildings should be, and if they were there, you couldn't see them . . . disorientation . . . I had already seen my third skyline in forty minutes."

Fire Department lieutenant Michael Cahill, on the period after the second Trade Center collapse. A time of "absolute panic . . . absolute panic . . . Most of us were just too tired . . . out of it . . . disorganized . . . Stuff in our eyes, cuts, bruises, equipment lost. Half the people we came with were lost."

Off-duty firefighters, former firefighters, men who worked in construction or salvage, all rushed to Ground Zero to help. One of them, crane operator turned fireman Sam Melisi, was one of the first would-be rescuers to pioneer routes through, over, and under the rubble. He had all the expertise and experience one could wish for, but was forced time and again to retreat.

It dawned on Melisi that the "tremendous devastation" of the Oklahoma City bombing, which he had worked six years earlier, had been nothing compared to this. "Visualize fiftyfold or a hundredfold, no matter where you turned . . . You can never quite prepare for something like this . . . on this magnitude. We started searching . . . We were hoping to find many live victims. But as time went on we realized there weren't going to be that many."

There were only a few. Twenty people were rescued after the collapses, all but one emerging in the first twenty-four hours. Two civilians, trapped at first in what had been a shopping mall beneath the plaza, managed to squeeze out through an opening. Next out were twelve firefighters, a civilian, and a Port Authority policeman—thanks to "the Miracle of Stairway B."

When the North Tower collapsed, Captain Jay Jonas and his crew had been four stories up the stairway, trying to help a woman who could walk no further. Swept away on an avalanche of rubble and steel, Jonas had thought, "This is how it ends." They ricocheted down to certain death, only to find themselves alive—the civilian included—still on or near the stairway.

The difference now was that they were in pitch darkness, at something like ground floor level, in what was rapidly to become known as "the pile." Jonas began hearing radio transmissions from firemen buried elsewhere: "Just tell my wife and kids that I love them." "Mayday. Mayday . . . I'm trapped and I'm hurt bad." The messages gradually petered out, for the men were dying.

Jonas kept sending his own Maydays. "It was a waiting game," he remembered. "We were trapped in there for over three hours . . . I heard one fireman on the radio saying, 'Where's the North Tower?' and I'm thinking to myself, 'We're in trouble if they don't even know where the North Tower is.' " Deep in the rubble, Jonas had no way of knowing the reality evident to everyone outside, that the tower had simply vanished.

He realized the truth only as the dust began to clear, when a beam of sunlight penetrated the darkness. It was coming through a hole that was to prove the group's salvation. "I survived," Jonas thought as he emerged. "All my men survived. And we have this small victory that is within us, that we brought somebody else out with us . . . We had a nice void. We had a nice little pocket. There's got to be hundreds of them. There's got to be a lot of people getting out of here."

In fact only three others were to be rescued. Port Authority engineer Pasquale Buzzelli had plunged down, also on a stairway, from the 22nd floor. The fall reminded him for a moment of an amusement park ride. Then he was hit on the head, saw stars, and fell unconscious. Buzzelli came to three hours later, covered in dust and reclining on a cement slab fifteen feet above the ground, there to be rescued by firemen. His only physical damage, a crushed right foot.

Two Port Authority police officers, Jimmy McLoughlin and William Jimeno, were found not by professional rescue workers but by two former U.S. Marines. Determined to be in the front line, they donned military fatigues, talked their way into Ground Zero, and clambered around hollering: "United States Marines! If you can hear us, yell or tap." After an hour of shouting, a muffled cry came back. The pair summoned help, and rescuers had Jimeno on the surface by midnight. McLoughlin, who was seriously injured, was extracted early the following morning.

There would eventually be an army of rescuers from all over the country, professionals with technical skills, volunteers with a contribution to make—and some who were no help at all. Every city has its cranks, but none outdid the fellow who jumped overboard, early in the aftermath, from a ferry evacuating people to New Jersey. The man then began swimming—back in the direction of the Trade Center. "I thought," he said as he was hauled out, "I could swim over to New York to help people." Not everyone on board wanted him rescued. "Shoot him!" someone shouted. "He may be a terrorist!"

HOSPITALS IN MANHATTAN and beyond, expecting an "onslaught of patients," had rushed to activate their disaster plans. Off-duty personnel, including a busload of surgeons attending a medical conference, dropped what they were doing and offered their services to the Fire Department. The expected flood of injured, however, never materialized. With most of those brought to hospitals released by midnight, the surgeons wound up loading water supplies.

On September 11 and for long afterward they found not survivors, not the injured, only the dead. Cadavers sometimes, but more often mere scraps of humanity. Those who found them saw things they will never forget.

"A person's torso, just no legs, no head, no arms, nothing, just chest and stomach area . . . Then like fifteen feet away I found a head to go with the torso . . . we tagged it."

"People had I-beams [steel joists] through them, and things like that."

"A woman's severed hand. You could still see the engagement ring on her finger . . . The constant smell of burnt flesh."

"The body of a young woman . . . her child underneath . . . an arm they found, a woman's, and when they pried open her fingers they found inside the fist of a baby."

"You couldn't walk more than a few feet in some areas without encountering body parts."

The charnel house that was the Trade Center would over time yield up 21,744 separate human remains. Chief medical examiner Dr. Charles Hirsch, whose task it would be to collect and identify them, was based on First Avenue, only two miles from the Trade Center. He and aides had rushed to a nearby site early on 9/11, to prepare a temporary morgue, and several of them had been injured by flying debris. Those still able to work then initiated the necessary, macabre process that—as this book goes to press—continues still.

Remains were brought to Dr. Hirsch's headquarters as they were found. They were analyzed, borne to a white tent nearby. There, a prayer was spoken over them. Then they were stored in refrigerated trailers pending identification. The operation would eventually require the installation of sixteen trailers.

To Hirsch, it came as no surprise that there should be so few complete bodies and so many thousands of body fragments. "If reinforced concrete was rendered into dust," he said, "it wasn't much of a mystery as to what would happen to people."

More remains would be found as the years passed—some as late as 2009—atop the damaged Deutsche Bank building, in manholes, under a service road at Ground Zero. An assortment of remains, from a complete cadaver dressed in a suit to tiny bone fragments, was found at a landfill on Staten Island, destination of the half million tons of debris removed from the site. The landfill's name, the name it had had since the late 1940s, was Fresh Kills.

Within ten months of 9/11, science and detective work would identify 1,229 of those killed. In the years since, 401 more victims have been identified. It has been an unparalleled forensic achievement. Even so, 1,122 men and women—41 percent of the total who died—remain unidentified. The families of more than a thousand people cannot bury their loved ones.

THERE IS ANOTHER REASON, though, that the true death toll will long remain elusive. Listen again to the voices of those who endured 9/11 on the streets and in the buildings of New York City.

"I see this fifty-, sixty-story dust rolling down the block." "The ambulances looked like they were covered with gray snow . . . so thick you couldn't see a sharp edge from a smooth edge." "People were just full of dust . . . looked like zombies."

"Nobody could breathe. Everything was stuck in their throats and their eyes, mouths, faces, and everything." "Everybody's coughing, breathing in mouthfuls of shit."

"Our face-pieces were on, because the probie [trainee firefighter] was having trouble with chest pains, having difficulty breathing." "My lungs were filling up with this stuff. I don't know what it was. I thought I was going to die." "The sergeant asked me, 'You think we could die from this stuff?' I'm like, 'Right now? No. But eventually? Yes.' "

Less than an hour after the second strike, a Fire Department operator had logged a phone call from a woman on Duane Street, near the Trade Center. At 9:59 the dispatcher noted:

FC—CONCERN ABOUT THE RESPIRATORY EFFECT OF THOSE PARTICLES

The person calling about the "particles" must have come across as a fusspot, her call a mere nuisance. Who had time to think, then, about the bits and pieces falling from the towers and wafting on the breeze? The material spewed out by the towers, however, did have significance—a significance that increased greatly once the towers had fallen and the walls of dust had roared up the canyons of Lower Manhattan.

"Dust" covers many evils. 9/11's dust contained: asbestos (tests after the attacks showed hazardous asbestos levels at sites up to seven blocks from Ground Zero), lead, glass fibers, dioxin, PCBs, and PAHs (potentially carcinogenic chemical compounds) and toxins from perhaps fifty thousand vaporized computers.

New York firefighters had reason, historically, to fear such pollutants. "We lost quite a few firemen back in the seventies in a telephone building fire," remembered Salvatore Torcivia. "They were exposed to PCBs when all the transformers in that building burned and they didn't have the proper equipment to protect themselves. Numerous guys died the first year from cancer. Over the next five to twenty years, all the guys from that job died. The majority went within the first ten years."

Torcivia worked at Ground Zero every day for two weeks. "There's gonna be a lot of people sick from this," he forecast later,

> and not just firemen. I wasn't wearing a mask the whole time . . . They issued us these paper masks used for painting, but they don't stop anything . . . From day one, everyone was complaining of the cough and the sore throats . . . The second day or third day I was getting told by private test groups at the site that the contaminants in the air were off the charts. They were so high they couldn't register them. But we were also being told by the city and the state that everything was within the range where it's not gonna harm anyone. That just wasn't so.

The firefighter coughed as he talked, a cough that seemed to come from deep inside his chest. He had begun having problems within a month of 9/11.

> Going on the normal runs, we noticed that a lot of us were getting winded more easily . . . On regular walk-ups, where I never had a problem before, I thought I was gonna have a heart attack. I couldn't catch my breath . . . I went to the Fire Department surgeon . . . They found out that I've dropped around 40 to 45 percent of my breathing capacity since the last time I was tested . . . I went to see a specialist. He explained to me that all the stuff that got into my body down at Ground Zero—I didn't just inhale it into my lungs and bronchial tubes—I *ingested* it . . . And everything working together is keeping it constantly inflamed and infected . . . There's four to five hundred guys with breathing problems.

Salvatore Torcivia's problems were far from unusual. A 2007 study by the Albert Einstein College of Medicine and the New York City Fire Department noted a huge increase in the number of firefighters suffering from the lung ailment sarcoidosis. Some two thousand fire-fighters had at that point reportedly been treated for serious respira-tory ailments.

"The World Trade Center dust," the college's Dr. David Prezant has noted, "is a combination of the most dense, intense particulate mat-ter [first responders] were ever exposed to in an urban environment."

The respiratory ailments have continued to increase, affecting not only firefighters but policemen, emergency medical personnel, and those who worked on the rubble removed from Ground Zero.

Many have succumbed to their illnesses. In a landmark decision in 2007, the New York medical examiner ruled that the 9/11 dust cloud contributed to the death as early as five months afterward of a young attorney from sarcoidosis. As in the case of all victims of the attacks, the cause of her death was registered as homicide.

According to figures published in late 2008 by the New York con-gressional delegation, 16,000 9/11 responders and 2,700 people who lived near Ground Zero were at that time "sick and under treatment."

Reports in 2009 suggested that some 479 people, from different walks of life, had died from illnesses that may be attributable to the condition of the air during and after the 9/11 attacks. One by one, news reports show, others continue to die.

In late 2010, when deaths from illness among first responders had risen to 664—many of them from causes suspected to be related to 9/11—Congress acknowledged the gravity of the problem.

The James Zadroga 9/11 Health and Compensation Act, named for a New York policeman who had died of pulmonary fibrosis at thirty-four, earmarked $4.2 billion to address the health needs of the long-term victims of 9/11.

"We will never forget the selfless courage demonstrated by the firefighters, police officers, and the first responders who risked their lives to save others," said President Obama when he signed the act. Back in September 2001, concern about the possible dangers of expo-sure to toxic dust and fumes had been swept aside. The Environmen-tal Protection Agency declared after two days that initial tests were "very reassuring." Five days later, Assistant Secretary of Labor John Henshaw said it was "safe to go back to work in New York's financial district." The Stock Exchange reopened on September 17, with EPA administrator Christine Todd Whitman reassuring New Yorkers the next day that their air was "safe to breathe."

There had been pressure from the start, from the very top, to get the financial district up and running. At a National Security Council meeting not twelve hours after the attacks, according to counterterrorism coordinator Richard Clarke, President Bush said, "I want the economy back, open for business right away, banks, the stock market, everything tomorrow."

Those who knew the situation on the ground knew that opening the next day was an impossible fantasy. The President, however, had been removed from the realities.

AFTER HASTILY LEAVING Sarasota airport in Florida, at 9:55 on the morning of 9/11, Bush had spent the rest of the day aboard Air Force One, with brief stops at two U.S. military bases. "The President is being evacuated," press secretary Ari Fleischer told reporters on the plane, "for his safety and the safety of the country."

Key civil and military aides were at Bush's side, but circumstances wreaked havoc with the concept of round-the-clock presidential grasp of the levers of power. For all his power and all the modern technology at his disposal, it is not evident that the President had much influence—if any—on the government's reaction to the day's events.

Accounts conflict mightily as to whether communications aboard Air Force One functioned well or appallingly badly. Bush spoke with Dick Cheney around the time of takeoff, but it is far from clear with whom, and how usefully, he spoke once the plane was airborne. In interviews conducted for the first anniversary of 9/11, chief of staff Andy Card repeatedly emphasized how efficiently the President had been able to communicate with the Vice President, National Security Adviser Condoleezza Rice, Defense Secretary Donald Rumsfeld, Transportation Secretary Norman Mineta, and the military.

Bush himself, though, said it proved difficult—time and again—to get through to Cheney. He recalled pounding his desk on the plane, shouting, "This is inexcusable! Get me the Vice President!" He "could not remain in contact with people," he was to say, "because the phones on Air Force One were cutting in and out." In Washington, senior aide Karen Hughes experienced the same difficulty getting through to the presidential plane. "The military operator came back to me and in—in a voice that sounded very shaken—said, 'Ma'am, I'm sorry. We can't reach Air Force One.' "

Given such contradictions, there is no way of knowing how Bush and Cheney or Bush and anyone else actually interacted that day. That issue, as will be seen, is central to the crucial matter of how the military responded to the hijackings.

Reporters traveling with the President watched the collapse of the towers on flickering television screens. At about 10:30, after the second tower fell, word came from the White House of a "credible," anonymous phone threat to "Angel," the insiders' word for Air Force One. Tension rose accordingly. Armed guards were posted at the cockpit door, and agents checked the identification of almost everyone on board. Reporters were told not to use their cell phones. F-16 fighters were soon to begin escorting Air Force One, and did so for the rest of the day. One escort plane flew so close, the President's press office would state, that Bush saluted through the window—and the F-16 pilot dipped a wing in reply. The warning of a threat to "Angel" had been just a baseless scare, but made a good story.

The President worried aloud about having literally vanished into the blue. "The American people," he reportedly said, "want to know where their dang President is." It was decided that he would land at Barksdale Air Force Base in Louisiana to make a television appearance. "Freedom itself," Bush said in a two-minute taped address at 1:20 P.M., "was attacked this morning by a faceless coward. And freedom will be defended." This was less than the reassurance he had wished to communicate, not least because the tape first hit the airwaves running backward.

Then the President was off again, this time heading for Offutt Air Force Base in Nebraska. Once aboard, in a conversation he did succeed in having with Cheney, Bush said: "We're at war, Dick. We're going to find out who did this and kick their ass." And: "We're not going to have any slap-on-the-wrist crap this time."

A rear admiral at Offutt, the underground headquarters of U.S. Strategic Command, would say he thought the President "very much in control . . . concerned about what was happening . . . calm . . . articulate . . . presidential." In mid-afternoon, Bush took part in a videoconference with National Security Council members in Washington—Cheney, Rumsfeld, Rice, CIA director Tenet, and FBI director Robert Mueller.

The President, however, was by now preoccupied with the thought that his continued absence from the capital made him look bad. The

Secret Service was still advising him to stay away from Washington. His staff wanted him to address the nation again from Offutt. Bush, however, would apparently have none of it.

"I'm not going to do it from an Air Force base," he reportedly said. "Not while folks are under the rubble." And, in another account, "I don't want a tin-horn terrorist to keep me out of Washington." Press secretary Fleischer agreed that the President's whereabouts was becoming "an increasingly difficult issue to deal with."

Air Force One at last made the return trip to the capital. From the helicopter carrying him to the White House, Bush got his first glimpse of the reality of 9/11. There in the evening light was the Pentagon, partly veiled in black smoke, a deep gouge in its west side. "The mightiest building in the world is on fire," Bush muttered, according to Fleischer. "That's the twenty-first century war you've just witnessed." Then he was down, landing on the South Lawn and walking back into the White House almost ten hours after the attacks had begun.

Political Washington had begun to show a brave face to the world. More than a hundred members of Congress had gathered on the steps of the Capitol in a display of unity. "We will stand together," declared Speaker of the House Dennis Hastert—now back on the Hill—and he and colleagues broke into a chorus of "God Bless America." An hour and a half later, once he was anchored back in the Oval Office, Bush delivered a four-minute address to the nation. It is said that he had an audience of eighty million people.

"Evil, despicable acts of terror," the President said, "have filled us with disbelief, terrible sadness, and a quiet, unyielding anger." Though he could not have known it, he ended by citing the same passage from the Twenty-third Psalm to which United 93 passenger Todd Beamer had turned in a moment of terror: "Even though I walk through the valley of the shadow of death, I fear no evil . . ."

The address also included something Bush had added himself just before going on air. "We will make no distinction," he said, after assuring Americans that those behind the attacks would be brought to justice, "between the terrorists who committed these acts and those who harbor them."

Afterward, in the underground bunker where Cheney and others had spent the day, Bush met with key officials—the group he was to call his "war council." The words "al Qaeda" and "Osama bin Laden" had been on everyone's lips for hours, and CIA director Tenet said al Qaeda and the Taliban in Afghanistan were essentially one and the same.

There was talk of reprisals and then, according to counterterrorism coordinator Clarke, Defense Secretary Rumsfeld came out with a remarkable comment. "You know," he said, "we've got to do Iraq."

PRESIDENT BUSH almost always went to bed early, and September 11 was no exception. He balked when the Secret Service asked him and the first lady to spend the night on a bed in the underground bunker, an old pullout couch. "The bed looked unappetizing," he recalled, "so I said no." The couple retired to their usual bedroom in the residence, only to be woken around 11:30 P.M. by a new security alert. "Incoming plane!" an agent told them. "We could be under attack. Come on. Right now!"

The President of the United States, he in T-shirt and running shorts and Mrs. Bush in her robe—with their dogs Barney and Spot—were rushed down to the basement to be confronted again by the unappetizing couch. The "incoming" plane, however, turned out to be merely a chartered airliner bringing FBI reinforcements from the West Coast. Back went the Bushes to their private quarters.

Two hundred and twenty-five miles away in New York City, in the glare of halogen lights, men worked on through the night in the tangle of steel and rubble that had once symbolized American prosperity. They were still looking hopefully for the living, and the hand of one more survivor—the last, as it turned out—would eventually appear through a hole to grasp that of a rescuer. It belonged to a young female clerk who had worked at the Trade Center and, though seriously injured, she was to recover.

That consolation aside, there would henceforth be only the dead, or fragments of the dead.

The pile at the scene of the attacks "heaved and groaned and constantly changed, was capable at any moment of killing again." The air smelled of noxious chemicals, and strange flames shot out of the ground, purple, green, and yellow. Fires were to burn on, underground, for three months to come.

An American apocalypse, a catastrophe with consequences—in blood spilled and global political upheaval—that continue to this day.

DISTRUST AND DECEIT

TEN

ONE CONSEQUENCE, A NATIONAL AND INTERNATIONAL PHENOMENON, is that countless citizens do not believe the story of September 11 as we have just told it.

We have striven in these chapters to recount what is firmly known. We have teased out detail, sorted the reliable from the dross, often gone back to original sources. Yet many would say our account is skewed, too close to the "official version," or just plain wrong.

9/11 is mired in "conspiracy theory" like no previous event in American history—more so even than President John F. Kennedy's assassination. Doubt and disbelief as to what really happened on 9/11, a *Time* magazine writer noted in 2006, is "not a fringe phenomenon. It is a mainstream political reality." By the end of George Bush's first term as President, a more iconoclastic writer—Matt Taibbi at *Rolling Stone*—concluded that Americans had "no dependable authority left to turn to, no life raft in the increasingly perilous informational sea. . . . Joe American has to turn on the Internet and tell himself a story that makes sense to him. What story is he going to tell?"

Americans, University of California history professor Kathryn Olmsted has said, "tend to be particularly receptive to anti-government conspiracy theories." Her study of conspiracy theory notes not only the evidence of the polls—that in 2006 a third of the U.S. population believed the Bush administration was involved in 9/11—but that a majority of that third were aged eighteen to twenty-nine.

Significant, too, given the continuing global upheaval, is the degree of 9/11 conspiracy belief among Arab Americans (of whom there are more than three million), American Muslims, and Arabs worldwide. Taibbi, doing interviews in Dearborn, Michigan, was shocked to hear "well-educated, pious Lebanese Americans regurgitating 9/11 conspiracy theories like they were hard news." One woman he interviewed "could not be budged from her conviction that Bush had bombed the Twin Towers." In much of the Arab world, the author and longtime Middle East resident Jean Sasson has written, "conspiracy theories dominate public opinion."

As recently as 2009, persistent belief in such theories so concerned the U.S. government that it issued a fact sheet for global consumption, seeking to rebut "unfounded . . . popular myths" about 9/11. It was an acknowledgment that the authors of conspiracy theory, the "skeptics" as they like to be characterized, were a force hard to ignore. What are their principal theories and speculations, and is there substance to them?

AT THE CORE of conspiracy theory is the idea that we were all hoodwinked, that what we thought we saw on 9/11 was not the full picture. The Twin Towers may have been struck by airliners filled with passengers—though some doubt even that—but it was not the planes that brought them crashing down. Explosives, planted explosives, had been used to achieve that. The same went for the total collapse later in the day, the skeptics claim, of World Trade Center Building 7. As for the Pentagon, there were claims by some that it had been struck not by a plane but by a missile.

Why perpetrate such gross trickery? The overarching suspicion— for some the conviction—is that people at the heart of the United States government were behind the attacks. The doubters belong, essentially, to one of two schools of thought, broadly defined by the acronyms MIHOP—Made It Happen On Purpose—and, the alternative, LIHOP—Let It Happen On Purpose.

LIHOP proposes that elements in the Bush administration, aware that a terrorist onslaught was likely, and motivated by the opportunities for foreign intervention it might provide, turned a blind eye to warning signs and let the attacks happen. MIHOP adherents suspect—argue strongly—that elements in the U.S. government and military actually engineered the attacks.

Those, then, are the central planks of conspiracy theory. As late as January 2011, National Geographic Channel was rebroadcasting programming that covered the theories plugged by the people some call 9/11 "truthers."

CONSPIRACY THEORIES are nothing new, in America and much of the rest of the world. The growth and durability of 9/11 skepticism, though, was inseparably intertwined with the rise and rise of the Internet. For better or worse and for the first time in history, the Internet permits citizens to propagate ideas faster than traditional media and beyond the control of government.

The electronic murmur that was to reach millions seems to have begun not six hours after the first strike on the Trade Center. Boston-based David Rostcheck, a software consultant with a physics degree, had spent the morning watching the drama on television. "Eventually," he recalled, "I went to see what people were saying online. I belonged to the set of people who had been on the Internet for most of my adult life, before there was a Web and before the Internet became a household presence. . . . No one seemed to be commenting on the unusual aspects of the building collapses, so I wrote up an analysis and posted it."

"Is it just me," Rostcheck asked on the Net that afternoon,

> or did anyone else recognize that it wasn't the airplane impacts
> that blew up the World Trade Center? To me, this is the most
> frightening part of this morning . . . look at the footage—
> those buildings were demolished. To demolish a building, you
> don't need all that much explosive but it needs to be placed in
> the correct places. . . . Someone had to have had a lot of ac-

cess to all of both towers and a lot of time to do this. . . . If, in a few days, not one official has mentioned anything about the demolition part, I think we have a REALLY serious problem.

There it was, almost instantaneously, the very first hint at the theory that for many has long since become an item of faith—that the fall of the Twin Towers was in reality caused by explosives planted within the buildings. Rapidly, the Internet became the forum for a great flood of skepticism.

"What happened after September 11," Rostcheck told the authors,

is that American society bifurcated into two groups—call them America 1 and America 2. America 1 makes up much of America. It is depicted by and shaped by broadcast media. It thinks it occupies what it would consider to be "conventional reality," which is to say it thinks it "is" America. It is barely aware of America 2, if at all.

America 2, by comparison, is what I'll roughly classify as the Internet domain. I don't mean that America 1 doesn't use the Internet—it does. . . . But America 2's concepts originate on the Internet, which is a different domain. . . . The two Americas live together, work together, interact together, but they are not quite the same and they are not necessarily going in the same direction anymore. What happened after September 11 is that a whole group of Americans found themselves abruptly dumped into America 2 . . . the population of America 2 became huge—likely tens of millions.

America 1 is only dimly aware of America 2, and reflexively consigns any elements of thinking from America 2 that it becomes aware of into one bin marked "crazy," then dismisses it. . . . By the standards of America 2, people from America 1 are profoundly and tragically uneducated—and reactionary.

Whatever one thinks of this concept of two Americas, the seeds of suspicion about 9/11 have flourished on the Internet ever since. Four years ago, it was said that almost a million Web pages were devoted to "9/11 conspiracy." As of early 2011, entering the phrase "9/11 conspiracy" into the Google search engine returned almost seven million hits.

"I don't believe the official story," wrote Jared Israel, a veteran anti–Vietnam War activist who had earlier started Emperor's Clothes—a website fired up by perceived American betrayal of the Serbs in Yugoslavia—within four days of the attacks. What he saw in "the semi-official *New York Times,*" he told his readers, raised grave questions. Why had President Bush gone on listening to a children's story about goats when a third hijacked plane was aimed at Washington, D.C.? Wasn't there something odd about the military response to the hijackings, or the lack of it? Israel said he smelled—and this may have been the first mention of the word in the context of 9/11—"conspiracy."

Even to peer into the world we now enter requires suspending disbelief, giving houseroom to a mind-boggling range of views. It includes the "no-planers," people who question whether commercial passenger jets crashed into the Trade Center and the Pentagon at all. Talk of that began just two days after 9/11 on a website run by a man named Peter Meyer and intended—he told readers—"for thinking people." Meyer and others would eventually be expressing doubt as to whether some or all of the planes involved on 9/11 really existed as genuine passenger flights.

By early October, one Carol Valentine was declaring that "there were no suicide pilots on those September 11 jets. The jets were controlled by advanced robotics." Her account, which ran to twelve pages, suggested that air traffic controllers' records had vanished, that the alleged Arab hijackers' names were missing from airline passenger lists, and that an alleged hijacker's passport—reportedly found in the street near the Trade Center—had been planted. She believed, moreover, that Flight 93 was "without a doubt" shot down, to prevent its "electronic controls" being examined and to ensure the silence of its crew and passengers.

A character named Joe Vialls, meanwhile, cast doubt on the belief that there had been air-to-ground phone calls from the "electronically hijacked" planes. How was it, a certain Gary North asked, that no names of Arab hijackers appeared on early published passenger lists? The omission was "very strange . . . peculiar."

Over the years, the plot thickened. An academic named Alex Dewdney suggested in 2003 that the four aircraft were not really hijacked but "ordered to land at a designated airport with a military presence." Two "previously-prepared planes," painted to look like an

American Airlines jet and a United Airlines jet, were "flown by remote control" along the designated flight paths of Flights 11 and 175 and on into the Twin Towers.

In Dewdney's version, it was a "fighter jet (under remote control), or a cruise missile" that crashed into the Pentagon. The passengers from the three genuine Boeings were transferred to Flight 93, which "flies towards Washington and is shot down by a U.S. Air Force jet over Pennsylvania." The three original Boeings were flown "by remote control out over the Atlantic," and then scuttled.

That is but a taste of the sort of theory many could read and some apparently believed—though there are more, yet more bizarre. Who are the theories' proponents? Dewdney is professor emeritus of computer science and adjunct professor of biology at Canada's University of Western Ontario. North holds a Ph.D. in history. Vialls, now deceased, said he was a "British aeronautical engineer." Valentine has described herself as a writer, researcher, and human rights activist. Meyer apparently holds a double honors degree in philosophy and mathematics from a leading Australian university.

There is more one should know about some of them. North describes himself as a Christian Reconstructionist and the magazine he edits as "an attempt to apply biblical principles to economic analysis." Cuba, Vialls declared as late as 2004, would "soon be used as 'point man' in a grand plan to deny American warships and other vessels safe transit through the Gulf of Mexico. . . . America will collapse in six months." The Southeast Asia tsunami that same year, he theorized, was a "nuclear war crime."

Carol Valentine, who ran a "Waco Holocaust Electronic Museum," claimed that Branch Davidian followers did not perish by fire in Texas in 1993. They had, rather, been secretly shot earlier, or shot while trying to escape, by the U.S. Army's Special Operations Command.

Peter Meyer, for his part, cheerfully acknowledges having indulged over a long period in the use of psychedelic drugs—including LSD. He developed computer software for "Timewave Zero," a program illustrating a "theory of time, history and the end of history" as revealed "by an alien intelligence." He reportedly "hopes to be present at the end of history in 2012."

• • •

AND THEN THERE ARE the books. As early as spring 2002 came one with a title that said it all—*9/11: The Big Lie*. This was the work of Thierry Meyssan, a Frenchman whose biographical note describes him as president of the Voltaire Network for freedom of speech and secretary of the Radical Left Party. According to the book's cover, *The Big Lie* was "based exclusively on documents published by the White House and the U.S. Department of Defense, as well as statements by American civilian and military leaders."

Meyssan's book was a best-seller, reportedly selling more than 200,000 copies in France and half a million internationally, and eighteen editions in other foreign languages. It was largely lambasted by the media in the West—ignored at first in France—and praised elsewhere, especially in the Middle East. In the United Arab Emirates, where Meyssan was invited to speak, he was introduced as a man "with the spirit of an investigative journalist, of a thinker." *Al Watan*, a prominent newspaper in Saudi Arabia, trumpeted the book on its front page.

The idea that the Pentagon had been struck by a Boeing airliner on 9/11, Meyssan claimed, was "nonsense," a "loony tale." "Only a missile of the United States armed forces transmitting a friendly code," he wrote, "could enter the Pentagon's airspace without provoking a counter-missile barrage."

The attacks on the World Trade Center had occurred "under the eye of the intelligence services, who observed but did not intervene." And: "We are asked to believe that these hijackers were Arab-Islamic militants. . . . The first question that should be asked is 'Who profits?'" Meyssan asked whether the ensuing FBI investigation was "meant to hide from view domestic American culpability and justify the military operations to follow." The 9/11 attacks, he concluded, were "masterminded from inside the American state apparatus."

That, the "truth" camp's dominant message, has been gotten over—couched in beguilingly moderate tones—by a theologian. David Ray Griffin, professor of religion and theology at Claremont School of Theology in California for more than three decades, has churned out no fewer than nine books on 9/11. He has become known as the "dean" of opposition to 9/11 orthodoxy.

Griffin makes stunning leaps, slipped in amidst phrases like "the evidence suggests" and "the many reasons to" in his books. The evidence on the destruction of the World Trade Center and other factors, he has said, "show that the attacks must have been planned by our own political and military leaders." He is evidently a full-fledged MIHOP man.

If the engine of the movement has been the Internet, it is the Web documentary film *Loose Change*—through its several incarnations since 2005—that has carried the message to a vast audience. The film is a fricassee of factoids, its ingredients largely clips from broadcast footage, laced with the voices of skeptics and served up over about two hours. While the film does not hand down a verdict in as many words, it makes no secret of its producers' belief in MIHOP. It is Ministry of Propaganda stuff delivered, ironically, via the Internet, the ultimate medium of free speech.

By mid-2010, the producers say, 125 million people had viewed *Loose Change* on Google alone. In the words of producer Korey Rowe, who served in the U.S. Army in Afghanistan and Iraq, "This is our generation's Kennedy assassination." Originally made for some $2,000 and available free on the Internet, the film has since gone into edition after edition. The latest update cost $1 million, and writer-director Dylan Avery moved to Los Angeles to write a feature film script.

In its most recent, 2009, edition, the makers of *Loose Change* no longer bothered to veil its message. They changed the title to *Loose Change 9/11—An American Coup*. "America was hijacked on September 11, 2001," an earnest voice intones at the end, "by a group of tyrants ready and willing to do whatever is necessary to keep their stranglehold on the United States of America. A group beyond any one man [a picture of President Bush appears on the screen], or any one administration [a picture of President Obama appears]. Until there is a new investigation into the events, we will not go away. We will not be silent. Ask questions. Demand answers."

David Griffin, usually careful to appear judicious, academically careful, at one stage acted as script consultant for *Loose Change*. He has, moreover, been quoted as saying he is doing what he can "to get the cabal who engineered 9/11 for imperialistic and plutocratic reasons stopped before they do still more damage to our country and our planet." The "cabal" he had in mind, Griffin had long since made clear, was the Bush administration.

Many who have voiced support for the professor, to one degree or another, have been educated, professional people. Richard Falk, Princeton University's Milbank professor emeritus of international law—and currently the United Nations' special rapporteur on human rights in the occupied territories of Palestine—lent credibility to Griffin's first book with a glowing foreword. Falk has written, "It is not paranoid to assume that the established elites of the American governmental structure have something to hide, and much to explain."

PROFESSIONALS WITH IDEAS like Griffin's have associated themselves with Internet groups reflecting their expertise—Scholars for 9/11 Truth, the Scientific Panel Investigating 9/11, Architects and Engineers for 9/11 Truth, Veterans for 9/11 Truth, Pilots for 9/11 Truth, Medical Professionals for 9/11 Truth, and so on. Such skeptics include men and women from differing fields of expertise, some distinguished, some even prominent. Here is a sample.

Scholars for 9/11 Truth, originally headed jointly by James Fetzer, now professor emeritus at the University of Minnesota—a specialist on the philosophy of science—and Steven Jones, professor emeritus of physics at Brigham Young University, focused specifically on the collapses. Following a series of disagreements and a split into two separate groups—with perhaps a thousand members between them—Fetzer and Jones offer differing perspectives.

According to Fetzer, members of his group "believe that the government not only permitted 9/11 to occur but may even have orchestrated these events to facilitate its political agenda." Fetzer claimed that his group has "established beyond reasonable doubt that the Twin Towers were destroyed by a novel form of controlled demolition from the top down . . . and that, whatever may have hit the Pentagon, multiple lines of argument support the conclusion that it was not a Boeing 757." Perhaps, he theorized, "high-tech weapons of the directed energy kind" were used against the Trade Center.

Dr. Jones has called for "discretion and discipline" and strict adherence to "the Scientific Method." He, too, however, espouses the hypothesis that the Trade Center was brought down by controlled demolition. He, too, asserts that 9/11 was an "inside job," that "the case for accusing ill-trained Muslims of causing all the destruction on 9/11 . . . just does not add up."

The academic doubters found apparently reputable allies in other walks of life. Glenn MacDonald, a former Army Reserve major who runs a Web journal called MilitaryCorruption.com, thought he could see something in the footage of the underside of Flight 175, as it tore toward the South Tower. "I have seen attachments that look like that—on military aircraft . . . It could have been even a missile. . . ."

Morgan Reynolds, who served as chief economist in the Department of Labor under President Bush, has described the official wisdom on the collapse of the Trade Center as "bogus," explicable only as "professional demolition." "We know," said Paul Roberts, an assistant secretary of the treasury under President Reagan who himself has some engineering training, that "it is strictly impossible for any building, much less steel-columned buildings, to 'pancake' at free fall speed. Therefore, it is a non-controversial fact that the official explanation of the collapse of the WTC buildings is false."

Seven CIA veterans have found fault with the official account. William Christison, a former director of the Agency's Office of Regional and Political Analysis, has been vocal on the collapses. In a lengthy article, he declared himself impressed by the "carefully collected and analyzed evidence" suggesting that the two Trade Center Towers and Building 7 "were most probably destroyed by controlled demolition charges placed in the buildings before 9/11." He had time, too, for the theory that the Pentagon was hit not by an airliner but perhaps by a "missile, a drone, or . . . a smaller manned aircraft."

Military men and members of parliaments in several foreign nations have raised questions about the towers' collapse. A bevy of show business figures and celebrities—including actors Charlie Sheen and Marion Cotillard, director David Lynch, comedian Rosie O'Donnell, and singer Willie Nelson—have drawn attention to the issue. So has former Minnesota governor turned television star Jesse Ventura, who showcased 9/11 on his television show *Conspiracy Theory*. Most significant, however, have seemed the views of professionals with seemingly relevant backgrounds.

Joel Hirschhorn, a former engineering professor who has often testified to congressional committees, believes that studies by scholars and professionals in relevant fields "reveal the collapse of the three World Trade Center buildings was not caused by the two airplanes exploding into the Twin Towers. . . . Why have the government and official investigations not come to the same controlled demolition conclusion?"

Dwain Deets, former director for aeronautical projects at NASA's Dryden Flight Research Center, stated that "The many visual images (massive structural members being hurled horizontally, huge pyro-clastic clouds etc.) leave no doubt in my mind explosives were in-volved." Larry Erickson, a retired aerospace engineer and research scientist for NASA; David Griscom, a research physicist for the Naval Research Laboratory; and Robert Waser, a former research and de-velopment engineer with the U.S. Naval Ordnance Laboratory, all joined their names to a petition signed by a thousand architects and engineers requesting a new investigation.

Because the attacks began in New York, because they killed so many people, and because the Twin Towers were iconic, the strike on Washington, D.C., has tended to take second place in the public mind. The crash at the Pentagon has also preoccupied the skeptics, though, and appearances suggest they are in impressive company.

Colonel George Nelson, U.S. Air Force (retired), a former air-craft accident investigator, commercial pilot, and airframe mechanic, said that—on the evidence as he saw it in 2006—"any unbiased ra-tional investigator" would conclude no Boeing 757 was involved in either the crash at the Pentagon or in Pennsylvania.

Air Force Lieutenant Colonel Jeff Latas, aerospace engineer, air-line captain, and former president of an Air Force accident board, found discrepancies between the Flight Data Recorder information on Flight 77 and the 9/11 Commission's account.

Former Army Captain Daniel Davis, who served with Air Defense Command before becoming a senior manager at General Electric Turbine [jet] Engine Division, declared himself puzzled by the seem-ing lack of substantial airplane wreckage at the Pentagon. "Where," he wanted to know, "are all of those engines?"

Former Air Force Lieutenant Colonel Karen Kwiatkowski, who was at the Pentagon when it was hit on 9/11, later went public with a lengthy essay expressing her suspicions. "There was a dearth of visible debris on the relatively unmarked lawn, where I stood only minutes after the impact," she wrote. "There was no sign of the kind of dam-age to the Pentagon structure one would expect from the impact of a large airliner. . . . It was, however, exactly what one would expect if a missile had struck the Pentagon."

From French author Thierry Meyssan to Lieutenant Colonel Kwiatkowski, that is the notion that has proved durable among the doubters. The Pentagon was hit not by an airliner but by a missile.

The perceived Pentagon mysteries have given the skeptics free rein. A group calling itself Citizen Investigation Team claimed in 2010 to have "proof" that "the plane that was seen flying low over Arlington on 9/11/01 did not in fact hit the Pentagon." Rather, it pulled up and flew over it at the last moment—all part, the authors would have us believe, of a "skilfully executed deception."

Only a tiny community of believers, perhaps, credit such bizarre hypotheses So influential have the skeptics proven, however, above all but not only thanks to the Internet, that many people are at least somewhat hooked.

The authors' contacts during the more than four years of work on this book—including both professional and social conversations with hundreds of people—seemed to confirm that many citizens, and not only young people, doubt that they have been given the full picture of what occurred on 9/11.

Such widespread doubt demands corroboration based on solid evidence—or rebuttal.

ELEVEN

THERE HAVE BEEN THREE MAIN OFFICIAL REPORTS ON THE NEW YORK collapses. First, the World Trade Center Building Performance Study, compiled in 2002 by the Federal Emergency Management Agency, the Structural Engineering Institute of the American Society of Civil Engineers, and other bodies. Second, there was the far more thorough—248 pages coupled to forty-two companion reports—2005 report by the National Institute of Standards and Technology (NIST). There is also the institute's eighty-eight-page report on the collapse of Trade Center Building 7, issued in 2008.

More than two hundred technical specialists, eighty-five from NIST and the others from the private sector and the academic world, worked on the institute's report on the Trade Center. Its conclusion as to why the towers collapsed in essence differed from FEMA's earlier finding only in the detail of its analysis.

The impact of the planes, NIST's experts said, severed steel support columns and dislodged fireproofing—a vital factor—and started fires that reached temperatures as high as 1,000 degrees Celsius. The intense heat had the effect of weakening floors to the point where they sagged and pulled inward until outer columns—on the south face of the North Tower and the east face of the South Tower—in turn bowed inward.

That is the process, according to the NIST, that led the towers to collapse. The institute found "no corroborating evidence" for theories that the towers were brought down by controlled demolition using explosives planted in advance. It said that even the perception that the towers "pancaked," as a cursory look at video footage might suggest—and as is associated with films of demolition using explosives—is inaccurate. NIST's reading of the evidence, moreover, is that there was no failure of the floors—falling down one upon another one by one—but rather that the *inward* bowing, as described in the previous paragraph, initiated collapse.

What ammunition do the conspiracy theorists have to challenge the NIST account, and what is it worth? We came across a study of just that, dedicated solely to Professor Griffin's criticism of the NIST reports on the Trade Center, and written by a NASA research scientist named Ryan Mackey—in language anyone can understand. In his analysis of Griffin's work, Mackey applies what the astrophysicist Carl Sagan called a "baloney detection kit."

Vital tools in the kit include independent confirmation of the facts, not confining oneself at the outset to a single hypothesis, and adherence to Occam's Razor—the principle that precedence should be given to the simpler of competing theories.

The approach of Professor Griffin, the conspiracy author who presents himself as reasoned and judicious, in Mackey's view "violates every single tenet" of the baloney detection kit. Mackey demonstrates as much, successfully in our view, over some three hundred pages. Errors made by Griffin regarding the NIST report, Mackey writes, "are so numerous and substantial as to discourage further analysis of his claims." Here, large and small, are examples of Griffin's claims, Mackey's rebuttals, and on occasion points of our own.

Contrary to the NIST's finding that fires so weakened the Twin Towers as to cause their collapse, Griffin has claimed that the fires were not especially hot, that there was no evidence that the heat was "breaking windows." In fact, video and photographs show hundreds of windows broken, with either flame or smoke visible.

Griffin, who on the one hand argues that the fires in the Twin

Towers were not hot enough to fatally weaken the steel columns, on the other hand asserts that molten steel was seen. For steel to have melted, he writes, "would be very strong evidence" that the columns were in fact "cut by explosives."

There is in fact no good evidence—*evidence*, as distinct from verbal eyewitness recollections—that any *steel*, as distinct from other metals like aluminum, melted. According to Mackey, moreover, explosives, "particularly those used in real controlled demolitions, do not melt steel. They destroy steel through impulse."

One possible scenario, Mackey writes, might support steel having melted at the very moment of collapse. That, he says, would fit not with the use of explosives but of "high-temperature incendiaries," such as thermite—the presence of which has been postulated by skeptic Dr. Steven Jones.

Jones has claimed to have discovered "thermitic" material in four samples of dust from Lower Manhattan. There are multiple problems with Jones's assertion, however, the first of them a problem that requires no scientific knowledge.

In all criminal investigations, a key factor is what detectives call the "chain of evidence" or "chain of custody." To be truly useful, evidence must have been handled with extreme care, to obviate questions as to its authenticity or origins. Dr. Jones's samples of dust emerged five years after 9/11, following an appeal by him for dust that might have been preserved.

One handful of dust reportedly came from a citizen who scooped it up on 9/11 from a handrail near the end of the Brooklyn Bridge, then preserved it in a plastic bag. Another was reportedly found the following day on a pile of laundry near an apartment window. Of the two other samples, both also picked up in Manhattan apartments, one had lain unretrieved—exposed to other particles entering through broken windows—for about a week.

To a detective—and in this case a scientist is indeed a sort of detective—such samples are interesting but much less than reliable. In a criminal case—and were the samples of, say, bloodstains containing DNA—they would be laughed out of court. There is no true chain of evidence in any of these instances.

Even were the provenance of the dust well established, moreover, some fellow scientists reject Jones's claim to have identified the incendiary thermite. Elements in the samples are as likely, they say, to have come from material one would *expect* to find in dust from the Trade Center—like paint.

There is disapproval, too, of the way Jones's thermite conclusions—grave, were they to be taken seriously—have been presented. The findings have not been subjected to peer review, the process under which a scholarly work is subjected to scrutiny by other experts in the same field. While most scientists consider peer review essential, Jones's thoughts on thermite seem first to have appeared in a paper he posted on a university website, then in the *Journal of 9/11 Studies*. The website of the *Journal*, of which Jones is coeditor, claims that it is "peer-reviewed." Fellow scientist Ryan Mackey dismisses that assertion as a "masquerade . . . cargo-cult science."

Thermite aside, Griffin and like-minded theorists espouse the idea that explosives of some sort were used to bring down the towers. They base their suspicion to a great degree on what witnesses said they saw and heard—understandably, or so one might think.

Wall Street Journal reporter John Bussey, for example, reported in a Pulitzer-winning article that from the *Journal* building near the South Tower he "heard metallic crashes and looked up out of the office window to see what seemed like perfectly synchronized explosions coming from each floor. . . . One after another, from top to bottom, with a fraction of a second between, the floors blew to pieces."

Bussey later recalled having seen "individual floors, one after the other exploding outward." "I thought to myself, 'My God, they're going to bring the building down.' And they, whoever they were, had set charges." "It just descended like a timed explosion," said Beth Fertig of WNYC Radio, "like when they are deliberately bringing a building down."

The skeptics also pounced early on what Van Romero of the New Mexico Institute of Mining and Technology—unlike the reporters an expert on explosives—told the *Albuquerque Journal* on the day of the attacks. "My opinion is, based on the videotapes," he said, "that after the airplanes hit the World Trade Center there were some explosive devices inside the buildings that caused the towers to collapse."

Ten days later, however, Romero reversed himself. It had initially looked to him as though explosives triggered the collapses, he said, but a further look at the videotapes led him to agree with colleagues that—essentially as the NIST would conclude four years later—the buildings fell because fire weakened their steel structures.

There's the nub. So many people, with less expertise in explosives than Romero or none at all, merely said what they *thought* they saw and heard. "Then we heard a loud explosion or what sounded like a loud explosion," Fire battalion chief John Sudnik recalled, "and looked up and I saw Tower Two start coming down." "First I thought it was an explosion," said firefighter Timothy Julian. "I thought maybe there was a bomb on the plane, but delayed type of thing, you know, secondary device."

"There was what appeared to be at first an explosion," said Chief Frank Cruthers, also describing the collapse of the South Tower. "It appeared at the very top, simultaneously from all four sides, materials shot out horizontally. And then there seemed to be a momentary delay before you could see the beginning of the collapse."

"The lowest floor of fire in the South Tower actually looked like someone had planted explosives around it," said battalion chief Brian Dixon. "Everything blew out . . . I thought, 'Jeez, this looks like an explosion up there.' "

Dr. Griffin seized on these accounts and more. On occasion, however, he was less than professorial in his editing. Griffin omitted, for example, what battalion chief Dixon said in his very next sentence, after recalling that he thought he was witnessing an "explosion." He had continued, "I guess in some sense of time we looked at it and realized, 'No, actually it just collapsed.' That's what blew out the windows, not that there was an explosion there."

Without having done a statistical study of the some five hundred formal interviews conducted with 9/11 emergency workers, it appears to the authors that the vast majority of them referred not to apparent explosions—as in detonations—but usually more vaguely, to loud bangs, thunder, rumbling, booms, or trainlike sounds.

There may even have been some actual explosions, but not ones indicating deliberate demolition. "You heard nothing but explosions all day," firefighter Salvatore Torcivia remembered. "The fires, the jet fuel burning. The nearby buildings had air conditioning and refrigerator units—they were all exploding from the super heat. It sounded like bombs going off. I believe the Secret Service had their armory in one of the towers. That stuff, ordnance, was going off."

After an analysis of Griffin's eye and ear witnesses to explosion, his critic Ryan Mackey notes that all were nonexperts, "relaying their impressions of a horrifically chaotic and deadly experience." There is no good reason to consider the witnesses' words evidence of the use of explosives.

To believe explosives were involved, moreover, one would have to account for how they were planted—in multiple locations—in advance of the attacks. Griffin states that demolition of the Twin Towers would have required more explosive than did that in 2000 of the Seattle Kingdome stadium—at the time the largest structure ever brought down by controlled implosion.

His tormentor Mackey, calculating that this would have meant bringing more than 60,000 kilograms of explosive into each tower, notes that the professor "produced no explanation of how such a staggering amount of explosives could have been smuggled into the Towers without detection, how it could have been placed without being seen, how many individuals would have been required to plant it all."

The 2005 report of the National Institute of Standards and Technology summed up the matter. Its experts had found no evidence, the report said, "for alternative hypotheses suggesting that the WTC towers were brought down by controlled demolition using explosives."

The authors have seen nothing, in all the verbiage of the skeptical literature, to persuade us otherwise.

In 2010, Dr. Griffin came out with yet another book, on what he described as "The Official Account's Achilles' Heel." The "smoking gun" that he and others see is the collapse on the evening of September 11 of the forty-seven-story World Trade Center Building 7.

Though not struck by an airplane, Building 7 was catastrophically damaged by chunks of debris from the collapsing North Tower, caught fire, and burned all day. When it in turn fell, WTC 7 became the first known instance in the world of a tall, modern, steel-reinforced building brought down apparently as a result of fire.

It was, *The New York Times* reported later, "a mystery that under normal circumstances would probably have captured the attention of the city and the world"—had its collapse not been eclipsed by that of the Twin Towers themselves. The *Times* said engineers expected to spend months piecing together the "disturbing puzzle." In the event, it took the NIST's experts seven years.

According to the NIST, in its 2008 report, WTC 7 was brought down by "fire-induced progressive collapse," a chain of events technically unlike those in the Twin Towers, beginning with the failure of one key structural column. The NIST "found no evidence supporting the existence of a blast event."

There has long been witness testimony militating against the notion that the WTC 7 collapse was triggered by explosions. Fire Department interviewees recalled having anticipated the collapse of WTC 7 from early in the afternoon of September 11. Frank Fellini, a senior chief, said the building was a "major concern" because of the hit it took from the fall of the North Tower. "When it fell, it ripped steel out from between the third and sixth floors . . . We were concerned that the fires on several floors and the missing steel would result in the building collapsing. So for the next five or six hours we kept firefighters from working anywhere near that building."

"Early on," Deputy Chief Peter Hayden said, "we saw a bulge in the southwest corner . . . a visible bulge, it ran up about three floors . . . by about 2 o'clock in the afternoon we realized this thing was going to collapse."

Daniel Nigro, who succeeded as head of the department following the death of Chief Ganci, said he personally ordered a collapse zone cleared around the building three hours before the building tumbled, at 5:20 P.M.

Conspiracy theories on the fate of WTC 7, Nigro wrote in 2007, "are without merit."

ON, THEN, to the idea that the Pentagon was hit not by American Flight 77 but by a missile. Food for that thought has been photographs taken after the initial explosion—and before the collapse of a major portion of the facade more than half an hour later. The pictures appear to doubters to show a hole, amidst the smoke, only some eighteen feet wide.

A Boeing 757 like American's Flight 77 has a wingspan of 124 feet 6 inches and a tail 44 feet 6 inches tall. "How could such a big airplane have created such a small hole?" asked Dr. Griffin. The missile theory, he thought, "fits the physical evidence much better."

The apparent size of the hole does at first glance seem odd. It seems curious, too, that photographs do not show sizable airplane debris scattered around outside the building. To draw conclusions from those visual oddities, however, is to ignore the mass of eyewitness testimony from people who saw a low-flying airliner roar toward the Pentagon. It is to reject a wealth of other evidence and to spurn the opinion of technical experts.

As in New York, no formal National Transportation Safety Board (NTSB) accident investigation report was issued on the Pentagon crash, because the disaster was treated from the start as a crime scene. There could and probably should have been one, not least because— unlike the scene in the aftermath of the New York attacks—there was initially a crash site that air transport investigators could have examined. Both the remains of the airplane and rubble from the building collapse, however, were removed early on—the airplane debris reportedly to an FBI warehouse—for storage as evidence.

The nearest thing to an investigative probe into the Pentagon strike is the 2003 report by a team from the American Society of Civil Engineers (ASCE). Its title, "The Pentagon Building Performance Report," reflects the group's brief—to focus on the damage done to the nation's defense headquarters. The seven-month probe, however, inevitably also involved close study of the crash itself, and the resulting report reflects absolutely no doubt that the catastrophe was caused by an airliner.

To say otherwise, says Professor Mete Sozen, a member of the ASCE team, is "hogwash." "To look at only the photograph of what some people see as the 'small' entry hole in the facade," Sozen told the authors in 2010, "is to see only part of the reality. Much of the facade is obscured by smoke in the photos, and our work—judging by the locations of broken or heavily damaged columns in the wall—showed that the real damage consisted of a ragged series of holes stretching to a width of some ninety feet."

Why, then, do the photographs taken before the facade's collapse not show more clearly the virtually wingtip-to-wingtip entry gashes seen when similar planes hit the World Trade Center on 9/11?

Another, long-ago, New York City plane crash may offer an insight. A plane that smashed into the Empire State Building in dense fog in 1945—a B-25 bomber with a sixty-five-foot wingspan—created a hole only twenty feet wide. The Empire State is a reinforced masonry structure, as is the Pentagon—which was built during World War II. The walls of both make substantial obstacles, more substantial than the relatively fragile glass and steel sides of the Twin Towers.

Here is what the ASCE team's Sozen, professor of structural engineering at Purdue University in Indiana, believes happened to the Boeing that smashed into the Pentagon:

> Think of the external shell of the plane as a sausage skin, and the function of the structural frame as being mainly to contain the internal pressure at altitude. The plane's structure doesn't have much strength. What creates the power generated on impact is what we call its "mass and velocity." And much of the mass in the case of a Boeing 757–200 is in the fuel-filled wings.
>
> On September 11, the Boeing was reported to have approached the Pentagon flying very low, just a few feet off the ground, at some 530 mph. Eyewitnesses said the right engine hit a portable generator on the ground outside, the left engine a steam vault. Then the nose cone hit the limestone facade, and the facade's columns cut into the fuselage. The right wingtip, which hit next, would have been cut by the columns. But when parts of the fuel-filled wing close to the fuselage impacted—given the speed at which it was traveling and its greater mass—it was the *columns* that would have been destroyed or badly damaged. The same series of events would have happened when the left wing impacted (though in reverse order because of the angle at which the plane hit the building). That is why the gash in the facade of the building was not as wide as the wingspan of the airplane.
>
> By the time the aircraft's mass had penetrated the building—by about its own length—it had been transformed into a violent flow of small and large projectiles of solid and fluid that ricocheted off the internal parts of the building. The ensuing fire, we concluded, devoured the flammable part of the airplane's debris inside the building. The Boeing's tall tail and rudder assembly would have been shattered when it impacted with the edges of building slabs on the upper levels.

That may seem a compelling, credible explanation of what befell Flight 77. The skeptics, however, have long made much of the supposed lack of debris at the crash site. Photographs published in "Pentagon 9/11," the account of the day's events by the Defense Department's Historical Office, however, do depict some debris outside the building: mangled pieces of metal, one clearly marked "AA," for American Airlines, another evidently a part of the fuselage bearing part of the airline's livery, and smaller material—fragments rather than chunks.

The ubiquitous Griffin has suggested that evidence may have been "planted." Dr. Fetzer, cofounder of Scholars for 9/11 Truth, went further and suggested *how* the planting may have been achieved. "Don't be taken in," he said. "Debris begins to show up on the completely clean lawn in short order, which might have been dropped from a C-130 . . . or placed there by men in suits who were photographed carrying debris with them."

Preposterous. Reports, and photographs taken before removal by the FBI, reflect the finding of significant remains of the aircraft *inside* the building: seats, including one from the cockpit still attached to a piece of floor, cockpit circuitry, pieces of Rolls-Royce turbofan engines, landing gear, pieces of the nose gear, a wheel hub, a piece of the nose cone, a piece "the size of a refrigerator," a tire. Some parts, reportedly, bore Boeing part numbers consistent with the airplane that crashed.

Try telling Tamara "T" Carter that the debris at the Pentagon was planted. Carter, herself an American Airlines flight attendant, went to the scene two days later as a volunteer to serve refreshments to the cleanup crews. She has recalled seeing recognizable parts of a plane, the internal American upholstery with which she was familiar—and body parts. She and family members were also shown photographs of items that they might recognize, jewelry, clothing, and the like. "I'm here to tell you," she said a year later, "that my friend's arm with a bracelet exactly like this"—Carter held up a bracelet—"was found. We buried it in Washington, D.C."

The friend, a close friend, had been fellow flight attendant Renee May, who on 9/11 got through by phone from Flight 77 to alert authorities to the hijacking. To Carter, who knew all the crew members killed that day, the loss was personal. "I saw pieces of our American Airlines 757," she said. "If anyone thinks the plane did not go in there, then what happened to all my friends and where did all those body parts come from? Every crew member's body was found."

A random check supports this. Renee May's ashes were divided between her parents, who scattered them on the sea off San Diego, and her fiancé on the East Coast. Fellow flight attendants, married couple Kenneth and Jennifer Lewis, were interred in Virginia. Another colleague, Michele Heidenberger, was buried in Maryland. Their captain, Charles Burlingame, lies in Arlington Cemetery.

Such facts, in the view of the authors, render the claims voiced by the skeptics outrageous, cruel insults to the memory of the dead. Human remains were painstakingly collected and identified for all but five of Flight 77's sixty-four passengers and crew, and for all of the 125 people killed at the Pentagon. Have the "no-planers" seen the horrific photographs of bodies and body parts at the Pentagon, as carbonized and petrified in death as the victims of the eruption that destroyed Pompeii? No retrieval of human remains was more poignant than that of one of the children on board.

"A stillness fell over the recovery workers as a child's pajamas were pulled from the debris," recalled Lieutenant Colonel William Lee, a chaplain. A Barbie doll was pulled out next, followed by the foot of a child—probably part of the torn remains of eight-year-old Zoe Falkenberg, who had been traveling on the plane with her parents and little sister, Dana. Dana, aged three, was one of the five victims for whom remains were not identified.

In light of such realities, Griffin's musings—along with those of others, such as Professor Dewdney and a woman named Laura Knight-Jadczyk, who runs an Internet site called "The Cassiopaean Experiment"—might be thought to sink to the level of obscenity. The professor expressed doubt that "the bodies of the crew and passengers were really found in the Pentagon wreckage. "For all we know," he opined, "human remains from two different sites could have been combined by FBI and military personnel."

So it goes, in the face of all the evidence. Griffin, Dewdney, and Knight-Jadczyk have insisted for years that phone calls reportedly made from the hijacked planes—including Flight 77—are fabrications. His research, Dewdney wrote, showed that technologically, "cell phone calls alleged to have been made by passengers were essentially impossible" in 2001.

The suggestion is that the two conversations said to have been conducted from Flight 77—by flight attendant Renee May to her mother and by Barbara Olson to her husband, Theodore, the solicitor general—are official concoctions.

The issue of whether it was possible to make cell phone calls from airliners at the time turns out to be irrelevant. Detailed AT&T records now available make it clear that Mrs. Olson and May used seat-back phones, not cell phones.

In a fatuous, callous account, Knight-Jadczyk suggests that Barbara Olson did not die on Flight 77, but may "have had a little plastic surgery and is waiting for Ted on that nice Caribbean island they have always wanted to retire to."

Theologian Griffin, who likes to write and talk about "voice transformers" and "voice morphing," techniques of flawlessly imitating voices that he thinks may have been used by the authorities on 9/11, does not emerge as having any consideration for the bereaved. Theodore Olson's account of having received calls from his wife on the morning of 9/11, he alleged, was only a claim.

"Either Ted Olson lied or else he, like many other people that day, was fooled by fake calls." The notion that the solicitor general told the truth, he said, "is based on the assumption that his wife Barbara Olson really died, and that he truly loved her."

The remains of Olson's wife, Barbara, were found in the ruins of the Pentagon, scattered in three separate locations. "It took a long time to provide an identification," her husband has said. "But finally they did release the remains of Barbara. And she's buried up in Door County, Wisconsin . . . because she loved that place so much. And she's there now."

Absent evidence for his claim about the Olson calls, Griffin resorted to innuendo. One "cannot ignore the fact," he wrote, "that the information about Barbara came from Ted Olson, that he was working for the Bush-Cheney administration." It is the notion on which Griffin and the rest harp over and over—in his words that there is "overwhelming" supporting evidence that 9/11 was "an inside job." There was "a *prima facie* case for assuming that the Bush administration was involved."

THE SKEPTICS MAKE much of a document issued exactly a year before the attacks by the Project for the New American Century, a right-wing group that included men soon to hold senior posts in the Bush administration—Cheney, Rumsfeld, Lewis "Scooter" Libby, Paul Wolfowitz, and George Bush's brother Jeb, the governor of Florida.

The paper, entitled "Rebuilding America's Defenses," envisaged the removal of "regional aggressors" in the Middle East, and a continuing U.S. military presence in the Persian Gulf—"unquestioned military pre-eminence." Achieving such ambitions would be a lengthy process, the document noted, "absent some catastrophic and catalyzing event—like a new Pearl Harbor."

The luminaries of the New American Century group, all now appointed to positions in the new administration, got their catalyzing event within eight months. In a diary entry on the night of the attacks, President Bush reportedly called 9/11 "the Pearl Harbor of the 21st century." Later, he would draw the parallel to 1941 in public. The catastrophe of September 11 did predispose the American public for great military initiatives abroad, wars in Afghanistan and in Iraq—to topple regional aggressor Saddam Hussein.

The skeptics do not believe the September 11 attacks occurred by happenstance. They infer, rather, that those around Bush who yearned for "unquestioned military pre-eminence" must have been involved in 9/11. "Who benefits?" asked Griffin. "Who had the motive? Who had the means? Who had the opportunity? Certainly the U.S. government benefited immensely from 9/11 and cannot therefore be dropped from any rational list of suspect organizations."

MIHOP—Made It Happen On Purpose—adherents suggest that 9/11 was a false flag operation, a fabrication to justify foreign wars, and rattle off a string of supposed precedents. They cite U.S. provocation as having triggered the Mexican-American War of 1846, resulting in the acquisition of vast new territories from Texas to California. They point to the mysterious sinking of the battleship *Maine* in 1898. Though perhaps just a tragic accident, the sinking was used to justify the ensuing war with Spain—leading to U.S. dominance over the Philippines, Guam, and Puerto Rico.

MIHOP disciples also recall the argument that the orthodox history of Pearl Harbor itself is incorrect, that—though President Franklin Roosevelt had prior intelligence of a coming attack—he took no preemptive action. Roosevelt's motive? According to revisionist theory, he *needed* the day of Japanese "infamy" to ensure support for taking America into the war.

MIHOP people cite, too, the Gulf of Tonkin incident during Lyndon Johnson's presidency. Exposés have shown that the administration greatly exaggerated the facts about skirmishes in the gulf between North Vietnamese and U.S. ships in 1964. The inflated story was used, all the same, as pivotal justification for committing the United States to war in Vietnam.

Those who think the false flag ploy may apply to 9/11 also pounced, within days of the attacks, on an authentic recent revelation. Documents made public just months earlier showed that, back in 1962, the U.S. Joint Chiefs of Staff had worked up plans to stage phony acts of terrorism—including the staged downing of a U.S. airliner—that could be blamed on Fidel Castro.

The object, then, had been to provoke an American invasion of Cuba and—though the project never got beyond the planning stage—news of its existence led to fevered speculation among 9/11 skeptics. "We must wonder," one Web theorist wrote, "if the inexplicable intelligence and defense failures [surrounding 9/11] claimed by U.S. government agencies are simply part of some elaborate cover story."

Wonder one may, but the authors have seen not a jot of evidence that anything like a false flag scenario was used on 9/11. Nor, after more than four years' research, have we encountered a shred of real information indicating that the Bush administration was complicit in 9/11. Subjected to any serious probing, the suspicions raised by Professor Griffin and his fellow "truthers" simply vanish on the wind.

The investigative writer David Corn, a longtime Washington editor of *The Nation*, was on many matters a harsh critic of the President and those around him. As a serious investigative writer who specialized in intelligence coverage, though, he had no time for the skeptics' fancies. "I won't argue," he wrote six months after 9/11,

> that the U.S. government does not engage in brutal, murderous skulduggery from time to time. But the notion that the U.S. government either detected the attacks but allowed them to occur, or worse, conspired to kill thousands of Americans . . . is absurd.
>
> Would George W. Bush take the chance of being branded the most evil president of all time by countenancing such wrongdoing? Aren't these conspiracy theories too silly to address? . . . Would U.S. officials be capable of such a foul deed? Capable, as in able to pull it off and willing to do so. Simply put, the spies and the special agents are not good enough, evil enough, or gutsy enough. . . . That conclusion is based partly

on, dare I say it, common sense, but also on years spent covering national security matters. . . .

Such a plot . . . would require dozens (or scores or hundreds) of individuals to attempt such a scheme. They would
have to work together, and trust one another not to blow their
part or reveal the conspiracy. . . .

This is as foul as it gets—to kill thousands of Americans,
including Pentagon employees. . . . (The sacrificial lambs
could have included White House staff or members of Congress, had the fourth plane not crashed in Pennsylvania.) This
is a Hollywood-level of dastardliness, James Bond (or Dr.
Evil) material. . . . There is plenty to get outraged about without becoming obsessed with *X Files*–like nonsense.

Corn's piece attracted a howl of rage on the Internet from the
busy scribblers he had characterized as "silly." Eight years of scrib-
bling and talk show jawing later, though, their theories still look silly.

THERE IS NO REASON to doubt that a team of terrorists targeted four airliners on September 11. No reason to doubt that the doomed planes
stood at their assigned gates, that passengers boarded, that the aircraft
took off, for some time flew their allotted flight paths, were hijacked,
and then—except for one that crashed following a brave attempt at
resistance by its passengers—crashed into targeted buildings in New
York and Washington. There is no good reason to suspect that the
collapse of the Twin Towers and nearby buildings, and the resulting
deaths, were caused by anything other than the inferno started by the
planes' impact. There is no reason, either, to suspect that the damage and death at the Pentagon was caused by anything other than the
plane striking the building.

The facts are fulsomely documented in the material available to
the public—not just the 9/11 Commission Report but the reams of
supporting documentation and the reports supplied by other agencies. The thousands of pages include: interviews of airline ground
staff on duty that day, interviews with crews' families, flight path studies prepared by the National Transportation Safety Board, Air Traffic Control recordings—transcripts of verbatim exchanges between
controllers and pilots—accompanying reports prepared by NTSB

specialists, radar data studies, the transcript of the one Cockpit Voice Recorder recovered in usable condition, the two Flight Data Recorders recovered, and interviews and transcripts of staff of the FAA Air Traffic Control Centers involved on the day.

All that material is now available, part of the approximately 300,000 pages released by the National Archives—with national security and privacy-related redactions—since 2009. The authors have read as much of it as was feasible, and it provides no support for the naysayers.

The legacy of the spurious doubts, though, has been that far too little attention has been given to the very real omissions and distortions in the official reporting. The conspiracy theorizing in which the skeptics indulged, David Corn has rightly said, "distracts people from the actual malfeasance, mistakes and misdeeds of the U.S. government and the intelligence community."

There were certainly mistakes, and there may have been wrongdoing.

TWELVE

ALMOST THREE YEARS AFTER THE ATTACKS, IN 2004, THE EXECUTIVE director of the 9/11 Commission—then in the final weeks of its work—dictated a memo. It was addressed to the inquiry's chairman and vice chairman, and it posed a very sensitive question. "How," Philip Zelikow wanted to know, "should the Commission handle evidence of possible false statements by U.S. officials?"

"Team 8," he reported, "has found evidence suggesting that one or more USAF officers—and possibly FAA officials—must have known their version was false, before and after it was briefed to and relied upon by the White House, presented to the nation, and presented to us. . . . The argument is not over details; it is about the fundamental way the story was presented. It is the most serious issue of truth/falsity in accounts to us that we have encountered so far."

The "story" that so provoked the Commission was the military and FAA version of their response to the 9/11 attacks, a response that failed utterly to thwart the terrorists' operation. The Commission's belief that it had been deceived would be lost in the diplomatic language of its final Report. Zelikow's memo on the subject would be withheld until 2009. The Commission's chairman, former New Jersey governor Thomas Kean, and the vice chairman, former congressman Lee Hamilton, however, gave a sense of their frustration in their later joint memoir. The military's statements, they declared, were "not forthright or accurate." To another commissioner, former congressman Tim Roemer, they were, quite simply, "false."

Former New Jersey attorney general John Farmer, who went on to become a senior counsel on the Commission, led Team 8's probe of the military's performance. He was shocked by the "deception," and explained why in a complex, mesmerizing account of his findings.

Farmer questioned not only how the military and the FAA had functioned on 9/11, but also the actions of the President and the Vice President. In his view, "The perpetuation of the untrue official version remains a betrayal of every citizen who demanded a truthful answer to the simple question: What happened?"

To ESTABLISH WHAT did happen, investigators found themselves plunging into a labyrinth of facts and factoids. Early official statements, made within days of the attacks, were clearly inconsistent.

Two days after the attacks, Air Force general Richard Myers testified to the Senate Armed Services Committee. Though the hearing had been scheduled before 9/11, questioning turned naturally to the crisis of the moment. For an officer of distinction, about to become chairman of the Joint Chiefs, Myers seemed confused as to when fighters had gone up to attempt to intercept the hijacked planes. Memory, he said vaguely, told him that fighters had been launched to intercept Flight 93, the plane that crashed before reaching a target. "I mean," he said, "we had gotten somebody close to it, as I recall. I'll have to check it out."

Twenty-four hours later, on the Friday, Deputy Defense Secretary Paul Wolfowitz seemed to confirm it. "We responded awfully quickly, I might say, on Tuesday," he said in a nationally broadcast interview, "and in fact we were already tracking in on that plane that crashed in Pennsylvania. I think it was the heroism of the passengers on board that brought it down, but the Air Force was in a position to do so if we had had to . . . it's the President's decision on whether to take an action as fateful as that."

The same day, though, another senior officer flatly contradicted Wolfowitz. Major General Paul Weaver, commander of the Air National Guard, gave reporters a detailed timeline of the military's reaction. According to him, no airplanes had been scrambled to chase Flight 93. "There was no notification for us to launch airplanes . . . We weren't even close."

What, moreover, asked Weaver, could a fighter pilot have done had he intercepted one of the hijacked airliners? "You're not going to get an American pilot shooting down an American airliner. We don't have permission to do that." The only person who could grant such permission was the President, the general pointed out, leaving the impression that Bush had not done so.

By week's end, however, that notion was turned on its head. Vice President Cheney, speaking on NBC's *Meet the Press*, said that George W. Bush had indeed made the "toughest decision"—to shoot down a civilian airliner if necessary. Fighter pilots, he asserted, had been authorized to "take out" any plane that failed to obey instructions to move away from Washington.

In spite of denials by General Myers and others, there were people who thought United 93 might in fact have been shot down. Bush himself had asked Cheney, "Did we shoot it down, or did it crash?" "It's my understanding," Cheney had told Defense Secretary Rumsfeld, that "they've already taken a couple of aircraft out." Transportation Secretary Norman Mineta, who was with the Vice President at the White House, recalled thinking, "Oh, my God, did we shoot it down?"

At one base, a crewman saw a fighter returning without missiles, surmised that it had shot down Flight 93—then learned that the plane had never been loaded with missiles in the first place. One F-16 pilot who flew that day heard that the aircraft had been downed—only to be told that the report was incorrect. Rumors would still be circulating years later.

In the absence of good evidence to the contrary, though, few now credit the notion that any pilot shot down an airliner filled with helpless civilians on September 11. No pilot would have fired without authorization, could not have done so without fellow officers, radio operators, and others being aware of it. There was no way such an action could have been kept secret.

Shoot-down aside, the statements by the military and political leadership raised a host of questions. Had fighters really gone up in time to intercept any of the hijacked planes? If they did get up in time, what had they been expected to do? Could they—would they—have shot a plane down? If pilots were cleared to shoot, was the order given in the way the Vice President described? If so, when did he issue the order and when did it reach military commanders?

Getting clear answers to these questions at first seemed a manageable task. Why would it not be, given that the military, the FAA, and the White House all kept logs and records and taped hours of phone and radio exchanges? The law establishing the Commission "required" those involved to produce all records on request. In the event, though, investigators were thwarted by delayed responses, irritating conditions, and actual obstruction.

The FAA said it had produced all relevant material, only for Commission staff to discover that was not true. It had failed to provide a large number of tapes and transcripts. What the Department of Defense and NORAD—North American Aerospace Defense Command—provided was, in the words of one Commission staff member, "incomplete, late, and inadequate to our purposes."

While key sources stalled, Commission investigators puzzled over further versions of what supposedly happened on 9/11—according to NORAD. Colonel William Scott suggested that fighters had been scrambled at 9:25 A.M., flying from Langley Air Force Base in Virginia to intercept the third hijacked plane, Flight 77, before it could reach Washington. Radar data, however, showed the fighters had headed *away* from Washington. As for the fourth plane, United 93, Scott appeared to corroborate the notion that the military had had notice of Flight 93's hijacking as early as 9:16, forty-seven minutes before it crashed at 10:03.

The senior officer who supervised NORAD's efforts on 9/11, Air Force Major General Larry Arnold, appeared to second what Scott had said about Flight 77—but in a very different context. "9:24," he said, "was the first time we had been advised of American 77 as a possible hijacked airplane. Our focus—you have got to remember that there's a lot of other things going on simultaneously here—was on United 93, which was being pointed out to us very aggressively, I might say, by the FAA." According to the general, fighters had been launched out of the base at Langley to "put them over the top of

Washington, D.C., not in response to American Airlines 77, but really to put them in position in case United 93 were to head that way."

There had been time to intercept Flight 93, Arnold indicated. The "awful decision" to shoot the plane down had been obviated only by the bravery of its passengers in storming the cockpit, and the ensuing crash. In one breath, however, General Arnold appeared to say that his airmen could have shot down planes as of 9:25, when all civilian airplanes were ordered to land, in another that shoot-down authority was not forthcoming until about 10:08, five minutes after the crash of Flight 93.

John Farmer and the Commission's Team 8 grew ever more leery of information offered by the military. Farmer stumbled on proof positive, too, that NORAD was failing to provide vital tapes. It took pressure at the very top, and a subpoena, to get them released. The more material team members obtained, the more they boggled in astonishment. Farmer heard one of his staffers, an Annapolis graduate named Kevin Schaeffer, muttering, "Whiskey tango foxtrot, man. Whiskey tango foxtrot." That phrase, Schaeffer and a colleague explained to Farmer, was a "military euphemism for 'What the fuck!'"

As the Commission zeroed in on the truth behind the military's failures, the phrase was used often.

THE MOST POWERFUL military nation on the planet had been ill-prepared and ill-equipped to confront the attacks. Time was, at the height of the Cold War, when NORAD could have called on more than a hundred squadrons of fighter aircraft to defend the continental United States. By September 2001, however, with the Soviet threat perceived as minimal—bordering on nonexistent—the number had dwindled to a token force of just fourteen "alert" planes based at seven widely scattered bases. Only four of those fighters were based in the Northeast Air Defense Sector—NEADS—which covered the geographical area in which the hijackings took place.

Practice runs aside, moreover, the airplanes had never been scrambled to confront an enemy. They were used to intercept civilian aircraft that strayed off course, suspected drug traffickers, planes that failed to file a proper flight plan. Hijackings were rare, and countermeasures were based on the concept of hijacking as it had almost always been carried out since the 1960s—the temporary seizure of an airliner, followed by a safe landing and the release of passengers and crew. FAA security had recently noted the possibility that suicidal terrorists might use a plane as a weapon—but only in passing, without putting new security measures in place.

The cumbersome protocol in place to deal with a hijacking involved circuitous reporting, up through the FAA and on to the Pentagon, all the way up to the office of the defense secretary. At the end of the process, if approval was granted, NORAD would launch fighters. The pilots' mission would then be to identify and discreetly follow the airplane until it landed. Nothing in their training or experience foresaw a need to shoot down an airliner.

On September 11, faced with swift-moving, complex information about multiple hijackings, the FAA was overwhelmed. The internal communications mix—multiple Air Traffic Control Centers, Eastern Region Administration, a command center in Herndon, Virginia, an operations center and FAA headquarters in Washington—proved too muddled to be effective.

There was some confusion over operational language. At the FAA, a "primary target" denoted a radar return. At NORAD, it meant a search target. In FAA parlance, to speak of a plane's "coast mode" was to project its direction based on its last known appearance on radar. On 9/11, one NEADS staff technician interpreted the word "coast" as meaning that one of the hijacked flights was following the coastline, the eastern seaboard. One senior FAA controller admitted having not even known, on September 11, what NORAD was.

NORAD, for its part, ran into problems when units not designated for defense were called in. Such units had different training, different regulations and equipment, used a different communications net. In one area, NORAD fighter pilots found themselves unable to communicate with airmen from other units. Of three relevant radio frequencies, none worked.

Transcripts of FAA and NEADS conversations, when finally obtained by the Commission, were found to feature exchanges like this:

NEADS VOICE: In that book . . . we used to have a book with numbers [Dial tone]
NEADS IDENTIFICATION TECHNICIAN: Wrong one [Beeps] I can't get ahold of Cleveland. [Sigh] [Dial tone, dialing, busy sig-

nal] . . . still busy. Boston's the only one that passed this informa-
tion. Washington [Center] doesn't know shit . . .
FAA BOSTON CENTER: . . . We have an F-15 holding . . . He's in
the air . . . he's waiting to get directions . . .
NEADS IDENTIFICATION TECHNICIAN: Stand by—stand by one.
Weapons? I need somebody up here that . . .

And so on. One NEADS technician would keep saying of Washington air traffic control, "Washington [Center] has no clue . . . no
friggin' . . . they didn't know what the hell was going on . . . What the
fuck is this about?" A staffer at the FAA's Command Center, speaking
on the tactical net, summed up the situation in four words: "It's chaos
out there."

"The challenge in relating the history of one of the most chaotic
days in our history," a Commission analyst wrote at one point in an
internal document, "is to avoid replicating that chaos in writing about
it." So copious is the material, so labyrinthine the twists and turns it
reflects, that a lengthy treatise would barely do it justice. Miles Kara,
a member of the team that analyzed the military's failures—himself
a former Army intelligence officer—was still producing learned essays on the subject as late as 2011. The Commission's basic findings,
however, were in essence straightforward, and—based on the incontrovertible evidence of the tapes and logs—revelatory.

THE NERVE CENTER for the military on September 11 was an unprepos-
sessing aluminum bunker, the last functional building on an otherwise
abandoned Air Force base in upstate New York. From the outside,
only antennas betrayed its possible importance. Inside, technicians
manned rows of antiquated computers and radar screens. They did
not, though, expect to have a quiet day on September 11. Their commander, Colonel Robert Marr, moreover, expected to have to respond
to a hijacking.

A simulated hijacking. For the Northeast Air Defense Sector's
headquarters was gearing up for its part in the latest phase of Vigilant Guardian, one of several large-scale annual exercises. This one,
old-fashioned in that it tested military preparedness for an attack by
Russian bombers, included a scenario in which an enemy would seize
an airliner and fly it to an unnamed Caribbean island.

At 8:30 that morning, the exercise proper had not yet got under way. The colonel was munching apple fritters. His mission control commander, Major Kevin Nasypany, was away from the ops floor—in his words, "on the shitter." The general to whom they answered, Larry Arnold, was at NORAD's regional command center in Florida.

On the ops floor at NEADS, Master Sergeant Maureen Dooley, Technical Sergeant Shelley Watson, and Senior Airman Stacia Rountree were chatting about furniture at the mall—wondering whether an ottoman and a love seat were on sale. To be sure, the orders for the day's training exercise provided for the team to be capable of responding to a "Real World Unknown," but no one expected much to happen.

Then the unknown arrived, in the form of a call from FAA controller Joe Cooper, at Boston Center, to Sergeant Jeremy Powell. It was 8:38.

> COOPER: Hi, Boston Center TMU [Traffic Management Unit]. We have a problem here. We have a hijacked aircraft headed towards New York, and we need you guys to, we need someone to scramble some F-16s or something up there, help us out.
> SGT. JEREMY POWELL: Is this real-world or exercise?
> COOPER: No, this is not an exercise, not a test.

The sergeant, and the women who moments earlier had been discussing home furnishings, needed some persuading. Fazed by the advent of real-life excitement, Shelley Watson even exclaimed, "Cool!" A moment later, after an "Oh, shit," she was all business. "We need call-sign, type aircraft. Have you got souls on board, and all that information? . . . a destination?" Boston Center could say only that the airplane seized was American 11—as would become clear, the first of the four hijacks. No one could have imagined the destination its hijackers had in mind.

By 8:41, Colonel Marr had ordered the two alert jets at Otis Air National Guard Base, on Cape Cod, to battle stations. At 8:46, having conferred with General Arnold, he ordered them into the air—to no avail. Absent any detailed data, they were assigned merely to fly to military-controlled airspace off the Long Island coast. In the same minute, 153 miles away, American 11 smashed into the North Tower of the World Trade Center.

The NEADS technicians, who had glanced up at a TV monitor, saw the tower in flames. "Oh, God," one technician said quietly. "Oh, my God . . ." A colleague at her side cried, "God save New York."

FAA controllers had meanwhile lost contact with the second hijacked plane, United 175. "It's escalating big, big time," New York Center manager Peter Mulligan told colleagues in Washington. "We need to get the military involved." The military was involved, in the shape of the two NEADS fighters, but impotent.

The Air Force knew nothing of the second hijack until 9:03, the very minute that Flight 175 hit the South Tower. News of that strike reached the Otis pilots Lieutenant Colonel Timothy Duffy and Major Dan Nash while they were still holding off the coast of Long Island.

Five minutes after the second strike, NEADS mission commander Nasypany ordered his fighters to head for Manhattan. Now, though, there was no suspect airliner in New York airspace to intercept. When the pilots began to fly a Combat Air Patrol over Manhattan, as soon they did, there was no enemy to combat. As catastrophe overwhelmed the city, they could only watch from high above. "I thought," Nash remembered, "it was the start of World War III."

The Air Force officers and the FAA controllers rapidly began to fear—correctly—that they had seen only the start of *something*, that there were more strikes to come. Where might they come from? It was perhaps no coincidence, they figured, that both the planes so far hijacked had started their journeys from Logan Airport. "We don't know how many guys are out of Boston," mused mission commander Nasypany. "Could be just these two—could be more." An FAA manager voiced the same thought. "Listen," he said, "both of these aircraft departed Boston. Both were 76s, both heading to LA."

"We need to do more than fuck with this," Nasypany told Colonel Marr, urging him to scramble the other alert fighters available to them—at the Langley base, three hundred miles south of New York. Marr agreed at first only to put Langley on standby. Then, at 9:21, came a call with information that changed the colonel's mind—and later led to lasting controversy.

The caller was Colin Scoggins, an FAA controller at Boston Center who—in part because of his own previous military service—had special responsibility for liaison with the Air Force. On the phone to NEADS, he shared stunning news:

Scoggins: Military, Boston. I just had a report that American 11 is still in the air, and it's on its way towards—heading towards Washington.
NEADS: OK. American 11 is still in the air?
Scoggins: Yes . . . It was evidently another aircraft that hit the tower . . . This is a report in from Washington Center. You might want to get someone on another phone talking to Washington Center.

One of the technicians did check with Washington, more than once—only to be told that they knew nothing about American 11 still being airborne. "First I heard of that," said one supervisor. The source could not be Washington Center, another said. He added, correctly, that "American 11 is the airplane, we're under the premise, that has already crashed into the World Trade Center." Scoggins, however, insisted that he had heard "from Washington" that American 11 was still in the air, going "southwest."

After Flight 11's transponder was switched off, FAA controllers at New York Center had entered a new "track" for the flight into the system in order to alert other controllers to the airliner's *projected* southerly direction. The track remained in the system for a while even after the real Flight 11 had crashed into the Trade Center. 9/11 Commission staff conjectured that it was that track, and emerging information about the loss of Flight 77, that sparked the rumor that Flight 11 was still airborne.

Scoggins never has been able to recall his source of the erroneous information—only that he picked it up while "listening on a Telcon with some people at Washington HQ, and other facilities as well, but I don't know who they were."

The information was a red herring. In the chaos of the moment, however, no one knew for certain that it was Flight 11—as opposed to some other aircraft—that had hit the North Tower. If it had not, and if hijackers were taking the captured plane southwest—as Scoggins suggested—their target had to be Washington, D.C. The realization galvanized NEADS.

"Shit!" exclaimed Nasypany. Then, "OK. American Airlines is still airborne, 11, the first guy. He's heading toward Washington. OK. I think we need to scramble Langley right now . . . Head them towards the Washington area."

So it was that at 9:30, chasing a plane that did not exist, three more Air National Guard fighters raced into the air—three, not just the two on alert duty, because NEADS had asked for every plane available. If a hijacked airliner was headed for Washington, Nasypany figured, he would send the fighters to the north of the capital, and block its way. NEADS duly ordered a course that would take them there, but the order was not followed. The tower at the base sent the fighters in another direction—east, out over the Atlantic. Where they were of no use at all.

Chaos prevailed. Four minutes into the fighters' flight, at 9:34, NEADS finally learned something American Airlines had known for more than half an hour and FAA controllers had known for even longer. "Let me tell you this," said Cary Johnson, the Washington Center operations manager. "We've been looking. We also lost American 77 . . . Indianapolis Center was working this guy . . . They lost contact with him . . . And they don't have any idea where he is."

Two minutes later, at 9:36, Scoggins came up on the phone again. "Latest report," he said. "Aircraft VFR [Visual Flight Rules, meaning the plane was not under the direction of Air Traffic Control], six miles southeast of the White House . . . We're not sure who it is." NEADS technician Stacia Rountree dialed Washington, only to be told, "It's probably just a rumor." This time, though, Scoggins's information was accurate. The plane maneuvering near the nation's capital was no phantom Flight 11. It was the very real, hijacked, American 77—lining up to strike.

In the NEADS bunker, mission commander Nasypany had no way of knowing that. What he knew, thought he knew, was that his Langley fighters were by now close to Washington, well positioned for an intercept. "Get your fighters there as soon as possible," he ordered.

Two minutes later, at 9:38, the major asked where the fighters were and learned that they were out over the ocean, 150 miles from where they were needed. Nasypany hoped against hope there was still time to respond. He urged them to fly supersonic—"I don't care how many windows you break." And, in frustration, "Why'd they go *there*? *Goddammit!* . . . OK, push 'em back!"

Too late, far too late. Even before Nasypany asked the whereabouts of his fighters, American 77 had scythed into the Pentagon.

Then, and even before the devastating news reached NEADS,

Colin Scoggins was back on the phone again from Boston Center—this time with information as misleading as had been his report that Flight 11 was still airborne. "Delta 1989," he said, "presently due south of Cleveland . . . Heading westbound." Delta 1989 was a Boeing 767, like the first two planes seized, and like them it had left from Boston. "And is this one a hijack, sir?" asked Airman Rountree. "We believe it is," Scoggins replied.

They believed wrong. Boston Center speculated that Delta 1989 was a hijack because it fit the pattern. It had departed Boston at about the same time as the first two hijacked planes. Like them it was a 767, heavily laden with fuel for a flight across the continent. Unlike them, however, it was experiencing no problems at all—until the false alarm.

NEADS promptly began tracking the Delta plane—easy enough to do because as a legitimate flight it was transmitting routine locator signals. It was the only airplane the military was able to tail electronically that day for any useful period of time. On seeing that Delta 1989 was over Ohio, NEADS sent a warning to the FAA's Cleveland Center. For the airliner's pilots, already jolted out of their routine by what little they had learned of the attacks, hours of puzzlement and worry began.

First came a text message, instructing Captain Paul Werner to "land immediately" in Cleveland. When the captain sent a simple acknowledgment, back came a second message reading, "Confirm landing in Cleveland. Use correct phraseology." A perplexed Werner tried again—more wordily, but still too casually for Cleveland. Phrases like "confirmed hijack" and "supposedly has a bomb on board" began flying across the ether. Information from Delta 1989, a controller would report, was "really unreliable and shaky."

By 9:45, only six minutes after his initial warning, Scoggins was saying the plane "might not be a hijack . . . we're just not sure." By then, though, the Air Force was busy trying to get fighters to the scene, Cleveland airport was in a state approaching panic, and 1989's pilots feared they might have a bomb on board.

"I understand," Cleveland control radioed Captain Werner meaningfully, "you're a *trip* today," The word "trip" was an established code for hijack, and Werner assured control he was not—only to be asked twice more. Once on the ground, at 10:18, he was ordered to taxi to the "bomb area," far from the passenger terminal. Passengers and crew would not be allowed to disembark for another two hours, and then under the wary eyes of gun-toting FBI agents and a SWAT team in full body armor.

It had all been, a Cleveland controller would recall, like a "scene out of a bad movie." Even before the innocent Delta 1989 landed, however, the latest phase of the aviation nightmare had become real-life horror—for Cleveland, for the Air Force team in its bunker, and, for the fourth time that day, for the nation. At 10:07, a phone call between the FAA's Cleveland Center and NEADS produced a revelation.

> FAA: I believe I was the one talking about that Delta
> 1989 . . . Well, disregard that. Did you? . . .
> NEADS: What we found out was that he was *not* a confirmed
> hijack.
> FAA: I don't want to even worry about that right now. We got a
> United 93 out here. Are you aware of *that*?

NEADS was completely unaware. During the wild-goose chase after Delta 1989, NEADS had been told nothing of the very real hijacking, also over Ohio, of United 93. An FAA controller had heard screams from Flight 93's cockpit, followed by a hijacker's announcement about a "bomb on board," some seven minutes before Scoggins alerted NEADS to the imagined problem aboard Flight 1989.

The controller had reported the new hijack promptly, and word had been passed to FAA headquarters. Cleveland control then came up again, purposefully asking whether the military had been alerted. A quarter of an hour later, nevertheless, the following pathetic exchange took place:

> FAA COMMAND CENTER: Uh, do we want to think, uh, about
> scrambling aircraft?
> FAA HEADQUARTERS: Uh, God, I don't know.
> FAA COMMAND CENTER: Uh, that's a decision somebody is
> going to have to make, probably in the next ten minutes.
> FAA HEADQUARTERS: Uh, you know, everybody just left the
> room.

Five minutes after that, at 9:53 and as United 93's passengers prepared to attack their captors, an FAA staffer reported that—almost twenty minutes after word of the hijack had reached the agency's headquarters—senior FAA executive Monte Belger and a colleague were discussing whether to ask for fighters to be scrambled. Belger would tell the 9/11 Commission that he "does not believe the conversation occurred."

At 10:03, ten minutes after the reported discussion, a full half an hour after FAA headquarters learned of the hijack, United 93's passengers and crew all died when the airliner plunged into the ground in Pennsylvania. NEADS knew nothing at all of the airliner's plight until several minutes later—and were then given only vague, out-of-date information.

"In a day when we were already frustrated," the FAA's Colin Scoggins recalled, "we were always a day late and a dollar short. We just could never catch up."

THAT, THE LOGS and documents clearly show, is the true story of the effort to defend America on 9/11. Why, then, did senior military and political men say otherwise? Why, within days, did General Myers and Paul Wolfowitz suggest that fighters had been in pursuit of Flight 93 and would have been able to bring it down? Why did senior officers, and in particular General Arnold—who had been in charge at the NORAD command center in Florida on the day—make similar claims to the 9/11 Commission?

"We believe," Arnold wrote as late as 2008, "we could have shot down the last of the hijacked aircraft, United 93, had it continued toward Washington, D.C." It was a statement founded on sand, one that airbrushed out of history the inconvenient facts of the general's previous claims. Four months after the attacks, he asserted that NORAD had already been "watching United Flight 93 wander around Ohio" at the time the Trade Center's South Tower was hit. That strike had occurred at 9:03, twenty-five minutes *before* Flight 93 had even been attacked.

Two years later, as noted earlier, Arnold would claim that NORAD's focus had been on Flight 93 by 9:24—when the hijack "was being pointed out to us very aggressively, I might say, by the FAA." This assertion also suggested a magical feat by the military, that the Air Force had been concentrating on United 93 before the plane was seized. The documented reality—damning to the FAA—is that no one at the agency reported the hijack to NORAD in any way, let alone "aggressively," until after it crashed.

General Arnold would eventually concede that his testimony had been inaccurate. What he, General Myers, and Deputy Defense Secretary Wolfowitz had said about Flight 93 had been nonsensical—though just how nonsensical would emerge only after the disentangling by Commission staff of a maze of logs and tapes—a prodigious task.

Why the officers initially told inaccurate stories is rather clear. In the fuzzy immediate aftermath of 9/11, before the facts and the timings could be analyzed, they conflated the flap over Delta 1989, the hijack that never was, with the very real hijack of Flight 93. That does not explain, however, why they continued to perpetuate the fiction long afterward, when there had been ample time to check the facts.

Former Commission analyst Miles Kara has likened NORAD's account to an attempt to solve a Sudoku puzzle—fated to fail if a single early mistake is made. He put the inaccurate story down to shoddy staff work and repeated misreadings of the logs.

Commission general counsel Daniel Marcus, though, pointed to disquieting discrepancies, including the "suspicious" omission of key times from an FAA document, the alteration of a NORAD press release, and a disputed claim about the reason for a supposed tape malfunction. Referring the matter to the inspectors general of both the Department of Defense and the Department of Transportation, he raised the possibility that the FAA and Air Force accounts were "knowingly false."

NORAD's commander-in-chief, General Ralph Eberhart, for his part, had assured the Commission he and his fellow officers "didn't get together and decide that we were going to cover for anybody or take a bullet for anybody."

Senator Mark Dayton, speaking at a hearing on the Commission's work, would have none of it. "NORAD's public chronology," he declared, "covered up . . . They lied to the American people, they lied to Congress, and they lied to your 9/11 Commission, to create a false impression of competence, communication, coordination, and protection of the American people . . . For almost three years now NORAD officials and FAA officials have been able to hide their critical failures, that left this country defenseless during two of the worst hours in our history."

The senator called on President Bush to fire "whoever at FAA or NORAD, or anywhere else who betrayed the public trust by not telling us the truth. And then he should clear up a few discrepancies of his own."

"At some level of the government, at some point in time . . . ," Commission counsel John Farmer has written, "there was a decision not to tell the truth about what happened." The troubling questions about the way the government really functioned on 9/11, Farmer made clear, also involved the White House.

THIRTEEN

WHILE THE FIRE AND SMOKE OF THE ATTACKS WERE STILL IN THE AIR, top Bush administration officials had hurried out statements on a highly sensitive issue—the decision made on 9/11 to shoot down civilian airliners if they appeared to threaten Washington. Who issued that momentous order, and when?

First there had been the flat statement by Deputy Defense Secretary Wolfowitz that—had United 93 not crashed—Air Force pilots had been poised to shoot it down. Next, on the Sunday, had come Vice President Cheney's account, in a *Meet the Press* interview, of how the shooting down of hijacked airliners had been authorized. Cheney said the "horrendous decision" had been made—with his wholehearted agreement—by the President himself. There had been moments, he said, when he thought a shoot-down might be necessary.

Bush took the decision during one of their phone calls that day, Cheney told *Newsweek*'s Evan Thomas. "I recommended to the President that we authorize . . . I said, 'We've got to give the pilots rules of engagement, and I recommend we authorize them to shoot.' We talked about it briefly, and he said, 'OK, I'll sign up to that.' He made the decision."

Bush himself, speaking with *The Washington Post*'s Bob Woodward, said Cheney had indeed suggested that he issue the order. His response, as he remembered it, had been monosyllabic. Just "You bet." Later still, speaking with the 9/11 commissioners, Bush recalled having discussed the matter in a call made to him by Cheney, and "emphasized" that it was he who authorized the shoot-down of hijacked aircraft.

By the time the President wrote his 2010 memoir, that call from the Vice President had become a call he made *to* Cheney. Bush's monosyllabic authorization, moreover, had transmogrified into a well thought-out plan.

"I called Dick Cheney as Air Force One climbed rapidly to forty-five thousand feet . . . ," the President wrote. "He had been taken to the underground Presidential Emergency Operations Center— the PEOC—when the Secret Service thought a plane might be coming at the White House. I told him that I would make decisions from the air and count on him to implement them on the ground.

"Two big decisions came quickly. The military had dispatched Combat Air Patrols—teams of fighter aircraft assigned to intercept unresponsive airplanes—over Washington and New York. . . . We needed to clarify the rules of engagement. I told Dick that our pilots should contact suspicious planes and try to get them to land peacefully. If that failed, they had my authority to shoot them down."

It would have been unthinkable for the U.S. military to down a civilian airliner without a clear order from the President, as commander-in-chief. In his absence, the authority belonged to the secretary of defense, Donald Rumsfeld. "The operational chain of command," relevant law decreed, ran "from the President to the Secretary of Defense," and on through the chairman of the Joint Chiefs to individual commanders. The Vice President was not in the chain of command.

The generals understood that. In an earlier exercise, one that postulated a suicide mission involving a jet aimed at Washington, they had said shooting it down would require an "executive" order. The defense secretary's authority, General Arnold told the Commission, was necessary to shoot down even a "derelict balloon." Only the President, he thought, had the authority to shoot down a civilian airliner.

The Commission made no overt statement as to whether it believed Cheney's assertion—that he recommended and Bush decided. Shown the final draft of the Report's passage on the shoot-down decision, however, Cheney was furious. For all its careful language, the Report dropped a clear hint that its staff had found Cheney's account—and Bush's—less than convincing.

"We just didn't believe it," general counsel Daniel Marcus declared long afterward. "The official version," John Farmer would say, "insisted that President Bush had issued an authorization to shoot down hijacked commercial flights, and that that order had been processed through the chain of command and passed to the fighters. This was untrue."

Why might a phony scenario have been created? "The administration version," Farmer noted, "implied, where it did not state explicitly, that the chain of command had been functioning on 9/11, and that the critical decisions had been made by the appropriate top officials. . . . None of this captures how things actually unfolded on the day."

THE POTENTIAL NEED to shoot down an airliner occurred to the man in the hot seat at NEADS, Major Nasypany, as early as 9:20 on 9/11 after two successful terrorist strikes and the realization that there might be more to come. "My recommendation if we have to take anybody out, large aircraft," he was taped saying, "we use AIM-9s [heat-seeking air-to-air missiles] in the face." Nasypany began asking his team whether they could countenance such an act. Everyone knew, though, that a shoot-down would require authorization from the top.

"I don't know," said Technical Sergeant Watson, on the line to the FAA, "but somebody's gotta get the President going." "I'm amazed," responded the operations manager at New York Center, "that we're not at a higher level of Defcon readiness already."

It was 9:30 by then. The President had yet to leave the school in Florida. Defense Secretary Rumsfeld, whose responsibility it was to set Defcon—the forces' Defense Condition, or military alert status— knew of the New York attacks but had so far taken no action. A few minutes later, when the Pentagon was hit at 9:37, that key figure in the chain of command would head off to view the damage—and have no contact with the President or Vice President until after 10:00.

Staff at the National Military Command Center, whose task it was to connect the President and the defense secretary to those charged with carrying out their orders, looked for Rumsfeld in vain. It was "outrageous," an unnamed senior White House official would later complain, for the man responsible for the nation's defense to have been "out of touch" at such a time.

Official reports disagree on what Rumsfeld did after leaving the scene of the crash and before his reappearance at the Pentagon's Executive Support Center around 10:15. Rumsfeld said in his Commission testimony that he had "one or more calls in my office, one of which I believe was with the President." The Defense Department's own report, however, states that he "tried without success to telephone the President."

When the President and Rumsfeld did finally speak, according to the secretary's communications assistant, the conversation covered only such questions as "Are you okay?" and "Is the Pentagon still intact?" The Commission decided that it was "a brief call, in which the subject of shoot-down authority was not discussed."

Rumsfeld was still "just gaining situational awareness"—as he put it—as late as 10:35, when he finally joined a conference call that included Vice President Cheney. Shoot-down authority had already been issued, Cheney said, and—as the transcript of the conversation makes clear—that was news to the defense secretary:

CHENEY: There's been at least three instances here where we've had reports of aircraft approaching Washington—a couple were confirmed hijack. And, pursuant to the President's instructions, I gave authorization for them to be taken out . . . [Long pause] Hello?

RUMSFELD: Yes, I understand. Who did you give that direction to?

CHENEY: It was passed from here through the [Operations] Center at the White House, from the PEOC [shelter beneath the White House].

RUMSFELD: OK, let me ask the question here. Has that directive been transmitted to the aircraft?

CHENEY: Yes, it has.

RUMSFELD: So we've got a couple of aircraft up there that have those instructions at this present time?

CHENEY: That is correct. And it's my understanding they've already taken a couple of aircraft out.

Later, interviewed for his own department's report, Rumsfeld was asked whether shoot-down authorization "had come from the Vice President." "Technically," he replied, "it couldn't. Because the Vice President is not in the chain of command. The President and he were talking, and the President and I were talking, and the Vice President and I were talking. Clearly he was involved in the process."

That fuzzy answer was of no use in establishing when and by whom the shoot-down authority was issued. Rumsfeld's public testimony to the 9/11 Commission was no more useful. The record of what he told staff in closed session is still withheld, and his 2011 memoir added no substantive detail.

The White House itself ought to have been the best source of information on communications between Bush and Cheney, but the White House proved unhelpful. Though the Commission did manage to get clearance to interview a few of the staff members who had been around the President and Vice President that morning, what they learned on the shoot-down issue was of virtually no use.

"Very little new information has been gained in the five White House meetings conducted thus far," a frustrated staffer noted in the final months of the Commission's work. "To a person, no one has any recollection of the circumstances and details surrounding the authorization to shoot down commercial aircraft. . . . Our sense is that the White House will take the position that it is not possible to reconstruct—with any degree of accuracy or reliability—what went on that morning."

Investigators also asked for interviews with relevant Secret Service agents, but the White House stalled. Then it offered limited access to some of them, with an attorney present. It was next to impossible, the staffer reported, to probe beyond the vague stories told by Bush and Cheney in their media interviews.

Faced with this obstruction, the Commission team concentrated on the paper trail. The White House famously keeps track of all high-level communications, maintains records of phone calls, logs of Secret Service operations, logs kept by military officers, a Situation Room log, a log of activity in the Presidential Emergency Operations Center—PEOC—the bunker in the bowels of the White House where Cheney spent much of the day on September 11, and logs kept aboard Air Force One. For the day of 9/11, there were also notes kept by individuals: President Bush's press secretary, Vice President Cheney's chief of staff, and his wife, Lynne Cheney.

Once again, however, the investigators found themselves stalled. White House personnel sought to limit the Commission's access to the contemporary record, while simultaneously insisting it was unreliable. Undeterred, Commission staff built a chronology as best they could from available logs and from what witness testimony they did manage to obtain.

The record, such as we have it, does not support the Bush/Cheney version of events, that the President gave Cheney shoot-down authorization during a phone conversation sometime soon after 10:00 A.M., after Cheney's arrival in the underground bunker.

The Bush/Cheney version, with its implication of the requisite line of command—Bush granted authority, Cheney transmitted it— does not mesh with events as they unfolded.

The emergency teleconferences that morning—one in the White House Situation Room, one at the Pentagon, another at the FAA— overlapped with one another, making for confusion rather than clarity. To participate in one, senior staff would temporarily have to drop out of another. The conference in the Situation Room—below the West Wing—was not linked to the part of the Pentagon dealing with the crisis, nor was it adequately linked to the Vice President in the PEOC, beneath the East Wing. "In my mind," one witness recalled of the teleconferences, "they were competing venues for command and control and decision-making."

It was not only the teleconferences that added to the fog. Some were to recall having seen staff members with a phone to each ear, reliance on runners to convey messages, and the use of personal cell phones to complete calls when landlines were unavailable. The cell phone system itself was at times overwhelmed.

Alerted to an aircraft approaching the city, just before Flight 77 struck the Pentagon, the Secret Service had hustled the Vice President toward the PEOC. Cheney had been logged in there at 9:58, having paused en route to use a phone in an adjacent passageway—and was to remain in the PEOC's conference room thenceforth.

It was from the PEOC, within moments of his arrival there, that the Vice President supposedly had his exchange with Bush about shoot-down authority. Yet, though many other key events of that morning are reflected in the contemporary record, there is no documentary evidence of the call. It is especially perplexing, moreover, that—assuming there was such a call and assuming the President did give shoot-down authority—the Vice President made no immediate move to pass on the order.

What the record does show occurred, at about the time the Cheney-Bush call is supposed to have been made, is that staff in the Situation Room received reports that further aircraft were missing, were told that a Combat Air Patrol had been established over Washington, and began attempting to reach the President.

At 10:03, in the Situation Room, NSC staffer Paul Kurtz made a note as follows: "asking Prez authority to shoot down a/c [aircraft]." That attempt to reach Bush, however, was apparently unsuccessful. The evidence is that calls reached not the President but only those with the Vice President in the PEOC. The weight of the written and spoken evidence indicates that it was beween 10:10 and 10:20—on being told of the progress of a suspect airplane supposedly headed for the Washington area—that Cheney twice rapped out a shoot-down order.

The Vice President's wife, Lynne, who was in the PEOC and not far from her husband, recorded some of the exchange about shoot-down authority in notes she made that morning.

Mrs. Cheney noted at "10:10":

Aircraft coming in from 80 miles out
Dick asked? Scramble fighters?

Navy commander Anthony Barnes, the senior military officer on duty in the PEOC that morning, told the authors in 2010, "A call comes into the PEOC. I'm talking to a general on a secure line. He asks for permission to engage confirmed terrorists on board commercial airplanes. I went into the conference room and I posed this question to the Vice President exactly the way it was posed to me. I received permission." Cheney's chief of staff, Scooter Libby, has recalled in an interview that the Vice President, asked whether fighters had authority to engage, barely paused before responding simply, "Yes."

At 10:12, Mrs. Cheney noted:

> *60 miles out—confirmed JOC [the Secret Service's Joint Operations*
> *Center]*
> *hijacked aircraft*
> *fighters cleared to engage*

The Vice President's wife would recall feeling "a sort of chill up my spine, that this is the kind of things you only read about in novels . . . We had to shoot down those planes if they didn't divert."

"I asked for confirmation on what I was being allowed to pass back to the general," Barnes recalled. "It was twice. I said it the first time and he answered straight up. . . . It wasn't indiscriminately: 'Splat everything airborne!' It was 'If you can confirm there's another terrorist aircraft inbound, permission is granted to take it out.' . . . I went back to the phone and said to the general, 'The Vice President has authorized you to engage confirmed terrorist aboard commercial aircraft.' "

At 10:14, a lieutenant colonel at the White House passed word to the Pentagon that the Vice President had "confirmed" fighters were "cleared to engage the inbound aircraft if they could verify that the aircraft was hijacked." It was, another officer said, a "pin-drop moment."

A Libby note, timed as "10:15–18," read:

> *Aircraft 60 miles out, confirmed as hijack—engage? VP: Yes. JB:*
> *Get President and confirm engage order*

The initials "JB" referred to Joshua Bolten, the White House deputy chief of staff—who was also with the Vice President in the bunker. He suggested that Cheney call Bush, he told the Commission, because he "wanted to make sure the President was told that the Vice President had executed the order. He said he had not heard any prior discussion on the subject with the President."

Nor had press secretary Ari Fleischer, who was at Bush's side aboard Air Force One and keeping a record of everything that was said—at the President's request. His notes up to that point—like those of Scooter Libby and Lynne Cheney at the White House—contain no reference to any conversation with Cheney about shoot-down authorization. They do show, however, that at 10:20—two minutes after a formally logged call from the Vice President—Bush told Fleischer that "he had authorized a shoot-down if necessary."

• • •

OTHER INFORMATION, reportable in detail now thanks to recent document releases, further suggests that the Vice President may have authorized the shooting down of suspect airliners without the President's say-so. It involves exchanges between Secret Service agents at the White House and Air National Guard officers at Andrews Air Force Base, just ten miles southeast of Washington. Though not an "alert" base, its units proudly styled themselves the "Capital Guardians."

Unlike the President—in his role as commander-in-chief—and those in the military chain of command, the Secret Service was not primarily concerned with countering the terrorist attacks. Its priority was the protection of the President and Vice President and those in the line of succession. On September 11, that meant trying to protect Air Force One and the White House itself from attack. On 9/11, according to Commission staff member Miles Kara, the missions of the military leadership—from the President as commander-in-chief on down—and the Secret Service were at times "mutually exclusive."

A Secret Service agent and his FAA liaison had, early on, after the two attacks on New York, discussed the need to get fighters over Washington. Once the Pentagon had been hit, the phones began ringing at Andrews. Brigadier General David Wherley, the National Guard commander at the base, arrived at a run to learn that Secret Service agent Ken Beauchamp had rung with the message, "Get anything you can airborne."

When he got back to Beauchamp, Wherley was helpful but cautious. He asked to speak with "someone a little higher up the food chain," and was passed first to another agent, Nelson Garabito. Garabito told him, "It's coming direct from the Vice President." Still not satisfied, the general then spoke with the agent in charge of the Presidential Protective Division, Rebecca Ediger. Ediger repeated the request—Wherley told the 9/11 Commission—"speaking for the Vice President."

The general asked to speak direct to Cheney, but Ediger said the Vice President was on another line. Wherley "wasn't going to get to talk to anyone he felt comfortable getting the order from," he realized. So he made do with Agent Ediger—and an "unidentified male voice who took the phone from Ediger" and asked him to "put aircraft over DC with orders to intercept any aircraft that approached within twenty miles and turn that aircraft around. If the aircraft would not change course, the interceptor should use 'any force necessary' to keep that aircraft from crashing into a building." Wherley felt the instructions were "understandable enough."

When did the Secret Service pass on this purported order from the Vice President? Of the various documents released, one heavily redacted Secret Service memo—dated less than a month after 9/11—is tantalizing. It states that:

> After the crash at the Pentagon, Commander [Anthony Barnes of the White House Military Office] in the PEOC advised . . . that the Vice President had authorized them to engage any other suspect aircraft. . . . It was at about this time, I began fielding calls from Andrews Air Force Base. I first got a call from [several words redacted]. I verified that they had been requested to do so with the PEOC. When I conveyed this to [words redacted] I told him the Vice President [words redacted] Commander [Barnes] was more than a little incredulous. He had me tell the General to get it from the NMCC [National Military Command Center].

While Barnes cannot today pin down at what time this exchange took place, an Andrews control tower transcript shows that, beginning at about 10:04, a controller began repeatedly transmitting a warning that unauthorized flights entering the closed airspace around Washington would be shot down. Though one cannot be conclusive, the genesis of the warning was likely an instruction passed from the Secret Service.

Cheney would later tell the 9/11 Commission that he had not even been "aware that that fighters had been scrambled out of Andrews at the request of the Secret Service and outside the military chain of command." *The Wall Street Journal*, however, has reported conflicting claims. While White House officials said the Secret Service "acted on its own," the Secret Service issued a statement denying that it did so. To the contrary, the *Journal* reported, senior agents insisted that "the agents' actions on September 11 had been ordered by the Vice President."

Did Cheney give a shoot-down order on his own initiative, before consulting the President? The available evidence suggests he may have. To have done so, moreover, would certainly have been more sensible than sinister. At a moment the capital seemed to be in imminent peril, the two men properly heading the chain of command were out of touch—the secretary of defense away from his post and the President only intermittently in contact because of shaky communications. Many might think that Cheney, on the spot and capable, would have been justified in short-circuiting the system.

If he did so, and had he and the President soon acknowledged as much, it would have been pointless to blame the Vice President. If he did so and then persistently told a false story, however—and if the eventual release of all the records were to prove it—history will be less generous.

WHOEVER REALLY ISSUED the shoot-down order, it came too late to have any effect on events. At Andrews, General Wherley had no immediate way to respond to it—no planes were ready to take off, let alone planes armed and ready. He had, moreover, come away from his exchanges with the Secret Service less than certain about the Vice President's order. He sent up the first plane available, an unarmed F-16 summoned back from a training exercise, to "check out" the situation over Washington—with no explicit instructions. Four more fighters took off a little later, one pair also without armament, the other—at 11:12 and after a rushed loading process—fully armed with heat-seeking missiles. Their instructions were to fly "weapons free," which left the decision to fire up to the pilots.

Even then, an hour or more after the shoot-down order came to him via the Secret Service, General Wherley still felt "uncomfortable with the situation." He did not receive formal, detailed rules of engagement from the Defense Department until long after the real action was over, five hours after the start of the attacks.

The vice presidential authorization to shoot down airliners, meanwhile, had made its way down the designated chain of command from the Pentagon to NEADS, NORAD's Northeast Air Defense Sector— the nerve center for the two "alert" bases, as distinct from General Wherley's outfit at Andrews—by 10:31. When the harried men in the NEADS bunker received the order, however, they hesitated:

MAJOR STEVE OVENS: You need to read this . . . The Region Commander has declared that we can shoot down aircraft that do not respond to our direction . . . Did you copy that?

Major James Fox, weapons director [a moment later]: DO [Director of Operations] is saying "No."

Ovens: No? . . . Foxy, you got a conflict on that direction?

Fox: Right now, no, but . . .

Ovens: OK? OK, you read that from the Vice President, right? . . . Vice President has cleared us . . .

Fox [reading]: . . . to intercept traffic . . . shoot them down if they do not respond.

NEADS's Robert Marr, and Major Nasypany commanding the fighters from Otis and Langley, were unsure of the order's ramifications, did not know quite how to proceed. No new order was sent to the pilots at that point. General Eberhart, moreover, in overall command of NORAD, directed that pilots should not shoot until satisfied that a "hostile act" was being committed.

Not until 10:53 did Nasypany order that his pilots be sent the following tentative message:

Any track of interest that's headed toward the major cities you will I.D. If you cannot divert them away from the major cities you are to confirm with me first. Most likely you will get clearance to shoot.

The stories told by Cheney, Deputy Defense Secretary Wolfowitz, the FAA, and the military all seemed to fit neatly together after 9/11. Yet they distorted historical truths. The Air Force would not, as Wolfowitz claimed, have been in a position to shoot down United 93, because—had it not crashed—the hijacked airplane would have reached Washington before any fighter pilot in the air received a shoot-down order. The military and FAA versions were similarly misleading or inaccurate—so arousing the Commission's suspicions that it referred the matter to their respective inspectors general for further investigation.

The FAA's acting deputy administrator, Monte Belger, told the 9/11 Commission that his officials reacted quickly, "in my opinion professionally," on September 11. This in spite of the fact that for a full half hour—in a crisis when every moment counted—the agency failed to alert the military to the plight of Flight 93.

"In my opinion," NORAD's General Myers was to say in his prepared statement, "lines of authority, communication and command were clear; and the Commander in Chief and Secretary of Defense conveyed clear guidance to the appropriate military commanders."

That was the message they all wanted the world to hear—that the men who held power in America had been on top of the situation. What is clear, in fact, John Farmer pointed out in 2009, is that "the top officials were talking mainly to themselves. They were an echo chamber. They were of little or no assistance to the people on the ground attempting to manage the crisis." A thoroughgoing analysis, in Farmer's view, "would have exposed the reality that national leadership was irrelevant during those critical moments."

The testimony offered after 9/11, Farmer wrote,

> was not simply wrong about facts; it was wrong in a way that misrepresented the competence and relevance of the chain of command to the response. . . . It was difficult to decide which was the more disturbing possibility. To believe that the errors in fact were simply inadvertent would be to believe that senior military and civilian officials were willing to testify in great detail and with assurance . . . without bothering to make sure that what they were saying was accurate. Given the significance of 9/11 in our history, this would amount to an egregious breach of the public trust. If it were true, however, that the story was at some level coordinated and was knowingly false, that would be an egregious deception.

"History," Farmer wrote later in his book, "should record that, whether through unprecedented administrative incompetence or orchestrated mendacity, the American people were misled about the nation's response to the 9/11 attacks."

PART III

AMERICA RESPONDS

FOURTEEN

Americans knew, instantly assumed they knew, who had attacked them on 9/11. The Arabs.

As soon as news of the attacks broke, before anything was known of the attackers, a woman phoned the FBI to report an experience she had had the previous evening. She had spotted a diary in a garbage can at Chicago's Midway Airport, she said, and the final entry had read: "Allah will be served." That, she thought, seemed sinister.

On an airliner en route to Australia, a flight attendant had kept an eye on a "Middle Eastern male passenger" who was busy on his laptop. Its screen carried a picture of a Boeing 747 and then, suddenly, the words "Mission failed." The attendant hurried to tell the captain. He in turn alerted the airline and the flight was diverted to the nearest airport—where it emerged that the swarthy passenger was from not the Middle East but Guatemala. The "suspicious" activity had been a video game.

In the turmoil at the Trade Center, even before the second tower fell, a New York fire chief witnessed what was almost certainly the first arrest of the day. As he led his men down to safety, Richard Picciotto remembered, he had come across a cluster of firemen and a police officer engaged in an encounter with "a middle-aged Middle Eastern man."

> The guy was dressed in a nice suit and carrying a nice brief-case, and as I pulled close to the commotion I could see there had been something of a struggle. . . . One of the firemen on the floor had grown concerned at the man's sudden appearance; the firefighter had once been a police detective, and he felt there was something fishy about this guy, something about his still being on such a high floor.
>
> All kinds of speculation had been bouncing around on our radios regarding responsibility for these terrorist attacks, and the sight of a transparently Middle Eastern individual was suspicious . . . plus he had a briefcase, which could have contained a bomb . . . the "suspect" was in handcuffs and crying uncontrollably. He was claiming innocence of any wrongdoing. . . . In all likelihood, this guy was guilty of nothing more than foolishness and slowfootedness, but here we were, escorting him down as he cried and as we fought back our own terrors. . . . It was little over an hour since the first attacks, and already we were running scared.

The Arab with the briefcase would neither be charged with anything nor heard of again. If he was roughly interrogated, though, if he was even held in jail for some time, he was one of many. Some five thousand foreign nationals, most of them of Arab descent, were taken into custody at some point in the two years after the attacks.

According to a Department of Justice inspector general's report, detainees picked up after 9/11 "remained in custody—many in extremely restrictive conditions of confinement—for weeks and months with no clearance investigations being conducted. . . . Those conditions included 'lock down' for at least 23 hours per day; escorts that included a '4-man hold' with handcuffs, leg irons, and heavy chains any time the detainees were moved . . . the evidence indicates a pattern of physical and verbal abuse by some correctional officers." None of those arrested in the United States was to be linked to the attacks, and only one man would be convicted of terrorism offenses. In the words of immigration commissioner James Ziglar, the period after 9/11 was "a moment of national hysteria."

Some innocent Arabs suffered humiliation or abuse simply on account of their ethnicity. In Brooklyn and Queens, districts where Arabs had long prospered, they suddenly faced open hostility from passersby. Anyone brown and foreign-looking was vulnerable, even at risk of physical violence. Four days after the attacks, a Sikh American was shot dead outside his convenience store by a man shouting that he was a "patriot." The previous day, the murdered man had made a donation to a charity for 9/11 victims.

Baseless prejudice aside, anything involving Arabs and air travel now triggered suspicion. An Egyptian pilot at a Manhattan hotel, overheard saying, "The sky's gonna change," faced a grueling interrogation. When the ban on civilian air travel was lifted, some passengers found themselves ordered off airliners before takeoff because they fit a profile—they were Arabs. On occasion, such incidents were defensible. For there were grounds for believing that, absent the order to ground all planes on 9/11, there would have been at least one more hijacking.

Several sources told of an incident that occurred at New York's Kennedy Airport that morning. It began as United Flight 23 waited its turn to take off, when an attendant told pilot Tom Mannello that there was something odd about "four young Arab men sitting in First Class." Mannello, for the moment busy responding to the decision to ground all planes, took the airliner back to the gate and told all his passengers that they had to leave the aircraft.

"The Muslims wouldn't disembark at first," a United official said. "The crew talked to the Muslims but by the time the Kennedy Airport police arrived the individuals had deplaned . . . they left the airport without being questioned." The Arabs' checked baggage, which they never reclaimed, reportedly contained "incriminating" material, including terrorist "instruction sheets."

One of the known 9/11 hijackers, Khalid al-Mihdhar, had reportedly told a cousin in Saudi Arabia sometime earlier that "five" hijacks were planned for September 11. "We think we had at least another plane that was involved," NORAD deputy commander Ken Pennie said later. "I don't know the target or other details. But we were lucky."

• • •

AROUND 1:00 P.M. on September 11, the President of the United States had a question for his CIA briefer on board Air Force One. "Who," he asked, "do you think did this?" "There's no evidence, there's no data," briefer Mike Morell replied, "but I would pretty much bet everything I own that the trail will end with al Qaeda and bin Laden."

In the Middle East as they spoke, some were celebrating. In contrast to most of their governments' expressions of sympathy, there were Arabs in Saudi Arabia, Egypt, and Lebanon who were openly jubilant. In Iraq, President Saddam Hussein said he thought Americans "should feel the pain they have inflicted on other peoples of the world." In Palestinian refugee camps across the region, men fired assault rifles into the air. People handed out candies to passersby, a tradition at times of joy. In the United Arab Emirates, a caller to a TV station claimed responsibility for the attacks in the name of the Democratic Front for the Liberation of Palestine. A DFLP spokesman swiftly issued a denial, surprising no one. For Arabs, knowledgeable or otherwise, shared the view of Bush's CIA briefer.

In the Gaza Strip, two men marched through the streets carrying an enormous blowup of Osama bin Laden. Messages circulated on Saudi mobile phones, according to a leading Saudi dissident, reading: "Congratulations. . . . Our prayers to bin Laden!" "This action," said Dr. Sayid al-Sharif, an Egyptian surgeon who had once worked with bin Laden in the underground, "is from al Qaeda."

Osama bin Laden.

Al Qaeda.

The day before the attacks, September 10th, the Congressional Research Service had published its 2001 report on terrorism in the Near East.

"Al Qaeda (Arabic for 'the base')," it said, "has evolved from a regional threat to U.S. troops in the Persian Gulf to a global threat to U.S. citizens and national security interests." It was "a coalition of disparate radical Islamic groups of varying nationalities to work toward common goals—the expulsion of non-Muslim control or influence from Muslim-inhabited lands." Cells had been identified or suspected in more than thirty-five countries, including the United States. On an activity scale of Low to High, al Qaeda was the only organization rated "Extremely High."

Osama bin Laden—"Usama bin Ladin" in officialese—got a page to himself in the report. It noted that he was forty-four years old, the seventeenth of twenty sons of a Saudi construction magnate. He "had gained prominence during the Afghan war against the Soviet Union," after which his "radical Islamic contacts caused him to run afoul of Saudi authorities. . . . As a result of bin Ladin's opposition to the ruling Al Saud family, Saudi Arabia revoked his citizenship in 1994 and his family disavowed him, though some of his brothers reportedly have maintained contact with him. . . .

"In May, 1996, following strong U.S. and Egyptian pressure . . . he returned to Afghanistan, under protection of the dominant Taliban movement. . . . Bin Ladin is estimated to have about $300 million in personal financial assets, with which he funds his network of as many as 3,000 Islamic militants." The report linked the bin Laden network to attacks on U.S. forces in Somalia in 1993 and to a dozen terrorist operations or plots—including the devastating bombing of the U.S. Navy destroyer the USS *Cole* the previous year. In 1999, it noted, "bin Ladin was placed on the FBI's 'Ten Most Wanted' list, and a $5 million reward is offered for his capture."

CBS News fingered bin Laden half an hour after the first strike on the World Trade Center. U.S. intelligence, it said, had "for some time been warning that Osama bin Laden has not been heard from . . . they believed it was only a matter of time." Half an hour after that, the National Security Agency—which spies on international communications—picked up the first indication that the intelligence had been accurate. A known bin Laden operative, talking on a phone in Afghanistan, was overheard speaking of having heard "good news." Also intercepted were the words: "We've hit the targets."

Airline computers were by now starting to disgorge printouts of passenger manifests for the hijacked flights. "Although in our collective gut we knew al Qaeda was behind the attacks, we needed proof," recalled CIA director George Tenet. "So CTC [the Agency's Counterterrorism Center] requested passenger lists . . . the initial response from some part of the bureaucracy (which parts since mercifully forgotten) was that manifests could not be shared with CIA. There were privacy issues involved. Some gentle reasoning, and a few four-letter words later, the lists were sprung."

The manifests satisfied Tenet "beyond a doubt" that al Qaeda was involved. For thousands of FBI agents, they opened the way to a massive investigation that was to last far into the future—but immediately bore fruit.

• • •

THE VERY FIRST LEAD was provided by the two flight attendants who phoned from Flight 11 in those last fraught minutes before the airplane hit the World Trade Center. Betty Ong and Amy Sweeney had between them provided the seat numbers of three of the five hijackers. "We could then go to the manifest," FBI director Robert Mueller said later, "find out who was sitting in those seats, and immediately conduct an investigation of those individuals, as opposed to taking all the passengers on the plane and going through a process of elimination."

The three passengers identified by the flight attendants were Satam al-Suqami and two brothers, Wail and Waleed al-Shehri, all Saudis. Among the Anglo, Russian, East European, and Latino names of the eighty-one passengers aboard Flight 11, two other names stood out: Moham—the computer had failed to complete the name "Mohamed"—Atta, and Abdul al-Omari.

A bright U.S. Airways employee in Portland, Maine, was already focusing on passengers Atta and Omari. On learning of the Trade Center crashes—two crashes at the same location in seventeen minutes had to be terrorism—security coordinator Diane Graney pulled the records to see if any passengers had left Portland for Boston that morning on the first leg of a longer journey. There were those two same names: Atta and Omari, booked to fly on to Los Angeles aboard American Flight 11.

Graney talked with the customer service representative who had checked in the two men. He remembered them, remembered that Omari had seemed not to know any English, that he had kept quiet and tagged along behind Atta. He remembered that, told he would have to check in again at Boston, Atta had "clenched his jaw . . . looked like he was about to get mad." He remembered, too, that Atta had checked two bags. Graney called her manager, and together they called corporate security.

Before 6:00 A.M., it would emerge, a security camera at Portland airport had recorded the pair, Atta in a blue shirt and dark pants, Omari in lighter clothing, retrieving hand baggage from the X-ray machine at the security point. Nothing about their demeanor, nothing in the expressions on their faces, had betrayed what they were about to do.

It would be a long time before the pieces of the jigsaw would be found and seen to make sense. From Portland, it would be discovered, Atta had called two key fellow conspirators; Marwan al-Shehhi, a citizen of the United Arab Emirates, whose name appeared on the manifest of United Airlines Flight 175, the second plane hijacked; and a Lebanese man named Ziad Jarrah, who had flown on Flight 93, the fourth plane hijacked.

The Nissan rental car Atta had used, found where he had left it in the parking lot, contained a rental agreement in Atta's name, maps of Boston and Maine, fingerprints and hairs—and a Chips Ahoy! cookie package. At other airports, however, and in other hotels and parking lots, there would be evidential treasure.

At Boston's Logan Airport, where two of the hijacker teams had boarded their target airliners, the FBI found two cars, a blue Hyundai Accent and a white Mitsubishi Mirage. The Hyundai had been rented in the name of "Fayez Ahmed," the two first names of Flight 175 hijacker Banihammad, from the United Arab Emirates. Phone records linked him, too, to Atta—they had spoken three times early on 9/11. Hotel stationery left in the Hyundai identified one of the Boston area hotels the hijackers had used, the Milner on South Charles Street. Banihammad had been ticketed for overstaying his time on a parking meter across the street from the hotel.

The white Mitsubishi at Logan was found rapidly, thanks to the man who had pulled up alongside and—as described earlier—reported the strange behavior of the three Arabs seated in it. The car had been rented by Flight 11 hijacker Wail al-Shehri, who had on the eve of the hijackings shared Room 433 at the Park Inn Motel near the airport with his brother Waleed and Satam al-Suqami. One of them, agents concluded, had slept in the bathtub.

Two comrades, Hamza and Ahmed al-Ghamdi—members of the same Saudi tribe but apparently not brothers—had stayed first at the upmarket Charles Hotel, just behind the John F. Kennedy School of Government, found it too pricey, and moved to a Days Inn. The Ghamdis were truly parsimonious. They tipped the driver of the cab that took them to the airport, on the way to hijack Flight 175, just 15 cents.

The contents of the cars at the airports and the hotel rooms, and the contacts the hijackers made, revealed an unexpected side of the Arabs—unexpected, that is, in supposed Muslim zealots. Muslims living according to their religious tenets are forbidden to engage in *zināa*—premarital sex or adultery. Even masturbation is *harām*—forbidden—except in certain circumstances. Anecdotal evidence suggests that some of the future hijackers respected these rules. In one of the rooms they had used at a seaside motel in Florida, a witness was to recall, two of the men draped towels over pictures on the wall of women in bathing suits. These were all young men, however—most of them in their twenties—and probably knew they were soon to die.

English-language reading the hijackers left behind ranged from what the FBI inventory calls "romance-type" books to an old copy of *Penthouse*, found under a bed. Among the toiletries found in one of the cars were a dozen Trojan condoms. It would turn out that several of the terrorists had sought out prostitutes in their last days alive.

Many other, evidentially significant, clues came out of Boston. From tracking the phone records, it early on began to look as though Atta had headed the operation in the field. In both Portland and Boston, agents got started on a key element in the case—the money trail. A FedEx bill in a trash can, calls to the United Arab Emirates, calls to Western Union, an attempt to send money from a TravelX office—all were clues that contributed to understanding how the 9/11 attacks had been funded. Much of the money had come through two key contacts in the Emirates and—faithful to the Muslim precept that prohibits squandering wealth—the men about to die were returning what was left over.

There were ominous indications, too, that the hijackers had had associates in the United States. Agents puzzled over a strange incident involving a hotel room the hijackers had used. "A maid at the Park Inn," an FBI report noted, advised "that an Arabic male answered the door of the room at approximately 11:00 a.m. on the morning of 9/11/01. The man asked her to come back later to clean because someone in the room was sleeping." Who was the unknown Arab still in a hijacker's room more than two hours *after* the hijackers had carried out their mission and gone to their deaths? And if there was a second man in the room, who was *he*? Were fellow terrorists, "sleepers," at large in the United States?

In one of the hijackers' cars, agents found a piece of paper with a name and a phone number, 589-5316, and—scrawled on a map in yellow highlighter—a second name and two numbers, 703–519–1947 and 703–514–1947. The names related to men who could be traced—leading to manhunts, arrests, and protracted investigations.

Washington's Dulles Airport, where the five American 77 hijackers had boarded, was replete with clues. Security camera pictures, and a detailed account by a security guard, seemed to indicate that several of the terrorists had reconnoitered a secure area of the airport the evening before the attacks. They may, too, have had the use of an electronic pass—another indication that the hijackers may have had accomplices.

There were major finds in the blue, California-registered Toyota Corolla found parked at Dulles. The vehicle was registered to Flight 77 hijack suspect Nawaf al-Hazmi, yet another Saudi, and he (and perhaps another man) had left their personal belongings in the vehicle. There was clothing—T-shirts, pants, shorts, belts, socks, and briefs. There were toiletries—Nivea cream, Dry Idea deodorant, Dr. Scholl's foot powder, Breath Remedy tongue spray, and Kleenex tissues. There was a broken pair of sunglasses, a hairbrush, an electric razor, no fewer than three alarm clocks, a compact disk entitled *The Holy Qur'an*, and worry beads.

As well as the bric-a-brac of daily life, though, there was also investigative treasure: fragments of torn paper relating to Flight 77, which, reassembled, revealed handwritten notes; a receipt for a driver's license issued to Hazmi in San Diego, banking information for him and fellow Saudi Hani Hanjour—another Flight 77 suspect—and a doctor's prescription written for Hazmi's Saudi comrade Khalid al-Mihdhar. There were mailbox receipts; a flyer for a library in Alexandria, Virginia; addresses in Virginia, Maryland, New Jersey, and Arizona; and a hand-drawn map pointing to an address in a suburb of San Diego.

Also, and this was a key to a whole world of information that would keep agents swarming across the country for months, here were the first traces of the suspects' involvement in aviation: Hanjour's ID card for the Pan Am International Flight Academy in Phoenix; a receipt from Caldwell Flight Academy in Fairfield, New Jersey; and four color diagrams of the instrument panels in a Boeing 757, the type of airliner that Nawaf al-Hazmi and his brother Salem, Hanjour, Mihdhar, and Majed Moqed—yet another Saudi—had boarded on 9/11.

There would be much more. Two duffel bags left at the Ayah Islamic Center in Laurel, Maryland—apparently by Hazmi and Mihdhar—contained pilot logbooks, evidence that they had attended a flight school as early as 2000, receipts for aviation headsets, and a chart kit. In the rental car at Portland Airport there was an Arabic-language flight manual and the name of another flight school, Huffman Aviation in Venice, Florida. Boeing 757 manuals would also be found at a motel the terrorists had used in Florida.

Even as news of the attacks was breaking, people at Huffman Aviation remembered their encounters with Atta and Shehhi. "Everybody was gathered around the hotel lobby television," said Mark Mikarts, a former Huffman instructor who had taught the pair, "and lo and behold there's Mohamed Atta's picture and Marwan al-Shehhi's picture up on the TV screen. I felt myself just pooling into a puddle . . . I was speechless, aghast. I just could not believe that these were the people I had sat next to, had given primary instruction to."

In southern England, former Huffman student pilot Ann Greaves recognized Atta's picture the moment it was shown on television. "It was the sort of face that once you'd seen it you would never forget it," she remembered. "His bearing was that of someone very much in command."

Rudi Dekkers, the Dutchman who ran Huffman, was soon besieged by journalists from around the world. He said he had assumed Atta and Shehhi had been at the school, like his many other foreign students, just to get their pilot's licenses. There had been no reason to inquire about their longer term plans.

By MIDNIGHT on September 11, agents had evidence that appeared to dispel any doubt as to the suspects' guilt and what their purpose had been—in Mohamed Atta's luggage. Atta and Omari had checked two suitcases when they arrived at Portland Airport, a green one and a black pull-along. When they made their connection to American 11 at Boston, however, the suitcases did not. The baggage reached the plane too late to be loaded. Atta, already on board and waiting for takeoff, had apparently been concerned about the bags—a flight attendant, presumably at his behest, had asked ground staff whether the bags safely made the transfer. If Atta did worry that the suitcases would be found later and searched, he worried with good reason.

Atta's pull-along bag turned out to be a window on his life—and on the nature of the 9/11 attacks. It contained his Egyptian passport and ID, which revealed his full name, a report card from the Faculty of Engineering at Cairo University, and an addressed envelope indicating that he had lived in Germany. There were videotapes of Boeing 747 and 757 operating procedures, flight simulator information, and a flight computer in a case. A copy of the Qur'an, a prayer schedule, and Atta's will—written and signed when he was only twenty-seven—revealed him to be intensely religious.

The significance of all that, however, paled beside that of another document. Seventeen days after the attacks, the FBI released four pages of Arabic script that had also been found in Atta's bag. Further copies were recovered, moreover, one in the car Hazmi abandoned at Dulles Airport, another—apparently a remnant—at the United 93 crash scene in Pennsylvania. Neither the 9/11 Commission Report nor a Commission staff document—released later—even mentions the find. An obscure footnote lists the various other contents of the retrieved baggage, but not the document.

The omission is extraordinary, unconscionable, for the telltale pages were important evidence. Scholars who have translated and analyzed them have described them as nothing less than a "Spiritual Manual" or "Handbook" for the 9/11 attacks. Intensely religious in tone from beginning to end, the document is a mix of counsel, comfort, inspiration, and practical instruction—complex in many ways, replete with references obscure to the non-Muslim Westerner—but its thrust is clear. The pages offered the hijackers detailed advice on how to prepare for the attacks—and for death.

The manual opens with instructions for its readers' "Last Night," a time to stay awake, to meditate, pray, renew the "mutual pledge to die," to contemplate "the eternal blessing God has prepared for the believers, especially for the martyrs."

As physical preparation, readers were reminded of the importance of "shaving off excess hair from the body and perfuming oneself" and "Performing the greater ritual ablution [washing thoroughly]." The manual urged the old custom of *nafth*—spitting—to bring protection. Readers were to spit on "the suitcase, the clothing, the knife . . . equipment . . . ID . . . *tdh* [probably an abbreviation of *tadhkira*, ticket] . . . passport . . . all your papers." "Each one of you must sharpen his knife."

The car journey to the "*m*" [the abbreviation, probably, of *matar*, airport] was to include further prayers, the prayer for travel, the prayer for arriving. Then the prayer: "O God, protect us from them . . . O God, we throw you against their throats and we seek refuge in you

The "Spiritual Manual," apparently written to steel the resolve of the hijackers for the 9/11 attack.

from their evil . . . Those who are enchanted by Western civilization are people who have drunk their love and reverence with cold water . . . Therefore do not fear them; but fear you Me, if you are believers" [Qur'an 3:175].

Readers were to recite repeatedly the first part of the Islamic creed, *lā ilāha illā llāh*—"There is no god but God." Care was to be taken, however, to appear to be silent, to ensure that "nobody takes notice." "Don't show signs of confusion or tension, but be happy, cheerful, bright and confident, because you carry out an action that God loves and approves . . . Smile in the face of death, young man, for you will soon enter the eternal abode.

"When you board the '*t*' [the abbreviation, probably, for *tā'ira* airplane]," the manual continued, "proceed with the prayer . . . and consider that it is a raid on the path [of God] . . . When the '*t*' begins to move slightly and heads for the '*q*' [perhaps standing for the Arabic word for 'takeoff position,' or perhaps for *Qiblah*, the direction of Mecca, toward which the planes did point once diverted], recite the prayer of travel because you are traveling to God the Most High, for you are traveling to Allah . . . This is the moment of the encounter of the two camps. Recite prayers . . . 'Our Lord, pour out upon us patience, and make firm our feet, and give us aid against the people of the unbelievers.'

"Pray for victory, assistance and the hitting of the target for yourself and for all your brothers, and don't be afraid. And ask God to grant you martyrdom . . . In close combat, strike firmly like heroes who do not wish to return to this world. Exclaim loudly *Allāhu akbar*, because the exclaiming of *Allāhu akbar* strikes fear into the unbelievers' hearts . . . the heavenly virgins are calling you, saying, 'O friend of God, come!'

"And when God grants any of you a slaughter," the text counseled, "you should dedicate it to your father and mother."

Those to be killed were the passengers and crews of the airliners. The Arabic word used for "slaughter" in the text is *dhabaha*—the word used for the cutting of an animal's throat.

"If everything has come off well, each of you is to pat his apartment brother on the shoulder. And in the *m* [airport] and in the *t* [plane] and in the *k* [perhaps the abbreviation for *kābīna*—cockpit] (each of you) should remind him that this operation is for the sake of God. . . .

"When the true promise and zero hour approaches," the manual's readers were told, "tear open your clothing and bare your chest, welcoming death on the path of God. Always mind God, either by ending with the ritual prayer—if this is possible—starting it seconds before the target, or let your last words be, 'There is no God but God, and

Muhammed is his Prophet.' After that, God willing, the meeting in the highest Paradise will follow."

So powerful is this document, so revelatory of the planning for the 9/11 hijackings—and the religious mind-set that drove them—it seems incomprehensible that the official U.S. account did not mention it at all. Professor Hans Kippenberg, coauthor of the most thorough study of the hijackers' manual, has a theory.

"To those who investigated the events of September 11," said Kippenberg, who is professor of Comparative Religious Studies at Jacobs University in Bremen, Germany,

> the terrorists were people without any conscience or moral compass, intentionally attacking civilians. In fact, far from being devoid of morality, the terrorists had an excess of it. They sought to bring summary justice to bear on those who— the way they saw it—inflicted injustice on their people.
>
> Civilians did die in the process. But the real targets, in the hijackers' minds, were the power centers of the United States: the financial hub by striking New York's Trade Center, the military hub by hitting the Pentagon, and—if as many think the plane that crashed in open country was meant to hit the Capitol or the White House—the heart of political power. I don't think the Americans could quite handle the concept that the attackers went ahead with what they did impelled by what they believed their religion required. No one who reads the hijackers' "manual," though, can do so without seeing that it, certainly, is totally driven by faith.

ALL OTHER EVIDENCE ASIDE, the "Spiritual Manual" must surely close off all doubt as to whether Atta and his comrades committed the hijacking. How the attacks were planned, and who was behind them, was another question. Was Osama bin Laden the éminence grise of 9/11, as President Bush's advisers had promptly told him?

In the days and weeks after 9/11, the man himself issued a string of denials, equivocations, and lofty comments. "We believe," bin Laden said the very day after in a message sent through an associate, "what happened in Washington and elsewhere against Americans, it was punishment from Almighty Allah. And they were good people who have done it. We agree with them." According to the go-between, bin Laden had "thanked Almighty Allah and bowed before him" on hearing the news, but had "no information or knowledge about the attack."

Four days later, on the Qatar-based television channel Al Jazeera, an announcer read out a first-person statement from the exiled Saudi: "I would like to assure the world that I did not plan the recent attacks, which seem to have been planned by people for personal reasons," it said. "I have been living in the Islamic emirate of Afghanistan and following its leader's rules. The current leader does not allow me to exercise such operations." A spokesman for the Taliban regime, for its part, said it accepted bin Laden's denial.

Late in September, he denied it yet again. "As a Muslim," he told a Pakistani newspaper, "I try my best to avoid telling a lie. I had no knowledge of these attacks. . . . Islam strictly forbids causing harm to innocent women, children and other people . . . even in battle. . . . We are against the American system, not against its people."

A few weeks later, though, the denial was blurred, the outright rejection of killing civilians dissipated. "Whenever we kill their civilians," he told Al Jazeera, "the whole world yells at us from East to West. . . . I say to those who talk about the innocents in America, they haven't tasted yet the heat of the loss of children and they haven't seen the look on the faces of the children in Palestine and elsewhere. . . . Who says our blood isn't blood and their blood is blood?"

For bin Laden, the 9/11 hijackers were heroes. "As concerns [America's] description of these attacks as terrorist acts," he said, "that description is wrong. These young men, for whom God has created a path, have shifted the battle to the heart of the United States. . . . We implore God to accept those brothers within the ranks of the martyrs, and to admit them to the highest levels of Paradise. . . . They have done this because of our words—and we have previously incited and roused them to action—in self-defense, defense of our brothers and sons in Palestine and in order to free our holy sanctuaries. If inciting for these reasons is terrorism, and if killing those that kill our sons is terrorism, then let history witness that we are terrorists."

Three weeks after 9/11, a single intelligence report—leaked to the media—seemed to speak as loud as the man's own denials. On the very eve of the attacks, *The New York Times* and NBC News reported, bin Laden had made a telephone call to his mother, Allia. He had always spoken affectionately of her, and she for her part had visited him in Afghanistan. She was on vacation in Syria in early September, and reportedly hoped he might be able to join her there. In the phone call, though, bin Laden said he would not be joining her.

"In two days," he reportedly told his mother, "you're going to hear big news." After the big news broke, he added, "You're not going to hear from me for a long time."

The story seemed loaded with sinister implication, but was it true? NBC could quote only "sources" who said the information— apparently gleaned by electronic eavesdropping—came from "a foreign intelligence service."

Just weeks later, in a rare interview, bin Laden's mother said the story was false. Her son had not risked phoning for the past six years. "I would never disavow him," she went on. "Osama has always been a good son to me . . . very kind, very considerate and very sweet . . . I love him and care about him." Allia was convinced, she said, that bin Laden was not responsible for 9/11.

In November, two months after the attacks, bin Laden gave the Pakistani newspaperman Hamid Mir a lengthy interview—one of only two interviews he granted in the past decade. He had talked with Mir twice before, seemed to think his reporting had been fair, and arranged for the journalist to be brought to him—trussed up and blindfolded during a lengthy jeep ride—at a secret hideout.

Bin Laden responded to most of the journalist's forty prepared questions, but on occasion made it clear he did not wish to go on the record. "I asked Osama whether he had done 9/11," Mir said in 2009, "and he asked me to turn off my recording machine. Then he said, 'Yes.' But when I turned on my machine again, he said, 'No.' "

FIFTEEN

THE TRUTH OFFICIALDOM GAVE US, THAT YOUNG MEN LOYAL TO al Qaeda and bin Laden were responsible for carrying out the attacks, is not the full story. The 9/11 Commission varnished the story for public consumption, spared the American people knowledge of troubling factors and issues—perhaps because they were highly sensitive, perhaps because pursuit of them involved banging on doors that seemed best left closed, perhaps simply because they remained unresolved.

The Nation's David Corn, rightly dismissive of most of the skeptics' ramblings, has made the point that serious matters have yet to be explained. "Without conspiracy theories," he wrote, "there is much to wonder about September 11th . . . Official answers ought not to be absorbed automatically without questions." Others agreed that what Corn saw as the failings of the U.S. government and the intelligence community should be exposed—and this well after publication of the 9/11 Commission Report.

No one at all, reportedly, has been held accountable for the missteps that preceded the September 11 attacks. There were no known dismissals, demotions, or even formal reprimands—at any level in the government or in government agencies. "No one has taken the fall for the failure to prevent attacks that killed 2,819 people," former Bush White House aide Richard Falkenrath noted following publication of the Report. "They could perhaps have been prevented . . . the starting point in any after the fact analysis should always be the concept of personal responsibility."

"Why did 9/11 happen on George Bush's watch," Senator Patrick Leahy asked in 2006, "when he had clear warnings that it was going to happen? Why did they allow it to happen?" Just what the President and his senior aides had been told, when they had been told it, and how they responded, had long been a vexatious issue. Why did CIA director Tenet tell the Commission that he had not briefed Bush in August 2001, only for it to emerge that he in fact saw him twice?

The previous month, according to Tenet, he and top aides had met with National Security Adviser Condoleezza Rice to deliver a dire warning that a major al Qaeda attack was imminent. According to one of America's most distinguished reporters, she responded by giving them the "brush-off." Rice said she could not recall the meeting. The record shows the 9/11 Commission was told of the meeting, but there was no mention of it in the 9/11 Commission Report. Why not?

"As each day goes by," Senator Max Cleland had said shortly before resigning as a member of the 9/11 Commission, "we learn that this government knew a whole lot more about these terrorists before September 11 than it ever admitted." Such doubts proved durable.

The agency most directly responsible for protecting the almost two million people who took flights every day in the States, the Federal Aviation Administration, seems to have been at best ineffectual, at worst fatally irresponsible, in the months and years before the attacks. The 9/11 Commission heard shocking testimony, which went unmentioned in its Report, from an experienced FAA team leader whose job it was to conduct undercover tests on airport security.

After September 11, said Bogdan Dzakovic, "officials from FAA as well as other government agencies made defensive statements such as, 'How could we have known this was going to happen?' The truth is, they did know. . . . FAA very deliberately orchestrated a dangerous facade of security. . . . They knew how vulnerable aviation security was. They knew the terrorist threat was rising, but gambled nothing would happen if we kept the vulnerability secret and didn't disrupt the airline industry. Our country lost that bet."

In the spring and summer of 2001, half of the FAA's daily summaries had mentioned bin Laden or al Qaeda. In July, it had "encouraged" all airlines to "exercise prudence and demonstrate a high degree of alertness." There was little or no real drive to ensure that better security was enforced, however, no sense of urgency at the level that mattered.

The US Airways ticket taker who checked in Atta and Omari in Portland for the first leg of their journey, Michael Touhey, would recall having had a "bad feeling" about them. They arrived just minutes before departure and carried expensive one-way, first-class tickets—though most business travelers fly round-trip. Had he received instructions to be more vigilant, he said later, he thought he would have acted differently. He might have ordered a search of the men's bags, which could have turned up suspicious items. There had been no such instructions, however, and Touhey let the men go on their way.

"I've been with American for twenty-nine years," said Rosemary Dillard, whose husband died aboard Flight 77. "My job was supervision over all the flight attendants who flew out of National, Baltimore or Dulles. In the summer of 2001, we had absolutely no warnings about any threats of hijacking or terrorism, from the airline or from the FAA." A key part of the FAA's mandate is to keep air travelers safe, and in that it signally failed.

The intelligence agencies failed, too, in ways that could perhaps have changed the course of history. The CIA and the FBI were both at fault, in part because of sheer inefficiency. The most scathing criticism of the FBI has come from insiders.

"September the 11th," said FBI agent Robert Wright, who had long been assigned to a Terrorism Task Force in Chicago, "is a direct result of the incompetence of the FBI's International Terrorism Unit. No doubt about that. . . . You can't know the things I know and not go public." Wright was joined in his protest—over the bungled handling of a counterterrorist operation two years earlier—by a fellow agent and a former assistant U.S. attorney.

In July 2001, exactly two months before the attack, an FBI agent in Phoenix had reported his suspicion that it was "more than a coincidence that subjects who are supporters of [bin Laden] are attending civil aviation universities/colleges in the state of Arizona. . . . Phoenix believes that it is highly probable that [bin Laden] has an established support network in place in Arizona." The memo recommended checks on flight schools and on the visa details of foreign students attending them, not only in Arizona but around the country.

After 9/11, the agent's apprehension was proven to have been entirely justified. One of the four hijacker pilots had indeed trained in Arizona, the other three at Florida flight schools. Two others, already known to the CIA as terrorist suspects, had for a while taken flight training in California. FBI headquarters, however, had virtually ignored the agent's prescient memo. No effective action was taken or planned.

Another, even more glaring FBI failure occurred just before the attacks, when agents in the Minneapolis field office reported their grave concern about a then-obscure French Moroccan flight student named Zacarias Moussaoui. The flight school at which he was studying had reported that he was behaving suspiciously, and a check with French intelligence revealed that he had links to extremism.

The Minneapolis agents, who wanted clearance to search the suspect's baggage, were rebuffed time and time again with legalistic objections sent from headquarters. Only on September 11, after the strikes on the Trade Center, was the search warrant approved. Moussaoui is now serving a life sentence for conspiracy to commit acts of terror and air piracy. Evidence found in his belongings and detainee statements would link Moussaoui to two of the most significant of the 9/11 conspirators.

Information that emerged in 2005 suggested that the Defense Intelligence Agency had failed to inform the FBI of intelligence on four of the future hijackers, including their leader, Mohamed Atta, when it was obtained in early 2000. The lead, provided by a U.S. Army officer, and initially supported by several other members of the DIA operation concerned, went nowhere. The Defense Department refused to allow those involved to testify to a Senate committee, and relevant documents have been destroyed. The Bush White House had allegedly been briefed on the matter within weeks of 9/11, as—much later—9/11 Commission staff had been. The episode went unmentioned, however, in the 9/11 Commission Report.

And then there is the CIA. The month before 9/11, the Agency's inspector general produced a report lauding the CIA's Counterterrorist Center as a "well-managed component that successfully carries out the Agency's responsibilities to collect and analyze intelligence on international terrorism." In 2007, however, and then only when Congress demanded it, the Agency belatedly produced an accountability review admitting that—before 9/11—the Counterterrorist Center had been "not used effectively."

It got worse. Most of those in the unit responsible for bin Laden, the inspector general reported, had not had "the operational experience, expertise and training necessary to accomplish their mission." There had been "no examination of the potential for terrorists to use aircraft as weapons," "no comprehensive analysis that put into context the threats received in the spring and summer of 2001."

Senator Bob Graham, who in 2001 was chairman of the Senate Intelligence Committee—and later chaired the House-Senate Joint Inquiry into the intelligence community's pre-9/11 failures—has cited a dozen "points at which the plot could have been discovered and potentially thwarted." "Both the CIA and the FBI," he wrote, "had information that they withheld from one another and from state and local law enforcement and that, if shared, would have cracked the terrorists' plot."

One item the CIA withheld from the FBI has never been satisfactorily explained. Agency officials had to admit—initially on the afternoon of 9/11 to a reportedly irritated President Bush—that the CIA had known a great deal about two of the future hijackers for the best part of two years. They had known the men's names, where they came from, the fact that they were al Qaeda operatives, that they had visas to enter the United States—and that one of them certainly, perhaps both, had long since actually arrived in the United States.

Why did the CIA hold this knowledge close, purposefully avoiding sharing it with the FBI and U.S. Immigration until just before the attacks? The CIA has attempted to explain the lapse as incompetence—human error. The complex available information on the subject, however, may suggest a different truth. Some at the FBI came to suspect that the Agency held what it knew close because it had hopes of turning the two terrorists, in effect recruiting them.

Or did the CIA contemplate keeping the men under surveillance following their arrival in the United States? Absent special clearance at presidential level, it would have been unlawful for the Agency to do that. Domestic surveillance is properly a task for the FBI. Alternatively, could it be that the CIA relied on an information flow from another, foreign, intelligence organization? If so, which organization?

One candidate, some might think, is the Israeli Mossad, a service uniquely committed to and experienced in countering Arab terrorism. Fragments of information suggest Mossad may indeed have had an interest in the 9/11 plotters before the attacks. Another candidate, though few would have thought it, is the General Intelligence Department—or GID—the intelligence service of Saudi Arabia. The Saudi element of the 9/11 story is multifaceted, complete with internal contradictions—and highly disquieting.

Saudi Arabia: leading supplier of oil to the United States in 2001, with reserves expected to last until close to the end of the century, a nation that has spent billions on American weaponry, in many ways America's most powerful Arab friend in the Middle East—and the birthplace of Osama bin Laden and fifteen of the nineteen 9/11 hijackers.

Though bin Laden was an exile, a self-declared foe of the regime, disowned in public statements by the Saudi royals and by his plutocrat brothers, many believed that was only part of the story—that powerful elements in his homeland had never ceased to support his campaign against the West in the name of Islam.

The Saudi GID, said since 9/11 to have fed information on the future hijackers to its counterparts in Washington, had long been regarded by the CIA's bin Laden specialists as a "hostile service." If the GID did share information, was it genuine? Or was it, by design, bogus and misleading?

The Saudi factor is one of the wild cards in the 9/11 investigation. Suspicion that Saudi Arabia had supported the hijack operation was rife for a while after 9/11, then faded—not so much because there was no evidence but because the suspicion was snuffed out. The possibility of Saudi involvement, a vital issue, will be a major focus in the closing chapters of this book.

In the immediate aftermath of September 11, only those in the inner councils of government and the intelligence services were mulling the deeper questions. The loud public call was for hitting back, striking those believed to have been the organizers, those who had been in direct command, hard and swiftly.

SIXTEEN

ON SEPTEMBER 14, 2001, THREE DAYS AFTER THE ATTACKS, THE words marching across the great, glittering signboard in Times Square had read: "BUSH CALLS UP 50,000 RESERVISTS." President Bush's motorcade drove past the sign that evening at the end of a day of prolonged high emotion—a memorial service at the National Cathedral in Washington, a visit to the pulverized ruins of the World Trade Center in New York, and a gut-wrenching two hours talking with relatives of the hundreds of firefighters and police who were missing and believed dead.

"After all the sadness and the hugging and the love and the families," the President's aide Ari Fleischer recalled thinking as the White House motorcade rolled down 42nd Street, "you could just feel the winds of war were blowing."

The way America would react to the al Qaeda assault had rapidly become clear. Evident within forty-five minutes of the first strike on the World Trade Center, when Bush spoke to the nation from the schoolroom in Florida, promising to "hunt down and to find those folks who committed this act." Evident two hours later at an Air Force base in Louisiana, away from the microphones, when he told aides, "We're gonna get the bastards." Evident in everything he said there-after, in private or in public.

The vast majority of the American people agreed that there must be severe retribution. The symbol of their resolve appeared within eight hours of 9/11, when a firefighter named Dan McWilliams took a national flag from a yacht moored in the Hudson nearby and—helped by fellow firemen—raised it high in the rubble at Ground Zero. The photographer who snapped them doing it realized instantly how the image would resonate. Right down to the angle of the flag as it went up, it resembled the raising of the Stars and Stripes by U.S. Marines during the battle of Iwo Jima in World War II.

At a memorial service on the 14th, with four U.S. presidents in the congregation, the National Cathedral reverberated to the roar of almost a thousand people singing "The Battle Hymn of the Re-public": "He hath loosed the fateful lightning of His terrible swift sword . . . the watch fires of a hundred circling camps . . . the trumpet that shall never call retreat . . . Let us die to make men free."

The September 11 onslaught had been an act of war, and the re-sponse was to be war. Many tens of thousands—the vast majority of them not Americans—were to die or be wounded in what Bush de-scribed as the coming "monumental struggle between good and evil." He made clear from the start that bin Laden and his followers would not be the only targets. Speechwriter Michael Gerson, briefed on the message the President wanted to convey in his address to the nation on the night of 9/11, has recalled writing in a draft that the United States would "make no distinction between those who planned these acts and those who permitted or tolerated or encouraged them."

Bush insisted that the language be clearer. In the final, amended version, he said the U.S. would "make no distinction between those who planned these acts and those who *harbor* them." Within an hour of the television appearance, he was discussing what that would mean with his war council—by now comprising Cheney, Rumsfeld, Secre-tary of State Colin Powell, Tenet, Rice, Richard Clarke, FBI director Robert Mueller, Attorney General John Ashcroft, key generals, and a few others.

In Afghanistan, by contrast, Taliban foreign minister Wakil Mut-tawakil had been asked whether he was certain bin Laden had not been involved in the attacks. "Naturally," he said. Were his government's restrictions on bin Laden's military activity on Afghan soil still in force? "Naturally," he said, and played down the likelihood of U.S. retaliation against Afghanistan.

Seven thousand miles away, though, the talk in the Situation Room at the White House was uncompromising. The Taliban were soon to propose trying bin Laden in Afghanistan or handing him over for trial in another Muslim country, but America was to turn a deaf ear. "We're not only going to strike the rattlesnake," Bush said at this time. "We're going to strike the rancher."

The administration never even considered negotiating with the Taliban, Rice said later. Washington would eventually issue a formal ultimatum—promptly rejected—demanding that Afghanistan hand over the Saudi exile, or "share in his fate."

The posture of Afghanistan's neighbor Pakistan—with its schizophrenic mix of ties to the Taliban, dependence on Washington, and divided religious and tribal loyalties—would now be pivotal. As Secretary of State Powell would recall it, Pakistan's president, Pervez Musharraf, "had to be told in no uncertain terms that it was time to choose sides." The way Musharraf remembered it being reported to him, those terms included being told that "if we chose the terrorists, then we should be prepared to be bombed back to the Stone Age." He bent to almost all the American demands for cooperation.

There were voices in Washington raising the notion of retaliation against nations other than Afghanistan. "Need to move swiftly," Rumsfeld's aide Stephen Cambone, noting the defense secretary's comments on the afternoon of 9/11, had jotted: "Near term target needs go massive—sweep it all up . . . need to do so to get anything useful . . . thing[s] related or not." "I know a lot," Rumsfeld would say publicly within days, "and what I have said, as clearly as I know how, is that states are supporting these people."

That first night at Bush's war council, the 9/11 Commission determined, Rumsfeld had "urged the President and the principals to think broadly about who might have harbored the attackers, including Iraq, Afghanistan, Libya, Sudan, and Iran." Though bin Laden was a Saudi and most of the hijackers Saudis, the possibility of that country's involvement was apparently not raised.

It was then, though, that Rumsfeld jumped at what he saw as the need to "do Iraq." "Everyone looked at him," Richard Clarke recalled. "At least I looked at him and Powell looked at him, like, 'What the hell are you talking about?' And he said—I'll never forget this—'There just aren't enough targets in Afghanistan. We need to bomb something else to prove that we're, you know, big and strong and not going to be pushed around by these kind of attacks.' And I made the point certainly that night, and I think Powell acknowledged it, that Iraq had nothing to do with 9/11.

"That didn't seem to faze Rumsfeld. . . . It shouldn't have come as a surprise. It really didn't, because from the first weeks of the administration they were talking about Iraq. I just found it a little disgusting that they were talking about it while the bodies were still burning in the Pentagon and at the World Trade Center."

President Bush kept the immediate focus on bin Laden and Afghanistan, but he did not ignore Rumsfeld. On the evening of the 12th, Clarke recalled, Bush quietly took aside his counterterrorism coordinator and a few colleagues to say, "Look . . . I want you, as soon as you can, to go back over everything, everything. See if Saddam did this. See if he's linked in any way . . . Just look. I want to know any shred."

"Absolutely, we will look . . . again," Clarke responded. "But, you know, we have looked several times for state sponsorship of al Qaeda and not found any real linkages to Iraq. Iran plays a little, as does Pakistan, and Saudi Arabia, Yemen."

Bush looked irritated. He replied, "Look into Iraq, Saddam," and walked away. Clarke's people would report that there was no evidence of cooperation between al Qaeda and Iraq. Pressure on the President to act against Iraq, however, continued. His formal order for military action against terrorism, a week after 9/11, would include an instruction to the Defense Department to prepare a contingency plan for strikes against Iraq—and perhaps the occupation of its oilfields.

THE WEEKEND FOLLOWING the attacks, after the frenzy of the first fearful days, Bush flew his war council to the presidential retreat at Camp David. Their deliberations began, as always during his presidency, with a moment of devotion. The meeting day before, the Friday, had opened with a prayer spoken by Defense Secretary Rumsfeld. He had asked the Lord for "patience to measure our lust for action," for resolve and patience. In the wooded peace of Camp David, nevertheless, the debate focused on the storm of violence that was coming.

Across the vast table from the President, CIA director Tenet and his counterterrorism chief Cofer Black briefed their colleagues on the Agency's plan for "Destroying International Terrorism." They described what they called the "Initial Hook," an operation designed to trap al Qaeda inside Afghanistan and destroy it. It was to be achieved by a numerically small CIA paramilitary component and U.S. Special Forces, working with Afghan forces that had long been fighting the Taliban. The chairman of the Joint Chiefs, General Hugh Shelton, outlined the crucial bomb and missile strikes that would precede and support the operation. "When we're through with them," Black had assured Bush, the al Qaeda terrorists would "have flies walking across their eyeballs."

The war planners dined that evening on what the President called "comfort food," fried chicken and mashed potatoes. Afterward, Attorney General Ashcroft accompanied Condoleezza Rice on the piano as she sang "Amazing Grace." Treasury Secretary Paul O'Neill sat in an armchair in the corner perusing the briefing documents the CIA had brought along that day. He read of measures to track and cut off the flow of money to terrorists, his special interest—and of draconian measures of a different sort.

The CIA proposed the creation of Agency teams to hunt down, capture, and kill terrorists around the world. It would have the authority to "render" those captured to the United States or to other countries for interrogation—effectively establishing a secret prison system. It would also be authorized to assassinate targeted terrorists. Two days later, the President signed a secret Memorandum of Notification, empowering the Agency to take such measures without the prior approval of the White House or any other branch of the executive.

Bush was by now referring to the coming fight as a "war on terrorism." By the following week, when he addressed a joint session of Congress, it had become the "war on terror"—the label for the conflict that was to endure until the end of his presidency.

So far as Osama bin Laden personally was concerned, the White House set the tone. "I want justice," the President told reporters on September 17, "and there's an old poster out West, I recall, that said,

'WANTED—DEAD OR ALIVE.' " Vice President Cheney said on television that he would accept bin Laden's "head on a platter." If he intended this figuratively, others did not.

Three days later, the CIA's Cofer Black gathered the team that was to spearhead the covert operation in Afghanistan. He dispensed with any notion of taking the terrorist leader alive. "Gentlemen, I want to give you your marching orders and I want to make them very clear. I have discussed this with the President, and he is in full agreement. . . . I don't want bin Laden and his thugs captured. I want them dead. Alive and in prison here in the United States, they'll become a symbol, a rallying point. . . . They must be killed. I want to see photos of their heads on pikes. I want bin Laden's head shipped back in a box filled with dry ice. I want to be able to show bin Laden's head to the President. I promised him I would do that."

"The mission is straightforward," Black told a colleague at headquarters. "We locate the enemy wherever they are across the planet. We find them and we kill them."

In the field, three men led the operations that targeted bin Laden, two veteran CIA officers, and a Special Forces officer with the unit popularly known as Delta Force. Their teams in the early months numbered only some seventy men, including a dozen Green Berets, Air Force tacticians, communications experts, and a small group of elite British commandos.

Asked by his wife why he was accepting the mission—he was on the verge of retirement—the CIA's Gary Schroen had picked up a newspaper with a picture of a Manhattan firefighter, his arm at the salute, tears running down his cheeks. "This is why I'm going," he said. "We all feel the pain. . . . Everyone wants to strike back." Schroen's successor, Gary Berntsen, told that some Afghan officers favored negotiating with al Qaeda, would merely snap, "Tell them your commander is from New York. I want them all dead!"

The U.S. generals' requirement, recalled Dalton Fury, the major in command of the military component, was a little less exorbitant than the demand for bin Laden's head in a box. "A cloudy photograph would do, or a smudged fingerprint. A clump of hair or even a drop of blood. Or perhaps a severed finger wrapped in plastic. Basically, we were told to go into harm's way and prove to the world that bin Laden had been neutralized, as in 'terminated with extreme prejudice.' In plain English: stone-cold dead."

Top Flight 11 passenger Daniel Lewin, probably the first to die on 9/11.

Above The Hanson family, passengers on Flight 175. On the phone to his father, Peter Hanson said: "Don't worry . . . If it happens, it'll be very fast."

Barbara Olson (*left*), known for her appearances on TV, was a passenger on Flight 77 – she managed to phone her husband, the US Solicitor General, to say the plane had been hijacked. Her name and those of sisters Zoe and Dana Falkenberg, aged eight and three respectively, are among those remembered at the Pentagon memorial (*below*). Dana's remains were not found.

Below Flight 93 flight attendant CeeCee Lyles's charred ID card, found after the crash. She had reached her husband to say the passengers were fighting back against the hijackers.

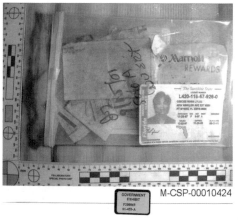

Office workers at windows of the Trade Center's North Tower. Trapped by fire, many jumped to their deaths.

Of those below the points of impact, most made their way to safety.

After the towers collapsed, New Yorkers ran pell-mell, a dust cloud at their heels. Hundreds have died, and many more are sick, from respiratory disease caused by the dust.

Two days after the attacks, firefighters and other rescue workers retrieve bodies from the rubble of the World Trade Center.

President Bush is told that a second plane has crashed.

In the Emergency Operations Center beneath the White House (*below*), Vice President Cheney speaks by phone with Bush. To the left of him is National Security Adviser Condoleezza Rice. To the left of her, kneeling, is Navy commander Anthony Barnes.

Left The facade of the Pentagon before it collapsed. Skeptics doubted that it could have swallowed a Boeing 757 airliner.

Above Investigators search the Pennsylvania field where Flight 93 crashed. In the foreground is the crater.

Right Wreckage at the Pentagon. Some skeptics suggested that evidence had been planted.

Right Flight 93's Cockpit Voice Recorder – hauntingly, minute by minute, it tracked the progress of the hijacking.

M-CSP-00017681

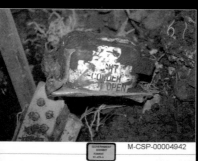

M-CSP-00004942

After, in New York.

Nine months later, draped in the flag, the last steel girder is removed from the ruins of the World Trade Center. It will stand in the memorial at Ground Zero.

The first CIA team was on the ground in Afghanistan just two weeks after 9/11, armed with not only their weapons but $3 million in $100 bills. "Money," Schroen has wearily noted, "is the lubricant that makes things happen in Afghanistan." The cash, lugged around in duffel bags, was used mostly to grease the palms of anti-Taliban warlords. For a mission that targeted the Taliban as much as bin Laden, buying their loyalty was essential. Brilliant American management of the warlords and their forces, combined with devastating use of airpower, would defeat and decimate the Taliban soldiers—though they were often valiant fighters—in little more than two months. Getting Osama bin Laden was another matter altogether.

He had continued to address the world as he had for years, by videotape. On October 7, the day of the first U.S. airstrikes, the terrorist leader was all defiance—and lauding the 9/11 attacks. "God has struck America at its Achilles' heel and destroyed its greatest buildings," he said. "What America is tasting today is but a fraction of what we [Arabs] have tasted for decades. . . . So when God Almighty granted success to one of the vanguard groups of Islam, He opened the way. . . . I pray to God Almighty to lift them up to the highest Paradise."

A few days earlier, in a letter to Taliban leader Mullah Omar that was to be retrieved later, bin Laden forecast that the coming U.S. campaign in Afghanistan would cause "great long-term economic burdens . . . force America to resort to the former Soviet Union's only option: withdrawal from Afghanistan." Two weeks on, with the bombing continuing, the Taliban's military commander—a longtime bin Laden ally—claimed his soldiers were holding their ground. Bin Laden was "safe and sound . . . in good spirits."

Thus far, the CIA team had only poor intelligence on bin Laden's whereabouts. There were attempts to persuade them that he had left the country soon after 9/11. Other reports put him either in the capital, Kabul, or at Jalalabad, nearer to the border with Pakistan. He was indeed in Kabul, or was there in early November, when he gave the first of his two post-9/11 interviews. Bin Laden was still talking tough, but his situation had clearly changed. He was in the capital that day to pay tribute to two comrades who had been killed, one of them his military chief—and close friend—Mohammed Atef. Enemy forces were closing on Kabul, and would take the city within the week.

Bin Laden did now head for Jalalabad, some ninety miles to the east. He and a large group of fighters were seen arriving in a convoy of white Toyota trucks. American bombs were already falling on the city, and their stay was brief. Dressed in the camouflage jacket familiar to Western television viewers, their leader appeared at the Saudi-funded Institute for Islamic Studies and addressed those brave enough to come to listen. "God is with us, and we shall win the war," he reportedly said. "Your Arab brothers will lead the way. . . . May God grant me the opportunity to see you and meet you again."

Bin Laden, said to have been upset, apparently spoke of wanting to stay and fight. He was dissuaded. The convoy left soon afterward, a Jalalabad witness later told the BBC, and it now consisted of as many as three hundred vehicles filled with tall, thin Saudis, muscular men who said they were from Egypt, and blacks who may have been from Sudan. They were, he said, "good Muslims, carrying the Qur'an in one hand and their Kalashnikov in the other." Bin Laden and his close companions, seated in the third vehicle, had covered their faces. At least one of those in the group said they were on their way "to their base at Tora Bora."

Tora Bora, which translates as "Black Widow," lies almost sixteen thousand feet above sea level on Towr Ghar—the "Black Dust"—a series of rocky ridges and peaks, ten precipitous miles from the border of Pakistan's Tribal Areas. A legend now, it was at the time a media fantasy. By November 27, a British newspaper was reporting that it was a "purpose-built guerrilla lair . . . 350 yards beneath a solid mountain. There are small rooms and big rooms, and the wall and floor are cemented. . . . It has its own ventilation system and its own power, created by a hydro-electric generator . . . driven by water from the peaks of the mountains."

The reality was far more primitive. Bin Laden's first wife, who had spent time there, remembered a place with no electricity and no running water, where life was hard at the best of times. In early December of 2001, in the icy Afghan winter, it became a desolate killing ground.

From their base at an abandoned schoolhouse, the pursuing Americans struggled with multiple obstacles. Tora Bora is not one place but a series of natural ramparts and cave complexes, a frustratingly difficult place to attack. Afghan generals, whose troops were key to the mission, were often intransigent, rarely dependable, and partial to negotiating with an al Qaeda enemy that the Delta Force and CIA commanders wanted only to destroy. The Afghan inhabitants of the mountains were at best uncertain sources of information. The Americans could dole out cellophane-wrapped cash from duffel bags, but these were people who had enjoyed bin Laden's largesse for years. Some locals had named their sons Osama, in his honor.

Berntsen, heading the CIA detachment, encountered reluctance when he begged for more U.S. military support. The operation to hunt down bin Laden, the team was told, was "flawed," too high-risk, and the reluctance to commit American ground forces was only going to get worse. What the United States could and did promptly deliver was the bludgeon of pulverizing airpower. Often guided by forward observation teams, waves of bombers flew from bases in the United States and carriers in the Persian Gulf to bombard the al Qaeda positions. AC-130 Spectre gunships, with their lethal firepower, pounded them by night.

The Americans became sure their quarry was there. A Lebanese-born former Marine with the CIA group, who had fluent Arabic and knew bin Laden's voice from tapes and intercepts, made a discovery on the morning of December 5. In the wreckage of a bombed encampment, he found a working radio clutched in the hand of a dead fighter. It was tuned to the al Qaeda frequency and soon, amidst the to-and-fro between harried men calling for water and supplies, he heard the familiar voice urging his followers to fight on.

On the 7th, a source who had been in among the enemy reported having encountered an "extremely tall" Arab—bin Laden was between six foot four and six foot six—near some large cave entrances. Berntsen called for the dropping of a BLU-82, the largest nonnuclear bomb in the U.S. arsenal, an eight-ton weapon the size of a Volkswagen Beetle. Used earlier to break Taliban lines on the plains, its primary target now was to be a single man in the mountains.

In the early morning of the 9th, CIA and Delta Force operatives watched through binoculars as an MC-130 airplane delivered the BLU-82. B-52s followed minutes later, dropping bombs guided by GPS. A desperate fighter was soon heard on a radio intercept saying, "Cave too hot. Can't reach others." There were calls for the "truck to move wounded." Another fighter, captured later, would speak of a "hideous" explosion that had vaporized men even deep inside the caves.

Decimated but not yet finally broken, the defenders held out a few days longer. Intercepts picked up an al Qaeda commander giving movement orders, ordering up land mines, exhorting his men to "victory or death." There was talk of "Father" moving to a different tunnel. Then, on the afternoon of December 13, Delta Force's Major Fury and his men listened to a voice they were sure was that of bin Laden. "His Arabic prose sounded beautiful, soothing, and peaceful," Fury recalled. "I paraphrase him . . . 'Our prayers have not been answered. Times are dire. . . . Things might have been different. . . . I'm sorry for getting you into this battle. If you can no longer resist, you may surrender with my blessing.' "

According to the ex-Marine expert at recognizing the Saudi's voice, bin Laden then gathered his men around him in prayer. There was the sound of mules, used for transport in the high mountains, and people moving around. Then silence.

BY THE TIME the bombing and the shooting stopped, Tora Bora was devastated, a wasteland of shattered rocks and broken trees. The detritus of war: spent ammunition, bloody bandages, torn fragments of documents in Arabic script—and not a trace of Osama bin Laden.

Had he died in the onslaught from the air? Or, in Fury's words, had a bomb "punched his ticket to Paradise"? Troops flown in months later by helicopter found the cave entrances impenetrably blocked by tons of rubble. Exhumations at a fighters' graveyard turned up nothing that was identifiable with bin Laden.

Long since convinced that their quarry escaped, those who risked their lives to kill him cast bitter blame on those from whom they had taken their orders. The Delta Force operatives, Fury said, had not been allowed to engage in "real war fighting." Had they been, he thought, things could have turned out differently. Being held back had been like "working in an invisible cage."

The CIA's Gary Berntsen had in vain requested a force of eight hundred U.S. troops—to block the "back door," the mountain escape route to Pakistan. "We need Rangers [Special Operations combat troops] now!" he had begged with increasing urgency. "The opportunity to get bin Laden and his men is slipping away!" He had been rebuffed every time.

Why were the troops refused, and who was responsible for the refusal? Military decisions were transmitted by the generals, directly to Berntsen by the officer commanding Joint Special Operations Command, Major General Dell Dailey, who in turn answered to General Tommy Franks, commander-in-chief at U.S. Central Command, the man running the Afghanistan operation.

"We have not said," Franks remarked at a press briefing just before the fighting at Tora Bora, "that Osama bin Laden is a target of this effort." It was a strange comment, even taking into account security considerations, given what Fury and Berntsen have said of the explicit orders they had been given. In a 2004 memoir, Franks skirted any discussion of the decision not to use U.S. troops to trap bin Laden. As recently as 2009, the general said he had doubted whether bin Laden was even at Tora Bora. Notwithstanding the certainty expressed by the CIA and Delta Force commanders on the spot, he claimed the intelligence had been "conflicting."

Delta Force's Major Fury placed responsibility elsewhere. "The generals," he said, "were not operating alone. Civilian political figures were also at the control panel. . . . I was not in those air-conditioned rooms with leather chairs when they came up with some of the strangest decisions I have ever encountered. . . . At times, we were micromanaged by higher-ups unknown, even to the point of being ordered to send the exact grid coordinates of our teams back to various folks in Washington."

The two civilian higher-ups involved with Franks in the decision making were Defense Secretary Rumsfeld and the man ultimately responsible as commander-in-chief, President Bush. Bush, who six days after 9/11 had indicated that he wanted bin Laden "dead or alive."

The President "never took his eye off the ball when it came to bin Laden," according to General Franks. Through October and into November, Bush had appeared still keen to "get" bin Laden. In late November, at a CIA briefing, he was told Tora Bora had become the focus, that Afghan forces were inadequate to do the job, that U.S. troops were required. "We're going to lose our prey if we're not careful," the CIA briefer warned. The President seemed surprised. In Afghanistan in early December, shortly before the massive BLU-82 bomb was unleashed on Tora Bora, those heading the fight in the field were told that POTUS had been personally "asking for details."

According to CIA sources, Bush would reportedly remain "obsessed" with the hunt for bin Laden even months after Tora Bora. In public, though, far from talking of getting him dead or alive, he seemed to downgrade his importance. "Terror's bigger than one person," the President said in March 2002. "He's a person who has been marginalized. . . . I don't know where he is. Nor, you know, I just don't spend that much time on him really, to be honest with you. . . . I truly am not that concerned about him."

THE RECORD, PERHAPS, explains the sea change in the priority given to the hunt for Osama bin Laden. On November 21, a couple of weeks before the final battles in the mountains and bin Laden's disappearance, the President had taken Rumsfeld aside for a conversation that he insisted must remain secret. He wanted a war plan for Iraq, and insisted that General Franks get working on it immediately.

Franks, already up to his eyes dealing with the conflict in Afghanistan, could barely believe what he was hearing. "Goddamn!" he exclaimed to a fellow general. "What the fuck are they talking about?" From then on, not least in early December, when there were repeated appeals for U.S. troops to block bin Laden's escape route, the general was constantly plagued with requests for plans as to how to attack Iraq. At a crucial stage of the Tora Bora episode, Bush's primary focus had begun to shift—and a shift in the commander-in-chief's focus meant distracting the attention of his overworked general from developments in Afghanistan.

FOR A LONG TIME, for almost three years, Osama bin Laden remained neither dead nor a prisoner—the options the President of the United States had initially contemplated—but an elusive, at times illusory, ghost.

A story in the Pakistan *Observer*, published on December 25, quoted a Taliban official as saying the fugitive had died "a natural and quiet death" of "serious complications in the lungs." He had supposedly been buried with military honors, according to his faith, in an unmarked grave. The story was clearly inaccurate—and perhaps a diversionary tactic, given that he in fact survived. A story that bin Laden made his escape after suffering a wound to the shoulder seems entirely possible.

Reports that became available in 2011, meanwhile, offer two versions of his escape. One holds that he headed north, to a remote part of Afghanistan, and remained there for months. The other suggests that, just as the CIA's man at Tora Bora had feared he would, he escaped over the snow-covered passes to Pakistan with the assistance of a Pakistani militant commander.

While the force guarding the border was commanded by a Pakistan army general, most of the troops involved were drawn from tribes in the region who answered to tribal chiefs, most of whom bin Laden had cultivated and who to one degree or another approved his cause.

Good evidence that he had survived came gradually: a handwritten letter, scanned and posted on islamonline.net in August 2002; weeks later, another letter; an audiotape, followed by two others in 2003— one of them, triumphal in tone, describing how "the forces of faith" had beaten back "the evil forces of materialism" at Tora Bora; in October 2003 a videotape urging on the fighters resisting the American occupation of Iraq, encouraging the people of Palestine to continue their struggle; in 2004 three further audiotapes and—on October 29, days before the U.S. presidential election—a videotape addressed to the American people.

Bin Laden wished to tell Americans, he said, how "to avoid another Manhattan." September 11 had been a response to the United States' "great injustices"—especially in Iraq and Israel. He invoked God's blessing on "the nineteen" [there had been nineteen hijackers on 9/11], and openly admitted his personal involvement. "We agreed with the general commander Mohamed Atta, may God bless his soul, to carry out all operations within twenty minutes, before Bush and his administration could be aware of them."

Until he saw that videotape, the former Delta Force commander at Tora Bora had not been sure what to think. Some had believed the previous bin Laden tapes authentic. Some had suspected they were fakes. Fury had preferred to think them fakes, until he saw the fall 2004 appearance.

"I knew immediately that the tape was the real thing. His posture, the voice, his thin body, and the aged beard that seemed frosted of snow were unmistakeable. Unfortunately, the man was still alive."

Not long before, far off in Afghanistan, a local militiaman named Faqir Shah had accompanied reporter Tim McGirk back to Tora Bora. "This was where Osama lived," Shah said as they walked the shattered battlefield. "We fought al Qaeda here for two weeks in the snow. . . . See that hole? An American soldier tossed a piece of concrete in there from the World Trade Center, because he thought al Qaeda was all finished. . . .

"I didn't think so."

PART IV

PLOTTERS

Two decades earlier, when the Twin Towers of the World Trade Center had been a relatively new phenomenon—years before the earliest official concern that they would make a prime target for terrorists—an improbably tall young Saudi, still in his early twenties, had flown into the United States with his pregnant wife and two infant children. His visit, in 1979, passed without notice, for he was neither famous nor infamous.

Osama bin Laden's activity in America appeared entirely peaceful. The fact that he came at all was not firmly established until 2009, when his wife Najwa—nine babies later and separated from her husband by force of circumstance—published a memoir. She recalled having thought that Americans in general were "gentle and nice . . . easy to deal with. . . . My husband and I did not hate America, yet we did not love it."

An incident on the final day of their stay, as the family sat in an airport departure lounge, showed Najwa how little some Americans knew of other cultures. "I saw an American man gawking at me . . . jaw dropped open in surprise, curious eyes growing as large as bugs popping from his skull. . . . I knew without asking that his unwelcome attention had been snagged by my black Saudi costume . . . face veil, head scarf, and *abaya*. . . . That man gave us a good laugh."

Bin Laden had been busy during the trip, but Najwa was the good Arab wife. "Since my husband's business was not my business, I did not ask questions." She asked no questions when bin Laden took off for Los Angeles for a week to talk with unknown men. Nor did she press for details when he said he was meeting—elsewhere—with "a man by the name of Abdullah Azzam."

By mentioning Azzam, bin Laden had provided a first pointer to the direction his life was going to take. Azzam lectured and led prayers in the mosque at King Abdul Aziz University in the Saudi city of Jeddah, where bin Laden was a third-year student of economics and management. Often described as a "cleric" or "scholar," Azzam was more than that. A Palestinian, whose village had been overrun by the Israelis in the Six Day War, he was on his way to becoming the "Emir of Jihad."

"Jihad" is a religious duty for Muslims. It can be interpreted in several ways—its basic sense is "struggle," or "striving"—but what Azzam meant by it was very clear. He preached the need for jihad to liberate Muslim lands from foreign occupation. "Humanity," he was to say, "is being ruled by Jews and Christians. The Americans, the British, and others. And behind them, the fingers of world Jewry."

In the late 1970s Azzam, an imposing figure and a fine speaker, was raging especially about Egyptian president Anwar al-Sadat's peacemaking visit to Israeli-occupied Jerusalem, a visit that millions in the Middle East saw not as statesmanship but betrayal.

With Azzam at Abdul Aziz University was Mohammed Qutb, brother of a writer and thinker who in death, following his execution in Egypt, became the guiding light of Islamic extremism. Sayid Qutb had been the leading voice of the Muslim Brotherhood, deplored the corruption of secular regimes in the Middle East, and advocated using violence to remove them. He excoriated Western society as he had seen it in the United States and poured verbal vitriol on the Jews and Zionism. Osama bin Laden read Sayid Qutb, and attended his brother's lectures.

Azzam and Qutb were free to spread their message at will in the Saudi Arabia of the 1970s, and what they said about Israel accorded perfectly with Saudi doctrine. For all his anti-Zionist speechifying, moreover, the United States welcomed Azzam. From 1979, the year the young bin Laden met with him in the States, he was perceived as an ally in a common cause, the struggle to expel Soviet forces from Afghanistan. For both Saudi intelligence—the GID—and the CIA, Azzam was useful, a man to manipulate.

An irony, then, that—after 9/11—Azzam's name would be joined to that of Osama bin Laden. The dedication to a so-called *Encyclopedia of Jihad*, a sort of how-to manual for terrorists in eleven volumes, would read: "To our much loved brother Abu Abdullah Osama bin Laden, who shared in the jihad of Sheikh Abdullah Azzam . . . Who has committed himself every day to jihad."

Azzam, bin Laden himself would say, was "a man worth a nation." For he, with bin Laden and a few comrades, was to found a movement that would shake the Western world and change history: al Qaeda.

In 1979, when the preacher from Palestine and the Saudi economics student got together in Indiana, the seeds were being sown. For the student, then and for the rest of his life, the driving force was always religion.

"GOD ALMIGHTY was gracious enough for me to be born to Muslim parents in the Arabian Peninsula in al-Malazz neighborhood, in al-Riyadh, in 1377 hegira . . ."

Bin Laden, perorating—he was always long-winded—on his early life and parentage. The year of his birth, 1377 hegira, is the Muslim calendar's rendering of the year most of the world refers to as 1957. The actual birthday appears to have been February 15.

Nineteen fifty-seven was the year that President Dwight Eisenhower took office for a second term, and that a rebel named Fidel Castro—previously rumored to have been killed—surfaced to fight on against the Cuban government. The nations of Western Europe began forming a unified economic bloc. The Soviet Union launched the Sputnik satellite into orbit and began catching up with U.S. missile technology.

The Saudi newborn's full name was Osama bin Mohammed bin Awad bin Aboud bin Laden al-Qatani—"bin" meaning "son of." He would one day tell his own children that "al-Qatani," which denotes those who trace their ancestry to Yemen, was their true family name.

"Osama" means "Lion," apt for a man who came to see himself as a warrior.

"I was named," bin Laden himself said, "after one of the venerable Companions of the Prophet, Osama bin-Zeid . . . He was someone whom the Prophet, God's peace and blessings be upon him, has loved and has loved his father before him." That Osama was an Islamic hero, a commander said to have defeated a Roman army.

"My father was born in Hadramaut," bin Laden said in 1999. "He went to work in Hejaz at an early age, more than seventy years ago. Then God blessed him and bestowed on him an honor that no other contractor has known. He built the holy Mecca mosque where the holy Ka'bah is located and at the same time, because of God's blessings to him, he built the Holy Mosque in Medina. . . . [Then] the Dome of the Rock in Jerusalem. . . . It is not a secret that he was one of the founders of the infrastructure of the Kingdom of Saudi Arabia."

The father, Mohamed bin Laden, had been a legend in his time. The Hadramaut was a sparsely populated region of what is now Yemen, which borders on Saudi Arabia, and the young Mohamed made his way the thousand miles to Jeddah penniless and hungry. He started out portering for pilgrims, moved on to lowly work in the construction trade, worked incessantly, thrived as a manager, and eventually—though almost illiterate, he had a phenomenal memory for facts and figures—rose to become a fabulously wealthy construction magnate.

The key to the rise of bin Laden Sr. was the patronage of the all-powerful Saudi elite, the rulers of a land that emerged from obscurity to gilded affluence in the space of a few decades. He hit his prime just as American money for Saudi oil began to bring the royal princes unparalleled riches. From the reign of King Abdul Aziz in the 1930s to that of King Faisal in the 1960s, he built palaces, roads across the desert, reservoirs, power stations. He catered to every royal whim, from providing the ramp that delivered the wheelchair-bound Abdul Aziz to his throne room to—a measure of his wealth—bailing out Faisal when the royal coffers ran dry for a while.

Nothing enhanced bin Laden Sr.'s prestige so much as his work on Islam's religious sites. "Religion in Saudi Arabia is like gravity," bin Laden family biographer Steve Coll has written. "It explained the order of objects and the trajectory of lives. The Qur'an was the kingdom's constitution and the basis of all its laws. The kingdom . . . evolved into the most devout society on earth."

Religion and Saudi royalty are inseparable. The Saud family had gained power in the eighteenth century thanks to a deal with a reformist preacher named Mohammed ibn Abdul Wahhab. He and his followers insisted on the most austere interpretation of Islam, banned the arts, music and dancing, celebration of holidays, and memorials to the dead.

The author Stephen Schwartz has defined Wahhabism as a "form of fascism" built on "a paramilitary political structure comparable to the Bolsheviks and Nazis" and "a monopoly of wealth by the elite, backed by extreme repression and a taste for bloodshed." In Saudi Arabia, someone who had lived there for many years told the authors, "Everything comes down to money. The extent of the greed is beyond the understanding of the ordinary Westerner."

Under the extreme form of shari'a—Islamic law—applied in today's Saudi Arabia, theft may be punished by amputation of a hand. Public beheading remains the designated penalty for murder, drug trafficking, rape, and adultery. In some cases a beheading is followed by crucifixion of the body, and placing of the head upon a pole. Human rights are severely limited. Women cannot attend university, have bank accounts, or take employment without permission of a male relative.

The Yemeni immigrant Mohamed bin Laden had no quarrel with Saudi ways. A devout Muslim himself, he would invite prominent clerics to his home to debate religion. His renovations and innovations at the three holy shrines of Medina, Mecca, and the Dome of the Rock in Jerusalem—before the Israeli occupation of 1967—earned him high honors in Saudi Arabia. He was appointed a minister of state by royal decree, and the letter appointing him to the Jerusalem work styled him "Your highness, Sheikh Mohamed bin Laden."

Mohamed's son Osama was the eighteenth of some two dozen sons sired by his series of some twenty-two wives. He was the product of a short-lived marriage to a Syrian girl named Allia who was fourteen years old to her husband's forty-nine. In the year Allia gave birth to Osama, her new husband fathered seven children.

Even by Saudi standards, Mohamed behaved bizarrely in the marital home. According to Osama, his mother confided that he had had "a shocking habit of asking his wives to take off their veils and stand in a line, sending for his male servants to look upon their faces . . . like harlots on view . . . and point out his most beautiful wife." Allia asked for a divorce, for reasons unknown, and went on to marry one of her husband's employees. Osama, who lived principally with her from then on, is said by his son Omar—one of the children of his first wife, Najwa—to have loved his mother "more than he loved his wives, his siblings, or his children."

Mohamed, Osama was to tell his own family, would usually summon his sons to see him as a group, and only a few times a year. "In my whole life," Osama said, "I only saw your grandfather five times . . . brief meetings, all but one with my large clan of brothers."

Mohamed had a strict rule, Osama told Omar, that "when he met with his sons, we must stand in a very straight line, organized according to height, rather than age. . . . Before I became a teenager, I was not the tallest . . . [One day] two of my older brothers, taller than me, locked me between them. . . . Your grandfather noticed. Furious, he marched to stand in front of me and without one word of warning struck me across the face with his strongest force. . . . I've never forgotten the pain." "Most of us were afraid of him," said Yeslam, one of Osama's half-brothers.

Bin Laden Sr. believed that Palestine belonged to the Arabs, not the Jews, and was accordingly "very, very, very anti-Israel, anti-Jewish." In June 1967, when Israel seized East Jerusalem and King Faisal made bellicose noises, Mohamed suggested a contribution he could make. He would, he said, convert the 250 bulldozers he used in his building operations into army tanks.

Three months later, Osama's father was dead. Ten thousand people reportedly attended the ceremonies that followed his death in an airplane crash. His myriad sons and daughters and wives, separated according to sex of course, gathered for the days of mourning. King Faisal, who said his protégé had been his "right arm," declared that he would henceforth act as father to the bin Laden children.

This was not only because the king had held the dead man in great affection. The bin Laden companies were important to ongoing government operations, and Faisal decreed that they must continue to function. The overall value of Mohamed's estate was in the region of $150 million, almost a billion dollars at 2010 values. His children, the sons as stipulated by law entitled to twice as much as the daughters, all instantly became millionaires.

The son named Osama, still in the care of his doting mother, was ten at the time. His most recent memory of his father was of a patriarch who—in spite of the boy's tender age—had recently given him a car as a present. Though of course not allowed to drive it, he remained crazy about cars for years to come.

The sparse memories of Osama's early life, however, recall a child who was "shy . . . aloof . . . gentle . . . polite . . . obedient . . . quiet, to the point of timidity." Briefly, before his father's death, he had been sent as a boarder to a Quaker school in Beirut. Not long afterward, back in his homeland, he began the first of eight years at a school for the Saudi elite founded by the king himself. An Englishman who taught there, Brian Fyfield-Shayler, remembered a pupil who was "extraordinarily courteous . . . not pushy in any way . . . pleasant, charming, ordinary, not very exceptional."

Fyfield-Shayler thought Osama's command of English mediocre, though a person who met him years later found him fluent enough in the language. His science teacher judged him "normal, not excellent." In arithmetic, he had inherited his father's flair. According to his son Omar, "No calculator could equal my father's remarkable ability, even when presented with the most complicated figures." Given the school's top national ranking, Fyfield-Shayler thought, Osama was probably "one of the top fifty students" in his age group.

Away from class, he was a boy like other boys. His schoolfriend Khaled Batarfi recalled him taking part in soccer games, near the Pepsi factory. Taller than most of his pals, Osama would "play forward to use his head and put in the goals." Off the pitch, he and his peers enjoyed watching cowboy and karate movies.

Batarfi recalled an incident when his friend was confronted by a bully. "I pushed him away from Osama, and solved the problem. But then Osama came to me and said, 'You know, if you waited a few minutes I would have solved the problem peacefully.' . . . This was the kind of guy who would always think of solving problems peacefully."

IN SUMMER during his childhood, Osama traveled to his mother's seaside home in Syria. There were camping trips, long hikes with a male cousin, and a special friendship with the cousin's young sister—Najwa. To her he seemed "soft-spoken, serious . . . delicate but not weak . . . a mystery—yet we all liked him." She had these impressions, by her account, before either child turned ten.

By the time Najwa turned thirteen, in 1972, "unanticipated emotions began to swirl" between her and Osama. He seemed "shyer than a virgin under the veil," said nothing directly to her. Instead he spoke to his mother and the respective parents spoke to each other. There was a wedding and a celebratory dinner—male and female guests carefully segregated, no music, no dancing—when Osama was seventeen and Najwa fifteen.

The teenage husband brought his wife home to Jeddah swathed in black, her face totally veiled. "Osama," she recalled in a 2009 memoir written with her son Omar, "was so conservative that I would also live in purdah, or isolation, rarely leaving the confines of my new home." Her husband explained "how important it was for me to live as an obedient Muslim woman. . . . I never objected because I understood that my husband was an expert regarding our faith."

It was decided that Najwa would no longer go to school. Instead she sat in the garden reading the Qur'an while Osama went to school. Her husband, she discovered, could recite the sacred texts by heart. Proudly, he took her to pray at the mosque in Mecca that his father had rebuilt. He fit attendance at school, and occasional arduous work for the family construction company, around praying at the mosque several times a day.

Najwa soon had a first baby, to be followed not long after by another. The obedient Muslim wife would bear eleven children over the years. The devout Muslim husband, meanwhile, observed his faith to the letter. Muslims should in principle avoid shaking hands with a person of the opposite sex or of a different religion, but Osama took things further than that. When a woman—his European sister-in-law Carmen bin Ladin—opened the front door of her home unveiled, he averted his gaze and ducked speaking to her. He did not allow Najwa to feed her baby from a bottle, because it had a rubber teat.

His rules extended to male company. Osama slapped one of his own brothers for ogling a female servant. He stared in disapproval when a male friend arrived in shorts, on the way to a soccer game. In the broiling heat of Saudi Arabia, he even urged his brothers not to wear short-sleeved shirts. In Syria, offended by the sound of a woman singing in a sexy voice, he ordered a driver to turn off the car radio.

"Around eighteen or nineteen or so," his half-brother Yeslam would say of Osama after 9/11, "he was already more religious than the average person or the average member of the family." Most Westerners might think that comment a gross understatement and dismiss Osama as having been an obsessive, a religious nut. To be super-strict about religion, however, was not—is not—unusual in Saudi Arabia. Far from alienating everyone, Osama's zealotry earned him respect. "His family revered him for his piety," his sister-in-law Carmen said. "Never once did I hear anyone murmur that his fervor might be a little excessive."

Osama would rise to pray even during the night, Batarfi remembered. It was not compulsory for Muslims, but it was "following the example of the Prophet." When he went on from school to university—he would start but not complete his economics degree—Osama became close to a fellow student named Jamal Khalifa, one day to become his brother-in-law. "I was almost twenty, and he was nineteen," Khalifa remembered. "We were religious . . . very conservative; we go to that extreme side."

Osama no longer watched movies. He did not watch television, except for news programs, and he avoided music with instruments, which some religious advisers deemed sinful. He disapproved of art, so no pictures hung on the walls. He avoided being photographed, though this was a matter on which he was to vacillate.

The shift to the extreme had not happened overnight. Looking back, Najwa remembered how—even while still at school—her husband had regularly gone out at night "for impassioned discussion of political or religious topics." Even before his marriage, a schoolfriend revealed, Osama and a half dozen other boys had begun studying Islam after school hours, taught by a Syrian teacher on the staff who was a member of the Muslim Brotherhood. It was at his urging that Osama memorized the Qur'an, under his tutelage that Osama and friends themselves began attending secret meetings of the Brotherhood.

In their impressionable teenage years, meanwhile, bin Laden and his contemporaries lived through a decade that destabilized the Arab world. The running sore of Palestine remained a concern for everyone. When Osama watched the news on television, he wept.

At his house, Batarfi recalled, they and their friends would "sing religious chants about Muslim youth and Palestine." The 1973 war, when Israel managed to beat back invading Arab forces, had been a great humiliation. Saudi Arabia's participation in the oil embargo that followed, the first use of the oil weapon against the West, had been a temporary consolation.

The year 1979, when Osama turned twenty-two, marked the start of a new century in the Islamic calendar, a time said to herald change.

Sure enough, upheaval piled on upheaval. First, and in the name of Islam, came the toppling of the monarchy in Iran, a monarchy that had long been sustained by the United States. Then, in November, came a bloody event in Saudi Arabia itself, one in which Osama may have played a minor role.

"For forty years," Osama would say years later, "my father kept on waiting for the appearance of Hazrat Mahdi. He had set aside some twelve million dollars for the Mahdi." The Mahdi, according to some Islamic texts, is an Islamic Messiah who will return to earth, bring justice in a time of oppression, and establish true Islamic government.

In 1979, a Saudi religious zealot claimed that the Mahdi had arrived—in the shape of his brother-in-law, a university drop-out named al-Qahtani. They and some five hundred heavily armed comrades then committed the unprecedented outrage of seizing the Grand Mosque in Mecca—one of the three holy places that bin Laden Sr. had renovated. They entered the mosque, indeed, through an entrance used by the bin Laden company, which was still completing construction within the complex.

This was more than sacrilege. It was sedition. The zealots accused the Saudi royal house of being pawns of the West, traitors to the faith. The government crushed the insurrection, but only after a bloody standoff that lasted for two weeks. Hundreds died in the battles, and sixty-eight prisoners were later beheaded.

The Mahdi did not survive to be executed. He had believed, until the fatal moment that he discovered otherwise, that he could pick up five live hand grenades and not be harmed.

THE MONTH AFTER the battle at the mosque, forty thousand Soviet troops began pouring into Afghanistan, the vanguard of an army that would eventually become a hundred thousand strong. The invasion marked the start of a savage conflict that would last almost a decade, kill a million Afghans, and drive some five million into exile. Long before it ended, it became a trial of strength between the Soviet Union and the United States—at the time underreported and minimally understood by the American public.

The war got scant attention not least because it did not involve the commitment of American troops. It was, rather, a purposeful, secret war to push back communism. Covertly, the United States committed cash and weaponry on a grand scale, using Afghans and foreign irregulars to do the fighting. Appropriately for a secret war, the conflict was orchestrated by the intelligence agencies of three nations: America, Pakistan, and Saudi Arabia.

So it was that, very relevantly for the 9/11 story, the Afghan saga that began in 1979 drew in two men, Osama bin Laden and Abdullah Azzam.

"MY FATHER," bin Laden would one day tell a visitor, "was very keen that one of his sons should fight against the enemies of Islam. So I am the one son who is acting according to the wishes of his father."

He had been called, he also believed, by a higher power. "Just remember this," he was to tell his son Omar. "I was put on this earth by God for a specific reason. My only reason for living is to fight the jihad. . . . Muslims are the mistreated of the world. It is my mission to make certain that other nations take Islam seriously."

IN 1979, the day bin Laden would be taken truly seriously was still more than two decades away. It was then, however, that—as his friend Batarfi has said, "the nightmare started."

EIGHTEEN

O N EVERY LEG OF THE JOURNEY TO 9/11 — OVER ALL THE TWENTY-ONE years that followed the Soviet invasion of Afghanistan—there would never be a time when several intelligence agencies were not involved.

Truth for public consumption is not a tool much favored by intelligence services. Those who direct the agencies prefer not to share information at all, except—in principle—with their own governments. It may, on occasion and in democracies, be useful to offer information to others—to investigating commissions, congressional and parliamentary committees, and the like, even to the media—but rarely can it be wholly relied upon.

Only rarely does an intelligence agency reveal facts inimical to its own interests. Most often, intelligence sources share only information that it is useful to share—in other words, self-serving. Such information is not necessarily truthful.

The natural impulse of the general public in the West may be to give credence to accounts provided by "our" intelligence—publicly and officially or through "sources." Such trust, though, may be misplaced. Like any story told by humans, an account given by an intelligence agency—domestic or foreign—may be only partially true. It may even be an outright lie.

WHAT IS CLEAR is that Saudi Arabia's intelligence service, the GID, reached out for bin Laden early in the Afghan confrontation with the Soviets—through his former school science teacher, Ahmed Badeeb. Badeeb had kept an eye on his pupil during his days on the school's religious committee, had liked him, thought him "decent . . . polite," and—now that bin Laden was in his early twenties—saw a role for him.

Badeeb had gone up in the world. He was no longer a science teacher but chief of staff to GID's director, Prince Turki al-Faisal. Turki was in the second year of what was to be a long career as chief of the agency. He was American-educated, a man who could relate easily to his U.S. counterparts. The GID and the CIA liaised closely with each other from the moment he became director—on his terms, not Washington's.

For the United States, the coming struggle with the Soviets was a pivotal confrontation in the Cold War. For the Saudi government in 1980, it was much more than that. Afghanistan was a fellow Muslim nation overwhelmed by catastrophe. Uncounted numbers of its citizens were swarming into Pakistan as refugees. To bring aid to the Afghans, and being seen to do it, was to aid the cause of Islam.

That aside, it was feared that the Soviet thrust heralded an eventual threat to Saudi Arabia itself. Prince Turki was soon shuttling between Riyadh and Pakistan, networking with Pakistan's Directorate for Inter-Services Intelligence—ISI—triggering a relief effort that was to last far into the future.

On another tack, and in great secrecy, the GID and the CIA worked together to support the Afghan rebels' fight against the Soviets. Thanks to huge sums of money funneled through a Swiss bank account, modern weaponry began to make the rebels a more viable fighting force.

"When the invasion of Afghanistan started," bin Laden once said, "I was enraged and went there at once. I arrived within days, before the end of 1979." At GID headquarters, Prince Turki and his aide

Badeeb noted bin Laden's potential. Youthful though he was, as a member of the bin Laden conglomerate he had clout. He had, above all, religious drive and commitment.

"To confront those Russian infidels," bin Laden said, "the Saudis chose me as their representative in Afghanistan. When they decided to participate actively in the Islamic resistance they turned to the bin Laden family . . . which had close links to the royal family. And my family designated me. I installed myself in Pakistan, in the frontier region bordering on Afghanistan. There I received the volunteers who arrived from Saudi Arabia and all the Arab and Muslim countries."

Prince Turki has admitted having met bin Laden a couple of times in that early period, while avoiding going into detail. His former chief of staff Badeeb has been more forthright. Bin Laden, he has said, "had a strong relation with the Saudi intelligence and with our embassy in Pakistan. . . . He was our man. . . . We were happy with him. . . . He had a good relationship with the ambassador, and with all Saudi ambassadors who served there. At times, the embassy would ask bin Laden for some things and he would respond positively. . . . The Pakistanis, too, saw in him one who was helping them do what they wanted done there."

According to one of the most well-informed sources on the conflict, the journalist Ahmed Rashid, Pakistan's ISI had wanted Turki "to provide a royal prince to lead the Saudi contingent." In bin Laden, with his family's links to the Saudi royals, they got the next best thing.

What was required of him in the early 1980s was not to fight but to travel to-and-fro, spread money around, cultivate Afghan contacts, make sure that cash got to the right people. Then his activities became entwined with those of Abdullah Azzam, the jihadist whose lectures he had attended at university. The duty of jihad "will not end with victory in Afghanistan," Azzam was heard to declare. "Jihad will remain an individual obligation until all other lands that were Muslim are returned to us."

With Saudi support, Azzam moved full-time to Pakistan, and so eventually did bin Laden—at his mentor's request. By 1986 they were running the office that processed Arab donations and handled recruits rallying to the cause. Funded with money from Saudi Arabia and the Gulf, and his own wealth, bin Laden ensured that arrivals were housed, cared for if they were sick or wounded, and fed Islamic propaganda.

Newcomers stayed initially at a building called Beit al-Ansar, which translates as Place of the Supporters. That was a reference to an episode in the story of the Prophet Mohammed, but it resonates today in another way. Twelve years later, some of the future 9/11 hijackers would give their apartment that name. Azzam, for his part, toured the United States regularly, raising funds and starting what eventually became a nationwide support system.

At some point, according to a source quoted by Barnett Rubin, now a senior State Department adviser on Pakistan and Afghanistan, the CIA "enlisted" Azzam. Did the Agency have any involvement with bin Laden himself?

The CIA had significantly ratcheted up its support for the anti-Soviet forces by the mid-1980s. U.S. funding, $470 million in 1986, continued to soar, and the agency saw to it that more and better weapons reached the Afghans. Under a supposedly strict, immutable arrangement, however—necessary to the United States to ensure deniability, to Pakistan to retain control—all this assistance was handled by the ISI, Pakistan's intelligence service. Officials of the day have played down the notion that there was American contact with bin Laden, or anyone else in the field.

Reputable authors have reported how the CIA on occasion circumvented the rules. While the bulk of the mujahideen were trained by Pakistani officers, some of the officers were trained in the States. U.S. and British Special Forces veterans entered Afghanistan and operated alongside the fighters. American cash went to at least one Afghan commander who collaborated with bin Laden.

Other voices claim there was an early link between the CIA and bin Laden himself. Michael Springmann, who in 1986 and 1987 headed the Non-Immigrant Visa Section at the U.S. consulate in Jeddah, said that the CIA forced him against his will to issue visas to people who would otherwise have been ineligible. "What I was protesting was, in reality, an effort to bring recruits, rounded up by [the Agency and] Osama bin Laden, to the U.S. for terrorists training by the CIA. They would then be returned to Afghanistan to fight against the Soviets."

Simon Reeve, a British author, cited a "former CIA official" as saying that "U.S. emissaries met directly with bin Laden." According to this source it was bin Laden, acting on advice from Saudi intelligence, who suggested that the mujahideen be supplied with the Stinger missiles that proved devastatingly effective against Soviet airpower.

"Bin Laden," wrote former British foreign secretary Robin Cook, "was a product of a monumental miscalculation of Western security agencies. Throughout the 80s he was armed by the CIA and funded by the Saudis to wage jihad against the Russian occupation of Afghanistan."

In a little-known interview, bin Laden himself appeared to offer a revelation. "I created my first camps," he said in 1995, "where these volunteers underwent training, instructed by Pakistani and *American officers* [authors' italics]. The arms were provided by the Americans and the money by the Saudis."

Then, a year later, bin Laden reversed himself. "Personally," he said in 1996, "neither I nor my brothers saw evidence of American help."

Statements by Osama bin Laden—and for that matter those of intelligence officials—rarely contribute much to historical clarity.

THE USE THE GID SAW for bin Laden initially put him nowhere near the combat zone. "The Saudi government," he would recall, had "officially asked me not to enter Afghanistan, due to how close my family is to the Saudi leadership. They ordered me to stay in Peshawar [Pakistan], because in the event the Russians arrested me that would be a proof of our support for the mujahideen. . . . I didn't listen to them, and went into Afghanistan for the first time."

Quite early in the 1980s, back in Jeddah, Najwa bin Laden heard her husband tell other family members that he had entered the Afghan war zone. He mentioned, too, that he had handled the controls of a helicopter. She began to probe a little but he merely said, "Najwa, stop thinking." As a dutiful Saudi wife, she knew it was not her place to ask what her husband did outside the home.

Many Arabs who answered the call to jihad never saw actual fighting, but bin Laden saw to it that some of them did. He eventually set up a base at Jaji, ten miles inside Afghanistan and not far from a Soviet base, and called it Maasada, or the Lion's Den. It was there that he and his Arabs had their baptism of fire.

One of Azzam's sons recalled how, greenhorn that he was, bin Laden initially reacted to explosions by running away. Soon, however, he and his men gained a reputation for breathtaking bravery in terrifying circumstances—for a reason that Westerners can barely begin to understand. One observer saw a man in tears because he *survived* an attack. For jihadis, Azzam would say, had a "thirst for martyrdom." The fact that he himself had not taken part in the fighting earlier, bin Laden said, "requires my own martyrdom in the name of God."

"As Muslims," he explained to the British journalist Robert Fisk, "we believe that when we die we go to heaven. Before a battle, God sends us *seqina*, tranquillity." "I was so peaceful in my heart," he said of one experience under bombing in Afghanistan, "that I fell asleep."

In 1989, after the deaths of more than a million Afghans and some fifteen thousand Soviets, the Russians pulled out of Afghanistan. With the Afghan communist regime still in place, however, the conflict merely entered a new phase. Bin Laden and an Arab force, who took part in an attempt to take the eastern city of Jalalabad, suffered appalling casualties. Their contribution had been botched and ill-planned, but Saudi propaganda mills continued to profile bin Laden as a champion of Islam.

He "took charge of the closest front lines to the enemy," trumpeted *Jihad* magazine, "started attacking with every hero that God gave him. Their number increased in view of their desire to take part in the deliverance of Jalalabad under the command of Osama bin Laden." And: "the land of Jalalabad swallowed one lion after another. Osama had pain every time he said goodbye to one mujahid. And every time he would say goodbye a new rocket would come and take another."

Bin Laden had for some time been having disagreements with his mentor, Azzam. That year, however, their differences became moot. Azzam and two of his sons were assassinated as they drove to the mosque to pray. Who was behind their murder was never established, let alone the motive. Bin Laden had left for Saudi Arabia a few weeks earlier, to be met with a hero's welcome.

He was greeted in Jeddah, by one account, by the crown prince himself, Abdullah bin Abdul Aziz. The great and the good of Jeddah feted bin Laden, threw feasts to celebrate his prowess. He gave talks on his experiences at the mosque and in private homes. Bin Laden recordings about the Afghan campaign circulated on audiocassette, and he featured largely in a film that was being made.

Heady stuff for a man who had just turned thirty-two. For a while, to Najwa's relief, he went back to work for the bin Laden construction company. Since the start of Osama's involvement in Afghanistan, there had been many changes in their domestic life.

He had taken a second wife, then a third, then a fourth. Though it is proper under religious law to take up to four wives, this had at first troubled Najwa. She reconciled herself to the new arrangements, she said, when her husband explained that "his aim was purely to have many children for Islam." Religion did dominate bin Laden's thinking, but—with male acquaintances—he joked about his polygamy. "I have four wives waiting for me," he would say. "Time for some fun."

The fun certainly produced his quota of bin Laden children for Islam. There were eleven children by late 1989, and more would follow. A total as of 2001—with one intervening divorce, an annulment, and one more wife along the way—of twenty.

His friend Jamal Khalifa thought bin Laden was good with his children. "I never saw him shouting at his kids, hitting his kids. Even his wives, they never say he has treated them bad . . . his wives, they like him so much." As time passed, meanwhile, it became clear that—wealthy though he might be—bin Laden believed that being "a good Muslim" required severe austerity. He decreed, Najwa has said, "that our home furnishings should be plain, our clothes modest in number." He considered Islamic beliefs to have been "corrupted by modernization," and forbade his wives to use the air-conditioning or the refrigerator. To ensure a supply of fresh milk, he kept cows.

Bin Laden was more severe with his children than Khalifa saw. "We were allowed to speak in his presence," recalled his son Omar, "but our voices must be kept low. . . . We were told that we must not become excited. . . . We should be serious about everything. . . . We were not allowed to tell jokes. . . . He would allow us to smile so long as we did not laugh. If we were to lose control of our emotions and bark a laugh, we must be careful not to expose our eye teeth. I have been in situations where my father actually counted the exposed teeth, reprimanding his sons on the number their merriment revealed."

The entire family was supposed to "live just as the Prophet had lived, whenever possible." Unless a family member were to become mortally ill, they were forbidden to use modern medicines. For asthma, which afflicted all the boys, bin Laden insisted on a natural remedy—breathing through a honeycomb rather than using an inhaler. Instead of toys, Omar recalled, "Father would give us some goats to play with, telling us that we needed nothing more than God's natural gifts to be happy. . . .

"From the time we were toddlers, he demanded that we be given very little water. . . . Our father would transport his sons into the dry desert . . . bin Laden sons must be physically immune to inhospitable desert heat." Bin Laden was teaching them, Khalifa has said, "how to be a mujahid, trying to bring them up on jihad, on jihad thinking." He had taken his eldest son, Abdullah, into the Afghan war zone when he was only ten years old.

The "shy" side of bin Laden was no longer so evident. His experience in Afghanistan had given him confidence. At meetings there, speaking clearly in elegant, classical Arabic, "like a university professor," he had sat at the head of the table handing down decisions. "We will do this," he would say. "We will do that . . ."

Canadian journalist David Cobain, who had encountered bin Laden outside Afghanistan, noted his "still, silent intensity," the way he would sit "gazing unblinkingly at everything. . . . He had the extraordinary quality of attracting and holding one's attention inactively, by his presence, by the impression he gave of other-worldliness."

As THE STRUGGLE against the Soviets ended, the CIA thought the most radical Islamic groups—backed by Pakistan's ISI—would be most effective in the effort to remove the residual communist regime. Far from showing gratitude for the U.S. contribution to beating the Soviets, however, the fundamentalists proved virulently anti-American.

Working with the United States, bin Laden was to say, had all along been only a "tactical alliance." America's motive in Afghanistan had merely been self-interest. "The United States was not interested in our jihad. It was only afraid that Russia would gain access to warm waters [i.e., the Gulf]. . . . The United States has no principles.

"In our struggle against the communists, our aim was the Islamic revolution, whoever our allies might be. . . . We got involved as Muslim fighters against Soviet atheism, not as American auxiliaries. The urgent thing was to deal with communism, but the next target was the United States. . . . I began by allying myself with them, and I finished without them."

"Every Muslim," bin Laden was to claim, "hates Americans, hates Jews, and hates Christians. This is a part of our belief and our religion. For as long as I can remember, I have felt tormented and at war, and have felt hatred and animosity for Americans."

Three firsthand accounts indicate that bin Laden was hostile to Westerners by the time the Soviets left Afghanistan.

Dana Rohrabacher, former Reagan White House aide and future congressman, recalled coming across an unusual encampment near Jalalabad. "We could see these tents, luxurious tents . . . more like a modern-day camping expedition by some rich people with SUVs than a mujahideen camp. . . . I was told immediately that that was the camp of the Saudis and that I should keep my mouth shut and no English should be spoken until we were far away . . . because they said there was a crazy man in that camp who hated Americans, worse than he hated the Soviets. . . . They said, 'That man's name is bin Laden.' "

A few months later, two experienced war reporters had separate encounters with bin Laden near Jalalabad. Edward Girardet, a Swiss American with long experience of the conflict, found himself confronted by "a tall, bearded man flanked by armed men," demanding in English, with a slight American accent, "to know who I was and what I, a *kafir* [infidel], was doing in Afghanistan. For the next forty-five minutes we had a heated debate about the war, religion, and foreigners. Haughty, self-righteous, and utterly sure of himself, he proceeded to lambast the West for its feebleness and lack of moral conviction." When Girardet held out his hand to say goodbye, the tall man refused to shake. Instead, he threatened, "If you ever come again, I'll kill you."

The BBC reporter John Simpson and his crew also had an unpleasant encounter with the tall, bearded figure. This time, the man actively urged the mujahideen present to kill Simpson and his colleagues. No one obliged—the group around bin Laden included more moderate Afghan fighters. The driver of an ammunition truck, offered $500 to run down the "infidels," also declined.

The murderous threats aside, Girardet and Simpson both thought there was something peculiar about the man in white. "The best description I can give," Girardet said, "is that he sort of came across as being a rather spoiled brat, like he was sort of 'playing at jihad.' Kind of an 'I'm here now, look at me,' sort of thing."

John Simpson, for his part, witnessed something bizarre. Toward the end of the encounter, when the tall Arab ran off toward the mujahideen sleeping area, the BBC crew followed—only to find their would-be nemesis "lying full-length on a camp-bed, weeping and beating his fists on the pillow."

Looking back, Simpson vividly remembered how the Arab who wanted him dead had looked at that moment. He remembered especially the eyes: with that "crazy, handsome glitter—the Desert Sheikh meets Hannibal Lecter."

Only years later, when the news was filled with stories and photographs of bin Laden, did Girardet and Simpson realize just who the menacing Arab had been.

THE MEN AROUND bin Laden had indeed long since deferred to him, as they had to his mentor, Azzam, before his death, as sheikh. Azzam had said jihad needed a "vanguard," a leadership that would give the dreamed-of future Islamic society a "strong foundation." The Arabic words he used for "strong foundation" were "*al-qaeda al-sulbah.*"

A few months later, in 1988, Azzam, bin Laden, and a handful of comrades had discussed plans for how to make progress once the Soviets finally left. Initially, they planned, they would maintain a militia of some three hundred men. Those who enlisted would make a pledge, "so that the word of God will be the highest and his religion victorious." The camps in which they would train would be "*al-qa'ida al'askariyya*"—the Military Base.

Those who do not understand Arabic—these authors included—might interpret these utterances as the birth of the dragon that the Western media now calls "al Qaeda." Not so, recent scholarship suggests. The word does mean "the foundation" or "the base"—and other things, for such is Arabic. More than one future bin Laden militant, though, would say he never heard the name "al Qaeda"—referring to an organization or fighting entity—before 9/11. Bin Laden himself would not refer to "members of al Qaeda" until shortly before 9/11.

"He rang me to explain," Saudi journalist Jamal Khashoggi said of a call from bin Laden after the anti-Soviet conflict. "He said al Qaeda was an organization to record the names of the mujahideen and all their contact details: a database. . . . So wherever jihad needed fighting, in the Philippines or Central Asia or anywhere in the world, you could get in touch with the fighters quickly."

All the same, a seed had been sown.

The ISI chief of the day, Hamid Gul, was asked in 1989 whether it had not been "playing with fire" to bring in Muslim radicals. "We are fighting a jihad," Gul replied. "The communists have their international brigades, the West has NATO, why can't the Muslims unite and form a common front?"

Gul was replaced as head of ISI by Benazir Bhutto, the moderate, Western-educated prime minister who had come to power in Pakistan the previous year. At a private meeting with President George H. W. Bush, she said, "I mentioned that in our common zeal to most effectively combat the Soviets in Afghanistan, our countries had made a strategic decision to empower the most fanatical elements of the mujahideen. . . . I sadly said to President Bush, 'Mr. President, I'm afraid we have created a Frankenstein's monster that could come back to haunt us in the future.' "

THE FUTURE CAST of 9/11's characters was now waiting in the wings. Ayman al-Zawahiri, a doctor by training, led a clique of militant Egyptians in Afghanistan. Though his specialty was eye surgery, he had dealt with every sort of injury and ailment during the conflict— including bin Laden's chronic low blood pressure. One day, he would become bin Laden's principal cohort. Bin Laden and Mohammed Atef, who would become his strategist and senior commander, had fought side by side. All three of them knew Omar Abdel Rahman, the incendiary preacher later to be known in the West as the "Blind Sheikh."

Khalid Sheikh Mohammed, who would one day claim to have been the principal planner of 9/11, was in his mid-twenties in 1989. Ramzi Yousef, who would lead a first attempt to destroy the World Trade Center, was still at college. Both of them were passionately hostile to the United States because of its support for Israel.

Mohamed Atta, who was to lead the 9/11 hijackers, was just twenty-one and studying architecture at Cairo University. His future fellow "pilots," Hani Hanjour, Ziad Jarrah, and Marwan al-Shehhi, were seventeen, fourteen, and eleven.

As a little boy, Jarrah had lived near the refugee camp where hundreds of Palestinian refugees had been slaughtered—by Christian militiamen with the knowledge of Israeli commanders—during Israel's 1982 invasion of Lebanon.

The plight of the Palestinians, the rise and rise of Israel, and America's consistent support of Israel preoccupied bin Laden from very early on. His mother has recalled him, as a teenager, being "concerned, sad, and frustrated about the situation in Palestine in particular." It was essential, bin Laden said even then, "to reclaim Palestine."

By the mid-1980s, bin Laden was already speaking out publicly about boycotting American products. He would not drink Coca-Cola, Pepsi, or 7-Up, or allow his children to drink such beverages. "The Americans take our money," he recalled saying, "and give it to the Jews so that they can kill our children with it in Palestine." "Our" children, because Palestinians were fellow Arabs, part of the wider Arab community. He was to raise the Palestine issue and excoriate American support for Israel time and again—until as recently as 2009.

The 1982 Israeli assault on Lebanon, bin Laden said after 9/11, made a lasting impression on him. "America allowed the Israelis to invade Lebanon," he declared. "They started bombing, killing and wounding many. . . . I still remember those distressing scenes: blood, torn limbs, women and children massacred. . . . It was like a crocodile devouring a child, who could do nothing but scream. . . . The whole world heard and saw what happened, but did nothing."

It was then, bin Laden asserted, that something like 9/11 first occurred to him. He watched, presumably on television, as Israel bombarded the high-rise apartment blocks that housed many Palestinians in Beirut. "The idea came to me," he asserted, "when things went just too far with the American-Israeli alliance's oppression and atrocities against our people in Palestine and Lebanon. . . . As I looked at those destroyed towers in Lebanon, it occurred to me to punish the oppressor in kind by destroying towers in America, so that it would get a taste of its own medicine."

"The events of Manhattan," he would say on an audiotaped message broadcast after 9/11, "were retaliation against the American-Israeli alliance's aggression against our people in Palestine and Lebanon."

PERHAPS so. While he was still the hero home from the war, though, a further grievance against the United States arose on his home territory—one that, for bin Laden and many other Saudis—loomed at least as large as Palestine.

NINETEEN

IN AUGUST 1990, OSAMA BIN LADEN STOCKED UP ON FOOD SUPPLIES, candles, gas masks, and portable communications equipment. In the event of the need for a quick getaway, he had a more powerful engine fitted to the boat he kept at the family marina. At home, he got his sons to help him cover the windows with adhesive tape. The tape, he explained, was in case of bombing, to protect the family from broken glass.

Bombing was a possibility. Saddam Hussein's army had overrun neighboring Kuwait and appeared poised to push on into Saudi Arabia. Bin Laden despised the Iraqi president, whom he considered an unbeliever. Saddam, he predicted, "will attack Saudi Arabia for possession of the oilfields in the eastern province."

Oil was what mattered, the one thing that really mattered, to all the nations involved. It was the only reason, certainly, that Saudi Arabia had ever mattered to the Americans. "The defense of Saudi Arabia," President Franklin Roosevelt had said back in 1943, "is vital to the defense of the United States." Half a century on and within twenty-four hours of the Iraqi invasion, the first President Bush now made a promise. "If you ask for help from the United States," he told Saudi ambassador Prince Bandar, "we will go all the way with you."

Four days later, at King Fahd's seaside palace in Jeddah, a senior U.S. delegation told the monarch what a request for help would mean. Some 300,000 Iraqi troops and almost three thousand tanks were threatening the border. To drive them back and throw them out of Kuwait, General Norman Schwarzkopf explained, would mean "flooding his airfields, harbors and military bases with tens of thousands more Americans than Saudi Arabia had ever seen."

To allow a foreign and overwhelmingly Christian army to enter the country—the sacred land of the Prophet—would be seen by much of the Saudi population as heinous sacrilege. Everything in the country, everything, revolved around religion. "This is something that a Westerner will never understand," one of the royals, Prince Amr, later explained to a foreigner. "Religion is the law. . . . It is rooted in the history. It is part of the DNA, if you like, of the Saudis."

At least a third of the Saudi school curriculum was devoted to religious study. Holy writ, children were taught, held that "the last hour won't come before the Muslims fight the Jews and the Muslims kill them." This was a land with a religious police, a Committee for the Promotion of Virtue and the Prevention of Vice, empowered to raid people's homes, make arrests, and use physical force to compel obedience to religious rules. Censors blacked out any part of a foreign newspaper or magazine that contained comment on Saudi Arabia, any reference to Israel—or illustrations that showed even an inch of a woman's limbs or neck.

This was a land where extremism ruled, from the preposterous to the barbaric: where oil dollars built a concert hall in which no performance was permitted, where Islamic courts ruled against the playing of music on phone recordings; where ownership of a Christian Bible could—and shortly would—lead to public execution by beheading.

According to the incumbent Grand Mufti, the nation's highest official of religious law, it was "a requirement of Muslims to be hostile to the Jews and the Christians and other polytheists." "The unbelievers," he wrote, "are the enemy, do not trust them."

The notion of inviting in an American army to fight off the Iraqis, then, was unthinkable. At the meeting with the U.S. delegation, the royals present held a brief animated exchange in Arabic.

Crown Prince Abdullah urged King Fahd not to make a decision until tribal and religious leaders had been consulted. Fahd, however, had already made up his mind. Better to take a risk domestically than to lose the throne, to lose the entire country, to Saddam Hussein. The king reportedly turned to Dick Cheney—then secretary of defense—and said, "Okay."

With those two syllables, Fahd had authorized a U.S. military presence that would eventually total half a million men—and not only men. How, in Saudi Arabia, to deal with the problem of female American soldiers—working in the heat—showing their *forearms* in public? Schwarzkopf promised that no female entertainers would be brought in to entertain the troops—only for the king to complain when CNN ran pictures of soldiers applauding female dancers. Only the dancers' legs were shown, but that was beyond the pale.

How to deal with Christmas carols in a Saudi war zone? Schwarzkopf solved the problem—more or less—by ensuring that only instrumental versions were broadcast. All Christian and Jewish emblems, he ordered, were to be concealed or removed from uniforms.

Where could Jewish soldiers serving with the U.S. force observe the Sabbath? The Americans told the Saudis they would ferry them to naval ships at sea for the occasion. Senior Saudis, for their part, agreed to turn a blind eye to American soldiers bringing Bibles into the country.

All those issues aside, the military offensive to oust the Iraqis had to be launched before March—the start of the Muslim holy month of Ramadan.

News of the decision to allow in U.S. troops stunned ordinary Saudis. For bin Laden, it came as a cultural thunderbolt. "Pollution," he said, hung in the air around anyone who was not a Muslim. As a renowned Afghan war hero, with a following of loyal veterans, he fooled himself into thinking he could offer a viable alternative.

Bin Laden obtained meetings with several royals, including Interior Minister Prince Naif and Defense Minister Prince Sultan. An imam present at one of the audiences, Professor Khalil-Khalil, recalled how bin Laden "kept asking the government officials in the room why they had brought the Americans into this war . . . said he wanted to fight alongside the Saudi army. The Prince asked bin Laden whether or not he had his own army. Bin Laden said that he did, and that he had a 20,000 person standing army, with 40,000 in reserves." His proposals were militarily preposterous on their face.

Not satisfied with seeing senior ministers, however, bin Laden requested an audience with the king himself. The request went no-where, not least because bin Laden had said that he "didn't care about King Fahd, only about Allah." He was sent on his way with a royal "Don't call us. We'll call you."

Bin Laden personally got away with this. The hundred or so war veterans he had brought into the country, however, and some of his personal staff were arrested. They were released only after bin Laden had made a string of calls to various princes. Unrepentant, he then began speaking out in public, arranging the distribution of flyers and audio-tapes that claimed Saudi Arabia was becoming "a colony of America."

The United States, meanwhile, leading a coalition of troops from thirty-two nations—including Saudi Arabia and several Muslim countries—duly recaptured Kuwait. Iraq was routed, at huge cost in men and matériel, in the brilliant operation remembered as Desert Storm. Even had bin Laden been able to resign himself to a temporary American presence, however, there was now a further affront. After the war, contrary to what he and like-minded objectors had hoped, some five thousand American troops and several bases remained. The American military did not leave Saudi Arabia.

IT WAS, FATEFULLY, bin Laden who departed. The precise reason that he left, and under what conditions, is lost in the fog of conflicting in-formation supplied by Saudi and CIA sources. The shapes in that fog may tell us something.

To at least some in the Saudi government, bin Laden had become a political pest at a difficult time. In the groundswell of protest over the U.S. presence, his very public dissent was galling. So was his at-tempt to use his veterans for a new jihad, against the communist re-gime that controlled part of neighboring Yemen. Bin Laden's passport was reportedly seized, his movements within Saudi Arabia restricted.

Then suddenly, in April 1991, he was cleared to travel. "One day," his son Omar recalled, "my father disappeared without telling us anything." He had gone to Pakistan—supposedly to attend an Is-lamic conference, or look after a business matter. "We didn't say, 'Get out!' " Prince Bandar has said. "He left because he thought it was getting to the point where what he was saying and doing was not going to be accepted."

The truth was probably not so simple. The whole purpose of confiscating bin Laden's passport, after all, had been to prevent him going abroad to make trouble. Why return it? One Saudi intelligence source said bin Laden was told he should leave because "the U.S. government was planning to kill him . . . so the royal family would do him a favor and get him out of the kingdom for his own protection." This makes no sense. Bin Laden had as yet perpetrated no crimes against the United States. As yet, Washington had no motive to want him dead.

Accounts vary as to the circumstances of bin Laden's departure. Former senior CIA officer Michael Scheuer has written that he managed to leave by "using the intervention of his brothers to convince the Saudi officials to let him travel on condition he would return. . . ." Author Lawrence Wright, for his part, wrote that many "prominent princes and sheikhs" interceded on his behalf. Interior minister Naif authorized the departure, but only after bin Laden signed "a pledge that he would not interfere with the politics of Saudi Arabia or any Arab country."

Out of the Kingdom, bin Laden would be free to pursue jihad. That, in the context of fighting for Islam, would be very much in line with Saudi foreign policy. If this scenario is accurate, the long-term implications are grave.

Just who did launch bin Laden on his career as international terrorist? In a little noted passage, the 9/11 Commission Report stated as fact that he had gotten out of Saudi Arabia "with help from a dissident member of the royal family." The Commission had this information from three of bin Laden's close associates. Some believe that there were dissidents among the royal princes, men who continued to sympathize with bin Laden's views and to support him for years to come. Until and perhaps even after 9/11.

Troubling clues that raise suspicion as to the true role of the Saudis, and particularly the activity of certain Saudi royals, proliferate throughout this story.

"Go to Sudan," a friend in the government had advised bin Laden. "You can organize a holy war from there."

An Islamic regime had recently come to power in Sudan, and bin Laden had been buying up land in that desperately poor North African country. So it was, in the summer of 1991, that he made Khartoum his destination. His four wives and their children—fourteen by now—arrived later direct from Saudi Arabia. They were whisked through the airport, ushered into luxury cars, and driven away in style. As a hero of jihad, and a very generous millionaire, bin Laden was the guest of Sudan's president.

Bin Laden and his family were to stay for five years. They took over several houses in a wealthy suburb of Khartoum, a three-story home and large garden for the wives and children, three houses for the servants and security men, an office, and a guesthouse where bin Laden received visitors. The family dwelling had some European furniture and a profusion of blue cushions laid out Arab-style but not a single picture to decorate the walls.

In this new setting, bin Laden continued to insist on austerity. Modern conveniences were to his mind contrary to Muslim law or just plain extravagant. On a visit to Sudan, the Saudi journalist Jamal Khashoggi asked him why his robe appeared all wrinkled. "You know how many kilowatts of electricity an iron consumes?" bin Laden asked. "I don't need an iron. I'm trying to live my life without electricity." He told his wives not to use the refrigerator, the electric stoves, or—in the searing heat—the air-conditioning.

Bin Laden's sons attended the best private school in Sudan, while the girls went to no school at all. Instead, they got rudimentary lessons at home, from an aunt. Bin Laden did not approve of formal education for girls. He had more time for his children now, though they might have preferred otherwise. Omar recalled how he and his brothers were punished. "His wooden cane was his favorite weapon. . . . It was not unusual for the sons of bin Laden to be covered with raised welts on our backs and legs."

If he thought his sons had defied him, bin Laden could turn apoplectic with rage. Once, when he told Omar to wash an honored guest's hands—in line with bin Laden's reading of the correct etiquette—the visitor demurred, saying he would wash himself. Omar handed over the water jug accordingly, only to have his father misconstrue what was happening. "Why do you embarrass me?" he bellowed. "Why should *he* wash *your* hands? You are a nobody!" So angry was his father, Omar recalled, that "spit spewed from his mouth."

Notwithstanding patriarchal explosions, first wife Najwa found a measure of contentment in Sudan. "My husband did not travel so much. . . . He had arrangements with high officials in the Sudanese government to build roads and factories. . . . Osama's favorite undertaking was working the land, growing the best corn and the biggest sunflowers. . . . Nothing made my husband happier than showing off his huge sunflowers."

Eighteen months later, in his first interview of substance with a Western journalist, bin Laden described himself as merely an "agriculturalist" and "construction engineer." Using the bulldozers and other equipment he had once used to build roads for the mujahideen in Afghanistan, he said, he and his men had undertaken a major highway project for the benefit of the Sudanese people.

The reporter, the British *Independent*'s Robert Fisk, looked carefully at his interviewee. With his high cheekbones and narrowed eyes, resplendent in a gold-fringed robe, he thought bin Laden looked "every inch the mountain warrior of mujahideen legend." Was there truth to the rumors, Fisk ventured, that he had brought his Arab veterans to the Sudan to train for future jihad? That, bin Laden said, was "the rubbish of the media."

Bin Laden had not, however, forgotten jihad. Several hundred of his jihadis had indeed migrated to the Sudan. This was a place and a time for training—and hatching plots.

Bin Laden's mentor, Azzam, had once called for worldwide war to recover all territory that had historically been part of Islam. "Jihad," he had written, "will remain an individual obligation until all other lands that were Muslim are returned to us . . . before us lie Palestine, Bokhara [part of Uzbekistan], Lebanon, Chad, Eritrea, Somalia, the Philippines, Burma, Southern Yemen, Tashkent [also in Uzbekistan] and Andalusia [the region of southern Spain that the Arabs had ruled until the late fifteenth century]."

If bin Laden's ambitions did not reach as far into a fantasy Islamic future as Azzam's, they were grand nonetheless. The task of the young men who joined jihad, bin Laden was to say, was to struggle in "every place in which non-believers' injustice is perpetrated against Muslims." With his approval and often with his funding, terrorism in the cause of Islam was on the rise.

• • •

AT ALMOST EXACTLY the time bin Laden arrived in Sudan, another man began working with a Muslim separatist group in the Philippines. He told his contacts he was an "emissary from bin Laden," acting on behalf of Blind Sheikh Omar Abdel Rahman—by then preaching jihad in the United States. He used many names, but the name by which the self-proclaimed "emissary" is known today is Ramzi Yousef.

Bin Laden was one day to claim he did not know Yousef. Yet the links were there. And soon, Yousef would lead the first attempt to bring down the World Trade Center.

TWENTY

HE WAS IN HIS MID-TWENTIES, LEAN, DIMINUTIVE. HE HAD DEGREES in chemistry and electrical engineering. At college in the United Kingdom, where he had studied, he was thought of as "hard-working, conscientious." A senior FBI official would one day describe him as "poised, articulate, well-educated." He spoke not only English but several other languages.

Ramzi Yousef was more political than he was fanatically religious. The Palestinian blood he claimed, he said, made him "Palestinian by choice," and he believed America's support for Israel gave all Muslims "the right to regard themselves as in a state of war with the U.S. government."

It had been the anti-Soviet war in Afghanistan, however, that first brought Yousef to jihad. In the Afghan training camps, during a break from his studies in Britain, he learned about explosives—learned so well, some said, that he rapidly became an instructor. Fellow trainees dubbed him "the Chemist."

Once America had become the enemy, Yousef's talent made him a deadly adversary. In midsummer 1992, speaking in code on the phone with a like-thinking friend, he referred to his "chocolate training." The friend did not at first understand so he said simply, "Boom!," adding that he was going to work in the United States. The friend got the gist.

In New York two years earlier, Blind Sheikh Rahman had preached the need to "break and destroy the morale of the enemies of Allah." It should be done, he said, by "exploding the structure of their civilized pillars . . . the touristic infrastructure which they are proud of, and their high buildings." He and those around him, an FBI informant recalled, often talked of "targeting American symbols."

The same month Yousef spoke of a mission to America involving explosives, the Blind Sheikh made a phone call to Pakistan. Within weeks, arriving on September 1, the Chemist and an accomplice flew First Class from Karachi to New York's Kennedy Airport.

The mission almost failed before it began, when the accomplice was stopped by Immigration. He was found to be carrying a false Swedish passport, a Saudi passport that had been altered, Jordanian and British passports, instructions on document forgery, rubber stamps for altering the seal on Saudi passports—and what turned out to be bomb-making instructions. Yousef also raised suspicions. In addition to an Iraqi passport, which turned out to be phony, he was carrying ID in the name of his traveling companion.

The companion was detained and would later be jailed. Yousef, who requested asylum on the grounds that he was fleeing persecution in Iraq, was admitted to the country pending a hearing. He headed at once, investigators later came to believe, for the Al Khifa center in Brooklyn, a focal point for Arabs bound for and returning from Afghanistan. A contact there took him, at least once, to see Blind Sheikh Rahman, the man who had called for exploding America's "high buildings."

Over the months that followed, in various apartments in Jersey City—just across the Hudson River from his target—Yousef the Chemist did the work he had come to do. He and accomplices acquired what he needed: 1,000 pounds of urea, 105 gallons of nitric acid, 60 gallons of sulfuric acid, three tanks of compressed hydrogen. At the apartment where the chemicals were mixed, walls became stained, metal items corroded.

By February 25, 1993, all was ready. Yousef and two accomplices loaded the bomb, packed in four large cardboard boxes, into a rented Econoline van. The cylinders of hydrogen, along with containers of nitroglycerine, blasting caps, and fuses, were laid alongside them.

Just after noon the following day, the bombers parked the van in a garage beneath the North Tower of the World Trade Center. Yousef lit the fuses with a cigarette lighter, closed the doors, and made his escape in a waiting car.

The bomb exploded just before 12:18 P.M. At 1,200 pounds, the FBI would rate it "the largest by weight and by damage of any improvised explosive device that we've seen since the inception of forensic explosive identification"—more than sixty years earlier.

A mile away, people thought there had been an earthquake. Beneath the ground—the Trade Center reached seven stories below the surface—the bomb opened a crater four stories deep. Burning cars hung from ruined parking levels "like Christmas tree ornaments." The explosion devastated an underground train station.

Above the explosion point, the blast rocketed upward, cut power, stopped elevators in mid-journey. One elevator, crammed with schoolchildren, was stranded for five hours. Smoke rose as high as the 82nd floor, and thousands of people rushed for the stairwells. Some crowded around windows as if planning to jump—eerily prefiguring the fatal plunges of almost a decade later.

Miraculously, for all the damage, only six people were killed—even though some hundred thousand people worked in or visited the Trade Center complex on an average weekday. More than a thousand were injured, however, sending more people to the hospital—it is said—than any event on the American mainland since the Civil War.

"If they had found the exact architectural Achilles' heel," an FBI explosives specialist said of the tower that was hit, "or if the bomb had been a little bit bigger—not much more, 500 lbs. more—I think it would have brought her down." Yousef would later tell investigators he had wanted to bring the North Tower crashing down on its twin, killing—he hoped—the quarter of a million people he imagined used the complex each day.

He had arranged for a communiqué to be mailed to the press in the name of the "Liberation Army," saying that the attack had been carried out in response to "the American political, economical, and military support to Israel. . . . The American people are responsible for the actions of their government."

When Yousef learned that the bombing had only partially succeeded, he phoned an accomplice to dictate a new ending to the communiqué. It read: "Our calculations were not very accurate this time. However, we promise you that the next time it will be very precise and the World Trade Center will continue to be one [of] our targets."

Yousef apparently phoned in the amendment from a First Class lounge at Kennedy Airport. An hour or so later he was gone, safe aboard an airliner bound for Pakistan.

Thanks to brilliant forensic work, most of the accomplices Yousef left behind were swiftly tracked down and jailed. The bomber himself, though identified, remained at large to plot new mayhem. By January 1995, he was back in the Philippines, with a dual focus. He intended a bombing during the visit to the Pacific region by Pope John Paul II, and—most fiendish and complex of all—a series of bombings of American airliners.

The plot against the Pope proved Yousef's undoing. The plot to bring down U.S. airliners—little understood at the time—was a turning point on the road to 9/11.

ON THE NIGHT of Friday, January 6, 1995, in Manila, smoke was reported billowing out of an apartment building just a block from the papal nunciature, where Pope John Paul would be staying. A patrolman reported that there was nothing to worry about—"Just some Pakistanis," he said, "playing with firecrackers."

Unconvinced, senior police inspector Aida Fariscal decided to take a look for herself. Told that the smoke had come from Suite 603 in the apartment building, and that its two tenants had fled during the initial panic, she asked to see inside. The apartment turned out to be crammed with chemicals in plastic containers, cotton soaked in acrid-smelling fluid, funnels, thermometers, fusing systems, electrical wiring, and explosives instructions in Arabic.

As Fariscal and the officers with her stared at their find, the doorman told them that one of the missing tenants had come back to retrieve something that had been left behind. He spotted the police and started running, but was caught and hauled back to headquarters. The man, who claimed he was "Ahmed Saeed," an innocent tourist, was handed over to agents at a military installation. They were not gentle with him.

According to reporting by two distinguished Filipino reporters, he was tortured over a period of more than two months. "Agents hit him with a chair and a long piece of wood, forced water into his mouth, and crushed lighted cigarettes into his private parts. They dragged him on the floor, from one corner of the interrogation room to the other. . . . They threatened to rape him. . . . His ribs were almost [all] broken."

A partial transcript of one taped session with the prisoner runs as follows:

INTERROGATOR: What will the bomb be made of?
PRISONER: That will be nitroglycerine . . . 5 milliliters of glycerine, 15 of nitrate, and 22.5 of sulphuric acid . . .
INTERROGATOR: What are your plans?
PRISONER: We are planning, I'm planning to explode this airplane. I have planning of of—just, I can't breathe, I can't breathe . . .
INTERROGATOR: What is your plan in America?
PRISONER: Killing the people there. Teach them . . .
INTERROGATOR: What do you do in . . . going to Singapore?
PRISONER: I'll put the bomb in the United Air . . .

The captive's real name was Abdul Murad, and he was the associate in whom Ramzi Yousef had confided before flying to New York to bomb the Trade Center. Torture notwithstanding, the evidence in Manila linked him firmly to the more recent terrorist activity. Extradited to the United States, in the hands of FBI agents, Murad told a cohesive story.

Yousef had told him the previous year, in Pakistan, of wanting "to blow up unnamed American airliners by placing explosives aboard the aircraft." Training sessions followed, with Murad making notes of formulas and instructions. Then, in December, Yousef had summoned him to the Philippines. They worked on methods of disguise—removal of the obligatory jihadi beard, L'Oréal dye to color the hair, and blue contact lenses—to look "more European."

They bought Casio watches for use as timing devices to trigger the airliner bombs. Yousef ran live experiments, the first time with a small device planted under a seat in a local movie theater. It worked perfectly, without causing serious injury—because the seat was unoccupied at the time. The second test, however, proved lethal.

In early December, posing as an Italian, Yousef boarded a Philippine Air flight bound for Tokyo with 273 passengers. He had with him one of the modified Casio watches, liquid explosive in a contact lens solution bottle, and minute batteries hidden in the heels of his shoes. He assembled the device in flight, concealed it under the seat cushion of Seat 26K, then left the plane at a scheduled stopover.

Two hours later, the bomb went off in mid-flight. Though it killed the unfortunate passenger in 26K and crippled the aircraft's controls, the plane landed safely thanks to the skill of its pilots. The operation had proved to Yousef, however, that his devices could work. He now prepared another bomb, intended for an American airplane.

Murad was to plant the bomb this time. He would avoid suspicion by using two carry-on bags, one to smuggle the liquid on board, the second for components. The detonator was to be concealed inside a Parker pen, the bomb placed in a restroom near the cockpit. Murad would escape by leaving the plane at a stopover, as had Yousef previously. The pair expected to "cause the destruction of the plane and the death of everyone on board."

A date had been picked, a flight chosen—United Airlines Flight 2 from Hong Kong to Los Angeles on January 14. Then on January 6, the plan fell apart—with the telltale smoke emanating from the conspirators' apartment, the police search that followed, and Murad's arrest. It was to retrieve Yousef's laptop computer that Murad had risked trying to return to the apartment. Now the police had it.

A file on the laptop revealed that the plot called for the bombing of not only United Flight 2 but of *eleven* other American airliners. A number of terrorists, identified on the laptop by pseudonyms, were to transport and plant the devices. Flights targeted included seven operated by United, three by Northwest, and one by Delta. Under the headings "TIMER" and "SETTING," Yousef had meticulously listed at precisely what time one of his Casio watches was to detonate each individual bomb.

The airlines were alerted, flights diverted and grounded, on orders direct from the Clinton White House. In the sort of security scare not to be seen again until after the Millennium, passengers in the Pacific region were searched, all liquids confiscated, for weeks to come.

Catastrophe had been averted thanks only to Inspector Fariscal's insistence on entering the apartment that served as Yousef's bomb factory. Had the plot succeeded, as many as four thousand people could have died—more than the total that were to be lost on 9/11.

The computer file on the plot bore a code name that at first meant nothing to investigators—"BOJINKA." It appears to be a Serbo-Croatian or Croatian word meaning "loud bang," "big bang"— or just "boom." "Boom," the word Yousef had used two and a half years earlier, in plain English, as verbal code for his coming attack on New York's World Trade Center.

Exactly a month after the discoveries in Manila, the bomber was finally betrayed and arrested in Pakistan. Extradited to the United States, thanks to a cooperative Prime Minister Bhutto, he faced trial twice—once for the airliner plot, once for the 1993 Trade Center bombing. Found guilty in both cases, Yousef was sentenced to a theoretical 240 years in jail.

"I am a terrorist and I'm proud of it," he had declared in court. "I support terrorism so long as it is against the United States government and against Israel." In 1995, on the final stage of his return from Pakistan, a helicopter was used to bring Yousef, shackled and blindfolded, to the Correctional Center in Lower Manhattan. As the helicopter approached the Twin Towers, an FBI agent pulled up the blindfold and pointed. "See," he said. "You didn't get them after all." The prisoner responded with a look and a curt "Not yet."

When the towers were finally destroyed, on 9/11, Yousef would prostrate himself in his prison cell and give praise to Allah. He had all along accepted responsibility for the 1993 bombing, but on one point he remained evasive. Was he or was he not the mastermind behind the operation? He would say only that Muslim leaders had inspired his work. Which Muslim leaders? He would not say.

As LATE AS 2004, a former CIA deputy director of intelligence—by then a senior staff member of the 9/11 Commission—would say there was "substantial uncertainty" as to whether Osama bin Laden and his organization had a role in either the Trade Center bombing or the plot to blow up U.S. airliners over the Pacific.

Available information suggests there was in fact a link to bin Laden. Yousef had learned about explosives in bin Laden–funded camps near the Afghan border. In 1991, when he reached the Philippines, he told separatists he was bin Laden's "emissary." The separatist with whom he had most contact was funded by bin Laden, had been close to bin Laden during the anti-Soviet conflict. The accomplice who tried to enter the United States with Yousef—but was refused admission—had carried a bomb manual headed "Al Qaeda," the name for the then-obscure entity headed by bin Laden.

Yousef made a huge number of long-distance calls while preparing to bomb the Trade Center. Checks on the calls after the attack reportedly indicated a link to bin Laden. During Yousef's stays in Peshawar, over several years, he stayed at the Beit Ashuhada [House of the Martyrs], which bin Laden funded. One of the operatives Yousef used in the Philippines was an Afghanistan veteran whom bin Laden has recalled as a "good friend," a man who had "fought from the same trenches" with him.

Bin Laden also connected to the Yousef operation through his own brother-in-law. This was his Saudi friend from university days, Jamal Khalifa, who married bin Laden's sister Shaikha and lived with bin Laden after the wedding. "Imagine how close we are," Khalifa would say after 9/11. "We never disagreed about anything."

By the early 1990s, Khalifa had long been active in the Philippines, fronting as a "missionary" or "philanthropist" and setting up charities to support Muslim causes. In 1992, according to an intelligence report, bin Laden himself visited the Philippines to bestow financial largesse.

Behind the facade, Khalifa spread money around in support of antigovernment rebels. By one report, moreover, he and bin Laden personally introduced one leading Filipino rebel leader to explosives expert Ramzi Yousef. Khalifa remained active in the Philippines until late 1994. Then he abruptly left the country, on the heels of a police report on Muslim groups and terrorism.

Just before Christmas that year, on the U.S. West Coast, Khalifa was arrested by FBI agents—at the very time that, back in the Philippines, Yousef was finalizing his plan to bomb eleven American airliners. In the Saudi's baggage, agents found: a phone book listing a number in Pakistan that Yousef had called from Manila; a beeper number for one of the accomplices Yousef planned to use to plant his bombs on American planes; the address of Yousef's bomb factory; documents related to explosives and weaponry—and a phone directory entry for Osama bin Laden.

There was more. Khalifa's business card was found both in

Manila—at the apartment of one of Yousef's accomplices—and in New York in a suitcase belonging to Blind Sheikh Rahman. One of Khalifa's aliases—he used several—was found on a document belonging to one of Yousef's accomplices. He would eventually be named as an unindicted co-conspirator in the 1993 bombing of the World Trade Center.

Inexplicably, there would not be a single reference to Khalifa in the 9/11 Commission report. Congress's Joint Inquiry report contained just one, characterizing him as the "alleged financier" of the plot to destroy American airliners. Khalifa would never be charged in the United States with any crime.

RAMZI YOUSEF's phone directory, meanwhile, also threw up a lead, a major clue that, successfully pursued, could perhaps have prevented the 9/11 catastrophe. The directory contained the name and contact information in Pakistan for one "Zahid Sheikh Mohammed," brother of a man named "Khalid"—both of them uncles to Yousef.

Zahid's name remains obscure, while Khalid would for years remain a will-o'-the-wisp, a quarry who would not be run to ground until 2003. Today, however, the name of Khalid Sheikh Mohammed sparks instant recognition.

By his own admission, he was the planner and organizer of many attacks—including 9/11. U.S. investigators have long since dubbed him, simply, KSM.

The information on Ramzi Yousef's computer implicated KSM in the Manila conspiracies and started the hunt for him. Investigators hurried to Zahid's home in Pakistan, to find photographs of bin Laden but no sign of either Mohammed brother. Clues proliferated, however, and much later—in captivity—he would fill in missing parts of the jigsaw.

Some of the many phone calls Yousef had made from New York, while planning the 1993 Trade Center bombing, had been to KSM. They had discussed procedures for mixing explosives on the calls, and the older man helped at least once by wiring his nephew money.

In Manila in 1994, KSM was at very least Yousef's senior accomplice, perhaps the plot's driving force. While Yousef found modest lodgings, KSM took a condominium at Tiffany Mansions, a rather grand address in an affluent part of town. Perhaps as part of their cover, perhaps by inclination, neither man lived the kind of life required of Islamic fundamentalists.

Some of the detail on the Philippines episode comes from the bar girls and dancers with whom uncle and nephew whiled away their nights—and whom they found useful. KSM bribed one of the girls to open a bank account and to purchase a sophisticated mobile phone. The account and the phone were in her name but for his use, ideal for shady financial transactions and unmonitored communication.

To Abdul Murad, the accomplice seized the night police raided the Manila bomb factory, KSM was "Abdul Majid"—one of his thirty-some aliases. Murad had met him once before in Pakistan, when Yousef was recovering from an injury incurred while handling explosives. Then, Yousef had told him "Majid" was a Saudi in the "electronics business." His uncle was in fact Kuwaiti-born and in the terrorism business.

In Manila, as final preparations were made to down U.S. airliners, KSM came repeatedly to the bomb factory. With chemicals and electronic components scattered in plain sight, Murad was to say that Mohammed "must have known that something was planned." "I was responsible," KSM would one day tell a U.S. military tribunal, "for the planning and surveying needed to execute the Bojinka Operation."

KSM was to tell the CIA that he thought of something else in Manila, a concept radically different from exploding bombs on airliners—the "idea of using planes as missiles." One potential target he and Yousef considered at that time was the CIA headquarters in Virginia. Another was the World Trade Center.

What KSM had to say on that, an indication that flying planes into buildings was under discussion long, long before 9/11, is on its own merely interesting. What sparked lasting controversy, though, is the suggestion that U.S. authorities learned early on what the plotters had in mind—and dropped the ball.

A Philippines police document cites Yousef's accomplice Murad as saying that they discussed a "plan to dive-crash a commercial aircraft at the CIA headquarters in Virginia. . . . What the subject has in his mind is that he will board any American commercial aircraft, pretending to be an ordinary passenger. Then he will hijack said aircraft, control its cockpit and dive it at the CIA headquarters."

No suggestion there that the terrorists discussed targets other than the CIA. One of the Philippines police officers who interrogated

Murad, however, has claimed otherwise. Colonel Rodolfo Mendoza told CNN that there was also talk of crashing a plane into the Pentagon. The Philippines presidential spokesman, Rigoberto Tiglao, went much further.

"The targets they listed," he said in 2001, "were CIA headquarters, the Pentagon, TransAmerica [the TransAmerica Tower, in San Francisco], Sears [the Sears Tower, in Chicago], and the World Trade Center."

Most credible, perhaps, is apparent corroboration from a source who does not cite Murad, whose statements were obtained under torture. Rafael Garcia, the Filipino computer analyst who examined Yousef's computer, recalls having discovered notes of a plan that called for crashing airliners into "selected targets in the United States." These included: "the CIA headquarters in Langley, Virginia; the World Trade Center in New York; the Sears Tower in Chicago; the TransAmerica Tower in San Francisco; and the White House in Washington DC."

The 9/11 Commission Report, which quoted none of these statements verbatim, consigned them to an obscure footnote and referred to them as mere "claims." Its investigation, it stated, found no indication that such information "was written down or disseminated within the U.S. government."

Congress's Joint Inquiry Report, however, said the FBI and the CIA did learn what Murad had said about a plan to crash a plane into CIA headquarters. The FBI, the report stated, later "effectively forgot all about it . . . ignored this early warning sign that terrorists had begun planning to crash aircraft into symbols of American power."

The Philippines National Police intelligence chief, Robert Delfin, said, "We shared that with the FBI. They may have mislooked [*sic*], and didn't appreciate the info coming from the Philippines police. . . . I believe there was a lapse."

Colonel Mendoza, who said he personally questioned Murad, insisted that he briefed the U.S. embassy on everything Murad told him. Another lead investigator on the Manila episode, police Colonel— later General—Avelino Razon, immediately called a press conference when news broke of 9/11. "We told the Americans about the plans to turn planes into flying bombs as far back as 1995," he said. "Why didn't they pay attention?"

Last word to Inspector Fariscal, the officer who discovered Ramzi

FD-302 (Rev. 3-10-82)

3536-B

- 1 -

FEDERAL BUREAU OF INVESTIGATION

Investigation on ___4/12-13/95___ at __Aircraft in Flight___   File # __265A-NY-252802 sub 302-47__

— SA FRANCIS J. PELLEGRINO, FBI
by SA THOMAS G. DONLON, FBI _____   Date dictated __4/19/95__

This document contains neither recommendations nor conclusions of the FBI. It is the property of the FBI and is loaned to your agency;
it and its contents are not to be distributed outside your agency.

> As for any future terrorist plans, MURAD advised that
> he and RAMZI discussed the possibility of bombing a nuclear
> facility in the United States. They also discussed additional
> attacks on American airline carriers such as United and Northwest
> Airlines. MURAD stated that RAMZI wanted to bomb El-Al Airlines
> but believed that security would be too difficult to penetrate.
> The underlying reason for these attacks would be to make the
> people of the U.S., and their government, "suffer" for their
> support of Israel. MURAD stated that America should remain
> neutral regarding the problems of the Middle East. MURAD advised
> that RAMZI wanted to return to the United States in the future to
> bomb the World Trade Center a second time.

Prisoner Murad said his principal accomplice planned a second attack on the World Trade Center—as early as 1995.

Yousef's bomb factory. "I still don't understand," she said after 9/11, "how it could have been allowed to happen. . . . The FBI knew all about Yousef's plans. . . . They'd seen the files. . . . The CIA had access to everything, too. . . . This should never have been allowed to happen."

AFTER THE WORLD TRADE CENTER bombing of 1993, well before the Philippines police discovered the Manila bomb factory, the U.S. Defense Department convened a panel to report on how vulnerable the nation might be to terrorism. Presciently, the group discussed the possibility of an airliner being deliberately flown into a public building.

"Coming down the Potomac in Washington," panelist Marvin Cetron recalled saying, "you could make a left turn at the Washington Monument and take out the White House, or you could make a right turn and take out the Pentagon." "Targets such as the World Trade Center," he wrote the following year, "not only provide the requisite casualties but, because of their symbolic nature, provide more bang for the buck. In order to maximize their odds for success, terrorist groups will likely consider mounting multiple, simultaneous operations with the aim of overtaxing a government's ability to respond."

That view did not appear in the published Defense Department report. "It was considered radical thinking," said Douglas Menarchik, the retired Air Force colonel who ran the study, "a little too scary for the times."

Khalid Sheikh Mohammed, who had plotted using planes as missiles to hit targets in the United States, was still at large, still plotting.

TWENTY-ONE

"**Y**OU NEED THE CHARISMATIC DREAMERS LIKE BIN LADEN TO MAKE a movement successful," a former intelligence analyst was to say. "But you also needed operators like Khalid Sheikh Mohammed who can actually get the job done." KSM's confederates dubbed him "Mukhtar"—an Arabic word to denote a leader, a man respected for his brain. The CIA came to consider him the "manager" of the September 11 plot.

He had been born in the mid-1960s in Kuwait, the son of immigrants from Baluchistan, a fiercely independent frontier region of Pakistan. His father was an imam, his mother a woman who got work preparing women's bodies for burial. The driving force for KSM, though, was the cause of Palestine. Kuwait teemed with Palestinian exiles, and antipathy toward Israel early on became part of KSM's makeup.

At eighteen, in 1983, Khalid traveled to the United States to study engineering at colleges in North Carolina. A fellow student remembered him as "so, so smart," focused on getting his degree—though he took part enthusiastically in amateur theater projects. He also spent a lot of time at his prayers, and tended to reproach contemporaries who strayed from the Muslim diet.

KSM disliked the America he saw. The student body of one of the colleges he attended was largely black, and life in the South showed him the face of discrimination. He went back to the Middle East with a degree in mechanical engineering and memories of a country that he deemed "racist and debauched."

Then, in 1987, he rallied to the fight to oust the Soviets from Afghanistan. At least one other brother, perhaps two—reports differ—were killed during the conflict. This was a family with a long-term commitment to jihad. At least half a dozen other relatives—KSM's nephew the Trade Center bomber Yousef aside—have been linked to al Qaeda in the years that followed. Most now languish in prison.

In the early 1990s the cause of jihad took KSM across the world, twice to Bosnia, where tens of thousands of Muslims had been slaughtered as the former Yugoslavia collapsed into chaos, to Malaysia, Sudan, China, even Brazil. By late 1994, as he hatched terrorism with Yousef in the Philippines, KSM was nudging thirty. He was short, somewhat overweight, balding, and often—though not always—sported a beard. The beard changed shape from time to time, useful for a man who wanted to confuse pursuers.

Pursuers there were, once Yousef and his would-be bombers had been caught, but KSM made good his escape to the oil-rich Gulf state of Qatar. He found employment there, and powerful support in the shape of Sheikh Abdullah bin Khalid al-Thani, then the minister for religious endowments and Islamic affairs. Sheikh Abdullah had underwritten one of KSM's visits to Bosnia. Now he reportedly saw to it that the fugitive was protected from the long arm of American justice.

Backed up as they were by the authority of a grand jury indictment, U.S. officials hoped Qatar's government would assist in getting KSM to America. An FBI team that flew to the region learned, however, that the quarry was gone. According to the Qatar police chief of the day—himself a member of the royal family—KSM had been tipped off to the danger, given temporary refuge at Sheikh Abdullah's private estate, then assisted in flying out of the country.

There was anger at the FBI and the CIA, and at Bill Clinton's White House, but no effective follow-up. In spite of the offer of a $5 million reward and an "Armed and Dangerous" lookout notice, KSM remained at large.

Half a decade on, the year before 9/11, U.S. analysts received intelligence on an al Qaeda terrorist named "Khalid al-Shaikh al-Balushi," (Khalid al-Shaikh from Baluchistan). The possible connection was noted at the CIA—it was common practice to refer to operatives by land of origin—but not pursued.

Two months before 9/11, KSM felt safe enough to apply for a visa to enter the United States, using an alias but his own photograph. The visa was granted the same day—just weeks after the CIA had received a report that he was currently "recruiting persons to travel to the United States to engage in planning terrorist-related activity."

"Based on our review," the director of Congress's Joint Inquiry concluded that U.S. intelligence had "known about this individual since 1995, but did not recognize his growing importance . . . there was little analytic focus given to him and coordination amongst the intelligence agencies was irregular at best." An executive summary by the CIA inspector general, grudgingly made public only in 2007, conceded there had been multiple errors, including a "failure to produce any [word redacted] coverage of Khalid Sheikh Mohammed from 1997 to 2001."

So IT WAS that KSM continued to range free until long after 9/11. His terrorist career would end only in the early hours of March 1, 2003, when a joint team of Pakistani and American agents cornered him at a middle-class home in the Pakistani city of Rawalpindi. A photograph taken at the scene of the arrest showed the prisoner bleary-eyed and unshaven, wearing an undershirt. "Nothing like James Bond," CIA director George Tenet noted, and saw to it that that was the image fed to the media.

Accounts differ as to how KSM had been tracked down. Suggestions have included betrayal by an al Qaeda comrade—there was by then a $25 million reward—an intercept by the National Security Agency of one of the terrorist's rumored ten mobile phones, or information gleaned from a high-level prisoner.

The capture of KSM was "wonderful," its importance "hard to overstate," said President Bush's press secretary. "This," House Intelligence Committee cochair Porter Goss exalted, "is equal to the liberation of Paris in the Second World War." "No person other than perhaps Osama bin Laden," the CIA's Tenet has said, "was more responsible for the attacks of 9/11 than KSM."

Sources let it be known that U.S. authorities "began an urgent effort to disorient and 'break' Mohammed." For the first two days in captivity, still in Pakistani custody, KSM had reportedly "crouched on the floor in a trance-like state, reciting verses from the Koran." He started talking only later, in the hands of the CIA.

The story the 9/11 Commission gave to the public of how the 9/11 plot evolved depended heavily on the accounts provided by KSM— and some other captives—in response to interrogation. The notes in the Commission Report reference his responses to interrogation 211 times. What readers had no way of knowing, though, is that most if not all of those responses were extracted by using measures the Bush Justice Department defined—in the words of a legal opinion provided to the CIA—as "enhanced interrogation techniques."

Vice President Cheney had hinted right after 9/11 at what was to come. The authorities, he said on *Meet the Press*, intended to work "sort of the dark side . . . It's going to be vital for us to use any means necessary at our disposal . . . we have to make certain that we have not tied the hands, if you will, of our intelligence communities."

A year after 9/11, a senior Justice Department official asserted in a memo to White House counsel Alberto Gonzales that "certain acts may be cruel, inhuman, or degrading, but still not produce pain and suffering of the requisite intensity to fall within Section 2340A's proscription against torture."

The International Committee of the Red Cross, which monitors the Geneva and U.N. Conventions on the treatment of "prisoners of war," long asked in vain for access to KSM and thirteen other detainees. When finally allowed to see them in 2006, the Red Cross reported that the prisoners had indeed been subjected to "torture." Two years later, when its report was leaked, the public learned the details.

Between them, the detainees alleged ill treatment that included "suffocation by water"—better known as waterboarding; prolonged stress standing naked, arms chained above the head for days at a time, often with toilet access denied; beatings and kicking; use of a neck collar to bang the head and body against a wall; confinement in a coffinlike box; enforced nudity for periods up to months; deprivation of sleep by enforcing stress positions, repetitive loud noise or music, or

SPECIAL REVIEW

Enhanced Interrogation Techniques

♦ The **attention grasp** consists of grasping the detainee with both hands, with one hand on each side of the collar opening, in a controlled and quick motion. In the same motion as the grasp, the detainee is drawn toward the interrogator.

♦ During the **walling** technique, the detainee is pulled forward and then quickly and firmly pushed into a flexible false wall so that his shoulder blades hit the wall. His head and neck are supported with a rolled towel to prevent whiplash.

♦ The **facial hold** is used to hold the detainee's head immobile. The interrogator places an open palm on either side of the detainee's face and the interrogator's fingertips are kept well away from the detainee's eyes.

♦ With the **facial or insult slap**, the fingers are slightly spread apart. The interrogator's hand makes contact with the area between the tip of the detainee's chin and the bottom of the corresponding earlobe.

♦ In **cramped confinement**, the detainee is placed in a confined space, typically a small or large box, which is usually dark. Confinement in the smaller space lasts no more than two hours and in the larger space it can last up to 18 hours.

♦ **Insects** placed in a confinement box involve placing a harmless insect in the box with the detainee.

♦ During **wall standing**, the detainee may stand about 4 to 5 feet from a wall with his feet spread approximately to his shoulder width. His arms are stretched out in front of him and his fingers rest on the wall to support all of his body weight. The detainee is not allowed to reposition his hands or feet.

♦ The application of **stress positions** may include having the detainee sit on the floor with his legs extended straight out in front of him with his arms raised above his head or kneeling on the floor while leaning back at a 45 degree angle.

♦ **Sleep deprivation** will not exceed 11 days at a time.

♦ The application of the **waterboard** technique involves binding the detainee to a bench with his feet elevated above his head. The detainee's head is immobilized and an interrogator places a cloth over the detainee's mouth and nose while pouring water onto the cloth in a controlled manner. Airflow is restricted for 20 to 40 seconds and the technique produces the sensation of drowning and suffocation.

SPECIAL REVIEW

95. (TS▓▓▓▓▓▓▓▓▓▓▓ An experienced Agency interrogator reported that the ▓▓▓▓▓▓▓▓ interrogators threatened Khalid Shaykh Muhammad ▓▓▓▓▓▓▓ According to this interrogator, the ▓▓▓▓▓▓▓▓▓▓ interrogators said to Khalid Shaykh Muhammad that if anything else happens in the United States, "We're going to kill your children." According to the interrogator, one of the ▓▓▓▓▓▓▓▓▓▓ interrogators said ▓▓ With respect to the report provided to him of the threats ▓▓▓▓▓▓▓▓▓ that report did not indicate that the law had been violated.

applications of cold water; exposure to cold; threats to harm a detainee's family; restriction of food; and—serious for Muslim men—forced shaving of the head and beard.

In the event of being taken prisoner, a captured al Qaeda manual showed, operatives had been advised to "complain of mistreatment . . . insist on proving that torture was inflicted." Though alert to false claims, however, the Red Cross was impressed by the consistency of the prisoners' allegations. A then-secret CIA inspector general's review, moreover, had acknowledged—even before the Red Cross reported—that "enhanced interrogation techniques" had indeed been used as described by the prisoners.

KSM told the Red Cross that his ill treatment had ranged right across the U.S. inventory of abuse. During his transfer around the planet, he said, "my eyes were covered with a cloth . . . a suppository was inserted into my rectum. . . . After arrival my clothes were cut off . . . photographs taken of me naked . . . made to stand on tiptoes for about two hours during questioning . . . the head interrogator (a man) and two female interrogators, plus about ten muscle guys wearing masks . . . a tube was inserted into my anus and water poured inside. . . . No toilet access was provided until four hours later."

At some point, physical coercion was compounded by psychological terror. "If anything else happens in the United States," KSM was allegedly told, "we're going to kill your children." KSM had some reason to fear this was true. His sons Yusuf and Abed, aged nine and seven, had been seized months before his own arrest. It has been claimed by another detainee that at some point even they were tormented—supposedly with insects—to scare the children into blabbing clues to their father's whereabouts.

Transported to Poland—KSM thought it was Poland because of a label on a water bottle he saw—three interrogators of non-American extraction told KSM they had approval from Washington to give him "a hard time." He would, they told him, be brought to the "verge of death and back again."

Waterboarding.

"I would be strapped to a special bed, which could be rotated. . . . A cloth would be placed over my face. Cold water from a bottle that had been kept in a fridge was then poured onto the cloth by one of the guards so that I could not breathe. . . . I struggled in the panic of not being able to breathe. . . . The harshest period of the interrogation was just prior to the end of the first month. . . . The worst day . . . my head was banged against the wall so hard that it started to bleed. . . . Finally I was taken for a session of waterboarding. The torture on that day was finally stopped by the intervention of the doctor."

The average time the CIA expected a subject to endure—before begging for relief and starting to talk—was fourteen seconds. KSM reportedly lasted as long as two to two and a half minutes before providing information. He was submitted to waterboarding 183 times.

THE WATERBOARD has a long history; it was a torture option for the Spanish Inquisition as early as the fifteenth century. In the twentieth century it was used by the British in the 1930s in Palestine, by the Japanese during World War II, by the North Koreans and by the French—in Algeria—in the 1950s, by the Americans in Vietnam in the 1960s, by the Khmer Rouge in Cambodia and the military regimes in Chile and Argentina in the 1970s.

In 1900, an American judge advocate general declared at an Army major's court-martial that waterboarding was "in violation of the rules of civilized war." In the late 1940s, when trying Japanese military personnel who had used waterboarding on American prisoners, the United States deemed them to be war criminals. They were executed.

To the Bush administration in 2006, however, waterboarding had become acceptable. "The United States does not torture," declared President Bush, conceding that the CIA had used an "alternative set of procedures" on detainees. "I cannot describe the specific methods used," he added, but the "separate program" was "vital."

In his 2010 memoir, the former President recalled having been asked by Director Tenet whether he had permission to use waterboarding and other techniques on KSM. "I thought about the 2,973 people stolen from their families by al Qaeda on 9/11," Bush wrote. "And I thought about my duty to protect the country from another act of terror. 'Damn right,' I said."

As Bush recalled it, when told earlier by legal advisers that certain "enhanced" interrogation techniques were legal, he had rejected two that he felt "went too far." Waterboarding, though, "did no lasting harm"—according to medical experts consulted by the CIA.

The "separate" interrogation program was essential, he had said in 2006, because it helped "take potential mass murderers off the streets before they were able to kill." KSM, he said by way of example, had provided information that helped stop a further planned attack on the United States. According to Vice President Cheney, "a great many" attacks had been stopped thanks to information obtained under the program.

Had only conventional interrogation techniques been used on KSM, Director of National Intelligence Mike McConnell said in 2008, he "would not have talked to us in a hundred years." Former CIA director Porter Goss has said the use of "enhanced" techniques produced "provable, extraordinary successes."

Others did not agree. FBI agents involved in the investigation thought ill treatment achieved little or nothing that skilled conventional questioning could not have achieved. Cheney's claim that the program obtained hard intelligence was "intensely disputed." On his first day in office, President Obama banned "alternative procedures."

Coerced admissions, meanwhile, are probably inadmissible in a court of law. "The use of torture," said Professor Mark Danner, who was instrumental in publishing the details of the Red Cross report on the prisoners' treatment, "deprives the society whose laws have been so egregiously violated of the possibility of rendering justice. Torture destroys justice."

THERE IS SOMETHING else, something especially relevant to the information extracted from Khalid Sheikh Mohammed. "Any piece of intelligence which is obtained under duress," said Lieutenant General John Kimmons, the Army's deputy chief of staff for intelligence, "would be of questionable credibility."

Is that the case with KSM, on whose statements much of the 9/11 Commission Report relies? The prisoner positively spewed information, and that is a part of the problem. At a rough count, he confessed to having carried out or plotted some thirty crimes—more than is plausible, surely, even for a top operative.

Transcripts of interrogation sessions with KSM were reportedly transmitted to Washington accompanied by the warning: "Detainee has been known to withhold information or deliberately mislead." In a combined confession and boast, the prisoner himself told the Red Cross: "I gave a lot of false information in order to satisfy what I believed the interrogators wished to hear in order to make the ill-treatment stop. . . . I'm sure that the false information I was forced to invent . . . wasted a lot of their time and led to several false red-alerts being placed in the U.S."

A parallel issue is what torture may have done to KSM's mental condition. His defense attorney at the initial military tribunal proceedings at Guantánamo in 2008, Captain Prescott Prince, thought KSM appeared to have suffered "some level of psychological impairment" as a result of the mistreatment.

When the 9/11 Commission was at work, KSM had yet to admit that he had lied under torture. Nor, at that time, did the Commission know that he or others had been tortured. "We were not aware, but we guessed," executive director Philip Zelikow has said, "that things like that were going on."

If Zelikow and senior colleagues guessed it, they seem not to have shared their guess with Commission members. "Never, ever did

INTERNATIONAL COMMITTEE OF THE RED CROSS

REGIONAL DELEGATION FOR
UNITED STATES AND CANADA

ICRC

"During the harshest period of my interrogation I gave a lot of false information in order to satisfy what I believed the interrogators wished to hear in order to make the ill-treatment stop. I later told the interrogators that their methods were stupid and counterproductive. I'm sure that the false information I was forced to invent in order to make the ill-treatment stop wasted a lot of their time and led to several false red-alerts being placed in the US."

SPECIAL REVIEW

---

225. (TS ▮▮▮▮▮▮▮) On the other hand, Khalid Shaykh Muhammad, an accomplished resistor, provided only a few intelligence reports prior to the use of the waterboard, and analysis of that information revealed that much of it was outdated, inaccurate, or incomplete. As a means of less active resistance, at the beginning of their interrogation, detainees routinely provide information that they know is already known. Khalid Shaykh Muhammad received 183 applications of the waterboard in March 2003 ▮▮▮▮▮▮▮▮▮▮▮▮▮▮

The 9/11 commissioners were not told that "enhanced techniques" were used to interrogate prisoners. The brutal treatment they received taints the prisoners' admissions.

I imagine that American interrogators were subjecting detainees to waterboarding and other forms of physical torture," Commissioner Richard Ben-Veniste has said. "No one raised such a possibility at a Commission meeting. In hindsight we were snookered."

The commissioners asked the CIA to allow its own staff access to detainees, only to meet with a flat refusal. If security was the issue, they then offered, staff could be taken to the prisoners' location wearing blindfolds. Could Commission people at least observe CIA interrogation sessions through a one-way observation window? The CIA blocked all such suggestions.

Commission senior adviser Ernest May thought the CIA's summaries of the results of interrogations "incomplete and poorly written." "We never," he wrote later, "had full confidence in the interrogation reports as historical sources." Former Commission counsel John Farmer warns that, even now, "reliance on KSM's version of events must be considered carefully."

The issue was and remains a huge problem, a blemish on the historical record. As the Report was being assembled, the Commission attempted to resolve the concern by inserting a paragraph or two on a page deep in the text—a health warning to the American public about the product of the CIA interrogations.

"Assessing the truth of statements by these witnesses," it read, "is challenging. . . . We have evaluated their statements carefully and have attempted to corroborate them with documents and statements of others."

THERE IS, however, a measure of considerable consolation. Long before they were caught, KSM and a fellow operative *freely* volunteered much the same version of events to an Arab television journalist. The scoop of a lifetime had come to Yosri Fouda, former BBC journalist and at the time star reporter for the satellite channel Al Jazeera—the way scoops are supposed to come, in a mysterious phone call to his London office.

Seven months after the 9/11 attacks, Fouda found himself listening to an anonymous male voice on the telephone proposing "something special for the first anniversary . . . exclusive stuff." Then, four days later, came a fax offering to provide him with "addresses of people" for a proposed documentary. Then another phone call, asking him to fly to Pakistan. Fouda did so, without confiding even in his boss.

After a harrowing process, an internal flight to Karachi, a change of hotels, a journey by car and rickshaw, then—in another car, blindfolded, the final leg—the reporter was ushered into a fourth floor apartment. The blindfold removed, Fouda found himself looking into the eyes of the fugitive who was being hunted more feverishly than anyone in the world except Osama bin Laden.

KSM and Ramzi Binalshibh, a key accomplice, told Fouda their story—the story, at any rate, as they wanted to tell it—over a period of forty-eight hours. "I am the head of the al Qaeda military committee," KSM said that first night, "and Ramzi is the coordinator of the Holy Tuesday operation. And yes, we did it."

After prayers together the following morning, the two men shared their version of the preparation and execution of 9/11. Their accounts largely match the version subsequently extracted from KSM by the CIA. Binalshibh pulled from an old suitcase dozens of mementos of the operation: information on Boeing airplanes, a navigation map of the American East Coast, illustrations on "How to perform sudden maneuvers"—a page covered in notations made, Binalshibh said, by the hijackers' leader, Mohamed Atta.

The interview over, blindfolded again, reporter Fouda was taken back to the airport. He had—and has—no doubt that the men he had met at the safe house in Karachi were who they said they were, that what they told him was credible. The three-page account of Fouda's work in the London *Sunday Times*, and his TV documentary, *The Road to 11 September*, on the Al Jazeera network, caused a sensation on the first anniversary of the attacks.

Unaccountably, 9/11 Commission staff failed to interview Fouda and mentioned his breakthrough interview only in an obscure footnote. It was included, however, in evidence presented during the military tribunal proceedings at Guantánamo. Two distinguished award-winning reporters, *The Wall Street Journal*'s Ron Suskind and CNN contributor Peter Bergen, who both interviewed Yosri Fouda, found his reporting of the Karachi encounter authentic and compelling.

During the reporter's meeting with KSM and Binalshibh, a mysterious visitor had arrived, a man who could not be named. He was,

Fouda was told, "a close companion of Sheikh Abu Abdullah, God protect him."

"Abu Abdullah" was one of the several names associates used to refer to Osama bin Laden.

Had al Qaeda been a company in the West, Fouda concluded from what he learned that day, KSM would have been its CEO. The post of chairman belonged to bin Laden.

TWENTY-TWO

AFTER FIRST MEETING TOWARD THE END OF THE ANTI-SOVIET CON-flict in Afghanistan, Bin Laden and KSM had for years followed separate trajectories. Until the mid-1990s, KSM plotted terror with his nephew Yousef, then traveled the world networking with fellow jihadis. Bin Laden stayed most of the time in Sudan, presenting an innocent face to the world.

To *Time* magazine's Scott Macleod, who saw him there, the Saudi seemed "very calm, serene, almost like a holy man. He wanted to show that he was a businessman, and he was a legitimate businessman." Major road-building projects aside, bin Laden's enterprises included a trucks and machinery importing company, a tannery, and more than a million acres of farmland. Rumor had it, too, that bin Laden produced a fabulous sum to capitalize a bank.

Bin Laden the tycoon tended his business empire, but bin Laden the jihadi was never far away. To his guesthouse in Khartoum came all manner of men, rich and poor, powerful and humble, all focused on Muslim causes. In 1992, following the collapse of the former Yugoslavia and the beginning of strife between Christians and Muslims, Bosnia became the cause of the moment. The embattled Bosnian regime accepted massive financial support from Saudi Arabia and volunteer fighters, Arab veterans of the war in Afghanistan.

Though bin Laden rarely ventured out of Sudan, he did visit Bosnia. Renate Flottau, of the German magazine *Der Spiegel*, encountered him, "a tall, striking Arab with piercing eyes and a long black beard," while waiting in President Alija Izetbegovic's anteroom. The Arab presented her with his card, but "Osama bin Laden" meant nothing to her then. In passable English, he described eagerly how he was bringing "holy warriors" into the country. The Bosnian president's staff treated him like a dignitary—bin Laden had reportedly been granted honorary citizenship.

Of the Arabs who rallied to the fight in Bosnia, three were to play key roles in the 9/11 operation. Khalid Sheikh Mohammed was in the country twice during the same period. Two others, Saudi fighters, went on to be 9/11 hijackers.

Through bin Laden, massive injections of funds also went to the Muslim separatists in Chechnya. It won him loyalty—there would be dozens of Chechens, it would be reported, among the holdouts who fought on with bin Laden, after 9/11, at Tora Bora.

In Sudan in the early 1990s those who plotted terror found a welcome. There was Ayman al-Zawahiri, the Egyptian doctor turned fundamentalist zealot who had been a close associate in Afghanistan. From Khartoum, he directed bombings and assassinations in his homeland. One attempt came close to killing then-President Hosni Mubarak himself.

There was also a younger man, whose name was never to be as familiar to the public as Zawahiri's. This was Abu Zubaydah, born in Saudi Arabia to a Palestinian father, still in his early twenties but already proving an effective manager of men and facilities. He was to be a key operative in the lead-up to 9/11.

At meetings in Khartoum, bin Laden sounded off regularly about the target he called the snake. "The snake is America, and we have to stop them. We have to cut their head off and stop what they are doing in the Horn of Africa."

In late 1992, in the Yemeni city of Aden, bombs exploded outside two hotels housing U.S. troops on their way to join the United Nations relief mission in Somalia—then, as now, a war-torn country on the east coast of Africa. Though botched—no American soldiers were killed—the attack was later linked to bin Laden.

Bin Laden would later claim that his men, fighting alongside Somalis, a year later played a leading role in the disastrous U.S. raid on a Somali warlord's headquarters. In that bloody fiasco, eighteen American soldiers were killed, seventy-eight wounded, and two Black Hawk helicopters shot down.

For a long time, there were no attacks in bin Laden's homeland, Saudi Arabia. Then, in 1995, a truck bomb exploded outside a National Guard facility in the capital, Riyadh. Seven were killed and sixty injured, and five of the dead were American Army and civilian trainers.

The only link to bin Laden at the time was that the four men accused of the bombing—who were executed—said they had read his writings on jihad. Information developed later, however, indicated that he supplied money to purchase the explosives, that the munitions were stored in a bin Laden warehouse, then moved onward to Saudi Arabia aboard a bin Laden–owned ship.

The attack, bin Laden has said since, was a noble act that "paved the way for the raising of voices of opposition against the American occupation from within the ruling family." He urged Saudis to "adopt every tactic to throw the Americans out of our territory."

Seven months later, a huge bomb exploded outside an American housing complex near Dhahran, in eastern Saudi Arabia. Inside at the time was a large number of troops, many of them personnel serving with the 4404th Fighter Wing at the time patrolling the no-fly zone over Iraq. Nineteen Americans were killed, 372 wounded.

It was the largest terrorist bomb ever to be used against Americans, more powerful than the device used in the 1983 bombing of the Marine barracks in Beirut, or a decade later in the destruction of the Alfred P. Murrah building in Oklahoma City. Who was behind the attack long remained the subject of controversy. A body of evidence indicated that Iran was responsible, but many believe bin Laden was at least complicit.

He had reportedly been in Qatar before the attack, arranging—again—for the purchase and delivery of explosives. In an interview the following year, he said al Qaeda had indeed been involved, that the bombers had been "heroes."

Even before the bombings in Saudi Arabia, bin Laden's life as an exile in Sudan had turned sour. The Saudi royals, and his own family, had tried to persuade him to change course. "They called me several times from the Kingdom," he recalled, "wanting me to return home, to talk about things. I refused. . . . They told me that the King would like me to act as intermediary between the different factions in Afghanistan. King Fahd himself called to try to win me over. . . . They sent my brother to try to convince me, but it didn't work."

The royals persuaded members of bin Laden's family—including his mother, his father's only surviving brother, and the half-brother who now headed the bin Laden company—to visit him in Sudan. "They beseeched him to stop his diatribes against Saudi and the Americans," a family source told the BBC. "Come back and we'll give you a responsible job in the company, one of the top five positions." When that suggestion was rebuffed, the Saudis' patience ran out.

That, at any rate, was the regime's official position. In the spring of 1994, the royal family declared bin Laden's citizenship revoked for "behavior that contradicts the Kingdom's interests." His family followed suit with a statement of "condemnation of all acts that Osama bin Laden may have committed." His share of the family fortune, which had earlier been placed in a trust, was sold off and placed in a frozen account.

Though this sounded draconian, the full picture may have been otherwise. The formal cutoff caused bin Laden only a temporary cash flow problem. Far into the future, he would have huge sums of money at his disposal.

Later, asked whether he had really been disowned, bin Laden would put his hand on his heart. "Blood," he said, "is thicker than water." The DGSE, France's intelligence service, which carefully monitored bin Laden over many years, took the view as late as 2000 that "Osama bin Laden has kept up contact with certain members of the family . . . even though it has officially said the contrary. One of his brothers would appear to be playing a role of intermediary in his professional contacts and the progress of his business."

It would be reported as late as 2006 that bin Laden's half-brother Yeslam had pledged to pay the cost of Osama's legal defense should he be captured. In the years before 9/11, female relatives were used to keep the money coming, perhaps because women in Saudi Arabia are treated as though they are invisible. "Some female members of bin

Laden's own family have been sending cash from Saudi Arabia to his 'front' accounts in the Gulf," Vincent Cannistraro, former CIA chief of operations and analysis, told a congressional committee after 9/11.

Major funding also came from others. Soon after his funding had officially been cut off, according to the DGSE report, $4.5 million went to bin Laden from "Islamic Non-Governmental Organizations" in the Gulf. Five years later, it was discovered that "at least $3,000,000" believed to be for bin Laden had been funneled through Saudi Arabia's National Commercial Bank. Those behind the payments, the CIA's Cannistraro testified, had been "wealthy Saudis." When the Commercial Bank connection was cut, they switched to "siphoning off funds from their worldwide enterprises in creative and imaginative ways."

The former head of the DGSE's Security Intelligence department, Alain Chouet, who had regular access to secret intelligence, has said that considerable evidence "points to a number of private donors in the Arabian Peninsula, as well as to a number of banks and charities with money pumped in from Saudi or Gulf funds. . . . What was expensive wasn't the terrorist operations themselves but all that's required for recruiting terrorists: financing the mosques, the clubs, the imams, the religious schools, the training camps, the maintenance of 'martyrs' ' families."

Funding for bin Laden's operational needs—weapons, camps, living expenses, operatives' travel—never dried up. As a 9/11 Commission report on terrorist financing noted, al Qaeda's budget in the years before 9/11 amounted to $30 million a year. It was money raised almost entirely from donations, especially from "wealthy Saudi nationals."

The DGSE's Alain Chouet dismissed the revocation of bin Laden's Saudi citizenship as merely a "subterfuge aimed at the gullible—designed to cover a continuing clandestine relationship." For years to come at least—according to Chouet—the Saudi government covertly manipulated bin Laden to act in its strategic interests, as he once had in the Afghan war against the Soviets.

There is information, to be reported later in these pages, that the "wealthy Saudi nationals" who continued to fund bin Laden included members of the ruling royal family.

• • •

By EARLY 1996, when U.S. ambassador to Sudan Timothy Carney sat down for talks with Sudanese foreign minister Ali Taha, the bin Laden problem was on the agenda. Washington, which had recently condemned Sudan for its "sponsorship of terror," claimed that bin Laden was directing and funding a number of terrorist organizations around the world.

Washington wanted Sudan to expel the troublesome exile. But to where? To the United States? What to do with him were he to be flown there? "We couldn't indict him then," President Clinton said after 9/11, "because he hadn't killed anyone in America." To Saudi Arabia? "We asked Saudi Arabia to take him," Clinton recalled. "The Saudis didn't want him back. . . . They were afraid it was too much of a hot potato."

Wherever bin Laden was to go, the Clinton White House believed it would be worthwhile just to get him out of Sudan. "My calculation was, 'It's going to take him a while to reconstitute,' " then–National Security Council counterterrorism director Steven Simon has said, "and that screws him up and buys time."

Following that line of thinking turned out to be a disastrous misjudgment. Not to have acted decisively against bin Laden in 1996, President Clinton would say—in private—after 9/11, was "probably the biggest mistake of my presidency." In Sudan, as former CIA station chief Milton Bearden has said, "perhaps we could have controlled or monitored him more closely, to see what he was doing."

The United States did not do that. It sat idly by when, in May that year, bin Laden returned to the remote, tragically chaotic country that he knew well and where Washington had virtually no leverage—Afghanistán. Allowing that to happen, the CIA's Bearden sardonically remarked, was "probably the best move since the Germans put Lenin in a boxcar and sent him to St. Petersburg in 1917."

"WE WERE WHISKED to a chartered Learjet," his son Omar has recalled. "My father and his party were treated as dignitaries, with no need for the formalities of passports and customs. Besides my father and me, there were only eight other male passengers. Brother Sayf Adel, my father's security chief, and Mohammed Atef, my father's best friend and top commander, were traveling with us."

The plane passed through Saudi airspace without difficulty, refueled in Iran, and landed at the eastern Afghan city of Jalalabad, near the border with Pakistan. Other members of bin Laden's family and entourage followed months later, again aboard a chartered jet.

"Our plane had two configurations: with fifty-six passengers and with seventy-nine," the captain recalled. "They wanted eighty-four. They asked how many extra seats we wanted. They installed the seats overnight. . . . We flew women, children, clothes, rickshaws, old bikes, mattresses, blankets."

After a brief stay in Jalalabad courtesy of a local warlord, bin Laden set up base for a while in the mountains at Tora Bora. Family members thought it a desolate place, but he called it "our new home," was excited to be back at a place he had known while fighting the Soviets.

A major concern, for some time, was how the Taliban—then gaining the upper hand in the civil war—would view his presence. Then their leader, Mullah Omar, sent word that he was welcome. It was by no means religious and ideological compatibility alone that was to ensure bin Laden a lasting welcome. Through him, the 9/11 Commission would calculate, between $10 and $20 million a year was to flow to the Taliban.

Visibly relaxed once he knew he had sanctuary, bin Laden began talking with his son Omar about his "mission in life." "I was put on this earth by God for a specific reason," he said. "My only reason for living is to fight the jihad and to make sure there is justice for the Muslims." He ranted on about America and Israel, and it was evident that there was no limit to what he imagined he could achieve.

"First," he said with the supreme self-confidence that only boundless faith or delusion can bring, "we obliterate America. By that I don't mean militarily. We can destroy America from within by making it economically weak, until its markets collapse. . . . That's what we did with Russia. When that happens, they will have no interest in supplying Israel with arms. . . . We only have to be patient. . . . This is God's plan."

The man who voiced this astounding ambition now lived in a makeshift wooden cabin. There bin Laden spent much of his time, reading deeply into his hundreds of books, most of them religious tomes, never far from his prayer beads, his copy of the Qur'an, and a radio that picked up the BBC's broadcasts from London. At his side, always, was his Kalashnikov assault rifle.

Bin Laden was interested in the techniques of mass communication, the distribution of propaganda by tape cassette and fax machine. He would shortly acquire a state-of-the-art satellite telephone. When the technology became available, his operatives would use the Internet as an everyday tool. Omar noticed that his father now spent much time recording his thoughts on a dictating machine.

The fruit of his latest thinking came in August 1996, with a fax transmission to the office of *al-Quds al-Arabi*—or *The Arab Jerusalem*—an Arabic-language newspaper published in London. It was a twelve-thousand-word message from the mountain, in bin Laden's words from "the summit of the Hindu Kush," one that at the time got little coverage in the West. Across the Middle East, where hundreds of thousands of copies were distributed in cassette form, it had a major impact.

Lengthy, couched in archaic language, replete with religious references, this was bin Laden's "Declaration of Jihad against the Americans occupying the Land of the Two Holy Places."

"Praise be to Allah, we seek his help and ask for his pardon," the declaration began, then launched into a catalogue of the iniquities imposed on Muslims by "the Zionist-Crusaders alliance." The greatest of the aggressions, bin Laden wrote, was the presence of the "American invaders" in Saudi Arabia, followed by U.S. exploitation of Arab oil and the "annexing" of Arab land by Israel.

"After Faith," he went on, "there is no more important duty than pushing the American enemy out of the holy land." Addressing U.S. Defense Secretary William Perry in person, he warned that his recruits to the cause made formidable enemies. "These youths love death as you love life. They inherit dignity, pride, courage, generosity, truthfulness and sacrifice. They are most effective and steadfast in war. . . . They have no intent but to enter Paradise by killing you."

Around the time he issued this proclamation of punishment to come, bin Laden sat down to confer with Khalid Sheikh Mohammed.

WHETHER THE TWO men had seen each other in the recent past remains unclear. According to KSM, he had hoped to meet with bin Laden in Sudan, but settled for seeing his military aide Atef instead. One intelligence lead suggests that he and bin Laden had traveled somewhere together—perhaps on one of the trips they both made to Bosnia. It seems certain, though, that they got together at Tora Bora in mid-1996.

At the meeting, which Atef also attended, KSM came up with a raft of ideas for terrorist attacks, most of them involving airliners. Atef, too, had recently been discussing the idea of attacking aircraft. Terrorist attacks on planes had usually followed a pattern—hijack a plane, have it land in a compliant nation-state, then make demands (often for the release of captured comrades). By the mid-1990s, however, bin Laden operatives had little prospect of finding a "friendly" place to land. For the men meeting at Tora Bora, the focus was simply on destroying planes.

Atef apparently favored finding ways to blow up airliners in mid-air, as in the 1988 downing of Pan Am 103 over Scotland. He and bin Laden listened, however, as KSM proposed a very different concept—using hijacked planes as weapons.

There are two versions of what he suggested. According to KSM himself, the notion he proposed was ambitious in the extreme. Ten planes would be hijacked, on the same day, to be crashed into target buildings on both coasts of the United States. He himself, as commander, would force a landing at an airport, kill all male passengers, then deliver a speech assailing American support for Israel and "repressive" regimes around the world. This, as the 9/11 Commission put it, would have been "theater, a spectacle of destruction with KSM as the self-cast star—the super-terrorist."

According to another detainee, KSM's proposal was more modest, a suggestion that the World Trade Center should be targeted again—this time not with a bomb but by small planes packed with explosives. This, the detainee said, prompted bin Laden to suggest a grander vision. "Why do you use an ax," he supposedly mused, "when you can use a bulldozer?"

KSM thought it was important to target civilian landmarks. Were only military or government buildings hit, he surmised, ordinary Americans "would not focus on the atrocities that America is committing by supporting Israel against the Palestinian people." The purpose of a further strike on the World Trade Center was to "wake people up."

KSM's proposal may have been premature. He got the impression that bin Laden's priority concern remained the situation in Saudi

Arabia. He told KSM he was "not convinced" of the practicality of the planes operation. For now, the discussion went no further.

Nevertheless, a further strike on the World Trade Center apparently remained on the drawing board. Months after the meeting at Tora Bora, a bin Laden operative in Europe traveled to America and shot videotape of various prominent buildings—including the Twin Towers. The footage, seized after 9/11, included shot after shot of the towers, taken from multiple angles.

There were five tapes, with pictures not only of the Trade Center but of the Statue of Liberty, the Brooklyn Bridge, San Francisco's Golden Gate Bridge, Chicago's Sears Tower, and Disneyland.

At his meeting with bin Laden, KSM had suggested sending operatives "to study in the U.S. flight institutes." Whether or not bin Laden ordered it, it seems that someone in the terrorist milieu was already making such preparations. The FBI had received information that "individuals with terrorist connections had requested and received training in the technical aspects of aviation."

One such individual was a young Saudi who, after a trip to Arizona to learn English, returned home seeming a "different person." He grew a full beard, shunned established friends, and spent most of his spare time reading books on religion and aviation. Then, in 1996, he returned to the Grand Canyon State—to learn to fly. The twenty-four-year-old seemed unsure of himself in the cockpit, even frightened, but he was to return again and again to flight school, even after he got his commercial pilot's license. The Saudi was Hani Hanjour, who in 2001 would fly a hijacked Boeing 757 into the Pentagon.

Mohamed Atta, who was to lead the 9/11 operation, turned twenty-seven the year of the Tora Bora meeting. In Germany, where he was now studying, he struck people—even those familiar with Muslim practices—as religiously obsessed.

In Afghanistan in 1996 bin Laden had asked the British reporter Robert Fisk to come to see him for a second time—less than three years after their first meeting in Sudan. The Saudi was nearing forty now and visibly aging. His beard was longer and starting to turn gray, the lines around his eyes deeper.

It was night when bin Laden met with the reporter. He talked on and on of how Saudi Arabia had become "an American colony," of how the "evils" of the Middle East were rooted in the policies of the United States. "Resistance against America will spread in many, many places in Muslim countries," he said. "We must drive out the Americans."

In the flickering light of a paraffin lamp, when his interviewee agreed to be photographed, Fisk saw in bin Laden's face the trace of a smile and what looked like vanity. He thought the man "possessed of that quality which leads men to war: total self-conviction. In the years to come I would see others manifest this dangerous characteristic . . . but never the fatal self-resolve of Osama bin Laden."

PART V

PERPETRATORS

Seven thousand miles and two continents away, very few people had yet sensed the real danger in the man.

According to the then-head of the CIA's Counterterrorist Center, Winston Wiley, in a recently released 9/11 Commission interview, President Clinton's administration actually reduced the focus on counterterrorism. Former Clinton officials, and the President himself, have insisted otherwise. One can only report claim and counterclaim, and cite the record.

Two months into the Clinton presidency, in 1993, bin Laden had been characterized in a CIA document as merely an "independent actor who sometimes works with other individuals or governments . . . to promote militant Islamic causes throughout the region." What the Agency told the White House ranged from dismissing bin Laden as "a flake" or—closer to reality—as a "terrorist financier," and the "Ford Foundation" of Sunni Muslim extremism.

In 1995, when the evidence had yet to link bin Laden firmly to any specific attack, a formal Clinton order—aimed at cutting off funding from named terrorist organizations—did not mention him.

In 1995 and 1996, however, the President made nine speeches mentioning terrorism or calling for tough action. He also issued a Presidential Decision Directive—PDD-39—designed to combat terrorism that targeted the United States. It included, for the first time, a provision for what was to become known as rendition, the forcible removal to the United States of captured terrorist suspects. Policy on the subject was henceforth to be coordinated from the White House.

Anthony Lake, Clinton's first national security adviser, and Richard Clarke—who eventually became national coordinator for counterterrorism—had been badgering the CIA for fuller information on bin Laden. One CIA official recalled having thought that Lake was positively "foaming at the mouth" about him. "It just seemed unlikely to us," Clarke recalled, "that this man who had his hand in so many seemingly unconnected organizations was just a donor, a philanthropist of terror."

CIA Director James Woolsey, who ran the agency until 1995, conceded after 9/11 that there was a period in the 1990s when U.S. intelligence was simply "asleep at the wheel." After the Clinton directive, which called for improving the agencies' performance, the CIA and the FBI responded.

In early 1996, with Lake's approval, a small group of CIA officers and analysts were formed into a unit that focused solely on bin Laden. Only a dozen strong at first, its number would in time grow to forty or fifty people—most of them women—supplemented by a small number of FBI employees. The Bureau staffers were there in the name of liaison, but the relationship was less than happy. The CIA attitude toward the FBI contingent was so hostile, one arriving Bureau supervisor thought, that he felt as though he had "walked into a buzz saw."

That said, the new unit did remarkable work. Working from a base away from CIA headquarters, near a shopping complex, they became passionately committed to the pursuit of bin Laden. They worked inordinate hours, rarely taking a day off, for a zealot of a boss who as often as not turned up for work at four in the morning. This was Michael Scheuer, whose idea the unit had been in the first place.

Reflecting the CIA's concept of bin Laden as a mere financier, the bureaucracy initially gave the project the acronym CTC-TFL—for Counterterrorism Center–Terrorist Financial Links. Scheuer saw the mission as far broader, more operational, and its function gradually shifted from data gathering to locating bin Laden and planning his capture. He changed the unit's moniker to "Alec Station," after one of his children.

Working around the clock, the unit began to get a clearer sense of what confronted them. Bin Laden's August 1996 "Declaration of Jihad" brought Scheuer up short. "My God," he thought as he perused the transcript, "it sounds like Thomas Jefferson. There was no ranting in it. . . . [It] read like our Declaration of Independence—it had that tone. It was a frighteningly reasoned document. These were substantive, tangible issues."

Scheuer concluded there and then that bin Laden was a "truly dangerous, dangerous man," and began saying so as often and as loudly as he could. Though for many months to come there were no new terror attacks, bin Laden's megaphone utterances, in interviews with journalists and in a second formal declaration in February 1998, could not have been clearer.

In the second declaration, presented as a religious ruling and co-signed by Zawahiri and others, he enumerated Muslim grievances and declared the killing of Americans—"civilians and military"—a duty for all Muslims. Time after time, with increasing clarity, he emphasized that civilians were vulnerable. "They chose this government and voted for it despite their knowledge of its crimes in Palestine, Lebanon and Iraq and in other places." And: "If they are killing our civilians, occupying our lands . . . and they don't spare any one of us, why spare any one of them?"

In the wake of Clinton's landmark 1996 Presidential Decision, the heads of relevant U.S. agencies—the Counterterrorism Security Group—had been mulling a possible "snatch" operation to capture bin Laden and bring him to the United States. With satellite surveillance as well as human intelligence, the CIA was to some extent able to track his movements.

Some valuable information came from eavesdropping on the Compact-M satellite phone he had purchased in 1996—number 00-873-682505331. Bin Laden was no longer at Tora Bora, but spending most nights with his family at a training camp near Kandahar.

The CIA developed a plan. A team of Afghans working with the

Agency would grab bin Laden while he was sleeping, roll him up in a rug, spirit him to a desert airstrip, and bundle him on board a CIA plane. He would be flown to New York aboard a civilian version of a C-130 airplane within which would be a container, inside which would be a dentist's chair designed for a very tall man.

The chair would be equipped with padded restraints designed to avoid chafing the captive's skin. In the event bin Laden had to be gagged, the tape used would have just the right amount of adhesive to avoid excessive irritation to his face and beard. There would be a doctor on the plane, with sophisticated medical equipment.

The Agency's plan was discussed, modified, and remodified. There were rehearsals. Intelligence agency attorneys conferred solemnly about the provisions for bin Laden's safety after capture. Then, in May 1998, the operation was scrapped.

CIA director Tenet has said he was responsible for the cancellation. The White House's Richard Clarke has said he thought it "half-assed," that he seconded the decision. In an internal memo, supposedly written at Tenet's direction, Alec Station's Scheuer wrote that the Clinton cabinet had been worried about potential fallout were bin Laden or others to die during the operation.

Scheuer thought the plan had been "perfect," that it should have gone ahead. According to him, it long remained difficult to persuade either the White House, or his superiors at the CIA, or the Defense Department, of the gravity of the bin Laden threat. "They could not believe that this tall Saudi with a beard, squatting around a campfire, could be a threat to the United States of America."

For any who could not see the danger, any last illusion was removed just after 3:30 A.M. Washington time on August 7, 1998. At that moment, a two-thousand-pound truck bomb exploded behind the American embassy in the Kenyan capital of Nairobi. Two hundred ninety-one people were killed, forty-four of them embassy employees. The embassy's city center location compounded the carnage, and some four thousand were injured. The five-story building was damaged beyond repair, an adjacent secretarial school totally destroyed.

Four minutes later at the U.S. embassy in Dar es Salaam, the capital of neighboring Tanzania, a terrorist detonated another truck bomb. Eleven were killed and eighty-five injured—lower casualties than in Nairobi because the building was on the city's outskirts. The explosion left part of the U.S. embassy roofless and damaged the missions of two other countries.

In terms of overall casualty figures, this had been the worst-ever terrorist attack on Americans. Clues as to who was responsible came fast, and pointed straight to the bin Laden organization. Instead of being blown to pieces, one of two suicide bombers in the Nairobi attack had jumped out and run at the last moment. He had suffered only minor injuries, and was captured within days. It emerged that the bomber was a Saudi, had trained at one of the camps in Afghanistan, and had met with bin Laden several times. He had believed all along that his mission was for bin Laden.

The Saudi gave investigators the number of a telephone outside Kenya that his controllers had told him he could call, and he had called it both the night before and an hour before the bombing. Using his satellite phone, bin Laden had also called the number before and after the attack. The number—967-1-200578—was a crucial lead, one that will become pivotal as this story unfolds.

Of the five men eventually tried and convicted in the United States for the bombings, the reported statement of another man, Saudi-born but of Palestinian origin, said it all. "I did it all for the cause of Islam," Mohamed Odeh told interrogators. Osama bin Laden "is my leader, and I obey his orders."

In Afghanistan on the morning of the bombings, bin Laden had been listening intently to the radio. When the news came through, his son Omar thought his father more "excited and happy" than he had ever seen him. "His euphoria spread quickly to his commanders and throughout the ranks, with everyone laughing and congratulating each other."

A Canadian teenager whose family had joined the jihadis, Abdurahman Khadr, witnessed the jubilation. "The leader of the guesthouse went outside and brought juice for like everybody. Jugs and jugs of juice. He was just giving it out. 'Celebrate, everybody!' And people were even making jokes that we should do this more often. You know, we'd get free juice."

Asked by reporters about the bombings, bin Laden vacillated between obfuscation and claiming credit. "Only God knows the truth," he would say, while praising the bombers as "real men . . . Our job is to instigate and by the grace of God we did that." Nairobi had been picked, he said, because "the greatest CIA center in East Africa is located at this embassy." American "plots" against countries in the region, he said, had been hatched there.

There appeared to be an opportunity for the United States to retaliate—or, with the niceties of international law in mind—"to respond." Bin Laden, the CIA learned, was shortly to attend a gathering of several hundred men at one of the training camps. On the day of his visit, it was decided, U.S. vessels—mostly submarines—would fire salvos of Tomahawk cruise missiles at six sites in Afghanistan. The camps aside, missiles would also strike a bin Laden–financed pharmaceutical factory in Sudan. The CIA believed it was producing the ingredients for nerve gas.

On the appointed day, August 20, the go-ahead was given. Security was exceptionally tight, with one significant exception. Because the missiles were to overfly Pakistan, it was deemed necessary to inform the Pakistani military. To avoid provoking an international incident, though, the Pakistan army was to be told—not consulted—and at the very last minute. The vice chairman of the Joint Chiefs of Staff, General Joseph Ralston, broke the news to a top Pakistani commander over dinner when the missiles were already on their way.

In Washington, Clinton went on television to tell the nation of the action he had taken. "Our target was terror," he said. "Our mission was clear: to strike at the network of radical groups affiliated with and funded by Osama bin Laden."

That was a circumlocution, to avoid mentioning publicly the fact that Clinton had signed memoranda designed to get around the long-standing legal ban on planned assassinations. After Kenya, however, the President was "intently focused," as he later wrote, "on capturing or killing [bin Laden] and with destroying al Qaeda."

In that, the U.S. attack failed miserably. The targets were hit and destroyed, and some people were killed at the camp where bin Laden was supposed to be. The man himself, however, remained very much alive. The factory in Sudan was destroyed, but there never was any proof that it had been more than a legitimate plant producing medicines. The CIA's intelligence had been shaky at best.

The strikes had been expensive in more ways than one. At $750,000 each, just the cost of the sixty-five Tomahawks fired amounted to about $49 million. The embassy bombings in Africa, to which the missiles had responded, are said to have cost around $10,000. Worse by far, the missile strikes and the failure to get bin Laden proved to be a propaganda victory for the intended target. Across the Muslim world, people began sporting Osama bin Laden T-shirts. Bin Laden's life had been spared, his followers were convinced, thanks to the direct intervention of Allah.

The truth was more mundane, as his son Omar revealed in 2009. Shortly before the strikes, he recalled, his father had received "a highly secret communication." "He had been forewarned," former U.S. Defense Secretary William Cohen was to tell 9/11 Commission staff, that "the intelligence [service] in Pakistan had a line in to him." The tight U.S. security had not been tight enough, a failing that one day in the distant future would be remedied—fatally for the target.

If the name Osama bin Laden had been slow to penetrate the American consciousness, it had now become—as it would remain—a fixture. "In 1996 he was on the radar screen," said Sandy Berger, who had succeeded Anthony Lake as national security adviser. "In 1998 he was the radar screen."

Before the embassy bombings, bin Laden had been secretly indicted merely for "conspiracy to attack." After the bombings, a two-hundred-page public indictment charged him with a litany of alleged crimes. A $5 million reward was offered for information leading to his arrest. The figure would rise to $25 million after 9/11, and was later doubled.

At the CIA after the bombings, combating the bin Laden threat was raised to "Tier 0" priority, one of the very highest levels. "We are at war," Director Tenet declared in a memo soon after. "I want no resources or people spared in this effort." President Clinton, for his part, signed a further "lethal force" order designed to ensure it was possible to circumvent the ban on targeted assassination. Nevertheless, and though operations against bin Laden were planned repeatedly during the two years that remained of the Clinton administration, none got the go-ahead.

Since 9/11, there have been bitter recriminations. "Policy makers seemed to want to have things both ways," Tenet wrote. "They wanted to hit bin Laden but without endangering U.S. troops or putting at significant risk our diplomatic relations."

In one year alone, former bin Laden unit head Scheuer wrote in 2008, the CIA presented Clinton with "two chances to capture bin Laden and eight chances to kill him using U.S. military air power."

The blame for failing to act on such occasions, according to Scheuer, lay in part with the White House and in part with his own boss. Quoting Clinton aides, he said, "Tenet consistently denigrated the targeting data on bin Laden, causing the President and his team to lose confidence in the hard-won intelligence . . . it spared him from ever having to explain the awkward fall-out if an attempt to get bin Laden failed."

Scheuer's most savage barb, however, was aimed at the President and aides Berger and Clarke. They, Scheuer would have it, "cared little about protecting Americans and were not manly enough to order such an attack, and their moral cowardice resulted in three thousand deaths on 9/11." The words "moral cowardice," in the context of Clinton and his people, occur no fewer than six times in Scheuer's book.

Richard Clarke, for his part, thought the CIA had proved "pathetically unable to accomplish the mission. . . . I still do not understand why it was impossible for the United States to find a competent group of Afghans, Americans, third-country nationals, or some combination, who could locate bin Laden in Afghanistan and kill him."

Comments by the former President and Berger on the failure to get bin Laden remain in closed Commission files. As recently as 2006, however, Clinton continued to insist that he "authorized the CIA to get groups together to try to kill him . . . I *tried*." The Commission's executive director, Philip Zelikow, agreed that one of the President's secret orders—still withheld today—was indeed a "kill authority." All the same, the Report noted, Clinton and Berger had worried lest "attacks that missed bin Laden could enhance his stature and win him new recruits."

Had the world been able to witness the way bin Laden conducted himself in August 1998, when told of the death and damage the missile attacks had caused, his image would surely not have been enhanced.

"My father," his son Omar recalled, "was struck by the most violent, uncontrollable rage. His face turned red and his eyes flashed as he began rushing about, repeatedly quoting the same verse from the Qur'an, The God kills the ones who attacked! . . . May God kill the ones who attacked! How could anyone attack Muslims? How could anyone attack Muslims? Why would anyone attack Muslims!' "

For a while after the missile attacks, bin Laden went to ground, rarely slept in the same place two nights running. He stopped using his satellite phone, which up to now had been a boon to those tracking him. Within a day of the U.S. onslaught, though, he had his military aide Atef risk a phone call to Abdel Atwan, editor of the London-based newspaper *Al-Quds al-Arabi*.

Having survived the missile strike, Atef said, bin Laden "wished to send this message to U.S. President Bill Clinton: that he would avenge this attack in a spectacular way and would deal a blow to America that would shake it to its very foundations, a blow it had never experienced before."

After the attack on the American embassy in Kenya, the bomber who had run for his life at the last moment—and fallen into U.S. hands—had said something both sinister and significant. A senior accomplice, he told his questioners, had confided that al Qaeda also had targets in America. "But things are not ready yet," the accomplice had added. "We don't have everything prepared yet."

NOT READY YET, but the concept was there. In late summer 1998 or soon after, Osama bin Laden summoned Khalid Sheikh Mohammed. Two years after rejecting KSM's idea of hijacking planes and crashing them into buildings, he now said he thought it "could work."

KSM, it seems, may have been back in the bin Laden camp for some time. An intelligence report suggests that he may have flown into Kenya, using an alias, before the bombing of the U.S. embassy there. There is a report that, two weeks later, he led a decoy operation designed to conceal bin Laden's whereabouts when America struck the training camps. It had been the East Africa bombings, KSM would say under interrogation, that persuaded him that bin Laden really was committed to attacking the United States.

The idea of flying hijacked airplanes into U.S. targets, bin Laden said at the renewed discussion, had his people's "full support." KSM thought it was probably Mohammed Atef, the military commander, who had led him to change his mind. Asked to run the operation, KSM agreed.

The initial notion was still to seize a number of American airliners and crash them into U.S. targets, so far as possible simultaneously. At a first targeting meeting, bin Laden said his hope was to hit the Pentagon, the White House, and the Capitol in Washington. The World Trade Center, one of KSM's preferences, was apparently raised later. Bin Laden had several operatives in mind for the hijackings and hoped KSM would come up with others.

Early in 1999, the "military committee" met and agreed once and for all that the project should go ahead. KSM thought it would take about two years to plan and execute. Those in the know began speaking of it as the "planes operation."

At some point that year, Omar bin Laden was taken aside by Abu Haadi, an aide of his father to whom he was close. Omar, now eighteen, had over a period become disillusioned, and was yearning for a way to get out of Afghanistan. Now Abu Haadi had a warning for him. "I have heard talk," he said, "that there is something very big in the works. You need to leave."

The something, he suggested, was "gigantic."

AT ABOUT THE TIME bin Laden summoned KSM, in the United States *Forbes* magazine published a thoughtful piece by the writer Peggy Noonan. "History," she wrote,

> has handed us one of the easiest rides in all the story of Man. It has handed us a wave of wealth so broad and deep it would be almost disorienting if we thought about it a lot, which we don't. . . . How will the future play out? . . . Something's up. And deep down, where the body meets the soul, we are fearful. . . . Everything's wonderful, but a world is ending and we sense it. . . . What are the odds it will happen? Put it another way: What are the odds it will not? Low. Non-existent, I think.
>
> When you consider who is gifted and crazed with rage . . . when you think of the terrorist places and the terrorist countries . . . who do they hate most? The Great Satan, the United States. What is its most important place? Some would say Washington. I would say the great city of the United States is the great city of the world, the dense 10-mile-long island called Manhattan. . . .
>
> If someone does the big, terrible thing to New York or Washington, there will be a lot of chaos. . . . The psychic blow—and that is what it will be as people absorb it, a blow, an insult that reorders and changes—will shift our perspective and priorities, dramatically, and for longer than a while. . . . We must press government officials to face the big, terrible thing. They know it could happen tomorrow.

TWENTY-FOUR

IN AFGHANISTAN ABOUT THIS TIME, OSAMA BIN LADEN WAS SERIOUSLY injured—horseback riding. "The mighty United States cannot kill me," he quipped as he lay in bed recovering, "while one little horse nearly killed me. Life is very mysterious."

The fall curbed his activities for months, but the 9/11 plot advanced. The first hurdle, a major one, was to find suitable candidates to lead the hijack teams. All the terrorists would need visas to enter the United States, and some would require flying skills.

Bin Laden had four men in mind, two Yemenis and two Saudis. It could be difficult for applicants from Yemen to get U.S. visas, not because of concerns about terrorism but because impoverished Yemenis were thought more likely to be would-be immigrants. Bin Laden's two Yemenis were to apply in vain, leading KSM to suggest dividing the operation into two parts. The Yemenis, he thought, could spearhead a group assigned to U.S. airliners on the Pacific route, not flying planes into targets but exploding them in midair. Bin Laden, however, eventually decided the entire thing was getting too complicated.

For a while, the two Saudis were the only two remaining candidates for the 9/11 operation. Khalid al-Mihdhar, aged about twenty-four, and Nawaf al-Hazmi, a year younger, had grown up in well-to-do families in Mecca, and may have been boyhood friends. Mihdhar, whose family originated in Yemen, was married to a young Yemeni woman whose family was directly involved in terrorism. His wife's family, as things would turn out, was related to another of the future 9/11 conspirators. Once again, just as Yousef the Chemist was related to KSM, terror ran in the family.

Young as they were, Mihdhar and Hazmi could claim to be veteran jihadis. Both had fought in Bosnia. A Saudi friend, "Jihad Ali" Azzam, had been killed the previous year driving the truck used to bomb the U.S. embassy in Kenya. Inspired by his sacrifice, according to KSM, they, too, yearned to die in a martyrdom operation against an American target. It was easy for them—as Saudis—to acquire U.S. visas, and they did so of their own accord even before traveling to Afghanistan.

Mihdhar and Hazmi had sworn *bayat*—the oath of loyalty to bin Laden—on previous visits. KSM, who himself put off taking the oath because he wanted to retain a measure of independence, later described the procedure to CIA interrogators.

Little ceremony was involved. A man pledging loyalty would stand with bin Laden and intone: "I swear allegiance to you, to listen and obey, in good times and bad, and to accept the consequences myself. I swear allegiance to you, for *jihad* and *hijrah* [redemption] . . . I swear allegiance to you and to die in the cause of God." A shake of the hand with bin Laden, and the oath was done. More than as a promise to any mortal, it was seen as a man's commitment to his God.

The Saudi pair notwithstanding, there was still a woeful shortage of suitable recruits for the 9/11 project. One day in 1999, Omar bin Laden has recalled, his father held a meeting to impress on his fighters "the joys of martyrdom, how it was the greatest honor for a Muslim to give his life to the cause of Islam." Osama even called his own sons together to tell them that there was a list on the wall of the mosque "for men who volunteer to be suicide bombers."

When one of the younger brothers ran off to sign the list, Omar dared to speak out in protest. His father's retort was brusque. Omar and the other sons, bin Laden said, held "no more a place in my heart than any other man or boy." "My father," Omar thought, "hated his enemies more than he loved his sons."

Few of the fighters who signed up for martyrdom, however, had the qualifications to enter and operate in enemy territory—the alien land of the United States. Perhaps, bin Laden ventured, KSM would locate such candidates in the area he knew well, the Gulf States. The evidence indicates that KSM traveled even further afield that year, to Italy and—on more than one occasion—to Germany. Not just to Germany but to Hamburg, the second largest city in the country, a port teeming with foreigners—including, we now know, three of the future pilot hijackers and a key accomplice.

THE FIRST OF those four Arabs to arrive in Germany is today a household name—more so, bin Laden aside, than anyone involved in 9/11. His name was Mohamed Mohamed el-Amir Awad el-Sayed Atta. His friends knew him as Amir, but in the public memory he is—indelibly—Mohamed Atta.

Egyptian-born, Atta had come to Europe in 1992 at the age of twenty-three, after studying architecture at Cairo University. His father, a lawyer who long worked for EgyptAir, has said that Atta's mother—from whom he was divorced—"never stopped pampering him," treated him as if he were a girl. The boy would snuggle up on his mother's lap, by one report, even in his teens. As a student, a contemporary remembered, he still had "child feelings, innocent, virgin." He became emotional, according to another, if an insect was killed. Islamic terrorists, Atta said as a young adult, were "brainless, irresponsible."

The Amirs also had daughters, bright, achieving young women—one qualified as a cardiologist, the other as a professor of geology. Their brother did all right at university, but his father nurtured higher aspirations for him. When he learned about two German teachers, visitors in Cairo for an educational exchange program, he arranged a meeting. The couple, Uwe and Doris Michaels, promptly invited young Atta to come to Hamburg and stay in their home. He had a grasp of German—having done a course in the language in Cairo—and accepted. He flew to Germany, and stayed with the Michaelses for about six months.

The couple rapidly discovered that their houseguest was "exceedingly religious . . . never missed his five prayer sessions per day." Atta insisted on preparing his own meals. Impossible to use the family's pots and pans, he said—they had previously been used to cook pork. The young man, they saw, was also a prude. He left the room while showing a video of his own sister's wedding—because it included a belly-dancer wearing a flesh-colored gown. If anything even a little risqué cropped up on television, he covered his eyes. If his middle-aged hostess failed to wear a blouse that covered her arms, the atmosphere became "unpleasant."

The family tolerated all this until the Ramadan daytime fasting period in early 1993, when Atta's obsession with religious observance became too much. After trying to put up with his nocturnal activity—hour after hour of cooking and moving about the house—the Michaelses asked him to leave. To their son, who was living at home, he had become "that person"—someone he didn't want to have anything to do with. Through it all, though, Doris Michaels has recalled, there had been no hint of violence in their student visitor. The problems of the Middle East, he would say, should be resolved peacefully with "words, not weapons."

When he did move to other accommodations, Atta's habits and prejudices again led to clashes. No one, least of all Westerners, could fail to notice his religious zeal and aversion to everything to do with female sexuality. His professor, however, who was familiar with Arab culture, thought Atta merely "a dear human being." He applied himself to his urban engineering and planning course at university, made periodic trips back to the Middle East, and the years slipped by.

In the fall of 1995, another young Arab arrived in Hamburg by ship. He said his name was Ramzi Omar, claimed to be a Sudanese student, spun a tale about having been imprisoned and tortured at home, and asked for political asylum. That was not his real name, and his story was a fabrication. Even so, "Omar" found a way to establish himself in Germany. He finagled phony documentation for himself as a student, then left for his real homeland—Yemen—only to return under his true name, Ramzi Binalshibh.

Though he said he aspired to an economics degree, Binalshibh studied almost not at all. Those who knew him described him as "in love with life . . . charming . . . very funny, made lots of jokes." All the same, he shared Atta's traits. At classes, he objected to the sight of women wearing blouses that showed cleavage. He thought that "disgusting." What distracted Binalshibh during math lessons, a fellow student recalled, was reading the Qur'an under the desk. He was more cheerful about his religion than Atta, to be sure, but faith was at the core of his being.

So it was, too, for a newcomer who was to become Atta's constant companion. Marwan al-Shehhi, just eighteen when he arrived from the United Arab Emirates, was the son of a muezzin—the man who called the faithful to prayer at the mosque in his hometown. In his teen years, before his father's recent death, he had sometimes had the task of switching on the prayer tape for his father.

Friends would remember Shehhi as "a regular guy," like Binalshibh "happy . . . always laughing and telling one joke after another," "dreamy . . . slightly spoiled." Spoiled not least because, after just six months in the military, he had been sent off to study marine engineering in Europe on an army scholarship of $4,000 a month. Happy perhaps, but—an echo of Atta and Binalshibh—he could "explode" with anger on "seeing a male friend looking at a woman." Shehhi never actually spoke to women unless he had to.

Probably thanks to his father the muezzin, Shehhi could recite Islamic texts on cue. Even at his tender age he yearned for the pleasures of Paradise, imagined himself sitting in the shade on the bank of a broad river flowing with honey. Binalshibh, for his part, would exclaim, "What is this life good for? The Paradise is much nicer." To these young men, heaven was no distant concept or possible consolation for the inevitability of death, but a real destination of choice.

The fourth man in the group, who arrived the same month as Shehhi, at first seems not to fit the pattern. Ziad Jarrah, who flew in with his cousin, had grown up in cosmopolitan Lebanon. The son of a well-to-do civil servant and a mother who worked as a French teacher, he had interesting relatives. A great-uncle, it would be reported after 9/11, had been recruited by a department of the former East Germany that handled espionage—and by Libyan intelligence. A cousin, according to *The New York Times* in 2009, confessed to having long spied for Israel—while posing as a supporter of the Palestinian cause.

If such odd details impinge not at all on Jarrah's own story, other factors marked him out. Though his family was Sunni Muslim, he had been sent to the best Christian schools. He had regularly skipped prayers, shown no special interest in religion, and was no stranger to alcohol. "Once," said Salim, the cousin who traveled to Germany with him, "we drank so much beer we couldn't go straight on a bike."

Jarrah enjoyed partying, thought the nightclubs in Europe tame compared to what he was used to in Lebanon—and he liked girls. When he met a strikingly lovely young Turkish woman, within weeks of arriving in Germany, he rapidly won her away from a current boyfriend. He and Aysel Sengün became lovers, beginning an on-off affair that was to endure until his death on 9/11.

For all that, and within months of his arrival, the twenty-two-year-old Jarrah also got religion—and a measure of political fervor he had never evinced before. Perhaps someone got to him during an early trip home to Lebanon, for it was when he got back that cousin Salim first noticed him reading a publication about jihad. Perhaps it was the influence of a young imam in Germany—himself a student—who badgered people he knew to attend the mosque, and pressed anyone who would listen to donate to Palestinian causes. The imam was suspected, the CIA would say later, of having "terrorist connections."

What is clear is that something happened to Jarrah that changed him, changed his directions. Aysel Sengün, herself a Muslim but of moderate bent, was troubled when—as she would tell the police later—he "criticized me for my choice of clothes, which he had not earlier. I was dressing in too revealing a manner for him. . . . He had also started to grow a full beard. . . . He started to ask me more and more frequently whether I would not want to pray with him."

Initially Jarrah had wanted to study dentistry, as did his lover, in the small town of Greifswald. Instead, after just over a year, he switched to an aeronautical engineering course—in Hamburg.

He and Aysel now had to travel to see each other and, when they met, she noticed that he had started talking about jihad. "Someone explained to me," she said after 9/11, that "jihad in the softer form means to write books, tell people about Islam. But Ziad's own jihad was more aggressive, the fighting kind."

Aysel became pregnant at this time, but had an abortion. She felt there were things that were not right about their relationship. She worried about being left with children were her lover to get involved "in a fanatic war." She was increasingly insecure, uncertain what Jarrah was up to, would surreptitiously comb through his papers looking for clues as to what he was doing. What he was doing was spending time in Hamburg with his future 9/11 accomplices. Their religion was inseparable from their politics. Shehhi, who could afford to live comfortably, moved to a shabby apartment with no television. Asked why, he said he was emulating the simple way the Prophet Mohammed had lived.

Given Atta's religious zeal, it may have taken little to add political extremism to the mix. Around 1995, reportedly, he spoke of a "leader" who was having a strong influence on his thinking. In the same time frame, a German student friend would recall, he talked angrily about Israel and America's protection of Israel. He was "always" linking other Muslim issues to "the war going on or the process going on, in Israel and Palestine, which he was very critical of."

In discussion with others, Atta carried on about the Jews' control of the banks and the media. These were not original thoughts, would normally have vanished on the air of heated debate in the mosques, apartments, and eating places in which they were voiced. The flame that was to make them combustible was waiting elsewhere, in Afghanistan. In 1998 or 1999—it is still not clear quite when or by whom—the connection was made.

The umbilical to activism for Atta was probably the Muslim Brotherhood, as once it had been for the young Osama bin Laden. For the Brotherhood, religion is indispensable at every level of existence, in government as in personal life. While the Brotherhood officially abjures violence, it makes exceptions—one of them the struggle in Palestine. The engineering department of Cairo University, where Atta first studied, was one of its known recruiting grounds.

Atta was a member of the engineering club, and he took two German friends there on a trip back to Cairo. The Brotherhood's influence was obvious even to them. In connection with his Hamburg university course, Atta also traveled twice to the Syrian city of Aleppo—where the Brotherhood has deep roots. It may be that he made connections there. Two older men from Aleppo—said to have been members of the Brotherhood and suspected of links to al Qaeda—were to associate with Atta and his little group back in Hamburg.

One of them, Mohammed Zammar, openly enthused about jihad and urged fellow Arabs to support the cause. The other, Mamoun Darkazanli, was filmed attending a wedding ceremony at a Hamburg mosque with the future hijackers. He has dismissed the connection as "coincidence."

• • •

IN THE WAKE OF 9/11, reporters for *Der Spiegel* magazine would discover boxes of books and documents in a room that had been used by an Islamic study group Atta started at college. In one of the books, a volume on jihad, was what amounted to an invitation. "Osama bin Laden," it read, "has said: 'I will pay for the ticket and trip for every Arab and his family who wants to come to jihad.' " Twice in two years, Atta took a trip—to somewhere.

In early 1998, Atta vanished from Hamburg for the best part of three months. When his professor asked where he had been, he claimed he had been in Cairo dealing with a family problem. Pressed, he deflected further questions with, in effect, "Don't ask." Soon afterward, he reported his passport lost and obtained a new one—a trick often pulled by those whose passports contain compromising visa stamps.

The speculation is that Atta, and months later Shehhi and Binalshibh, made trips to Afghanistan that year. Whether they did or not, they would certainly have taken note of the statement bin Laden made in February, calling for war on America. In a list of grievances, U.S. support of Israel, and Israel's occupation of Arab Jerusalem, ranked high. America's wars, he said, "serve the interests of the petty Jewish state, diverting attention from the occupation of Jerusalem."

The 9/11 Commission Report was to duck the issue of what motivated the perpetrators of 9/11. Afterward, in a memoir, Chairman Thomas Kean and Vice Chair Lee Hamilton explained that the commissioners had disagreed on the issue. "This was sensitive ground," they wrote. "Commissioners who argued that al Qaeda was motivated primarily by a religious ideology—and not by opposition to American policies—rejected mentioning the Israeli-Palestinian conflict in the Report. In their view, listing U.S. support for Israel as a root cause of al Qaeda's opposition to the United States indicated that the United States should reassess that policy.

"To Lee, though, it was not a question of altering support for Israel but of merely stating a fact that the Israeli-Palestinian conflict was central to the relations between the Islamic world and the United States—and to bin Laden's ideology and the support he gained throughout the Islamic world for his jihad against America." The commissioners resolved their differences by settling on vague language that circumvented the issue of motive.

All the evidence, however, indicates that Palestine was the factor that united the conspirators—at every level. Bin Laden, who repeatedly alluded to it, would at one point try to get KSM to bring forward the 9/11 attack date to coincide with a visit to the White House by Israeli prime minister Ariel Sharon.

For KSM, concern about Palestine had been a constant ever since his return from college in the United States. He believed a 9/11-style attack would make Americans focus on "the atrocities that America is committing by supporting Israel." Separately, in captivity, he has claimed responsibility for the planning or execution of seven attacks on buildings, planes, and other targets, either in Israel or because they were Israeli or "Jewish."

KSM's nephew Ramzi Yousef, the 1993 Trade Center bomber, said in the only interview he has been allowed that he believed he—and Palestinians—were "entitled to strike U.S. targets because the United States is a partner in the crimes committed in Palestine. . . . It finances these crimes and supports them with weapons."

"If you ask anybody," Yousef's accomplice Abdul Murad told police in the Philippines, "even if you ask children, they will tell you that the U.S. is supporting Israel and Israel is killing our Muslim brothers in Palestine. The United States is acting like a terrorist, but nobody can see that."

Palestine was certainly the principal political grievance—the only clearly expressed grievance—driving the young Arabs in Hamburg. As reported earlier in this chapter, Atta regularly sounded off about the Palestine issue. So did Binalshibh, who would speak of a "world Jewish conspiracy." A woman with whom he had a brief affair recalled how stridently he condemned the United States for its support for Israel. His "great-grandparents, his grandparents, his parents," he said, "hated the Jews and if he should have children, they would hate them too."

Shehhi, though generally a cheery fellow, could on occasion appear saturnine. Asked by an acquaintance why he and Atta seemed rarely to laugh, he responded with a question of his own. "How can you laugh," he wondered, "when people are dying in Palestine?"

Jarrah also felt strongly about the Palestine issue. "He enlightened me," his lover Aysel Sengün would remember, "about the problems Muslims have in the Middle East. He also spoke about the intifada. I wouldn't have known what the intifada meant at that time, because I don't have a political background. When I asked, Ziad explained it was the freedom struggle of the Palestinians against Israel."

In his set-piece statement in 1998, bin Laden had issued a call to arms. "With God's permission," he had said, "we call on everyone who believes in God . . . to kill the Americans and their allies—civilians and military—is an individual duty incumbent on every Muslim in all countries . . . in order to liberate the Al Aqsa Mosque [in Jerusalem] . . . wars are being waged by the Americans for religious and economic purposes, they also serve the interests of the petty Jewish state, diverting attention from its occupation of Jerusalem."

In October 1999, at the mosque for the marriage of a member of their group, Binalshibh made a speech—political in spite of the happy occasion—that echoed bin Laden. "The problem of Jerusalem is the problem of the Muslim nation . . . the problem of every Muslim everywhere. . . . Every Muslim has the aim to free the Islamic soil from the tyrants and oppressors."

By that fall, Binalshibh and Atta and their group had become closer than ever. They met together, prayed together, did jobs to earn money together, and spent much of their time together at the three-room apartment on Marienstrasse in Harburg that Atta had rented late the previous year. They called it Dar al-Ansar—House of the Followers—entered the name in their phone books, even scrawled it on the monthly rent check. It mirrored, almost exactly, the name of the guesthouse bin Laden had established, long ago, to house recruits in Pakistan.

These were young men who had long talked of martyrdom. "It is the highest thing to do, to die for jihad," Binalshibh would say. "The mujahideen die peacefully. They die with a smile on their lips, their dead bodies are soft, while bodies of the killed infidels are stiff." Jarrah, in some ways the odd man out, had declared early on that he was "dissatisfied" with his life, hoped to find some meaning—"not leave Earth in a natural way."

The notion of dying for the faith was parroted at the mosque all the time. These men, however, were eager not merely to talk but to act. Jarrah left behind clear evidence on that score, evidence that shows he had long since been hanging on bin Laden's every word.

Hamburger Mietvertrag für Wohnraum

_____ als Vermieter

Vor- und Zuname

wohnhaft ____ Hamburg
Straße, Hausnummer, Ort

vertreten durch_____████████████████████

Said Bahaji   15.07.1975   Student

und Mohamed El-Amir   01.09.1968   Student
Vor- und Zuname   geb. am   Beruf

sowie Ramzi Binalshibh   01.05.1972   Student
Vor- und Zuname   geb. am   Beruf

wohnhaft 1.Bunatwiete 6, 2.Harburger Chaussee 115, 3.Etzter Heller 10a, HH als Mieter
Straße, Hausnummer, Ort

schließen, vermittelt durch _____

folgenden Mietvertrag:

(Unter Mieter und Vermieter werden im folgenden die Mietparteien auch dann verstanden, wenn sie aus mehreren Personen bestehen. Alle genannten Personen müssen den Mietvertrag unterschreiben. Soweit einzelne der nachfolgenden Bestimmungen ganz oder teilweise nicht gelten sollen, sind sie jeweils im Einvernehmen der Vertragspartner zu streichen. Gegebenenfalls sind andere bzw. ergänzende Vereinbarungen einzufügen.)

§ 1 Mieträume

1. Zur Benutzung als Wohnung

werden im Hause _____ Marienstraße 54 in 21073 Hamburg
(Straße, Hausnummer, Ort)

vermietet. _____ I. OG links
(Geschoß Mitte/rechts/links)

Three years earlier, in his Declaration of "Jihad" against the Americans, bin Laden had spoken of the brave young Muslims who "love death as you love life," who "have no intent but to enter Paradise by killing you."

In a note dated October 1999, found among his possessions after 9/11, Jarrah used almost the identical phrase: "The morning will come," he wrote. "The victors will come, will come. We swear to beat you. The earth will shake beneath your feet." And then, days later: "I came to you with *men who love the death as you love life*. . . . Oh, the smell of Paradise is rising" (authors' italics).

"Paradise," Atta and Binalshibh would say, "is overshadowed with swords." A South African–born Muslim convert who hung out with the group, Shahid Nickels, questioned all the talk about fighting for

the cause of Palestine. "Muslims," he said, "are too weak to do anything against the U.S.A."

"No, something can be done," replied Atta. "There are ways. The
U.S.A. is not omnipotent." The exchange took place in November
1999, and—that month and early the next—Atta, Binalshibh, Shehhi,
and Jarrah did do something.

They left for bin Laden's headquarters in Afghanistan.

THE FUTURE HIJACKERS traveled separately, probably for security reasons, to Karachi in Pakistan and on to Kandahar in Afghanistan. There
is no doubt they were there. A former bin Laden bodyguard has recalled meeting Atta, Jarrah, and Shehhi. Another jihadi, a man who
had also come from Germany, recalled encountering Binalshibh. A
handwritten note on Atta was recovered after 9/11 in the bombed-out
ruins of a house military chief Mohammed Atef had used.

Apparent proof that the German contingent went to Afghanistan—a link in the chain that the 9/11 Commission did not have—is a
videotape reported to be in the hands of the U.S. government. Almost
an hour long, it is said to show Atta and Jarrah at Tarnak Farms near
Kandahar—the very camp where the CIA had once hoped to have bin
Laden kidnapped and spirited away to the United States.

In still photos reportedly taken from the footage, both men are
shown neatly bearded and smiling widely—in Atta's case, an image
utterly unlike the grim visage the world was shown after 9/11. Jarrah wears a white robe, apparently over Western clothing, Atta dark
trousers and a brown sweater. Atta dons an Afghan-style hat, looks
at the camera, takes the hat on and off, then chucks it away. Then he
reads to the camera for perhaps ten minutes, to be followed by Jarrah
doing likewise.

The video is reportedly silent, but the pair were evidently recording statements to be preserved until after their deaths. The words
"al wasiyyah," Arabic for "will," can be clearly seen on a paper that
Jarrah holds up for the camera before speaking. As he does so, he and
Atta both laugh. Then they turn serious as they read out their statements. Clearly recognizable on the tape, seated on the ground among
a crowd of about a hundred, is Ramzi Binalshibh.

A segment of the footage depicts the arrival of a very tall, robed
figure, surrounded by bodyguards. Bin Laden, of course. If authentic,

the videotape is unique evidence of the future hijackers' presence in Afghanistan.

BOTH KSM and Binalshibh, the sole survivor of the group from Germany, have described the visit to Afghanistan. Except for Shehhi, who left early—he had been suffering from a stomach ailment—they stayed for several weeks, weeks that put them irreversibly on course for 9/11.

For bin Laden, Atef, and KSM, the trio must have seemed, in the true sense of that phrase, sent from God. KSM had only "middling confidence" in Mihdhar and Hazmi, the two remaining pilot hijacker candidates that bin Laden had initially picked. Committed and courageous though they might be, they spoke virtually no English, had no experience of life in the West. The men from Hamburg, by contrast, did have linguistic ability, were far more likely to be able to operate effectively in the United States.

In a series of meetings with bin Laden, Atef, and KSM, the trio took the oath to bin Laden—"I swear allegiance to you and to die in the cause of God"—before learning the nature of the mission. Bin Laden considered appointing Binalshibh leader, then plumped for Atta instead. He was now the emir—commander—of the operation.

Atta was included in the meeting to select targets. Dozens were discussed, with bin Laden emphasizing that he wanted one target to be military, one political, one economic. It was eventually decided that the team "must hit" the Pentagon, the Capitol—"the perceived source of U.S. policy in support of Israel"—and both towers of the World Trade Center.

Atta was free to choose in addition one other potential target—the White House, the Sears Tower in Chicago, or a foreign embassy in Washington. The name of the embassy has not been released, but it was surely that of Israel. Atta himself suggested a strike on a nuclear power station in Pennsylvania—Three Mile Island?—and bin Laden agreed.

After the talking, the training. There was some fieldwork—Jarrah cheerfully endured long hours on guard duty—but KSM thought the military side of things irrelevant. The new recruits learned the tricks of the terrorist trade—how to remove telltale stamps from passports, the importance of secure communications, of keeping phone calls short. With their very specific mission in mind, they also learned how to read airline schedules.

In a real sense, in counterpoint to its eventual success, the 9/11 operation was amateurish. KSM and bin Laden had thought initially that no special skills were needed to be a pilot, that "learning to fly an airplane was much like learning to drive a car . . . easily accomplished." Totally wrong, as KSM admitted in captivity.

His maxim, though, that "simplicity was the key to success," was in many ways probably right. He urged team members "to be normal to the maximum extent possible in their dealings, to keep the tone of their letters educational, social, or commercial." Though averse to the unnecessary use of codes, he did develop some. If telephone numbers had to be used in correspondence, KSM directed, they were to be rendered so that the real numeral and the coded one totaled ten. His own number in Pakistan—92-300-922-388—thus became 18-700-188-722.

For Atta, some of the preparation for the mission took the form of what to others counts as fun. He was to be seen "playing video games on a PlayStation—flying a plane." KSM thought Atta "worked hard, and learned quickly." He gave him sufficient authority to be able to make decisions on his own, to press ahead without having to consult too often. One of the Saudis bin Laden had originally chosen, Nawaf al-Hazmi, was to be his deputy.

Each of the five early team members was honored with a *kunyah*, an honorific prefaced by *Abu*—meaning, literally, "father," though the bearer of the name need not have children. In this case, all the *kunyahs* harked back to the days of the Prophet. As Binalshibh remembered them: Atta was "Father of the servant of the Beneficent, the Egyptian," one of the followers to whom the Prophet pledged the certainty of Paradise; Shehhi was *Abu'l'Qaqa'a al-Qatari*, literally "the sound of clashing swords, from Qatar" (though he was in fact a citizen of the United Arab Emirates); and Jarrah was *Abu Tareq al-Lubnani*, literally, "Father of the one who knocks at the door, the Lebanese"—probably after an Arab commander celebrated for his conquests in North Africa and southern Spain.

Bin Laden was keen for all the future hijackers to be on their way to the United States as soon as possible—including the two Saudis, Nawaf al-Hazmi and Khalid al-Mihdhar. Hazmi was to be *Rab'iah al*

Makki, to whom the Prophet promised anything he should ask. Mih-dhar was to be *Sinan*, "the Spear." They were to be the trailblazers of the 9/11 operation.

AT THE TURN of the year, on the night of the Millennium, President Clinton had watched a fireworks display and hosted a large dinner at the White House. "It was a wonderful evening," he recalled, "but I was nervous all the time. Our security team had been on high alert for weeks due to numerous intelligence reports that the United States would be hit with several terrorist attacks. . . . I had been focused in-tently on bin Laden."

The Millennium, a cause for celebration for millions, also seemed just the moment the terrorists might strike. On December 6, in Jor-dan, a group of terrorists had been caught while preparing to bomb a hotel used by American and Israeli tourists. They had been overheard on a telephone intercept talking with bin Laden's aide Abu Zubaydah.

On December 14, concern about a coming attack on the United States turned to a permanent state of alarm. The driver of a Chrys-ler sedan, waiting to enter Washington State from a ferry arriving from Canada, caught the attention of an alert Customs officer. There was something about the man. He was fidgeting, sweating profusely, would not look her in the eye. Hidden in the car, officers discovered, were bomb-making materials—RDX and HMTD explosives, chemi-cals, and Casio watch timing devices.

The man turned out to be Ahmed Ressam, an Algerian who was to admit—much later—that his intended target had been Los Ange-les International Airport. The plan, he said, had been to explode the bomb on or about the day of the Millennium. He had learned about explosives in bin Laden's Afghan training camps, and he, too, had had contact with Abu Zubaydah. He had planned the foiled attack himself, Ressam said, but bin Laden had been "aware" of it.

After the Ressam arrest, and with the Millennium looming, ev-eryone thought there was more to come. A round of frenzied activi-ty began. Clinton rang Pakistan's President Musharraf to demand that a way be found to stop bin Laden's operations. National Security Adviser Berger and intelligence chiefs, often with Attorney General Janet Reno present, met almost daily at the White House. A record number of wiretap orders were issued. "Foreign terrorist sleeper cells are present in the U.S.," counterterrorism coordinator Clarke's staff warned, "and attacks in the U.S. are likely."

Berger and Clarke spent the morning of Christmas Day at FBI headquarters and the afternoon at the CIA. Nothing happened. Come the night of the Millennium, thousands of law enforcement agents and military personnel were on duty. FBI director Louis Freeh and Attorney General Reno kept vigil in their offices—Reno would sleep the night on a couch at the Justice Department. In New York's Times Square, local FBI counterterrorism chief John O'Neill waited for the famous ball to fall at midnight.

The ball fell, and no catastrophe came. "I think we dodged the bullet," Berger said when he rang Clarke after midnight. Clarke said he would wait three more hours, until New Year's came in Los Angeles. At 3:00 A.M., when all was still well, he went up to the roof of the White House and "popped open a bottle."

The FBI told Berger after the Millennium, he was to recall, that al Qaeda did not after all have active cells in the U.S. "They said there might be sleepers, but they had that covered. They were saying this was not a big domestic threat."

No ONE THAT New Year's spoke publicly about a specific danger, that an attack in the United States might come in the shape of airplane hijackings. Many months earlier, however, bin Laden had spoken of just that. "All Islamic military," he had boasted, "have been mobilized to strike a significant U.S. or Israeli strategic target, to bring down their aircraft and hijack them."

In 1998, indeed, the White House had quietly held an exercise involving a scenario in which terrorists flew an explosives-laden jet into a building in Washington. In December that year, the CIA had told Bill Clinton of intelligence suggesting that "bin Laden and his allies are preparing for attack in the U.S., including an aircraft hijacking."

During 1999, Britain's foreign intelligence service warned its American counterparts that bin Laden was planning attacks in which airliners could be used in "unconventional ways." Two U.S. bodies, moreover, produced prophetic warnings.

"America," the congressionally mandated Commission on National Security forecast in its initial report, "will become increasingly vulnerable to hostile attack on our homeland. . . . Americans will likely die on American soil, possibly in large numbers." The same month, a report by the Library of Congress's Federal Research Division, which had wide circulation within the government, said al Qaeda could be expected to retaliate for the cruise missile attack on bin Laden's camps.

"Suicide bombers belonging to al Qaeda's Martyrdom Battalion," the report went on to say, "could crash-land an aircraft packed with high explosives (C-4 and Semtex) into the Pentagon, the headquarters of the Central Intelligence Agency, or the White House."

IN NOVEMBER 1999, just months after bin Laden had decided on the 9/11 operation, two young Saudi students had boarded as Coach Class passengers on an America West Flight 90 from Phoenix, Arizona, to Washington, D.C. During the flight, one of them—in the words of a flight attendant—"walked into the First Class section and continued walking towards the cockpit door. He tried to open the door. He was very subtle in his actions." A passenger in First Class also saw the Arab man "try to get into the cockpit."

The cockpit door was locked, and the man claimed he had mistaken it for the lavatory. The behavior of the passenger and his traveling companion had made the flight attendants uneasy, though, and they alerted the captain. At a routine stopover in Ohio, the plane had taxied to a remote parking place and the two men had been taken away in handcuffs. After four hours of interrogation and a search of their baggage, they were eventually allowed to continue their journey.

Since 9/11, the suspicion has strengthened that this had been, as one FBI agent put it, a "casing operation." It turned out, according to a Commission memorandum, that both the Saudi passengers were " 'tied' to Islamic extremists." One of those extremist associates, interviewed at home by the FBI before 9/11, had said openly that he thought America a legitimate target. On the wall, in plain sight, was a poster of bin Laden.

Intelligence on the companion of the man who tried the cockpit door indicated that after leaving the United States he received "explosive and car bomb training" in Afghanistan. One of his friends had studied flying in the United States and was arrested after 9/11 along with top bin Laden aide Abu Zubaydah. The traveling companion, moreover, has admitted having met one of the future pilot hijackers.

The America West incident may indeed have been a reconnaissance mission. According to KSM, as many as four bin Laden units made early exploratory trips to the United States.

In 1999, and the previous year, reports reached the FBI that terrorists were planning to send men to learn to fly in the United States. "The purpose of this training was unknown," the 1999 report said, "but the [terrorist] organization leaders viewed the requirement as 'particularly important' and were reported to have approved an open-ended amount of funding to ensure its success."

The FBI's Counterterrorism Division responded to the reports by asking field offices to investigate. Congress's Joint Inquiry, however, found no indication that any investigation was conducted. Paul Kurtz, who at that time was a senior official on the National Security Council, said dealing with the Bureau was "very frustrating," at some levels "totally infuriating." Overall, he said, the FBI was a "freaking black hole."

In November 1999, moreover, when the Bureau's Counterterrorism Division asked the Immigration and Naturalization Service to share data on relevant arrivals in the country, the INS did not respond to the request.

November was the month of the suspicious incident aboard America West Flight 90. It was also the month that, in Afghanistan, KSM and bin Laden assembled the future hijacker pilots and ordered them to head for the United States. As the FBI and the INS dithered, the enemy was at the gate.

TWENTY-FIVE

HAZMI AND MIHDHAR, BIN LADEN'S FIRST CHOICES FOR THE "PLANES operation," had undergone months of preparation in Afghanistan. With other select fighters, they had undergone an intensive course at an old Soviet copper mine used as a training camp. It involved endurance exercises, man-to-man combat, and night operations—most of which KSM deemed, reasonably enough, of little use for the challenge awaiting them.

Once in KSM's hands, the advance guard received tuition in relevant subjects. They perused aviation magazines, were introduced to the mysteries of airline timetables, and viewed flight simulation software. Like Atta, they played computer games involving aviation scenarios. They watched Hollywood movies about hijackings, but with sequences featuring female characters carefully edited out. How instructive that can have been, given the ubiquity of female flight attendants on airliners, remains a question.

Hazmi and Mihdhar, KSM decided, were to stay initially in California. He had yellow and white phone directories, supposedly found in a Karachi market, and tried to teach the men how to use them. The directories would help, KSM thought, in locating apartment rental agencies and language schools—and places to take flying lessons. They also tried to grasp some basic words and phrases in English.

The two young men were coached separately. Mihdhar, who was married to a Yemeni wife, left early. Hazmi trained with the two Yemenis bin Laden had picked but who had been refused U.S. visas. One of them, Walid bin Attash, has recalled talks on choosing the optimal moment to hijack an airplane. They were to take careful note of flight attendants' and pilots' movements, the routine attendants followed when taking meals to the cockpit, the comings and goings to the lavatory of the pilots.

Attash was assigned to do a dry run. He flew first to Kuala Lumpur, the capital of Malaysia, a largely Muslim nation that did not require visas for travelers from certain other Muslim states. Then he flew to Bangkok and onward, aboard an American airliner, to Hong Kong. He took the flight to Hong Kong on December 31, 1999, Millennium Eve, the same day on which U.S. officials were beside themselves with worry about a possible bin Laden attack.

Attash learned a good deal from these rehearsal flights. It was not enough, he realized, just to travel First Class. It was important to reserve a seat with a clear view of the cockpit door. Second, he discovered it was possible to board a plane carrying a box cutter or razor knife. Were the knife to trigger a metal detector, he realized, toiletries that came in metallic tubes or containers—like toothpaste or shaving cream—were probably enough to fool inspectors at security checks. In the event of awkward questions, and to account for the box cutter, Attash also carried art supplies. His bag was opened and he was questioned, but the ploy worked every time.

The reconnaissance completed, Attash, Hazmi, and Mihdhar—and several other terrorists—spent a few days at a condominium complex on the outskirts of Kuala Lumpur. Then they traveled on to Bangkok, the last stop for Hazmi and Mihdhar before the real start of the 9/11 mission. On January 15, 2000, the pair boarded a United Airlines flight bound for Los Angeles. Armed with the entry visas obtained the previous year, they had no problem at all at Immigration. They were admitted to the U.S. as "tourists."

KSM was to claim "no al Qaeda operative or facilitator" was ready and waiting to help the two future hijackers on arrival. The Commission, however—usually careful not to raise doubt where there was none—did not believe him. With reason.

On the routine form they filled out on arrival, Hazmi and Mihdhar stated they would be staying initially at a Sheraton in Los Angeles. Intensive inquiries after 9/11, however, would produce no trace of them there or at any other hotel or motel. Where did they stay?

A driver who said he did chauffeuring work for the Saudi consulate was to give a detailed account of having chauffeured "two Saudis." Someone else, he indicated, had met them at the airport, then taken them to "an apartment . . . that had been rented for them" on Sepulveda Boulevard. An imam at the King Fahd mosque, near the consulate, had introduced the driver to the new arrivals. The driver gave them a tour, to the beach at Santa Monica and over to Hollywood. Shown a number of photographs of young Arabs, the driver picked out Hazmi and Mihdhar—only to back off and nervously deny having known them.

Knowing that the pair spoke virtually no English and "barely knew how to function in U.S. society," KSM has said, he had "instructed" them—unlike the more sophisticated accomplices who were later to arrive from Germany—to feel free to ask for assistance at a local mosque or Islamic center. That is what Hazmi and Mihdhar appear to have done, but they likely had more specific guidance than KSM admitted. Another captured terrorist said KSM was in possession of at least one address in the States, perhaps in California.

If there was such a contact, KSM managed to conceal it. The CIA concluded that his principal goal, even under torture, was to protect sleepers—operatives already in the United States. In doing so, he seems to have sought to lay a false trail. On the one hand he claimed under interrogation that he had shown Hazmi and Mihdhar a phone directory that "possibly" covered Long Beach, near Los Angeles, and that they tried to enroll in various language schools in the L.A. area. On the other hand, he referred to definitely having had directories for San Diego and having noted that there were language schools and flight schools in that city. KSM's "idea," he said, was that Hazmi and Mihdhar should base themselves in San Diego.

At any rate, whatever guidance they may have received at the Saudi consulate and mosque in Los Angeles, it was to San Diego that they headed. The man who invited them there and arranged housing for them was to become a major focus of the investigation.

Forty-two-year-old Omar al-Bayoumi was a mystery in his own right. According to a rental application form he filled out, he was a student receiving a monthly income from relatives in India. In fact he was an employee of a subsidiary of a contractor for the Saudi Civil Aviation Authority—paid but, as a colleague put it, a "ghost"—not required to work. He had time on his hands, and spent much of it helping to run a mosque near San Diego.

According to Bayoumi and a companion, they met Hazmi and Mihdhar on February 1, 2000, two weeks after their arrival in the United States. According to the companion, an American Muslim convert named Caysan bin Don, he and Bayoumi drove first to Los Angeles. Bayoumi, he said, met for thirty minutes with a man at the Saudi consulate, then went on to the nearby King Fahd mosque. Bayoumi, for his part, denied that they stopped at the mosque.

Both agreed that they went to eat at the Mediterranean Café, a restaurant that served food suitable for Muslims. As they were waiting to be served, they said, Hazmi and Mihdhar walked in. On hearing them speaking Arabic, Bayoumi invited them to come join them at their table. He did so, according to a *Los Angeles Times* account, after first dropping a newspaper on the floor and bending to retrieve it.

What led Hazmi and Mihdhar to express interest in moving to San Diego, Bayoumi claimed, was his "description of the weather there." They duly showed up in the city, sought him out at the Islamic Center, and—with his assistance—moved for a while into the apartment next door to his own.

The way Bayoumi and bin Don told it, it had been pure chance that they met the two future terrorists. There are factors, though, that suggest it did not happen that way: a witness who quoted Bayoumi as saying before going to Los Angeles that he was on his way "to pick up visitors"; phone records that indicate frequent contact between him and the imam said to have arranged for the "two Saudis' " car tour around Los Angeles; phone records indicating that Hazmi and Mihdhar used Bayoumi's cell phone for several weeks; the fact that Bayoumi appeared to have written jihad-type material; that Bayoumi's salary was approved by the father of a man whose photo was later found in a raid on a terrorist safe house in Afghanistan; and that there was a mark in his passport that investigators associated with possible affiliation to al Qaeda.

"We do not know," the 9/11 Commission Report would conclude,

"whether the lunch encounter occurred by chance or design." The
staff director of Congress's Joint Inquiry, Eleanor Hill, told the authors she thought Bayoumi's story "very suspicious." An unnamed
former senior FBI official who oversaw the Bayoumi investigation was
more trenchant. "We firmly believed," he told *Newsweek*, "that he had
knowledge . . . and that his meeting with them that day was more than
coincidence."

The man most likely to have been a primary contact for Hazmi
and Mihdhar is a man who has since gained global notoriety—Anwar
Aulaqi. American-born Aulaqi, then twenty-nine, was imam at a San
Diego mosque familiar to most of the cast of characters mentioned in
this chapter. On the day the two terrorists arranged to move in next
door to Bayoumi, four phone calls occurred between Bayoumi's telephone and Aulaqi's.

Hazmi and Mihdhar attended the mosque where Aulaqi preached
and were seen there in his company. Witnesses told the FBI that the
trio had "closed-door meetings." According to a later landlord, Hazmi
said he respected Aulaqi and spoke with him on a regular basis.

Aulaqi, for his part, admitted to the FBI after 9/11 that he had
met Hazmi several times, enough to be able to assess him as a "very
calm and extremely nice person." Congress's Joint Inquiry Report was
to characterize Aulaqi as having been the future hijackers' "spiritual
adviser."

In the context of holy war, that is to say a good deal. The following year, the year of 9/11, all three men—Aulaqi and, subsequently,
the two terrorists—relocated to the East Coast. Hazmi and one of the
hijacking pilots attended his mosque in Virginia. He claimed that he
had no contact with them there.

The Bureau had looked hard at Aulaqi even before the future hijackers came to California, and also while they were there. One lead
investigated was the suggestion that he had been contacted by a "possible procurement agent for bin Laden." There had been nothing,
however, to justify prosecuting the imam. The 9/11 Commission described Aulaqi as "potentially significant."

By 2011, Aulaqi would have the world's total attention. At large
in Yemen following a brief spell in prison—at the belated request of
the United States—the former San Diego imam was suspected of involvement in four serious recent terrorist attacks aimed at the United
States. Two had involved attempts to explode bombs on aircraft.

The chairwoman of the House Subcommittee on Intelligence, Jane Harman, has called Aulaqi "Terrorist No. 1."

IN SAN DIEGO in early 2000, Hazmi and Mihdhar appear to have at first sought to pass themselves off as long-stay visitors interested in seeing the sights—as KSM had suggested. Hazmi bought season passes to the San Diego Zoo and SeaWorld. They opened bank accounts, bought a Toyota sedan, obtained driver's licenses and state IDs. When they moved on from Bayoumi's apartment complex, to accommodations elsewhere, Hazmi even allowed his name, address, and telephone number to appear in the Pacific Bell phone directory for San Diego.

```
ALHARK Akram ................... 619 303 7629
  Akram 9716 Osage Sp Vly .......... 619 303 7632
ALHASAN Majed ................... 619 590 0358
AL-HASSAN Hekmat
  1000 S Mollison Av El Caj ........ 619 444 0021
ALHASSOON Omar .................. 619 294 7790
ALHAZMI Nawaf M ... Mount Ada Rd . 858 279 5919
ALHMERI Ahmed
  8633 La Mesa Bl La Mesa ......... 619 460 8615
AL-HOSINY Aqel
  1041 N Mollison Av El Caj ........ 619 593 1178
```

Hazmi seems to have been pleasant enough and sociable, and joined a soccer team in San Diego. Mihdhar was a darker, "brooding" character. Early on, told that renting an apartment would involve putting down a deposit, so violently did he fly off the handle that the landlord thought him "psychotic." Not clever for a terrorist living undercover—it was the kind of thing people remembered.

A Muslim acquaintance vividly recalled an exchange he had with Mihdhar. When Mihdhar reproached him for watching "immoral" American television, the acquaintance retorted, "If you're so religious, why don't you have facial hair?" To which Mihdhar replied meaningfully, "You'll know someday, brother."

Had their tradecraft been better, the two men would not have used long-distance communication as much as they did. KSM, concerned about their ability to function in the West, had told them to contact him with urgent questions. Once they had acquired their own cell phones, however, they often used them to call not KSM but relatives in Saudi Arabia and Yemen. They sent emails—both had addresses on

Yahoo.com—using their landlord's computer and those provided free at San Diego State University.

Hazmi and Mihdhar failed utterly to live up to bin Laden's early expectations. Though Hazmi enrolled in English classes, he learned hardly anything. Mihdhar apparently did not even start the course. The pair's effort to learn to fly, meanwhile, was tardy, short-lived when it did get started, and hopeless.

More than two months after arriving, the pair attended a one-hour introductory session at a local San Diego flight school. A month later, at another school, they bought equipment and took a few lessons. They said from the start that they wished to fly jets—Boeing airliners—although they had no previous experience. They had no interest in takeoffs or landings. When taken up in a Cessna, one of them began praying loudly.

"They just didn't have the aptitude," instructor Rick Garza would recall. "They had no idea. . . . They were like Dumb and Dumber." He told bin Laden's chosen men that flying was simply not for them. That was the end of that.

On June 9, less than five months after arriving and soon after hearing that his wife had given birth to their first child, Mihdhar dropped out and flew back to the Middle East. By any standard, it was an unforgivable lapse. When KSM said as much, though, he was overruled by bin Laden. The operatives' pathetic bumbling, KSM was to tell the CIA, was not really a disaster. His planning was progressive, a step-by-step affair, he said, and the next step had already been taken.

As Mihdhar left the United States, more competent accomplices arrived.

ONCE BACK in Germany from Afghanistan, the Hamburg-based conspirators had changed so much as to be unrecognizable. To outward appearances, they were no longer the obvious fundamentalists they had been before leaving. They shed the clothing and the beards that marked them out as Muslim radicals, no longer attended the mosques known as haunts of extremists.

Atta fired off emails to thirty-one U.S. flight schools. "We are a small group of young men from different Arab countries," he wrote in March 2000. "We would like to start training for the career of professional pilot." The future hijackers declared their passports "lost," received new ones, and applied for visas to enter the United States.

As a Yemeni with no proof of permanent residence, Ramzi Binalshibh was turned down. His hopes of becoming a pilot hijacker frustrated, he was thenceforth to function as fixer and middle man, liaison to KSM. Binalshibh's three companions, however, encountered no problems.

Marwan al-Shehhi flew into New York first, at the end of May 2000, with Atta following soon after. Beyond the fact that they took rooms in the Bronx and Brooklyn, how they spent the month that followed remains a mystery. Atta bought a cell phone and calling card—the first of more than a hundred cards the team was to use during the operation. Ziad Jarrah, the last to arrive, headed straight for a flight school in Florida. He had signed up while still in Germany, having seen its advertisement in a German aviation magazine.

Florida Flight Training Center, still in business today, sits beside the runway of the airport at Venice, a quiet retirement community on the Gulf Coast near Sarasota. It was a small operation, and Jarrah got on well with the man who ran it. "He was," Arne Kruithof was to remember ruefully, "the kind of guy who wanted to be loved. . . . I remember him bringing me a six-pack of beer at home when I hurt my knee one time." Jarrah himself, Kruithof said, liked an "occasional bottle of Bud."

Jarrah's course was geared to obtaining a Private Pilot License to fly single-engine aircraft. He already had a handle on the theory, having studied aviation mechanics in Germany, and he made quiet, steady progress. A fellow student, Thorsten Bierman, however, found Jarrah self-centered and uncooperative when they flew together. "He wanted to do everything single-handed."

Atta and Shehhi had left New York and traveled first to look at a flight school in Norman, Oklahoma, at which one of bin Laden's personal pilots had once trained to fly. As early as 1998, the FBI's regional office had been alerted to the large number of Arabs learning to fly in the area.

After a tour of that school, however, Atta and Shehhi decided not to enroll. They made their way instead to Venice, Florida, and Huffman Aviation, just a block from the school where Jarrah was already at work. No reliable source, however, has spoken of seeing Jarrah with Atta and Shehhi in Venice. Their tradecraft was superior to that of the inept fellows who had arrived earlier in California.

UNITED STATES OF AMERICA VISA

Issuing Post Name
BERLIN

Control Number
20001389580003

Surname
ATTA

Given Name
MOHAMED MOHAMED ELAMIR

Visa Type /Class
R   B1/B2

Passport Number
1617066

Sex
M

Birth Date
01SEP1968

Nationality
EGYP

Entries
M

Issue Date
18MAY2000

Expiration Date
16MAY2005

1011

34137932

**

VNXGEATTA<<MOHAMED<MOHAMED<ELAMIR<<<<<<<<<<<<
1617066<<3EGY6809010M0005186B3207202B2F45192

Mohamed Atta's visa, which got him into the United States in spring 2000, was issued without any prior interview. Ziad Jarrah's charred visa (below) was recovered at the site of the crash of United Flight 93.

Rudi Dekkers, who ran Huffman, would have nothing good to say about Atta. The hijackers' team leader, he said, "had an attitude, like he was standing above everybody . . . very, very arrogant." Shehhi, by contrast, was a "likeable person, he had fun, he was laughing . . . this is a male environment, so we talk about girls, planes. But Atta was never socializing."

Their first flying instructor, Mark Mikarts, was at first just a little nonplussed at the sight of Atta. "When you do flight training," Mikarts said, "you tend to get a little bit dirty—there's oil and fuel. You're sweating. He was always immaculately dressed, with the $200 Gucci shoes, silk shirts, double-hemmed pants. He always overdressed."

Teaching Atta to handle a Cessna 172, meanwhile, turned out to be a nightmare. "Generally," said Mikarts,

> the first five to ten hours is where a student learns to fly by visual references. Using outside visual references, we'd keep the horizon at a certain part of the windshield. He had a very difficult time learning that. He would always over-rotate, or he couldn't keep the reference. . . . But he would not listen. . . . It was like he had to do it his way.
>
> Then finally one day he over-rotated the airplane and I thought, "I'm going to let him do whatever he wants to do. Let's see what happens." He pitches the airplane way up. . . . The engine is screaming. The stall horn is blaring. The air speed's bleeding away. We're about to stall and tumble out of the air. I'm saying, "Nose down!" Next time, louder. Third time, I said, "Nose down!" in a rather nasty tone. [Then] I took my hand and shoved the control wheel forward and stamped on the rudder pedal to get it back where it's supposed to be. We pitched down so abruptly that he popped out of his seat from the negative g's—hit his head on the ceiling.
>
> He turned his head towards me and gave me a look like, "You infidel . . . " or something. Like he wanted to kill me. That's it, we turned back and he went and complained to my chief pilot. . . . I said, "If he's going to be that much of a baby about it and not follow instructions, let him go someplace else. Not worth me breaking my neck and you losing an instructor."

Things were no better in September, when Atta and Shehhi tried another flight school. They failed an instrument rating, argued about how things should be done, even tried to wrest control of the airplane from their instructor. They were asked to leave—and got Huffman to take them back again.

Ann Greaves, a student from England, asked the instructor they shared how the two Arabs were getting on. He replied with "a gesture of the hand. Nothing was said. It was sort of, you know, 'So so . . . ' " The instructor told her that Atta had connections to Saudi royalty, that Shehhi, who seemed to follow behind, was supposedly his body-guard. Once, when Greaves reached out to retrieve her seat cush-ion—Atta, who was short and also needed a cushion, had appropriated it—Shehhi rushed to place himself between them. Royalty and their staff, Greaves thought, ought to have better manners.

What led Shehhi to respond the way he did probably had nothing to do with manners—and everything with the fact that Greaves was a woman. Islam dictates that men and women not married or related to each other may not touch, not even to shake hands. Atta abhorred the idea of proximity to women, even after his death. In his will, writ-ten long since at the age of twenty-seven, he had stipulated: "I don't want a pregnant woman or a person who is not clean to come and say goodbye to me . . . I don't want women to come to my house to apologize for my death . . . I don't want any women to go to my grave at all, during my funeral or on any occasion thereafter."

In Venice, they all remembered Atta's hang-up about women. "We had female dispatchers at the flight school," Mikarts recalled. "He would order them around, tell them this, tell them that. I'd pull him aside and say, 'I don't know how you treat women in your country, but you don't talk to her that way.' " Ivan Chirivella, who taught Atta and Shehhi during their brief stint at another school, remembered that they were both "very rude to the female employees."

The pair were never seen in a woman's company at the Outlook bar, where flight students gathered at the end of the working day. Lizsa Lehman, who worked there, remembered the two of them well. She liked Shehhi, thought him "fun, inquisitive, friendly," while Atta rarely exchanged a word with her. He always stood with his back to the bar, Shehhi explained, because he did not approve of female bartenders.

Atta did break one Muslim taboo. If he did deign to address her,

Lehman said, it was to utter the words "Bud Light." There appears to be no truth to allegations made after 9/11 that several of the terrorists, including Atta, drank alcohol to excess. Lehman's clear memory, though, is that Atta and Shehhi were partial to a beer at the end of the day. "Two, maybe, but they never—ever—overindulged."

IN EARLY AUGUST, the diligent Ziad Jarrah was awarded his Private Pilot License. In contrast to Atta, the love of a woman was on his mind. He headed back to Germany in the fall to spend several weeks with his girlfriend, Aysel. They went to Paris together, had themselves photographed up the Eiffel Tower. "I love you . . . don't worry," Jarrah wrote when he got back, then indulged himself a little. He bought a red Mitsubishi Eclipse, spent a weekend in the Bahamas. Over Christmas, he took a week-long trip to Lebanon to see his family.

By late December, and in spite of Atta's obstreperous behavior, both he and Shehhi had qualified to fly not only small private planes but also multi-engine aircraft. Professional, however, the pair were not. The day before Christmas, when their rented plane stalled on the taxiway at Miami Airport, they simply abandoned it and walked away. That fiasco reportedly marked the end of their relationship with Huffman Aviation.

Atta's mind was racing ahead. Even before receiving his certification, he had sent off for flight deck videos for Boeing airliners. In the last week of December, at a training center near Miami, he and Shehhi paid for six hours on a Boeing 727 simulator. "They just wanted to move around in mid-air," said the instructor who supervised the session, "not take off or land. I thought it was really odd. I can see now what I was allowing them to do. It's a terrible thing to live with."

Some have argued that the hijacking pilots did not have the skills required to pull off the maneuvers performed on 9/11. Given that they would not have to face the complexities of takeoff and landing, though, and given the further practice they were to have in the remaining months, their abilities apparently sufficed for their deadly purpose.

On New Year's Eve, at another school, Atta and Shehhi trained on a Boeing 767 simulator. It would be a 767, with Atta at the controls, that eight months later crashed into the North Tower of the World Trade Center.

• • •

FAR OFF in Afghanistan, seemingly oblivious to what he was asking of the men he had sent to America, Osama bin Laden had become impatient. In the fall of 2000, when they were still at flight school, he had pressed KSM to launch the operation. It would be enough, he said, simply to bring airliners down, not necessarily to strike specific targets. This was at the time of the second Palestinian intifada, or uprising, that followed then Israeli opposition leader Ariel Sharon's provocative visit to Jerusalem's Temple Mount. Bin Laden, KSM said, wanted to be seen to retaliate against Israel's principal supporter.

As he would time and again, KSM resisted bin Laden's pressure. Lack of readiness aside, there was a cogent new reason not to rush matters. A new pilot hijacker candidate had materialized. Twenty-nine-year-old Hani Hanjour, the son of a well-to-do family in the Saudi city of Ta'if, already had flying qualifications. After years of travel back and forth to American flight schools, he had succeeded in getting his commercial pilot's license. After trying in vain to get work flying for an airline in his own country, however, he had resorted to pretending to his family that he had a job as a pilot in the United Arab Emirates. This was a frustrated young man.

The key to understanding the direction Hanjour now took, though, lies elsewhere. Though described by those who knew him well as "frail," "quiet," "a little mouse," he could show another side. When alcohol was available, this conspirator reportedly went drinking on occasion. Afterward, however, filled with guilt, he would devote an entire day to praying. So moved would he become during prayers that one witness recalled seeing him in tears. Religion figured large for him. Ever since a first trip to Afghanistan at the age of seventeen, he had wanted to make jihad.

In 2000, when Hanjour turned up in one of the Afghan camps and let it be known that he was a qualified pilot, bin Laden's aide Atef sent him to KSM. KSM saw his potential, gave him a basic briefing on how to act in the field, and dispatched him—equipped with a visa obtained in Saudi Arabia—to join Nawaf al-Hazmi in San Diego. They would not stay there long, but would head off to yet another flight school—in Arizona.

Given Hanjour's flying experience, KSM thought his target should be the Pentagon—relatively hard to hit because it is only five stories high. On reaching the States, one of Hanjour's calls would be to a flight school owner he knew from previous visits. He now wanted, he said, to learn how to fly a Boeing 757. The instructor suggested he first get some experience on a smaller business airplane, but Hanjour persisted. "No," he said, "I want to fly the 757." On 9/11, he would be aboard the 757 that hit the Pentagon.

The first name "Hani" means "content." Hanjour liked to say, however, that it meant "warrior," in line with the name that he—like all the hijackers—had been given before setting off for the States. Bin Laden dubbed him "'Orwah al-Ta'ifi," after a follower of the Prophet who had died in a shower of arrows in Hanjour's hometown—giving thanks to God for allowing him martyrdom.

IN OCTOBER 2000, as KSM prepared Hanjour for his mission, Atta and Shehhi were well into their course at Huffman Aviation. They and fellow students had to use a computer provided by the school to prepare for a written test, and people often had to wait their turn. One day, however, as Ann Greaves waited outside for Atta and Shehhi to emerge from the computer room, she realized they were not working on the test at all. She heard hushed voices talking in Arabic, then an outburst of what sounded like delight.

"I went into the room," she recalled, "and they were hugging each other and sort of slapping each other on the back . . . I have no way of knowing what it was that made them so happy." What would certainly have made Atta and Shehhi happy was the news—on the 12th of the month—that came out of Yemen.

At 11:18 A.M. local time that morning, the guided missile destroyer USS *Cole* was about to complete refueling in the port of Aden. Its captain, Commander Kirk Lippold, was preparing to leave harbor. Small craft had been buzzing around, delivering fresh food, clearing the ship's garbage. One such boat, carrying two men in Yemeni dress, approached the destroyer, smiled and waved, then stood as if to attention.

"There was a tremendous explosion," Lippold remembered. "You could feel the entire 8,400 tons of ship violently thrust up and to the right. It seemed to hang in the air for a second before coming back into the water. We rocked from side to side. . . . Then it was dead quiet and there was a wave of smoke and dust that washed over me."

Moments later, on deck, the captain looked down at the hull of his vessel.

"The best way to describe it," he said, "would be that it was like someone had taken their fist and literally punched a forty-foot hole all the way in the side of the ship—all the way through, shoving everything out of the way until it came out of the starboard side. . . . The force of an explosion like that does terrible things to a human body."

The men in Arab dress in the small boat had detonated a massive, lethal charge of Semtex explosive and the effect on the *Cole* was devastating. Seventeen of the sailors on deck or below, waiting for chow in the canteen, were killed. Thirty-nine were injured. The average age of the dead was nineteen.

True to previous form, bin Laden would deny that he was behind the bombing, but praise the perpetrators. Later, during the wedding festivities for one of his sons, he would recite a poem he had written:

> *A destroyer, even the brave might fear . . .*
> *To her doom she progresses slowly, clothed in a huge illusion,*
> *Awaiting her is a dinghy, bobbing in the waves.*

And:

> *The pieces of the bodies of infidels were flying like dust particles,*
> *Had you seen it with your own eyes you would have been very pleased,*
> *Your heart would have been filled with joy.*

In a recruitment video that circulated the following year, bin Laden spelled out his grand theory. "With small means and great faith, we can defeat the mightiest military power of modern times. America is much weaker than it seems."

SIX DAYS AFTER the bombing of the *Cole*, President Clinton spoke at a memorial service for the dead. "To those who attacked them we say, you will not find a safe harbor. We will find you. And justice will prevail."

"Let's hope we can gather enough intelligence to figure out who did the act," said George W. Bush, then in the last weeks of his campaign for the presidency. "There must be a consequence."

A cabinet-level White House meeting after the attack, however, had decided to take no immediate action, to wait for clear evidence as to who was responsible. Michael Sheehan, the State Department representative on the Counterterrorism Security Group, seethed with rage as he talked with Richard Clarke afterward. "What's it gonna take, Dick?" he exploded. "Who the shit do they think attacked the *Cole*, fuckin' Martians? . . . Does al Qaeda have to attack the Pentagon to get their attention?"

No one doubted bin Laden and his people were behind the bombing. In the final days of the administration, however, and with fresh memories of the failed missile attack following the embassy bombings in Africa, there was going to be no action without clear evidence.

In public and in private, the President had been hot on the issue all year long. Terrorism, Clinton had said in his State of the Union address, would be a "major security threat" far into the future. In February, when sent a memo updating him on efforts to locate bin Laden, he responded with a scrawled note in the margin—"not satisfactory . . . could surely do better."

The Air Force had done better. By September, Clarke and others had sat in amazement as an Air Force drone—an unmanned craft named Predator—beamed back pictures taken from the air over Afghanistan. Not merely pictures but, on two occasions, pictures of a tall man in a white robe—surrounded by what appeared to be bodyguards—at one of bin Laden's camps. The Afghan winter was coming, however, and photography would soon become impossible. Besides, the Predator could not be used to hit bin Laden. It was as yet unarmed.

In late fall, American negotiators were in secret negotiations with the Taliban that reportedly included talk of the possible handover of bin Laden. In December, a U.N. Security Council resolution called for the Saudi's extradition. To no avail.

On December 18, CIA director Tenet warned Clinton that there was increased risk of a new bin Laden attack. The best information indicated it would occur abroad, he said, but the United States itself was also vulnerable. Intelligence had been coming in of terrorist plans similar to what was actually being planned.

A Pakistani recently arrived in the States had told the FBI of having been recruited in England, flown to Pakistan, and given training on how to hijack passenger planes. His instructions, he said, had been to join five or six other men—they included trainee hijacking pilots— already in America. On arrival in New York, however, he had gotten cold feet and turned himself in. Though the man passed FBI lie detector tests, no action was taken. He was simply returned to London.

In Italy in August, a bug planted by Italian police had picked up a chilling conversation between a Yemeni just arrived at Bologna airport and a known terrorist operative. Asked how his trip had been, the Yemeni replied that he had been "studying airplanes." He spoke of a "surprise strike that will come from the other country . . . one of those strikes that will never be forgotten" engineered by "a madman but a genius . . . in the future listen to the news and remember these words. We can fight any power using airplanes."

Such intelligence was routinely shared with other Western intelligence agencies, according to a senior Italian counterterrorism officer interviewed by the authors. How long this fragment of information took to reach American analysts, however, remains unclear.

In September, there was fear of a 9/11-style attack during the Olympic Games in Sydney, Australia. Fighters patrolled overhead, ready to intercept any aircraft that might be used to target the stadium. The principal perceived source of the threat, security chief Paul McKinnon has said, was bin Laden.

The FBI and the Federal Aviation Administration, however, downplayed the notion that an attack was possible within the United States. "FBI investigations," a joint assessment said in December 2000, "do not suggest evidence of plans to target domestic civil aviation." Further investigation of activity at American flight schools, the Bureau's headquarters unit told field offices, was "deemed imprudent."

CIA OFFICIALS had briefed candidate George Bush and his staff on the terrorist threat two months before the election, bluntly warning that "Americans would die in terrorist acts inspired by bin Laden" in the next four years. In late November, after the election but while the result was still being contested, President Clinton authorized the Agency to give Bush the same data he himself was receiving.

The election once settled, Vice President–elect Cheney, Secretary of State–designate Colin Powell, and National Security Adviser–designate Condoleezza Rice received detailed briefings on bin Laden and al Qaeda. "As I briefed Rice," Clarke recalled, "her facial expres-

sion gave me the impression she had never heard the term before."
Asked about that, Rice said acidly that she found it peculiar that Clarke
should have been "sitting there reading my body language." She told
the 9/11 Commission that she and colleagues had in fact been quite
"cognizant of the group." Clarke, for his part, claimed most senior
officials in the incoming administration did not know what al Qaeda
was.

Clinton's assistant secretary of defense for special operations,
Brian Sheridan, told Rice that al Qaeda was "not an amateur-type
deal . . . It's serious stuff, these guys are not going away." Rice listened
but asked no questions. "I offered to brief anyone, anytime," Sheridan
recalled. No one took him up on the offer.

The Commission on National Security, which had been at work
for two and a half years, was about to issue a final report concluding
that an attack "on American soil" was likely in the not-too-distant
future. "Failure to prevent mass-casualty attacks against the American
homeland," the report said, "will jeopardize not only American lives
but U.S. foreign policy writ large. It would undermine support for
U.S. international leadership and for many of our personal freedoms,
as well. . . . In the face of this threat, our nation has no coherent or
integrated government structures."

So seriously did Commission members take the threat that they
pressed to see Bush and Cheney even before the inauguration. They
got no meeting, however, then or later.

Bush, for his part, met with Clinton at the White House. As Clinton was to recall in his 2004 autobiography, he told the incoming
president that Osama bin Laden and al Qaeda would be his biggest
security problem.

Bush would tell the 9/11 Commission he "did not remember
much being said about al Qaeda" during the briefing. In his 2010
memoir, he dealt with the subject by omitting it altogether. According
to Clinton, Bush "listened to what I had to say without much comment, then changed the subject."

TWENTY-SIX

"WE ARE NOT THIS STORY'S AUTHOR," GEORGE BUSH TOLD THE American people in his inaugural speech on January 20, 2001. God would direct events during his presidency. "An angel," he declared, citing a statesman of Thomas Jefferson's day, "still rides in the whirlwind and directs this storm."

In the months and years since the whirlwind of 9/11, statesmen, intelligence officers, and law enforcement officials have assiduously played the blame game, passed the buck, and—in almost all cases—ducked responsibility. No one, no one at all, would in the end be held to account.

The Clinton administration's approach, Condoleezza Rice has been quoted as saying, had been "empty rhetoric that made us look feckless." The former President, for his part, staunchly defended his handling of the terrorist threat. "They ridiculed me for trying," Clinton said of Bush's people. "They had eight months to try. They did not try."

"What we did in the eight months," Rice riposted, "was at least as aggressive as what the Clinton administration did. . . . The notion [that] somehow for eight months the Bush administration sat there and didn't do that is just flatly false."

Quite early in the presidency, according to Rice, Bush told her: "I'm tired of swatting at flies. . . . I'm tired of playing defense. I want to play offense. I want to take the fight to the terrorists." Counterterrorism coordinator Clarke, who was held over from the Clinton administration, recalled being sent a presidential directive to "just solve this problem."

The record shows, however, that nothing effective was done.

JUST FIVE DAYS after the inauguration, Rice received a memorandum from Clarke headed "Presidential Policy Initiative/Review—the al Qaeda Network." It had two attachments, a "Strategy for Eliminating the Threat" worked up especially for the transition to the new administration, and an older "Political-Military" plan that had the same aim.

Al Qaeda, the memo stressed, was "not some narrow little terrorist issue." It was an "active, organized, major force. . . . We would make a major error if we underestimated the challenge al Qaeda poses." A meeting of "Principals"—cabinet-level members of the government—Clarke wrote, was "*urgently*" required. The italicization and the underlining of the word "urgently" are Clarke's in the original.

Suggestions for action aside, the material said al Qaeda had "multiple, active cells capable of launching military-style, large-scale terrorist operations," that it appeared sleeper agents were active within the United States. It proposed an increased funding level for CIA activity in Afghanistan. It asked, too, when and how the new administration would respond to the attack on the USS *Cole*—the indications, by now, were that al Qaeda had indeed been responsible.

Condoleezza Rice would claim in testimony to the 9/11 Commission that "No al Qaeda plan was turned over to the new administration." Nor, she complained, had there been any recommendation as to what she should do about specific points. The staff director of Congress's earlier Joint Inquiry into 9/11, Eleanor Hill—a former inspector general at the Defense Department—was shocked to hear Rice say that.

"Having served in government for twenty-some years, I was horrified by that response," Hill said. "She is the national security adviser.

30009

NATIONAL SECURITY COUNCIL
WASHINGTON, D.C. 20504

January 25, 2001

C

INFORMATION

MEMORANDUM FOR CONDOLEEZZA RICE

FROM: RICHARD A. CLARKE

SUBJECT: Presidential Policy Initiative/Review -- The Al-
                 Qida Network

Steve asked today that we propose major Presidential policy
reviews or initiatives. We _urgently_ need such a Principals
level review on the al Qida network.

Just some Terrorist Group?

As we noted in our briefings for you, al Qida is not some
narrow, little terrorist issue that needs to be included in
broader regional policy. Rather, several of our regional
policies need to address centrally the transnational challenge
to the US and our interests posed by the al Qida network.   By
proceeding with separate policy reviews on Central Asia, the
GCC, North Africa, etc. we would deal inadequately with the need
for a comprehensive multi-regional policy on al Qida.

al Qida is the active, organized, major force that is using a
distorted version of Islam as its vehicle to achieve two goals:

        --to drive the US out of the Muslim world, forcing the
withdrawal of our military and economic presence in countries
from Morocco to Indonesia;

*Within a week of President Bush's inauguration, counterterrorism coordinator Clarke called
for top-level action. By 9/11, eight months later, none had been ordered.*

She can't just sit there and wait. . . . Her underlings are telling her that
she has a problem. It's her job to be a leader and direct them . . . not
to sit there complacently waiting for someone to tell her, the leader,
what to do."

The Clarke submission had in fact made a series of proposals for
action. The pressing request, however, was for the prompt meeting of
cabinet-level officials. Far from getting it, Clarke found that he himself was no longer to be a member of the Principals Committee. He
was instead to report to a Committee of Deputy Secretaries. There
were to be no swift decisions on anything pertinent to dealing with al
Qaeda.

Though candidate Bush had declared there should be retaliation for the *Cole* attack, there would be none. Rice and Bush wanted something more effective, the former national security adviser has said, than a "tit-for-tat" response. By the time the Bush team took over, she added, the attack had become "ancient history."

As for the deputy secretaries, they did not meet to discuss terrorism for three full months. When al Qaeda was addressed, at the end of April, Deputy Defense Secretary Paul Wolfowitz was deprecatory about the "little terrorist in Afghanistan." "I just don't understand," he said, "why we are beginning by talking about this one man bin Laden."

It was a tetchy, inconclusive meeting, which agreed only on having more papers written and more meetings held. Not until July would the deputies produce the draft of an overall plan for action.

It was not only Clarke sounding the tom-tom of alarm. The former deputy national security adviser, Lieutenant General Donald Kerrick, who stayed on for a few months in 2001, wrote in a memo, "We are going to be struck again." He received no reply, and would conclude that Bush's people were "gambling nothing would happen."

The chairman of the National Commission on Terrorism, Paul Bremer, said in a speech as early as February that the new administration seemed "to be paying no attention to the problem of terrorism. What they will do is stagger along until there's a major incident and then suddenly say, 'Oh, my God, shouldn't we be organized to deal with this?' That's too bad. They've been given a window of opportunity with very little terrorism now, and they're not taking advantage of it."

"The highest priority must invariably be on those things that threaten the lives of Americans or the physical security of the United States," CIA director Tenet told the Senate Intelligence Committee the same month. "Osama bin Laden and his global network of lieutenants and associates remain the most immediate and serious threat."

A scoop article in 2007 in France's newspaper of record, *Le Monde*, made public a large batch of French intelligence documents. Copies of the documents, which the authors have seen, include a January 2001 report stating that bin Laden and others had been planning an airplane hijacking for the past twelve months.

Seven airlines had been considered as potential targets under the plan as initially discussed, the report said, five American, Air France, and Lufthansa. The U.S. airlines mentioned included American and

United, the two airlines that were to be hit on 9/11. According to French intelligence sources, the report was passed on to the CIA at the time.

The CIA and the FBI shared at least the gist of perceived threats with the FAA, the body responsible for supervising the safety of the flying public. Bin Laden or al Qaeda, or both, would be mentioned in more than fifty of about a hundred FAA daily summaries issued between the early spring and September 2001. The FAA took no preventative action, however, ordered no new measures to safeguard cockpit security, did not alert the crews who flew the planes to anything special about the situation.

On most days, at his own request, President Bush met with CIA director Tenet. Every day, too, the President received a CIA briefing known as the PDB—the President's Daily Brief. Between the inauguration and September 10, bin Laden was mentioned in forty PDBs.

THE TERRORIST OPERATION, of course, continued throughout the period. As Bush prepared for the presidency, Atta had made a brief January trip outside the United States, flying to Europe for a secure meeting with Binalshibh. Each of the hijack pilots, he was able to report, had completed their training and awaited further orders.

Marwan al-Shehhi traveled to Morocco for reasons unknown. Ziad Jarrah reentered the United States—this time accompanied by his lover, Aysel. He introduced her around the flight school in Florida and—equipped as he now was with his new pilot's license—flew her to Key West and back. Aysel had had her suspicions about what her lover was up to in the United States, had wondered whether he really was learning to fly. Now she believed him.

Any travel outside the United States was a risk for the terrorists, as there was always the possibility that they would not be allowed back in. Jarrah, with his Lebanese passport and a girlfriend on his arm, encountered no problem and was readmitted as a tourist.

Reentry was not so easy for Atta and Shehhi. Atta, whose visa status was out of order, faced the hurdle of seeing two immigration inspectors. He was allowed in as a tourist all the same—a decision that, after 9/11, would be ruled as having been "improper." Improperly admitted or not, the hijackers' leader was back in the country.

Shehhi, too, almost blew it. When he was referred to a second inspector—because his visa status also looked dubious—he balked at going to the inspection room. "I thought he would bolt," the immigration man was to recall. "I told someone in secondary to watch him. He made me remember him. If he had been smart he wouldn't have done that." Nevertheless, Shehhi was readmitted.

One after another, the systems designed to protect the United States had failed—and would fail again.

In the weeks that followed, Atta and Shehhi turned up in Florida, in Georgia, possibly in Tennessee, and in Virginia. Their movements in those states remain blurred, their purpose unclear. On several occasions, they rented single-engine airplanes. Witnesses who believed they encountered them would say Atta asked probing questions about a chemical plant, about crop duster planes, about a reservoir near a nuclear facility. KSM had left Atta free to consider optional targets.

The fourth of the future hijacking pilots, Hani Hanjour, stayed put in Arizona, devoting himself to learning more about big airliners at a flight training center. Though not deemed a promising student, he received a training center certificate showing that he had completed sixty hours on a Boeing 737–200 simulator. Hazmi, who never succeeded as a pilot at any level, stayed close to Hanjour. On Hanjour's behalf presumably, he sent off for videos from Sporty's Pilot Shop. He received information on Boeing flight systems, and advice on "How an Airline Captain Should Look and Act."

Following a trip to the Grand Canyon, Hazmi and Hanjour headed for the East Coast—and a vital appointment. In early May they were at Washington's Dulles Airport to greet two of the "muscle hijackers," the thirteen additional men trained for the violent, bloody work ahead.

All but one of the new arrivals were Saudis aged between twenty and twenty-eight, from the southwest of their country. None had more than a high school education, an education in which they had been inculcated with authorized government dogma such as "The Hour will not come until Muslims will fight the Jews and Muslims will kill all the Jews."

Saudi officials, on whom American investigators had to rely after 9/11, said only one of the muscle recruits had held a job. He taught physical education. Some were devout—one had acted as imam at his local mosque—but none had been considered zealots. One had suffered from depression, his brother said, until he consulted a religious adviser. Two, according to the Saudis, had been known to drink alcohol. All wound up in a bin Laden training camp, some of them after starting out with plans to join the jihad in Chechnya.

Osama bin Laden himself picked many of these young men for the 9/11 operation, according to KSM. Size and strength were not a primary qualification—most were no more than five foot seven. What was essential was the readiness to die as a martyr—and the ability to obtain a U.S. visa. Before final training, all the Saudis had been sent home to get one.

In Saudi Arabia, with its special relationship to the United States, getting a visa was astonishingly easy—easier by far than the arduous process that had long been the norm for citizens of friendly Western countries. Visa applications were successful even when not properly filled out, let alone when they were literately presented. One future hijacker described his occupation as "teater." Two said they were headed for a city named as "Wasantwn" to join an employer or school identified only as "South City."

Obtaining a visa turned out to be even easier for the last four of the muscle hijackers to apply. Under a new U.S. program named Visa Express, applicants could merely apply through a travel agency, with no need even to appear at the consulate. The in-joke was that "all Saudis had to do was throw their passports over the consulate wall." The then American consul general in Riyadh, Thomas Furey, told the 9/11 Commission he "did not think Saudis were security risks."

Now that the recruits had visas in hand, the final phase of training involved hijacking techniques, advice on how to deal with sky marshals, and lessons in killing. The men bound for America were issued Swiss knives. Then, by way of rehearsal for the slaughter of passengers and aircrew, they used them to butcher sheep and camels.

According to KSM, trainees were also obliged to learn about hijacking trains, carrying out truck bombings, and blowing up buildings. This was "to muddy somewhat the real purpose of their training, in case they were caught while in transit to the U.S." The men were told they were to take part in an airborne suicide operation, KSM said, only when they reached Dubai en route to the United States.

The muscle hijackers arrived during the late spring and early summer, traveling mostly in pairs. Except for one man, who was supposedly on business as "a dealer," the word often used by Saudi applicants to signify "businessman," they masqueraded as tourists. Several had unsatisfactory documentation—one called himself by different names on different forms—yet none had real difficulty getting into the United States. The rickety system was failing still.

By prior arrangement with Atta, some flew into Washington or New York, the others into airports in Florida. Atta looked after logistics in the South, while Hazmi—at this stage viewed as second-in-command—made arrangements in the North. With the newcomers came a fresh supply of money to feed and maintain the terrorists as the countdown to 9/11 began.

As had most of those who preceded them, the thirteen had recorded videotaped martyrdom messages in Afghanistan. "We left our families," one said, "to send a message the color of blood. The message says, 'Oh Allah, take from our blood today until you are satisfied.' The message says: 'The time of humiliation and subjugation is over.' It is time to kill Americans in their homeland, among their sons and near their forces and intelligence."

The hijackers' videotapes would not be released until after 9/11.

WARNINGS THAT something specific was afoot were now reaching the outside world with increasing frequency. Bin Laden's archenemy in Afghanistan, Ahmed Shah Massoud, the most prominent military figure still undefeated by the Taliban, brought a blunt message with him on a visit to Europe in April.

At a press conference at the European Parliament in Strasbourg, Massoud made a wide-ranging appeal for assistance. "If President Bush doesn't help us," he said in response to a reporter's question on al Qaeda, "then these terrorists will damage the United States and Europe very soon, and it will be too late." Though the comment received little if any coverage in the media, the CIA was paying close attention. Two agency officers, sent from Washington for the express purpose, had a private meeting with Massoud in France. The full detail of what he told them remains classified, but a heavily redacted intelligence document reveals that he had "gained limited knowledge of the intentions of the Saudi millionaire, bin Laden, and his terrorist organization, al Qaeda, to perform a terrorist act against the U.S., on a scale larger than the 1998 bombing of the U.S. embassies in Kenya and Tanzania [two lines deleted]."

CIA director Tenet, for his part, has revealed significantly more about Massoud's warning. He told his Agency visitors that "bin Laden was sending twenty-five operatives to Europe for terrorist activities. The operatives, he said, would be traveling through Iran and Bosnia." The intelligence was not far off target. "Twenty-five" was close to nineteen, the actual number of terrorists dispatched on the 9/11 mission, and some of them did travel through Iran.

Around the time Massoud talked with the CIA officers, ominous information came in from Cairo. Egyptian intelligence, itself ever alert to the threat from the Muslim Brotherhood—and aware that Ayman al-Zawahiri, the long-distance element of that threat, was in Afghanistan at bin Laden's side—had managed to penetrate al Qaeda. "We knew that something was going to happen," President Mubarak would recall, "to the United States, maybe inside the United States, maybe in an airplane, maybe in embassies." Imprecise though it was, the warning was passed to the CIA's station in Egypt.

When he addressed a class at the National War College that month, the CIA's Cofer Black said he believed "something big was coming, and that it would very likely be in the U.S." He also spoke of his foreboding at a meeting with executives at the FBI Academy at Quantico.

The Bureau's director, Louis Freeh, raised the subject of terrorism, that same day, with Attorney General John Ashcroft, to be told, according to one account—which has since been denied by a Justice Department spokesperson—that Ashcroft "didn't want to hear about it." It was not the last time, reportedly, that the attorney general would speak in that vein.

Exactly what warnings CIA director Tenet personally passed to President Bush, what was in the Daily Briefs the President received, and how he responded, we do not know. With one exception, the Bush administration briefs remain classified. Very similar briefing documents, however, went each morning to other very senior officials. Commission staff who read them learned that, in April and May alone, such senior officials received summaries headed "Bin Laden Planning Multiple Operations," "Bin Laden Public Profile May Presage Attack," and "Bin Laden's Networks' Plans Advancing."

That the CIA and other intelligence agencies were getting a stream of intelligence is not surprising. Al Qaeda's security was constantly being breached, notably by Osama bin Laden himself. His "public profile," to use the Agency's wording, reflected in part the fact that the terrorist leader had been making triumphalist speeches to his followers. He was also hopelessly indiscreet.

A young Australian recruit to the cause, David Hicks, got off letter after gushing letter to his mother back home. "They send a lot of spies here," he wrote in May. "One way to get around [the spies] is to send a letter to 'Abu Muslim Australia'. . . . By the way, I have met Osama bin Laden about twenty times, he is a lovely brother. . . . I will get to meet him again. There is a group of us going."

A follower who served bin Laden as bodyguard, Shadi Abdalla, would recall his leader boasting of plans to kill thousands of people in the United States. "All the people [in the camp] knew that bin Laden said that there would be something done against America . . . America was going to be hit."

Even one of the future hijackers was blabbing. Khalid al-Mihdhar, still in the Middle East following his impetuous return home to see his wife and newborn baby, chattered to a cousin in Saudi Arabia. Five attacks were in the works, he said—close to the eventual total of four—and due by summer's end. He quoted bin Laden as having said, "I will make it happen even if I do it by myself."

Bin Laden himself went even further, asking a crowd in one of the camps to pray for "the success of an attack involving twenty martyrs." Had Ramzi Binalshibh not been refused a visa, and had it not proved impossible to replace him, there would have been twenty hijackers on 9/11.

"It's time to penetrate America and Israel and hit them where it hurts," said bin Laden. "Penetrate."

The Taliban regime, worried in part about the potential consequences, asked bin Laden to moderate his outbursts. Their guest got around that by calling in an MBC—Middle East Broadcasting Corporation—TV reporter and telling him—off camera and off mic—that there would soon be "some news." Then he sat back as an aide, Atef, said: "In the next few weeks we will carry out a big surprise, and we will strike or attack American and Israeli interests." Others told the reporter that the "coffin business will increase in the United States." Asked to confirm the nature of the "news"—again off camera—bin Laden just smiled.

Behind the scenes with KSM, he had again become impatient. He was a man with a penchant that many in his culture shared, for auguries and superstition. At one point that spring, with no more justification than that the number 7 was by tradition auspicious, bin Laden urged KSM to bring forward the hijackings and strike on May 12. That date, he pointed out, would be exactly seven months after the successful attack on the *Cole*. KSM told him the team was not yet ready.

In mid-June, following reports in the media that Israel's prime minister Ariel Sharon was within days due to visit President Bush at the White House, bin Laden bombarded KSM with requests for the operation to be activated at once. The MBC television team had been told during their recent visit that the coming strike would be "a big gift for the intifada."

A strike coinciding with the Sharon trip—not least when Palestinian leader Yasser Arafat had pointedly received no invitation from the White House—must have seemed highly desirable. KSM, however, again persuaded bin Laden that precipitate action would be ill-advised.

All this was terrible tradecraft, amateurish folly that could have doomed the 9/11 plan to failure.

IN WASHINGTON, meanwhile, Richard Clarke still pressed in vain for expeditious action. Fearing that he was becoming "like Captain Ahab with bin Laden as the White Whale," he had long since thought he should consider finding other work. Yet he was still there at the end of May, still worrying.

A recently released Commission staff note, written following a review of National Security Council files, observes that it was clear that "Clarke was driving process in the new Bush Administration, not Condi Rice or Steve Hadley. Not much was going on at their level against AQ. Highest levels of government were not engaged, were not driving the process."

"When these attacks occur, as they likely will," Clarke wrote Rice on May 29, "we will wonder what more we could have done to stop them."

The following day, Rice asked George Tenet and CIA colleagues to assess the gravity of the danger. On a scale of one to ten, she was told, it rated a seven.

Two weeks later, a report reached the CIA that KSM was "recruiting people to travel to the United States to meet with colleagues already there." On June 21, with the wave of threat information continuing, the intelligence agencies—and the military in the Middle East—went on high alert. As the month ended, with the July 4 holiday approaching, the National Security Agency intercepted terrorist traffic indicating that something "very, very, very, very big" was imminent. Clarke duly advised Rice.

The holiday passed without incident, but the anxiety remained. On July 10, according to Tenet, his counterterrorism chief, Cofer Black, delivered a threat assessment that made his hair stand on end. With Black and the head of the bin Laden unit at his side, the director rushed immediately to see Rice at the White House. There followed a deeply unsatisfactory encounter—one the 9/11 Commission Report failed to mention.

The CIA chiefs told Rice flatly: "There will be a significant terrorist attack in the coming weeks or months." The bin Laden unit head went through the bald facts of the intelligence. His colleagues described CIA ploys that might disrupt and delay the attack. Then they urged immediate decisions on measures that would tackle the overall problem. The slow, plodding deliberations of the deputy secretaries were taking too long.

Rice asked Richard Clarke, who was also present, whether he agreed. Clarke, according to Tenet, "put his elbows on his knees and his head fell into his hands and he gave an exasperated yes." "The President," Tenet told Rice, "needed to align his policy with the new reality." Rice assured them that Bush would do that.

She did not convince the deputation from the CIA. According to the *Washington Post*'s Bob Woodward, writing in 2006, they "felt they were not getting through to Rice. She was polite, but they felt the brush-off. . . . Rice had seemed focused on other administration priorities, especially the ballistic missile defense system that Bush had campaigned on. She was in a different place. . . . No immediate action meant great risk."

In Cofer Black's view, Woodward wrote, "The decision to just keep planning was a sustained policy failure. Rice and the Bush team had been in hibernation too long." "Adults," Black said, "should not have a system like this."

Black had been sure for months that catastrophe was coming. Sure, too, that as counterterrorist head he would take the flak for it, he had long had his resignation signed and ready in his desk. The bin

Laden unit head—his name is still officially withheld—and Michael Scheuer, his predecessor, were also now talking of resigning.

The same day the CIA chiefs tried to get action from the White House, an FBI agent in Arizona sent a memo to a number of head-quarters officials, including four members of the Bureau's own bin Laden unit. Agent Kenneth Williams reported: "The purpose of this communication is to advise the Bureau and New York of the possibility of a coordinated effort by Osama bin Laden to send students to the United States to attend civil aviation universities and colleges. Phoenix has observed an inordinate number of individuals of investigative interest who are attending or who have attended. . . . These individuals will be in a position in the future to conduct terror activity against civil aviation targets."

Over eight pages, Williams laid out the reasons for his concern. One man he named was a known contact of bin Laden's senior accomplice Abu Zubaydah. Another connected to the two Saudis who two years earlier had come under suspicion for their behavior during an America West flight. Investigators were later to conclude that the same man's associates had included Hani Hanjour—the 9/11 hijacking pilot who had trained in Arizona.

Agent Williams recommended checking on flight schools around the nation. Yet he got no response, and his prescient message received minimal circulation. FBI officials worried that the checks he proposed would risk accusations of "racial profiling."

Only a week earlier, all FBI regions had been alerted to the terrorist threat and urged to "exercise extreme vigilance." "I had asked to know if a sparrow fell from a tree," counterterrorism coordinator Clarke would write long after 9/11. "Somewhere in FBI there was information that strange things had been going on at flight schools. . . . Red lights and bells should have been going off."

Had the FBI recipients of Williams's memo been aware of the attitude of the man who headed the Bush Justice Department, their torpor might have been more understandable. Acting Director Thomas Pickard has said that, following Director Freeh's resignation that June, he tried repeatedly to get Attorney General Ashcroft to give the terrorist threat his attention. When he approached the subject for the second time, on July 12, Ashcroft abruptly cut him off—as he reportedly had Freeh back in the spring.

"I don't want to hear about that anymore," snapped the attorney general, according to Pickard. "There's nothing I can do about that." Pickard remonstrated, saying he thought Ashcroft should speak directly with his CIA counterpart, but the attorney general made himself even clearer. "I don't want you to ever talk to me about al Qaeda, about these threats. I don't want to hear about al Qaeda anymore."

"Fishing rod in hand," CBS News noted two weeks later, "Attorney General John Ashcroft left on a weekend trip to Missouri aboard a chartered government jet." Asked why he was not using a commercial airline, the Justice Department cited a "threat assessment," saying he would fly only by private jet for the remainder of his term. Asked whether he knew the nature of the threat, Ashcroft himself responded, "Frankly, I don't."

Late on July 20, when President Bush arrived in Italy to attend a G8 summit, antiaircraft guns lined the airport perimeter. He and other leaders slept not on land but on ships at sea. Next day, Bush had an audience with the Pope not at the Vatican but at the papal residence outside Rome. Wherever he went, the airspace was closed and fighters flew cover overhead. Egypt's President Mubarak, acting on an intelligence briefing, had warned of a possible bin Laden attack using "an airplane stuffed with explosives."

TWENTY-SEVEN

IN THE UNITED STATES, MEANWHILE, THE TERRORISTS HAD CONTINUED to move toward their goal. On July 4, as Americans celebrated the holiday and security officials fretted, Khalid al-Mihdhar had flown back into JFK Airport—unchallenged. It should not have been that way.

The CIA had identified Mihdhar as a prime suspect eighteen months earlier—it was to emerge after 9/11—when the Saudi flew to join fellow terrorists in Kuala Lumpur. While he was on his way there, during a stopover in Dubai, the local intelligence service broke into his hotel room at the request of the CIA. His passport, which was copied, had given the Agency two superb leads. It now knew not only Mihdhar's full identity but also the fact that he had a valid entry visa for the United States.

Even so, and although the CIA firmly believed he and his companions in Kuala Lumpur were terrorists, it had not placed Mihdhar on the TIPOFF list of known and suspected terrorists. And it had withheld what it knew from the FBI. The CIA's handling of its intelligence on Mihdhar—and the almost identical information on the companion with whom he arrived in the States, Nawaf al-Hazmi—had allowed the first of the 9/11 operatives to enter the States under their own names and live openly in California in the months that followed.

The CIA's action—or failure to take appropriate action—had also allowed Mihdhar to depart freely in mid-2000, when he returned to the Middle East for an extended period. Then in summer 2001, and because the CIA continued to withhold what it knew about him from U.S. Immigration, he had easily obtained yet another entry visa to get back into the country.

So it was, on July 4, that Mihdhar was able to breeze back into America and join his accomplices as they made final preparations for the 9/11 operation. His return brought the hijackers' numbers up to nineteen, the full complement of those who were to attack on 9/11. Had the CIA's performance been merely an appalling blunder, as it would later claim? Or, as another theory holds it, does the Agency's explanation hide an even more disquieting intelligence truth? That possibility will be considered later.

The team was now divided into two groups, north and south. Mihdhar made the short trip to Paterson, New Jersey, where Hazmi, Hanjour, and three of the muscle hijackers were already based. Six of them lived there, crammed into a one-bedroom apartment, during this phase of the operation. The other operatives settled in Florida, mostly around Fort Lauderdale. There are clues to how some of them spent their private time.

Hazmi had earlier been trawling the Internet for a bride. Some Muslims hold that marriage is obligatory under Islam—being married is seen as a central statement of one's faith. Even Atta, who behaved as though he loathed everything about women, had told his first German hosts that it was difficult for him to be unmarried at the age of twenty-four. Then, he had said he expected to return to Egypt and marry and have children there. When he stayed on in Germany, however, and a fellow student looked for a suitable wife for him, Atta turned out not to be interested.

None of this means that he was not heterosexual. Sexual self-denial can be a feature of the committed jihadi life. One al Qaeda operative, it was recently reported, recommended that his comrades take injections to promote impotence—as he did himself—to avoid being distracted by the female sex.

Marriage had continued to be a goal for Hazmi, though, even when he was in the United States and launched on a mission in which he knew he was going to die. KSM encouraged the aspiration, promising a $700-a-month stipend should he succeed. The hijacker-to-be even advertised for a wife on muslimmarriage.com, letting it be known that he was open to taking a Mexican bride—apparently hoping that a Hispanic woman would at least somewhat fit the bill.

Hazmi apparently lost interest, however, when only one person responded to the post, an Egyptian woman he apparently deemed unsuitable. A morsel of documentary evidence suggests that he fell back on more leisurely pursuits in spring 2001. He went to Walmart and bought fishing equipment.

Over the final months, others—Muslim zealots though they might be, they shared the lusts of ordinary mortals—sampled the offerings of the American sex industry. A witness at Wacko's strip club in Jacksonville said she recognized Jarrah—from photographs—as having been a customer. On a trip to Nevada, Shehhi reportedly watched lap dancing at the Olympic Garden Topless Cabaret. He also turned up at a video store in Florida, accompanied by one of the muscle hijackers who was to fly with him, and bought $400 worth of pornographic movies and sex toys. In Maryland, where two of the team spent a few days, another of the terrorists returned repeatedly to the Adult Lingerie Center. He purchased nothing, just flipped through the smut on offer, looked "uncomfortable," and left.

Ziad Jarrah, the only pilot hijacker known to have had a long-term relationship with a woman, went back and forth between the United States and Germany to see his lover, Aysel Sengün. When in the States, he took a series of lessons in one-on-one combat. His trainer was Bert Rodriguez, of the US-1 Fitness Center in Dania, Florida, who had previously taught a Saudi prince's bodyguard.

Jarrah "was very humble, very quiet . . . in good shape," Rodriguez remembered. "Ziad was like Luke Skywalker. You know when Luke walks the invisible path? You have to believe it's there. And if you do believe, it *is* there. Ziad believed it." In four months, he gave Jarrah more than ninety lessons. They discussed fighting with knives. "It's always good policy to bleed your opponent," Rodriguez advised. "Try to cut him so that he sees where he's cut. If you have a choice, cut under the arm."

Over the months, the evidence would show, several of the hijackers attended fitness classes. Some would buy knives—or utility tools, like box cutters, that would serve their deadly purpose just as well as knives.

Jarrah, who also worked at his flying, went up to Hortman Aviation near Philadelphia hoping to rent a light aircraft. He flew well enough, but proved inept at landing the plane and using the radio. Accompanying him was a man he said was his "uncle," an older Arab whose identity has never been established. Hortman's owner would recall that Jarrah wanted to fly the Hudson River Corridor—a congested route known to pilots as a "hallway"—which passed several New York landmarks, including the World Trade Center.

Hani Hanjour, apparently still striving to become a competent pilot, did manage to fly the Hudson Corridor with an instructor. Presumably because he made errors, he was turned down when he asked to fly the route again. Later, however, he had a practice flight that took him near Washington, D.C.—where weeks later he would pilot the 757 that struck the Pentagon.

Four of the hijacker pilots, and one of the muscle men, took time to familiarize themselves with the routine on transcontinental flights within the United States. Shehhi first, then Jarrah, followed by Atta—twice, in his case—muscle hijacker Waleed al-Shehri, Hazmi, and Hanjour all made trips to Las Vegas. All flew First Class aboard Boeing 757s and 767s, the aircraft types that would be downed on 9/11.

THERE WERE GLITCHES. On July 7, an apparently frantic Atta dialed a German cell phone seventy-four times. It had been decided earlier that he and intermediary Binalshibh, who had been in Afghanistan taking instructions from bin Laden, needed to talk at this critical point—and in person—to avoid the risk of a communications intercept. Then, after Atta made contact to say he could not make it to Southeast Asia, they settled on a rendezvous in Europe—though not in Germany. Too many people knew them there, and they feared being seen together.

Last-minute problems disentangled, they arranged to get together in Spain. During a stopover in Zurich Atta bought two knives, perhaps to check that he could get away with taking them on board on the onward leg to Madrid. He and Binalshibh conferred for days when they finally met up.

Binalshibh arrived with the now familiar message. Bin Laden

wanted the attacks to go forward as rapidly as possible, and this time not merely because he was impatient. With so many operatives now in holding positions in the United States, he had become understandably anxious about security. Binalshibh also came with a reaffirmation of the preferred targets. All were to be "symbols of America," the World Trade Center, the Pentagon, the Capitol, and hopefully the White House. Given the option, bin Laden "preferred the White House over the Capitol."

Atta thought the White House might be too tough a target—he was waiting for an assessment from Hani Hanjour. Were he and Shehhi not able to hit the World Trade Center, he said, they would crash the planes they had hijacked into the streets of Manhattan. Final decisions on targeting, KSM has said since, were left "in the hands of the pilots."

At Atta's request, Binalshibh had brought necklaces and bracelets from Southeast Asia. Atta hoped that by wearing them on the day, the hijackers would pass as wealthy Saudis and avoid notice. Binalshibh returned to Germany once their business was done. Once there, as agreed, he organized himself for the communications that would be necessary in the weeks to come.

He obtained two new phones, one for contacts with Atta and the second for liaison with KSM. The evidence would suggest they had agreed on using simple codes for security purposes.

Atta, meanwhile, flew back to the United States, to be admitted yet again without difficulty—in spite of the fact that, given his travel record, he should have faced probing questions.

He returned to what appeared to him to be a crisis in the making. There had been growing tension between himself, the single-minded authoritarian, and Ziad Jarrah. Atta found his fellow pilot's repeated trips out of the country disquieting. Was a key member of the team about to drop out?

Jarrah may indeed have been wavering between devotion to the cause and the love of a woman. He telephoned Aysel Sengün more than fifty times during the early part of July, then decided to take off for Germany to see her again—without making a return reservation.

Binalshibh, whom Atta had told of his concern during the meeting in Spain, had in turn mentioned it to KSM. KSM responded with alarm. A "divorce," he said, apparently referring to the difficulties between Atta and Jarrah, would "cost a lot of money." As though keeping a close eye on him, Atta went to the airport to see Jarrah off when he left for Europe. Binalshibh met him on arrival at Düsseldorf.

During an "emotional" exchange, Binalshibh urged Jarrah not to abandon the mission. Jarrah's priority, however, appeared to be to get to Aysel as rapidly as possible. The lovers, she would remember, spent almost two weeks with each other. "We spent the entire time together," she recalled. "I did not study, but spent all the time alone with him."

In the end, Jarrah's commitment to the mission proved more potent than the pull of Aysel's love for him. On August 5, he flew back to Florida and the apartment that he was renting all summer. Outside the house, on a quiet street in Fort Lauderdale, hung a wind chime with the message "This House Is Full of Love."

Jarrah made an out-of-the-blue call to his former landlady in Germany that month, and surprised her by saying that he was in America learning to fly "big planes." So he was. Purchases he made included a GPS system, cockpit instrument diagrams for a Boeing 757, and a poster of a 757 cockpit.

In an ideal world, had the law enforcement and intelligence system functioned to perfection, the 9/11 operation might by now have run into problems—for the most mundane of reasons. Mohamed Atta and his second-in-command, Nawaf al-Hazmi, had been noticed, or should have been noticed, or had actually been stopped by the police, many times that year.

It had been routine, when Atta was pulled over for speeding in Florida in July, for the officer who stopped him to run a check on his name. The check should have told him that there was a bench warrant out for Atta's arrest—he had failed to appear in court in connection with a previous violation. Hazmi, for his part, had been stopped for speeding in April, had possessed the gall to report that he had been attacked by a mugger in May, and had rear-ended a car on the George Washington Bridge in June. His driving, moreover, had also caught the attention of a traffic policeman in New Jersey.

Because the CIA had long since identified Hazmi as a suspected terrorist, because the Agency knew he was likely in the United States, there should long since have been an alert out for him. As there should have been for his comrade Mihdhar, when he slithered back into the country on July 4.

"Every cop on the beat needs to know what we know," CIA director Tenet was to say. But that would be after the fact of 9/11—when all was lost. The Agency had shared what it knew with no one in law enforcement.

At their meeting in Spain, when Binalshibh told Atta that bin Laden wanted the operation to go forward rapidly, the hijackers' leader had responded that he was not yet quite ready. He would come up with a date for the attacks, he said, in "five or six weeks." As the first week of August ended, three of those weeks had passed.

Atta had recently tapped out a message to several associates in Germany. It read: "Salaam! Hasn't the time come to fear God's word? Allah. I love you all."

In Washington, warnings of impending attack had been coming in all summer. From France's intelligence service, the DGSE; from Russian counterintelligence, the FSB; and—again—from Egypt. Citing an operative inside Afghanistan, the Egyptian report indicated that "20 al Qaeda members had slipped into the U.S. and four of them had received flight training."

The most ominous warning, had it been heeded, reached the State Department from a source uniquely well placed to get wind of what bin Laden was hatching. The Taliban foreign minister, Wakil Muttawakil, had sent an emissary across the border into Pakistan to seek out a U.S. official to whom he could pass information.

Muttawakil, according to the emissary, had learned from the leader of one of the fundamentalist groups working with bin Laden of a coming "huge" attack on the United States. Already worried about the activities of Arab fighters in Afghanistan, the foreign minister now feared they were about to bring disaster down on his country in the shape of American retaliation. "The guests," as he put it, "are going to destroy the guesthouse."

So it was, in the third week of July, that the Taliban emissary met at a safe house with David Katz, principal officer of the U.S. consulate in the border town of Peshawar. Also present, reportedly, was a second, unnamed American. The emissary did not reveal exactly who in the Taliban regime had dispatched him on the mission. Muttawakil was taking a great risk in sending the message at all.

The bin Laden attack, the emissary said, "would take place on American soil and it was imminent. . . . Osama hoped to kill thousands of Americans. . . . I told Mr. Katz they should launch a new Desert Storm, like the campaign to drive Iraq out of Kuwait, but this time they should call it Mountain Storm and they should drive the foreigners out of Afghanistan."

According to diplomatic sources quoted in 2002, principal officer Katz—an experienced diplomat—did not pass on the warning to the State Department. "We were hearing a lot of that kind of stuff," one of the sources said. "When people keep saying the sky's going to fall in and it doesn't, a kind of warning fatigue sets in."

The CIA and counterterrorism coordinator Clarke, fielding incoming intelligence in July, reported up the line that bin Laden's plans seemed to have been temporarily postponed. One CIA brief for senior officials read: "Bin Laden Plans Delayed but Not Abandoned," another: "One Bin Laden Operation Delayed. Others Ongoing." Intelligence on a "near-term" attack had eased, Clarke said in an email to Rice, but it "will still happen."

New York Times reporter Judith Miller, busy working on a series of articles about al Qaeda, had been finding her Washington contacts unusually open about their worries. Officials, she was to recall, had recently been "very spun-up . . . I got the sense that part of the reason I was being told of what was going on was that the people in counterterrorism were trying to get word to the President or the senior officials through the press, because they were not able to get listened to themselves."

The desperately slow progress of the Deputy Secretaries Committee, charged with deciding on a course of action against bin Laden, had been frustrating Clarke all year. In July, however, the deputies had finally decided on what to recommend to cabinet-level officials. "But the Principals' calendar was full," Clarke would recall, "and then they went away on vacation, many of them in August, so we couldn't meet in August."

PRESIDENT BUSH and Vice President Cheney were among those on vacation. Both, it was reported, planned to spend a good deal of time fishing. Bush was expected to spend the full month on his 1,583-acre ranch in Texas, not returning until Labor Day. "I'm sure," said his press secretary, "he'll have friends and family over to the ranch. He'll do a little policy. He'll keep up with events." This would tie with the longest presidential vacation on record in modern times, enjoyed by Richard Nixon, and 55 percent of respondents to a CNN/*USA Today/* Gallup poll thought that "too much."

For a president, however, there is no getting away from the CIA's daily intelligence brief—the PDB. The one Bush received on August 6 was to haunt him for years to come. CBS News would be first to hint at what it contained, in a story almost a year after 9/11. Apparently thanks to a leak, national security correspondent David Martin was to reveal that Bush had been warned that month that "bin Laden's terrorist network might hijack U.S. passenger planes."

Bombarded with questions the following day, White House press secretary Ari Fleischer would say the August 6 PDB had been a "very generalized" summary brought to the President in response to an earlier request. In a follow-up, he told reporters the PDB's heading had read: "Bin Laden Determined to Strike U.S." Condoleezza Rice, in her own separate briefing, made no reference to the title of the document. She went out of her way, however, to say the PDB had been "not a warning" but "an analytic report that talked about bin Laden's methods of operation, talked about what he had done historically." She characterized the document repeatedly as having been "historical," that day and in the future.

Rice said there had indeed been two references to hijacking in the PDB, but only to "hijacking in the traditional sense . . . very vague." No one, she thought, "could have predicted that these people would take an airplane and slam it into the World Trade Center, take another one and slam it into the Pentagon—that they would try to use an airplane as a missile."

In spite of efforts to slough it off, though, the August 6 PDB became the story that would not go away, the center of a two-year struggle between the Bush administration and panels investigating 9/11. The White House line was that, as the "the most highly sensitized classified document in the government," the daily briefs had to remain secret. The CIA, for its part, refused even to provide information on the way in which a PDB is prepared.

The nature of the daily briefs was in fact no mystery, for several of those delivered to earlier presidents had been released after they left office. A PDB consists of a series of short articles, enclosed in a leather binder, delivered to the President by his ubiquitous CIA briefer. It has been described as a "top-secret newspaper reporting on current developments around the world" and "a news digest for the very privileged." A PDB may contain truly secret information, but can as often be less than sensational, even dull.

Congress's Joint Inquiry was to press in vain for access to all relevant PDBs delivered to both Presidents Bush and Clinton. The 9/11 Commission would return to the fray—not least so as to be seen to have resolved the celebrated question that had once been asked about President Nixon during Watergate: "What did the President know and when did he first know it?" The more the Bush White House stonewalled, however, the more the commissioners pressed their case. "We had to use the equivalent of a blowtorch and pliers," Commissioner Richard Ben-Veniste recalled.

They did get to the PDBs in the end. The section of the August 6 brief on 9/11, just one and a half pages long, was finally released in April 2004 with redactions only of sources of information. This established a number of things that earlier White House flamming had obscured.

The heading of the August 6 PDB had not read, as Bush's press secretary had rendered it: "Bin Laden Determined to Strike U.S." Not quite. Inadvertently or otherwise, the secretary had omitted a single significant two-letter word. The actual title had been "Bin Laden Determined to Strike in U.S." The headline had itself been a clarion message to President Bush that bin Laden intended to attack on the U.S. mainland.

The very first sentence of the PDB, moreover, had told the President—in italicized type—that secret reports, friendly governments, and media coverage had indicated for the past four years that bin Laden wanted to attack within the United States. He had even said, according to an intelligence source—identity redacted—that he wanted to attack "in Washington."

In another paragraph, the PDB told the President that al Qaeda had personnel in the United States and "apparently maintains a support structure that could aid attacks." FBI information, the PDB said, "indicates patterns of suspicious activity in this country consistent with preparations for hijackings or other types of attacks, including recent surveillance of federal buildings in New York."

The day after the release of the PDB, President Bush told reporters that the document had "said nothing about an attack on America. It talked about intentions, about somebody who hated America. Well, we knew that . . . and as the President, I wanted to know if there was anything, any actionable intelligence. And I looked at the August 6th briefing. I was satisfied that some of the matters were being looked into." This particular PDB, he said, had been produced for him by the CIA at his own request.

Later the same month, Bush agreed to meet the full 9/11 Commission—on condition Vice President Cheney was also present. They received the commissioners in the Oval Office, seated beneath a portrait of George Washington. They had insisted it be a "private interview," with no recording made and no stenographer present. We rely, therefore, principally on an account by commissioner Ben-Veniste, drawing on his scribbled notes and published in a 2009 memoir.

Prior to the August 6 PDB, the President said, no one had told him al Qaeda cells were present in the United States. "How was this possible?" Ben-Veniste wrote later. "Richard Clarke had provided this information to Condoleezza Rice, and he had put it in writing." Indeed he had, on two occasions. Three weeks earlier, Ben-Veniste had asked Rice whether she told the President prior to August 6 of the existence of al Qaeda cells in the United States. After much prevarication, she replied: "I really don't remember."

As for the reference in the PDB to recent surveillance of buildings in New York—known to relate to two Yemenis who had been arrested after taking photographs—the President quoted Rice as having told him the pair were just tourists and the matter had been cleared up. If so, that, too, was strange. The FBI had not cleared the matter up satisfactorily. Agents tried in vain to find the man who, using an alias, had asked that the photographs be taken. The unidentified man had wanted them urgently, even asking that they be sent to him by express mail.

What then, Ben-Veniste asked, did the President make of his national security adviser's claim that nobody could have foreseen terrorists using planes as weapons? How to credit that, in light of the warnings in summer 2001 that the G8 summit in Genoa might be attacked by airborne kamikazes? Had Bush known about the Combat Air Patrol enforced over cities he visited in Italy? Had he known about the Egyptian president's warning? No, Bush said, he had known nothing about it.

If there had been a "serious concern" in the weeks before 9/11, Bush volunteered, he would have known about it. Ben-Veniste re-

Bin Ladin Determined To Strike in US

Clandestine, foreign government, and media reports indicate Bin Ladin since 1997 has wanted to conduct terrorist attacks in the US. Bin Ladin implied in US television interviews in 1997 and 1998 that his followers would follow the example of World Trade Center bomber Ramzi Yousel and "bring the fighting to America."

> After US missile strikes on his base in Afghanistan in 1998, Bin Ladin told followers he wanted to retaliate in Washington, according to a ████████████ service.

> An Egyptian Islamic Jihad (EIJ) operative told an █████ service at the same time that Bin Ladin was planning to exploit the operative's access to the US to mount a terrorist strike.

The millennium plotting in Canada in 1999 may have been part of Bin Ladin's first serious attempt to implement a terrorist strike in the US. Convicted plotter Ahmed Ressam has told the FBI that he conceived the idea to attack Los Angeles International Airport himself, but that Bin Ladin lieutenant Abu Zubaydah encouraged him and helped facilitate the operation. Ressam also said that in 1998 Abu Zubaydah was planning his own US attack.

> Ressam says Bin Ladin was aware of the Los Angeles operation.

Although Bin Ladin has not succeeded, his attacks against the US Embassies in Kenya and Tanzania in 1998 demonstrate that he prepares operations years in advance and is not deterred by setbacks. Bin Ladin associates surveilled our Embassies in Nairobi and Dar es Salaam as early as 1993, and some members of the Nairobi cell planning the bombings were arrested and deported in 1997.

Al-Qa'ida members—including some who are US citizens—have resided in or traveled to the US for years, and the group apparently maintains a support structure that could aid attacks. Two al-Qa'ida members found guilty in the conspiracy to bomb our Embassies in East Africa were US citizens, and a senior EIJ member lived in California in the mid-1990s.

> A clandestine source said in 1998 that a Bin Ladin cell in New York was recruiting Muslim-American youth for attacks.

We have not been able to corroborate some of the more sensational threat reporting, such as that from a ██████████████ service in 1998 saying that Bin Ladin wanted to hijack a US aircraft to gain the release of "Blind Shaykh" 'Umar 'Abd al-Rahman and other US-held extremists.

> — Nevertheless, FBI information since that time indicates patterns of suspicious activity in this country consistent with preparations for hijackings or other types of attacks, including recent surveillance of federal buildings in New York.

> The FBI is conducting approximately 70 full field investigations throughout the US that it considers Bin Ladin–related. CIA and the FBI are investigating a call to our Embassy in the UAE in May saying that a group of Bin Ladin supporters was in the US planning attacks with explosives.

strained himself from pointing out that the CIA brief of August 6 had been headed "Bin Laden Determined to Strike in U.S." Had the President not rated that as "serious"?

Ben-Veniste asked Bush whether, after receiving the PDB, he had asked National Security Adviser Rice to follow up with the FBI. Had she done so? The President "could not recall." Nor could he remember whether he or Rice had discussed the PDB with Attorney General Ashcroft.

There is another, bizarre and unresolved, anomaly. Rice—and Bush—have said the national security adviser was not present during the August 6 briefing at the President's ranch. She was in Washington, she said, more than a thousand miles away. CIA director Tenet, however, told the Commission in a formal letter that Rice *was* present that day.

Finally, and for a number of reasons, there is doubt as to whether the Agency produced the relevant section of the August 6 PDB because—as Rice indicated and Bush flatly claimed—he had himself "asked for it."

Had he really requested the briefing? It is reliably reported that, having received it, Bush responded merely with a dismissive "All right. You've covered your ass now." Ben-Veniste has made the reasonable point that if the President himself had called for the briefing, his response would hardly have been so flippant.

The President had indeed asked over the weeks whether available intelligence pointed to an internal threat, Director Tenet was to advise the Commission in a formal letter. But: "There was no formal tasking."

According to Ben-Veniste's account, the two analysts who drafted the PDB told him that "none of their superiors had mentioned any request from the President as providing the genesis for the PDB. Rather, said Barbara S. and Dwayne D., they had jumped at the chance to get the President thinking about the possibility that al Qaeda's anticipated spectacular attack might be directed at the homeland."

The threat, they thought, had been "current and serious." CIA officials, sources later told *The New York Times*'s Philip Shenon, had called for the August 6 brief to get the White House to "pay more attention" to it.

The Agency analysts, Ben-Veniste reflected, "had written a report for the President's eyes to alert him to the possibility that bin Laden's words and actions, together with recent investigative clues, pointed to an attack by al Qaeda on the American homeland. Yet the President had done absolutely nothing to follow up."

WHAT THEN of the time between August 6 and September 11, the precious thirty-six-day window during which the terrorists could conceivably perhaps have been thwarted? There were two major developments in that time, both of which—with adroit handling, hard work, and good luck—might have averted catastrophe.

The first potential break came on August 15, when a manager at the Pan Am International Flight Academy in Minneapolis phoned the local FBI about an odd new student named Zacarias Moussaoui. Thirty-three-year-old Moussaoui, born in France to Moroccan parents, had applied for a course at the school two months earlier, saying in his initial email that his "goal, his dream" was to pilot "one of these Big Bird." That he as yet had no license to fly even light aircraft appeared to discourage Moussaoui not at all. "I am sure that you can do something," he had written, "after all we are in AMERICA, and everything is possible."

It happened on occasion that some dilettante applied to buy training time on Pan Am's Boeing 747 simulator. Moussaoui himself was to say that the experience would be "a joy ride," "an ego boosting thing." The school did not necessarily turn away such aspirants. Moussaoui arrived, paid the balance of the fee—$6,800 in cash he pulled out of a satchel—saying that he wanted to fly a simulated flight from London to New York's JFK Airport. At his first session he asked a string of questions, about the fuel capacity of a 747, about how to maneuver the plane in flight, about the cockpit control panel—and what damage the airliner would cause were it to collide with something.

Sensing that this student was no mere oddball, that he might have evil intent, the school's instructors agreed that the FBI should be contacted. The reaction at the Minneapolis field office was prompt and effective. Moussaoui was detained on the ground that his visa had expired, and agents began questioning him and a companion—a Yemeni traveling on a Saudi passport. They learned rapidly that Moussaoui was a Muslim, a fact he had denied to his flight instructor.

The companion, moreover, revealed that the suspect had fundamentalist beliefs, had expressed approval of "martyrs," and was "preparing himself to fight." Within the week, French intelligence responded to a request for assistance with "unambiguous" information that Moussaoui had undergone training at an al Qaeda camp in Afghanistan.

One of the Minneapolis agents, a former intelligence officer, felt from early on "convinced . . . a hundred percent that Moussaoui was a bad actor, was probably a professional mujahideen" involved in a plot. Though he and his colleagues had no way of knowing it at the time, their suspicions were well founded. KSM would one day tell his interrogators that Moussaoui had been slated to lead a second wave of 9/11-type attacks on the United States. In a post-9/11 climate, KSM had assumed, the authorities would be especially leery of those with Middle Eastern identity papers. In those circumstances, and though Moussaoui was a "problematic personality," his French passport might prove a real advantage. Osama bin Laden, moreover, favored finding a role for him.

Before flying into the States, the evidence would eventually indicate, Moussaoui had met in London with Ramzi Binalshibh. Binalshibh had subsequently wired him a total of $14,000. Binalshibh's telephone number was listed in one of Moussaoui's notebooks and on other pieces of paper, and he had called it repeatedly from pay phones in the United States.

In August 2001, however, the agents worrying about Moussaoui knew nothing of the Binalshibh connection, were not free to search the suspect's possessions. In spite of a series of appeals that grew ever more frantic as the days ticked by—the lead agent wound up sending Washington no fewer than seventy messages—headquarters blocked the Minneapolis request to approve a search warrant.

In late August, in response to a tart comment from headquarters that he was just trying to get people "spun up," the Minneapolis supervisor agreed that was exactly his intention. He was persisting, he said with unconscious prescience, because he hoped to ensure that Moussaoui did not "take control of a plane and fly it into the World Trade Center."

"That's not going to happen," a headquarters official retorted. "You don't have enough to show that he is a terrorist."

THE SECOND DEVELOPMENT, of enormous potential importance, had meanwhile been evolving—and aborting—on the East Coast. The episode centered on the prickly relationship between the FBI and the CIA, a blot on good government since anyone could remember. While in theory the two agencies liaised on counterterrorism, in practice they coexisted at best awkwardly. From early in 2001, according to the sequence of events published in the 9/11 Commission Report, some in the CIA's bin Laden unit had been looking again at the case of Khalid al-Mihdhar.

New information indicated that Mihdhar, whom the Agency had identified as a terrorist the previous year, who it had known had a visa to enter the United States—yet had failed to share the information with the FBI or Immigration—was linked to bin Laden through his trusted operative Walid bin Attash. Yet still the FBI was kept in the dark about Mihdhar.

In the spring of 2001, a CIA deputy chief working liaison with the Bureau's terrorism unit in New York—now known to have been Tom Wilshire—reportedly reconsidered the overall picture on Mihdhar. The suspect with a U.S. visa was an associate of Nawaf al-Hazmi, who—the CIA knew—definitely had entered the United States many months earlier. With growing indications that an attack was coming, it is said to have occurred to Wilshire that "Something bad was definitely up." When he asked a CIA superior for permission to share what he knew with the FBI, however, he got no reply.

In late July, apparently on his own initiative, Wilshire suggested to Margarette Gillespie, an FBI analyst working with the CIA's bin Laden unit, that she review files on the terrorist meeting in Malaysia back in January 2000—the meeting that had first brought Mihdhar to CIA attention. Gillespie did so, and—piece by piece, week by week— began putting together the alarming facts about Mihdhar, his visa, and his plan to visit the United States.

On August 21, she found out about his accomplice Hazmi's arrival in the United States. Within twenty-four hours, when she consulted the INS, she made a startling discovery. Not only that Hazmi was probably *still* in the country, but that Mihdhar had very recently been readmitted. "It all clicked for me," Gillespie was to recall.

The final days of August were a combination of rational action and bureaucratic confusion. On the 22nd, at Gillespie's request, the CIA drafted a message asking the FBI, INS, the State Department, and Customs to "watchlist" Mihdhar and Hazmi. The watchlisting, though, applied only to international travel, not to journeys within the United States—and the FAA was not informed at all.

Gillespie's colleague Dina Corsi, meanwhile, sent an email to the FBI's I-49 unit—which handled counterterrorism—requesting an investigation to find out whether Mihdhar was in the United States.

At that point the process became tied up in much the same red tape as the push in Minnesota to find out what Moussaoui was up to. Mihdhar could not be pursued as a criminal case, Corsi stipulated, only as an intelligence lead. This was a misinterpretation of the rules, but—even though only one intelligence agent was available—Corsi and a CIA official insisted on the condition. One I-49 agent was angered by their insistence. "If this guy is in the country," Steve Bongardt said acidly during a call to colleagues on August 28, "it's not because he's going to fucking Disneyland!"

Within twenty-four hours, Bongardt's frustration surfaced again. "Someday," he wrote in an email, "someone will die . . . the public will not understand why we were not more effective and throwing every resource we had at certain 'problems.' "

The job of finding Mihdhar, nevertheless, went to an intelligence agent, Robert Fuller, working on his own. Corsi marked the assignment "Routine" because—she would later tell investigators—she "assigned no particular urgency to the matter." The designation "Routine" gave Fuller thirty days to get under way. It was August 29.

LIKE PRESIDENT BUSH, CIA director Tenet had spent part of August on vacation—again like the President, fishing. By his own account, however, he kept very much abreast of developments. That month, he wrote in 2007, he had directed his counterterrorism unit to review old files—and thus took part of the credit for the "discovery" that Mihdhar and Hazmi might be in the United States.

Tenet, too, had been briefed on the detention of the suspect flight student in Minneapolis. The FBI early on sent fulsome information on Moussaoui to the Agency, and the details went to Tenet on August 23 in the form of a document headed "Islamic Extremist Learns to Fly." The director's staff took the matter very seriously, urging that the Bureau give it real attention. "If this guy is let go," one CIA officer wrote on the 30th to a colleague liaising with the Bureau, "two years from now he will be talking to a control tower while aiming a 747 at the White House."

Did Tenet share the developments on Mihdhar and Hazmi, and the alert over Moussaoui, with the President? It would seem surprising had he not done so—especially in the month Bush had received a Daily Brief entitled "Bin Laden Determined to Strike in U.S." When the President was asked the question, Commissioner Ben-Veniste recalled, his "brow furrowed." Bush said he recalled no mention of Moussaoui, that "no one ever told him there was a domestic problem."

Tenet, for his part, stumbled badly in an appearance before the Commission. He claimed in sworn testimony that he had not seen Bush in August. "I didn't see the President," he said. "I was not in briefings with him during this time. . . . He's in Texas and I'm either here [in Washington] or on leave [in New Jersey]." "You never get on the phone or in any kind of conference with him to talk," asked commissioner Tim Roemer, "through the whole month of August?" "In this time period," replied Tenet, "I'm not talking to him, no."

It seemed astonishing, and for good reason: it was not true. Hours after Tenet had testified, CIA spokesman Bill Harlow told reporters that the director had in fact briefed the President in person twice in August, at the Texas ranch on August 17 and in Washington on August 31.

Could Tenet possibly have forgotten his one trip to see Bush in August, the very first time he had visited the ranch, in the sweltering heat of Texas? Roemer thought it possible that Tenet had lied.

Writing in 2007, Tenet made no mention of the lapse. Instead, he said he had indeed traveled to Texas, "to make sure the President stayed current on events." According to the known record, the director would not have known of the Moussaoui and Mihdhar-Hazmi developments on the 17th. Both were well under way, however, by the time he saw the President on the 31st. Would they not have fit within the frame of keeping the President "current on events"? In a private interview, Tenet told the Commission that he did "not recall any discussions with the President of the domestic threat during this period."

"THE QUESTION," Michael Hirsh and Michael Isikoff wrote in *Newsweek*, is in the end "not so much what the President knew and when he knew it. The question is whether the administration was really paying much attention."

In her testimony to the Commission, Rice rejected any notion that the administration let things slide. "I do not believe there was a lack of high-level attention," she said. "The President was paying attention to this. How much higher level can you get?"

Lawrence Wilkerson, a trusted aide to Secretary of State Colin Powell, worked with a colleague on the preparation of Rice's testimony. The job, he said, had been "an appalling enterprise. We would cherry-pick things to make it look like the President had been actually concerned about al Qaeda. . . . They didn't give a shit about al Qaeda. They had priorities. The priorities were lower taxes, ballistic missiles, and the defense thereof."

Commissioner Ben-Veniste, for his part, came away from his work on the Commission drawing the gravest possible conclusion. "There was no question in my mind," he has written, "that had the President and his National Security Advisor been aggressively attentive to the potential for a domestic terrorist attack, some of the information already in the possession of our intelligence and law enforcement agencies might have been utilized to disrupt the plot."

TWENTY-EIGHT

HELLO JENNY,
Wie geht's dir? Mir geht's gut . . .
Wie ich Dir letze mal gesagt habe die Erstsemester wird in drei
wochen beginn kein Aendrugen!!!!!! . . .

The start of a coded email message written in broken German
that Atta sent to Binalshibh in the third week of August. It is phrased
as though it were a letter to his girlfriend Jenny. Translated, the entire
message reads:

DEAR JENNY,
How are you? I'm fine . . .
As I told you in my last letter, the first semester starts in three
weeks. No changes!!!!!! Everything's going well. There's high
hope and very strong thoughts for success!!! Two high schools
and two universities . . . Everything is going according plan. This

summer is for sure going to be hot. I want to talk to you about some details. Nineteen certificates for specialized studies and 4 exams. . . . Regards to your professors . . .
Until then . . .

The key part of the message is the reference to "high schools" and "universities." In an earlier discussion of targeting—Atta and Binalshibh had still been discussing the option of striking the White House—they had used "architecture" to refer to the World Trade Center, "arts" to mean the Pentagon, "law" the Capitol, and "politics" to denote the White House.

The true meaning of the message, Binalshibh would explain in the interview he gave before he was captured, was:

Zero hour is going to be in three weeks' time. There are no changes. All is well. The brothers have been seeing encouraging visions and dreams. The Twin Towers, the Pentagon and Capitol Hill. Everything is going according to plan. This summer is for sure going to be hot. I want to talk to you about some details. Nineteen hijackers and four targets. Regards to Khalid [KSM]/ Osama.
Until we speak.

In the early hours of August 29, in Germany, Binalshibh was woken by the telephone. The caller was Atta, his Egyptian-accented voice instantly recognizable.

Atta had a riddle for Binalshibh, a joke as he put it: " 'Two sticks, a dash, and a cake with a stick down' . . . What is it?" Binalshibh, half asleep, was stumped for a moment. Then—presumably he was expecting such a call—he figured out the answer. The puzzle, he told Atta, was "sweet."

"Two sticks" signified "11." The "dash" was a dash. A "cake with a stick down" was a "9."

11–9—the way most of the world renders the days of the calendar. Or, as Americans render them:
9/11
The date was set.

• • •

BINALSHIBH PASSED on the date to KSM, and the hijackers' operation entered its final phase. Everything now depended on Atta's organizing ability and success in maintaining security. An effort to bring the total number of terrorists up to twenty—four five-man teams, one for each target—had recently risked wrecking the entire endeavor.

In early August, at Orlando, Florida, a U.S. immigration inspector had had his doubts about a newly arrived young Saudi. Standing instructions were to take it easy on Saudis—they were a boost to tourism—but this man had no return ticket and had not filled out customs and immigration forms. The inspector sent the man on for a "secondary," a grilling that was to last two hours.

The would-be "tourist," twenty-five-year-old Mohamed el-Kahtani, said that, though he would be staying only a few days, he did not know where he would be going next. He first said that someone due to arrive from abroad would be paying for his onward travel, then that another "someone" was waiting for him in Arrivals. Secondary inspector José Meléndez-Pérez noted, too, that the subject was belligerent.

"He started pointing his finger . . . Whatever he was saying was in a loud voice—like 'I am in charge—you're not going to do anything to me. I am from Saudi Arabia.' People from Saudi think they are untouchable . . . He had a deep staring look . . . [like] 'If I could grip your heart I would eat it' . . . This man intimidated me with his look and his behavior."

The inspector felt in his gut that Kahtani had evil intent—he thought he might be a hit man—and recommended that he be sent back to Saudi Arabia. This was the one occasion, after a series of inefficiencies involving the terrorists, that an alert INS official had really done his job. KSM was to admit under interrogation that the suspect had indeed been sent to the States to join the terrorist team—to "round out the number of hijackers."

It is rational to think that, but for the inspector's acumen, there would have been five rather than four hijackers aboard United Flight 93. With Kahtani's additional muscle—Meléndez-Pérez remembered him as having looked trim, "like a soldier"—they might have been better able to resist the passengers' attempt to retake the cockpit. Instead of plunging to the ground in Pennsylvania, Flight 93 might have stayed on course and struck its target in Washington.

There had indeed been a "someone" waiting to meet Kahtani at

Orlando. Evidence gathered after 9/11 established to a virtual certainty that Mohamed Atta had been at the airport that day. He did not leave, parking records showed, until it was clear that the new recruit was not going to emerge from Immigration. Had those handling Kahtani taken the investigation of him one step further, had they thought the suspect might be engaged in terrorism, the leader of the operation might himself have come under the microscope. Atta might have been unmasked.

As it was, Atta remained free, putting thousands of miles on rental cars, flying hither and thither, coordinating communications, the whirl of logistics involved in getting nineteen men—most of them with minimal familiarity with the West or the English language—in place and ready for the appointed day.

Most of the time in August, the terrorists stayed in their apartments and motels. They did what in other men would have been everyday activities: in Florida, exercising, two of them, at a Y2 Fitness Center; going shopping—for jewelry at a store called the Piercing Pagoda, for a dress shirt at Surreys Menswear; getting clothes cleaned at a Fort Dixie Laundry.

There were some signs of movement. The men crowded into the apartment in Paterson, New Jersey, moved out, leaving behind a few items of clothing, glasses in the bathroom—and flight manuals. Crowded they remained, though. By late that month five of them were squeezed into one room at the Valencia Motel, a cheap joint in Laurel, Maryland. They seemed rarely to leave the room, opening the door to the maid only to take in fresh towels. Guests who used a next-door room "thought they were gay."

Mostly, the men avoided attracting attention. An exception was the day at the end of August in Delray Beach, Florida, when a woman named Maria Simpson was startled by two men tugging unceremoniously at the door of her condominium. To her relief it turned out that, without asking permission, they were merely trying to retrieve a towel that had fallen from their balcony on the floor above. Simpson was to recognize them later, when she looked at FBI mug shots, as two of the muscle hijackers who took down United Flight 93. Their faces looked harder in the photographs, she thought, than she remembered them.

There was little about the hijackers—with the exception on occasion of Atta—that struck people as sinister. Richard Surma, who ran the Panther Motel in Fort Lauderdale, rented rooms to groups of them twice in the final weeks. "They looked young," he recalled, "like they're trying to make it, like students."

Brad Warrick, the boss of a rental car company at Pompano Beach, supplied cars several times to Shehhi and Atta. Warrick prided himself on his "gut check," the eye he ran over new customers to see if they gave him a bad feeling. "Didn't have it with those guys," he would remember. "They were just great customers. . . . They both spoke very well, of course with an accent. . . . Atta was a very normal, nice guy. Nothing weird about him. Never had an eerie feeling."

Ziad Jarrah, however, whose resolve had seemed to Atta to be wavering, may have been getting edgy. A man who resembled him, along with a companion, asked to use the Internet at the Longshore Motel in Hollywood, Florida, but left in a huff within hours. Manager Paul Dragomir asked the pair to use the line in his office—he was worried about the bill they might run up—and they had angrily objected. "You don't understand," the man he later thought had been Jarrah exclaimed. "We're on a mission."

The manager put the "mission" remark out of his mind until after 9/11. Jarrah, if it was Jarrah, may just have been overtired, having trouble with his English. In other ways, though, the operation was less than secure.

Hijacker Nawaf al-Hazmi, the terrorist who spent the longest time in the States, may have been seriously indiscreet—or shared news of what was coming with a loose-lipped associate, not himself one of the hijackers. Investigators came to suspect that in late August, as final preparations for the attacks were being made, Hazmi phoned a Yemeni student friend in San Diego named Mohdar Abdullah.

Abdullah had known Hazmi and Mihdhar early on, had helped them apply for driving lessons and flying lessons. Evidence found later on a computer, moreover, suggested that he in turn was in contact with an activist fervently opposed to U.S. support for Israel. His circle of friends also included another man, himself linked to Hazmi, who had Osama bin Laden propaganda.

When he was detained after the attacks, Abdullah's belongings were found to include a spiral notebook with references to "planes falling from the sky, mass killings and hijacking." In late August 2001, about the time of the supposed call from Hazmi, Abdullah reportedly stayed away from work and school, began "acting very strange," appeared "nervous, paranoid, and anxious."

In the weeks before the strikes, Atta had his men working on their personal documentation. Some of the terrorists had only passports, and young men with Arab passports might have prompted closer scrutiny at airport security. With the help of individuals prepared to vouch for them—in return for a bribe—several now obtained state IDs.

Even before Atta passed the date of the planned strikes up the line, the terrorists had already begun making airline reservations and purchasing tickets for September 11. Over the phone or using the Internet, sometimes from computers at small-town libraries, on different days and in different places, all would acquire their tickets before the end of the first week of September.

Atta and Mihdhar, perhaps keen to appear to be ordinary travelers, set up frequent flier accounts. The Shehri brothers made reservations, then changed their seat assignments—so as to sit on the side of the First Class aisle that afforded the best view of the cockpit door. Hamzi and his brother Salem ordered special meals suitable for the Muslim diet, meals they knew they would never eat. Perhaps to avoid appearing to be in a group, seven terrorists booked to travel on beyond the destinations of their targeted flights—by which time they would be long dead.

All the flights booked, of course, were for transcontinental flights scheduled to depart in the morning. Transcontinental, in part because they would take off heavily laden with fuel. The more fuel in an airplane's tanks, the greater the explosive force on impact. In the morning, at a time, Atta thought, when most people in the target buildings would have arrived in their offices.

Key operatives, meanwhile, had shopped around for weapons. Using a Visa card at a Sports Authority store, Shehhi purchased two short black knives, a Cliphanger Viper and an Imperial Tradesman Dual Edge model. Each of the knives had a four-inch-long blade, the maximum length permitted aboard planes under FAA regulations. Fayez Banihammad and Hamza al-Ghamdi, who were to fly with Shehhi, bought a Stanley two-piece snap knife and a Leatherman Wave multi-tool. Nawaf al-Hazmi also picked Leatherman knives.

Atta, who two weeks earlier had purchased two knives in Europe, had been at a Dollar House, looking for box cutters with Hazmi and Jarrah. Days later, at a Lowe's Home Improvement Warehouse, he, too, picked up a Leatherman. Atta also had a large folding knife, but that would not be carried on board on 9/11.

For the men who had practiced slaughter techniques on sheep and camels, there would be a sufficiency of knives.

ON SEPTEMBER 4, as the hijackers completed their ticketing arrangements, Bush cabinet-level officials—the Principals—convened at the White House for the long-delayed, very first meeting to discuss the bin Laden problem. They had in front of them the draft National Security Presidential Directive the deputies had agreed on before the August vacation. It outlined measures—long-term measures—designed to destroy the terrorists in their Afghan sanctuary.

The State Department had already told the Taliban regime that the United States would hold it responsible, as the host government, for any new bin Laden attack. That line of approach was to be stepped up, along with forging closer links to forces still resisting the Taliban. There was some talk of one day perhaps using U.S. forces on the ground, but nothing decisive.

There was debate at the meeting, but no decision, about use of the Predator, the unmanned drone that had long since proven capable of stunningly clear air-to-ground photography. Prolonged experiment—a model of a house bin Laden was known to frequent was used for target practice—had established that the Predator could be transformed into a pinpoint-accurate, missile-bearing weapon. Were the drone to get bin Laden in its sights, as it had as long ago as fall 2000, there was every likelihood he could be killed almost instantly.

At the September 4 meeting, though, Chairman of the Joint Chiefs General Myers and CIA director Tenet merely dueled over whether handling the Predator should be the mission of the military or of the CIA. "I just couldn't believe it," counterterrorism coordinator Clarke remembered. "This is the Chairman of the Joint Chiefs and the Director of the CIA sitting there, both passing the football because neither one of them wanted to go kill bin Laden." Their argument, apparently, was primarily about which agency was to foot the bill for operating the Predators. All that was resolved was that the CIA should consider using the Predator again for reconnaissance purposes.

As for the directive as a whole, Clarke came away from the meeting as frustrated as ever. All the things he had recommended back in January 2001, he was to tell the Commission, were to get done—after

9/11. "I didn't really understand," he said, "why they couldn't have been done in February."

Clarke had been trying in vain, his aide Paul Kurtz recalled, to get Bush officials to "grasp the enormity of this new, transnational, networked foe . . . people thought he was hyping it up." "It sounds terrible," Clarke's then-deputy Roger Cressey recalled, "but we used to say to each other that some people didn't get it—it was going to take body bags."

Hours before the September 4 meeting, Clarke had sent National Security Adviser Rice a strongly worded note, with several passages underlined. The real question before the participants that day, he wrote, was: "Are we serious about dealing with the al Qaeda threat? . . . Is al Qaeda a big deal? . . . Decision makers should imagine themselves on a future day when the CSG [Counterterrorism Security Group] has not succeeded in stopping al Qaeda attacks and hundreds of Americans lay dead in several countries, including the U.S. . . . What would those decision makers wish that they had done earlier? That future day could happen at any time . . . You are left waiting for the big attack, with lots of casualties."

September 4 ended with the Presidential Directive approved subject to just a few final adjustments by the Deputies Committee. It would be ready for the president's signature—soon.

A THOUSAND MILES to the south, Atta found time for a matter of financial integrity. He told Binalshibh on September 5 that he and his men had money left over. Since they would soon have no further need of it, it should be reimbursed. For the hijackers, FBI investigators were to conclude, not to have returned remaining funds would have been to die as thieves.

In dribs and drabs over the next few days, by Western Union, bank transfer, and express mail, the terrorist team arranged for some $36,000 to be sent to the accomplice in Dubai who had been handling funds. The entire 9/11 operation, the Commission was to calculate, cost al Qaeda and Osama bin Laden less than $500,000.

Across the world, accomplices and men with guilty knowledge were by now running for safety. The "brothers," as Binalshibh put it later, "were dispersed." He himself flew from Germany to Spain, was met by a Saudi who furnished him with a phony passport, then took off on an airborne marathon that took him via Greece, the United Arab Emirates, and Egypt to Pakistan.

Soon after he arrived, Binalshibh would tell his interrogators, a messenger set off overland with a status report for the leadership in Afghanistan. "The message was great news for Sheikh Abu Abdallah," Binalshibh said, using one of the many names followers used for bin Laden. "May Allah protect him."

ACCORDING TO a British government source, communications intercepts at this time picked up messages between bin Laden and senior comrades. One of them, probably a contact with KSM in Pakistan, "referred to an incident that would take place in America on or around September 11"—and the repercussions that might follow.

Egyptian intelligence, with its penetration agent inside al Qaeda, received and passed on "information about some people planning an operation in the United States." "It was one week before," recalled President Mubarak. "The wheels were going."

On September 6, oblivious to such specifics, former senator Gary Hart attended a meeting at the White House. Having tried in vain in January to get the Bush administration to pay real attention to the warnings of the Commission on National Security he had cochaired, he had begun to think there was movement at last.

President Bush had said in the spring that he was establishing a new office, supervised by Vice President Cheney and devoted to "preparedness" for all forms of terrorist strikes on American soil. He himself, the President said, would periodically chair meetings to review the office's work. That had not happened, but now here was Hart at the White House in early September, offering his commission's expertise to help with the project. Rice, he was to recall, merely "said she would pass on the message."

Their vacations over, President Bush and CIA director Tenet met six times in the first eight days of September. It is not known what they discussed.

AT AN FBI OFFICE in New York, meanwhile, the lone FBI agent charged with looking for Hazmi and Mihdhar was just getting started. Agent Robert Fuller had not been instructed that the matter was especially urgent, nor that the two men posed a serious threat. On a request form he sent to another agency about Mihdhar, he did not even tick the box to indicate that the subject was wanted in connection with "security/terrorism."

He did put out some tentative feelers. Mihdhar had written on his most recent immigration form that he planned to stay at a Marriott hotel in New York City. Unsurprisingly, checks showed that no one with his name had registered at any of the six local Marriotts.

Mihdhar and Hazmi had both used their own names while in the States, and several commonly used databases might well have thrown up information on them. By his own account, Fuller did check the National Crime Information Center, the NCIC, credit and motor vehicle records, and—with a colleague's help—the ChoicePoint service. Whether he in fact trawled all those sources, though, has been questioned.

While Mihdhar had been out of the country for much of the past year, Hazmi had for months been on the East Coast. Had the hunt for him been treated seriously—had his case been given the priority of, say, the search for a wanted bank robber—tracking him would not have been a hopeless quest. Three days before Agent Fuller received his assignment, Hazmi had come to the notice of a traffic policeman while driving a rental car in Totowa, New Jersey. The patrolman had reportedly taken down the license plate and entered it as a matter of routine in the NCIC.

As reported earlier in these pages, moreover, Hazmi had also featured in three other traffic episodes: another recent "query" by police in Hackensack, New Jersey, a collision outside New York City, and a speeding ticket in Oklahoma. He had even filed a police report in Washington, D.C, using his own name, complaining of having been mugged. One or more of this total of five incidents ought to have made it to the NCIC.

All that aside, Hazmi and Mihdhar had for more than eighteen months lived in the United States—in plain sight—leaving a trail of credit card, bank account, telephone, and accommodations records behind them. Yet Agent Fuller turned up nothing on them. Having made a start on September 5, it appears that he then let the matter drop—until the day before the attacks.

• • •

WITH U.S. INTELLIGENCE and law enforcement in a state of paralysis, the terrorists were moving into position. On September 6, if a later FBI analysis is correct, those in Florida held some sort of get-together. According to the manager and bartender at Shuckums, a sports bar in Hollywood, Atta, Shehhi, and a companion spent three hours there relaxing.

There may be truth to the story. Atta and Shehhi were in the state that day, had long been close, and may have chosen to have a last evening together. It may even be true that the man thought to have been Atta, faced with a sizable bill, declared arrogantly that he was an airline pilot and could well afford to pay.

What is less likely is that, as the press first reported, the trio all got drunk on vodka and rum—contrary to the dictates of Islam. Shehhi, known to have enjoyed a beer and knowing that he was not long for this world, may perhaps have downed spirits. For Atta to have gotten inebriated, though, would have been out of character. In a later version of the story, he merely drank cranberry juice and nibbled on chicken wings.

The following day, Friday the 7th, Atta sold his car, a 1989 Pontiac Grand Prix, for $800. Ziad Jarrah sold his, a 1990 Mitsubishi with 97,000 miles on the clock, for $700. They both then headed north, to Baltimore and Newark, respectively. Omari and Suqami, Saudis in their twenties who were to fly with Atta aboard American 11, had arrived earlier at a hotel in Boston. They seized a last opportunity to dally with earthly pleasures.

According to an FBI report, the Sweet Temptations escort agency supplied the two young men with prostitutes that night. Two days later, according to the person who drove her, a woman from another Boston escort service—it advertised escorts for "the most important occasion"—visited one of the terrorists twice in a single day. Four of the men reportedly wanted to indulge, but decided the price for the service—$100 apiece—was too high. One man made do with a pornographic video piped into his hotel room. Another, in New Jersey, paid a dancer $20 to dance for him in a go-go bar.

By early on the 9th, all but one of the terrorists were in hotels in or near Boston, Washington, and New York. Only Marwan al-Shehhi, who had probably helped manage the movement north, remained at the Panther Motel near Fort Lauderdale. Then he in turn flew up to Boston, where two of the hijack crews were gathered. The Panther was a mom-and-pop operation, and owners Richard and Diane Surma themselves cleared up the room Shehhi and his comrades had used.

In the drawer of a dresser, they found a box cutter. In the garbage, there was a tote bag from a flight school containing a German-English dictionary, three martial arts books, Boeing 757 manuals, an eight-inch-thick stack of aeronautical charts, and a protractor. There was also a syringe with an extraordinarily long needle. The Surmas puzzled over these items, then put them aside.

The previous night, on I-95 in Maryland, a state trooper had stopped a man driving at ninety miles per hour. It was Ziad Jarrah in a rental car heading toward Newark, New Jersey, where his hijack crew was billeted. The officer noted that he seemed calm and cooperative, gave him a speeding ticket, and let him go.

Jarrah had his family on his mind, as well as his lover, Aysel Sengün. In the past week alone, he had called his family in Lebanon nine times and Aysel three. There were family matters to discuss with his father. Money his father had recently sent him, $2,000 "for his aeronautical studies," had arrived safely. Having failed to get back to Lebanon for the recent wedding of one of his sisters, he said, he intended to be home for another family wedding in just two weeks' time. He would definitely be there, he promised, with Aysel at his side. He had even bought a new suit for the occasion.

Soon after, Jarrah prepared a package for Aysel. He enclosed his FAA Private Pilot License, his pilot logbook, a piece of paper with his own name written over and over, a postcard of a beach—and a four-page handwritten letter. Written in German interspersed with Arabic and Turkish, it read in part:

> SALAMUALYAKUM, CANIM, AYSELIM, [PEACE BE UPON YOU, MY SOUL, MY AYSEL]
> First, I want you really to believe and be very sure that I love you with all my heart . . . I love you and I will love you for all eternity; my love, my life, my love, my soul, my heart—are you my heart? I do not want you to be sad. I am still alive somewhere else where you cannot see and hear me, but I will see you . . . I will wait for you until you come to me. There comes a time for everyone to make a move. I am to blame for giving you so many hopes about marriage, wedding, children, family . . . I did not flee from you, but did what I was supposed to do. You ought to

بسم الله الرحمن الرحيم

Salamualyokum Ganim Ayselim

Aller erstens ich will, daß Du ganz fest glaubst, und ganz

sicher gehst, daß ich Dich vom ganzen Herzen liebe.

Du darfst keinen Zweifel daran haben. Ich liebe Dich

und ich werde Dich Immer lieben bis zur Ewigkeit;

Habibi, Hayatim, Askim, Ganim, Albi; inte Habibi?

ich will nicht, daß Du traurig wirst, ich lebe noch

ich bin deinen Prinz und Ich werde Dich

Abholen

Auf wiedersehen !!

Deinen mann für immer

Ziad Jarrah

10-9-2001

Hijacker Jarrah's farewell letter to his lover—he misaddressed it.

be very proud of it, because it is an honor and you will see the outcome and everybody will be glad . . . Until we meet again, and then we'll have a beautiful eternal life, where there are no problems and no sorrow, in palaces of gold and silver . . . I thank you and apologize for the wonderful, hard five years that you have spent with me.

Your patience will be rewarded in Paradise, God willing.
I am your prince and I will come for you.
Goodbye!
Your husband for ever,
Ziad Jarrah

The letter did not reach Aysel but was returned through the mail, for Jarrah had misaddressed this last sad letter of his short life. It wound up in the hands of the FBI, and she would be told of it only months later. For a while she would hope against hope that Ziad might still be alive, had not after all died on 9/11 and would turn up at her door as he had in the past—with gifts and an apologetic grin.

A packet Khalid al-Mihdhar had hoped would reach his wife, Hoda, in Yemen had also ended up with the FBI. A letter in it, sent with a bank card for an account containing some $10,000, expressed his love for her and their daughter and his desire for her to have the money.

Atta had told the hijackers not to contact their families. He himself, though, apparently placed a call to his father in Cairo on September 9.

In Afghanistan, Osama bin Laden and KSM were taking precautions. KSM crossed over into Pakistan. Bin Laden ordered some followers to disperse, others to stay on high alert. His son Omar had left Afghanistan for good months earlier, disillusioned and following a further warning by the jihadi he trusted that the "big plan" was ongoing, that it was time for him to be "far, far away." Omar had urged his mother, Najwa, the wife who had borne bin Laden eleven children, to leave as well. "My mother," he had urged her, "come back to real life."

Najwa asked her husband for permission to leave, and he agreed on one condition. She was to leave behind several of their sons and daughters, the youngest aged only eight and eleven. On the morning she left, she gave her husband a ring as a remembrance of their long life together. Then, with her two youngest children and a twenty-three-year-old son who was mildly retarded, she climbed into a vehicle to be driven to the border and safety.

Najwa and Osama had been together for almost thirty years, since they were children. Then, he had been the "soft-spoken, serious boy" not yet in his teens. Now, at forty-four, he was the most wanted man in the world, accused of multiple mass murders.

On her way out of Afghanistan, Najwa has said, she prayed for peace.

PART VI

TWENTY-FOUR HOURS

TWENTY-NINE

SEPTEMBER 10, LESS THAN TWENTY-FOUR HOURS BEFORE THE ON-slaught.

In New York, after five days of inaction on the case, the FBI began again the leisurely search for Hazmi and Mihdhar. Having failed to find Mihdhar at any Marriott hotel in Manhattan, Agent Fuller now hoped to find a trace of them in Los Angeles. Both men, immigration records showed, had said when they first arrived eighteen months earlier that they planned to stay at a "Sheraton hotel" in the city. Checking records in Los Angeles was a job for the local field office, so Agent Fuller wrote up a routine request.

The request was not sent, merely drafted, to be transmitted only the following day—September 11. Had anyone looked, and looked in a timely fashion, Hazmi and Mihdhar had left tracks all over the place in California. There was Hazmi's name, address, and phone number of the day, bold as brass in the 2000–2001 Pacific Bell White Pages directory for San Diego. Better yet, there were their names on bank records, driver's license and car registration records, which could have enabled investigators to leapfrog onto traffic police records in New Jersey and elsewhere—even to the purchase of tickets for the flight they were soon to hijack.

But these are "what ifs." The hunt for the two terrorists, if it can be described as a hunt, was all too little too late. So it went, too, with the great lead the FBI had been handed almost a month before in Minneapolis, with the detention of Zacarias Moussaoui, a flight student who—the information they learned led them to believe—might be planning to hijack a Boeing jumbo jet. By September 10, local case agents had been begging headquarters, again and again over a period of three weeks, for clearance to search the prisoner's belongings. Only to be blocked by headquarters, time and time again, with legal quibbles.

By mid-afternoon on the 10th, in deep despond, the Minneapolis agent running the case in Minneapolis, Harry Samit, shared his feelings about the deadlock with a headquarters official who had shown herself to be sympathetic to his appeals for action. It could even become necessary, he wrote in an email, to set Moussaoui free. The official, Catherine Kiser, emailed back:

> HARRY,
> Thanks for the update. Very sorry that this matter was handled the way it was, but you fought the good fight. God Help us all if the next terrorist incident involves the same type of plane.
> take care,
> Cathy

Permission to search Moussaoui's possessions was to be granted only the following day, after the attacks.

It happened that on the 10th, as the Moussaoui probe ran into the ground, Attorney General Ashcroft formally turned down an FBI request for additional funding and agents to fight terrorism—even though the number of agents working on counterterrorism had not increased since 1996. The Bureau of 2001, a new FBI director was to admit months later, was a "very docile, don't-take-any-risks agency."

Warnings had meanwhile continued to reach the United States from friendly countries. Just days before the attacks, according to CNN—some weeks earlier in another account—Jordanian intelligence reported having intercepted a terrorist communication that referred to an operation code-named "al Urous al Kabir": "The Big Wedding." This was apparently code for a major attack on U.S. territory in which "aircraft would be used." France had also reportedly passed threat intelligence to the CIA.

Those in the United States still trying to get the attention of the White House included U.S. senator Dianne Feinstein, who served on two committees that dealt with terrorist issues and had gone public with her worries two months earlier. "One of the things that has begun to concern me very much," she told Wolf Blitzer on CNN, "is as to whether we really have our house in order. Intelligence staff have told me that there is a major probability of a terrorist incident within the next three months."

So concerned had Feinstein been in July that she contacted Vice President Cheney's office to urge action on restructuring the counterterrorism effort. On September 10, she tried again. "Despite repeated efforts by myself and staff," she recalled, "the White House did not address my request. I followed this up . . . and was told by Scooter Libby [then Cheney's chief of staff] that it might be another six months before he would be able to review the material. I did not believe we had six months to wait."

Just overnight, savage news had come out of Afghanistan. The most formidable Afghan military foe of the Taliban—and of Osama bin Laden—Ahmed Shah Massoud, had been assassinated. The killers had posed as Arab television journalists, then detonated a bomb in the camera as the interview began. The "journalists' " request to see Massoud, it would later be established, had been written on a computer bin Laden's people used.

No one doubts that bin Laden ordered the Massoud hit—the widow of one of the assassins was later told as much. Doing away with Massoud, bin Laden well knew, was more than a favor to the Taliban. Were the imminent attack in the United States to succeed, the murder of Massoud would deprive America of its most effective military ally in any attempt to retaliate.

Massoud dead. Massoud, who just months ago had warned CIA agents in private that something was afoot, who had publicly declared, "If President Bush doesn't help us, then these terrorists will damage the United States and Europe very soon, and it will be too late."

People with specialist knowledge in America saw the turn things were taking. The legendary counterterrorism chief at the FBI's New

York office, John O'Neill, had warned publicly long ago that religious extremists' capacity and will to strike on American soil was growing. In mid-August, frustrated and exhausted after heading the probe into the bombing of the USS *Cole*, he had resigned from the Bureau after thirty years' service—to become head of security at the World Trade Center.

On the night of September 10, having just moved into his new office in the North Tower, O'Neill told a colleague, "We're due for something big. I don't like the way things are lining up in Afghanistan." He was to die the following morning, assisting in the evacuation of the South Tower.

In Russia, President Vladimir Putin was jolted by the news of Massoud's murder. "I am very worried," he told President Bush in a personal phone call on the 10th. "It makes me think something big is going to happen. They're getting ready to act."

The chief of the CIA's bin Laden unit had learned of the assassination within hours in a call from one of Massoud's aides. CIA officials discussed the development with Bush on the morning of the 10th during his daily briefing, and analyzed the implications. In his 2010 memoir, however, the former President refers neither to the Putin call, nor to the Agency briefing, nor to how he himself reacted to Massoud's murder at the time.

That day at the White House, at long last, the Deputies Committee tinkered with the Presidential Directive one last time and finalized the plan to eliminate bin Laden and his terrorists over the next three years. The directive, White House chief of staff Andy Card was to say, was "literally headed for the President's desk. I think, on the 10th or 11th of September." Condoleezza Rice was to tell Bob Woodward she thought the timing "a little eerie."

For Bush, September 10 was a day filled largely by meetings with the prime minister of Australia. Then, in early afternoon, he boarded a helicopter at the Pentagon to head for Air Force One and the journey to Florida to publicize his campaign for child literacy. By early evening he was settling in at the Colony Beach and Tennis Resort on Longboat Key, near Sarasota—the ocean to one side, a perfectly groomed golf course to the other. Bush enjoyed a relaxed evening, dined Tex-Mex, on chili con queso, with his brother Jeb and other Republican officials, and went to bed at 10:00.

The President's public appearance the next morning—reading

with second graders at Emma E. Booker Elementary—was, in White House schedulers' parlance, to be a "soft event."

At the National Security Agency outside Washington that evening—as yet untranslated—were the texts of two messages intercepted in recent hours between pay phones in Afghanistan and individuals in Saudi Arabia.

The intercepts would not be translated until the following day. Analysts would realize then that a part of the first of the intercepts translated as: "Tomorrow is zero hour."

The second contained the statement: "The match begins tomorrow."

To SOME INTIMATES of the terrorists, the event that was coming was no secret. On the morning of the 10th in California—around noon East Coast time—a group of Arabs gathered at the San Diego gas station where Nawaf al-Hazmi had worked for a while the previous year. It was rare for them to get together in the morning, but six did that day. One, according to a witness interviewed by the FBI, was Mohdar Abdullah, the friend who had helped Hazmi settle in the previous year. The mood was "somewhat celebratory," and the men gave each other high fives. "It is," the witness remembered Abdullah saying, "finally going to happen."

Just outside Washington that afternoon, Hazmi and Mihdhar and the other members of their unit checked into a hotel near Dulles Airport. In and around Boston and Newark, most of their accomplices were in position at their various hotels. In the afternoon, however, the remaining two terrorists—Atta and Abdul Aziz al-Omari—took a car journey north.

They drove from Boston to Portland, Maine, a distance of more than a hundred miles, then checked into a Comfort Inn near the airport. Security camera tapes retrieved later would show that they withdrew a little money from ATMs, and stopped at a gas station and a Walmart—a witness recalled having seen Atta looking at shirts in the men's department. They had bought a takeout dinner at a Pizza Hut—the pizza boxes, removed from their room the next morning by a maid, would be found in the Dumpster behind the hotel.

Phone records established that Atta made and received a number of telephone calls while in Portland. He called Shehhi's mobile phone from a pay phone at the Pizza Hut, and ten minutes later called Jarrah at his hotel. The terrorists' emir was apparently busy organizing to the last, checking that everyone was in place.

Why, though, did Atta go to Portland at all? Neither the 9/11 Commission nor anyone else has ever located evidence that would explain that last-minute journey. Of various hypotheses, two in particular got the authors' attention. Former Commission staff member Miles Kara, who has continued over the years to study the hijackers' plan of attack, suggests Atta may have seen the diversion to Portland as his Plan B. Were other hijackers due to leave from Boston stopped for some reason, he and Omari—arriving seemingly independently from Portland—might still succeed alone.

An alternative speculation—made by Mike Rolince, a former FBI assistant director who specialized in counterterrorism—is that Atta went to Portland to meet with someone. But with whom? What could possibly have made the time-consuming diversion necessary on the very eve of the 9/11 operation?

Whatever the reason for the Portland trip, it was a risky expedition. The flight Atta and Omari were to take in the morning, to get back to Boston's Logan Airport in time for the American Airlines flight they were to hijack, involved a tight connection. Had their plane been just a little late, the leader of the 9/11 gang—the man from whom the others all took their lead—would have blown the plan at the last moment. Portland must have been important.

In Boston, meanwhile, solemn ritual had been under way behind the door of Room 241 of the Days Inn on Soldiers Field Road. It was the ritual called for in the hijackers' "spiritual manual," copies of which were to be recovered in Atta's baggage, Hamzi's car, and—a partial copy—in the wreckage in Pennsylvania.

A maid admitted to clean the room "noticed large amounts of water and body hair on the floor . . . all body lotion provided for the room had been used. . . . Room occupants [had] slept on top of the bed sheets and placed light silk cloth over the pillows." In the final hours, there was also a great deal of praying to be done.

Pray, remain awake, renew "the mutual pledge to die," think about God's blessing—"especially for the martyrs." Spit on the suitcase, the clothing—the knife. Then, moving through the phases as instructed, prayers on the way to the airport, avoiding any sign of confusion at the airport. Prayers and more prayers.

"Smile in the face of death, young man, for you will soon enter the eternal abode." Ramzi Binalshibh was to say that, shortly before the end, Atta told him with assurance that their next meeting would be, "God willing, in Paradise." Binalshibh responded with a request to Atta. "I asked him [that] if he was to see the Prophet Mohammed, peace be upon Him, and reach the highest place in Heaven, he should convey our *salaam* to Him."

Atta promised he would do so, then shared something his comrade Marwan al-Shehhi had told him:

"Marwan had a beautiful dream, that he was flying high in the sky surrounded by green birds not from our world, that he was crashing into things, and that he felt so happy."

Green birds. In a passage in the Qur'an, it is said that in Paradise people "will wear green garments of fine silk." Green is said to have been the Prophet Mohammed's favorite color. During the Crusades, to distinguish themselves from the Christians, Arab soldiers wore green into battle.

SEPTEMBER 11,

the way Ramzi Binalshibh would remember that morning:

When the news started and we heard the news of the collision of the first aircraft, as it was wrecking the World Trade Center, guided by our brother Mohamed Atta—may Allah have mercy on his soul—the brothers shouted "Takbir!"—"Allah is Greatest!" . . . And they prostrated themselves to Allah in gratitude and they wept.

The brothers thought that this was the one and only part of the operation, so we said to them, "Patience, patience!" And suddenly our brother Marwan was wrecking the southern tower of the World Trade Center in a very fierce manner. I mean, in an unimaginable way we were witnessing live on air. We were saying, "Oh, Allah, show us the right way, show the right way" . . . So the brothers prostrated themselves in thanks to Allah . . . and they sometimes wept for joy and at other times from sadness for their brothers. . . .

They thought it was over. We said to them, "Follow the news. The matter is not over yet. Make prayers for your brothers. Pray for them . . ." Imagine! Within forty-five minutes, in the space of this record time, the [third] aircraft was wrecking the Pentagon building, the building of the American Defense Ministry. The aircraft was guided by our brother Hani Hanjour. . . . The joy was tremendous. . . .

Then came the news of the aircraft which was flown by our brother Ziad Jarrah, which was downed in the suburbs of the capital, Washington. At this the brothers shouted "Allah is Greatest!" and they prostrated themselves and embraced. . . .

It was a sign from Allah for the whole world to see. . . . Allah the Almighty says: "Did they not travel through the earth and see the end of those before them who did evil. Allah brought utter destruction on them, and similar fates await those who reject Allah." [Qur'an, Surah 47, Verse 10]. The divine intervention was without a doubt very clear and palpable. . . . Praise and gratitude be to Allah!

The blessed day of Tuesday, 11 September in Washington and New York was one of the glorious days of the Muslims . . . it represents a calamitous defeat for the greatest power on earth, America . . . a fatal blow in her heart, which is filled with animosity and hatred for Islam. . . . Allah the Almighty has decided to inflict upon her a punishment—to be executed by the hands of this group of believing mujahideen, whom Allah has chosen and ordained for this mighty task. Praise and glory be to Him!

PART VII

UNANSWERED QUESTIONS

THE STORY OF SEPTEMBER 11, 2001—THAT OF THE VICTIMS AND OF the terrorists—is told. The identity of the perpetrators is not in doubt. As told in these pages, the essential elements are as described in the conclusions of the two official inquiries.

There are two areas, though, on which the 9/11 Commission fudged or dodged the issue: the full truth about U.S. and Western intelligence before the attacks; and whether the terrorist operation ten years ago had the support of other nation-states or of powerful individuals within those nation-states. There remain multiple and serious questions and yawning gaps in our knowledge of which the public knows little or nothing.

A case in point, one that we include because it is not covered at all in the Commission Report—and because our interviews indicate that there may possibly be some substance to it—is a report that surfaced seven weeks after the attacks in the leading French newspaper *Le Figaro*. It was carried by major news agencies and newspapers, denied by the CIA, then forgotten. If the *Le Figaro* story was correct, U.S. intelligence officials had had a face-to-face meeting with Osama bin Laden in early July 2001, sitting down with a deadly foe, a man wanted for the mass murder of Americans.

According to the report, bin Laden that month traveled secretly from Pakistan to Dubai in the United Arab Emirates, a destination that until 9/11 remained relatively friendly territory for him. He spent several days there reportedly, in private accommodations at the prestigious American Hospital. The ostensible reason for the visit was to undergo medical tests related to his kidney function, long said to have caused him problems. Such tests may have been conducted, but the claim is that he also agreed to meet with a locally based CIA agent and—reportedly—a second official sent in from Washington.

The reporter who originated the story, Alexandra Richard, told the authors that she happened on the story during a visit to the Gulf weeks before 9/11. Checks she made in Dubai, with a senior administrator at the American Hospital, with an airport operative at the point of origin of bin Laden's alleged journey—Quetta in Pakistan—and with a diplomatic contact she consulted, convinced her that the episode did occur.

The then–head of urology at the hospital, Dr. Terry Callaway, declined to respond to reporter Richard's questions. Hospital director Bernard Koval was reported as having flatly denied the story.

The authors, however, spoke with Richard's original source, who said he spoke from firsthand knowledge. The source said he had been present when the local CIA officer involved in the meeting—who, the witnesses interviewed have said, went by the name Larry Mitchell—spoke of the bin Laden visit while out for a social evening with friends. That a professional could have been so loose-lipped seems extraordinary, if not entirely unlikely. It remains conceivable, though, that the bin Laden visit to Dubai did occur. A second kidney specialist, an official source told the authors, described the visit independently, in detail, and at the time. The specialist was able to do so because he, too, was flown to Dubai to contribute to bin Laden's treatment.

Seeming corroboration of the CIA–bin Laden meeting, meanwhile, came to the authors in a 2009 interview with the official who headed the Security Intelligence department of France's DGSE, Alain Chouet, who is cited elsewhere in this book.

Did Chouet credit the account of the contact in Dubai? He replied, "Yes."

Did the DGSE have knowledge at the time that CIA officers met with bin Laden? "Yes," Chouet said. "Before 9/11," Chouet observed. "It was not a scoop for us—we weren't surprised [to learn of it]. We did not consider it something abnormal or outrageous. When someone is threatening you, you try to negotiate. Our own service does it all the time. It is the sort of thing we are paid to do."

The Dubai episode, Chouet noted, would have occurred "at the time of the Berlin negotiations—through interested parties—between the U.S. and the Taliban. The U.S. was trying to send messages to the Taliban. We didn't know whether [the meeting with bin Laden] was to threaten or to make a deal."

There were contacts with the Taliban through intermediaries that July, the latest stage in a long series of approaches. At initial meetings in Europe organized by the United Nations, American emissaries—not speaking officially for the U.S. government—had suggested the possibility of improved relations, cooperation on a strategically important oil pipeline project, and long-term assistance. They had also urged the Taliban to hand over bin Laden.

According to the *Le Figaro* report, the Dubai contact between bin Laden and U.S. intelligence occurred between July 4 and 14. The final contact, DGSE's Chouet believes, was on the 13th. According to Chouet, the United States had a twofold approach. At the discussions in Germany, negotiators would both attempt to cool down relations between Washington and the Taliban and ask for the handover of bin Laden. The contact in Dubai, Chouet surmises, was arranged through Saudi Arabia's intelligence chief, Prince Turki—whose agency had handled bin Laden during the anti-Soviet war in the 1980s.

The hope, Chouet said, was to persuade bin Laden "not to oppose the negotiations in Berlin, and above all to leave Afghanistan and return to Saudi Arabia with a royal pardon—under Turki's guarantee and control. In exchange, the U.S. would drop efforts to bring him to justice for the attacks in Nairobi and Dar es Salaam and elsewhere in Arabia."

Chouet believes the overtures to bin Laden were bluntly rebuffed. At the forthcoming U.N.-sponsored meetings in Berlin, between July 17 and 21, former U.S. diplomat Tom Simons pressed even harder for the handover of bin Laden. Should he not be handed over, and should solid evidence establish that the terrorist leader had indeed been behind the attack on the USS *Cole*, he indicated, the United States could be expected to take military action.

If that was the threat, nothing came of it. After the 9/11 attacks in early fall, of course, there would be no more serious discussion. The Taliban did not give up bin Laden, and were rapidly ousted.

There is nothing in the 9/11 Commission Report about a July meeting with bin Laden in Dubai, but there is what may conceivably be a small clue. At a May 29 meeting with CIA officials, the report notes, National Security Adviser Rice had asked "whether any approach could be made to influence bin Laden."

The genesis of these straws in the historical wind about a purported meeting between CIA officers and bin Laden in summer 2001 may have been disinformation spread for some political purpose. The 9/11 Commission, though, should have investigated the matter and been seen to have done so.

OTHER PUZZLES remain, some of them with serious implications, as to what Western intelligence services knew about the hijackers before 9/11.

Very soon after 9/11, major newspapers on both sides of the Atlantic ran stories stating that Western intelligence had known about Mohamed Atta for some time. The *Chicago Tribune* reported as early as September 16 that Atta had been "on a government watchlist of suspected terrorists." Kate Connolly, a reporter for the British newspaper *The Guardian*, vividly recalls being told by German officials that operatives "had been trailing Atta for some time, and keeping an eye on the house he lived in on Marienstrasse."

No evidence was to emerge of Atta having been on a watchlist. It is evident, though, that both German intelligence and the CIA had long been interested not merely in Islamic extremists in Germany but—at one stage—in the men on Marienstrasse. Congress's Joint Inquiry Report aired a little of this, but the Commission Report virtually ignored the subject.

So far as can be reconstructed, the sequence of events was as follows. Well before the future terrorists rented the Marienstrasse apartment, German intelligence took an interest in two men in particular. The first was Mohammed Zammar, who seemed to be facilitating jihadi travel to Afghanistan. The name of a second man, a Hamburg businessman named Mamoun Darkazanli, came up repeatedly—especially when a card bearing his address was found in the possession of a suspect in the 1998 East Africa embassy bombings. There was intermittent physical surveillance of both men, and Zammar's telephone was tapped.

It was an incoming call, picked up by the Zammar tap in January 1999, that first drew attention to the apartment on Marienstrasse. A German intelligence report of the call, a copy of which is in the authors' possession, shows that the name of the person calling Zammar was "Marwan." The conversation was unexciting, an exchange about Marwan's studies and a trip Zammar had made. In a second call, a caller looking for Zammar was given the number of the Marienstrasse apartment—76 75 18 30—and the name of one of its tenants, "Mohamed Amir." On a third call, in September, Zammar sent "Mohamed Amir" his greetings.

Amir, of course, was the last name most used—prior to his departure for the United States—by the man who was to become known to the world as Mohamed Atta.

Those tapped calls are of greatest interest today in the context of the CIA's performance. The Germans reportedly thought the "Marwan" lead "particularly valuable," and passed the information about it to the CIA. The caller named "Marwan," they noted, had been speaking on a mobile phone registered in the United Arab Emirates. According to George Tenet, testifying in 2004 to the Senate Intelligence Committee, the CIA "didn't sit around" on receipt of this information, but "did some things to go find out some things."

According to security officials in the UAE, the number could have been identified in a matter of minutes. The "Marwan" on the call is believed to have been UAE citizen Marwan al-Shehhi, who in 2001 was to fly United 175 into the World Trade Center's South Tower. Was Shehhi's mobile phone ever monitored by the CIA? Queried on the subject in 2004, U.S. intelligence officials said they were "uncertain."

The CIA on the ground in Germany did evince major interest in the Hamburg coterie of Islamic extremists. In late 1999, an American official who went by the name of Thomas Volz turned up at the office of the Hamburg state intelligence service—the Landesamt für Verfassungsschutz—with a pressing request.

Though he used the cover of a diplomatic post, Volz was a CIA agent. The Agency believed that Mamoun Darkazanli "had knowledge of an unspecified terrorist plot." Volz's hope, he explained, was that the suspect could be "turned," persuaded to become an informant and pass on information about al Qaeda activities.

The Germans doubted that Darkazanli could be induced to do any such thing. They tried all the same, and failed. Volz, however, repeatedly insisted they try again. So persistent was he, reportedly, that the CIA's man eventually tried approaching Darkazanli on his own initiative. To German intelligence officials, this was an outrageous intrusion, a violation of Germany's sovereignty.

All this at the very time, and soon after, that Atta and his comrades—whom Darkazanli knew well—had traveled to Afghanistan, sworn allegiance to bin Laden, and committed to the 9/11 operation. What really came of Volz's efforts remains unknown.

The 9/11 Commission Report did not mention the Volz episode. The public remains uninformed, moreover, as to what U.S. intelligence may have learned of the hijackers before they left Germany and became operational in the United States.

THE LEAD on Shehhi arising from the Hamburg phone tap aside, there is information suggesting there was early U.S. interest in his accomplice Ziad Jarrah. In late January 2000, on his way back from the future hijackers' pivotal visit to Afghanistan, Jarrah was stopped for questioning while in transit at Dubai airport.

"It was at the request of the Americans," a UAE security official was to say after 9/11, "and it was specifically because of Jarrah's links with Islamic extremists, his contacts with terrorist organizations." The reason the terrorist was pulled over, reportedly, was "because his name was on a watchlist" provided by the United States.

During his interrogation, astonishingly, Jarrah coolly told his questioners that he had been in Afghanistan and now planned to go to the United States to learn to fly—and to spread the word about Islam.

While the airport interview was still under way, according to the UAE record, the Dubai officials made contact with U.S. representatives. "What happened," a UAE official elaborated in 2003, "was we called the Americans. We said, 'We have this guy. What should we do with him?' . . . their answer was, 'Let him go, we'll track him.' . . . They told us to let him go."

At the relevant date in FBI task force documents on Jarrah, and next to another entry about the terrorist's UAE stopover, an item has been redacted. The symbol beside the redaction stands for: "Foreign Government Information."

Was there also interest in Mohamed Atta before *his* arrival in the United States? Several former members of a secret operation run by the DIA, the U.S. military's Defense Intelligence Agency, went public four years after 9/11 with a disquieting claim. The names of four of the hijackers-to-be, Atta, Shehhi, Hazmi, and Mihdhar, they claimed, had appeared on the DIA's radar in early 2000, even before they arrived in the United States.

According to the lieutenant colonel who first made the claim, Anthony Shaffer, the names came up in the course of a highly classified DIA operation code-named Able Danger. He and his staff had carried out "data mining," under a round-the-clock counterterrorist program Shaffer described as the "use of high-powered software to bore into just about everything: any data that was available—and I mean anything. Open-source Internet data, e-mails believed to be terrorist-related, non-secret government data, commercial records, information on foreign companies, logs of visitors to mosques."

According to Shaffer, such data also drew on U.S. visa records. If so, and given the reference to information obtained from mosques, it would seem that Able Danger perhaps could have picked up information on the named terrorists—even before they arrived in the United States.

Atta had applied for a U.S. green card in late 1999. Shehhi had gotten his U.S. entry visa by January 2000. Hazmi and Mihdhar had arrived that same month, having applied for and obtained their visas in the summer of 1999. All these documents were in the record.

All the documentary evidence involved, however, was destroyed well before 9/11 because of privacy concerns by Defense Department attorneys. Absent a future discovery of surviving documentary evidence, the Able Danger claims depend entirely on the memories—sometimes rusty memories—of those involved in the operation.

IN GERMANY, and as an outgrowth of surveilling the extremists in Hamburg, a border watch—or Grenzfahndung—was ordered on at least two of the men who frequented the Marienstrasse apartment. The routine was not to arrest listed individuals, but discreetly to note and report their passage across the frontier. It is hard to understand why, if the names of two of the Marienstrasse group were on the list, those of Atta and Shehhi would not have been. If they were under border watch, their departure for the United States ought to have been noted.

German federal officials were unhelpful when approached by the authors for interviews on the subject of either monitoring the terrorists or on the relationship with U.S. agencies before 9/11. "Sadly," said an official from Germany's foreign intelligence service, the Bundesnachrichtendienst, "due to considerations of principle, your request cannot be granted. We ask for your understanding."

The official who was in 2001 and still is deputy chief of Hamburg domestic intelligence, Dr. Manfred Murck, was in general far more cooperative. He had no comment, however, on the subject of collaboration with U.S. intelligence.

The Islamic affairs specialist with the domestic intelligence service in Stuttgart, Dr. Herbert Müller, for his part, offered a small insight into where the Germans' monitoring of the men at Marienstrasse had led them. "Atta," he said, "was going through the focus of our colleagues. . . . He came to their notice."

Did the Germans share with the United States everything they learned about the future hijackers? "Some countries," a 9/11 Commission staff statement was to state tartly, "did not support U.S. efforts to collect intelligence information on terrorist cells in their countries. . . . This was especially true of some of the European services." Information gathered by Congress's Joint Inquiry, and what we have of a CIA review, make it clear that there was intermittent friction between the U.S. and German services.

A former senior American diplomat, on the other hand, cast no aspersions on the Germans. "My impression the entire time," former deputy head of mission in Berlin Michael Polt told the 9/11 Commission, "[was] that our level of interaction with counterterrorism and cooperation with the Germans was extremely high and well coordinated. . . . And the reason the Germans would want to share those concerns with us [was] because they were expecting from us some information that they could use to go ahead and go after these people."

For all that, German officials the authors contacted remained either evasive or diplomatic to a fault. Were they concealing the failures of their own intelligence apparatus, or courteously avoiding placing the blame on the ally across the Atlantic?

"They lied to my face for four years, the German secret service," said Dirk Laabs, a Hamburg author who has reported on the 9/11 story for the *Los Angeles Times* and the *Frankfurter Allgemeine Zeitung*. "Then I found information that they passed on everything to the CIA. . . . We only know a little bit of the true story, what really went on."

The release to the authors in 2011 of a single previously redacted sentence on a 9/11 Commission staff document makes crystal clear what was left fuzzy in the Commission Report. The document summarized the coded conversation between KSM and Binalshibh not long before the attacks—described in an earlier chapter—as to whether lovelorn Ziad Jarrah would stay the course.

The sentence that heads the document's summary of the exchange, now made public for the first time, reads:

> *On July 20, 2001, there was a call between*
> *KSM and Binalshibh. They used the codewords*
> *Teresa and Sally.*

The only way the authorities could have known of such a phone call, on a known date and in great detail, was thanks to a telephone intercept. The call was intercepted and recorded while it was in progress.

That certainty leads to a string of further questions.

Which intelligence service tapped the call? The only probable candidates are those of the United States or of Germany. If the intercept was American, which service was responsible? The CIA or the NSA—the National Security Agency? It is the NSA's mission to spy on international communications, yet its pre-9/11 performance is only minimally reported in the Commission Report.

If the intercept cited above was made in Germany by the Germans, was the take passed to the Americans at the time—or only after 9/11?

The questions do not end there. What other conversations between key 9/11 players were tapped into during the run-up to the attacks? If other conversations were captured, were they all in code that was incomprehensible at the time? Did such intercepts result in any action being taken?

A breakthrough answer on the German intelligence issue came to the authors from a very senior member of the U.S. Congress, a public figure with long experience of intelligence matters, who has held high security clearances, speaking not for attribution.

"We were told by the German intelligence," the member of Congress said of a visit to Berlin following 9/11, "that they had provided U.S. intelligence agencies with information about persons of interest to them who had been living in Hamburg and who they knew were in, or attempting to get into, the United States. The impression German intelligence gave me was that they felt the action of the U.S. intelligence agencies to their information was dismissive."

Sour grapes, or an accurate account of the American response to pertinent intelligence?

THIRTY-ONE

THE CIA CERTAINLY HAD KNOWN EARLY ON ABOUT TWO OF THE 9/11 terrorists.

The way it gained that intelligence speaks to the Agency's operational efficiency, in a brilliant operation a full twenty months before the attacks. Its subsequent performance, however, reflects disastrous inefficiency, perhaps the greatest fiasco in CIA history. Depending on how the evidence is interpreted, it points to something even more culpable.

This is a scenario that began to unravel for the CIA on 9/11 itself, just four hours after the strikes. Soon after 1:00 P.M. that day, at Agency headquarters, an aide hurried to Director Tenet with a handful of papers—the passenger manifests for the four downed airliners. "Two names," he said, placing a page on the table where the director could see it. "These two we know."

Tenet looked, then breathed, "There it is. Confirmation. Oh, Jesus . . ."

A long silence followed. There on the Flight 77 manifest, allocated to Seats 5E and 5F in First Class, were the names of Nawaf al-Hazmi and his brother Salem. Also on the list, near the front of the Coach section at 12B, was Khalid al-Mihdhar's name.

The names Hazmi and Mihdhar were instantly familiar, Tenet has claimed, because his people had learned only weeks earlier that both men might be in the United States. According to his version of events, the CIA had known of Mihdhar since as early as 1999, had identified him firmly as a terrorist suspect by December that year, had had him followed, discovered he had a valid multiple-entry visa to allow him into the States, and had placed him and comrades—including Hazmi—under surveillance for a few days. Later, in the spring of 2000, the Agency had learned that Hazmi had arrived in California.

Yet, the director had claimed in the wake of 9/11, the CIA had done absolutely nothing about Mihdhar or Hazmi. It had not asked the State Department to watchlist the two terrorists at border points, had not asked the FBI to track them down if they were in the country, until nineteen days before 9/11.

Tenet blamed these omissions solely on calamitous error.

"CIA," he wrote in 2007, "had multiple opportunities to notice the significant information in our holdings and watchlist al-Hazmi and al-Mihdhar. Unfortunately, until August, we missed them all. . . .

"Yes, people made mistakes; every human interaction was far from where it needed to be. We, the entire government, owed the families of 9/11 better than they got."

But was it just that CIA "people made mistakes"? Historical mysteries are as often explained by screwups as by darker truths. Nevertheless, senior Commission staff became less than convinced—and not just on the matter of Mihdhar and Hazmi—that Tenet was leveling with them.

When the director was interviewed, in January 2004, on oath, he kept saying "I don't remember" or "I don't recall." Those with courtroom experience among the commissioners reflected that he was "like a grand jury witness who had been too well prepared by a defense lawyer. The witness's memory was good when it was convenient, bad when it was convenient."

Executive Director Philip Zelikow was to say later of Tenet, "We just didn't believe him anymore." Tenet, for his part, declared himself outraged by the remark, and insisted that he had told the truth about everything.

What is known of the evidence on Hazmi and Mihdhar, however, makes it very hard for anyone to swallow the screwup excuse. Not least because, the CIA version of events suggests, its officials blew the chance to grab the two future hijackers not once, not twice, but time and time again.

This is a puzzle that has confounded official investigators, and reporters and authors, for a full decade now. It will not be solved in these pages, but readers may perhaps see its stark outline, its striking anomalies, its alarming possible implications, more clearly than in the past. To trace the chapter of supposed accidents we must start with a pivotal development that occurred as long as five years before 9/11.

SOMETIME IN 1996, the National Security Agency—which intercepts electronic communications worldwide—had identified a number in Yemen that Osama bin Laden called often from his satellite telephone in Afghanistan. The number, 967-1-200-578, rang at a house in the capital, Sana'a, used by a man he had first known in the days of the anti-Soviet war in Afghanistan. The man's name was Ahmed al-Hada, and—a great benefit for bin Laden, who in Afghanistan had no access to ordinary communications systems—his house had long served as an al Qaeda "hub," a link to the wider world.

The NSA did not immediately share this information either with the CIA or with other agencies—a symptom of the interagency disconnect that long plagued U.S. intelligence. The CIA did learn of the intercepts, however, and eventually obtained summaries of intercepted conversations. It was the start of a period of frustratingly sporadic, incomplete access granted by the NSA to material harvested from the hub.

Hada's telephone also came to loom large for the FBI. One of the Kenya bombers called the number before and after the 1998 attack on Nairobi, and—once agents learned that the number also took calls from bin Laden's sat-phone on the day of the bombing and the following day—they had a vital evidentiary link between the East Africa attacks and al Qaeda.

The intercepts of Hada's phone conversations were a priceless resource, and in 1999 yielded the first factual pointer to the preparations for 9/11. Hada's daughter, U.S. intelligence learned at some stage, was married to a young man named "Khalid"—full name, as we now know, Khalid al-Mihdhar. In December 1999, crucially, the NSA reported to both the CIA and the FBI that it had intercepted an especially interesting call on the Hada telephone, one that mentioned an upcoming trip by "Khalid" and "Nawaf" to Malaysia.

From the start, CIA officers guessed that this was no innocent excursion. Its purpose, one staffer suspected, was "something more nefarious." The travel, one cable stated, "may be in support of a terrorist mission." The men were referred to early on as members of an "operational cadre" or as "terrorist operatives."

The episode that was eventually to bring the Agency lasting shame began as textbook undercover work. As foreshadowed in an earlier chapter, Mihdhar's Saudi passport was photographed during the stopover in Dubai—leading to the startling revelation that the terrorist had a visa valid for travel to the United States.

As veteran FBI counterterrorism specialist Jack Cloonan was to say, "This is as good as it gets. . . . How often do you get into someone's suitcase and find multiple-entry visas? How often do you know there's going to be an organizational meeting of al Qaeda anyplace in the world? . . . This is what you would dream about."

Intelligence bounty continued to rain down on the CIA following the look inside Mihdhar's passport. The suspect was tracked as he traveled on to the Malaysian capital, Kuala Lumpur. He was watched, starting on January 5, as he met and talked with fellow suspects—including his associate Nawaf al-Hazmi. Courtesy of Malaysia's Special Branch, the men were covertly photographed, observed going out to pay phones, surveilled when they went to an Internet café to use the computers. The computers' hard drives were reportedly examined afterward.

The whirl of suspicious activity was of interest not merely to CIA agents in the field, nor only to CIA headquarters at Langley. For it all occurred in the very first days of January 2000, the post-Millennium moment when Washington was more than usually on the alert—at the highest level—for any clue that might herald a terrorist attack. Regular situation reports went day by day not only to the directors of the CIA and the FBI but also to National Security Adviser Sandy Berger and his staff, who included Richard Clarke, at the White House.

Three days later, on January 8, Mihdhar and two of his comrades—one of them later to be identified as having been Hazmi and the other as senior bin Laden henchman Tawfiq bin Attash—took the brief two-hour flight from Kuala Lumpur to the Thai capital Bang-kok. There, according to the CIA, and though communication with a Bangkok hotel was logged on one of the pay phones used by the suspects in Kuala Lumpur, the trail was lost.

Nothing would be known of the operatives' whereabouts, the available record indicates, until two months later. Only then, accord-ing to the known record, did Thai authorities respond to a January CIA request to watch for the suspects' departure. At last, however, in early March, two Agency stations abroad reported a fresh develop-ment. Their message said that Hazmi and an unnamed comrade—only later to be named as Mihdhar—had flown out of Bangkok as long ago as January 15, bound for Los Angeles. The men, the cables noted, were "UBL [bin Laden] associates."

This was stunning information, information that should have triggered an immediate response. Yet, we are asked by the CIA to believe, no one reacted. No one did anything at all. The first cable to arrive with the news was marked "Action Required: None."

This in spite of the fact that, just before the Millennium, Director Tenet had told all CIA personnel overseas, "The threat could not be more real. . . . The American people are counting on you and me to take every appropriate step to protect them."

Tenet's Counterterrorist Center had circulated an unambiguous instruction just a month before the al Qaeda meeting in Kuala Lum-pur. "It is important," the document had warned, "to flag terrorist personality information in DO [Directorate of Operations] reporting for the [State Department watchlist program] so that potential terror-ists may be watchlisted."

Yet in March 2000, although it had learned that Hazmi, a bin Laden operative, had entered the country, the CIA did not alert the State Department. Nor, back in January, had it alerted State to the fact that Mihdhar had a U.S. entry visa. The Agency was not to re-quest that either man be watchlisted until late August 2001.

While the Kuala Lumpur meeting was still under way, a 9/11 Commission document notes, top FBI officials had been told that the CIA "promised to let FBI know if an FBI angle to the case developed." The CIA is prohibited from undertaking operations in the United States, and the FBI has responsibility for domestic intelligence and law enforcement.

Even so, with the revelation that Mihdhar had a U.S. visa—very much an FBI angle—the CIA left the Bureau in the dark just as it did the State Department. It certainly should have alerted the FBI the moment it learned that Hazmi had entered the United States. Information that, if shared, may have led to an earlier hunt for Hazmi and Mihdhar.

After 9/11, when its horrendous failure to do any of these things came out, the CIA would attempt to claim that it had not been quite like that. Later investigations by Congress's Joint Inquiry and the Department of Justice's inspector general were to produce vestigial portions of emails and cables written right after the discovery that Mihdhar had a U.S. entry visa. The picture that emerged is not immediately clear.

The very day the CIA learned that Mihdhar had a U.S. visa, a CIA bin Laden unit desk officer—identified for security reasons only as "Michelle"—informed colleagues flatly that his travel documents, including the visa, had been copied and passed "to the FBI for further investigation."

In an email to CIA colleagues the following day, an Agency officer assigned to FBI headquarters—identified as "James"—wrote of having told two senior FBI agents what had been learned of Mihdhar's activity in Malaysia. He had advised one of them: "as soon as something concrete is developed leading us to the criminal area or to known FBI cases, we will immediately bring FBI into the loop."

Were one to know only that about the CIA record, it might seem that the FBI *was* given the crucial visa information. Serious doubt sets in, though, on looking at the wider picture. In an email to CIA colleagues, the Justice Department inspector general discovered, "James" had "stated that he was detailing 'exactly what [he] briefed [the FBI] on' *in the event the FBI later complained* that they were not provided with all of the information about al-Mihdhar. This information did not discuss al-Mihdhar's passport or U.S. visa [authors' italics]."

"James," the inspector general noted, refused to be interviewed.

The inspector general was given access to "Michelle," the desk officer who had written flatly that Mihdhar's passport and visa had been passed to the FBI. She prevaricated, however, saying she could not remember how she knew that fact. Her boss, Tom Wilshire, the deputy chief of the CIA's bin Laden unit, said that for his part he had no knowledge of the "Michelle" cable. He "did not know whether the information had been passed to the FBI."

Other documents indicate that the opposite was the case, that Wilshire had deliberately ensured that the information would *not* reach the FBI. This emerged with the inspector general's discovery of a draft cable—one prepared but never sent—by an FBI agent on attachment to the CIA's bin Laden unit.

Having had sight of a CIA cable noting that Mihdhar possessed a U.S. visa, Agent Doug Miller had responded swiftly by drafting a Central Intelligence Report, or CIR, addressed to the Bureau's bin Laden unit and its New York field office. Had the CIR then been sent, the FBI would have learned promptly of Mihdhar's entry visa.

As regulations required, Agent Miller first submitted the draft to CIA colleagues for clearance. Hours later, though, he received a note from "Michelle" stating: "pls hold off on CIR for now per [Wilshire]."

Perplexed and angry, Miller consulted with Mark Rossini, a fellow FBI agent who was also on attachment to the CIA unit. "Doug came to me and said, 'What the fuck?,' " Rossini recalled. "So the next day I went to [Wilshire's deputy, identity uncertain] and said, 'What's with Doug's cable? You've got to tell the Bureau about this.' She put her hand on her hip and said, 'Look, the next attack is going to happen in South East Asia—it's not the FBI's jurisdiction. When we want the FBI to know about it, we'll let them know.' "

After eight days, when clearance to send the message still had not come, Agent Miller submitted the draft again directly to CIA deputy unit chief Wilshire along with a note asking: "Is this a no go or should I remake it in some way?" According to the CIA, it was "unable to locate any response to this e-mail."

Neither Miller nor Rossini was interviewed by 9/11 Commission staff. Wilshire was questioned, the authors established, but the report of his interview is redacted in its entirety.

In July 2001, by which time he had been seconded to the FBI's bin Laden unit, Wilshire proposed to CIA colleagues that the fact that Mihdhar had a U.S. entry visa should be shared with the FBI. It never happened.

Following a subsequent series of nods and winks from Wilshire, the FBI at last discovered for itself first the fact that Mihdhar had had a U.S. entry visa in 2000, then the fact that he had just very recently returned to the country. Only after that, in late August, did the FBI begin to search for Mihdhar and Hazmi—a search that was to prove inept, lethargic, and ultimately ineffectual.

An eight-member 9/11 Commission team was to reach a damning conclusion about the cable from CIA officer "Michelle" stating that Mihdhar's travel documents had been passed to the FBI. "The weight of the evidence," they wrote, "does not support that latter assertion." The Justice Department inspector general also found, after exhaustive investigation, that the CIA had failed to share with the FBI two vital facts—"that Mihdhar had a U.S. visa and that Hazmi had travelled to Los Angeles."

In 2007, Congress forced the release of a nineteen-page summary of the CIA's own long-secret probe of its performance. This, too, acknowledged that Agency staff neither shared what they knew about Mihdhar and Hazmi nor saw to it that they were promptly watchlisted. An accountability board, the summary recommended, should review the work of named officers. George Tenet's successor as CIA director, Porter Goss, however, declined to hold such a review. There was no question of misconduct, he said. The officers named were "amongst the finest" the Agency had.

THE EXCUSE for such monstrous failures? According to the CIA's internal report, the bin Laden unit had had an "excessive workload." Director Tenet claimed in sworn testimony, not once but three times, that he knew "nobody read" the cable that reported Hazmi's actual arrival in Los Angeles. Wilshire, the officer repeatedly involved, summed up for Congress's Joint Inquiry: "All the processes that had been put in place," he said, "all the safeguards, everything else, they failed at every possible opportunity. Nothing went right."

There are those who think such excuses may be the best the CIA can offer to explain a more compromising truth. "It is clear," wrote the author Kevin Fenton, an independent researcher who completed a five-year study of the subject in 2011, "that this information was not withheld through a series of bizarre accidents, but intentionally. . . . Withholding the information about Mihdhar and Hazmi from the FBI makes sense only if the CIA was monitoring the two men in the U.S. itself."

That notion is not fantasy. The CIA's own in-house review noted that—had the FBI been told that the two future hijackers were or might be in the country—"good operational follow-through by CIA and FBI might have resulted in surveillance of both Mihdhar and

(S) Separately, in March 2000, two CIA field locations sent to a number of addressees cables reporting that al-Hazmi and another al-Qa'ida associate had traveled to the United States. They were clearly identified in the cables as "UBL associates." The Team has found no evidence, and heard no claim from any party, that this information was shared in any manner with the FBI or that anyone in UBL Station took other appropriate operational action at that time.

(C) In the months following the Malaysia operation, the CIA missed several additional opportunities to nominate al-Hazmi and al-Mihdhar for watchlisting; to inform the FBI about their intended or actual travel to the United States; and to take appropriate operational action. These included a few occasions identified by the Joint Inquiry as well as several others.

(C) The consequences of the failures to share information and perform proper operational followthrough on these terrorists were potentially significant. Earlier watchlisting of al-Mihdhar could have prevented his re-entry into the United States in July 2001. Informing the FBI and good operational followthrough by CIA and FBI might have resulted in surveillance of both al-Mihdhar and al-Hazmi. Surveillance, in turn, would have had the potential to yield information on flight training, financing, and links to others who were complicit in the 9/11 attacks.

The CIA kept to itself the fact that it knew long before 9/11 that two of the future hijackers—known to be terrorists—had U.S. visas, and that one had definitely entered the United States.

Hazmi. Surveillance, in turn, would have had the potential to yield information on flight training, financing and links to others who were complicit in the 9/11 attacks."

If the FBI had known, then–New York Assistant Special Agent in Charge Kenneth Maxwell has said, "We would have been on them like white on snow: physical surveillance, electronic surveillance, a special unit devoted to them." After 9/11, and when the CIA's omissions became known, some of Maxwell's colleagues at the FBI reacted with rage and dark suspicion.

"They purposely hid from the FBI," one official fulminated, "purposely refused to tell the FBI that they were following a man in Malaysia who had a visa to come to America. . . . And that's why September 11 happened. . . . They have blood on their hands. They have three thousand deaths on their hands."

Could it be that the CIA concealed what it knew about Mihdhar and Hazmi because officials feared that precipitate action by the FBI would blow a unique lead? Did the Agency want to arrange to monitor the pair's activity? The CIA's mandate does not allow it to run operations in the United States, but the prohibition had been broken in the past.

The CIA had on at least one occasion previously aspired to leave an Islamic suspect at large in order to surveil him. When 1993 Trade Center bomber Ramzi Yousef was located in Pakistan two years later, investigative reporter Robert Friedman wrote, the Agency "wanted to continue tracking him." It "fought with the FBI," tried to postpone his arrest. On that occasion, the FBI had its way, seized Yousef, and brought him back for trial.

With that rebuff fresh in the institutional memory, did the CIA decide to keep the sensational discovery of Mihdhar's entry visa to itself? Or did it, as some Bureau agents came to think possible, even hope to recruit the two terrorists as informants?

The speculation is not idle. A heavily redacted congressional document shows that, only weeks before Mihdhar's visa came to light, top CIA officials had debated the lamentable fact that the Agency had as yet not penetrated al Qaeda: "Without penetrations of OBL organization . . . [redacted lines] . . . we need to also recruit sources inside OBL's organization. Realize that recruiting terrorist sources is difficult . . . but we must make an attempt."

The following day, CIA officers went to the White House for a meeting with a select group of top-level National Security Council members. Attendees discussed both the lack of inside information and how essential it was to achieve "penetrations." Many "unilateral avenues" and "creative attempts" were subsequently to be tried. Material on those attempts in the document has been entirely redacted.

President Clinton himself aside, the senior White House official to whom the CIA reported at that time was National Security Adviser Sandy Berger. After 9/11, while preparing to testify before official inquiries into the attacks, Berger was to commit a crime that destroyed his shining reputation, a folly so bizarre—for a man of his stature—as to be unbelievable were it not true.

On four occasions in 2002 and 2003, Berger would make his way to the National Archives in Washington, the repository of the nation's most venerated documents—including the Declaration of Independence, the Constitution, and the Bill of Rights. This trusted official, alumnus of Cornell and Harvard, former lawyer and aide to public officials, a former deputy director of policy planning at State, had crowned his career by becoming national security adviser during President Clinton's second term.

It was at Clinton's request, and in his capacity as one of the very few people allowed access to the former administration's most secret documents, that Berger went to the Archives to review selected files. Given his seniority, he was received with special courtesy and under rather less than the usual stringent security conditions. All the more astounding then that on his third visit a staff member "saw Mr. Berger bent down, fiddling with something that could have been paper, around his ankle."

Under cover of asking for privacy to make phone calls, or in the course of uncommonly frequent visits to the lavatory, the former national security adviser was purloining top secret documents, smuggling them out of the building hidden in his clothing, and taking them home. He was caught doing so, publicly exposed, forced to resign from his senior post with the 2004 Democratic campaign for the presidency, charged with taking classified documents, and—a year later—fined $50,000 and sentenced to one hundred hours of community service.

What had possessed Berger? What seemed so compromising to himself or to the Clinton administration—or so essential to be hidden from 9/11 investigators—as to drive him to risk national disgrace?

What is known is that Berger took no fewer than five copies of the Millennium After Action Review, or MAAR, a thirteen-page set of recommendations that had been written in early 2000, focused mostly on countering al Qaeda activity inside the United States. While the MAAR is still classified, it seems somewhat unlikely that it is the item that Berger deemed potential dynamite. It may have been handwritten notes on the copies that he thought potentially explosive, former 9/11 Commission senior counsel John Farmer has surmised. That would account for the former official's apparently frantic search for additional copies.

The National Archives inspector general and others worried about what other documents Berger may have removed from the Archives. Short of a further admission on his part, the director of the Archives' presidential documents staff conceded, we shall never know. Whatever he took, Farmer pointed out, it made him appear "desperate to prevent the public from seeing certain papers."

"What information could be so embarrassing," House Speaker Dennis Hastert asked, "that a man with decades of experience in handling classified documents would risk being caught pilfering our nation's most sensitive secrets? . . . Was this a bungled attempt to rewrite history and keep critical information from the 9/11 Commission?"

The question is all the more relevant when one notes that, so far as one can tell, Berger's focus was on the period right after the CIA's resolve to "penetrate" bin Laden's terrorist apparatus, or "recruit" inside it, an aspiration followed in rapid order by the discovery of Khalid al-Mihdhar's U.S. entry visa—and the highly suspect failure to share that information with the State Department and the FBI.

THOUGH FRAGMENTARY, there are pointers suggesting that the CIA did not promptly drop its coverage of Mihdhar. On January 5, 2000—the day of the discovery of Mihdhar's visa, and in the same cable that claimed the FBI had been notified—desk officer "Michelle" noted that "we need to continue the effort to identify these travelers and their activities." As late as February, moreover, a CIA message noted that the Agency was still engaged in an investigation "to determine what the subject is up to."

Mihdhar was to tell KSM, according to the CIA account of KSM's interrogation, that he and Hazmi "believed they were surveilled from

Thailand to the U.S." KSM seems to have taken this possibility seriously—sufficiently so, the CIA summary continues, that he "began having doubts whether the two would be able to fulfil their mission." Later, in 2001, two other members of the hijack team sent word that they thought they, too, had been tailed on a journey within the United States.

The hijackers may have imagined they were being followed. Given their mission, it would have been a natural enough fear. There is another relevant lead, though, that has more substance.

In the early afternoon of September 11, the senior aide to Defense Secretary Rumsfeld penned a very curious handwritten note. Written by Deputy Under Secretary Stephen Cambone at 2:40 P.M., following a phone call between Rumsfeld and Tenet, it appears in a record of the day's events that was obtained in 2006 under the Freedom of Information Act.

The note reads:

AA 77—3 indiv have been followed since Millennium & Cole
1 guy is assoc of Cole bomber
3 entered US in early July
(2 of 3 pulled aside and interrogated?)

Though somewhat garbled, probably due to the rush of events in those hectic hours, the details more or less fit. Mihdhar, Hazmi, and Hazmi's brother were hijackers aboard American Flight 77, the airliner that was flown into the Pentagon. Mihdhar had been an associate of USS *Cole* planner Attash, the most significant of the fellow terrorists with whom he met in Kuala Lumpur. Mihdhar, certainly, had entered the United States—for the second time, after months back in the Middle East—in "early July," on July 4.

Cambone's note on three individuals having "been followed" could be interpreted in two ways. Had Tenet meant during his conversation with Secretary Rumsfeld merely to convey the fact that three of the terrorists had at an earlier point *come to the notice* of the intelligence community? Or had he—conceivably—meant what the note says he said, that the terrorists' movements had indeed been monitored?

Was it Tenet's knowledge of some intelligence operation that had targeted Mihdhar and Hazmi—whether in the shape of monitoring them or attempting to recruit them—that led to the director's flash of

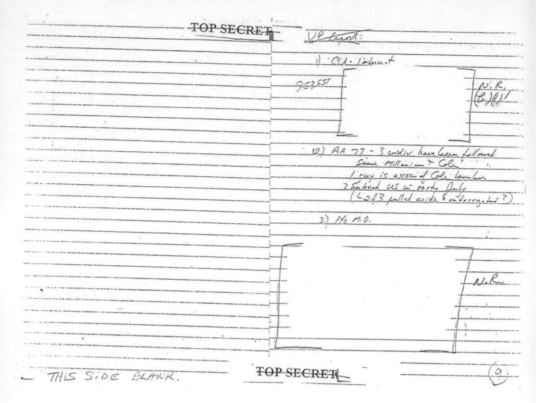

recognition and his "Oh, Jesus" exclamation on seeing their names on the Flight 77 manifest?

If an operation had been attempted, contrary to the rules that govern CIA activities, to whom was it entrusted? To try to answer that question is to fumble in the dark. There are pointers, though, in the evidence as to whether any foreign nation-state—other than Afghanistan, where the Taliban played host to bin Laden—had responsibility at any level for the 9/11 attacks.

THIRTY-TWO

A QUESTION THE 9/11 COMMISSION SOUGHT TO ANSWER, ITS CHAIRmen Thomas Kean and Lee Hamilton recalled, was "Had the hijackers received any support from foreign governments?"

"The terrorists do not function in a vacuum," Defense Secretary Donald Rumsfeld had told reporters the week after 9/11. They "live and work and function and are fostered and financed and encouraged, if not just tolerated, by a series of countries. . . . I know a lot, and what I have said, as clearly as I know how, is that states are supporting these people." Pressed to elaborate, Rumsfeld was silent for a long moment. Then, saying it was "a sensitive matter," he changed the subject.

Three years later, the 9/11 Commission would consider whether any of three foreign countries in particular might have had a role in 9/11. Two were self-avowed foes of the United States—Iran and Iraq. The third was the country long since billed—by both sides—as a close friend of the United States, Saudi Arabia.

Iran, the Commission found, had long had contacts with al Qaeda and had allowed its operatives—including a number of the future hijackers—to travel freely through its airports. The Commission Report, however, said there was no evidence that Iran "was aware of the planning for what later became the 9/11 attack." The commissioners urged the government to investigate further.

There is nothing to indicate that federal agencies have probed further. In late May 2011, however, it was reported that a suit filed by lawyers for bereaved U.S. family members would include revealing testimony from three Iranian defectors. Former senior Commission counsel Dietrich Snell was quoted as saying in an affidavit that there was now "convincing evidence the government of Iran provided material support to al Qaeda in the planning and execution of the 9/11 attack." As this book went to press, however, the evidence could not be evaluated. It had yet to surface, and the three defectors who had testified remained unidentified.

The 9/11 commissioners had stated, meanwhile, that they had seen no "evidence indicating that Iraq cooperated with al Qaeda in developing or carrying out any attacks against the United States."

By contrast, there was no finding in the 9/11 Commission Report that categorically exonerated America's "friend" Saudi Arabia—or individuals in Saudi Arabia—from all involvement in the 9/11 plot. The decision as to what to say about Saudi Arabia in the Report had been made amid discord and tension.

Investigators who had probed the Saudi angle believed their work demonstrated a close link between hijackers Mihdhar and Hazmi and the Saudi government. Their written findings reflected that.

Then, late one night, as last-minute changes to the Report were being made, the investigators received alarming news. Senior counsel Snell, their team leader, was at the office, closeted with executive director Zelikow, making major changes to their material and removing key elements.

The lead investigators, Michael Jacobson and Rajesh De, hurried to the office to confront Snell. With lawyerly caution, he said he thought there was insufficient substance to their case against the Saudis. They considered the possibility of resigning, then settled for a compromise. Much of the telling information they had collected was to survive in the Report—but only in tiny print, hidden in the endnotes.

Prince Bandar, then still Saudi ambassador to Washington, expressed delight when the Commission Report was published. "The

clear statements by this independent, bipartisan commission," he declared, "have debunked the myths that have cast fear and doubt over
Saudi Arabia." Quotations from the Report favorable to Saudi Arabia
were posted on the embassy's website and remained there still in early
2011.

Foremost among the quotes Prince Bandar liked was a Commission finding that it had located "no evidence that the Saudi government as an institution or senior Saudi officials individually funded"
al Qaeda. The full quote, which was not cited, was less satisfying.

"Saudi Arabia," the same paragraph said, "has long been considered the primary source of al Qaeda funding," and—the Report
noted—its conclusion "does not exclude the likelihood that charities with significant Saudi government sponsorship diverted funds to
al Qaeda . . . al Qaeda found fertile fund-raising ground in Saudi
Arabia."

Another major passage did not appear on the embassy site. "Saudi
Arabia," it read, "has been a problematic ally in combating Islamic
extremism. At the level of high policy, Saudi Arabia's leaders cooperated with American diplomatic initiatives . . . before 9/11. At the
same time, Saudi Arabia's society was a place where al Qaeda raised
money directly from individuals and through charities . . . the Ministry of Islamic Affairs . . . uses *zakat* [charitable giving, a central tenet
of Islam] and government funds to spread Wahhabi beliefs throughout the world. . . . Some Wahhabi-funded organizations have been
exploited by extremists to further their goal of violent jihad against
non-Muslims."

The long official friendship between the United States and Saudi
Arabia, the Report said, could not be unconditional. The relationship
had to be about more than oil, had to include—this in bold type—"a
commitment to fight the violent extremists who foment hatred."

For a very long time, there had been no such clear commitment
on the part of the Saudis. More than seven years before 9/11, the first
secretary at the Saudi mission to the United Nations, Mohammed
al-Khilewi, had defected to the United States—bringing with him
thousands of pages of documents that, he said, showed the regime's
support for terrorism, corruption, and abuse of human rights. At the
same time, he addressed a letter to Crown Prince Abdullah, calling
for "a move towards democracy." The Saudi royals, Khilewi said, responded by threatening his life. The U.S. government, however, of-

fered little protection. FBI officials, moreover, declined to accept the documents the defecting diplomat had brought with him.

In support of his claim that Saudi Arabia supported terrorism, Khilewi spoke of an episode relevant to the earliest attempt to bring down the Trade Center's Twin Towers. "A Saudi citizen carrying a Saudi diplomatic passport," he said, "gave money to Ramzi Yousef, the mastermind behind the [1993] World Trade Center bombing" when he was in the Philippines. The Saudi relationship with Ramzi Yousef, the defector claimed, "is secret and goes through Saudi intelligence."

The reference to a Saudi citizen having funded Yousef closely fit the part played by Osama bin Laden's brother-in-law, Jamal Khalifa. He was active in the Philippines, fronted as a charity organizer at the relevant time, and founded a charity that funded Yousef and KSM during the initial plotting to destroy U.S. airliners. There was telephone traffic between Khalifa's cell phone and an apartment the conspirators used.

When Khalifa eventually returned to Saudi Arabia in 1995—following detention in the United States and subsequent acquittal on terrorism charges in Jordan—he was, according to CIA bin Laden unit chief Michael Scheuer, met with a limousine and a welcome home from a "high-ranking official." A Philippines newspaper would report that it had been Prince Sultan, then a deputy prime minister and minister of defense and aviation, today the heir to the Saudi throne, who "allegedly welcomed" Khalifa.

Information obtained by U.S. intelligence in that period, veteran investigative reporter Seymour Hersh has written, had been the very opposite of the 9/11 Commission's verdict of "no evidence" that senior Saudi officials funded al Qaeda.

"Since 1994 or earlier," Hersh noted, "the National Security Agency has been collecting electronic intercepts of conversations between members of the Saudi Arabian royal family. . . . The intercepts depict a regime increasingly corrupt, alienated from the country's religious rank and file, and so weakened and frightened that it has brokered its future by channeling hundreds of millions of dollars in what amounts to protection money to fundamentalist groups that wish to overthrow it. The intercepts had demonstrated to analysts that by 1996 Saudi money was supporting Osama bin Laden's al Qaeda. . . ."

" '96 is the key year," Hersh quoted an intelligence official as saying, "Bin Laden hooked up to all the bad guys—it's like the Grand Alliance—and had a capability for conducting large-scale operations." The Saudi regime, the official said, had "gone to the dark side."

Going to the dark side, by more than one account, began with a deal. In June 1996, while in Paris for the biennial international weapons bazaar, a group of Saudi royals and financiers is said to have gathered at the Royal Monceau hotel near the Saudi embassy. The subject was bin Laden, and what to do about him. After two recent bombings of American targets in Saudi Arabia, one of them just that month, the fear was that the Saudi elite itself would soon be targeted.

At the meeting at the Monceau, French domestic intelligence reportedly learned, it was decided that bin Laden was to be kept at bay by payment of huge sums in protection money. To the tune, one account had it, of hundreds of millions of dollars. The *Los Angeles Times* was in 2004 to quote 9/11 Commission member Senator Bob Kerrey as saying that officials on the Commission believed Saudi officials had received assurances of safety in return for their generosity, even if there was no hard specific evidence.

In years to come, senior Saudi princes would deride reports of payoffs or simply write them out of the script of history. "It's a lovely story," Prince Bandar would say, "but that's not true." GID's Turki, for his part, recalled exchanges with the Taliban about bin Laden in 1996 during which he asked them to "make sure he does not operate against the Kingdom or say anything against the Kingdom." In 1998—and at the request of the United States—according to Turki, he made two unsuccessful secret visits to try to persuade the Taliban to hand over bin Laden.

Others say Turki actually traveled to Afghanistan in both 1996 and 1998. In sworn statements after 9/11, former Taliban intelligence chief Mohammed Khaksar said that in 1998 the prince sealed a deal under which bin Laden undertook not to attack Saudi targets. In return, Saudi Arabia would provide funds and material assistance to the Taliban, not demand bin Laden's extradition, and not bring pressure to close down al Qaeda training camps. Saudi businesses, meanwhile, would ensure that money also flowed directly to bin Laden.

Turki would deny after 9/11 that any such deal was done with bin Laden. One account has it, however, that he himself met with bin Laden—his old protégé from the days of the anti-Soviet jihad— during the exchanges that led to the deal. Citing a U.S. intelligence source, the author Simon Reeve reported as much in 1999—well before it became an issue after 9/11.

Whatever the truth about Turki's role, other Saudi royals may have been involved in a payoff. A former Clinton administration official has claimed—and U.S. intelligence sources concurred—that at least two Saudi princes had been paying, on behalf of the Kingdom, what amounted to protection money since 1995. "The deal was," the former official said, "they would turn a blind eye to what he was doing elsewhere. 'You don't conduct operations here, and we won't disrupt them elsewhere.' "

American and British official sources, speaking later with Simon Henderson—Baker fellow at the Washington Institute for Near East Policy—named the two princes in question. They were, Henderson told the authors, Interior Minister Naif and the minister of defense and aviation, Prince Sultan. The money involved in the alleged payments, according to Henderson's sources, had amounted to "hundreds of millions of dollars." It had been "Saudi official money—not their own."

Unlike other surviving monarchies, the Saudi royal family comprises a vast number of princes—modest estimates put their number at some seven thousand. All are hugely wealthy, though only a much smaller number have real clout. There were Saudi royals, some came to believe, whose relations with bin Laden extended to active friendship.

Four-star General Wayne Downing, who headed the task force that investigated the 1996 bombing in Saudi Arabia, said he learned of princes who went to Afghanistan and fraternized with bin Laden. "They would go out and see Osama, spend some time with him, talk with him—you know—live out in the tents, eat the simple food, engage in falconry . . . ride horses. And then be able to have the insider secret knowledge that, 'Yes, we saw Osama, and we talked to him.' "

At the State Department, the director of the Office of the Coordinator for Counterterrorism concluded that the relationship with some royals went way beyond recreational pursuits. "We've got information about who's backing bin Laden," Dick Gannon was saying by 1998, "and in a lot of cases it goes back to the royal family. There are certain factions of the royal family who just don't like us."

In the years and months before 9/11, American officials visiting Riyadh usually discovered that it was futile to ask the Saudis for help in fighting terrorism. George Tenet, who had become CIA director during Bill Clinton's second term, has vividly recalled an audience he was granted by the crown prince's brother Prince Naif. Naif, who as interior minister oversaw domestic intelligence, began the exchange with "an interminable soliloquy recounting the history of the U.S.-Saudi 'special' relationship, including how the Saudis would never, ever keep security-related information from their U.S. allies."

There came a moment when Tenet had had enough. Breaching royal etiquette, he placed his hand on the prince's knee, and said, "Your Royal Highness, what do you think it will look like if someday I have to tell the *Washington Post* that you held out data that might have helped us track down al Qaeda murderers?" Naif's reaction, Tenet thought, was what looked like "a prolonged state of shock."

Vice President Al Gore, who saw Crown Prince Abdullah soon afterward, renewed an existing request for access to a captured al Qaeda terrorist, a man known to have information on al Qaeda funding. "The United States," the 9/11 Commission was to note dourly, "never obtained this access."

So it went, year after year. Robert Baer, a celebrated former CIA field officer in the Middle East, recalled that Prince Naif "never lifted a finger" to get to the bottom of the 1996 bomb that killed and injured U.S. servicemen in Saudi Arabia. Baer pointed out, too, that it was Naif—in 1999—who released from prison two Saudi clerics long associated with bin Laden's cause.

Congress's Joint Inquiry was to note that it had been told "the Saudi government would not cooperate with the United States on matters relating to Osama bin Laden [name and information censored]." Words, perhaps, out of the mouth of Michael Scheuer, former chief of the CIA's bin Laden unit.

"As one of the unit's first actions," Scheuer recalled in 2008, "we requested that the Saudis provide the CIA with basic information about bin Laden. That request remained unfulfilled." The U.S. government, he bitterly recalled, "publicly supported a brutal, medieval Arab tyranny . . . and took no action against a government that helped ensure that bin Laden and al Qaeda remained beyond the reach of the United States." To Scheuer, looking back, America's supposed ally had in reality been simply a "foreign enemy."

On a flight home from Saudi Arabia in the late 1990s, FBI director Louis Freeh told counterterrorism chief John O'Neill that he thought the Saudi officials they had met during the trip had been helpful. "You've got to be kidding," retorted O'Neill, a New Jersey native who never minced his words. "They didn't give us anything. They were just shining sunshine up your ass."

Several years later, in two long conversations with an investigator for a French intelligence agency, O'Neill was still venting his frustration. "All the answers, all the clues that could enable us to dismantle Osama bin Laden's organization," he said, "are in Saudi Arabia."

The answers and the clues, however, remained out of reach. In part, O'Neill told the Frenchman, because U.S. dependence on Saudi oil meant that Saudi Arabia had "much more leverage on us than we have on the Kingdom." And, he added, because "high-ranking personalities and families in the Saudi Kingdom" had close ties to bin Laden.

The conversations took place in June and late July of 2001.

A YEAR AFTER 9/11, former Saudi intelligence chief Prince Turki—the longtime head of GID—expounded at length on his service's relationship with the CIA.

From around 1996, he said, "At the instruction of the senior Saudi leadership, I shared all the intelligence we had collected on bin Laden and al Qaeda with the CIA. And in 1997 the Saudi Minister of Defense, Prince Sultan, established a joint intelligence committee with the United States to share information on terrorism in general and on bin Laden and al Qaeda in particular."

That the GID and U.S. services had a long if uneasy understanding on sharing intelligence is not at issue. A year after his initial comments, though, by which time he had become ambassador to London, Turki spoke out specifically about 9/11 hijackers Mihdhar and Hazmi.

In late 1999 and early 2000, he said—when Mihdhar and Hazmi were headed for the terrorist meeting in Malaysia—GID had told the CIA that both men were terrorists. "What we told them," he said, "was these people were on our watchlist from previous activities of al Qaeda, in both the [East Africa] embassy bombings and attempts to smuggle arms into the Kingdom in 1997."

The Saudi ambassador to the United States, Prince Bandar, had hinted right after 9/11 that the intelligence services had known more about the hijackers in advance than they were publicly admitting. Then, his remarks had gone virtually unnoticed.

In 2007, however, by which time he had risen to become national security adviser to former crown prince—now King—Abdullah, Bandar produced a bombshell. He went much further than had Prince Turki on what—he claimed—GID had passed to the CIA.

"Saudi security," Bandar said, had been "actively following the movements of most of the terrorists with precision. . . . If U.S. security authorities had engaged their Saudi counterparts in a serious and credible manner, in my opinion, we would have avoided what happened."

The same week, speaking not of 9/11 but of the 2005 London Underground train bombings that killed more than fifty people and injured some eight hundred, King Abdullah made astonishing remarks. "We have sent information before the terrorist attacks on Britain," the king said, "but unfortunately no action was taken . . . it may have been able to avert the tragedy."

Such claims might be rejected out of hand, were it not that they came from Saudis at the very top of the power structure. A British government spokesman publicly denied King Abdullah's remarks, saying that information received from the Saudis had been "not relevant" to the London bombings and could not have been used to prevent the attacks. The comments about Mihdhar and Hazmi led to a mix of denial, rage—and in one case, a curious silence.

"There is not a shred of evidence," the CIA's Bill Harlow said of Turki's 2003 claim, "that Saudi intelligence provided CIA any information about Mihdhar and Hazmi prior to September 11 as they have described." Harlow said information on the two hijackers-to-be had been passed on only a month *after* the attacks.

Prince Turki stood by what he had said, while eventually acknowledging that it had not been he himself who had given the information to the Americans. The prince's former chief analyst, Saeed Badeeb, said it was he who briefed U.S. officials—at one of their regular liaison meetings—warning that Mihdhar and Hazmi were members of al Qaeda.

There was no official reaction to the most stunning allegation of all, Prince Bandar's claim that the GID had followed most of the future hijackers, that 9/11 could have been averted had U.S. intelligence responded adequately. The following year, the CIA's earlier bin Laden unit chief Michael Scheuer dismissed the claim—in a book—as a "fabrication." By failing to respond to it publicly, he wrote, U.S. officialdom had condoned the claim.

Though senior 9/11 Commission staff interviewed Prince Bandar, they did so well before he came out with his claim about the Saudis having followed most of the hijackers "with precision." The record of what the prince told the Commission—even at that early stage—remains classified on grounds of "national security."

As interesting, of course, would be to know what former Saudi intelligence chief Prince Turki told the Commission—if indeed he was interviewed. On finding no reference to any Turki contact in listings of Commission documents—even if only referred to as withheld—the authors sent an inquiry to the National Archives. The response was remarkable, one that the experienced archivist with whom we dealt said she had never had to send before.

"I can neither confirm nor deny the existence of a Prince Turki Memorandum for the Record," the archivist wrote in early 2011. "I'm not allowed to be any clearer. . . . I can't tell you, or I'm revealing more than I'm allowed to. . . . If we have an MFR for Prince Turki, it would also be withheld in full."

Legal advice to the authors is that the umbrella nature of the withholding—under which the public is not allowed to know whether a document on a subject even *exists*—is rare. Information about the GID, and what really went on between the Saudi and U.S. intelligence services before 9/11, apparently remains highly sensitive.

WITH THE U.S. authorities blocking access to information, one can but sift the fragments of information that have surfaced. Did the GID "follow" Mihdhar and Hazmi, or indeed any of the terrorists?

A former head of operations and analysis at the CIA Counterterrorist Center, Vincent Cannistraro, has said that—as one might expect—Saudi intelligence had in the past "penetrated al Qaeda several times." A censored paragraph on Hazmi in Congress's Joint Inquiry states that the future hijacker

> returned to Saudi Arabia in early 1999, where [words withheld], he disclosed information about the East Africa bombings.
>
> Al Mihdhar's first trip to the Afghanistan training camps was in early 1996. [three lines withheld] In 1998, al Mihdhar traveled to Afghanistan and swore allegiance to Bin Laden.

Hazmi "disclosed information"? To whom—to the GID? That possibility aside, there is a clue in a 9/11 Commission staff report. Mihdhar and Hazmi and Hazmi's brother "presented with their visa applications passports that contained an indicator of possible terrorist affiliation."

Depending how one reads a footnote in the Commission Report, all fifteen Saudi hijackers were vulnerable due to the fact or likelihood that their passports "had been manipulated in a fraudulent manner" by al Qaeda. According to the author James Bamford, however, Mihdhar's two passports "contained a secret coded indicator, *placed there by the Saudi government* [authors' emphasis], warning of a possible terrorist affiliation."

What then of the claims by Princes Turki and Bandar that the Saudis shared information on Mihdhar and Hazmi with the CIA? Two years after the attacks, the authors Joseph and Susan Trento suggested a mind-boggling possible answer to that question. They claimed that a former CIA officer, once based in Saudi Arabia, had told them, "We had been unable to penetrate al Qaeda. The Saudis claimed they had done it successfully. Both Hazmi and Mihdhar were Saudi agents."

Citing not only that officer but other CIA and GID sources, the Trentos have written that Mihdhar and Hazmi—assumed at the time to be friendly double agents—went to the January meeting of terrorists in Kuala Lumpur "to spy on a meeting of top associates of al Qaeda associates. . . . The CIA/Saudi hope was that the Saudis would learn details of bin Laden's future plans."

As noted earlier, the CIA knew even before Mihdhar reached Kuala Lumpur that he had a multiple-entry visa for the United States—a fact it said it discovered when his passport was photographed en route to Malaysia.

The reason the CIA did not ask the State Department to watchlist Mihdhar and Hazmi, according to the Trento account, was that the men "were perceived as working for a friendly intelligence service"— the GID. In any case, the Trentos quote one of their sources as saying that CIA operations staff allowed names to go forward to the watchlist only with reluctance. "Many terrorists act as assets for our case officers," the source said. "We do deal with bad guys and, like cops protect snitches, we protect ours . . . none of those guys is going to show up on the no-fly list."

The reason the FBI was not told anything about Mihdhar and

Hazmi, the Trentos quote a source as telling them, was "because they were Saudi assets operating with CIA knowledge in the United States."

Then the kicker. According to the Trentos, Mihdhar and Hazmi had not been thoroughly vetted by either the CIA or the GID. "In fact they were triple agents—loyal to Osama bin Laden." And so it was, months later, that catastrophe followed.

Is this mere disinformation? Early on in his career, Joe Trento worked for the columnist Jack Anderson, famous in his day for breaking big stories, often without naming his sources. He has also worked for CNN. The Trentos have long written on intelligence, and have repeated their claim about the handling of Mihdhar and Hazmi in another book, in a 2010 article, and in a conversation with the authors.

The scenario they paint, though, bumps up against known events and evidence. It seems likely that the Trentos' intelligence sources fed them morsels of fact mixed in with deliberate disinformation—a common enough ploy. Their account, though, does prompt a much closer look at the interplay between the CIA and the Saudi GID.

The CIA's own inspector general, reporting in 2005, found that its bin Laden station and "[name redacted] were hostile to each other and working at cross purposes for a number of years before 9/11." In context, it is clear that the redacted name refers to the GID. Pulitzer-winning *New York Times* reporter James Risen, who, writing later, revealed that—as early as 1997—Alec Station, the CIA unit that specifically targeted bin Laden, had seen its GID counterparts as a "hostile service."

The signs were, Risen reported, that intelligence given to the GID about al Qaeda was often passed on to al Qaeda. Once CIA staff shared intercepts with the GID, they found, al Qaeda operatives would abruptly stop using the lines that had been monitored. Congress's Joint Inquiry Report hinted at the true picture. "On some occasions," one passage read—followed by several redacted lines— "individuals in some [foreign] liaison services are believed to have cooperated with terrorist groups."

The legal defense fund of Blind Sheikh Omar Abdel Rahman, on trial in the mid-1990s for plotting to bomb New York landmarks, had been supported with GID money. Osama bin Laden himself, who had made his name under GID direction during the anti-Soviet war in Afghanistan, remained a hero for many.

A number of Saudi officials, a friendly intelligence service told the CIA well before 9/11, used bin Laden's picture as the screen saver on their office computers. Little was to change. Even three years *after* the attacks—following the shock of serious al Qaeda attacks inside Saudi Arabia, and severe reprisals by the regime—one senior Arab source would still be telling the London *Times* that Saudi intelligence was "80% sympathetic to al Qaeda."

In 2001, sympathy for al Qaeda and bin Laden was widespread across the spectrum of Saudi society. It extended, even, to approval of the strikes on America.

THIRTY-THREE

At first on September 11, early estimates had been that as many as tens of thousands might have died in the New York attacks alone. There was a universal sense of catastrophe across the Western world. In Saudi Arabia, as in a number of countries across the region, many expressed delight.

Drivers honked their horns. In Internet cafés, many young men adopted shots of the blazing Twin Towers as screen savers—and restored the photographs if proprietors removed them. Students in class seemed "quite proud." Some people killed sheep or camels and invited friends to a feast.

Satisfaction over the blow to the United States was not confined to the street. The hostess at a lunch for society women was shocked to hear many of her guests evince the sentiment that, at last, "somebody did something."

There was a tangible feeling abroad that the attacks had been a good thing, that "someone had stood up to America." At King Fahd National Guard Hospital in Riyadh, one foreign doctor had a unique

insight into the reaction of ordinary patients and medical professionals alike.

Dr. Qanta Ahmed, a British-born Muslim of Pakistani origin, had
trained in Britain and the United States. Like millions of others, she
had spent the hours after the attacks watching satellite television news
in horror, phoning friends in New York to ask if they were safe. On
arriving at the hospital next morning, though, what she sensed was an
atmosphere of "muted exaltation . . . relish in the face of destruction."

On the general medical and surgical wards, nurses told her, Saudi
patients had clapped and cheered as TV pictures showed the Twin
Towers crumbling. What had outraged one fellow foreigner most,
though, was when two Saudi obstetricians sent out to the Diplomat
Bakery for cakes—the sort of cakes customarily used at moments of
mabrouk, when congratulation or celebration is due. When the cakes
arrived, they passed out slices to their colleagues and to the patients
who had clapped.

"So, they lost thousands of Americans," a New York–trained Pakistani doctor said. "They are guessing three thousand right now. Do
you have any idea how many people die in Palestine every day, Qanta?
The loss of these lives is hardly equal to the daily losses of lives in the
Muslim world in past years."

The mood was pervasive and lasting. Later that week, at the gro-
cery in the hospital complex, the man at the checkout was eager as
usual to chat. "This news in New York has been very good, Doctora!"
he said. And then: "The Americans deserved it."

A month later, a survey of educated Saudi professionals found
that 95 percent of respondents favored bin Laden's cause. Asked to
comment, Crown Prince Abdullah's half-brother, Prince Nawwaf
bin Abdul Aziz, opined that this reflected the "feelings of the people
against the United States . . . because of its unflinching support for
Israel against the Palestinians."

Several years later, conducting interviews in Saudi Arabia, 9/11
Commission staff interviewed several dozen young to middle-age
men said to be "moderates." "Almost unanimously," Commission
chairmen Kean and Hamilton noted, the men were "harshly critical of
the United States. . . . They did not defend crashing planes into buildings, but they believed strongly that the United States was unfair in
its approach to the Middle East, particularly in its support for Israel.

"These feelings were not surprising, but hearing them firsthand from so-called moderates drove home the enormous gap between how we see ourselves and our actions in the Middle East, and how others perceive us."

AT HIS RESIDENCE outside Washington on the morning of 9/11, Saudi ambassador Prince Bandar had been in his bedroom when the planes hit the Trade Center. He became aware of the first of the crashes, he recalled, when—as he glanced up at one of his ten television screens— he saw flames erupting from the North Tower. Then, when a second plane struck the South Tower, he realized that America was being attacked. He said he had hoped "they were not Arabs."

"My God," he said he thought later, on seeing pictures that showed Palestinians apparently celebrating in the street. "The whole impression this nation is going to have of us, the whole world, will be formed in the next two days."

Each for their own complex mix of reasons, the Saudis and the Bush administration were suddenly struggling to keep the fabled U.S.-Saudi "friendship" from falling apart. Bandar rushed out a statement of condolence. The kingdom, an embassy statement said, "condemned the regrettable and inhuman bombings and attacks which took place today. . . . Saudi Arabia strongly condemns such acts, which contravene all religious values and human civilized concepts; and extends sincere condolences."

Behind the political scenery, and on the festering subject of Israel, relations between Riyadh and Washington had very recently become unprecedentedly shaky. Crown Prince Abdullah had long fumed about America's apparent complacency over the plight of the Palestinians. In the spring, he had pointedly declined an invitation to the White House. Three weeks before 9/11, enraged by television footage of an Israeli soldier putting his boot on the head of a Palestinian woman, he had snapped. His nephew Bandar had been told to deliver an uncompromising message to President Bush.

"I reject this extraordinary, un-American bias whereby the blood of an Israeli child is more expensive and holy than the blood of a Palestinian child. . . . A time comes when peoples and nations part. . . . Starting today, you go your way and we will go our way. From now on, we will protect our national interests, regardless of where America's interests lie in the region." There was more, much more, and it rocked the Bush administration. The President responded with a placatory letter that seemed to go far toward the Saudi position of endorsing the creation of a viable Palestinian state. As of September 7, it looked as though the situation had stabilized. Then came the shattering events of Tuesday the 11th.

In Riyadh, and within twenty-four hours, Abdullah pulled the lever that gave his nation its only real power, the economic sword it could draw or sheathe at will. He ordered that nine million barrels of oil be dispatched to the United States over the next two weeks. The certainty of supply had the effect, it is said, of averting what had otherwise been a possibility at that time—an oil shortage that would have pushed prices through the roof and caused—on top of the real economic effects of the 9/11 calamity—a major financial crisis.

On the night of Wednesday the 12th, though, a CIA official phoned Ambassador Bandar with the news that fifteen of the hijackers had been Saudis. As Bandar recalled it, he felt the world collapsing around him. "That was a disaster," Crown Prince Abdullah's foreign affairs adviser Adel al-Jubeir has said, "because bin Laden, at that moment, had made in the minds of Americans Saudi Arabia into an enemy."

All over the country, royal and rich Saudis scrambled to get out of the United States and home. These were people used to being able to travel at will, if not aboard their own jet, then by chartered airplane. This was no normal time, however, and U.S. airspace was closed. Seventy-five royals and their entourage, ensconced at that wholly un-Islamic venue, Caesars Palace hotel and casino in Las Vegas, had decamped within hours of the attacks to the Four Seasons. They felt "extremely concerned for their personal safety," they explained to the local FBI field office, and bodyguards apparently deemed the Four Seasons more secure.

On the other side of the country, Saudis who wished to leave included members of the bin Laden family. One of Osama's brothers, never named publicly, had hastily called the embassy wanting to know where he could best go to be safe. He was installed in a room at the Watergate Hotel and told to stay there until advised that transportation was available. Across the country, more than twenty bin Laden family members and staff were getting ready to leave.

In Lexington, Kentucky, the thoroughbred racing mecca of America, Prince Ahmed bin Salman—a nephew of King Fahd—had been attending the annual yearling sales. After the attacks, Ahmed began quickly to round up members of his family for a return to Saudi Arabia. He ordered his son and a couple of friends, who were in Florida, to charter a plane and get themselves to Lexington to connect with the plane he was taking home.

Prince Ahmed's son was at first unable to charter a plane, because U.S. airspace was closed. On September 13, however, he and his group did succeed in getting to Kentucky. They managed it, one of them told the security man hired for the flight, because "his father or his uncle was good friends with George Bush Sr."

In spite of the fact that it was known that fifteen of those implicated in the attacks had been Saudis, President George W. Bush did not hold the official representative of Saudi Arabia at arm's length. He kept a scheduled appointment to receive Saudi ambassador Prince Bandar at the White House. The two men, who had known each other for years, reportedly greeted each other with a friendly embrace. They smoked cigars together on the Truman Balcony and conversed, looking relaxed, with Cheney and Rice.

Later that night, Bandar's assistant rang the FBI's assistant director for counterterrorism, Dale Watson. He needed help, the assistant said, in getting bin Laden "family members" on a flight out of the country. Watson said Saudi officials should call the White House or the State Department. The request found its way to counterterrorism coordinator Richard Clarke.

The confluence of events—the White House meeting and the subsequent calls—would set off a firestorm of criticism when it became known. A photograph of Bush's September 13 meeting on the balcony with Prince Bandar was published in a 2006 book by Bob Woodward. When the authors asked for a copy of the photograph before publication of this book, however, the George W. Bush presidential library responded that the former President's office was "not inclined to release the image from the balcony at this time."

Had Ambassador Bandar used his influence and connections to whisk Saudi citizens—some of whom had links to Osama bin Laden himself—out of the country? There was speculation, too, that some Saudis were allowed to fly before U.S. airspace reopened, perhaps on the authority of President Bush. Had they, others asked, all been properly investigated before departure?

Richard Clarke, who has acknowledged that he gave the go-ahead for the flights, said he had "no recollection" of having first cleared it with anyone more senior in the administration.

One flight especially queried—on the grounds that it had supposedly occurred before U.S. airspace opened—was the charter flight from Tampa, Florida, to Lexington, Kentucky, on the afternoon of September 13. Contrary to previous reporting, however, FAA and other records show that U.S. airspace had by the time of the plane's takeoff opened not only to commercial flights but also to charters.

Prince Ahmed and his party would stay on in Kentucky until the weekend, when they left the country aboard a 727 so luxurious that it could accommodate only twenty-six passengers. By then, with the press in full cry over the news that most of the 9/11 hijackers had been Saudi nationals, all or most of the frightened Saudi elite were on their way home.

It may be that none of the flights carrying Saudis occurred contrary to the emergency closure of U.S. airspace. The FBI's checks on those who boarded the charter flights, though, were less than thorough. The 9/11 Commission found no evidence, for example, that the names of any of some 144 people who departed on charters within days of the airspace reopening had been checked against the State Department's watchlist. Nor were most of those leaving questioned by the FBI before departure.

The Bureau did speak—albeit, it seems, briefly—with almost all of the bin Laden relatives involved in the exodus, including one of Osama's nephews, Omar Awadh bin Laden.

Omar had once shared an address in Falls Church, Virginia, with his brother Abdullah bin Laden. The Bureau had briefly investigated Abdullah in the late 1990s because of his role in running a suspect Saudi organization known to preach extreme Islamism. The investigation had been closed after he produced a Saudi diplomatic passport. Questioned after 9/11, his brother Omar said he had had no contact with his uncle Osama and knew none of the Arabs suspected of involvement in the attacks, and he was allowed to go on his way.

An FBI memo written two years after the exodus appears to acknowledge that some of the departing Saudis may have had information pertinent to the investigation. "Although the FBI took all possible steps to prevent any individuals who were involved in or had knowledge of the 9/11/01 attacks from leaving the U.S. before they could be interviewed," the memo reads, "it is not possible to state conclusively that no such individuals left the U.S. without FBI knowledge."

It is a point on which the Bureau and the Saudi government seem to agree. Asked on CNN the same year whether he could say unequivocally that no one on the evacuation flights had been involved in 9/11, Saudi embassy information officer Nail al-Jubeir responded by saying he was sure of only two things, that "there is the existence of God, and then we will die at the end of the world. Everything else, we don't know."

This was not an answer likely to satisfy anyone in the United States.

EVEN AS THE SAUDI aristocracy fled homeward, the embassy was mounting a propaganda campaign to counter the perception that Saudi Arabia was in any way responsible for 9/11. Millions of dollars—more than $50 million over the next three years—were to flow to public relations firms to restore the country's image as friend, ally, and Middle East peacemaker. Another firm was paid to get the Saudi message to members of Congress.

Ambassador Bandar got the Saudi line over on *Larry King Live*. "We feel what happened to the United States—the tragedy and the cowardly attack on the United States—was not against the United States at all. It's really against all civilized people in the world. . . . Our role is to stand shoulder-to-shoulder with our friends."

It had soon become evident that, far from confronting the Saudis, the Bush administration wanted rapprochement. The President invited Crown Prince Abdullah to visit the United States, pressed him to come when he hesitated, and—when he accepted—welcomed him to his Texas ranch in early 2002. Vice President Cheney was there, as were Secretary of State Powell, National Security Adviser Rice, and First Lady Laura Bush. The Saudi foreign minister and Ambassador Bandar, with his wife, Princess Haifa, accompanied the crown prince.

9/11, it seems, barely came up during the discussions. The principal topic was the Saudi concern over Palestine, which had led to such tension the previous summer. Speaking with the press afterward, the President cut off one reporter when he started to raise the subject of the fifteen Saudi hijackers. "Yes, I—the Crown Prince has been very strong in condemning those who committed the murder of U.S. citizens," Bush said. "We're constantly working with him and his government on intelligence-sharing and cutting off money . . . the government has been acting, and I appreciate that very much."

The President was being economical with the facts. Saudi spokesmen had from early on waxed equivocal as to whether any of the hijackers had even been Saudi nationals. Two days after Ambassador Bandar had been told of the CIA's estimate that some fifteen of the hijackers were Saudi, his spokesman said the terrorists had probably used stolen identities.

In Saudi Arabia, historian Hatoon al-Fassi has said, "most people were in denial" over the American claim that their compatriots had been responsible. "They thought that, 'Here's Americans and the CIA trying to fabricate . . .'" Senior officials encouraged that notion.

"There is no proof or evidence," claimed Sheikh Saleh al-Sheikh, minister of Islamic affairs, "that Saudis carried out these attacks." Defense Minister Prince Sultan doubted whether only bin Laden and his followers were responsible, and hinted that "another power with advanced technical expertise" must have been behind 9/11. As of December 2001, Interior Minister Naif—a half-brother to the crown prince—was saying he still did not believe fifteen hijackers had been Saudis.

Not until February 2002 was Naif to acknowledge the truth. "The names we have got confirmed [it]," he then conceded. "Their families have been notified. I believe they were taken advantage of in the name of religion, and regarding certain issues pertaining to the Arab nation, especially the issue of Palestine."

Sultan and Naif were still not done, however. They began pointing to a familiar enemy. "It is enough to see a number of [U.S.] congressmen wearing Jewish yarmulkes," Sultan said, "to explain the allegations against us." In late 2002, Naif blamed the "Zionists," saying "we put big question marks and ask who committed the events of September 11 and who benefited from them. . . . I think they [the Zionists] are behind these events."

As for cooperation over the investigation of 9/11, the Saudis had been less than helpful. "We're getting zero cooperation," former CIA counterterrorism chief Cannistraro said a month after the attacks. Requests for name checks and personal information on the hijackers and other suspects were turned down. "They knew that once we started asking for a few traces the list would grow," a U.S. source said. "It's better to shut it down right away." American investigators were not allowed access to the suspects' families.

Three months after 9/11, a senior Bush administration official was saying that the Saudis were prepared only to "dribble out a morsel of insignificant information one day at a time." Contrary to what the President would imply after his meeting with the crown prince, moreover, the Saudis reportedly delayed or blocked attempts to track the sources of terrorist funding in their country. "It doesn't look like they're doing much," former FBI assistant director Robert Kallstrom said in spring 2002, "and frankly it's nothing new."

As FOR THE ATTACKS themselves, Saudi Arabia would long remain a black hole for U.S. investigators. Also confronting them, obstruction and obfuscation aside, was the vast cultural gulf and the language gap; pathetically few staff in any agency had fluent Arabic. What they did begin to accumulate, as they looked for a possible umbilical linking the largely Saudi hijacking team to forces in Saudi Arabia, were some fragmentary clues and some suspects.

The suspects were the men believed to have met with or helped Mihdhar and Hazmi when they first arrived in California—as outlined in an earlier chapter. The blur of witness accounts permits the following scenario:

The imam named Fahad al-Thumairy, an accredited diplomat appointed by the Saudi Ministry of Islamic Affairs to liaise with the huge nearby mosque, served at the time at the Saudi consulate in Los Angeles. According to one witness, Thumairy had at the relevant time arranged for two men—whom the witness at first identified from photographs as having been the two future terrorists—to be given a tour of the area by car. A fellow Saudi, a San Diego resident named Omar al-Bayoumi, who was said to have had frequent contact with Thumairy, stated—according to a person interviewed by the FBI—that he was going to Los Angeles "to pick up visitors."

Bayoumi did make the trip north, accompanied by an American Muslim named Caysan bin Don. On the way there, Bayoumi mentioned that he was accustomed to going to the consulate to obtain religious materials. They did stop at the consulate, where—according to bin Don—a man "in a Western business suit, with a full beard—'two fists length' "—greeted Bayoumi and took him off to talk in an office for a while. Bayoumi emerged some time later, carrying a box of Qur'ans. Bayoumi described the encounter differently, said he was "uncertain" whom he met with and "didn't really know people in Islamic Affairs."

After that, the two men have said, they went to a restaurant and—this is the crucial moment in their story—met and talked with the two new arrivals, future hijackers Mihdhar and Hazmi. Was the encounter really, as Bayoumi and bin Don were to tell the FBI, merely a chance encounter? The reported detail, that Bayoumi dropped a newspaper on the floor, bent to retrieve it, and *then* approached the two terrorists, may—with a bow to espionage cliché—indicate otherwise.

The rest requires no lengthy retelling. Bayoumi urged Mihdhar and Hazmi to come south to San Diego, assisted them in finding accommodations, and stayed in touch. On the day they moved into the apartment they first used, an apartment next door to Bayoumi, there were four calls between his phone and that of Anwar Aulaqi—the local imam, who, as this book goes to print in 2011, is in Yemen, plotting attack after attack on America.

There is another factor in this tangled tale, one that involves money flow—and yet another local Saudi. Bayoumi's income, paid by a Saudi company—though he did no known work—reportedly increased hugely following the future hijackers' arrival. Also on the money front, enter another Saudi named Osama Basnan. A three-page section of Congress's Joint Inquiry Report, containing more lines withheld than released, tells us only that he was a close associate of Bayoumi in San Diego, who at one point lived across the street from Mihdhar and Hazmi.

According to former U.S. senator Bob Graham, cochair of the joint investigation, and to press reports, regular checks paid to Basnan's wife at some point began flowing from the Basnans to Bayoumi's wife. The payments, ostensibly made to assist in paying for medical treatment, originated with the Saudi embassy in Washington.

Thumairy, Bayoumi, and Basnan all have suspect backgrounds. Thumairy, who had a reputation as a fundamentalist, was to be refused reentry to the United States—well after 9/11—on the grounds that he "might be connected with terrorist activity." Bayoumi had first attracted the interest of the FBI years earlier, and the Bureau later learned he had "connections to terrorist elements." Bayoumi left the country two months before the attacks.

As for Basnan, his name had come up in a counterterrorism inquiry a decade earlier. He had reportedly hosted a party for Blind Sheikh Omar Abdel Rahman when he visited the United States, and had once claimed he did more for Islam than Bayoumi ever did. He is said to have celebrated 9/11 as a "wonderful, glorious day." A partially censored Commission document suggests that—after Mihdhar and Hazmi and the hijacker pilots arrived in the United States to learn to fly—a Basnan associate was in email and phone contact with accused key conspirator Ramzi Binalshibh. A year after 9/11, Basnan was arrested for visa fraud and deported.

Available information suggests two of the trio were employed by or had links to the Saudi regime—Thumairy through his accreditation to the Ministry of Islamic Affairs and Bayoumi through his employment by a company connected to the Saudi Civil Aviation Authority. Several people characterized Bayoumi as a Saudi government agent or spy. The CIA, former senator Graham has said, thought Basnan was also an agent. The senator cited an Agency memo referring to "incontrovertible evidence" of support for the terrorists within the Saudi government.

IN 2003 and 2004, but only following a high-level request from the White House, 9/11 Commission staff were able to make two visits to Saudi Arabia to interview Thumairy, Bayoumi, and Basnan. All interviews were conducted in the presence of officials from Prince Naif's internal security service.

The U.S. questioners, a recently released Commission memo notes, believed Thumairy was "deceptive during both interviews. . . . His answers were either inconsistent or at times in direct conflict with information we have from other sources." Most significantly, he denied knowing Bayoumi, let alone Mihdhar and Hazmi. Shown a photograph of Bayoumi, he did not budge. He knew no one of that name, he said. Then, prompted by a whispered interjection from one of the Saudi officials present, he said he had heard of Bayoumi—but only from 9/11 news coverage.

At a second interview, told by Commission staff that witnesses had spoken of seeing him with Bayoumi, Thumairy said perhaps he had been mistaken for someone else. Perhaps, too, there were people who might "say bad things about him out of jealousy." Finally told that telephone records showed numerous calls between his phones and Bayoumi's phones, just before the arrival of Mihdhar and Hazmi in the United States to boot, Thumairy was stumped.

Perhaps, he ventured, his phone number had been allotted to somebody else after he had it? Perhaps the calls had been made by someone else using Bayoumi's phone? He flailed around in vain for an explanation. Everything Thumairy came up with, his Commission questioners noted, was "implausible."

Bayoumi, who was interviewed earlier—though not by staff with firsthand experience of the California episode—had made a more favorable impression. He stuck to his story about having met Mihdhar and Hazmi by chance. He said he had rarely seen Mihdhar and Hazmi after they came to San Diego, that they had been his neighbors for only a few days. Bayoumi said he had then decided he did not want to have much to do with them. Commission executive director Zelikow, who was present during the interview, did not think Bayoumi had been a Saudi agent.

The Commission Report, however, was to note that Bayoumi's passport contained a distinguishing mark that may be acquired by "especially devout Muslims"—or be associated with "adherence to al Qaeda." Investigators had also turned up something else, something disquieting. Bayoumi's salary had been approved by a Saudi official whose son's photograph was later found on a computer disk in Pakistan—a disk that also contained some of the hijackers' photographs.

The son, Saud al-Rashid, was also produced for interview in Saudi Arabia. He admitted having been in Afghanistan—and to having "cleansed" his passport of the evidence that he had traveled there. He said, though, that he had known nothing of the 9/11 plot. Commission staff who questioned him thought Rashid had been "deceptive." They noted that he had had "enough time to develop a coherent story . . . even may have been coached."

Finally, there was Basnan. The Commission's interview with him, senior commission counsel Dietrich Snell wrote afterward, established only "the witness' utter lack of credibility on virtually every material subject." This assessment was based on "a combination of confrontation, evasiveness, and speechmaking . . . his repudiation of statements made by him on prior occasions," and the "inherent incredibility of many of his assertions when viewed in light of the totality of the available evidence."

Two men did not face Commission questioning in Saudi Arabia. One of them, a Saudi religious official named Saleh al-Hussayen, certainly should have, although his name does not appear in the Commission Report. Hussayen, who was involved in the administration of the Holy Mosques in Mecca and Medina, had been in the States for some three weeks before 9/11. For four days before the attacks, he had stayed at a hotel in Virginia.

Then on September 10, the very eve of the attacks, he had made an unexplained move. With his wife, he had checked into the Marriott Residence Inn in Herndon, Virginia—the very hotel at which Mihdhar and Hazmi were spending their last night alive.

Commission memos, one of them heavily censored, state that FBI agents arrived at Hussayen's room at the Marriott after midnight on the 11th. As questioning began, however, he began "muttering and drooping his head," sweating and drooling. Then he fell out of his chair and appeared to lose consciousness for a few moments. Paramedics summoned to the room, and doctors who examined Hussayen at a local hospital, found nothing wrong. An FBI agent said later that the interview had been cut short because—the agent suggested—Hussayen "feigned a seizure."

Asked by one of the Bureau agents why they had moved to the Marriott, Hussayen's wife said it was because they had wanted a room with a kitchenette. There was no sign, however, that the kitchenette in the room had been used, and the fridge was empty. Asked whether she thought her husband could have been involved in the 9/11 attacks in any way, the wife replied—oddly, the agents thought—"I don't know."

Agents never did obtain an adequate interview with Saleh al-Hussayen. Instead of continuing with his tour of the United States, he flew back to Saudi Arabia—and went on to head the administration of the two Holy Mosques. It remains unknown whether he had contact with Mihdhar and Hazmi on the eve of 9/11, or whether his presence at the Marriott—that night of all nights—was, as Bayoumi claimed of his meeting with the two terrorists, just a matter of chance.

As Hussayen left Virginia for home, other FBI agents in the state were interviewing the imam Anwar Aulaqi. As reported earlier, he did not deny having had contact with Mihdhar and Hazmi in California and later—with Hazmi—in Virginia. He could not deny that his own move from San Diego to the East Coast had paralleled theirs. Yet he made nothing of it—and U.S. authorities apparently pursued the matter no further at that time.

Aulaqi, almost uniquely for a suspect in this story, is American-born, the son of a former minister in the government of Yemen. Hard to credit though it is in light of what we now know of him, he had reportedly preached in the precincts of the U.S. Capitol shortly before 9/11. Not long afterward, moreover, he had lunched at the Pentagon—in an area undamaged by the strike in which his acquaintances Mihdhar and Hazmi had played such a leading role. The reason for the lunch? An outreach effort to ease tensions between Muslim Americans and non-Muslims.

Aulaqi remained in the United States for more than a year before departing, first for Britain and eventually for Yemen. He had been allowed to move about unimpeded, even though the phone number of his Virginia mosque had turned up in Germany in the apartment of 9/11 conspirator Ramzi Binalshibh. Only seven years later, starting in 2009, did he at last begin to become known around the world.

Aulaqi's name was associated with: the multiple shootings by a U.S. army major at Fort Hood, an almost successful attempt to explode a bomb on an airliner en route to Detroit, a major car bomb scare in Times Square, and a last-minute discovery of concealed explosives on cargo planes destined for the United States.

When Aulaqi's name began to feature large in the Western press, Yemen's foreign minister cautioned that—pending real evidence—he should be considered not as a terrorist but as a preacher. Briefed on the intelligence about him, President Obama took a different view. In early 2010, he authorized the CIA and the U.S. military to seek out, capture, or kill the Yemeni—assigning Aulaqi essentially the same status as that assigned at the time to Osama bin Laden.

Commission staff had never had the opportunity to interview Aulaqi. Executive Director Zelikow, however, had long thought he merited more attention. Aulaqi remains, as Zelikow memorably noted when his name finally hit the headlines, "a 9/11 loose end."

Taken together, the roles and activities of Thumairy, Bayoumi, Basnan, Hussayen, and Aulaqi—and the dubious accounts some them have given of themselves—heightened suspicion that the perpetrators of 9/11 had support and sponsorship from backers never clearly identified.

. . .

CONGRESS'S JOINT INQUIRY, its cochair former senator Bob Graham told the authors, found evidence "that the Saudis were facilitating, assisting, some of the hijackers. And my suspicion is that they were providing some assistance to most if not all of the hijackers. . . . It's my opinion that 9/11 could not have occurred but for the existence of an infrastructure of support within the United States. By 'the Saudis,' I mean the Saudi government and individual Saudis who are for some purposes dependent on the government—which includes all of the elite in the country."

Those involved, in Graham's view, "included the royal family" and "some groups that were close to the royal family." Was it credible that members of the Saudi royal family would knowingly have facilitated the 9/11 operation? "I think," the former senator said, "that they did in fact take actions that were complicit with the hijackers."

9/11 Commission executive director Zelikow—always cautious, and in the view of some of his staff reluctant to chase down the full truth in some areas—also concluded that there was "persuasive evidence of a possible support network" for Mihdhar and Hazmi in San Diego. In his view, though, the Commission "did not find evidence to make the case that it involved 'Saudi government agents.'"

In the alien terrain of the Saudi world, where hard information is so scarce, proof was always going to be a mirage.

AT PAGE 396 of the congressional Joint Inquiry's report on 9/11, the final section of the body of the Report, a yawning gap appears. All twenty-eight pages of Part Four, entitled "Finding, Discussion and Narrative Regarding Certain Sensitive National Security Matters," have been redacted. The pages are there but—with the rare exception of an occasional surviving word or fragmentary, meaningless clause—they are entirely blank. While many words or paragraphs were withheld elsewhere in the Report, the decision to censor that entire section caused a furor in 2003.

Inquiries established that, while withholdings were technically the responsibility of the CIA, the Agency would not have obstructed release of most of the twenty-eight pages. The order that they must remain secret had come from President Bush himself.

REPORT

OF THE

U.S. SENATE SELECT COMMITTEE ON INTELLIGENCE

AND

U.S. HOUSE PERMANENT SELECT COMMITTEE ON INTELLIGENCE

PART FOUR—FINDING, DISCUSSION AND NARRATIVE REGARDING
CERTAIN SENSITIVE NATIONAL SECURITY MATTERS

20. Finding: [Through its investigation, the Joint Inquiry developed information
suggesting specific sources of foreign support for some of the September 11 hijackers while
they were in the United States. The Joint Inquiry's review confirmed that the Intelligence
Community also has information, much of which has yet to be independently verified,
concerning these potential sources of support. In their testimony, neither CIA nor FBI

[Given the serious national security implications of this information, however, the
leadership of the Joint Inquiry is referring the Joint Inquiry Staff's compilation of relevant
information to both the FBI and the CIA for investigative review and appropriate investigative
and intelligence action].

*The start of the final section of the Joint Inquiry's Report. Its focus is reportedly the
matter of support for the hijackers from Saudi Arabia. The material was withheld
from the public on the orders of President Bush.*

The Democratic and Republican chairmen of the Joint Committee, Senators Graham and Richard Shelby, felt strongly that the bulk of the withheld material could and should have been made public. So did Representative Nancy Pelosi, the ranking Democrat for the House. "I went back and read every one of those pages thoroughly," Shelby said. "My judgment is that 95% of that information could be declassified, become uncensored, so the American people would know."

Know what? "I can't tell you what's in those pages," the Joint Committee's staff director, Eleanor Hill, was to say. "I can tell you that the chapter deals with information that our Committee found in the CIA and FBI files that was very disturbing. It had to do with sources of foreign support for the hijackers." The focus of the material, leaks to the press soon established, had been Saudi Arabia.

There were, sources said, additional details about Bayoumi, who had helped Mihdhar and Hazmi in California, and about his associate Basnan. The censored portion of the Report had stated—even then, years before he came to haunt the West as a perennial threat—that Anwar Aulaqi, the imam, had been a "central figure" in a support network for the future hijackers.

There had been, an official let it be known, "very direct, very specific links" with Saudi officials, links that "cannot be passed off as rogue, isolated or coincidental." The *New York Times* journalist and author Philip Shenon has written that Senator Graham and his investigators became "convinced that a number of sympathetic Saudi officials, possibly within the Islamic Affairs Ministry, had known that al Qaeda terrorists were entering the United States beginning in 2000 in preparation for some sort of attack. Graham believed the Saudi officials had directed spies operating in the United States to assist them."

Most serious of all, the information uncovered by the investigation had reportedly drawn "apparent connections between high-level Saudi princes and associates of the hijackers." Absent release of the censored pages, one can only surmise as to what the connections may have been.

One clue is the first corroboration—in an interview with a former CIA officer for this book—of an allegation relating to the capture in Pakistan, while the Joint Inquiry was at work, of senior bin Laden aide Abu Zubaydah. Many months of interrogation followed, including, from about June or July 2002, no less than eighty-three sessions of

Osama bin Laden and his "holy war" against the United States, acclaimed by crowds in Pakistan after 9/11.

Khalid Sheikh Mohammed (*centre right*) claimed credit for the plot. Ramzi Binalshibh (*upper left*) acted as a go-between for the hijackers. Abu Zubaydah (*right*), a key al Qaeda logistics man, was gravely wounded during his arrest.

How reliable are their confessions, obtained under "enhanced" interrogation?

REWARD
$2,000,000

KHALED SHAIKH MOHAMMAD
ALIASES: KHALED SHAIKH, SALEM ALI, ABU-KHUALA, ASHRAF REFAT NABIAH HENIM

1993-1994   October 1995

DESCRIPTION: EYES: Brown
DATE OF BIRTH: April 14, 1965 or March 1, 1964   BUILD: Slightly overweight to medium
PLACE OF BIRTH: Kuwait or Pakistan   COMPLEXION: Olive or Light Skinned
HEIGHT: 165 cm   CHARACTERISTICS: Long shaped face, wears
WEIGHT: 60 kg   a full beard, a trimmed beard and clean shaven.
HAIR: Dark Brown/Black   Has been known to wear glasses.

On January 6, 1995, a fire broke out in an apartment in Manila occupied by KHALED SHAIKH MOHAMMAD. The information developed from the investigation into this small fire, ultimately saved the lives of thousands of people.

The investigation revealed that in August 1994 through January 1995 in this apartment and elsewhere, KHALED SHAIKH MOHAMMAD unlawfully and willfully conspired to bomb U.S. civilian airliners by placing explosive devices on twelve airliners flying over the Pacific Ocean during a two day period in January 1995.

Had any of these devices exploded, innocent lives would have been lost. People should not have to live under the fear of terrorism. KHALED SHAIKH MOHAMMAD has been indicted for his involvement in this deadly conspiracy and must stand trial for his crimes.

The United States is offering a reward of up to $2,000,000 for information leading to the arrest or prosecution of KHALED SHAIKH MOHAMMAD. If you have any information about KHALED, contact the nearest U.S. embassy or consulate. In the United States, you may call your local Federal Bureau of Investigation or contact the Department of State Diplomatic Security Service at 1-800-HEROES-1, or write to:

HEROES ■ Post Office Box 96781 ■ Washington, D.C. ■ 20090-6781 U.S.A.
www.heroes.net ■ e-mail: bsmith@heroes.net

Mohamed Atta, the hijackers' leader, and Flight 93 hijacker Ziad Jarrah in Afghanistan (*below left*) preparing to videotape martyrdom statements. The beards came off on their return to Europe. Atta as a youngster, (*below right*) with his sisters.

Waleed M. Alsheri

Mohammed Atta

Wail M. Alshehri

Abdulaziz Alomari

Satam M. A. al-Suqami

Ahmed Alnami

Ahmed Ibrahim A. al Haznawi

Ziad Samir al-Jarrah

Saeed Alghamdi

Khalid Almihdar

Majed Moqed

Nawaf Alhazmi

Salem Alhazmi

Hani Hanjour

Marwan Alshehhi

Ahmed Alghamdi

Mohand Alshehri

Hamza Alghamdi

Fayez Rashid
Ahmed Hassan
al-Qadi Banihammad

The nineteen hijackers,
sixteen of whom were Saudis.
To some, they were heroes.
A poster (*right*), produced
two years after the attacks,
glorified the terrorists.

The men believed to have been at the controls of three of the hijacked airliners: Marwan al-Shehhi (*above left*), Hani Hanjour (*above centre*), and Ziad Jarrah, with his lover Aysel Sengün (*above right*), and in the cockpit of a light aircraft – he had recently completed pilot training.

Below right Anwar Aulaqi, an American-born imam, at a mosque after 9/11. He is characterized as having been "spiritual adviser" to two future hijackers. Now in Yemen, he is considered a possible successor to bin Laden.

Above Saleh al-Hussayen, a Saudi religious official. On the eve of 9/11, he stayed at the same hotel as two lead hijackers.

Khalid al-Mihdhar (*above left*) and Nawaf al-Hazmi (*above right*) were the first future hijackers to arrive in the United States.

Omar al-Bayoumi, a Saudi living in California (*below left*), and American-born Caysan bin Don (*below centre*), said they met future hijackers Mihdhar and Hazmi in a restaurant by chance. Did Mohdar Abdullah (*below right*), who also befriended the terrorists, get advance information that an attack was coming?

CIA Director George Tenet (*centre*), had a standing arrangement that ensured effective liaison with his counterpart in Saudi Arabia, GID chief Prince Turki (*left*) – in theory. Saudi Interior Minister Prince Naif (*right*), who dealt with domestic security, was to say he did not believe most hijackers had been Saudis. It has been alleged that Naif paid protection money to bin Laden.

Saudi Prince Bandar (*rear left*) meeting at the White House with President Bush, Vice President Cheney, and National Security Adviser Rice, two nights after the attacks.

Seven months after 9/11, Bush invited Saudi Crown Prince Abdullah to his Texas ranch (*left*). He again welcomed Abdullah, soon to become King, in 2005 (*above*).

Left The joint chairmen of Congress's probe, Senators Bob Graham (*centre*) and Richard Shelby (*right*), with their Report in 2003. They pointed out that many pages had been suppressed, on President Bush's orders. The pages are still withheld today.

Below 9/11 Commission members and staff watching video of the Twin Towers burning, at a hearing in 2004.

Left Some of the bereaved who pressed for the Commission's creation and closely followed its progress rejected its findings.

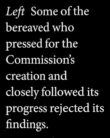

Reserved for
11 Families

Reserved for
9-11 Families

Re:
9-1

Left Osama bin Laden, apparently pictured here in hiding in Pakistan, was shot dead by US commandos in May 2011.

Americans celebrated the feared terrorist's death, yet faced an uncertain future.

waterboarding. Zubaydah was the first al Qaeda prisoner on whom that controversial "enhanced technique" was used.

John Kiriakou, then a CIA operative serving in Pakistan, had played a leading part in the operation that led to Zubaydah's capture—gravely wounded—in late March. In early fall back in Washington, he informed the authors, he was told by colleagues that cables on the interrogation reported that Zubaydah had come up with the names of several Saudi princes. He "raised their names in sort of a mocking fashion, [indicating] he had the support of the Saudi government." The CIA followed up by running name traces, Kiriakou said.

Zubaydah had named three princes, but by late July they had all died—within a week of one another. First was Prince Ahmed bin Salman bin Abdul Aziz, the leading figure in the international horse-racing community whose name came up earlier in the authors' account of Saudis hurrying to get out of the United States after 9/11. Ahmed and a nephew of both then-King Fahd and defense and aviation minister Prince Sultan, died of a heart attack at the age of forty-three, following abdominal surgery, according to the Saudis. Prince Sultan bin Faisal bin Turki bin Abdullah al Saud, also a nephew of the then-king and his defense minister though not a top-rank prince, reportedly died in a car accident. A third prince, Fahd bin Turki bin Saud al-Kabir, a more distant family member whose father was a cousin of Fahd and Sultan, was said to have died "of thirst."

In his interview for this book, former CIA officer Kiriakou said his colleagues told him they believed that what Zubaydah told them about the princes was true. "We had known for years," he told the authors, "that Saudi royals—I should say elements of the royal family—were funding al Qaeda."

In 2003, during the brouhaha about the redacted chapter in the Joint Inquiry Report, Crown Prince Abdullah's spokesman, Adel al-Jubeir, made a cryptic comment that has never been further explained. The regime's own probe, he said, had uncovered "wrongdoing by some." He noted, though, that the royal family had thousands of members, and insisted that the regime itself had no connection to the 9/11 plot.

Joint Inquiry cochair Bob Graham did not share that view. What Zubaydah is reported to have said about the princes, he told the authors, is credible. Graham has said publicly, meanwhile, that the hijackers "received assistance from a foreign government which further facilitated their ability to be so lethal." The assistance, a very senior Committee source told the authors, "went to major names in the Saudi hierarchy."

In all, more than forty U.S. senators clamored for the release of the censored pages. Committee cochairs Graham and Shelby aside, they included John Kerry, Joe Lieberman, Charles Schumer, Sam Brownback, Olympia Snowe, and Pat Roberts.

Nothing happened.

Graham, with his long experience in the field as member and co-chair not only of the 9/11 probe but of the Intelligence Committee, has continued to voice his anger over the censorship even in retirement. President Bush, he wrote in 2004, had "engaged in a cover-up . . . to protect not only the agencies that failed but also America's relationship with the Kingdom of Saudi Arabia. . . . He has done so by misclassi-fying information on national security data. While the information may be embarrassing or politically damaging, its revelation would not damage national security."

Graham's Republican counterpart on Congress's probe, Senator Shelby, concluded independently that virtually all the censored pages were "being kept secret for reasons other than national security."

"It was," Graham thought, "as if the President's loyalty lay more with Saudi Arabia than with America's safety." In Graham's view, Bush's role in suppressing important information about 9/11, along with other transgressions, should have led to his impeachment and removal from office.

Within weeks of his inauguration in 2009, Bush's successor, Barack Obama, made a point of receiving bereaved relatives of 9/11. The widow of one of those who died at the World Trade Center, Kristen Breitweiser, has said that she brought the new President's attention to the infamous censored section of the Joint Inquiry Report. Obama told her, she said afterward, that he was willing to get the suppressed material released. As of this writing, two years later, the chapter re-mains classified.

"If the twenty-eight pages were to be made public," said one of the officials who was privy to them before President Bush ordered their removal, "I have no question that the entire relationship with Saudi Arabia would change overnight."

THIRTY-FOUR

THE 9/11 COMMISSION REPORT BLURRED THE TRUTH ABOUT THE Saudi role. By the time it was published in July 2004, more than a year had passed since the invasion of Iraq, a country that—the report said—had nothing to do with 9/11.

In the eighteen months before the invasion, however, the Bush administration had persistently seeded the notion that—Saddam Hussein's other sins aside—there *was* an Iraqi connection to 9/11. While never alleging a direct Iraqi role, President Bush had linked Hussein's name to that of bin Laden. Vice President Cheney had gone further, suggesting repeatedly that there had been Iraqi involvement in the attacks.

Polls suggest that the publicity about Iraq's supposed involvement affected the degree to which the U.S. public came to view Iraq as an enemy deserving retribution. Before the invasion, a Pew Research poll found that 57 percent of those polled believed Hussein had helped the 9/11 terrorists. Forty-four percent of respondents to a Knight-Ridder poll had gained the impression that "most" or "some" of the hijackers had been Iraqi. In fact, none were. In the wake of the invasion, a *Washington Post* poll found that 69 percent of Americans believed it likely that Saddam Hussein had been personally involved in 9/11.

Of the many reports and rumors circulated alleging an Iraqi role, two dominated. One, which got by far the most exposure, had it that Mohamed Atta had met in spring 2001 in Prague with a named Iraqi intelligence officer. The Iraqi officer later denied it, a fact that on its own might carry no weight. The best evidence, meanwhile, is that Atta was in the United States at the time.

A second allegation, persistently propagated before and after 9/11 by Laurie Mylroie, a scholar associated with the conservative think tank American Enterprise Institute, proposed that Ramzi Yousef—the terrorist responsible for the 1993 World Trade Center bombing—had been an Iraqi agent using a stolen identity. Investigation by others, including the FBI, indicated that the speculation is unsupported by hard evidence.

Mylroie, meanwhile, appeared to believe that Saddam Hussein had been behind multiple terrorist attacks over a ten-year period, from the East Africa embassy bombings to Oklahoma City and 9/11. "My view," said Vincent Cannistraro, a former head of the CIA's Counterterrorist Center, "is that Laurie has an obsession with Iraq." Mylroie's claim about Yousef nevertheless proved durable.

None of the speculative leads suggesting an Iraqi link to the attacks proved out. "We went back ten years," said former CIA bin Laden unit chief Michael Scheuer, who looked into the matter at the request of Director Tenet. "We examined about 20,000 documents, probably something along the line of 75,000 pages of information, and there was no connection between [al Qaeda] and Saddam."

A CIA report entitled "Iraqi Support for Terrorism," completed in January 2003, was the last in-depth analysis the Agency produced prior to the invasion of Iraq in March. "The Intelligence Community," it concluded, "has no credible information that Baghdad had foreknowledge of the 11 September attacks or any other al Qaeda strike."

After exhaustive trawls of the record, official probes have concluded that senior Bush administration officials applied inordinate pressure to try to establish that there was an Iraqi connection to 9/11, and that American torture of al Qaeda prisoners was a result of such pressure. CIA analysts noted that "questions regarding al Qaeda's ties to the Iraqi regime were among the first presented to senior op-

erational planner Khalid Sheikh Mohammed following his capture."
KSM was one of those most persistently subjected to torture.

The CIA's Charles Duelfer, who was in charge of interrogations
of Iraqi officials after the invasion, recalled being "asked if enhanced
measures, such as waterboarding, should be used" on a detainee who
had handled contacts with terrorist groups and might have knowledge
of links between the Hussein regime and al Qaeda.

The notion was turned down. Duelfer noted, however, that it
had come from "some in Washington at very senior levels (not in the
CIA)" who thought the detainee's interrogation had been "too gentle." Two U.S. intelligence officers, meanwhile, have said flatly that
the suggestion came from Vice President Cheney's office.

"There were two reasons why these interrogations were so persistent and why extreme methods were used," a former senior intelligence official said in 2009. "The main one is that everyone was worried
about some kind of follow-up attack [after 9/11]. But for most of 2002
and into 2003, Cheney and Rumsfeld, especially, were also demanding proof of the links between al Qaeda and Iraq that [former Iraqi
exile leader Ahmed] Chalabi and others had told them were there."

A former U.S. Army psychiatrist, Major Paul Burney, told military investigators that interrogators at the Guantánamo Bay detention center were under "pressure" to produce evidence of ties between
al Qaeda and Iraq. "We were not successful," Burney said in interviews for the Army's inspector general, but "there was more and more
pressure to resort to measures that might produce more immediate
results."

In the absence of evidence, according to the author and Pulitzer winner Ron Suskind, it was in one instance fabricated. Suskind
has reported that in fall 2003—when the U.S. administration was still
struggling to justify the invasion of Iraq—the White House asked the
CIA to collaborate in the forgery of a document stating that hijacker
leader Atta had spent time training in Iraq.

The forgery took the form of a purported memo to Saddam Hussein from the former head of the Iraqi intelligence service. The memo
was dated two months before 9/11—the actual former intelligence
chief was prevailed upon to put his signature to it long after its supposed writing—and it stated that Atta had just spent time training
in Iraq "to lead the team which will be responsible for attacking the
targets that we have agreed to destroy."

The story of this fakery raised a brief media storm and a spate of denials. Rebuttals included a carefully phrased statement from Suskind's primary source, a former head of the CIA's Near East Division named Rob Richer—to which Suskind responded by publishing a transcript of one of his interviews with Richer.

Another former CIA officer, Philip Giraldi, meanwhile, placed responsibility for the fabrication on the Pentagon's Office of Special Plans, at the instigation of Vice President Cheney. According to Giraldi, the Pentagon, unlike the CIA, had "no restrictions on it regarding the production of false information to mislead the public" and had "its own false documents center."

If it happened, the forgery was the most flagrant attempt, in a long line of such maneuvering, to blame 9/11 on Iraq—and it has never been officially investigated.

A former deputy director of the CIA's Counterterrorist Center, Paul Pillar, has called the case against Iraq "a manufactured issue."

In 2008, by a bipartisan majority of ten to five, the Senate Intelligence Committee produced its "Report on Whether Public Statements Regarding Iraq by U.S. Government Officials Were Substantiated by Intelligence Information." "Unfortunately," said its chairman, John D. Rockefeller,

> our Committee has concluded that the administration made significant claims that were not supported by the intelligence. In making the case for war, the administration repeatedly presented intelligence as fact when in reality it was unsubstantiated, contradicted, or even non-existent.
>
> It's my belief that the Bush administration was fixated on Iraq and used the 9/11 attacks by al Qaeda as justification for overthrowing Saddam Hussein. To accomplish this, top administration officials made repeated statements that falsely linked Iraq and al Qaeda as a single threat and insinuated that Iraq played a role in 9/11. Sadly, the Bush administration led the nation into war under false pretenses.

IN THE SEVEN YEARS since the invasion of Iraq, reputable estimates indicate, more than 4,000 American soldiers have died and 32,000 have suffered serious injury as a result of the invasion and the violence that followed. Some 9,000 Iraqi men in uniform were killed, and 55,000 insurgents. Figures suggest that more than 100,000 civilians died during and following the invasion.

A total of some 168,000 people, then, have died—and tens of thousands have been injured—as the result of an attack on a nation that many Americans had been falsely led to believe bore some if not all of the responsibility for the attacks of September 11.

The 3,000 who died in New York, Washington, and the field in Pennsylvania, the many hundreds who have died since from exposure to the toxins they breathed in at Ground Zero, and all their grieving relatives, deserved better than to have had their tragedy manipulated in such a way.

THIRTY-FIVE

IN THE YEARS THAT THE CONFLICT IN IRAQ HAD THE WORLD'S ATTEN-
tion, the real evidence that linked other nations to Osama bin Laden
and 9/11 faded from the public consciousness. This was in part the
fault of the 9/11 Commission, which blurred the facts rather than
highlighting them. It was, ironically, a former deputy homeland security adviser to President Bush, Richard Falkenrath, who loudly expressed that uncomfortable truth.

The Commission's Report, Falkenrath wrote, had produced only
superficial coverage of the fact that al Qaeda was "led and financed
largely by Saudis, with extensive support from Pakistani intelligence."
Saudi Arabia's murky role has been covered in these pages. The part
played by Pakistan—not least given the stunning news that was to
break upon the world in spring 2011—deserves equally close scrutiny.

Pakistan has a strong Islamic fundamentalist movement—it was,
with Saudi Arabia and the United Arab Emirates, one of only three
nations that recognized the Taliban. Bin Laden had operated there
as early as 1979, with the blessing of Saudi intelligence, in the first

phase of the struggle to oust the Soviets from neighboring Afghanistan. The contacts he made were durable. "Pakistani military intelligence," the Commission Report did note, "probably had advance knowledge of his coming, and its officers may have facilitated his travel" when he returned to Afghanistan in 1996. Pakistan "held the key," the Report said, to bin Laden's ability to use Afghanistan as a base from which to mount his war against America.

Time was to show, moreover, that Pakistan itself was central not only to the terrorist chief's overall activity but also to the 9/11 operation itself. Al Qaeda communications, always vulnerable and often impractical in Afghanistan, for years functioned relatively safely and certainly more efficiently in Pakistan. Pakistan, with its teeming cities and extensive banking system, also offered the facilities the terrorists needed for financial transactions and logistical needs.

As reported in this book, World Trade Center bomber Ramzi Yousef had family roots in Pakistan. He traveled from Pakistan to carry out the 1993 attack, and it was to Pakistan that he ran after the bombing. Yousef would eventually be caught in the capital, Islamabad, in 1995. His bomb-making accomplice Abdul Murad, though seized in the Philippines, had lived in Pakistan.

It was through Pakistan that the future pilot hijackers from Europe made their way to the Afghan training camps, and to their audiences with bin Laden. The first two Saudi operatives inserted into the United States, Mihdhar and Hazmi—and later the muscle hijackers—were briefed for the mission in the anonymity of Karachi, Pakistan's largest city.

The family of the man who briefed the hijackers and who was to claim he ran the entire operation, Khalid Sheikh Mohammed, hailed from Baluchistan, Pakistan's largest province. Though high on the international "most wanted" list, he operated with impunity largely from Pakistan over the several years devoted to the planning of 9/11. KSM, though in Afghanistan when the date for the attacks was set, then left for Pakistan. He remained there, plotting new terrorist acts, until his capture in 2003—in Rawalpindi, headquarters of the Pakistan military command.

Ramzi Binalshibh, who had functioned in Germany as the cutout between KSM and lead hijacker Atta, ran to Pakistan on the eve of the attacks. In the spring of 2002, at a safe house in Karachi, he and KSM had the effrontery to give a press interview boasting of their part in

9/11. It was in the city's upmarket Defense Society quarter that he was finally caught later that year. Abu Zubaydah, the first of the big fish to be caught after 9/11, had been seized in Faisalabad a few months earlier.

What bin Laden himself had said about Pakistan two years before 9/11 seemed to speak volumes. "Pakistani people have great love for Islam," he observed after the U.S. missile attack on his camps in the late summer of 1998, in which seven Pakistanis were killed. "And they always have offered sacrifices for the cause of religion." Later, in another interview, he explained how he himself had managed to avoid the attack. "We found a sympathetic and generous people in Pakistan . . . receive[d] information from our beloved ones and helpers of jihad."

Then again, speaking with *Time* magazine in January 1999: "As for Pakistan, there are some governmental departments which by the grace of God respond to the Islamic sentiments of the masses. This is reflected in sympathy and cooperation." The next month, in yet another interview, he praised Pakistan's military and called on the faithful to support its generals.

"Some governmental departments." "The generals." Few doubt that these were allusions to bin Laden's support from within the Inter-Services Intelligence Directorate, or ISI, Pakistan's equivalent to the CIA. The links went back to the eighties and probably—some believe certainly—continue to join al Qaeda to elements of the organization today.

PAKISTAN, CHAIRMAN OF the U.S. Joint Chiefs of Staff Mike Mullen reflected in a recent interview, is "the most complicated country in the world." The bin Laden/ISI connection had been made during the Afghan war against the Soviets, when the CIA—working with the ISI and Saudi intelligence—spent billions arming and training the disparate groups of fighters. Once the short-term goal of rolling back the Soviets had been achieved, the United States had walked away from Afghanistan. Pakistan had not.

It saw and still sees Afghanistan as strategically crucial, not least on account of an issue of which many members of the public in the West have minimal knowledge or none at all. Pakistan and India have fought three wars in the past half-century over Kashmir, a large disputed territory over which each nation has claims and that each partially controls, and where there is also a homegrown insurgency. Having leverage over Afghanistan, given its geographical position, enabled Pakistan to recruit Afghan and Arab volunteers to join the Kashmir insurgency—and tie down a large part of the Indian army.

The insurgents inserted into Kashmir have by and large been mujahideen, committed to a cause they see as holy. As reported earlier, the man who headed the ISI in 1989, Lieutenant General Hamid Gul, himself saw the conflict as jihad. Osama bin Laden made common cause with Gul and—in the years that followed—with like-minded figures in the ISI. ISI recruits for the fight in Kashmir were trained in bin Laden camps. Bin Laden would still be saying, as late as 2000, "Whatever Pakistan does in the matter of Kashmir, we support it."

Such action and talk paid off in ways large and small. The ISI at one time even reportedly installed the security system that protected bin Laden in one of the houses he used in Afghanistan.

The tracks of the ISI and al Qaeda converged in other ways. Months after the Taliban had begun hosting bin Laden in 1996, they had been, as *Time* magazine put it, "shoehorned into power" by the ISI—thus ensuring Pakistan's influence over most of Afghanistan. The need to keep things that way, and to fend off rebellion on its own border, a Pakistani official told the State Department in 2000, meant that his government would "always" support the Taliban.

So powerful was the ISI in Afghanistan, former U.S. special envoy Peter Tomsen told the 9/11 Commission, that the Taliban "actually were the junior partners in an unholy alliance"—ISI, al Qaeda, and the Taliban. As it grew in influence, the ISI liaised closely with Saudi intelligence—and the Saudis reportedly lined the pockets of senior Pakistani officers with additional cash.

The ISI over the years achieved not only military muscle but massive political influence within Pakistan itself—so much so that some came to characterize it as "the most influential body in Pakistan," a "shadow government."

The United States, caught between the constraints of regional power politics and the growing need to deal with bin Laden and al Qaeda, long remained impotent.

By the late nineties, former U.S. ambassador to Pakistan Thomas Simons has recalled, American efforts to bring pressure on the Pakistanis and the Taliban over bin Laden resulted only in "a sense of helplessness." Concern about the tensions between India and Pakistan loomed larger at the State Department than Islamic extremism—not least after both those nations tested nuclear weapons.

In 1999, then–Pakistani prime minister Nawaz Sharif held out the possibility of working with the CIA to mount a commando operation to capture or kill bin Laden. Nothing came of it, the National Security Agency reported, because the plan was compromised by the ISI. In early 2000, though, after General Pervez Musharraf seized power, Washington made a serious effort to ratchet up the pressure.

President Clinton insisted on making a visit to Islamabad, the first by an American head of state in more than thirty years. He did so in spite of CIA and Secret Service warnings that a trip to Pakistan would endanger his life. Air Force One arrived without him, as a decoy, while he flew in aboard an unmarked jet. At a private meeting with Musharraf, Clinton recalled, he offered the Pakistani leader "the moon . . . in terms of better relations with the United States, if he'd help us get bin Laden." Nothing significant came of it. Clinton had avoided pushing too hard about bin Laden at an earlier meeting— because ISI members were in the room.

The following month, when then–ISI director General Mahmoud Ahmed was in Washington, Under Secretary of State Thomas Pickering warned that "people who support those people [bin Laden and al Qaeda] will be treated as our enemies." Later, at Pakistan's interior ministry, Pickering confronted a senior Taliban official with evidence of bin Laden's role in the embassy bombings in East Africa. The official said the evidence was "not persuasive."

About this same time, Assistant Secretary of State Michael Sheehan suggested giving Pakistan an ultimatum: Work with the United States to capture bin Laden or face a cutoff of vital financial aid. Fears of the possible consequences—that Pakistan might opt out of talks to ensure that it did not share its nuclear know-how with rogue nations—loomed larger than concerns about terrorism. Sheehan's idea went nowhere.

Come early 2001, the start of the Bush presidency, and his warning memo to Condoleezza Rice about al Qaeda, counterterrorism coordinator Richard Clarke stressed how important it was to have Pakistan's cooperation. He noted, though, that General Musharraf had spoken of "influential radical elements that would oppose significant Pakistani measures against al Qaeda." Musharraf had cautioned, too, that the United States should not violate Pakistani airspace when launching strikes within Afghanistan.

Nothing effective was achieved by the Bush administration. At the CIA, director Tenet sensed a "loss of urgency." It had been obvious for years, he wrote later, that "it would be almost impossible to root out al Qaeda" without Pakistan's help. The Pakistanis, moreover, "always knew more than they were telling us, and they had been singularly uncooperative." "We never did the Full Monty with them," another former senior CIA official has said. "We don't trust them. . . . There is always this little dance with them."

On September 11, however, the dancing and the diplomatic dithering stopped. While no hard evidence would emerge that Pakistan had any foreknowledge of the attacks—let alone an actual role in the plot—Washington now issued a blunt warning. It was then—according to ISI director Ahmed, who was visiting Washington at the time—that U.S. deputy secretary of state Richard Armitage said the United States would bomb Pakistan "back to the Stone Age" should it now fail to go along with seven specific American demands for assistance.

Musharraf weighed up the likely consequences of failure to comply, not the least of them the fact that the U.S. military could pulverize his forces. With a couple of reservations—he says he could not accept the U.S. demands for blanket rights to overfly Pakistan and have the use of all its air bases and port facilities—he cooperated as required. "We have done more than any other country," the former president has said, "to capture and kill members of al Qaeda, and to destroy its infrastructure in our cities and mountains." Musharraf's administration indeed cracked down on extremism, at a terrible cost in human life that persists to this day. In one year alone, 2009, 3,021 Pakistanis died in retaliatory terrorist attacks—approximately the same number as the American dead of 9/11. Musharraf's army thrust into the tribal badlands near the Afghan border, and some 700 purported al Qaeda operatives were rounded up across Pakistan. As of 2006, according to Musharraf, 369 of them had been handed over to the United States—for millions of dollars in bounty money paid by the CIA.

The former CIA station chief in Islamabad, Robert Grenier, recently confirmed that Pakistani cooperation against al Qaeda did improve vastly after 9/11. The arrests of the three best-known top al Qaeda operatives—Abu Zubaydah, Ramzi Binalshibh, and Khalid

Sheikh Mohammed—were, it seems, made by Pakistani intelligence agents and police, in some if not all cases working in collaboration with the Agency.

Former CIA officer John Kiriakou, who was involved in operations on the ground in Pakistan during the relevant period, told the authors that this statement by Musharraf was "generally accurate." He said, however: "The truth is, we allowed the Pakistanis to believe they were taking the lead. Certainly they were the first through the door, but on those high-profile captures we never told them who the target was. We were afraid they would leak the information to al Qaeda and the target would escape. The information leading to the captures was a hundred percent CIA information. The Pakistanis had no role in the intelligence."

The biggest name of all, of course, long eluded pursuit. Last on the list of Washington's post-9/11 demands, as Musharraf recalled it, had been to help "destroy bin Laden." "We have done everything possible to track down Osama bin Laden," Musharraf wrote in 2006, "but he has evaded us."

No one, according to Musharraf, had been more anxious than the Pakistanis to resolve the mystery of bin Laden's whereabouts. As the months and years passed, however, there were those who believed otherwise.

FROM THE TIME America routed al Qaeda after 9/11, information indicated that the ISI continued to remain in touch with bin Laden or aware of his location. ISI officials, former special envoy Tomsen told the 9/11 Commission, were "still visiting OBL [bin Laden] as late as December 2001"—and continued to know his location thereafter. In 2007 Kathleen McFarland, a former senior Defense Department official, spoke of bin Laden's presence in Pakistan as a fact. "I'm convinced," military historian Stephen Tanner told CNN in 2010, "that he is protected by the ISI. I just think it's impossible after all this time to not know where he is."

Why would the ISI have allowed bin Laden to enjoy safe haven in Pakistan? The ISI, Tanner thought, would see him as a trump card—leverage over the United States in the power play involved in Pakistan's ongoing dispute with India.

It went deeper, and further back than that. "You in the West," the veteran London *Sunday Times* reporter Christina Lamb has recalled former ISI head General Gul telling her twenty years ago, "think you can use these fundamentalists and abandon them, but it will come back to haunt you." It was clear to Lamb that "For Gul and his ilk, support for the fundamentalist Afghan groups, and later the Taliban, was not just policy but also ideology." In spite of the vast sums in U.S. aid doled out to Pakistan, a 2010 poll suggested that a majority of Pakistanis viewed the United States as an enemy.

There was special suspicion of the S Section of the ISI, which is made up of personnel who are officially retired but front for certain ISI operations. S Section, *The New York Times* has quoted former CIA officials as saying, has been "seen as particularly close to militants."

In Washington, trust in the Pakistanis had long since plummeted. "They were very hot on the ISI," said a member of a Pakistani delegation that visited the White House toward the end of the Bush presidency. "When we asked them for more information, Bush laughed and said, 'When we share information with you guys, the bad guys always run away.'"

The lack of trust notwithstanding, policy on Pakistan did not appear to change. Better to do nothing and have some cooperation, the thinking in the new Obama administration seemed to be, than come down hard and get none. In early 2011, on Fox News, former government officials called on the administration to take a tougher line with Pakistan.

Obama had vowed during his campaign for the presidency, "We will kill bin Laden. . . . That has to be our biggest national security priority." In office, he made no such public statements. The hunt for bin Laden, meanwhile, seemed to be getting nowhere—and not to be a high priority. In retrospect, though, there was a trickle of fresh information that suggested otherwise.

General David Petraeus, commander of U.S. and NATO forces in Afghanistan, was asked on *Meet the Press* in 2010 whether it was now less necessary to capture bin Laden. "I think," he replied, "capturing or killing bin Laden is still a very, very important task for all of those who are engaged in counterterrorism around the world."

For those who doubted that bin Laden was still alive, late fall 2010 brought two new bin Laden audio messages. There had been intercepts of al Qaeda communications, CIA officials told *The New York Times*, indicating that he still shaped strategy. Then, within weeks, CNN was quoting a "senior NATO official" as saying that bin Laden and his deputy Zawahiri were believed to be hiding not far from each other in northwest Pakistan, and not "in a cave." The same day, the New York *Daily News* quoted a source with "access to all reporting on bin Laden" as having spoken of two "sightings considered credible" in recent years—and even of "a grainy photo of bin Laden inside a truck." The sources were vague, though, as to where bin Laden might have been. Defense Secretary Robert Gates, for his part, was at pains in an ABC interview to suggest that it had been "years" since any hard intelligence had been received on bin Laden's likely location.

In late March 2011, out of Hong Kong, came a story suggesting that the CIA had "launched a series of secret operations in the high mountains of the Hindu Kush . . . consistent reports have established that Osama bin Laden has been on the move through the region in recent weeks."

It is a fair guess that much if not all of this was disinformation, planted to suggest to the quarry that U.S. intelligence had lost the scent, had no strong lead as to where precisely bin Laden might be, and had no plan for an imminent strike against him.

At 10:24 P.M. on the night of Sunday, May 1, 2011—an improbable hour—this bulletin came over the wires:

Breaking News Alert: White House says Obama to make late-night statement on an undisclosed topic.

Soon after, there was this from *The Washington Post*:

Osama bin Laden has been killed in a CIA operation in Pakistan, President Obama will announce from the White House, according to multiple sources.

At 11:35 P.M., the President appeared on television screens across the globe to say:

Tonight I can report to the American people and to the world that the United States has conducted an operation that killed Osama bin Laden, the leader of al Qaeda and a terrorist who's responsible for the murder of thousands of innocent men, women and children. . . .

The images of 9/11 are seared into our national memory. . . . And yet we know that the worst images are those that were unseen to the world. The empty seat at the dinner table. Children who were forced to grow up without their mother or their father. Parents who would never know the feeling of their child's embrace. Nearly three thousand citizens taken from us. . . .

Osama bin Laden avoided capture and escaped across the border into Pakistan. . . . Shortly after taking office I directed Leon Panetta, the director of the CIA, to make the killing or capture of bin Laden the top priority of the war against al Qaeda. . . . Then, last August, after years of painstaking work by our intelligence community, I was briefed on a possible lead to bin Laden. . . . I met repeatedly with my security team as we developed more information about the possibility that we had located bin Laden hiding within a compound deep inside of Pakistan. And finally, last week, I determined that we had enough intelligence to take action. . . .

Today, at my direction, the United States launched a targeted operation. . . . A small team of Americans carried out the operation with extraordinary courage. . . . No Americans were harmed. . . . After a firefight, they killed Osama bin Laden and took custody of his body.

It was a momentous victory. Jubilant Americans thronged in front of the White House, in Times Square, and at Ground Zero. For many days, there was wall-to-wall coverage in newspapers, television, and radio. The Internet hummed with information.

In its haste to break the news to the world, apparently before personnel involved in the strike against bin Laden had been fully debriefed, U.S. government officials put out information that would turn out to have been inaccurate. An initial claim that bin Laden had used a woman as a human shield, and that she had been shot dead as a result, proved to be unfounded. A woman did die in the assault, but elsewhere in the compound.

Contrary to an early statement giving the impression that bin Laden was armed and died fighting, presidential spokesman Jay Carney later said he had been unarmed. "Resistance," Carney said, "does not require a firearm." The al Qaeda leader had been in his night-clothes when confronted, it was reported later, clothing that could conceivably have concealed a weapon or explosives. The U.S. commandos involved, said CIA director Leon Panetta, "had full authority to kill him."

The rush to get the story out, albeit raw and insufficiently checked, had not been merely for maximum impact. U.S. officials had in part rushed to get their version out, it was reported, "before the Pakistanis pushed theirs."

The version of events that emerged from Pakistan was indeed different. A twelve-year-old daughter of bin Laden, who survived, was quoted as saying her father had been "captured alive and shot dead by the U.S. Special Forces during the first few minutes . . . in front of family members." That provocative quote, significantly, was sourced as coming from "senior Pakistani security officials."

Pakistan was compromised by the strike, for bin Laden had been living—by all accounts for years, comfortably housed and well protected—in not just any Pakistani city. He had been living in the pleasant town of Abbottabad, where many serving and retired military officers live, and within shouting distance of the nation's most prestigious military academy—the equivalent of America's West Point. The ISI also had a presence there.

Officials in Washington did not mince their words when these facts became public. The Pakistanis, CIA director Panetta said, had been either "involved or incompetent." The President's counter-terrorism advisor, John Brennan, thought it "inconceivable" that bin Laden had not had a "support system" in Abbottabad. On CBS's *60 Minutes,* Obama himself speculated "whether there might have been some people inside of government, people outside of government, [supporting bin Laden] . . . that's something we have to investigate, and more importantly the Pakistani government has to investigate."

Bin Laden, Pakistan's President Zardari said helplessly, "was not anywhere we had anticipated he would be." The ISI, long the principal object of U.S. suspicion, denied that it had shielded the terrorist or had known where he was. Former ISI chief Hamid Gul, the veteran supporter of jihad, declared it "a bit amazing" that bin Laden could have been living in Abbottabad incognito.

Bin Laden had been tracked to Abbottabad, U.S. sources revealed as this book went to press, thanks to information on his use of couriers to hand-carry messages to his associates. Unmentioned in the coverage these authors have seen are facts about the link between Abbottabad and al Qaeda that former president Musharraf made public as long ago as 2006—five years before the U.S. caught up with bin Laden and killed him.

Pakistan's 2005 capture and transfer to U.S. custody of another very senior bin Laden aide—Khalid Sheikh Mohammed's successor, Abu Faraj al-Libi—Musharraf had written, had been achieved after a prolonged pursuit by Pakistani investigators. In the course of the hunt, according to Musharraf, the investigators discovered that Libi used no less than three safe houses—in Abbottabad. Far from being a place where one would not expect a top terrorist to be hiding, it turns out, Abbottabad has a track record for being exactly that.

America's eventual success in tracking down bin Laden, it is clear from the reporting, grew out of the intelligence gained from Libi back in 2005. It is possible—if the Musharraf account turns out to be accurate, and whatever role Pakistan may have played in the years that followed—that Pakistan deserves at least some of the credit for the outcome in 2011.

According to CIA director Panetta, U.S. authorities gave the Pakistanis no advance notice of the 2011 strike that led to bin Laden's demise—though the operation involved a highly sensitive incursion, an overflight of Pakistan's airspace, and action on the ground deep inside Pakistani territory. "It was decided," Panetta told *Time* magazine, "that any effort to work with the Pakistanis could jeopardize the mission. They might alert the targets."

Both U.S. and Pakistani officials, however, initially suggested that Pakistan may have been informed—"a few minutes" in advance. Some sources in the Pakistani capital claimed that they had been cooperating with the United States, and had been keeping the building in Abbottabad under surveillance.

There is another wrinkle, one that may eventually illuminate the truth about the attitude of those in authority in Pakistan—whatever knowledge some Pakistani element may have had of bin Laden's presence in the town. Ten days after the strike against bin Laden, it was reported that a decade ago—after 9/11—President Bush struck a deal with then–Pakistan president Musharraf. Under the deal, should bin Laden be located inside Pakistan's borders, the U.S. would be permitted unilaterally to conduct a raid.

"There was an agreement," a former senior U.S. official was quoted as saying, "that if we knew where Osama was, we were going to come and get him. The Pakistanis would put up a hue and cry, but they wouldn't stop us." Musharraf has denied that the reported deal was made. A Pakistani official, however, reportedly offered corroboration for the story. "As far as our American friends are concerned," he said, "they have just implemented the agreement."

Pakistan did, sure enough, protest the violation of its sovereignty after bin Laden was killed. Should anything similar occur in the future, Prime Minister Yousaf Gilani said sternly, his country would be within its rights "to retaliate with full force." That, though, according to the U.S. source of the story, was merely the "public face" of the arrangement. Gilani himself had reportedly long since said of similar possible American action: "I don't care if they do it, so long as they get the right people. We'll protest in the National Assembly and then ignore it."

A full, authoritative account of the painstaking hunt for the world's most wanted man, and an accurate telling of the circumstances surrounding his bloody end, lies in the future. Meanwhile, the certainty must be that Osama bin Laden is dead.

His cadaver has not been seen publicly—U.S. officials say it was rapidly disposed of at sea following Muslim funeral rites. As of early June 2011, no photographs had been publicly released—President Obama said displaying "trophies" was not his administration's way. Some members of the Congress, however, are said to have seen photographs and to accept that the face of the dead man depicted resembles that of bin Laden. DNA analysis has established the identification, according to the administration.

In a statement on the websites on which it habitually posted messages, moreover, al Qaeda acknowledged that bin Laden is dead. His blood, it threatened, will not have been spilled in vain. "We will remain, God willing, a curse chasing the Americans and their agents. . . . Soon, God willing, their happiness will turn to sadness. Their blood will be mingled with their tears."

AFTERWORD

IN THE TEN YEARS SINCE THE ATTACKS ON THE UNITED STATES—THE last four and more of them dominated for us by the writing of this book—there have been momentous events that grew out of the catastrophe—and resolution of virtually nothing.

"We are sure of our victory against the Americans and Jews, as promised by the Prophet," bin Laden had said three years before 9/11. In 2009, in a letter to the military judges at Guantánamo, Khalid Sheikh Mohammed said the attack had been "the noblest victory known to history over the forces of oppression and tyranny."

Victory? Amid all his flowery verbiage, the essential elements of what bin Laden demanded are clear. He called for: the "complete liberation of Palestine"; an end to the American "Crusaders' occupation of Saudi Arabia"; an end to the U.S. "theft" of Arab oil at "paltry prices"; and the removal of [Arab] governments that "have surrendered to the Jews."

A decade on, we are witnessing a great upheaval across the Middle East. Two Arab dictatorships have been toppled, six others to one degree or another rocked by rebellion or protest. Oil, which bin Laden had variously said should retail at $144 a barrel and "$100 a barrel at least," at one point since 2001 peaked at $146. In early spring 2011, it stood at $124.

As for the presence of U.S. forces in Saudi Arabia, all were gone by fall 2003. Only conditional upon a subsequent pullout, reportedly, had Crown Prince Abdullah permitted the use of Saudi bases for the invasion of Iraq. The Palestine issue, though—a constant in bin Laden's rhetoric from the start and so far as one can tell the primary motivation for KSM and the principal operatives involved in the 9/11 attacks—festers on.

How much the activity of bin Laden and al Qaeda had to do with what has changed is another matter. Though rumors swirl, there is no good evidence that Islamist extremism is playing an important role in the latest turmoil across the region. The price of oil vacillates not so much according to doctrine as according to the law of supply and demand. On the other hand, the threat of more terrorist attacks—in both America and Saudi Arabia—was surely a factor in the decision to remove the U.S. military from Saudi territory.

The decade has seen some American pressure applied to Israel over its persistent occupation of Palestinian territory and its overall treatment of the Palestinians. It has been ineffectual pressure, though, and the United States' commitment to Israel seems undiminished. Few people, it seems, are even aware that the Palestine issue was a primary motivation for the perpetrators of 9/11.

The true effect of the 2001 onslaught is less what it achieved than what it triggered. Bin Laden and some of those closest to him had fervently hoped to goad the United States into retaliating. "We wanted the United States to attack," his military chief Mohammed Atef said after an earlier attack. ". . . They are going to invade Afghanistan . . . and then we will start holy war against the Americans, exactly like the Soviets." The notion was that the United States could be bled into defeat, literally and financially, as the Soviets had been in Afghanistan, and bin Laden shared it.

Then there was Iraq. "I am rejoicing," he said in 2003, "that America has become embroiled in the quagmires of the Tigris and Euphrates. Bush thought that Iraq and its oil would be easy prey, and now here he is, stuck in dire straits."

A decade after 9/11, even with bin Laden dead we cannot know the end of the story. The invasion of Afghanistan that some al Qaeda leaders had desired brought disruption and death both to the organization and to the country that hosted it. In both Afghanistan and Iraq, however, the United States and its allies remain bogged down—though not necessarily as fatally as bin Laden hoped. Human casualties aside, however, the dollar cost of the "war on terrorism"—Afghanistan, Iraq, and other post-9/11 operations—was as of last year estimated to have been $1.15 trillion. That, a Congressional Research Service report indicated, made it second only to the cost of World War II, even with adjustments for inflation.

A recent Pew Research survey indicated that support for the cause bin Laden and al Qaeda have espoused had faded in the Muslim countries studied. "Brand bin Laden," a U.S. business journal reported of a previous poll, is "dying fast." Those fighting terrorism are not banking on it.

National Counterterrorism Center director Michael Leiter believed even before the strike on bin Laden that the greatest terrorist threat to the United States was posed by Anwar Aulaqi—the "spiritual adviser" to two key 9/11 terrorists who professed innocence and ignorance after the attacks, then made a getaway at his leisure.

Aulaqi eventually took refuge in Yemen, where he was still believed to be active as of spring 2011. Days after bin Laden was killed, Aulaqi was targeted by a U.S. drone. He reportedly got away.

AT HOME in recent times, there has been crass posturing and prolonged squabbling, with predictably tragic results.

In Florida, after months of threatening to do so—and after many appeals that he desist, including one by President Obama—the pastor of a fringe church he calls the Dove World Outreach Center burned a copy of the Qur'an. He had earlier held a mockery of a "trial" at which the Muslims' holy book was found guilty of "crimes against humanity." A "jury" convened by the pastor, Terry Jones, had chosen burning over three other ways of destroying the sacred text: shredding, drowning, or firing squad.

In Afghanistan, when news of the burning of the Qur'an spread, thousands of protesters took to the streets. Seven United Nations employees were killed, two of them by beheading, when a mob overran one of the organization's compounds. Violence over three days resulted in further deaths and dozens of injuries. Back in Florida, Jones said that he did not feel responsible, and that the time had come "to hold Islam accountable."

In New York City, there has been protracted discord over whether a new mosque and Muslim community center should be allowed on a site two blocks from Ground Zero. Its sponsors say it will be a symbol "that will give voice to the silent majority of Muslims who suffer at the hands of extremists." Opponents say the center would be "sacrilege on sacred ground," a "gross insult to the memory of those that were killed." As of the spring of this year, the dispute was unresolved.

So were more melancholy disagreements centered on what really is and always will be hallowed ground—the memorial at Ground Zero, with which we opened this book. Seventy feet below ground, in what will be the September 11 Museum, the steel bases of the Twin Towers stand exposed at the point of bedrock, preserved by order of the federal government. Nearby, sheathed in a climate-controlled covering, will stand the last steel column removed from the debris of the World Trade Center, a column that in the aftermath of 9/11 served as a memorial in and of itself.

The plan, as of this writing, is that the museum will hold something else, the collection of some 9,000 fragments of humanity, the remains of the 1,122 people whose body parts cannot be identified. They would repose, hidden from the public eye yet hauntingly present. The plan's proponents maintained that the presence of the remains would enhance the sanctity of the memorial, making it a place where generations would come to pay their respects and reflect. Its opponents objected to what is left of their loved ones being turned into what they saw as a lure for tourists. Placement in the museum space, relatives thought, was tantamount to creating "a freak show" put on for "gawkers."

Two thousand miles away, in Phoenix, Arizona, state senators were voting to remove wording on the city's 9/11 memorial that they deemed objectionable. A memorial, one senator said, should display only "patriotic, pro-American words." The inscribed words he and others found upsetting included "VIOLENT ACTS LEADING US TO WAR"; "MIDDLE EAST VIOLENCE MOTIVATES ATTACKS IN US"; "YOU DON'T WIN BATTLES OF TERRORISM WITH MORE BATTLES"; "FEELING OF INVINCIBILITY LOST"; "MUST BOMB BACK"; "FOREIGN-BORN AMERICANS AFRAID"; and "FEAR OF FOREIGNERS."

The fury that flamed across America after 9/11 was shot through with fear, fear of a foe few citizens could even begin to understand, fear of the unknown, fear that more was coming. Wisdom still holds, as that three-term President told the nation almost eighty years ago, that the only thing to be feared is fear itself. Yet fear, unspoken, remains pervasive, in airports and train stations, in the places where great issues are debated, in the living rooms of families across the nation.

In its fury and its fear, some say, America lost its way. Perhaps it did. On the other hand, the extreme measures its terrorist enemies espouse will lead not to utopia for anyone, only to further horrors. Crammed together on a small planet beset with desperate problems, the more than three hundred million non-Muslim Americans, the world's 1.65 billion Muslims, and the billions of others of differing religions and none must find other ways to resolve what divides them.

In New York, there has been quibbling over even the quotation from Virgil's *Aeneid* chosen for the wall at the Ground Zero memorial behind which the unknown dead would lie. Should the quotation survive the debate, it at least will—however unintentionally—remain valid for both the murdered victims of 9/11 and their murderers. It reads:

"No day shall erase you from the memory of Time."

ACKNOWLEDGMENTS

This is the eighth heavily researched book project we have undertaken. All involved difficult challenges or required us to tackle intractable questions. Sometimes we have managed to answer the questions. Often, we hope, we have managed to clear up historical muddle or confusion. Nothing, however, quite prepared us for the tangle of fact, fallacy, and fantasy that enmesh this dark history.

We were reminded at every step of the way that the story on which we were embarked was freighted with human suffering: that of those who died on September 11 itself, of those killed in earlier and subsequent attacks, and of the more than 100,000 people who have died and continue to die in the ensuing conflicts—and those left grieving across the world.

In this Acknowledgments section of our book, then, we honor first and foremost those who will never be able to read it.

Writing *The Eleventh Day* has been a task for which we needed more than usual guides to people and places, nations and cultures, that do not readily reveal themselves. Our personal thanks, then, to those we can name: Hugh Bermingham, who has lived and worked in Saudi Arabia for almost thirty years; the author Jean Sasson, who also lived there and who has the trust of the first wife and the fourth son of Osama bin Laden; Flagg Miller, associate professor of religious studies at the University of California at Davis, who has analyzed bin Laden's writing in unique depth; editor and author Abdel Atwan, who interviewed bin Laden and reads the galloping pulse of history in the Middle East with rare expertise; and Alain Chouet, former head of security intelligence with the DGSE—France's foreign intelligence service—and an accomplished Arabist in his own right.

Others with a variety of backgrounds shared experience or special knowledge: Captain Anthony Barnes, who on 9/11 was deputy director of presidential contingency planning in the White House Military Office; Jean-Charles Brisard, lead investigator for lawyers representing families bereaved on 9/11, who opened up his vast archive of documents to us; John Farmer, former senior counsel to the 9/11 Commission, now dean of Rutgers University Law School, who was an eminently informative source on the military response to the attacks; former U.S. senator and Florida governor Bob Graham, onetime chairman of the Senate Committee on Intelligence and cochair of the House-Senate Joint Inquiry into intelligence activities before and after September 11, 2001, who gave us time in Florida, Massachusetts, and London, and who champions truth-telling in a milieu where truth is so often a stranger; Simon Henderson, who heads the Gulf and Energy Policy Program at the Washington Institute for Near East Policy; Eleanor Hill, a former Defense Department inspector general and the Joint Committee's relentless staff director; former FBI intelligence analyst Mike Jacobson, who served with both the Joint Committee and the 9/11 Commission and surfaced facts that others preferred suppressed; Miles Kara, a former career intelligence officer with the U.S. Army, who also served on both official probes—with a special focus on the FAA and NORAD while on the Commission team—and who was endlessly patient and responsive to our queries; Ryan Mackey, research scientist at NASA's Jet Propulsion Laboratory and author of a paper on conspiracy theories about 9/11, who applied a "baloney detection kit" to great effect; Sarandis Papadopoulos of the Naval Historical Center, who conducted research and interviews and coauthored the report on the Pentagon attack for the Office of the Secretary of Defense; Mete Sozen, professor of structural engineering at Purdue University in Indiana, who explained in a way we could understand—and believe—how it appeared that American Flight 77 was swallowed up by the Pentagon; teacher and literacy coach Dwana Washington, who vividly described for us the September 11 visit by President Bush to the Emma E. Booker Elementary School in Sarasota, Florida.

Like so much of history, work on this project has been a paper chase. We owe sincere thanks to the National Archives, where the hugely able Kristen Wilhelm handled document applications and dealt with difficult questions with skill and evident integrity—wondrously refreshing for authors inured over the years to sustained obstruction to the public's right to know. In 2010 and 2011, as we labored on far from Washington, and as tens of thousands of 9/11 Commission documents became available for the first time, we enjoyed the generous collegiate help of Erik Larson. The National Security Archive at George Washington University, which collects and publishes material obtained through the Freedom of Information Act, was often useful.

In Europe, too, we learned much. In Germany, Dr. Manfred Murck, who before 9/11 and since has been deputy chief of Hamburg's domestic intelligence service, put up with persistent quizzing for longer than we could have expected and, when obliged to limit what he could tell us, was frank about doing so; from Stuttgart, Dr. Herbert Müller, Islamic affairs specialist at the parallel organization in that city, gave ready assistance; Hamburg attorney Udo Jacob helped document the story of the young Islamists who gathered in the cause of jihad before 9/11—and who included several of the 9/11 perpetrators. Without his help we could not have gained admission to Fuhlsbüttel prison to visit Mounir Motassadeq, who is serving fifteen years for his supposed role as accessory to the murders of those aboard the four hijacked airliners on 9/11. Motassadeq, for his part, put up with our questions over a period of hours. It is not clear to us that he is guilty as charged, and should we not return to his case ourselves, we hope other investigators will. Also in Germany, Hans Kippenberg, professor of comparative religious studies at Bremen's Jacobs University, and Dr. Tilman Seidensticker, professor of Arab and Islamic studies at Jena's Friedrich Schiller University, helped with interpretation and translation of the hijackers' "manual" and of Ziad Jarrah's farewell letter to his Turkish lover.

In Milan, Italy, deputy chief prosecutor and counterterrorism coordinator Armando Spataro gave us a first glimpse of the brutal injustices meted out in the name of the War on Terror; Bruno Megale, deputy head of counterterrorism, described police surveillance operations in northern Italy before 9/11. While we failed to get to Spain, our friend Charles Cardiff's reading of the Spanish dossier—accumulated by Judge Baltasar Garzón—persuaded us of al Qaeda's pre-9/11 reach in that country.

The fellow journalists who helped us are too numerous to name. Of their number, we thank especially Thomas Joscelyn, Gerald Posner, Jeffrey Steinberg, and Joseph Trento in the United States; Guillaume Dasquié, Richard Labévière, and Alexandra Richard in France; and Josef Hufelschulte in Germany. Also in Germany, we much appreciated the hard-earned knowledge and professionalism of Dirk Laabs, an all-around reporter and practitioner of the time-honored school of shoe-leather journalism.

Yosri Fouda, the brave reporter who interviewed Khalid Sheikh Mohammed, was helpful to us from Cairo—as was his colleague Nick Fielding, who subsequently worked with him on a book about the experience.

We have on our shelves more than three hundred books that relate one way or another to 9/11, al Qaeda, and the roots from which al Qaeda sprang. Those of Peter Bergen, Steve Coll, Jim Dwyer and Kevin Flynn, former 9/11 Commission senior counsel John Farmer, Yosri Fouda and Nick Fielding, William Langewiesche, Jere Longman, Terry McDermott, Philip Shenon, and Lawrence Wright are essential reading. No one who wishes to explore the intelligence angles should miss the works of J. M. Berger, Peter Lance, and former senior CIA officer Michael Scheuer; Kevin Fenton's deconstruction of the roles of the CIA, the FBI, and the 9/11 Commission—soon to be published as this book went to press, but kindly made available to us by the author—is valuable and provocative. Paul Thompson's encyclopedic *The Terror Timeline* and, above all, his "Complete 9/11 Timeline," updated regularly on the Net, were indispensable. The author Peter Dale Scott has taken his scalpel to the jugular of the story of President Bush and the aides who surrounded him.

On the "skeptical" front, we thank author Daniel Hopsicker, investigator of the hijackers' activities in Florida. He introduced us to Venice, shared his time unstintingly, and trusted us down the months—long after it became clear that where he saw conspiracy we saw coincidence or happenstance. There was something to be learned, as in the past, from John Judge, a veteran of alternative history in Washington, D.C.

These days more than ever, nonfiction authors must head down the long research trail on shrunken budgets. It has been all the more rewarding, then, to have the loyalty and commitment of a new colleague. Hannah Cleaver, a Berlin-based journalist with prior expertise and knowledge of the case, made it clear that the story itself and the comradeship were as important to her as professional gain. The inquiring mind of intern Stefani Jackson produced useful research.

The efficient Sinéad Sweeney, in Ireland, has long been far more valuable to us than a mere assistant. Moss McCarthy of LED Technology rescued us from more than one computer crisis. Martina Coonan helped out on the last lap, when every hour was precious. Pauline Lombard and Ann Dalton put up with our demands yet again. We thank, too, Ger Killalea, who keeps the office functioning, and Jason Cairns, who cheerfully turns his hand to anything under the sun.

The Eleventh Day would not exist without the initial interest and backing of our publishers at Random House. Group president Gina Centrello and Ballantine publisher Libby McGuire in New York, and Transworld's Bill Scott-Kerr in London, kept us going along a bumpy trail.

Our editors, Mark Tavani and Simon Thorogood, were there for us in the final months with skill and good judgment. Where they saw clutter, they pointed the way to clarity. Our agent, Jonathan Lloyd, also reads everything we write with a keen editorial eye—a bonus for us—for he is himself a former publisher. He has steadied us, once again, with his combination of common sense and uncommon good humor.

We thank our good friends and neighbors, who have been endlessly supportive. Our neglected children heroically put up with the neglect—though one has asked, "When are we going to be a family again?"

The Eleventh Day is dedicated to our steadfast friends Chris and Gaye Humphreys—who know why—and to Angela Amicone, who turns ninety-five this year. Angela has been teaching children to read since 1940, and has no intention of giving up now.

Anthony Summers and Robbyn Swan
Ireland, 2011

NOTES AND SOURCES

ABBREVIATIONS USED IN NOTES AND SOURCES

AP   Associated Press

BG   *Boston Globe*

CF   Files of the National Commission on Terrorist Attacks upon the
            United States, held at the National Archives, Record Group 148.
            Cited documents are listed here, as they are at the Archives, by
            folder name, box [B] and team [T] numbers. Many documents were
            supplied to the authors by an independent researcher, and others
            obtained on line via www.scribd.com or directly from the Archives.

CO   Website of the National Commission on Terrorist Attacks upon the
            United States, archived at http://govinfo.library.unt.edu/911/about
            .html

conv.   conversation

corr.   Authors' correspondence

CR   Final Report of the National Commission on Terrorist Attacks upon
            the United States, NY: W. W. Norton, 2004

FBI IG   Review of the FBI's Handling of Intelligence Information Related
            to the September 11 Attacks, Office of the Inspector General, U.S.
            Department of Justice, November 2004

FEMA   Federal Emergency Management Agency, U.S. Department of
            Homeland Security

int.   interview (by authors unless otherwise noted)

INTELWIRE	FBI documents sourced in the notes of the 9/11 Commission Report, obtained by Intelwire under FOIA (Freedom of Information Act) and available on its website, www.intelwire.com
JI	Joint Inquiry into Intelligence Community Activities Before and After the Terrorist Attacks of September 11, 2001, House Permanent Select Committee on Intelligence and Senate Select Committee on Intelligence, 107th Congress, 2nd Session
KSM SUBST	Substitution for the Testimony of Khalid Sheikh Mohammed, Defense Exhibit 941, *U.S. v. Zacarias Moussaoui*, Cr. No. 01-455-1, U.S. District Court for the Eastern District of Virginia
LAT	*Los Angeles Times*
MFR	Memorandum for the Record of 9/11 Commission staff interviews, available on National Archives website, http://www.archives.gov/legislative/research/9-11/commission-memoranda.html
NARA	National Archives and Records Administration
NIST	National Institute of Standards and Technology, U.S. Department of Commerce
NTSB	National Transportation Safety Board
NYT	*New York Times*
OBL	Osama bin Laden
TF	Oral histories of 503 first responders conducted by the Fire Department, City of New York, archived by *The New York Times* at http://graphics8.nytimes.com/packages/html/nyregion/20050812_WTC_GRAPHIC/met_WTC_histories_full_01.html
WP	*Washington Post*
WSJ	*Wall Street Journal*

PREFACE

3–4   **memorial:** *NY Daily News*, 8/20/01, *NYT*, 6/10/09, www.wtcsitememorial.org, www.national911memorial.org/site, int. Michael Frazier for National September 11 Memorial and Museum; **disease:** AP, 6/24/09.

4   **tens of thousands:** Documenting the number of dead in any conflict is difficult, fraught as such figures are with political ramifications. Americans in particular, given the lingering specter of the Vietnam War, are sensitive to rising casualty counts among servicemen and women. Nor does any military readily accept responsibility for civilian casualties. The issue is further complicated by determining which deaths qualify as having been the result of war—does one, for example, include deaths due to disease or starvation—conditions brought about by conflict? In citing the figure of many tens of thousands of dead, the authors have relied on casualty counts from the U.N. Assistance Missions in Afghanistan and Iraq, and the websites icasualties.org and iraqbodycount.org.

4   **graves/remains:** AP, 4/1/09, www.911research.wtc7.net, *Israel National News*, 2/1/08, *NYT*, 2/23/08, MFR 03009720; **Riches:** *NYT*, 11/5/02, 4/21/08, www.NY1.com, 4/17/08,

NY Post, 4/13/02; **McIntyre:** AP, 5/19/06, *Independent on Sunday* (U.K.), 10/7/07; **Dillard:** Arlington historian Thomas Sherlock to authors, 9/11/09, *WP,* 5/26/07, *NY Observer,* 6/20/04; **Breitweiser:** Kristen Breitweiser, *Wake-up Call,* NY: Warner, 2006, Preface, 110, 240.

4   **Martin:** *WP,* 11/2/06, *Newsweek,* 12/25/06, transcript, 9/12/01, FBI 265D-NY-280350, report, 9/12/01, FBI 265D-NY-280350-CE, courtesy of INTELWIRE. Though Martin suffered serious injuries early in the first hijacking, it is probable that a First Class passenger—Daniel Lewin—was the first to die. See Ch. 1, p. 15.

5–7   **safe to breathe:** "EPA's Response to the World Trade Center Collapse," Office of the Inspector General, U.S. Environmental Protection Agency, 8/21/03, 4; **Riches ill:** www .NY1.com, 4/17/08, www.sohoblues.com, citing *Time;* **"dead or alive":** CNN, 9/17/01; **backtrack:** press release, 3/13/02, www.whitehouse.gov; **Obama:** *NY Post,* 2/7/09; **Zubaydah:** *NY Daily News,* 9/10/06, & see later refs.; **Dillard questions:** CNN, 3/28/04, ACLU statement, 12/12/08; **Breitweiser testimony/questions:** testimony, 9/18/02, JI, Breitweiser, 100–, int. Kristen Breitweiser, *St. Petersburg Times,* 8/12/05; **CIA/two hijackers:** see later refs.; **kept secret:** Bob Graham with Jeff Nussbaum, *Intelligence Matters,* NY: Random House, 2004, 228, 231; **Breitweiser/Obama:** *NYT,* 6/24/09; **Commission Final Report received:** Philip Shenon, *The Commission,* NY: Twelve, 2008, 415–; **Kean/Hamilton:** *NYT,* 12/8/07 & 1/2/08, www.rawstory.com, 12/24/07, *International Herald Tribune,* 12/8/07; **Kerrey:** *Newsweek,* 3/23/09, Air America radio, 3/2/08; **Cleland:** *Salon,* 11/21/03, *NYT,* 10/26/03; **"first draft":** CBC transcript, 8/21/06; **CBS poll:** www .angus-reid.com/polls, www.alternet.com, 9/16/06; **Scripps poll:** Scripps Howard News Service, 11/23/07; **Zogby poll:** Zogby International, Aug. 2007; **sixteen thousand:** Reuters, 9/10/08, www.alternet.com, 9/16/08; **Iraq/attacks:** *NYT*/CBS News polls cited at www.angus-reid.com; **Angus Reid poll:** released 3/17/10, www.angus-reid.com; **criticism: (senators)** Lincoln Chaffee, Mark Dayton, Mike Gravel, Patrick Leahy, Charles Schumer; **(representatives)** Dennis Kucinich, Cynthia McKinney, Ron Paul, Curt Weldon; **(governor)** Jesse Ventura; **(deputy attorneys general)** Roy Andes, Philip Berg, Donald Bustion; **(state legislators)** Peter Allen, Peter Espiefs, Karen Johnson, Barbara Richardson, Charles Weed, Suzi Wizowaty; **(public officials/diplomats/engineers/ officers)** see https://patriotsquestion911.com; **Texas candidates:** "Texas GOP Gubernatorial Candidate Questions Government Involvement in 9/11," Fox News, 2/12/10, "Shami Questions US Involvement in 9/11 Attack," KTBS TV, 2/14/10; **CIA/FBI:** e.g., letter to Congress regarding the 9/11 Commission Report signed by twenty-five military, intelligence, and law enforcement veterans, 9/13/04, National Security Whistleblowers Coalition; **Freeh:** *WSJ,* 11/17/05, CNN, 11/30/05; **Mondale:** int. Minnesota, "We Are C.H.A.N.G.E.," 2/3/08, www.youtube.com; **Clark:** *This Week with George Stephanopoulos,* ABC News, 3/5/06; **Graham:** ints. Bob Graham, *Salon,* 9/9/04, Graham with Nussbaum.

8   **300,000 pages:** corr. Kristen Wilhelm, 2011. Only some 35 percent of the Commission documents held by the National Archives had been reviewed for release as of February 2011. Of the documents reviewed, 15 percent remain classified, largely under national security and privacy restrictions. The remaining 20 percent, some 300,000 documents, are available to researchers.

Part I: ATTACK

CHAPTER 1

11–12   **recognized:** Martin Gilbert, *Israel,* London: Black Swan, 1999, 189; **day in 1938:** Robert Lacey, *The Kingdom,* NY: Avon, 1983, 262; **40,000 planes:** Jane Garvey testi-

mony, 1/27/04, CO; **Rosenzweig/Mladenik/Gordenstein/Theodoridis/Iskandar/
Filipov:** "DOJ Documents Requests #35–13," B13, T7, CF, "AAL Misc. Folder—AA11
and AA77," B18, T7, CF; **Cuccinello:** eds. *Der Spiegel* magazine, *Inside 9–11*, NY: St.
Martin's, 2001, 37; **Gay:** AP, 9/25/01, Raytheon press release, 9/10/07; **Morabito:**
Post-Standard (Syracuse, NY), 10/20/07; **Berenson:** Richard Bernstein, *Out of the Blue*,
NY: Times Books, 2002, 171; **Angell:** *People*, 5/17/04; **Lewin:** *BG*, 9/12/01.

12 **five young men:** *BG*, 9/13/01. Some have raised questions about the identities of the
hijackers. The issue will be covered in Ch. 14 and its related notes.

12 **Ogonowski:** Bernstein, 110–, James Ogonowski remarks at Safety Awards Banquet,
9/11/02, "Ogonowski Legacy," Public Radio International, 9/13/02.

12–15 **5:00 A.M.:** Unless otherwise indicated, all times in this book are rendered as the times
in use by civilians on the U.S. East Coast on the day in question (i.e., EDT)—as opposed to the times used by the military or the aviation industry, or in other time zones;
McGuinness: website of Cheryl McGuinness (widow), www.beautybeyondtheashes
.com; **"turn-around":** MFR 04016228, 2/10/04; **take off due:** CR, 2; **cleaners/fuel-
ers:** "FBI 302s of Interest Flight 11," B17, T7, CF, "FBI 302s Arestegui," B10, T7, CF;
flight attendants: "FBI 302s Homer Folder re Kathleen Nicosia," B10, T7, CF; **"organized":** *NYT*, 12/9/01; **backup:** "FBI 302s Arestegui," B10, T7, CF; **joked:** *Cape Cod
Times*, 9/14/01; **sick/standby:** "FBI 302s Arestegui," B10, T7, CF; **odd incident:** Staff
Report, "The Four Flights and Civil Aviation Security," note 22, CF, MFR 04020636,
2/2/04, MFR 03007050, 8/15/03, *Miami Herald*, 9/22/01; **Filipov/"suspicious":** "DOJ
Documents Requests 35–13," B13, T7, CF; **Howland:** "FBI 302s Cockpit and American and Hijacker," B11, T7, CF; **profiling system:** CR 4, MFR 04018154, 11/24/03,
Staff Report, "The Four Flights and Civil Aviation Security," 2, 77, CF, John Raidt
comments, 1/27/04, CO; **crutch:** *BG*, 11/10/01; **"sweating bullets":** *World Net Daily*,
9/21/01; **last to board:** MFR 04020636, 2/2/04; **greeted by Martin/final checks:** "FBI
302s Arestegui," B10, T7, CF; **seating:** CR, 2, *BG*, 9/13/01; **Sweeney call:** *NY Observer*,
2/15/04, FBI 302 Michael Sweeney, 9/21/01, INTELWIRE; **switch off phones:** "FBI
302s Arestegui," B10, T7, CF; **pushed back/takeoff:** Joseph Gregor, "Air Traffic Control Recording," NTSB, 12/21/01, CR, 2, 4; **"severe clear":** Lynn Spencer, *Touching
History*, NY: Free Press, 2008, 3; **air-to-ground exchanges:** Gregor, 2–, & see FAA
Memo, Full Transcript: Aircraft Accident AA11, New York, NY, 9/11/01, "Boston Cen-
ter, Shirley Kula," B3, T8, CF; **"a brief unknown sound":** "Summary of Air Traffic
Hijack Events, Sept. 11, 2001, FAA," Report on Investigation of 9/11 Commission Staff
Referral, Dept. of Transportation, Office of Inspector General, Appendix 3; **Ong to
Reservations:** quotes attributed to Ong & nature of her call come from FBI 302 of
Vanessa Minter, 9/12/01, FBI 302 of Craig Marquis, 9/16/01, & "Charlotte to Direc-
tor," FBI 265D-NY-280350-CE, 9/13/01, "Flight Call Notes," & Transcript of 9/11
Telephone Calls, "AA Phone Calls," B13, T7, CF, FBI 302 of Nydia Gonzalez, 9/12/01,
"FBI 302s—Knife and American Flight 11," B11, T7, CF, FBI 302 of Winston Sadler,
9/13/01, INTELWIRE, Nydia Gonzalez testimony, 1/27/04, CO.

15 **"sterile cockpit":** The interjection appears on the transcript but is only partially audible
on the tape version as heard by the authors; **Lewin dead?:** Lewin was an American-Israeli
citizen who as "Daniel Levin" had served in the Israel Defense Forces as a member of
Sayeret Matkal—in its Unit 269, which specializes in counterterrorism (FBI 302 of Anne
Lewin, 9/21/01, "Flight Calls Notes," B13, T7, CF, UPI, 3/6/02, ints. Tom Leighton,
Marco Greenberg, *Ha'aretz*, 9/15/06).

15–16 **man in 10B:** Ong also identified the passengers in Seats 2A and 2B as hijackers, while
her colleague Sweeney—whose call was not recorded—is variously reported as identifying hijackers in 9B, 9C, 9D, 9E, 9G, 10B, and 10C. 2A, 2B, and 10B were indeed
the assigned seats of three of the five Arab passengers traveling. (Ong re 2A/2B: Tran-

scripts of 9/11 Telephone Calls, "AA Phone Transcripts," & Charlotte to Director, FBI 265D-NY-280350-CE, 9/13/01, "Flight Call Notes," B13, T7, CF; Sweeney re Seats: FBI 302 of Michael Woodward, 9/14/01, & of James Sayer, 9/13/01, "FBI 302s—Olsen," B10, T7, CF); **Sweeney/Woodward call:** Quotes attributed to Sweeney & nature of her call come from CR, 453n32, FBI 302 of Michael Woodward, 9/14/01, & of James Sayer, 9/13/01, "FBI 302s—Olsen," B10, T7, CF, Staff Report, "The Four Flights and Civil Aviation Security," 14, CF.

16   **borrowed card:** The calling card was provided to Sweeney by another flight attendant, Sara Low—who also passed information on the hijackers' seat location to colleagues (*NY Observer*, 6/20/04, AP 3/5/09, ABC News, 7/18/02).

16–17 **keys:** CR, 5, 453n26, FBI 302 of Michael Sweeney, 9/21/01, INTELWIRE, John Farmer, *The Ground Truth*, NY: Riverhead, 2009, 109; **"no warning":** *NY Observer*, 6/20/04; **"refrain":** Staff Report, "The Four Flights and Civil Aviation Security," 81, CF; **not panicky/"static":** ABC News, 7/18/02.

CHAPTER 2

18   **data processor:** (Chuck Allen), eds. *Der Spiegel, Inside 9–11*, 46–; **steelworker:** (Joe Libretti), Wayne Barrett and Dan Collins, *Grand Illusion*, NY: Harper, 2006, 245; **construction workers/composer:** (Juan Suarez & "Artie" & composer Jim Farmer) Bernstein, 199; **student:** *9/11: Dust & Deceit at the World Trade Center*, documentary, www .dust.org.

19   **8:46 A.M.:** 8:46 A.M. is the generally accepted time of the impact on the North Tower. Scientists measuring seismic data at the Lamont-Doherty Earth Observatory at the New Jersey Palisades, twenty-one miles from New York City, initially—in 2001—calculated the impact time as 8:46:26. In 2005, they adjusted the estimate to 8:46:29. The 9/11 Commission, meanwhile, relied on the flight path study for Flight 11 provided by the NTSB, reckoning the impact time as 8:46:40. (Similar discrepancies appear in times given for the subsequent crash into the South Tower.) While too complex to detail here, several plausible explanations have been offered for this anomaly. Though minimal, the discrepancies have been used by critics of the conventional account to bolster the notion that—in addition to the planes—explosives were used in the attacks on the Twin Towers. The differing timings supplied by the seismic station, the critics claim, reflect explosions in the towers *before* the impact of the airplanes. That theory does not hold, however, because the seismic data reflect only a single event. Had there been first an explosion, then an impact, the seismic instruments would have registered *two* events. They did not ("Seismic Waves Generated by Aircraft Impacts and Building Collapses at World Trade Center," by Won-Young Kim et al., www.ldeo.columbia.edu, "Federal Building and Fire Safety Investigation of the WTC Disaster," NCSTAR1–5A, NIST, 22–, CR, 7, 454n39, "Seismic Proof—9/11 Was an Inside Job," by Craig T. Furlong & Gordon Ross, www .journalof911studies.com, "On *Debunking 9/11 Debunking*," by Ryan Mackey, 5/24/08, 79–, authors' corr. Dr. Won-Young Kim & NTSB's Ted Lopatkiewicz, 2009).

19–23 **Rubenfien:** Leo Rubenfien, *Wounded Cities*, Göttingen, Germany: Steidl, 2008, 32–; **Naudet:** David Friend, *Watching the World Change*, NY: Farrar, Straus & Giroux, 2006, 185–; **Naudet image:** *9/11*, documentary film, Jules & Gedeon Naudet et al., CBS Television, 2002; **Allen:** eds. *Der Spiegel*, 48, Chuck Allen profile on LinkedIn .com; **Gartenberg:** WABC (NY), 9/11/01, videotape on www.youtube.com, eds. *Der Spiegel*, 89; **93rd and 99th floors:** CR, 285; **10,000 gallons:** "Visual Evidence, Damage Estimates, and Timeline Analysis, Federal Building and Fire Safety Investigation of the World Trade Center Disaster," NIST, released April 2005, liii; **Fireballs:** CR, 285, 292; **"The windows"/"I just didn't":** Friend, 188, Naudet documentary, Jim Dwyer & Kevin Flynn, *102 Minutes*, NY: Times Books, 2005, 280; **milling around:** Brian Jenkins and Frances Edward-Winslow, "Saving City Lifelines: Lessons Learned in the 9/11 Terrorist Attacks," Mineta Transportation Institute report, 9/03, 11; **1,344 souls:** *NYT,* 1/15/04; **stairways blocked:** CR, 285; **Meehan:** Dwyer & Flynn, 36, *NYT,* 9/25/01, www.damianmeehan.org (family website); **San Pio Resta:** Bernstein, 177; **Richards:** *The Independent* (U.K.), 9/24/01, *Village Voice,* 6/6/02, *Art News,* 11/01; **Fred Alger:** *NY Sun,* 9/11/06; **Marsh:** *Insurance Journal,* 9/6/04; **"Oh, my God!":** Dwyer & Flynn, 14; **remains:** ibid., 20; **658 people:** www.cantor.com/public/charities; **Wittenstein:** eds. *Der Spiegel,* 51; **Rosenblum:** Bernstein, 212; **van Auken:** CNN, 9/13/01; **dead staffer:** William Langewiesche, *American Ground,* NY: North Point, 2002, 134; **Windows:** ibid., 56–; **meetings:** Dwyer & Flynn, 11; **Risk Waters:** ibid., 12, Bernstein, 175; **Kane:** Dwyer & Flynn, 14; **calls/Olender/Heeran:** ibid., 38–, 138, 127, 277, James Bamford, *A Pretext for War,* NY: Doubleday, 2004, 21–, Bernstein, 205–, *Times Union* (Albany), 8/20/06; **Wortley:** Dwyer & Flynn, 130; **two helicopters:** CR, 291–; **blocked:** Thomas Kean & Lee Hamilton, *Without Precedent,* NY: Alfred A. Knopf, 2006, 220, "Crisis Management," Staff Statement 14, CO, Dwyer & Flynn, 126–41–; **cut:** MFR 03003644, 7/21/03, CF; **"Be advised":** Dwyer & Flynn, 58; **"We got jumpers"/too shocking:** Friend, 188, 128–, *Esquire,* 9/03.

23–24 **Reiss:** Dwyer & Flynn, 18 & cf. 136–; **Naudet:** *9/11,* documentary; **clutching briefcase/skirt:** *Economist,* 5/6/06; **burning shirt:** Dwyer & Flynn, 32; **groups/paratroopers:** Friend, 134, int. of Jason Charles, TF, 1/23/02, *New Yorker,* 9/24/01; **Smiouskas:** Dwyer & Flynn, 137; **"As the debris":** int. Kevin McCabe, TF, 12/13/01; **"looked like":** int. Derek Brogan, TF, 12/28/01; **"We started":** Bernstein, 5.

24   **"Christ!":** "Why No Rooftop Rescues on September 11?," ABC News, 11/8/01.

CHAPTER 3

25   **"We have *some planes*":** ATCR-AA11, 7–.

25   **Zalewski/colleagues:** MFR 04016801, 9/22/03, CR, 6. On the second transmission, at 8:24 A.M., the hijacker said: "Nobody move. Everything will be okay. If you try to make any moves you'll endanger yourself and the airplane. Just stay quiet." There would also be a third transmission. At 8:33, the hijacker said: "Nobody move, please. We are going back to the airport. Don't try to make any stupid moves." Contrary to the notion that this was an inadvertent blunder by the American 11 hijacker, Commission staff member Miles Kara ventures the thought that the transmission was deliberate—a way of letting his accomplice aboard United 175, who could listen in to radio traffic on cabin channel 9, know that the operation had begun. (MFR 04016801, 9/22/03, corr. Miles Kara, 2011.)

26–29 **Horrocks:** www.michaelroberthorrocks.com; **Saracini:** *NYT,* 12/31/01; **attendants:** CR, 454n41, www.afanet.org, www.airlineride.org; **usual mix:** FBI 302, 10/01/01, "FBI 302s, Arestegui," B10, T7, CF, Bernstein, 180, INN.com, 2/1/08, *The Sun* (Ireland), 9/11/06, *Northeastern University Voice,* 12/11/01; **Arabs First or Business:** UA175 manifests, "Flight 175 Misc. Manifest—Check in—Boarding," B17, T7, CF & Exhibit P200018, *U.S. v. Zacarias Moussaoui,* Cr. No. 01-455-A, U.S. District Court for the Eastern District of VA; **boarding card:** FBI 302 re int. of [name redacted], 9/12/01, "Flight 175 Info.," B16, T7, CF; **buy ticket:** FBI 302 re Gail Jawahir, 9/21/01, INTEL-WIRE; **in line:** FBI 302 re Mike Castro, 9/15/01, "302s of Interest Flight 175," B17, T7, CF; **Flight 175 course/We figured/suspicious:** "Flight Path Study—UA Flight 175," NTSB, 2/19/02, MFR 04016823, 10/1/03. As noted above, none of the hijacker transmissions from Flight 11 heard by ground control included these precise words; **Channel 9:** *Time,* 9/14/01, *PRWeek,* 3/10/08 & see Farmer, 124, 143; **Allentown:** MFR 04016828, 10/1/03; **Policastro:** MFR 04017221, 11/21/03, MFR 04017218, 11/21/03; **Hanson:** FBI 302 re Lee Hanson, 9/11/01, "FBI 302—Mace and Flight," B11, T7, CF, Bernstein, 7; **"We might":** MFR 04016823, 10/1/03, MFR 04016828, 10/1/03, "Flight

Path Study—UA Flight 175," NTSB, 2/19/02, map; **8:58:** FBI 302 re [name redacted], 9/28/01, INTELWIRE, *NY Daily News*, 3/9/04, but see CR, 8; **Sweeney:** *Hyannis News*, 9/13/01, *Metrowest Daily News*, 9/18/01, *WP*, 9/14/01; **Peter Hanson 2nd call:** FBI 302 of Lee Hanson, 9/11/01, "FBI 302—Mace and Flight," B11, T7, CF; **"planes, as in plural":** Position 15, Parts 2 & 3, "ATCSCC Tape Transcript," B1, T8, CF, CR, 23, 460n131; **"He's going in":** *WP*, 9/17/01; **Statue of Liberty:** Peter Lance, *1000 Years for Revenge*, NY: Regan, 2003, 12; **rocked:** Bamford, *Pretext*, 28.

29   **Mosiello:** int. Steven Mosiello, TF, 10/23/01. Mosiello was one of 503 firefighters, paramedics, and emergency medical technicians who contributed oral history interviews after 9/11. The interviews were released by city authorities—and transcripts were published by *The New York Times* as "World Trade Center Task Force" interviews—in 2005. They will be cited frequently—sourced as "TF"—in the chapters that follow (*NYT*, 8/12/08).

29–30 **O'Clery:** Conor O'Clery, *May You Live in Interesting Times*, Dublin: Poolbeg, 2009, 4; **Praimnath:** *NYT*, 5/26/02, Staff Statement 13, CO, Dwyer & Flynn, 92; **Clark:** "A Survivor's Story," transcript, PBS *Nova*, Bernstein, 222, CR, 293, CTV News (Canada), 9/6/02, CNN, 9/9/02; **Many others:** "Final Report on the Collapse of the World Trade Center," NCSTAR 1, NIST, 23,41.

CHAPTER 4

31–32 **CNN break:** transcript, 09/11/01, www.transcripts.cnn.com, Bamford, *Pretext*, 16; **Sawyer/Gibson:** transcript, "ABC News Special Report: Planes Crash into World Trade Center," 09/11/01, & tape on www.youtube.com; **"stupidity":** "Five Years Later: Media Recollections of 9/11," 9/11/06, citing Dorian Benkoil, www.mediabistro.com; **pilot drunk:** Dwyer & Flynn, 86; **Hayden:** James Bamford, *The Shadow Factory*, NY: Doubleday, 2008, 86.

32   **Tenet:** Bob Woodward, *Bush at War*, NY: Simon & Schuster, 2002, 3–. Tenet reversed the sequence of the attacks in his book, inaccurately indicating that the first plane crashed into the South Tower of the Trade Center, the second into the North Tower. What he meant, though, becomes clear as one reads on. (George Tenet with Bill Harlow, *At the Center of the Storm*, NY: HarperCollins, 2007, 161–).

32   **Rumsfeld:** int., Larry King show, CNN, 12/6/01, & testimony, 5/23/04, www .defenselink.mil, notes of int. Rumsfeld, B7, T2, CF; **Clarke:** Richard Clarke, *Against All Enemies*, NY: Free Press, 2004, 1; **Cheney:** ibid., 2, *Meet the Press*, NBC, 9/16/01, *WSJ*, 8/15/07; **Rice:** *Newsweek*, 12/31/01.

32   **Bush in Sarasota:** *Sarasota Magazine*, 11/01. In the early hours of the morning of September 11, a police report shows, a Sudanese man had contacted Sarasota police to say he feared an associate and two companions then visiting Sarasota might pose a threat to the President—who was staying at the Colony resort hotel on nearby Longboat Key. The associate, it was later reported, had links to the Sudanese People's Liberation Army. Officers and Secret Service agents went to an address on 32nd Street in Sarasota, a law enforcement source told the authors, and found eleven Arab men up and about— "apparently at morning prayer." One of the men had a card for a resort not far from the President's—the Longboat Key Club. The men were questioned, held until the President had left, then released. There was nothing to indicate they were linked to the 9/11 plotters, the source told the authors. There appears to be no substance to other reports of threats to the President at Longboat Key (Incident Report, Sarasota Police Dept., 4:07 A.M., 9/11/01, obtained by authors, conv. Monica Yadav, ABC 7 [affiliate], int. Sheriff's Dept. source, ints. Carroll Mooneyhan, Murf Klauber, Katy Moulton).

32   **Draper:** *Albuquerque Tribune*, 9/10/02; **Morell:** Tenet, 165–.

33   **President first learned:** At 9:17 that morning, in a conversation live with presenter Peter Jennings, reporter John Cochran stated from Sarasota that as Bush "got out of

his hotel suite this morning, was about to leave, reporters saw the White House chief of staff, Andy Card, whisper into his ear. The reporter said to the President, 'Do you know what's going on in New York?' He said he did, and he said he will have something about it later. His first event is [in] about half an hour at an elementary school in Sarasota." This report has been taken to indicate that President Bush was already aware of the first impact on the Trade Center as he left his hotel. This would be impossible, however, as the President reportedly left his hotel at 8:35, some eleven minutes *before* the crash of American Flight 11. Bush did tell a reporter he would "talk about it later," but at a later stage, well into his visit to Booker Elementary, after the second airplane had hit and just before 9:17 when Cochran spoke to Peter Jennings. The authors conclude that, in the rush of unfolding events, Cochran conflated disparate events—perhaps not reporting all of them firsthand (Cochran: "ABC News Special Report: Planes Crash into World Trade Center," transcript, 9/11/01 & tape on www.youtube.com; 8:35 at hotel: *WP*, 1/27/02; "talk . . . later": ABC News, 6/22/04).

33   **Loewer:** AP, 11/26/01; **Card:** Rep. Adam Putnam in *GW Hatchet*, 4/8/02; **"The first report":** *Washington Times*, 10/7/02; **"I thought":** CBS, 9/10/03; **"We're going":** AP, 8/19/02.

33–35 **three alarms:** Dwyer & Flynn, 47–; **first responders:** Staff Statement 13, 14, CO; **"twenty-four hours":** int. Richard, World Trade Center Task Force, 10/10/01; **Instructions not heard:** Staff Statement 13, CO; **"no need":** Dwyer & Flynn, 72; **9:02:** CR, 289; **4,000 people:** *USA Today*, 12/20/01; **On Channel 5:** *NYT*, 8/27/10; **"One plane's":** Bamford, *Pretext*, 92, 89; **Rumsfeld:** Torie Clarke, *Lipstick on a Pig*, NY: Free Press, 2006, 217–, int. Torie Clarke on WBZ (Boston), 9/16/01, int. Donald Rumsfeld by Alfred Goldberg and Rebecca Cameron, 12/23/02, "Rumsfeld on Intel," B7, T2, CF; **"With all hell":** Tenet, 162; **Clarke:** Richard Clarke, 1–; **"Get ready":** footage of Bush's visit to Booker Elementary is viewable on www.youtube.com; **phonics-based:** *New Yorker*, 7/26/04.

35   **picked up readers:** The President held his book the correct way up, contrary to persistent claims that he held it upside down. A photograph purporting to show him holding a book upside down—on another occasion—was doctored. In the original AP photograph of that occasion, Bush was clearly holding the book the correct way up (claims: e.g., refs. to the "Pet Goat" story on Google, Jude Cowell blog, 11/19/08, www.judecowell.wordpress.com, *Asia Times*, 10/30/04; doctored: "Dubya, Willya Turn the Book Over?" 11/16/02, www.wired.com).

35   **news coverage:** Televisions were available at the school. President Bush would be excoriated, later, for appearing to claim—in Florida in December 2001 and subsequently—that he had seen TV coverage of the *first* plane hitting the Trade Center. What he said in December was: "And I was *sitting outside the classroom waiting to go in* [authors' italics], and I saw an airplane hit the tower—the television was obviously on, and I used to fly myself, and I said, 'There's one terrible pilot.' " Bush was in error in saying that he saw one of the strikes on TV before entering the classroom. There was no live footage of the first strike on the Trade Center. The footage of Flight 11's impact, shot by documentary filmmaker Jules Naudet, was on video and not shown until much later. Bush, moreover, would be in the classroom with the schoolchildren—not watching television—when the TV showed live pictures of the second plane flying into the Trade Center. The footage of the second strike, however, was shown again and again in the minutes and hours that followed. What Bush recalled having seen on TV at the school was surely one of the reruns, transmitted *after* he had left the classroom. A photograph taken at the school features Bush standing near a TV screen—one that appears to show smoke billowing from the Trade Center. Given the tumultuous events that followed on September 11 and later, and given the President's infamous propensity to muddle his utterances, there is no reason to attach

significance to his error in saying he saw one of the strikes on television before entering the classroom (there were TVs: Summers tour of school, int. Dwana Washington; "And I was *sitting*": interview George Bush, 12/04/01, www.whitehouse.gov; much later: Paul Thompson, *The Terror Timeline*, NY: Regan, 2004, 388, & see Friend, 187; photo: AP).

35   **Marine:** *Sarasota Herald-Tribune*, 9/10/02.

35   **"It took me"/"Captain Loewer says":** AP, 11/26/01.

35   **"A second plane":** CR, 38. To calculate the timing of the classroom session and when Bush was informed of the second strike, the authors studied the footage of the session available on YouTube and in the relevant section of Michael Moore's *Fahrenheit 9/11*, which includes specific time points. The authors' calculation as to the delay before Bush was told of the second strike—"ninety seconds"—would mean that Card interrupted him somewhat after 9:04—a little earlier than the 9:05 timing cited in the Commission Report. The delay was in any case minimal (*Fahrenheit 9/11*, Sony Pictures, 2004, CR, 38).

35   **Brian Clark:** Bernstein, 224–; **emergency calls:** *NY Daily News*, 9/30/01.

36   **Compton:** ABC News, 9/11/02; **Daniels:** *St. Petersburg Times*, 9/8/02; **Jones-Pinkney/Radkey:** AP, 9/11/06; **"Can you get":** *St. Petersburg Times*, 7/4/04; **"The Pet Goat":** eds. Siegfried Engelmann & Elaine Bruner, *Reading Mastery 2, Storybook 1*, NY: McGraw-Hill, 1995; **"DON'T SAY":** *Washington Times*, 10/7/02.

36   **Gartenberg/Puma:** WABC (NY), 9/11/01, eds. *Der Spiegel*, 85–, 212–.

38–39 **Flight 77:** Farmer, 160–, 186, "Air Traffic Control Recording," NTSB, 12/21/01, CR, 8–, 24–; **"Whose plane":** MFR 04017175, 11/20/03, CF; **Ballinger/Boston warned:** Staff Report, "The Four Flights and Civil Aviation Security," 8/26/04, CF, CR, 455n67; **Command Center failed:** ibid.; **Boston advised/NY issued:** CR, 23, "Staff Report"; **"Beware":** CR, 11. One such message went to Flight 175, which, still unknown to Ballinger, had already crashed; **4,546:** Pamela Freni, *Ground Stop*, NY: iUniverse, 2003, 59.

39   **May call:** Las Vegas to Dallas, 9/12/01, Dallas to Las Vegas, 9/11/01, Dallas to Dallas, 9/11/01, "Misc. Comms from 4 Flights," B13, T7, CF; **mother got through:** "Through My Eyes," by Toni Knisley, submission for National September 11 Memorial & Museum, http://ns11makehistory.appspot.com, MFR 04017206, 11/19/03; **some wondered:** Farmer, 162; **videoconference:** CR, 36; **"I need":** Stephen Hayes, *Cheney*, NY: HarperCollins, 2007, 331–; **"The Cabinet":** Barton Gellman, *Angler*, London: Allen Lane, 114.

39–40 **"very aware":** *Newsweek*, 12/3/01; **Cheney/Rice:** CR, 39, 463n204, *St. Petersburg Times*, 9/8/02.

CHAPTER 5

41–42 **Olson calls:** FBI 302 of Lori Keyton, 9/14/01, "Flight Call Notes and 302s," B13, T7, CF, FBI 302 of Ted Olson, 9/11/01, INTELWIRE, int. Ted Olson on *Larry King Weekend*, CNN, 1/6/02, Farmer, 163; **undetected:** Staff Monograph, "The Four Flights and Civil Aviation Security," 8/26/04, CF; **speeding east/notified Reagan/Secret Service:** Flight 77 map and timeline, "Timelines 9-11, 1 of 2," B20, T7, CF.

42–43 **Ladies and gentlemen:** AP, 9/11/01; **"We're under":** *Clear the Skies*, BBC documentary, 9/1/02.

43   **"We've got":** Alfred Goldberg et al., *Pentagon 9/11*, Washington, D.C.: Office of the Secretary of Defense, 2007, 13; **agents acted:** CR, 39–, 464n209, Gellman, 114–, int. of Dick Cheney on *Meet the Press*, NBC, 9/16/01. Questions have been raised about the timing of Cheney's move from his office to the underground shelter—to be reported in Ch. 13.

43–44 **P-56/O'Brien:** Spencer, 145–; **horrified controllers:** ibid., 158, *USA Today*, 8/11/02; **fire engine crew:** "Arlington County After-Action Report," www.co.arlington.va.us/

fire/edu/about/pdf/after_report.pdf, Annex A, A-4; **policeman:** Goldberg et al., 13; **priest:** Penny Schoner, "Analysis of Eyewitness Statements on 9/11, American Airlines Flight 77 Crash into the Pentagon," www.ratical.org, pt. 8; **Anderson/Benedetto/ Riskus:** ibid., pts. 13, 18, 3; **"I looked out":** "Personal Experience at the Pentagon on September 11, 2001," by Penny Elgas, Smithsonian Institution.

44–45 **Jester:** Goldberg et al., 151–; **Boger:** ibid., 27, 64–; **Others heard:** ibid., 137, 134; **fuel/mph/had struck:** ibid., 16–; **"simply melt":** statement of Penny Elgas, http://americanhistory.si.edu.

45 **"I saw":** The source of this quote is blogger Rebecca Gordon, a resident of Virginia, writing as "Skarlet" on www.punkprincess.com (corr. Rebecca Gordon, 2009, column at Gordon's blog www.meanlouise.com).

45–46 **"I expected":** Christopher Hilton, *The Women's War,* Stroud, U.K.: History Press, 2003; **impact:** Goldberg et al., 17; **dead/injured:** ibid., 23–, 49, 117–, 123; **Morrison/Cruz/ Kurtz/Moody/Gallop:** ibid., 28–; **Marines:** ibid., 53–; **firefighters:** ibid., 64–, 78–, 93–.

46–47 **CIA briefer/room shaken:** interview of Donald Rumsfeld by Alfred Goldberg & Rebecca Cameron, "Rumsfeld on Intel," B7, T2, CF; **left office/"it was dark":** Andrew Cockburn, *Rumsfeld,* NY: Scribner, 2007, 1–; **"hundreds":** int. of Rumsfeld; **"people lying":** transcript of Rumsfeld int. for *Parade* magazine, 10/12/01, www.defenselink.mil & see Donald Rumsfeld, *Known and Unknown,* NY: Sentinel, 2011, 336–; **examined/ gurney:** Cockburn, 2; **photographed:** Goldberg et al., photo section 82–; **"suit jacket":** Torie Clarke, 221. Victoria "Torie" Clarke, whose timing of 10:15 we have used, took notes of events that day. Rumsfeld himself believed he was back inside the Pentagon from the crash site "shortly before or after 10:00," and then used the phone before proceeding to the Executive Support Center (took notes: int. of Rumsfeld; "shortly before or after": testimony of Donald Rumsfeld, 3/23/04, CO).

47 **news reached/escort to advise:** CR, 39, 463n206; **President hurried:** Bamford, *Pretext,* 62; **"Sounds like":** CR, 39; **"They were taxiing":** int. law enforcement officer, now member of Joint Terrorism Task Force, who asked not to be identified; **"like a rocket":** CBS News, 9/10/03; **northeast/west:** corr. Miles Kara, 2011, Stephen Hayes, 341, *St. Petersburg Times,* 7/4/04; **Instead of returning:** CR, 39, 325.

CHAPTER 6

48 **Melodie/Leroy Homer:** int. of Melodie Homer on *American Morning,* CNN, 9/11/06, CR, 11, 456n70, FBI 302 of Tara Campbell, "FBI 302s ACARS," B11, T7, CF; **Dahl nonplussed:** CR, 11, 456n70.

48–49 **"Mayday!"/"Ladies and gentlemen":** "Air Traffic Control Recording," NTSB, 12/21/01. The hijackers' transmission is rendered with minor variations—though essentially the same—in the 9/11 Commission Report, the NTSB's "Air Traffic Control Recording," and the transcript of the Cockpit Voice Recorder prepared for the trial of Zacarias Moussaoui in 2006. We have used the latter (CR, 12, "Air Traffic Control Recording," Government Exhibit P200056T 01-455-A [ID], "Transcript of the Flight Voice Recorder for UA Flight 93, Commission Copy," B17, T7, CF).

49 **panting:** Jere Longman, *Among the Heroes,* NY: Perennial, 2003, 70, 83; **Some investigators:** CR, 12.

49 **Recorder survived:** Every commercial aircraft is required to carry two black boxes that record data about each flight—a Cockpit Voice Recorder (CVR) and a Flight Data Recorder (FDR). Skeptics have raised questions as to the whereabouts of the recorders that were aboard the four flights that crashed on 9/11. Both of Flight 93's recorders were recovered in readable condition. The CVR for Flight 93 ran on a loop, constantly recording over itself, represented by the thirty-one surviving minutes of sound that we have from inside the cockpit.

The recorders from Flight 77 were found, but only the FDR contained usable data—its CVR was too badly burned to be decipherable.

Both the NTSB and the FBI have said that none of the four recorders from Flights 11 and 175 was located during the cleanup at Ground Zero. A 2003 book reported a claim by former firefighter Nicholas DeMasi to have found three of the four black boxes at Ground Zero during the recovery operation. His account of having found the boxes was corroborated by Mike Bellone, who also worked on the recovery operation. Something that NTSB spokesman Ted Lopatkiewicz told the authors may explain the DeMasi claim. The agency sent several dummy black boxes to Ground Zero, he recalled, specimens to help nonexpert volunteers in the hunt for the real ones. It may be the dummy boxes that DeMasi described (boxes general/re four flights: "Cockpit Voice Recorders & Flight Data Recorders," www.ntsb.gov, CR, 456n76, corr. Ted Lopatkiewicz, 2009; DeMasi: Gail Swanson, *Behind the Scenes at Ground Zero*, NY: TRAC Team, 2003, 108–; Bellone: *CounterPunch*, 12/19/05, *NYDN*, 9/28/05, *NY Post*, 4/5/04, "Black Box Cover-Up," 12/12/04, www.AmericanFreePress.net; FBI/NTSB denied: *CounterPunch*, 12/19/05).

49   **partial record:** The authors have drawn on the transcript as released in 2009; **Welsh:** CR, 455n62, *NYT*, 3/27/02, www.unitedheroes.com; **Green:** CR, 455n62.

49   **cockpit key/coded knock:** Longman, 6. Accounts vary as to whether United attendants carried keys. The FBI was told that "some flight attendants used to carry the cockpit key on their security badge neck chains." Jere Longman, a *New York Times* reporter who has written an excellent book on the Flight 93 hijacking, suggests that attendants did not carry keys (FBI 302 of [name redacted], 12/19/01, "FBI 302s Arestegui," B10, T7, CF, Longman, 6).

49–50   **forty-nine/tough, etc.:** ibid., 25–, www.flightattendants.org, *Post-Gazette* (Pittsburgh), 10/28/01; **Green doubled:** ibid.; **Basmala:** "An Exegesis of the Basmala," http://muslimmatters.org, "Bismillah," defined at http://wahiduddin.net.

50   **voice not heard again:** The 9/11 Commission concluded that the voice recorder data indicated that a flight attendant was "killed or otherwise silenced." United Airlines officials would later tell Deborah Welsh's husband, Patrick, that an attendant was stabbed early in the hijacking, implying that the victim was his wife (CR, 12, *NYT*, 3/27/02).

50   **"We are going back":** As before, the terrorist's words were heard not as intended by the passengers but by ground control and by other aircraft.

50–51   **Bradshaw/Starfix:** MFR re Richard Belme, 11/21/03, "DOJ Doc. Request 35," B12, T7, CF, MFR 04020029, 5/13/04, MFR 04017218, 11/21/03, "Ref. Lead Control No. SFA62," FBI int. of [name redacted], 9/11/01, INTELWIRE, FBI 302s of Richard Belme, Ray Kime, & Andrew Lubkemann, 9/11/01, "Key 302s," B19, T7, CF. Starfix was the same United facility that had earlier taken a call from an attendant on hijacked Flight 175—see p. 28.

51   **"knives were":** Timeline compiled by Joe Vickers, "Timelines 9-11, 2 of 2," B20, T7, CF.

51   **"lying on the floor":** This information derives from accounts of the phone call made from the plane by passenger Todd Beamer, who from 9:43 used a seatback phone to hold a long conversation with Verizon supervisor Lisa Jefferson. Jefferson said afterward that Beamer was being passed information by a flight attendant whose voice sounded "African-American." Of the two African-American flight attendants on Flight 93, Wanda Green and CeeCee Lyles, the attendant who spoke to Beamer is more likely to have been Lyles—who worked to the rear of the plane (MFR 04020031, 5/11/04, FBI 302 of [name redacted], 9/22/01, INTELWIRE, Lisa Jefferson and Felicia Middlebrooks, *Called*, Chicago: Northfield, 2006, 36, recording of conversation, 5/10/04, "Flight #93 Calls—Todd Beamer," B12, T7, CF).

51   **Sliney first day:** *USA Today*, 8/12/02; **Delta flight:** Spencer, 167, MFR 04017314m, 10/2/03, CR, 10, 455n68, 28; **bomb/"ground stop":** CR, 25, 28.

51   **"Order everyone":** *USA Today*, 8/12/02. There has been controversy over the origin of this order. Secretary of Transportation Norman Mineta, testifying later to a congressional committee, said *he* "immediately called the FAA, told them to bring all the planes down. . . . [It] was the right thing to do." Bob Woodward and Dan Balz, writing in *The Washington Post*, attributed the decision to land all planes to Mineta. The book *Out of the Blue*, by *The New York Times*'s Richard Bernstein, states that the order was issued by FAA administrator Jane Garvey. Joshua Green, for *Slate*, reported that the decision was in fact taken by the FAA's acting deputy administrator, Monte Belger. The 9/11 Commission credited Sliney, citing the Command Center traffic transcript. In an interview with the authors, FAA spokeswoman Laura Brown emphasized that the decision was collaborative—taken not only by Ben Sliney but also by facility manager Linda Schuessler and other senior staff at the Command Center. Schuessler said as much in a 2001 interview (testimony of Norman Mineta, 5/23/03, CO, *WP*, 1/27/02, Bernstein, 188, *Slate*, 4/1/02, CR, 29, 461n165, int. Laura Brown, *Aviation Week & Space Technology*, 12/17/01, see also Freni, 65, testimony of Monte Belger and Ben Sliney, 6/17/04, CO, MFR 04018154, 4/20/04, MFR 04017327, 7/22/03).

51–52 **4,540:** Freni, 59; **By 12:16:** *WSJ*, 3/22/04.

52   **Clarke's videoconference:** The Commission Report states that the White House teleconference began around 9:25. Information the authors have learned, however, suggests that it started with some—but not all—officials on line at about 9:37. At the Pentagon, a "significant event" conference call—already under way for some minutes—was upgraded to an "air threat" conference call at around the same time. The FAA, for its part, had begun its own teleconference at about 9:20. The White House teleconference, and Clarke's desire to have the most senior representative of each agency participating, had the effect of "decapitating" the agencies at various points. Taking part in the White House conference call meant that individual agency heads were away from the very people from whom they could receive the most accurate incoming information, and to whom they needed to give moment-by-moment instructions (CR, 36–, corr. Miles Kara, 2011); **Defense:** Farmer, 184–, Tenet, 163; **first matter:** Tenet, 163; **contingency/ Hastert:** Bamford, *Pretext*, 70–, 80–, transcript, *9/11*, ABC News, 9/11/02, *WP*, 3/2/02; **Byrd:** corr. Jesse Jacobs, 2010; **people pouring:** int. Eleanor Hill; **White House evacuation:** testimony of Norman Mineta, 5/23/02, CO, Richard Clarke, 8, CNN, 9/11/01, *Newsweek*, 9/24/01; **"CNN says"/"Does it":** Richard Clarke, 9; **humor:** Dwyer & Flynn, 175.

53   **golf club/computers:** Dwyer & Flynn, 175–; **"There's another":** int. Edward Chacia, TF, 12/6/01; **"They hit":** int. James Canham, TF, 12/18/01; **"What happened?":** Dwyer & Flynn, 178.

53   **locked doors:** CR, 294. Any faint possibility of going up had vanished at 9:30, when security officers tried and failed to activate a lock release programmed to open all doors— including doors leading to the roof—as explained on p. 22; **Beyea:** Dwyer & Flynn, 178, 243; **Lillo:** int. Manuel Delgado, 10/21/01, TF, *NY Post*, 9/21/01; **"The Chief said"/ Suhr:** int. Paul Conlon, TF, 1/26/02, *NY Daily News*, 11/1/01.

54   **"We didn't have":** Staff Statement 13, CO. The World Trade Center did have such a radio repeater system, but most chiefs were unable to use it on the day—either because it was malfunctioning or because they failed to use it properly. To bridge the communications gap, chiefs attempted to use shorter range equipment available—sometimes even their own cell phones—with little success. This left the chiefs in the lobby or outside the towers largely in the dark about the progress of the units moving up and around the building ("FDNY Fire Operations Response on September 11," www.nyc.gov, CR, 188).

54   **"People watching"/men struggled:** Staff Statement 13, CO.

54   **towers' casualties/survivors:** "Federal Investigators Classify WTC Victims' Loca-

tions," 7/20/04, NIST, Staff Statement 13, CO, Dwyer & Flynn, 252, 312. Estimates vary as to the number of people in the Twin Towers at the time of the attacks. We have here drawn on numbers cited in *102 Minutes*, by Jim Dwyer and Kevin Flynn—which take into account not only the 2005 Final Report of the National Institute of Standards and Technology, but also of figures supplied by the Port Authority of New York (Dwyer & Flynn, 280, "Final Report on the Collapse of the World Trade Center Towers," Washington, D.C.: National Institute of Standards and Technology, Sept. 2005, 19, 34, 37–, 48).

54–55 **Clark/Praimnath:** Bernstein, 225- ; **Rooney:** Banford, *Pretext*, 32–58; **70th floor:** Staff Statement 13, CO; **Palmer:** Dwyer & Flynn, 206; **PEOPLE TRAPPED:** *NY Daily News*, 9/30/01; **overwhelmed:** Staff Statement 13, CO; **"Some of them":** int. Roberto Abril, TF, 1/17/02.

56   **Turi wondered:** int. Albert Turi, TF, 10/23/01, CR, 302, 549n134—the chief is not identified in line with the 9/11 Commission's agreement with the city of New York, corr. Kristen Wilhelm, 2010.

56–57 **He shared:** int. Peter Hayden, TF, 10/23/01, & see Staff Statement 13, CO; **"The potential"/"I think":** int. Peter Hayden, TF, 10/23/01, Dennis Smith, *Report from Ground Zero*, NY: Viking, 2002, 33; **"Everything above":** *New Yorker*, 2/11/02; **"Tommy":** int. Richard Carletti, TF, 1/2/02; **"I believe":** Dwyer & Flynn, 149–, De Martini's comments were made in an interview for the History Channel, *NYT*, 8/29/03; **707/"low on fuel":** *Seattle Times*, 2/27/93, *MedServ*, 9/11/01, "Painful Losses Mount in the Construction Family," 10/1/01, www.construction.com, "WTC Building Performance Study," FEMA, 5/02, Ch.1.17; **drooping/molten metal:** "World Trade Center Investigation Status," 12/03, & "Investigation of the Sept. 11 World Trade Center Disaster—FAQs," 8/30/06, NIST, "World Trade Center Building Performance Study," Ch. 2., Pt. 2.2.3, FEMA, May 2002; **"large pieces":** CR, 304, 321, 549n148; **9:37 call:** *NY Daily News*, 9/30/01, "Increasing FDNY Preparedness," FDNY report, 8/19/02, 46–.

CHAPTER 7

58   **over Ohio/Flight 93:** "Flight Path Study—United Flight 93," 2/19/02, NTSB, ed. James Boyd, *After September 11*, Saddle River, NJ: Prentice Hall, 2003, 88; **managed to telephone:** MFR 04020029, 5/13/04—detailed study of phone records, used throughout chapter, Moschella to Marcus (& attachments), 4/26/04, "Flight 11 Calls—DOJ Response," B13, T7, CF. In addition to the passengers named in the text, several others succeeded in making or attempted to make calls to the ground. Three who did get through were Linda Gronlund, Lauren Grandcolas, and Joseph DeLuca. Two others, Andrew Garcia and Waleska Martinez, got through only momentarily (several others: MFR 04020029, 5/13/04, Longman, 190).

58   **Bingham:** This is what Bingham said to his aunt by marriage, the first family member to get to the phone. Some, who question the authenticity of the calls from the air on 9/11, have made much of the fact that—when afterward his mother came on the line—he reportedly said, "Hello, Mom, this is Mark *Bingham* [authors' italics] . . ." No one, the skeptics suggest, would address his own mother with such formality. There is no tape or transcript of the call so far as the authors know—the earliest version of the quote is in an FBI report. Bingham's mother, Alice Hoglan, however, herself remembered her son greeting her that way. To her, she said, it merely showed that he was a "little rattled" and fell back on the way that—as a young businessman—he regularly introduced himself on the phone. One cannot hang any significant doubt on the reported formality—least of all the idea, as some suggest, that the Bingham call itself is part of some complex fabrication. The call, like the other calls from Flight 93, is included in a list of air and cell phone calls compiled with the help of GTE engineers and released in 2009. For further discussion of the "fake calls" issue, see Ch. 11 ("This is Mark"/"*Bingham*": FBI 302 of ints. Alice

Hoglan, Carol Phipps, & Kathy Hoglan, 9/11/01, "Flight 93 Calls," B12, T7, CF, FBI 302s of [names redacted], 9/19/01 & 9/23/01, INTELWIRE; doubt: David Ray Griffin, *Debunking 9/11 Debunking*, Northampton, MA: Olive Branch, 2007, 89–, James Fetzer cited in "Osama Tape Appears Fake," PR Web, 5/30/06; "little rattled"/repeatedly: transcript of int. Hoglan, *Newsnight*, 2001, www.bbc.co.uk, int.of Hoglan, *The Flight That Fought Back*, Brook Lapping Productions for Discovery Channel, 2005).

58   **Burnett:** FBI 302 of int. Deena Burnett, 9/11/01, INTELWIRE, Longman, 107, MFR 04020024, 4/26/04.

59   **knife point/bomb:** Burnett also told his wife that he thought one of the hijackers had a gun. His wife believed this, because her husband was familiar with guns. Fellow passenger Jeremy Glick, however, specifically told his wife that he saw no guns on the hijackers, only knives. Janet Riffe, an FAA security inspector assigned to American Airlines on 9/11, told the 9/11 Commission that she was told by an American employee that day of a flight attendant's report that Flight 11 passenger Daniel Lewin had been shot. Riffe said she was later told she had been wrongly informed. A partly redacted FBI summary states that passenger Peter Hanson, who phoned his father from Flight 175, said he had seen a flight attendant shot. Available reports of what Hanson said include no such reference. The presence of guns aboard any of the hijacked flights would of course indicate a grave security lapse. The 9/11 Commission concluded that the reports of guns were mistaken, that the weight of the evidence indicated that knives were the only weapons the hijackers brought on board (Burnett told: MFR 04020024, 4/26/04, Longman, 108; very familiar: *The Times* [London], 8/11/02, bio at www.tomburnettfoundation.org; Glick: *Reader's Digest* [U.K.], 9/06, MFR 04020025, 4/22/04, "FBI Documents—Inc. Joanne Makely Call Transcript," B13, T7, CF; Riffe: MFR 03007067, 9/11/03, "Flight 11 Gun Story," B16, T7, CF; Hanson: Chicago to Director, 9/12/01, FBI 265D-NY-280350-CG, INTELWIRE; Commission: CR 13, 452n25, 457n82).

59–60 **Glick:** *Reader's Digest* (U.K.), 9/06, FBI 302 of Lyzbeth Glick, 9/12/01, INTELWIRE, Longman, 146; **told him/"My God"/"A group":** FBI 302 of int. Deena Burnett, 9/11/01, INTELWIRE, Longman, 110–; **"I'm going":** *Reader's Digest* (U.K.), 9/06; **equipped:** Longman, 19, 108–, 114, 27–,137–, 132–; **Beamer:** ibid., 17–, 200, 202; **Jefferson account:** Jefferson & Middlebrooks, 29–; **"Shit!":** "Recording of Conversation," 9/15/01, "Flight 93 Calls," B12, T7, CF; **"Oh, my God":** Jefferson & Middlebrooks, 44–; **Flight Data Recorder:** "Study of Autopilot, Navigational Equipment, and Fuel Consumption Activity Based on UA Flight 93 and AA Flight 77 Digital Flight Recorder Data," 2/13/02, www.ntsb.gov; **23rd Psalm:** Longman, 200; **"We just lost":** Joseph Gregor, "Air Traffic Control Recording," NTSB, 12/21/01, int. John Werth.

60   **executive jet:** transcript of audiotape, FAA Cleveland Air Traffic Control Center—Lorain position, 9/11/01, int. John Werth, CR, 30. There had not yet been time to comply with the nationwide grounding order. The FAA transcript indicates that the plane that sighted Flight 93 was Executive Jet 956. The authors' reading of relevant sources, including a transcript of the Cleveland Air Traffic Control recording, suggests the Jet 956 sighting occurred soon after 9:41. The 9/11 Commission Report, meanwhile, refers to a sighting of Flight 93 by an aircraft at about 9:53. The sources cited in the Report do not make entirely clear whether this reference is to a sighting by Executive 956 or by another airplane (CR, 29–, 461n167, Full Transcription, "Air Traffic Control System Command Center, National Traffic Management Officer, East Position, 9/11/01," B1, NY Office files, CF, int. John Werth).

60   **navigational aid:** CR, 457n85.

60–61 **Britton:** Interviewed by the FBI after the attacks, Britton's friend Frank Fiumano said he "assumed she had borrowed a cell phone from another passenger" to make her call because Britton's own cell phone was not working. Records released in 2009 make clear, however, that Britton used a seatback phone (Britton's friend: FBI 302 of [name re-dacted], 9/20/01, & Pittsburgh to Pittsburgh, 9/22/01, INTELWIRE, Longman, 162; 2009 records: United Airlines Flight 93, Telephone Calls, "Flight 11 Calls—Response to DOJ Documents Requests," B13, T7, CF); **plane turning:** "Flight Path Study—United Flight 93," 2/19/02, NTSB; **"I know":** *Reader's Digest* (U.K.), 9/06; **"to jump":** Jefferson & Middlebrook, 52–; **"the impression":** MFR 04020031, 5/11/04; **Greene:** Chicago to Counterterrorism Baltimore et al., 10/4/01, "Flights 175 and 93 Load Patterns," B20, T7, CF, Longman, 182–. Another passenger on Flight 93, Andrew Garcia, had served in the California Air National Guard and trained as an air traffic controller. Even with his limited knowledge of aviation, he might have been of some help in the cockpit. As to the possibility that Greene could conceivably have landed the plane, the authors consulted Gerry Humphries, a working pilot with thirty-five years' experience who regularly flies a plane similar to a King Air (Garcia: *Post-Gazette* [Pittsburgh], 10/28/01, Humphries: int. Gerry Humphries); **Boeing:** "757–200 Technical Characteristics," www.boeing .com; **flying erratically:** "Flight Path Study—United Flight 93," 2/19/02, NTSB; **"commotion":** Longman, 204; **"Are you guys":** MFR 04020031, 5/11/04, FBI 302 of Lisa Jefferson, 9/11/01, INTELWIRE, Longman, 202; **"OK":** *Reader's Digest* (U.K.), 9/06; **Wainio:** www.elizabethwainio.com, Longman, 168, 171–, FBI 302 of [name redacted], 9/12/01, INTELWIRE; **Bradshaw:** MFR of Philip Bradshaw, 6/15/04, "Flight 93 Calls," B12, T7, CF, FBI 302 of int. Philip Bradshaw, 9/11/01 & 9/12/01, INTELWIRE.

61 **Lyles:** Longman, 180. Lyles had phoned her police officer husband earlier. He had been asleep, after coming home from a night shift, and she had left a message on the answering machine (FBI 302 of int. Lorne Lyles, 9/17/01, "FBI 302s Homer," B10, T7, CF).

62–63 **"I think":** FBI 302 of [name redacted], 9/12/01, INTELWIRE; **Burnett's wife recognized:** MFR 04020024, 1/26/04, **rolling.** "Flight Path Study—United Flight 93," 2/19/02, NTSB; **"The wings started":** pilot Bill Wright cited at Longman, 192–, *Flight 93's Last Moments*, WTAE TV, 9/19/01, & see CR, 30; **Glick's father-in-law/"roller coaster":** *Reader's Digest* (U.K.), 9/06; **"wind sounds":** FBI 302 of int. [name redacted], 9/12/01, INTELWIRE.

63–64 **scrapyard:** *St. Petersburg Times*, 9/12/01; **"nosediving":** *WP*, 9/16/01; **"sort of whistling":** *St. Petersburg Times*, 9/12/01; **"barely fifty":** *The Mirror* (U.K.), 9/12/02.

64 **It was 10:03:** For the time Flight 93 crashed, the authors have relied—as did the 9/11 Commission—on the impact time established by the combination of the Cockpit Voice Recorder, the Flight Data Recorder, and Air Traffic Control and radar data. In 2002, geologists at the Lamont-Doherty Earth Observatory produced a report—based on seismic data—that put the impact time of Flight 93 as some three minutes later, at 10:06. In the years since, the scientists themselves have stressed that the seismic signals cited in respect to Flight 93 were too weak and speculative to be relied upon. It should be noted, too, that the NTSB does not characteristically rely on seismic data to establish crash time. Commission staff considered the Lamont-Doherty time of 10:06 to be a significant anomaly and therefore asked for the time according to satellite infrared imaging—as a "tiebreaker." This further established the 10:03 time for the crash of UA 93. The timing discrepancy has been seized on by those who suggest the U.S. military shot down Flight 93, an issue that will be addressed in Ch. 12 (CR, 30, 461n168, Won-Young Kim & Gerald Baum, "Seismic Observations During September 11, 2001 Terrorist Attack," Spring 2002, corr. Won-Young Kim, Ted Lopatkiewicz, 2009, & see Terry Wallace cited in "Cockpit Voice Recording Ends Before Flight 93's Official Time of Impact," 9/16/02, www.phillynews.com, corr. Terry Wallace, 2010, Miles Kara, 2011).

65 **strip mine/"Where's the plane":** "Flight 93 Crash Site Left Most of the Horror to the Imagination," KDKA radio, 2006; **crater burning/couple of feet:** *Post-Gazette* (Pittsburgh), 9/12/01; **recorder buried:** *WP*, 9/15/01; **clothing:** *Post-Gazette* (Pittsburgh),

9/12/01. All sorts of identifiable bits and pieces would eventually be collected at the crash site. Douglass personal effects administrators would circulate a list and photographs of many personal items that had belonged to those aboard Flight 93—pieces of jewelry, snapshots, clothing, and shoes. Jeremy Glick's widow, Lyz, recognized a picture of a pair of black briefs as her husband's. An American Express personal organizer was returned to her, with notes in Glick's still legible handwriting (*Reader's Digest* [U.K.], 9/06).

65   **"shiny stuff"**: *WP*, 9/14/01; **Lisa Beamer:** Longman, 220–; **Lyz Glick/father:** Moschella to Marcus (& attachments), 4/26/04, & see *Reader's Digest* (U.K.), 9/06.

CHAPTER 8

66–67   **Peruggia/instructions:** int. John Peruggia, TF, 10/25/01. The Office of Emergency Management was in the building known as World Trade Center 7, which would itself collapse later in the day. Mayor Rudolph Giuliani apparently never made it to the OEM that morning, because the building was being evacuated. He set up a temporary base elsewhere (CR, 283–, 293, 301–, 305, 311, Rudolph Giuliani with Ken Kurson, *Leadership*, NY: Hyperion, 2002, 5–, but see also Barrett & Collins, 5–); **engineer/Peruggia/Zarrillo:** int. Peruggia, int. Richard Zarrillo, TF, 10/25/01, Dwyer & Flynn, 203–; **command and control:** CR, 301–.

67   **"We stared"/"You know":** *A Survivor's Story*, www.pbs.org/wgbh/nova/wtc/above .html.

67   **Cosgrove/911:** *Newsday*, 4/10/06, Dwyer & Flynn, 207; **Rooney:** *Chicago Tribune*, 10/31/01.

68   **"Listen":** int. Zarrillo, int. Steven Mosiello, TF, 10/23/01.

68   **"started to lean":** int. Richard Carletti, TF, 1/21/02; **"bulge out"/"snapping sounds":** *NY Daily News*, 9/11/01; **"real loud"/"groaning":** e.g., entry for 9:59 A.M., September 11, 2001, "Some Witnesses Hear Explosions," www.cooperativeresearch.org, Jim Marrs, *The Terror Conspiracy*, NY: The Disinformation Co., 2006, 47. Critics of official accounts of 9/11 have used such references to "explosions" to suggest that the Twin Towers collapsed at least partially as the result of explosive devices planted in the buildings. Those claims will be covered in Chapter 11.

68   **"The entire":** *The Independent* (U.K.), 9/12/01.

69   **Jennings/Dahler:** transcript & video on YouTube, "ABC News Special Report: Planes Crash into World Trade Center," 9/11/01, *9/11*, ABC News, 9/11/02; **9:59:** CR, 305—more precisely, 9:58:59. The 9/11 Commission Report used the figure of ten seconds. For the collapse time of some twenty seconds, the authors have relied on explanations by the National Institute of Standards and by scientist Ryan Mackey, who estimated that it took fifteen to twenty seconds for the tower's roof to hit the ground (CR, 305–, "NIST's Investigation of the Sept. 11 World Trade Center Disaster—FAQ," 8/30/06, http://wtc .nist.gov, Ryan Mackey, "On *Debunking 9/11 Debunking*," 5/24/08, www.jod911.com); **"From a structure":** int. James Cannon, TF, 12/18/01.

69–71   **garages:** int. Pedro Carrasquillo, TF, 10/16/01; **"I took":** int. Zarrillo; **"I grabbed":** int. Peruggia; **"Everybody's like":** int. Jody Bell, TF, 12/15/01; **"smoked"/"Everything started":** int. Timothy Brown, TF, 1/15/02; **16 firefighters:** CR, 308; **Marriott sliced:** "The 9/11 Hotel, pt. 3 of 5" documentary on www.youtube.com; **"stared in awe":** "A Survivor's Story"; **"huge tidal":** *The Independent* (U.K.), 9/12/01; **"all the walking":** *NY Daily News*, 9/11/01.

71   **few aware:** Staff Statement 13, CO, int. Joseph Pfeifer, TF, 10/23/01; **"We felt it":** int. Michael Brodbeck, TF, 12/10/01; **"You just":** int. Derek Brogan, TF, 12/28/01; **"It didn't register":** int. James Canham, TF, 12/18/01; **"To think that":** Staff Statement 13, CO; **burst of energy:** Dwyer & Flynn, 242; **pitch black:** int. Peter Hayden, TF, 10/23/01; **fatally for some:** Smith, 30–; **Judge:** *USA Today*, 2/19/03, Bernstein, 231;

Pfeifer: int. Pfeifer, int. Joseph Callan, TF, 11/2/01, Smith, 42–; **evacuation:** Staff Statement 13, CO.

72 **"get the fuck":** The 9/11 Commission credited Picciotto both with the "Get the fuck out!" initiative and with the radioed instructions. He himself said words to that effect on a CBS television show days after 9/11. His autobiographical accounts of events later in the day, however, have been rebutted by colleagues ("Get!"/radioed: CR, 307, 550n165; CBS show: transcript of int., *Montel Williams Show*, 9/17/01; autobiography: Richard Picciotto with Daniel Paisner, *Last Man Down*, NY: Berkley, 2002; rebutted: *NY Daily News*, 11/26/02, *New York*, 9/11/03).

72 **"knew that he had men":** int. Mosiello; **"We're not fucking":** CR, 310, 552n183; **McGinnis:** Dwyer & Flynn, 237.

72 **"What we didn't":** "Emergency Preparedness & Response," Staff Statement 13, CO; **blind:** int. Callan, Staff Statement 13, CO.

72 **"There was gas":** int. Derek Brogan, TF, 12/28/01. The Twin Towers were sheathed in aluminium (e.g., see "Cladding Fragment," exhibit description, Division of Work & Industry, National Museum of American History).

72 **"littering":** int. Robert Byrne, TF, 12/7/01; **Pilots:** ibid., NYPD Call Routing & Message Dispatch Report, 7/23/02, "NYPD folder," B9, NY Office files, CF, CR, 309, 551n176.

73 **10:28:** CR, 311; **"do a little rock":** int. Carletti; **"explosions"/"pop"/"thunderous":** int. Craig Carlsen, TF, 1/25/02, int. Pfeifer; **"the entire":** int. Dean Beltrami, TF, 12/17/01; **"looking like":** int. Bell; **"I opened up":** int. James Basile, TF, 10/17/01; **"This beautiful":** Staff Statement 13, CO; **twenty seconds:** see note at source entry for "9:59," above.

73–74 **alarms:** Lance, 419; **343:** CR, 311; **firefighters killed:** Smith, 193; **Ganci:** int. Mosiello, Bernstein, 149, 231; **brother Kevin:** http://americanhistory.si.edu/September11, www.septembereleven.net; **families:** Smith, 33, 53, 15, 44, 349, Damon DiMarco, *Tower Stories*, NY: Revolution, 2004, 189, Langewiesche, 70, 131–, 145–; **Port Authority/NYPD dead:** CR, 311; **Morrone:** Port Authority press release, 8/13/02, www.PANYNJ.gov; **5 dead PAPD:** William Keegan with David Bart, *Closure*, NY: Touchstone, 2006, 67; **policewoman:** Smith, 67, *NY Daily News*, 3/24/02, www.irishtribute.com entry for Moira Smith.

74 **"The number":** transcript of press conference, CNN, 9/11/01; **7,000:** John Ashcroft cited in MFR 04020543, 12/17/03, & see Knight Ridder report, 10/11/01.

74 **2,760:** The authors' rendering of the total number of 9/11 deaths in New York City includes the ten hijackers of the two planes that hit the Trade Center. The figure used in the 9/11 Commission Report did not include the hijackers, nor did it include three victims injured that day whose deaths were registered later outside New York. The total used here does not include those deemed to have died of illnesses contracted as a result of 9/11, an issue that will be covered elsewhere (CR, 311, 552n188, "World Trade Center Operational Statistics," Office of the Chief Medical Examiner, 1/30/09, *NYT*, 7/22/04, ed. Robyn Gershon, *High Rise Building Evacuation*, Chicago: Univ. of Chicago Press, 2006, 19, CR, 552n188); **other countries:** *NYT*, 4/19/02; **immigrants:** *Hoy*, cited by *AM New York*, 9/7/06.

74–75 **Ground Zero:** The term "Ground Zero" appears to have been used for the first time on the evening of 9/11, by CBS reporter Jim Axelrod (CBS News, 9/11/01, video at www.archive.org); **"All that remained"/final throes:** Langewiesche, 6, 4, www.national911memorial.org; **lesser giants:** frontispiece, ibid., "World Trade Center Building Performance Study," Washington, D.C.: FEMA, May 2002, 3–.

75–76 **WTC 7:** "Final Report on the Collapse of World Trade Center Building 7," Federal Building and Fire Safety Investigation of the World Trade Center Disaster, Washington,

D.C.: NIST, 11/08, NCSTAR 1A, 4.2. There has been a long-running controversy about the collapse of WTC 7—the thrust of it being the suggestion that the building collapsed not solely because of fire and damage but, skeptics suggest, because explosives were used. The controversy will be covered in Ch. 11; **Verizon:** MFR 04018174, 2/25/04, DiMarco, 302–, Smith, 198–; **NY Stock Exchange:** MFR 03013078, 12/11/03, MFR 04016224, 1/21/04; **American Stock Exchange:** MFR 04014516, 1/14/04; **"visiting":** MFR 04017265, 12/18/03; **NASDAQ:** MFR 04014517, 1/14/04; **Federal Reserve NY:** MFR 04016224, 1/21/04; **Greenspan:** MFR 04014512, 1/9/04, MFR 04018180, 1/20/04, MFR 04016224, 1/21/04; **liquidity/ATMs:** MFR 04014512, 1/9/04, MFR 04016224, 1/21/04, MFR 04018180, 1/20/04; **$83/95 billion:** *Real Estate Weekly*, 9/11/02.

CHAPTER 9

77   **"Ambulances going":** int. Michael Cahill, TF, 10/17/01; **Melisi:** "America Rebuilds," transcript of int. Melisi, www.pbs.org.

78   **Two civilians:** They were Tom Canavan, who had worked at First Union Bank on the 47th floor of the North Tower, and a second, unknown man who escaped with him (*USA Today*, 9/5/02).

78–79 **Jonas & rescued group:** "A Day in September," www.recordonline.com, "World Trade Center Survivors," http://911research.wtc7.net, Picciotto with Paisner, 128–, *New York*, 11/26/02; **Buzzelli:** *USA Today*, 9/5/02, Langewiesche, 103–; **McLoughlin/Jimeno/ Marines:** *Slate*, 9/10/02, *NY Post*, 8/7/06, *Times Herald-Record*, 1/18/02. The two former Marines were David Karnes, at the time an accountant with Deloitte Touche, and Jason Thomas, who on 9/11 was attending the John Jay College of Criminal Justice in New York City.

79   **fellow overboard:** Langewiesche, 62.

79–80 **"onslaught":** MFR 04018541, 4/15/04; **personnel/surgeons:** int. Dr. Glenn Asaeda, TF, 10/11/01; **by midnight:** "DOD Medical Support to the Federal Response Plan," Washington, D.C.: Office of the Inspector General, Dept. of Defense, 5/10/02, 7; **"A person's torso":** int. Benjamin Badillo, TF, 1/24/02; **"I-beams":** int. Charles Blaich, TF, 10/23/01; **"A woman's":** DiMarco, 270; **"The body":** eds. *Der Spiegel*, 243; **"You couldn't":** Barrett & Collins, 248; **21,744:** *New York*, 1/7/10; **medical examiner:** *NYT*, 7/14/02, & see "World Trade Center Operational Statistics," Office of the Chief Medical Examiner, NYC, 9/9/03; **2009:** update, "DNA Testing of Remains," 2/1/09, Office of the Chief Medical Examiner, www.nyc.gov; **Deutsche Bank:** "Deutsche Bank Building—FAQ," Lower Manhattan Development Corporation, www.renewny.com; **manholes/road:** AP, 4/8/08.

80   **Fresh Kills:** *NYT*, 3/24/07. According to a sworn affidavit by Eric Beck, a supervisor for Taylor Recycling, the process at Fresh Kills involved creating a mixture used to pave city streets and fill potholes. Troubled by the implication that fragments of their loved ones may have become part of this mixture, relatives of the dead went to federal court in 2007 to plead that the sifted debris be removed from the site and reburied in a more appropriate setting on a site nearby. In 2009, a judge dismissed the families' suit, citing in part the city's intention of redeveloping the now closed Fresh Kills landfill into a park and nature reserve that would include a memorial to the 9/11 victims (*NYT*, 3/24/07, *Staten Island Advance*, 7/7/08, *NY Post*, 7/8/08); **1,229:** *NYT*, 7/14/02; **401:** authors' calculation based on figures in *NYT*, 7/14/02, 5/12/11, and ABC News, 5/13/11.

81–83 **"I see this":** int. Jason Charles, TF, 1/23/02; **"The ambulances":** int. Michael Cahill, TF, 10/17/01; **"People were":** int. Richard Broderick, TF, 10/25/01; **"Nobody could":** int. David Blacksberg, TF, 10/23/01; **"Everybody's coughing":** int. Jody Bell, TF, 12/15/01; **"Our face-pieces":** int. Paul Bessler, TF, 1/21/02; **"My lungs were":** int. Paul Adams, TF, 11/1/01; **"The sergeant asked":** int. Jason Charles, TF, 1/23/02; **9:59/**

FC: *NY Daily News,* 9/30/01; **asbestos, etc., in dust:** "EPA's Response to the World Trade Center Collapse," Washington, D.C., Office of the Inspector General, Environmental Protection Agency, 8/21/03, Cate Jenkins [EPA] to Monona Rossol, 11/15/01, www.whitelung.org, *NYT,* 9/14/01, *Newsweek,* 10/5/01, *Der Spiegel,* 12/20/06, DiMarco, 130, Gail Sheehy, *Middletown, America,* NY: Random House, 2003, 41; **seven blocks:** *Village Voice,* 7/31/07; **"We lost"/Torcivia:** DiMarco, 191–, *St. Petersburg Times,* 2/3/02; **2007 study:** UPI, 5/9/07; **2,000 firefighters:** *Guardian* (U.K.), 1/28/08; **"The World Trade Center dust":** Voice of America, 4/8/10; **young attorney:** (Felicia Dunn-Jones) "NYC Links First Death to Toxic Dust," www.msnbc.com, 5/23/07; **"sick and under":** Fact Sheet, http://stws.org, *Sacramento Bee,* 1/6/11; **479 people:** *NY Post,* 9/6/09; **One by one:** e.g., *WSJ,* 12/9/10, *Dallas Morning News,* 11/29/10, *New York Post,* 1/10/11, *NY Daily News,* 3/30/11; **risen to 664:** *NY Post,* 9/12/10; **James Zadroga Act/ $4.2 billion/"We will never":** *USA Today,* 2/2/11, H.R. 847 James Zadroga 9/11 Health & Compensation Act 2010, http://thomas.loc.gov; **"very reassuring":** "EPA's Response to the WTC Collapse"; **"safe to go":** ibid., *NYT,* 9/18/01.

83   **"safe to breathe":** "EPA's Response to the WTC Collapse." John Henshaw has since explained that a decision not to enforce safety regulations was made because of the delay that would have caused: "We had to deploy a strategy that achieved compliance as soon as the hazard was recognized so corrective action was immediate." Christine Todd Whitman, for her part, told a congressional committee that allegations that she misled New Yorkers about air quality in lower Manhattan were "outright falsehoods." She said that reassurances that air quality was safe applied to lower Manhattan, not to Ground Zero itself (*EHS Today,* 6/27/07).

84   **"I want":** Richard Clarke, 24. The President also discussed the closure of the markets with his assistant for economic policy, Larry Lindsey, urging a "return to normal as soon as possible." Lindsey discussed with the EPA's Christine Todd Whitman "the need to get the financial markets open quickly." Whitman has denied that Lindsey pressured her. The EPA's own inspector general, meanwhile, has said that the Agency's press releases were "influenced" by the White House Council on Environmental Quality. According to the EPA's Tina Kreischer, there was "extreme pressure from the White House" (Lindsey: MFR 04018180, 1/20/04, Whitman denied: CR, 555n13; "influenced"/"extreme pressure": "EPA's Response to the WTC Collapse," 7, 16–, CR, 555n13).

84–85 **9:55:** CR, 325; **"The President":** *9/11,* transcript, ABC News, 9/11/02; **Card:** White House transcripts of ints. of Andy Card for ABC, 8/12/02, CNN, 8/12/02, NBC, 8/15/02, CBS, 8/16/02; **Bush said:** CR, 40, 464n212; **"inexcusable":** *60 Minutes,* transcript, CBS News, 9/11/02; **"could not remain":** Kean & Hamilton, 265; **"The military":** *60 Minutes,* 9/11/02; **flickering TV:** *9/11,* ABC News; **"credible" threat/Armed guards:** CR, 325, 554n1, *60 Minutes,* Bill Sammon, *Fighting Back,* Washington, D.C.: Regnery, 2008, 128; **cell phones:** *Salon,* 9/12/01; **saluted:** Spencer, 255–.

85   **baseless scare:** The Secret Service tracked down the source of the "threat" within hours, and concluded that the flap had arisen because of a watch officer's misunderstanding. Even so, press secretary Fleischer would still be talking of the threat at a press briefing the next day—and describing it as having been "real and credible" (CR, 554n1).

85–87 **"The American people":** *60 Minutes;* **"faceless coward":** CNN, 9/12/01; **running backward:** int. Dan Alcorn, *Salon,* 9/12/01; **"We're at war":** *60 Minutes,* 9/11/02; **"very much in control":** *World-Herald* (Omaha), 2/27/02; **took part:** Sammon, 122; **"I'm not going":** *Telegraph* (U.K.), 12/16/01; **"tin-horn terrorist":** *60 Minutes,* 9/11/02; **"increasingly difficult":** *Telegraph* (U.K.), 12/16/01; **"The mightiest":** *9/11,* ABC News; **"We will stand":** CNN, 9/12/01, Graham with Nussbaum, 100; **Bush address:** *60 Minutes,* 9/11/02, BBC News, 9/12/01; **key officials:** CR, 330; **al Qaeda/Taliban:** *WP,* 1/27/02.

87   **"You know":** The authors have here cited Clarke's interview with *Vanity Fair* in 2009, in which he stated that Rumsfeld made these remarks on the night of September 11. In his 2004 memoir, however, Clarke appeared to indicate that the remarks were made at a meeting the following day (*Vanity Fair,* 2/09, Richard Clarke, 31).

87   **bed early:** *Telegraph* (U.K.), 1/15/08; **He balked, etc.:** *Newsweek,* 12/3/01, Sammon, 133–; **"Incoming plane!":** Spencer, 282, 279; **Ground Zero:** DiMarco, 269–.

87   **one more survivor:** This was Genelle Guzman, who had worked for the Port Authority in the North Tower and was found in the same area as was Pasquale Buzzelli earlier. She suffered serious leg injuries, but recovered in the hospital (*Time,* 9/1/02, Langewiesche, 107).

87   **"heaved":** Langewiesche, 72; **flames:** Barrett & Collins, 247; **would burn:** ABC News, 12/19/01.

Part II: DISTRUST AND DECEIT

CHAPTER 10

91–92 **"not a fringe":** *Time,* 9/3/06; **"no dependable":** Matt Taibbi, *The Great Derangement,* NY: Spiegel & Grau, 2009, 189; **"tend to be"/poll:** *San Diego Union Tribune,* 12/4/06; **18 to 29:** "Questions with Kathryn Olmsted," 4/13/09, http://theaggie.org; **Arab Americans/Arabs worldwide:** *NY Post,* 5/23/07, "Muslim Public Opinion on US Policy, Attacks on Civilians and al Qaeda, 2007" & "No Public Consensus on Who Was Behind 9/11, 2008," www.worldpublicopinion.org; **"well-educated, pious":** Taibbi, 171; **"conspiracy theories dominate":** Najwa bin Laden, Omar bin Laden, and Jean Sasson, *Growing Up bin Laden,* NY: St. Martins, 2009, 290; **"unfounded":** "The Top September 11 Conspiracy Theories," 5/5/09, www.america.gov.

93   **MIHOP/LIHOP:** BBC News, 7/4/08, *Vanity Fair,* 8/06; **As late as 2011:** *Conspiracy vs. Science,* National Geographic Channel, & see re first aired *NY Post,* 9/2/09.

93–96 **Rostcheck/"Is it just":** corr. David Rostcheck, 2010, Rostcheck message on USAttacked@topica.net, 9/11/01, 3:12 P.M., cited on www.serendipity.li, Rostcheck profile, www.linkedin.com, Rostcheck to Ira Glasser, ACLU, 7/4/01, www.keepand beararms.com; **million Web pages:** *NY Post,* 9/12/06; **"I don't believe"/"conspiracy":** "Who We Are," & "Criminal Negligence or Treason," www.emperors-clothes.com; **"for thinking people":** See the "About" page on Meyer's website, www.serendipity.li; **doubt expressed:** "Reply to Popular Mechanics," www.serendipity.li; **Valentine:** Valentine articles, "Operation 911: No Suicide Pilots," 10/6/01, www.public-action.com, "Internet Censorship and Jewish Destiny," http://library.flawlesslogic.com, "Waco Holocaust Electronic Museum: Fire," www.public-action.com, & "Waco Suits for Waco Suckers," www.web-ak.com; **Vialls/"electronically hijacked":** "Flight 93 Saddest Flight of All," and various Vialls articles at www.vialls.homestead.com, "Home Run, Electronically Hijacking the WTC Attack Aircraft," 10/01, www.geocities.com; **"very strange":** "Reality Check," No. 82, 10/12/01, www.ratical.org; **Dewdney:** "Ghost Riders in the Sky," 1/22/02, www.ilaam.net; **"ordered to land":** "Operation Pearl," 8/03, www.serendipity.li; **Dewdney professor:** Dewdney bio. on University of W. Ontario website, www .csd.uwo.ca; **North Ph.D:** www.garynorth.com; **"aeronautical engineer":** www.vialls .homestead.com; **Valentine:** "About" page on www.comeandhear.com; **Meyer degrees:** "Interzine" int. of Meyer at www.deoxy.org; **Christian/"attempt to apply":** see masthead of North's periodical *Remnant Review* & see Gary North & Gary DeMar, *Christian Reconstructionism: What It Is, What It Isn't,* Tyler, TX: Institute for Christian Economics, 1984; **Cuba "soon":** "China Backs Iran Against the Great Satan," 12/22/04, www.web

.archive.org, "Why the March 8.7 Quake Did Not Cause a Tsunami," www.whale.to; **Waco Museum/shot:** "Waco Holocaust Electronic Museum: Catalogue of Evidence," www.public-action.com, "Internet Censorship & Jewish Destiny," 11/8/98, http://library.flawlesslogic.com; **Meyer indulged/"Timewave Zero":** "Interview of TWZ Programmer Peter Meyer," *Interzine*, issue 2, http://deoxy.org, "DMT & Hyperspace," & "Interpretations of the Experience" by Peter Meyer, *Psychedelic Monographs & Essays*, no. 6, www.lycaeum.org.

97–98 **The Big Lie:** Thierry Meyssan, *9/11: The Big Lie*, NY: Carnot, 2002, esp. 24, 28, 39, 56, 60, 139, www.effroyable-imposture.net, eds. David Dunbar & Brad Reagan, *Debunking 9/11 Myths*, NY: Hearst, 2006, 60. The book was first published in France as *L'Effroyable Imposture*, which translates as *The Appalling Deception*; **Griffin bio/"dean" of opposition:** e.g., Griffin as "high priest of the 'truther' movement," *The News Statesman* (U.K.), 9/24/09; **"show that the attacks":** Griffin speech, University of Wisconsin, 4/18/05, *BookTV*, C-SPAN2; **Loose Change:** viewable on www.youtube.com in various editions—the authors have primarily viewed *Loose Change—The Final Cut* (Louder Than Words, 2007) and *Loose Change 9/11—An American Coup* (Collective Minds Media, 2009); **125 million:** "Fact Sheet," www.loosechange911.com; **"This is our":** *Vanity Fair*, 8/06; **$2,000/$1 million:** "Fact Sheet"; **Avery:** "Bios," www.loosechange911.com; **"to get the":** Barrie Zwicker, *Towers of Deception*, Gabriola Island, B.C.: New Society, 2006, 303.

98–99 **Falk/foreword:** to U.S. edition of David Ray Griffin, *The New Pearl Harbor*, Northampton, MA: Interlink, 2004, foreword also posted at www.transnational.org, & see *Jerusalem Post*, 1/27 & 1/31/11; Falk has praised the professor's work as "objective and compelling" as recently as 2008—and his comments on 9/11 were still causing controversy in early 2011. He referred then to "the apparent cover up" (Richard Falk, "9/11: More than Meets the Eye," 11/9/08, www.journal-online.co.uk, Sky News, 1/29/11, "Interrogating the Arizona Killings from a Safe Distance, 1/11/11," http://richardfalk.wordpress.com).

99 **Internet groups:** David Ray Griffin, *The Mysterious Collapse of World Trade Center* 7, Northampton, MA: Olive Branch, 2010, 5; **skeptics:** e.g., "Reply to Scientific American's Attempted Debunking of 9/11 Skeptics," www.serendipity.li.

99 **Fetzer/Jones:** Fetzer bio, www.d.umn.edu; Jones CV, www.physics.byu.edu, *Deseret News* (Salt Lake City), 10/22/06. Fetzer's group retains the name Scholars for 9/11 Truth, while Jones' group took the name Scholars for 9/11 Truth and Justice. The appellation "Scholars" is loose—the membership ranges from people with Ph.D.'s in anything from physics to classics to French, medical doctors and dentists, attorneys, college students, and a yoga instructor. In a public statement in 2005, Jones's department and college administrators at Brigham Young University said they were "not convinced that his analyses and hypotheses [on 9/11] have been submitted to relevant scientific venues that would ensure rigorous technical peer review." Jones took early retirement in 2007 (membership ranges: "Full Member List," www.911scholars.org, "Members," http://stj911.org; Jones: "BYU Discredits Prof. Jones for 9/11 WTC Paper!," by Greg Szymanski, 11/29/05, www.rense.com, Jones CV, *Deseret News* [Salt Lake City], 10/22/06).

99–101 **members "believe"/"established"/"high-tech":** "Scholars for 9/11 Truth—Who Are We?" & "Scholars: On Its First Anniversary," www.9/11scholars.org; **"discretion"/ "Scientific":** "What Is the Goal of the 9/11 Truth Community?," by Steven Jones, http://stj911.org; **"inside job":** *Guardian* (U.K.), 9/5/06; **MacDonald:** cited at www.patriotsquestion911.com; **Reynolds:** "Bush Insider Says WTC Collapse Bogus," by Greg Szymanski, undated 2005, www.americanfreepress.net; **Roberts:** "What We Don't Know About 9/11," by Paul Roberts, 8/16/06, www.informationclearinghouse.info; **CIA veterans:** "Seven CIA Veterans Challenge 9/11 Commission Report," 9/23/07, www.opednews.com; **Christison:** "Stop Belittling the Theories About September 11," 8/14/06, www.dissidentvoice.org; **Charlie Sheen:** int. on *Alex Jones Show*, 3/20/06; **Co-**

tillard: "Plus Fort Que Thierry Meyssan," 2/29/08, www.marianne2.fr; **Lynch:** int. on *Wereldgasten,* VPRO (Dutch TV), 12/3/06; **O'Donnell:** *The View,* ABC News, 3/29/07; **Nelson:** int. on *Alex Jones Show,* 2/4/08; **Ventura:** "9/11," *Conspiracy Theory with Jesse Ventura,* 12/9/09, www.trutv.com, int. on *Alex Jones Show,* 4/2/08; Jesse Ventura with Dick Russell, *American Conspiracies,* NY: Skyhorse, 2010; **Hirschhorn:** "Painful 9/11 Truth," by Joel Hirschhorn, www.blogcritics.org, bio on http://word.world-citizenship .org; **Deets:** profile on www.ae911truth.org—the adjective "pyroclastic" is used to refer to material formed by volcanic or igneous action; **Erickson:** profile on www.ae911truth .org; **Griscom:** Griscom blog, www.impactglassman.blogspot.com; **Waser:** profile on www.ae911truth.org; **thousand architects & engineers:** Examples of others who have made their views known on the collapses, or joined their names to petitions, include:

In the United States:

Dr. Robert Bowman, formerly an Air Force lieutenant colonel who served as director of Advanced Space Programs Development, questioned the towers' collapses and called for a new investigation (bio on www.thepatriots.us)

Major Jon Fox, former Marine Corps fighter pilot and pilot for Continental Airlines, thought research "proved" the use of explosives (statement to http://patriots question911.com)

Former Navy commander Dennis Henry, who worked as a civil engineer for thirty-four years, doubted the simple collapse account (profile on www.ae911truth.org)

Commander Ralph Kolstad, former fighter pilot and commercial airline captain, said the collapse story did not "make any sense" (statement to http://patriotsquestion911.com)

Joel Skousen, a fighter and commercial airplane pilot, thought there was "significant evidence that the airplane impacts did not cause the collapse" ("Debunking the Debunkers," by Joel Skousen, 2/14/06, www.rense.com)

Roy Andes, a former assistant attorney general of the state of Montana, signed a petition on the collapses (petition at www.ae911truth.org)

Barbara Honegger, a senior military affairs journalist at the Naval Postgraduate School, suggested that "the U.S. military, not al Qaeda, had the sustained access weeks before 9/11 to also plant controlled demolition charges throughout the superstructures of WTC 1 and WTC 2, and in WTC 7, which brought down all three buildings" ("The Pentagon Attack Papers," by Barbara Honegger, www.physics911.net)

Karen Johnson, a member of the Arizona state legislature, expressed doubt about the collapses and joined her name to a call for a new investigation (*Arizona Republic,* 5/3/08, petition at www.ae911truth.org)

William Nugent, former assistant director of research for Technology Services at the Library of Congress, thought "controlled demolition the only scientifically plausible explanation" of the collapses (statement at www.ae911truth.org)

Lon Waters, a former staff member of a Defense Department–funded computing and research facility in Hawaii, signed the architects and engineers' petition on the collapses (petition at www.ae911truth.org)

Outside the United States:

In Denmark: Commander Jens Claus Hansen, of the Danish Defense Academy, thought "bombs must have been placed inside the Trade Center towers" (http://patriots question911.com)

In Finland: Heikki Kurtila, a veteran in the investigation of pressure-vessel explosion accidents, said the "great speed of the [Building 7] collapse and the resistance factor strongly suggest controlled demolition" ("Collapse Examination of WTC7," by Heikki Kurtila, 11/18/05, www.syyskuun11.ja)

In Japan: Yukihisa Fujita, a member of the upper house of the Diet, included doubt about the collapses in a forty-minute presentation to the Committee on Foreign Affairs in 2008 (http://patriotsquestion911.com)

In Malaysia: Former prime minister Tun Mahathir bin Mohammad expressed doubts about the collapses and said he "could believe" the U.S. government would organize the strikes to have an excuse for war in Iraq ("No Place for War Criminals," 10/6/07, www .globalresearch.ca)

In Norway: Lieutenant Commander Rolf Hustad, a navy weapons specialist, said the statistical likelihood of the "only three steel-framed buildings ever to collapse [due to fire] . . . is just too remote to grasp" (profile at www.ae911truth.org)

In Switzerland: Lieutenant Colonel Albert Stahel, senior lecturer in strategic studies at the Federal Institute of Technology, has raised questions about the collapses, and especially about Building 7 ("Je Mehr Wir Forschen, Desto Mehr Zweifeln Wir," 9/15/06, www .blick.ch)

Celebrities:

Actors Ed Asner, Juliette Binoche, Janeane Garofalo, and Woody Harrelson have expressed doubts in a more general sense (*Post Gazette* [Pittsburgh], 11/27/06, Asner letter, 4/26/04, www.septembereleventh.org, *Telegraph* [U.K.], 9/1/07, http://patriots question911.com)

101   **Nelson:** "Aircraft parts and the Precautionary Principle," www.physics911.net, bio. at www.patriotsquestion911.com.

101–2 **Latas:** bio. at www.latasgroup.com, int. of Jeff Latas for Pilots for 9/11 Truth, audio on www.youtube.com; the Flight Data Recorder from Flight 77 was recovered from the ruined section of the Pentagon, in decipherable condition. The voice recorder, though also recovered, was reportedly so badly damaged as to be of no use (corr. NTSB's Ted Lopatkiewicz, 2010, "Specialist's Factual Report of Investigation Digital Flight Data Recorder, NTSB no. DCA01MA064," 1/31/02, www.ntsb.gov); **Davis:** www.patriotsquestion911 .com; **Kwiatkowski:** eds. David Ray Griffin & Peter Dale Scott, *9/11 and American Empire*, Northampton, MA: Olive Branch, 2007, 28–; **Citizen Investigation Team:** www .citizeninvestigationteam.com.

CHAPTER 11

103–6 **200, etc.:** FAQ, 8/30/06, http://wtc.nist.gov; **NIST/FEMA conclusions/"no corroborating":** Executive Summary, "World Trade Center Building Performance Study," FEMA, Washington, D.C., 2002, & Executive Summary, "Final Report on the Collapse of the World Trade Center Towers," NIST, Washington, D.C., 9/05; **"pancaked"/"bowing":** FAQ, 8/30/06; **Mackey:** "On *Debunking 9/11 Debunking*: Examining Dr. David Ray Griffin's Latest Criticism of the NIST World Trade Center Investigation," 5/08, corr. Ryan Mackey, 2009, 2010; **"baloney"/"violates":** cited in Mackey, 137–,147; **"are so numerous":** ibid., 2; **"breaking":** David Ray Griffin, *Debunking*, 157, Mackey, 25; **"would be very":** Griffin, *Debunking*, 248–, 181–; **no good evidence/"particularly"/ "high-temperature":** Mackey, 82–, 86; **Jones's four samples:** Niels H. Harrit, Jeffrey Farrer, Steven E. Jones, et al., "Active Thermitic Material Discovered in Dust from 9/11 World Trade Center Catastrophe," *Open Chemical Physics Journal*, Vol. 2 (April 3, 2009): 7–31, www.bentham.org; **fellow scientists:** corr. Ryan Mackey, 2010, "Active Thermitic Material Claimed in Ground Zero Dust May Not Be Thermitic at All," 4/13/09, http:// undisettembre.blogspot.com, "Steven Jones," article at www.ae911truth.info; **university website:** Steven Jones, "Why Indeed Did the WTC Buildings Collapse?," http://web .archive.org; *Journal:* Steven Jones, "Why Indeed Did the WTC Buildings Completely Collapse?," www.journalof911studies.com; **coeditor/"peer-reviewed":** "Home" page, http://www.journalof911studies.com; **"masquerade":** Mackey, 13, 40, Mackey corr. 2010, but see Dr. Jones's riposte to such criticism in "An Open Letter to Dr. Steven Jones by James Bennett, with Replies by Steven Jones," www.journalof911studies.com. When Jones's and his colleagues' most recent take on thermite was published in 2009, in *The Open Chemical Physics Journal*, the person whose name appeared on the masthead as "editor" promptly disassociated herself from the publication. The article, said Marie-Paule Pileni, a highly distinguished French scientist, had been printed without her knowledge. She characterized the periodical itself as "sheer nonsense ... I do not want my name associated with this kind of stuff" ("sheer nonsense": "Chefredaktor skrider efter kontroversiel artikel om 9/11," videnskab.dk, 4/28/09, excerpts translated from the Danish by Marianne Gurnee, 2010, corr. Marie-Paul Pileni, 2010).

106   **"heard":** *WSJ*, 4/8/02; **"individual floors":** Bussey cited in Cathy Trost & Alicia Shepard, *Running Toward Danger*, Lanham, MD: Rowman & Littlefield, 2002, 87; **"It just descended":** Judyth Sylvester & Suzanne Hoffman, *Women Journalists at Ground Zero*, Lanham, MD: Rowman & Littlefield, 2002, 19—in his article "Explosive Testimony," www.911truth.org, Griffin rendered the text's word "*im*plosion" as "*ex*plosion."

106–7   **Romero:** *Albuquerque Journal*, 9/11/01, 9/21/01. Undeterred, skeptics resorted to innuendo. One coupled Romero's retraction to a "rumor" that he had "since found preferment from the federal government." Griffin has written that Romero had been "a very successful lobbyist for Pentagon contracts." "Saying that the government got to me," Romero has said, "is the farthest thing from the truth." In his initial comment, he would insist, he had "only said that that's what it looked like" ("rumor": Webster Griffin Tarpley, *9/11: Synthetic Terror*, Joshua Tree, CA: Progressive, 2005, 225; "very successful": Griffin, *Debunking*, 255; "Saying that"/"looked": eds. Dunbar & Reagan, 49); **"Then we":** int. John Sudnik, TF, 11/7/01; **"First I":** int. Timothy Julian, TF, 12/26/01; **"There was":** int. Frank Cruthers, TF, 10/31/01; **"The lowest":** int. Brian Dixon, TF, 10/25/01.

107   **Griffin seized:** Griffin, "Explosive Testimony." In his quote of *Journal* reporter Bussey, Griffin omitted the reporter's description of the initial sounds he heard as having been "metallic." He also left out a sentence in which the reporter, amending what he had at first assumed about the use of planted explosives, added, "In fact, the building was imploding down." Griffin attributed the quote starting "individual floors ..." to "another *Wall Street Journal* reporter"—as distinct from Bussey. In fact, the source makes clear, Bussey is the source of both quotes used (Griffin, "Explosive Testimony" & see source for "individual floors," above).

107   **formal interviews:** published online by the *NYT* at http://graphics8.nytimes.com. Griffin cited Professor Graeme MacQueen, who did study all 503 Fire Department statements, as finding that 118 of them—some 23 percent of the group—"appear to have perceived, or thought they perceived, explosions that brought down the towers." Our reading of the actual study suggests it is flawed. For example, MacQueen acknowledged having excluded from his analysis "a host of similes and metaphors referring to freight trains, jet planes and the like." Significantly, he has glossed over the fact that—even under his own criteria—the majority of the 503 witnesses do *not* claim to have heard explosions. The authors note, too, that MacQueen's analysis wrongly suggests—and he makes a point of this—that "fire chiefs on the scene thought the collapse of the towers was impossible." As the authors have noted, the possibility of partial collapse was discussed by fire chiefs early on, see Ch. 6 (Griffin, *Debunking*, 76, Graeme MacQueen, "118 Witnesses: The Firefighters' Testimony to Explosions in the Twin Towers," 8/21/06, www .journalof911studies.com).

107–8   **bangs:** e.g., int. Julio Marrero, TF, 10/25/01; **thunder:** e.g., int. Mark Stone, TF, 10/12/01, int. Eric Hansen, TF, 10/10/01, int. Jody Bell, TF, 12/15/01; **rumbling:** e.g., int. Patricia Ondrovic, TF, 10/11/01, int. Scott Holowach, TF, 10/18/01, int. John Delendick, TF, 12/6/01, int. John Picarello, TF, 12/6/01, int. Anthony DeMaio,

TF, 1/28/02; **trainlike:** e.g., int. Louis Giaconelli, TF, 12/6/01, int. Paul Curran, TF, 12/18/01, int. Mark Ruppert, TF, 12/4/01, int. Joseph Fortis, TF, 11/9/01, int. Dominick Muschello, TF, 12/6/01; **"You heard":** int. Salvatore Torcivia cited in DiMarco, 188; **"relaying":** Mackey, 75; **Griffin on Kingdome:** Griffin, *Debunking*, 188, & see *U.S. News & World Report*, 6/22/03, www.controlled-demolition.com/seattle-kingdome; **"produced no":** Mackey, 94; **"for alternative":** Executive Summary, NIST, xxxviii.

108   **"Achilles' Heel"/ "smoking gun":** Griffin, *Mysterious*, xi; see pp. 97–99; **first known/"a mystery":** *NYT*, 11/29/01.

108   **"fire-induced":** "Final Report on the Collapse of World Trade Center Building 7," Federal Building & Fire Safety Investigation of the World Trade Center Disaster, National Institute of Standards and Technology, Washington, D.C., 11/08, ES-3, xxxvi. Author Griffin wrote off that finding as "scientific fraud," claiming that the institute's experts ignored numerous items of physical evidence, fabricated and falsified evidence, and ignored a recommendation that their documentation should be peer-reviewed. Evidence ignored, the professor asserted, included in particular the evidence in dust of thermitic material—Griffin thought the "most likely explanation" was that WTC 7, like the Twin Towers, was brought down by explosives ("scientific fraud," etc.: Griffin, *Mysterious*, 245–; "most likely": ibid., xii).

109   **"When it fell":** int. Frank Fellini, TF, 12/3/01; **Hayden:** *Firehouse*, 4/02, Smith, 31–, 159–, int. Ray Goldback, TF, 10/24/01, int. Richard Banaciski, TF, 12/6/01, int. Robert Sohmer, TF, 1/17/02, int. Frank Cruthers, TF, 10/31/01.

109   **Nigro:** int. Daniel Nigro, TF, 10/24/01, "Chief of Department FDNY (ret.) Daniel Nigro Addresses Conspiracy Theories," http://guide.googlepages.com/danielnigro. Brent Blanchard, a senior writer on *ImplosionWorld*, an online magazine for the demolition industry, has written, "Any detonation of explosives within WTC 7 would likely have been detected by seismographs monitoring ground vibration. . . . To our knowledge, no such telltale 'spike' or vibratory anomaly was recorded. . . . Several demolition teams had reached Ground Zero by 3:00 P.M. on 9/11, and these individuals witnessed the collapse of WTC 7 from within a few hundred feet. . . . We have spoken with several who possess extensive experience in explosive demolition, and all reported hearing or seeing nothing to indicate an explosive detonation precipitating the collapse." Readers who wish to delve deeper could consult Blanchard's paper; Ryan Mackey's paper, at p. 112–; the BBC documentary film *The Conspiracy Files: 9/11—The Third Tower*, July 6, 2008; and of course Dr. Griffin's book *The Mysterious Collapse of World Trade Center 7*. (Brent Blanchard, "A Critical Analysis of the Collapse of WTC Towers 1, 2 and 7 from an Explosives and Conventional Demolition Industry Viewpoint," www.implosionworld .com).

109   **photos:** credited to Corporal Jason Ingersoll, USMC; Goldberg et al., 159, 245n30, & see photo section, photos also at http://911research.wtc7.net; **18 feet/"How could":** David Ray Griffin, *The 9/11 Commission Report: Omissions and Distortions*, Gloucestershire, U.K.: Arris, 2005, 34; **wingspan/tail:** Goldberg et al., 17fn; **"fits":** Griffin, *Omissions*, 38.

109   **Eyewitnesses:** e.g., see p. 44. Many more such witnesses are on record.

110–12   **evidence/opinions:** Paul Mlakar et al., "The Pentagon Building Performance Report," Reston, VA: American Society of Civil Engineers, 1/03, 1–; **removed/FBI warehouse:** ibid., 24, *Libération*, 3/30/02, "Arlington County After-Action Report," www .co.arlington.va.us/fire/edu/about/pdf/after_report.pdf, Annex C, 53–; **report concluded:** Mlakar et al., 58; **"hogwash"/"To look":** corr. Mete Sozen, 2010; **Empire State:** "B-25 Empire State Building Collision," www.aerospaceweb.org, "Ask the Pilot," *Salon*, 5/19/06; **photos:** Goldberg et al., photo section; **"planted":** Griffin, *Debunking*, 265.

112   **"Don't be taken in":** "New Study from Pilots for 9/11 Truth: No Boeing Hit the Pentagon, *Global Research*, 6/24/07. Fetzer was impressed by the suggestion from James Hanson, a retired attorney, who claimed that he had traced the debris that was found at the Pentagon to an American Airlines 757 that crashed in Colombia in 1995! (ibid. & *Idaho Observer*, 2/8/05); **aircraft remains:** "Photos of Flt 77 Wreckage Inside the Pentagon," by Sarah Roberts, www.rense.com (referred to the authors by Sarandis Papadopoulos, an editor of *Pentagon 9/11*, whom Roberts consulted), "Pentagon & Boeing 757 Engine Investigation," www.aerospace.org, "Airplane Fragment in Patriotic Box," exhibit description, http://americanhistory.si.edu, *Libération*, 3/30/02.

112   **Carter:** address at Coalition on Political Assassinations conference, 2002. The ashes given to May's fiancé are interred in Maryland.

112   **Flight 77 crew remains:** Submission by Toni Knisley, American Airlines flight service administration manager, National September 11 Memorial & Museum, http://ns11make history.appspot.com, Burlingame bio. at www.arlingtoncemetery.net. Forensic work on the Pentagon victims was done by the Armed Forces Institute of Pathology at Dover, Delaware. Remains of five individuals also found at the crash scene, and believed to be those of the hijackers, were eventually handed over to the FBI (Goldberg et al., 183, 178).

113   **remains identified:** Goldberg et al., 177–, 183, 204, "Attack on the Pentagon," www .arlingtoncemetery.net; **photos:** Exhibits P200042, P200045, P200047, P200048, *U.S. v. Zacarias Moussaoui*, www.vaed.uscourts.gov; **"A stillness":** Goldberg et al., 195; **"the bodies"/"For all we know":** Griffin, *Debunking*, 268–.

113   **"cell phone calls":** "Operation Pearl," 8/03, www.serendipity.li. Wireless and cell phone industry sources have said cell phone calls from planes were possible—even from high altitudes—at the time of 9/11, though connections were sporadic (e.g., *NYT*, 9/14/01, "Final Contact," 11/1/01, www.connectedplanet.com, eds. Dunbar & Reagan, 83–, David Aaronovitch, *Voodoo Histories*, London: Jonathan Cape, 2009, 224).

114   **seatback not cell phone:** In May's case, the skeptics' claims grew out of early news reports that the attendant used her cell phone to call home—the record shows she did not. Solicitor General Theodore Olson, for his part, made it clear in a Fox News interview after 9/11 that he simply did not know what sort of phone his wife had used to call. The records now available show that *only* seatback phone calls, or attempted calls, were made from Flight 77.

        The skeptics have claimed flatly that American Airlines 757s "were not equipped with seatback phones." Though the airline had apparently decided to discontinue seatback phone service prior to 9/11, analysis indicates that such phones were still in use on some flights as late as March 2002. That they were still in use on 9/11 is evident from the phone records alone.

        The skeptics have also claimed that the reports of passengers' calls from Flight 93—see Ch. 7—are suspect. Griffin even suggests that Todd Beamer's long call to operator Lisa Jefferson did not occur. Beamer's call, however, is listed in the telephone company records now available. As in the case of Flight 77, early reports of "cell phone calls" made from Flight 93 sowed confusion. Deena Burnett, widow of Flight 93 passenger Tom Burnett, told the FBI that her husband made a series of three to five calls home on his cell phone. The records show that Burnett made three calls on a seatback phone. There is no way of knowing whether Mrs. Burnett simply misremembered the exact number of calls she got from her husband, or whether he did use his cell phone to make some of the calls. The records show that many Flight 93 calls, initially described as being by cell phone, in fact originated from seatback phones (early news: *Las Vegas Review Journal*, 9/13/01; made it clear: Olson, Fox News, 9/14/01; *only* seatback phone: DOJ "Briefing on Cell and Phone Calls from AA77," 5/20/04, in "Flight 93 Calls" folder [inc. details on other flights], B12, T7, CF, & Moschella to Marcus [& attachments], 4/26/04, in

"Flight 11 Calls folder—Calls from AA11, AA77, UA175, & UA93, ATT Wireless & GTE Airphones," B13, T7, CF; "were not equipped": Griffin, *Debunking*, 266–; discontinue/analysis: "Airline Grounds In-Flight Phone Service," 2/6/02, www.news.cnet.com, *Business Week*, 9/30/02, AA spokesman John Hotard cited at "American Airlines Flight 77 Calls," www.911myths.com; suspect: e.g., Griffin, *Debunking*, 86–, 292–; Griffin re. Beamer: "The Ultimate 9/11 Truth Showdown," 10/6/08, www.alternet.org; Burnett: FBI 302 of int. Deena Burnett, 9/11/01, INTELWIRE, Moschella to Marcus [& attachments], 4/26/04, records show: MFR 04020029, 5/13/04, CF, FBI 302 of int. Mark Rugg, 7/1/02, "Key 302s," B19, T7, CF).

114   **"have had a little"**: "Comments on the Pentagon Strike," www.cassiopaea.org; **"transformers"/"morphing"**: Griffin, *Debunking*, 89, 86; **"Either Ted"/"is based on"**: "The Ultimate 9/11 Truth Showdown, www.alternet.org; **scattered in three:** Exhibit P200318, *U.S. v. Zacarias Moussaoui.*

114   **"It took"**: transcript, *Larry King Weekend*, CNN, 1/6/02; Mrs. Olson is indeed interred in Door County, at Ellison Bay Cemetery. Had Dr. Griffin cared to check, he could have established this long before he made his most recent suggestion, in 2008, that she might be alive. (Ellison Bay Cemetery: int. Mayor's Office, Liberty Grove, WI, Barbara K. Olson listing, www.findagrave.com).

114   **"cannot ignore"**: Griffin, *Debunking*, 266, & see Griffin, *New Pearl Harbor: Disturbing Questions About the Bush Administration and 9/11*, Moreton-in-March, U.K.: Arris, 2009, 28; **"overwhelming"/"an inside"**: Griffin, *Debunking*, 1, 309, & see Griffin & Scott, *Empire*, 12; **"a prima facie"**: Griffin, *New Pearl Harbor*, 2009, 131.

114   **Project:** "Rebuilding America's Defenses," Washington, D.C.: Project for the New American Century, Sept. 2000, 10, 4, 51, "Statement of Principles," www.newamerican century.org.

115   **"the Pearl Harbor"**: *WP*, 1/27/02; This part of the passage echoed almost word for word testimony before the Senate Armed Services Committee in 1999. The then–executive director of the Center for Strategic and Budgetary Assessments, Andrew Krepinevich, spoke of the difficulties in transforming the U.S. military, "in the absence of a strong external shock to the United States—a latter-day 'Pearl Harbor' of sorts" (testimony of Andrew Krepinevich, 3/5/99).

115   **in public:** Sammon, 205, 316; **"Who benefits?"**: Griffin & Scott, *Empire*, 103; **precedents:** e.g., Zwicker, multiple refs. to false flag ops., & Griffin in ed. Ian Woods, *9/11*, Vol. 2, Ontario: Global Outlook, 2006, 15; **Roosevelt:** Zwicker, 273, & see "FDR Knew Pearl Harbor Was Coming," *New York Press*, 6/14/01.

116   **false flag/pounced:** "11 September 2001—Another Operation Northwoods?," 9/17/01, www.blythe.org, & see "Operation 911: No Suicide Pilots," 10/6/01, www.public-action .com. The reference was to Operation Northwoods, which was revealed in the book *Body of Secrets* by the author James Bamford (NY: Doubleday, 2001—see 82–, 300–).

116–17   **"We must"**: "11 September 2001—Another Operation Northwoods?"; **Corn objected:** *LAT*, 7/3/02, "Van Jones & the 9/11 Conspiracy," http://motherjones.com; **"I won't"**: "When 9/11 Conspiracy Theories Go Bad," by David Corn, 3/1/02, www .zcommunications.org; **howl of rage:** *Nation*, 5/31/02.

117   **thousands of pages:** see refs in sourcing for Chs. 1–9; Some skeptics suggest that the absence of formal NTSB investigations on Flights 11 and 175—as well as the other two hijacked flights—is suspicious. From the outset, however, these crashes were deemed to have been "criminal acts," which meant jurisdiction fell not to the NTSB but to the FBI. Within two days of the attacks, though, the FBI requested technical assistance from the NTSB. According to the NTSB's chairman, some sixty NTSB experts worked "around the clock in Virginia, Pennsylvania, New York, and at our headquarters in Washington, D.C., assisting with aircraft parts identification, searching for and analyzing flight record-

ers." Some of the research done by NTSB experts has emerged in recent years, especially with the 2009 opening of 9/11 Commission files and absence of reports: e.g., notation on NTSB DCA01MA060 [Flight 11], www.ntsb.gov; (suspicious: e.g., "A Little Known Fact About the 9/11 Planes," http://sabbah.biz, "Flight 77 Black Boxes," http://911review .org; "criminal acts"/FBI requested: NTSB Advisory, 9/13/01, www.ntsb.gov; "around the clock": Testimony of NTSB Chairman Marion C. Blakey, 6/25/01, Committee on Commerce, Science & Transportaion, U.S. Senate, www.ntsb.gov, corr. NTSB's Ted Lopatkiewicz, 2009).

118   **300,000:** corr. NARA's Kristen Wilhelm, 2011; **"distracts people":** *Nation,* 7/12/02.

CHAPTER 12

119–21   **memo/"How," etc.:** Philip to Tom & Lee, 9/6/04, "Farmer Memo re False Statements," B4, Dana Hyde files, CF; **chairman/vice chairman:** Kean & Hamilton, 25; **Roemer/"false":** int. Roemer on *American Morning,* CNN, 8/2/06; **shocked:** *WP,* 8/2/06; **"deception":** Farmer, 4; **Farmer questioned:** Farmer, 4–, 227–; **Meyers confused/had launched:** Testimony of General Richard Myers, Hearings, U.S. Senate Armed Services Committee, 107th Cong., 1st Ses., 9/13/01; **"We responded awfully":** transcript, OnLine NewsHour, 9/14/01, www.pbs.org; **Weaver timeline/"There was no":** *Dallas Morning News,* 9/15/01, *Seattle Times,* 9/16/01; **Cheney/"toughest decision":** transcript, *Meet the Press,* 9/16/01, www.msnbc.msn.com; **"Did we shoot":** cited by Bob Woodward and Dan Balz in "10 Days in September," a series of articles based on interviews with Bush, Cheney, and other official sources, *WP,* 1/27/02; **"It's my understanding":** CR, 43, 465n233; **"Oh, my God":** Testimony of Norman Mineta, 5/23/03, CO; **never missiles:** Spencer, 277; **report incorrect:** *Cape Cod Times,* 8/21/02.

121   **Rumors circulating:** A retired Army colonel, Donn de Grand-Pre, claimed in 2004 that Flight 93 was shot down by a pilot flying for the North Dakota National Guard. He named the pilot supposedly responsible and said he had sent a report on the matter to a named general. Flight records reportedly show that the alleged pilot was on other duties at the relevant time—and the general denied even knowing de Grand-Pre. A contributor to a 2008 blog, posted by a person identifying himself only as a former Langley Air Force Base mechanic, quotes a colleague at second hand as having said, "They shot one down . . . One of those 16s came back with one less missile than it left with." The claim has no value as information—it is anonymous, and the supposed veteran did not himself speak with the original source of the quote. Conspiracy theorists, meanwhile, seized on the alleged content of a 911 call made from Flight 93 by passenger Edward Felt shortly before the airliner crashed. According to a staffer at the emergency center that took the call, Felt mentioned that there been an explosion on board, and "white smoke." The dispatcher who actually took the call, however, denied that Felt said anything about an explosion. The call was recorded, and there is no such reference in the transcript. David Griffin refers in his books to "considerable evidence" that 93 was shot down—yet cites none of substance (De Grand-Pre: eds. Dunbar & Reagan, 77–; blog: "The US Air Force Shot Down Flight 93," 4/11/08, http://georgewashington.blogspot.com; Felt: FBI 302 of [name redacted], 9/19/01, Pittsburgh to Counterterrorism, New York, 9/17/01, & FBI 302 of [name redacted], 9/11/01, INTELWIRE, transcript of call 9/11/01, "Flight 93 Calls," B12, T8, CF; Griffin: e.g., *Debunking,* 70, & David Griffin, *The New Pearl Harbor Revisited,* Northampton, MA: Olive Branch Press, 2008, 127–).

122–23   **Commission "required":** Public Law 107–306, 11/27/02, www.archives.gov; **delays/obstruction/tapes withheld/recalcitrant:** Kean & Hamilton, 83–, 258–, Shenon, 203–; **"incomplete":** corr. Miles Kara, 2011; **Scott timeline/"9:24"/"awful decision"/ In one breath, etc.:** Testimonies of Larry Arnold & Alan Scott, 5/23/03, CO, Farmer,

262–; **leery/proof/subpoena:** Shenon, 203–, Kean & Hamilton, 88, 260; **"Whiskey tango foxtrot":** Farmer, 265.

123–25   **NORAD/more than 100 squadrons/14 "alert"/intercepts:** CR, 16–, Spencer, 286–; **planes as weapons:** Staff Monograph "The Four Flights and Civil Aviation Security," 55–, CF, Farmer, 98–; **hijacking protocol:** CR, 17–, Farmer, 117; **multiple Centers:** e.g., Miles Kara, "Archive of the 'Transponders and Ghosts' Category," www .oredigger61.org—Centers involved were Boston, New York, D.C., Indianapolis, and Cleveland; **"primary target":** MFR 04016798, 9/22/03, "Aeronautical Information Manual," 2/11/10, www.faa.gov; **"coast mode"/coastline:** *Avionics*, 6/1/05, Farmer, 135, 9/11 NEADS Tape Transcription, "NEADS-CONR-NORAD, NEADS Transcripts Channel 4," B3, NYC files, CF, MFR 04016774, 10/27/03; **not know NORAD:** MFR 04017316, 10/2/03; **units different training:** MFR 04020720, 3/11/04; **unable to communicate/frequencies/none worked:** MFR 040176171, 10/2/03; **Transcripts/In that book, etc.:** Farmer, 215–; **"Washington [Center] has no clue":** 9/11 NEADS Tape Transcription, "NEADS-CONR-NORAD Transcripts, NEADS Transcripts Channel 7," B3, NYC files, CF; **"It's chaos"/"The challenge"/Kara:** Miles Kara, "Chaos Theory and 9–11, Some Preliminary Thoughts," 6/12/09, www.oredigger61.org, & see Archives, 911 Revisited, www.oredigger61.org, Kara Career Summary, 12/12/02, "Commission Meeting 4/10/03, Tab 7," B1, Front Office files, CF.

125   **evidence of tapes and logs:** In writing this account of the FAA/military response to the attacks, the authors relied—as did the 9/11 Commission—on the tapes and transcripts of conversations between the various FAA and NORAD sites. As the Commission's Miles Kara wrote in 2009, the "complete set of information needed to attempt any analysis of the events [of that morning] includes the radar files and the software to run them, time-stamped tapes, and any transcripts that were made" (Commission account: Miles Kara, "Archive for the NEADS files category," www.oredigger61.org; NORAD audio files are available at the National Archives, B82 & B110, GSA Files, CF, but—for ready availability—at http://911depository.info).

125   **nerve center:** *Vanity Fair*, 9/06, Spencer, 2.

125   **Marr/hijacking/Vigilant Guardian:** *Vanity Fair*, 9/06, CR, 458n116. The military exercise scheduled for September 11, and several others that took place earlier in the year, have been the source of speculation. Some thought aspects of the exercises indicated U.S. government foreknowledge of the manner and timing of the 9/11 attacks. Others suggested that September's Vigilant Guardian exercise had a negative effect on NORAD's ability to react to the attacks. The 9/11 Commission found that the timing of the drill may have had a positive impact, because more personnel were on duty that day. The tapes and transcripts, though, reflect temporary confusion within NORAD as to whether the attacks were part of the war game or were real-world (Miles Kara, "9–11 Training, Exercises, and War Games, Some Collected Thoughts," 9/11 Revisited, www.oredigger61 .org, "Exclusive Report: Did Military Exercises Facilitate the 9/11 Pentagon Attack?," by Mathew Everett, 7/06, www.911truth.org, *Aviation Weeks & Space Technology*, 6/3/02, "NORAD Exercises Summary," Team 8 files, posted on www.scribd.com, CR, 458n116).

126   **"on the shitter":** NEADS audiotape, DRM1, CH2, www.oredigger61.org; **Arnold in FL:** MFR 04016749, 2/3/04; **Dooley et al.:** 9/11 NEADS Tape Transcription, "NEADS-CONR-NORAD Transcripts, NEADS Channel 4," B3, NYC files, CF; **"Real World Unknown":** Memorandum for CC et al. from NEADS Sector/CVX, 8/23/01, "RDOD 03013146, Entire Contents, Vigilant Guardian," B116, GSA files, CF.

126   **Cooper call:** MFR 04016791 & 04016790, 9/22/03, CR, 20. Disregarding the official FAA/military protocol, Boston Center had made two earlier attempts to contact the military on a "freelance" basis. The first such call, which went to the New Jersey Air National

Guard's 177th Fighter Wing at Atlantic City, got nowhere because the wing was not on alert status. Boston's second early attempt to reach the military—through the FAA's Cape Cod facility—did eventually lead to an alert being passed to NEADS, but only after the call made by the FAA's Cooper. These calls were made at the initiative of Boston Center's traffic management supervisor, Dan Bueno. Bueno—who was aware of the protocols in place—told the Commission that his actions were based on the "urgency of the situation." Cooper's use of "F-16" was a misspeak for "F-15" (CR, 20, Position 15, pts. 2 & 3, "ATC-SCC Tape Transcription," B1, T8, CF, *Bergen Record* [N.J.], 12/5/03, MFR 04016791, 9/22/03, MFR 04016790, 9/22/03, MFR 03012969, 9/30/03, CF, Spencer, 22–).

126–27   **"Cool"/all business/Boston could say:** 9/11 NEADS Tape Transcription, "NEADS-CONR-NORAD Transcripts, NEADS Channel 4," B3, NYC files, CF, *Vanity Fair*, 9/06; **8:41 battle stations:** CR, 20, Farmer, 123; **conferred Arnold/ordered:** "Conversation with Maj. Gen. Larry Arnold," www.codeonemagazine.com, 1/02, CR, 20; **without direction/assigned:** CR, 20; **"Oh, God":** 9/11 NEADS Tape Transcription, "NEADS-CONR-NORAD Transcripts, NEADS Channel 4," B3, NYC files, CF; **Mulligan:** Full Transcript: Command Center; NOM Operational Position, Sept. 11, 2001, 10/14/03, "NOM Operation Position (5)," B1, NYC files, CF, CR 22.

127   **Air Force knew nothing:** Some skeptics have seized on an early NORAD chronology that appeared to suggest that the FAA notified the military of the hijacking of Flight 175 at 8:43 A.M., claiming that this was evidence that U.S. forces failed to react promptly—even "stood down"—as the attacks unfolded. The contention is spurious—the 8:43 notification time in the NORAD chronology was simply incorrect. Although 8:43 A.M. does approximate the time the plane was hijacked, that fact was not at the time known to the FAA (critics: Griffin, *The New Pearl Harbor Revisited*, 8–; 8:43 notification: Chronology of the September 11 Attacks & Subsequent Events Through Oct. 24, 2001, "Timelines, 1 of 2," B20, T7, CF, "FAA Believed Second 9/11 Plane Heading Towards New York for Emergency Landing," & linked FAA document 4, 9/5/05; time incorrect: www.gwu.edu, Miles Kara, "Chaos Theory & 9/11," 9/11 Revisited, www.oredigger61.org, corr. Miles Kara, 2010).

127   **Otis pilots holding:** *Cape Cod News*, 8/21/02, *BG*, 9/11/05, *Vanity Fair*, 9/06. The speed at which the fighters traveled and their exact route to New York has been the subject of some debate. Available tapes, and Commission interviews with the pilots and the mission commander, make clear that when they were first launched the flights headed for military-controlled airspace where they stayed in a holding pattern until after NEADS learned the second tower had been hit. The fighters then proceeded to New York, where they established a Combat Air Patrol (CAP) over the city at 9:25. The F-15 fighter, when new and stripped of its armament, is capable of doing a speed of Mach 2.5—some 1,650 miles per hour. Pilot Nash told the Commission that he and Duffy never exceeded Mach 1.1 (727 mph) as they flew toward New York. Duffy estimated that the fighters had reached between Mach 1.1 and 1.3, but said the pair "throttled back" on learning of the second strike—to conserve fuel. While it is possible that the Otis fighters went supersonic on the final leg of the journey to New York, radar data showed that the pair averaged a less-than-supersonic speed of Mach.86 (debate: see refs, "Complete 9/11 Timeline," www.historycommons.org; record scanty: CR, 459n120; available tapes/interviews: transcripts from Voice Recorder, 11/9/01 1227Z-1417Z, Channel 24, "Trip 2 of 3, NEADS Transcript Color Coded," B20, T8, CF, 9/11 ATCSCC Tape Transcription, "NEADS-CONR-NORAD Transcripts, NEADS Channel 5," B3, NYC files, CF, MFR 04016778, 1/22 & 1/23/04, MFR 03012972, 10/14/03, MFR 04016756, CF, CR, 21–, 23–, corr. Kris Wilhelm, Miles Kara, 2010).

127   **Long Island:** Full Transcript: Command Center; NOM Operational Position, Sept. 11, 2001, 10/14/03, "NOM Operation Position (5)," B1, NYC files, CF, CR 22; **Five minutes**

after: CR, 23–; **"I thought":** *Cape Cod Times,* 8/21/02; **"We don't know"/"We need"/ urged/Marr at first:** 9/11 NEADS Tape Transcription, "NEADS-CONR-NORAD Transcripts, NEADS Channel 2," B3, NYC files, CF & re Boston, authors' check of audiotape, CR, 460n137; **"Listen":** Position 15, Parts 2 & 3, "ATCSCC Tape Transcript, Position 15," B1, T8, CF.

127–28 **9:21 call/Scoggins/checked D.C./"First I heard"/Scoggins insisted:** MFR 04016798, 9/22/03, 9/11 NEADS Tape Transcription, "NEADS-CONR-NORAD Transcripts, NEADS Channel 7," B3, NYC files, CF. Scoggins has said he is "99% certain the person who made that call on the Telcon [about Flight 11 still being airborne] was Dave Cannoles." The FAA's Cannoles told 9/11 Commission staff that he did not recall doubt as to whether Flight 11 had crashed into the Trade Center. Another staff member, Doug Davis, thought the chief of staff for the director of air traffic at FAA headquarters, Mary Ellen Kraus, said Flight 11 was still airborne. Kraus denied it ("Losing Flight 77," www.911myths.com, handwritten notes of Dave Canoles interview, 3/25/04, "Dave Canoles, FAA WOC," B2, Dana Hyde files, CF, MFR of int. Mary Ellen Kraus, 4/27/04, "FAA HQ—Mary Ellen Kraus," B6, T8, CF).

128 **new "track":** Miles Kara, "Archive for the 'Transponder & Ghosts' Category," 9/11 Revisited, www.oredigger61.org, Traffic Situation Display (TSD) Demo, 4/13/04, "FAA HQ Floor Position Maps—Herndon," B19, T8, CF; **"listening on a Telcon":** int. of Colin Scoggins at www.911myths.com; **"Shit!":** 9/11 NEADS Tape Transcription, "NEADS-CONR-NORAD Transcripts, NEADS Channel 2," B3, NYC files, CF, CR, 461n149.

129 **9:30 fighters into air:** CR, 27.Two planes on alert duty were ready and loaded with live missiles, while the third—the "spare"—had only its 20mm gun. The pilots were Major Lou Derrig, Captain Dean Eckmann, and—piloting the spare—Captain Craig Borgstrom (Spencer, 115–, 142–).

129 **Nasypany figured:** MFR 04016778, 1/22 & 23/04, MFR 04016771, 10/27/03.

129 **NEADS ordered/tower sent:** "Staff Statement 17," CO, MFR 04016771, 10/27/03. The Commission Report offers three explanations for the change of course. One, that the scramble order had given no distance to the target, nor where it was. Two, that the pilots followed a "generic" flight plan designed to get them out of local airspace. Three, that the lead pilot and the local FAA controller assumed that the Langley tower's instruction superseded the order received from NEADS. According to author Lynn Spencer, who interviewed members of the unit involved, Captain Dean Eckmann assumed the fighters were "being vectored eastward in order to fly around the traffic in their way. He doesn't second-guess the instructions. . . . The jet's targets are customarily out over the ocean." There is, however, no mention of traffic on the Air Traffic Control tapes (CR, 27, Spencer, 143–; corr. Miles Kara, 2011).

129–30 **NEADS finally learned:** American Airlines executive vice president Gerard Arpey had been told at 9:00 A.M. that communications with American 77 had been lost. As reported in Ch. 4, the FAA controller at Indianapolis Center had his last routine contact with Flight 77 as early as 8:54 (CR, 8–); **"Let me tell":** 9/11 ATCSCC Tape Transcription, "NEADS-CONR-NORAD Transcripts, NEADS Channel 5," B3, NYC files, CF; **"Latest report"/"not sure"/"rumor":** 9/11 NEADS Tape Transcription, "NEADS-CONR-NORAD Transcripts, NEADS Channel 7," B3, NYC files, CF; **"Get your fighters":** "Transcripts from Voice Recorder, Channel 14," B20, T8, "NEADS Transcripts color-coded," CF; **asked where fighters/"I don't care":** 9/11 NEADS Tape Transcription, "NEADS-CONR-NORAD Transcripts, NEADS Channel 2," B3, NYC files, CF; **Scoggins back/"Delta 1989"/"And is this one?":** Chronology of Events at Mission Coodinator Position, 9/24/03, "Boston Center—Colin Scoggins," B3, T8, CF, 9/11 NEADS Tape Transcription, "NEADS-CONR-NORAD Transcripts, NEADS

Channel 7," B3, NYC files, CF. Based on a Commission staff timeline, the authors have taken 9:39 as the time Scoggins warned NEADS about Delta 1989—even though the Commission Report uses a time of 9:41. ("Timeline of the Events of the Day," www .scribd.com, & see MCC log, "Miles Kara trips," B19, T8, CF, Farmer, 193– v. CR, 28).

130   **Boston speculated:** Miles Kara, "Archive for the Delta 1989 category," 9/11 Revisited, www.oredigger61.org, & see Position 15, Parts 2 & 3, "ATCSCC Tape Transcription," B1, T8, CF. In a chronology he gave the Commission of the day's events, Scoggins noted that an "Open Telcon reports that DAL1889 [*sic*] is NORDO [no radio]" and described his own subsequent action as "call NEADS to advise" suggesting that his concern about 1989 was piqued only after hearing of it from others. In an interview much later, Scoggins said he thought Delta 1989 might have become suspect because it "missed a frequency transfer" or "didn't make a transmission back" when given a frequency change ("Open Telcon": Chronology of Events at Mission Coordinator Position, 9/24/03, "Boston Center—Colin Scoggins," B3, T8, CF, & see Position 15, Parts 2 & 3, "ATCSCC Tape Transcription," B1, T8, CF; later interview: "Q & A with 9/11 Boston Air Traffic Controller," http://sites.google.com).

130   **NEADS tracked:** MFR 04016777, 10/28/03, Miles Kara, "Archive to the 'Transponders & Ghosts' Category, 9/11 Revisited," www.oredigger61.org, Kara to Brinkley, 1/26/04, "Misc. Loose Documents re. Delta 1989," B5, T8, CF, UA93 & Andrews Timeline, "Andrews AFB Logs—Timelines, UA93 & Andrews," B4, Dana Hyde files, CF.

130–31   **only plane able to tail:** NEADS had also been able briefly to pinpoint and track Flight 77, even though the FAA alerted it to the problem with the airliner only at 9:34, only some three minutes before it struck the Pentagon (Miles Kara, "Archive for the 'Transponders & Ghosts' Category, 9/11 Revisited, www.oredigger61.com); **"land immediately"/"Confirm"/"unreliable"/Cleveland panic/pilots feared/"you're a *trip*"/ assured/"bomb area"/"bad movie":** Dave Dunlap (copilot) memoir, "September 11, 2001," www.3dlanguage.net, DAL 1989 Order of Events, "FAA Subpoena Compendium, Delta 1989 Timeline," B15, T8, CF, int. John Werth, MFR 04017313, 10/2/03; **Scoggins, "might not be":** 9/11 NEADS Tape Transcription, "NEADS-CONR-NORAD Transcripts, NEADS Channel 7," B3, NYC files, CF, Summary [slugged as Timeline of Events of the Day], "Boston Center—Colin Scoggins," B3, T8, CF, Farmer, 211.

130   **trying to get fighters:** MFR 04016778, 1/22 & 23/04, MFR 04016771, 10/27/03, 9/11 NEADS Tape Transcription, "NEADS-CONR-NORAD Transcripts, NEADS Channel 2," & ATCSCC Tape Transcription, "Channel 5," B3, NYC files, CF, Staff Report, "The Four Flights and Civil Aviation Security," 8/26/04, CF, 101n391. NEADS asked two additional bases to provide fighters—Selfridge, in Michigan, and Toledo, in Ohio. Contrary to reports at the time, it appears that they were unable to help during the Delta episode. The Selfridge Air National Guard fighters were in the air, but had expended all their ammunition on a training exercise. They did not land until 10:29. Two Toledo F-16s were to take off, but—according to Colonel Marr—only after the Delta 1989 episode was over and after United 93 had been shot down ("The Unthinkable Had Happened," 2007, www.candgnews.com, *The Wolverine*, Fall 2006, Spencer, 178–, *Toledo Blade*, 12/9/01, MFR 03012970, 10/27/03).

131–32   **I believe:** ATCSCC Tape Transcription, "Channel 5"; **NEADS told nothing:** ibid., 9/11 NEADS Tape Transcription, "NEADS-CONR-NORAD Transcripts, NEADS Channel 2," B3, NYC files, CF, MCC Log, "Miles Kara Trips," B19, T8, CF, CR, 30; **controller heard/reported promptly:** int. John Werth, CR, 28, FAA Memo, "Full Transcription: Air Traffic Control System Command Center, National Traffic Management Officer, East Position, 9/11/01," B1, NYC files, CF; **Uh, do we want to think?/FAA staffer reported/"does not believe":** ibid., MFR 04018154, 11/24/03, CR, 461n167.

132 **NEADS knew nothing:** MCC/T Log, "Miles Kara Trips—MCC Log," B19, T8, CF. Ironically, this was the one time during the morning that U.S. forces might have been in a position to intercept one of the hijacked flights. In the words of Commission staffer Kara, "it was only because of a proactive error by Boston air traffic controller Colin Scoggins [suggesting that Flight 11 might still be aloft] . . . that the nation's air defenders had any real chance to defend against Flight 93." The flap over the nonexistent Flight 11 got fighters from Langley in the air, where they established a Combat Air Patrol over Washington by 10:00. It was a patrol at that stage, however—an impotent patrol. It had no rules of engagement, no knowledge of the real flight that was missing, United 93 ("Archive for the Andrews Fighters Category," www.oredigger61.org); **"we were always":** int. of Colin Scoggins (under his Internet name of Cheap Shot), "Q&A with Boston Center Air Traffic Controller," http://sites.google.com.

132 **"We believe":** Spencer, 286; **"watching United":** "Conversation with Maj. Gen. Larry Arnold," www.codeonemagazine.com, 1/02.

132–33 **magical feat/no one reported:** The FAA's call alerting the military to United 93's situation was at 10:07, and the airliner had crashed at 10:03. Seven minutes later, NEADS was told that the plane was down. (9/11 ATCSCC Tape Transcription, "NEADS-CONR-NORAD Transcripts, NEADS Transcripts Channel 5," B3, NYC files, CF, MCC Tech logbook, "Miles Kara FAA HQ 3 of 3," B19, T8, CF).

133 **Arnold concedes:** Testimony of Larry Arnold, 6/17/04, CO, MFR 04016749, 2/3/04, *Vanity Fair*, 9/06 & see re officers conceding same MFR 04016769, 1/23/04.

133 **conflated Delta 1989:** Miles Kara, "Archive for Delta 1989 Category," 9/11 Revisited, www.oredigger.com—with which the authors concur, int. John Werth, & see MFRs 04016769, 1/23/04, 04016749, 2/3/04. Colonel Marr, the NEADS battle commander, also offered inaccurate information about NEADS and Flight 93. The Air Force's official 9/11 history, published as *Air War over America* in January 2003, quoted him as saying he and colleagues called in fighters from the airbase at Selfridge "so they could head 93 off at the pass . . . get in there, close on him, and convince him to turn." The request to Selfridge was made, however, at about 9:43, before NORAD knew anything about Flight 93. The request was made, rather, in connection with Delta 1989, which—as discussed in the text—had not in fact been hijacked ("so they could": Staff Monograph, "The Four Flights and Civil Aviation Security," 8/26/04, CF, 100n391; Selfridge request: 1989: 9/11 NEADS Tape Transcription, "NEADS-CONR-NORAD Transcripts, NEADS Transcripts Channel 2," B3, NYC files, CF, Staff Monograph, "The Four Flights and Civil Aviation Security," 8/26/04, CF, 101n391).

133 **Sudoku/shoddy work:** Miles Kara, "NORAD's Sudoko Puzzle, a Failure to Tell the Truth" & "Archive of the 'May 23, 2003 Hearing' Category," 9/11 Revisited, www .oredigger61.org.

133–34 **Marcus pointed:** Marcus to Schmitz & Mead plus attachments, 7/29/04, "Referral of False Statements by Government Officials to FAA & DOD Inspectors General," CF; Kara, for his part, told the authors that in his view the press release in question had been a "rush to judgment" by NORAD, that NORAD had simply wanted to "get out in front of FAA before the upcoming White House meeting to sort things out"; the tape malfuntion referred to, Kara said, did indeed occur (corr. Miles Kara, 2011); **"didn't get together":** Testimony of Ralph Eberhart, 6/17/04, CO; **"NORAD's public chronology"/"whoever at FAA":** "Sen. Dayton's 'NORAD Lied' Transcript," www.scoop.co.nz; **"At some":** Farmer, 4–.

CHAPTER 13

135–36 **Wolfowitz:** Online NewsHour, 9/14/01, www.pbs.org; **"horrendous decision":** *Meet the Press*, NBC, 9/16/01; **"I recommended":** Office of the Vice President Internal

Transcript, Telephone Interview of the Vice President by *Newsweek*, "Farmer—Misc.," B9, NYC files, CF; **"You bet":** *WP,* 1/27/02; **"emphasized":** CR, 40, 464n214; **2010 memoir:** Bush, 129–.

136   **"The operational chain":** Dept. of Defense Directive 5100.1, 9/25/87. The authors have here referred to the directive effectuating the Goldwater-Nichols Department of Defense Reorganization Act of 1986, the relevant law on 9/11. Other Defense Department regulations in force in 2001 stated—on the matter of military cooperation with civilian authorities (like the FAA)—that the defense secretary had to approve "any request for potentially lethal support," and that "only the President" could request the use of the military to respond to domestic terrorism. It was "understood" in 2001, the 9/11 Commission stated, that a shoot-down order would have to come from the National Command Authority—"a phrase used to describe the President and the Secretary of Defense." Dr. David Griffin, the prominent skeptic, has suggested that the military did not in fact require authorization—that they could act at once in cases requiring "immediate responses." The authors' reading of the regulation Griffin cites is that in certain circumstances and "where time does not permit" prior approval, the military could indeed take "necessary action." The sort of action it could take, however, is very specifically described and does *not* include the use of force ("understood": CR 17, 43; Griffin: *New Pearl Harbor Revisited,* 265n12; regulation: DOD Directives, "Military Assistance to Civil Authorities," 3025.1, 1/15/93, 3025.15, 2/18/97, Joint Chiefs of Staff Instructions, "Aircraft Piracy [Hijacking] and Destruction of Derelict Airborne Objects," 3610.01, 7/31/97, 3610.01A, 6/1/01).

136–37   **generals understood/exercise:** Testimony of Larry Arnold & Craig McKinley, 5/23/03, CO, CR 457n98; **"derelict balloon"/Only President:** MFR 04016749, 2/3/04, Testimony of Larry Arnold, 5/23/02, CO, CR 457n98; **Cheney furious:** Shenon, 267, 411–, but see Kean & Hamilton, 261; **clear hint:** CR, 40–, 464n213–216; **"We just didn't":** Shenon, 265; **"The official version":** Farmer, 255.

137–38   **"My recommendation":** 9/11 NEADS Tape Transcription, "NEADS-CONR-NORAD Transcripts, NEADS Channel 2, B3, NYC files, CF; **Nasypany began asking:** *Vanity Fair,* 9/06; **"I don't know":** 9/11 NEADS Tape Transcription, "NEADS-CONR-NORAD Transcripts, NEADS Channel 4," B3, NYC files, CF, FAA Memo, Full Transcript, Aircraft Accident: UAL175; New York, NY, 9/11/01, "AAL 11, UAL 175: FAA Produced documents, Transcripts used in interviews," B2, NYC files, CF; **Rumsfeld movements from 9:37:** see Ch. 5; **NMCC looked:** CR, 37–; **"outrageous":** Cockburn, 3–; **"one or more calls":** Testimony of Donald Rumsfeld, 3/23/04, CO; **"tried without success":** Goldberg et al., 131; **"Are you okay?":** ibid., 131, 240n6. The assistant was Major Joseph Wassel, who set up the call. Wassel was interviewed for the Defense Department's "Pentagon 9/11" report, but not by the staff of the 9/11 Commission. Wassel described an initial attempt to call the President through the White House Situation Room—a call he came to believe did not go through. Sometime later—Wassel could not pinpoint the time, but placed it as being when Rumsfeld was back in his Pentagon office, having returned from the crash site—the President called the defense secretary from Air Force One (Goldberg et al., 131, 240n6, *AF News,* 3/8/01, Fenner to Campagna & attachments, 12/21/03, "DOD Documents Produced," B22, T2, CF, int. of Joseph Wassel by Alfred Goldberg, 4/9/03, B115, GSA files, CF).

138   **"brief call"/"just gaining"/10:35/There's been;** CR, 43–, 465n234, Farmer, 230, "Dana Hyde Notes of Air Threat Conference Call," released to authors under Mandatory Declassification Review 2011. The text of this conversation is taken from the Defense Department transcript of the "Air Threat" teleconference that began at 9:37 A.M., a key document in the context of establishing the time of the actions and knowledge of senior officials. The Defense Department and Commission staff held that the transcript

had a three-minute margin of error. The authors obtained the release of Commission staffer Dana Hyde's detailed notes on the Air Threat call, which support the timeline in the Commission's Report. The transcript of the teleconference remains classified as of this writing (CR, 37, 462n194, Levin to Zelikow, 8/22/03, "Air Threat Call," B1, Daniel Marcus Files, CF, "Dana Hyde Notes of ATC Call," CF, corr. Kristen Wilhelm, 2010).

139   **"had come"/"Technically"/testimony/withheld:** "Interview with Donald Rumsfeld, 12/23/02," B7, T2, CF, Goldberg et al., 131, testimony of Donald Rumsfeld, 3/23/04, CO, corr. NARA's Kristen Wilhelm, 2010. The defense secretary's full testimony on the point was: "In the National Military Command Center (NMCC), I joined the Air Threat Conference call in progress. One of my first conversations during the Conference Call was with the Vice President. He informed me of the President's authorization to shoot down hostile aircraft coming toward Washington, D.C." In the 2011 memoir, Rumsfeld said Cheney told him there had been "at least three instances" of reports of planes approaching Washington—"a couple were confirmed hijack. And, pursuant to the President's instructions, I gave authorization for them to be taken out" (Rumsfeld, 339).

139–40   **"Very little"/"To a person":** Hyde to Front Office, 3/2/04, "Daniel Marcus," B8, T8, CF; **White House keeps track:** Shenon, 265; **notes by individuals:** CR, 464n216; **sought to limit/record unreliable:** Hyde to Front Office, 3/2/04, "Daniel Marcus," B8, T8, CF; **teleconferences/"In my mind"/cell phones:** CR, 36–, 463n190, int. Anthony Barnes, int. Joseph Wassel by Alfred Goldberg, 4/9/03, B115, GSA files, CF, *Sunday Times* (U.K.), 9/5/10.

140   **logged in 9:58:** Hyde to Front Office, 3/2/04, Dan Marcus Files, CF. Much-publicized recollections, particularly those of former transportation secretary Norman Mineta, appear to suggest that Cheney was moved to the PEOC before 9:30 A.M. According to the authors' analysis, they are in error. Mineta himself, moreover, was not logged into the PEOC until 10:07.

140–41   **disputed call:** CR, 40. Cheney had also called Bush minutes earlier, from a wall phone in a tunnel on the way to the bunker. In that call, he said, they discussed principally the matter of whether the President should return to Washington. Cheney's aide, Scooter Libby, who arrived in the tunnel during the call, thought the gist of it was "basically conveying what was happening." Neither he nor Mrs. Cheney, who was also there, heard any discussion of the shoot-down issue. It is evident from a Defense Department transcript that a White House official requested a Combat Air Patrol over the capital at about that time, but made no mention of a shoot-down order. Counterterrorism coordinator Clarke, moreover, was still talking of "asking the President for authority to shoot down aircraft."

Neither Libby's notes, however, nor Mrs. Cheney's, reflect contact with Bush at the time mentioned by Cheney. National Security Adviser Condoleezza Rice did tell the Commission she heard Cheney's end of a conversation with the President at that time. While she recalled a reference to a Combat Air Patrol, however, she did not hear Cheney recommend the shoot-down of hijacked airliners. A separate statement by Rice, moreover, mightily diminishes her credibility. She told ABC News that shoot-down authority was "requested through channels, by Secretary Rumsfeld, Vice President passed the request, the President said, 'Yes.' " Far from requesting shoot-down authority, Rumsfeld—as reported in the text—learned of the shoot-down order only after the fact, from Cheney (Cheney called: CR 40, 464n211/213, Interview of Scooter Libby by *Newsweek*, 11/16/01, & Interview of Mrs. Cheney by *Newsweek*, 11/9/01, "Farmer Misc.," B10, NYC files, CF; transcript: CR 38, 463n201; "asking": CR 36, 463n191, MFR 04018415, 12/16/03, CF; Libby/Cheney notes/Rice: CR 40–, 43; "requested": "9/11," ABC News, 9/11/02, transcript at http://s3.amazonaws.com, Farmer, 259).

141   **staff received/Kurtz:** CR, 36, MFR 04018415, 12/16/03, CF.

141   **suspect aircraft:** The reports of inbound aircraft originated, as Mrs. Cheney's notes suggest, as information from the Secret Service's Joint Operations Center (JOC), which was in turn getting its information directly from the FAA. The incoming aircraft was likely United 93, which the Secret Service and its FAA contact were tracking on a screen that showed its *projected* path. Both were unaware that, as of 10:03, the flight that appeared on the screen to be approaching the capital had in fact already crashed. Within a minute or so of the confusing reports about Flight 93, the fighters out of Langley—just arriving over Washington—were also briefly mistaken as a threat (CR, 40–, Staff Statement 17, CO, Miles Kara, "9-11: Rules of Engagement," www.oredigger61.org).

141   **Mrs. Cheney noted:** notes, "Office of the VP Notes," B1, Dana Hyde files, CF. The content of Mrs. Cheney's notes come from a handwritten digest done by Commission staff, which was released in 2009. Mrs. Cheney's original notes, like those of Scooter Libby, have not been released at the time of writing, nor has the Commission staff's record of its interview of Josh Bolten. Bolten has disputed the way he was reported in the Commission Report. According to Cheney biographer Stephen Hayes, he said "he suggested Cheney call Bush not because the Vice President had overstepped his authority, but as a reminder that they should notify the President." In his November interview with *Newsweek*, Libby would say, "I wouldn't be surprised that there were—that there had already been discussion with the President about getting CAP [Combat Air Patrol] up. . . . I'm almost certain that they had already had discussions . . . as I say, I was not on those phone calls." (Mrs. Cheney's notes: "OVP Notes," B1, Dana Hyde files, CF; Cheney/Libby/Bolten notes: corr. NARA's Kristen Wilhelm, 2010; Bolten disputed: Hayes, 546n20; "I wouldn't": int. Libby by *Newsweek*, 11/16/01).

141   **"I'm talking":** int. Anthony Barnes. According to Barnes, it was not he who warned Cheney of an approaching aircraft. That information reached the Vice President from someone else. The Commission Report identifies the source of the "aircraft 80 miles out" report only as a "military aide." The aide could perhaps have been the Vice President's military aide, Douglas Cochrane, who was also in the PEOC at some point (CR, 40–).

141–42   **Libby/"Yes":** int. Libby by *Newsweek*, 11/16/01; **lt. col. "confirmed":** CR 42, 465n227; **"pin-drop":** MFR 04020719, 4/29/04; **Libby note:** CR, 465n220; **"wanted to make sure":** CR, 41.

142–43   **Fleisher kept record:** Ari Fleischer, *Taking Heat*, NY: William Morrow, 2005, 141, transcript *60 Minutes*, CBS, 9/11/02. The note Fleischer made on 9/11, which firmly timed the President's comment as having been made at 10:20, remains classified. The press secretary's memoir—published after the Commission's Report came out—refers to the timing of the authorization only vaguely, as "shortly after we took off" (classified: corr. Kristen Wilhem, 2010, "shortly": Fleischer, 141); **"he had authorized":** CR, 41, 465n221; **not "alert":** Cherie Gott, "Brief Look at the Effect of Considering Prior Years' More Robust Alert Facility Architecture on Events of 11 Sep 2001," www.scribd.com; **"Capital Guardians":** "Andrews AFB Guide," www.dcmilitary.com.

143   **SS/FAA contact early on:** CR, 464n208. Secret Service agent Nelson Garabito had first discussed how to react with his usual FAA liaison, Terry Van Steenbergen, who said what was needed was "fighters airborne." Van Steenbergen initiated contacts with the National Guard at Andrews. Told by a colleague at the base of the approach, Major Daniel Caine in turn called another Secret Service agent, Ken Beauchamp, asking whether he could be of assistance. Though Beauchamp initially made no request, he phoned back later—after the Pentagon was hit at 9:37. (Garabito/Van Steenbergen: MFR of int. Terry Van Steenbergen, 3/30/04, "FAA HQ," B6, T8, CF, MFR 04017326, 7/28/03, CR, 464n208, USSS Statements & Interview Reports, 7/28/03, "Secret Service Requests," B5, Dana Hyde files, CF; Caine/Beauchamp: MFR 04020717, 3/8/04, Spencer, 124).

143   **Pentagon/Wherely at run:** MFR 03005418, 8/28/03, *WP*, 4/8/02.

143   **"Get anything":** Wherley Interview, "Andrews AFB Logs-Timelines," B4, Dana Hyde files, CF. This wording fits closely with a "Memo for Record" written on September 16 by Andrews's Aircraft Generation Squadron Commander, Lieutenant Colonel Charles Denman. "At 10:10," he noted, "we received word to 'Get something up.' " "10:10" may or may not be a correct timing—a time Denham gave for a later event in the Andrews sequence seems inconsistent with other information (Memo for Record, 9/16/01, "Andrews AFB Timelines," B4, Dana Hyde files, CF).

143–44   **"someone a little higher"/"It's coming"/Ediger:** "Andrews AFB Timelines," BH, Dana Hyde files, CF, MFR 03005418, 8/28/03; **asked to speak/"wasn't going"/made do/"unidentified male":** MFR of int. David Wherley, 2/27/04, "General Wherley," B1, Dana Hyde, CF; **"put aircraft"/"any force"/"understandable":** MFR 03005418, 8/28/03; **After the crash:** Prewitt (USSS) to Monaghan re FOIA 20080330 & 20080331 & attachments, 4/23/10, "USSS Memos & Timelines," www.scrib.doc re [Barnes] USSS Interview notes, 7/28/03, "USSS Requests & Notes," B5, Dana Hyde files, CF, int. Anthony Barnes, MFR 03005418, 8/28/03, National Society of Black Engineers press release, "Igniting the Torch," 2008.

144   **Barnes cannot pin down:** A further document, a Commission memo on the Secret Service records, suggests the contacts with Barnes took place at about the time Cheney was arriving at the PEOC—linking it to efforts to protect the White House. "All air traffic," the document indicates, "would be halted and forced to land" (memo, 7/28/03, "USSS Requests & Notes," B5, T8, CF); **10:04:** Relevant Andrews Transmissions, 2/17–18/04, "Andrews AFB Logs," B4, Dana Hyde files, CF, corr. Miles Kara, 2011.

144   **Cheney would deny/"aware that":** CR, 44; **"acted on its own"/"the agents' ":** *WSJ*, 3/22/04.

144   **On own initative?:** While there is no documentary evidence of a call between Bush and Cheney in which Bush authorized a shoot-down, Commission notes released to the authors in 2011 do indicate that the Vice President felt the need to get Bush's authorization at a later point. At 10:44, while speaking with Defense Secretary Rumsfeld about raising the military's alert status to Defcon 3, Cheney told Rumsfeld, "I'll have to run that by him [Bush] and let him make the call." It is arguable that Cheney would have felt the same need for authority to engage hijacked airliners ("Dana Hyde Notes of Air Threat Conference Call," CF, corr. Miles Kara).

145   **sec. def. out of touch/intermittent contact:** As reported earlier, the President recalled that it repeatedly proved difficult to get through to Cheney on 9/11. Richard Clarke described Cheney, in the PEOC, complaining, "The comms [communications] in this place are terrible." Presidential press secretary Ari Fleischer recalled the President saying, "The communications equipment was good, not great, as he often had to wait to get people on the phone. After September 11, Air Force's One's communications equipment received a major modernization." (Bush recalled: see Ch. 9; "The comms": Richard Clarke, 19; "The communications": Fleischer, 141).

145   **Wherley no immediate way:** Miles Kara, "The Andrews Fighters": An Expeditionary Force, Not an Air Defense," 9/11 Revisited, www.oredigger61.org, CR, 44, Charles J. Gross, Memo for the Record, 9/19/01, "Andrews AFB Logs-Timelines," B4, Dana Hyde files, CF.

145   **less than certain/"check out":** MFR 03005418, 8/28/03, MFR of int. David Wherley, 2/27/04, "General Wherley," B1, Dana Hyde files, CF. This first fighter to go up from Andrews carried no missiles, and its gun was loaded only with training rounds. Its pilot, Major Billy Hutchison, would later claim that the general told him to "intercept [an] aircraft coming toward D.C. and prevent it from reaching D.C." Another officer at the base, however, Major David McNulty, said Hutchison was tasked to do nothing more than

identify an aircraft approaching along the Potomac. (That plane, it later turned out, had been just a helicopter.) Senior Commission counsel John Farmer in 2009 roundly rejected an account that suggested Hutchison located United 93 on his radar and considered ramming it—Hutchison did not even take off until 10:38, more than half an hour after Flight 93 had crashed ("intercept": Hutchison [typed notes of int.] & MFR of Hutchinson, "Billy Hutchinson Andrews AFB," B3, Dana Hyde files, CF; McNulty: MFR 04020718, 3/11/04; Farmer rejected: Farmer, 375, & see Miles Kara, "The Scott Trilogy: Cutting to the Chase," 9/11 Revisited, www.oredigger61.org; considered ramming: Spencer, 219–; 10:38: Relevant Andrews Timelines, "Miles Kara Docs 3," B8, T8, CF).

145   **Four more fighters:** ibid., MFR 04020720, 3/11/04, Charles Gross, Memo for the Record, UA 93 and Andrews Timeline, & transcript ints. Igor Rasmussen & Leslie Filson, 9/18/03, "Andrews AFB Logs-Timelines," B4, Dana Hyde files, CF.

145   **"weapons free"/"uncomfortable":** MFR of int. David Wherley, 2/27/04, "General Wherley," B1, Dana Hyde files, CF, Staff Statement 17, CO, transcript ints. McNutz/Thompson/Sasseville, & ints. Thompson & Penney, undated, "Andrews AFB Logs-Timelines," B4, Dana Hyde files, CF, & see Kara to Hyde & Azzarello, 5/25/04. The general may have had reason to feel uncomfortable. According to NORAD commanding general Eberhart, Wherley "did not have the authority to give a 'weapons-free' order." Wherley said later that he "didn't feel comfortable until he heard Vice President Cheney's interview with Tim Russert [on September 16, on *Meet the Press*]" (Eberhart: MFR 04018141, 3/1/04; "didn't feel": MFR of int. David Wherley, 2/27/04, "General Wherley, Zelikow Notes & MFRs," B1, Dana Hyde files, CF; "had not been aware": CR, 44).

145–46   **formal rules:** MFR of int. David Wherley, 2/27/04, "General Wherley," B1, Dana Hyde files, CF, CR, 465n234; **made its way/10:31/You need to read:** 9/11 NEADS Tape Transcription, "NEADS-CONR-NORAD Transcripts, NEADS Channel 2," B3, NYC files, CF, & Channel 2 audio at B82 & B110, GSA files, CF, Spencer, 240–, Shootdown references, "Miles Kara and Dana Hyde Work Papers," B8, T8, CF, CR, 4; **Marr/Nasypany unsure:** CR, 43; **"hostile act":** MFR 0401841, 3/1/04.

146   **Any track:** Kara to Hyde et al., 5/24/04. It is not clear whether the voice on the tape is that of Nasypany or that of his weapons officer, Major James Fox (CF, DH, B5, "Langley Pilots Interviews Fdr.—email thread re Flight 93—NEADS Tapes," B5, Dana Hyde files, CF).

146   **Wolfowitz/FAA & military versions:** see earlier refs in Chapters 12 & 13; Farmer, 245, 251, 255, CR, 31–.

146   **referred to inspectors general:** The inspectors general of both the Defense Department and the Department of Transportation delivered their reports in 2006. Neither conceded that there was evidence that either department's officials connived to reconstruct the story on events on 9/11. The Commission's John Farmer—as a former attorney general of New Jersey a man well used to weighing evidence—challenged that finding. "There is no question," he has written, "that the official version . . . served the interest of every institution involved. . . . It is impossible to conclude honestly, from the two Inspector General reports, that the official version of the events of 9/11 was the result of mere administrative incompetence; too many questions remained unanswered." The full body of evidence is extremely complex, too complex to be dealt with in this book. The authors suggest that interested readers consult Commission general counsel Marcus's referral letter to the inspectors general, the resulting IG reports, and Farmer's 2009 book, *Ground Truth* (referral: Marcus to Schmitz and Mead & attachments, 7/29/04; IG reports: "Memorandum for Under Secretary of Defense of Intelligence," 9/12/06, "Results of OIG Investigation of 9/11 Commission Staff Referral," Todd Zinser to Acting Secretary, FAA, 8/31/06; "There is no question": Farmer, 287–).

146–47   **"in my opinion":** Testimony of Monte Belger, 6/17/04, CO; **"In my opinion":** Testimony of Richard Myers, 6/17/04, CO; **"were talking mainly"/"leadership was irrelevant"/"was not simply wrong:** Farmer, 186–, 290, 277, 288–.

Part III: AMERICA RESPONDS

CHAPTER 14

151–52   **garbage can/"Allah will be":** Chicago to Director, 9/12/01, FBI 265D-NY-280350-CG, INTELWIRE; **kept an eye/"Mission failed":** FBI 302 of int. Grant Besley, 9/16/01, B11, T7, CF, Chronology ADA-30, Operations Center, Terrorist Attacks NYC-DC 9/11/01, "FAA 3 of 3 Chronology ADA Ops Center," B19, T8, CF; **Picciotto/The guy:** Picciotto, 75–.

152   **5,000/"remained in custody":** "The September 11 Detainees: A Review of the Treatment of Aliens Held on Immigration Charges in Connection with the Investigation of the September 11 Attacks," Washington, D.C.: U.S. Dept. of Justice, Office of the Inspector General, 6/03. The figure of 5,000 is taken from the study by Professors David Cole and Jules Lobel, which is in turn derived from official U.S. government reports. *The Washington Post* reported that 1,182 "potential terror suspects" had been detained by November 2001. In addition, some 4,000 were detained under two post-9/11 INS initiatives, the Special Registration and Alien Absconder programs. "The vast majority" of the 5,000, Professor Cole told the authors, were detained "on immigration charges, ranging from overstaying a visa to working without a permit or even to failing to file a notice of change of address" (corr. David Cole, 2010, *LAT*, 11/18/07, *WP*, 11/6/01, 6/16/04, Anjana Malhotra, "Overlooking Innocence," www.aclu.org, & see "The September 11 Detainees," Office of the Inspector General, U.S. Department of Justice, 4/03, 2–, CR, 327–, 556n17, Philip Heymann, "Muslims in America after 9/11: The Legal Situation," conference paper, 12/15/06, www.ces.fas.harvard.edu).

152   **conditions included/abuse:** The abuse occurred especially at the Federal Bureau of Prisons' Metropolitan Detention Center in Brooklyn ("The September 11 Detainees," 4–).

152–53   **only one convicted:** As of 2009 the only post-9/11 detainee convicted was Ali al-Marri, who had been arrested in December 2001. Marri was sentenced to eight years for plotting with and materially supporting al Qaeda. Zacarias Moussaoui, who is serving life without the possibility of parole for conspiracy to commit acts of terrorism and air piracy, had been arrested before 9/11 (Marri: corr. David Cole, 2010, AP, 10/30/09, *LAT*, 5/1/09; Moussaoui: AP, 9/25/09, BBC News, 5/4/06, AFP, 1/4/10, CR, 247); **Ziglar/"a moment":** MFR 04016455, 11/14/03; **anti-Arab hostility/Sikh shot:** *New Republic*, 9/24/01, *Queens Tribune*, 9/18/01; **Egyptian pilot:** DiMarco, 314–.

153   **Flight 23/"four young Arab":** Spencer, 102–, MFR 04020009, 4/14/04, CBS News, 9/14/01. The account of the Flight 23 incident is drawn principally from notes of a Commission interview with Ed Ballinger, the United dispatcher in charge of the airline's transcontinental flights that day, and from Lynn Spencer's book *Touching History*. Ballinger cited what he had been told by United's chief pilot, and Spencer apparently interviewed Flight 23 crew members. There were other, less well documented reports of possible threats to planes on 9/11. Flight attendants told the Commission of Arab passengers having behaved in a way they thought suspicious aboard United Flight 962 from Los Angeles to Washington, D.C. A passenger who flew aboard yet another United plane, Flight 915 from Paris to Washington, D.C., told the Commission there had been

a major security alert at Charles de Gaulle Airport before takeoff—and before the attacks began in the United States—and that guards removed a suspect from the terminal. In the States, the FBI reportedly searched for passengers who had been aboard another grounded airliner, American Flight 43. In Canada, authorities detained a Yemeni arrested aboard a U.S.-bound plane that had been diverted to Toronto. He was reportedly carrying several different passports, had papers with Arabic writing sewn into his clothing, and his baggage contained Lufthansa crew uniforms. A U.S. Justice Department spokesman said box cutters, similar to those used as weapons on the hijacked planes, were later found on other aircraft. Though the authors surmise that few if any of these accounts relate to real threats, the incident involving United 23 may indeed have been serious (Ballinger/Spencer: MFR 04020009, 4/14/04, Spencer, 102–; UA962: FBI 302, ints. Elizabeth Anderson & Elizabeth Henley, 9/20/01, "FBI 302s—ACARS," B11, T7, CF, MFR 03007051, undated, 8/03; AA43: BBC News, 9/18/01; Yemeni: CBS News, 9/14/01, *Hamilton Spectator* [Canada], 9/26/01; box cutters: CNN, 9/24/01, & see MFR 04017172, 9/29/03, MFR 04019897, 7/29/03, FBI 302, 9/15/01, *Chicago Tribune*, 9/23/01, *Guardian* [U.K.], 10/13/01).

153   **Mihdhar:** Bamford, *Shadow Factory*, 64; **"We think we had":** *Globe and Mail* (Toronto), 6/13/02.

154–55   **"Who do you think":** Ronald Kessler, *The Terrorist Watch*, NY: Crown, 2007, 8–; **some Arabs celebrate:** Fox News, 9/12/01, "Bulls-Eye Say Egyptians as They Celebrate Anti-US Attacks," AFP, 9/11/01, *NYT*, 9/13/01, 9/26/01, 10/27/01; **"should feel":** CNN, 9/18/01; **Palestinians/rifles/candy:** Fox News, 9/12/01, *New Yorker*, 9/24/01, BBC News, 9/14/01, *The Times* (London), 9/11/01, Reuters, 9/12/01; **caller/DFLP:** BBC News, 9/12/01, "Sept. 11 One Year On," www.rte.ie, 9/11/02, CNN, 9/11/01; **Osama poster:** AP, 9/14/01; **"Congratulations":** The dissident was Saad al-Fagih, of the Movement for Islamic Reform in Arabia, transcript, *Frontline:* "Saudi Time Bomb," 9/15/01, www.pbs.org, & see Corbin, 250; **"This action":** *New Yorker*, 6/2/08; **CRS report:** Kenneth Katzman, "Terrorism: Near Eastern Groups and State Sponsors, 2001," Washington, D.C.: Congressional Research Service, 9/10/01; **17th:** an approximation. Osama's father reportedly had some twenty-two wives over the years, and at least four other sons were born during the year of Osama's birth. It is safe to say, though, that he fell between sons number seventeen and twenty-one (Steve Coll, *The Bin Ladens*, London: Allen Lane, 2008, 72–); **$300 million:** For a more detailed analysis of bin Laden's fortune, see Chapter 22; **"for some time":** CBS News, 9:12–9:54 A.M., 9/11/01, www .archive.org; **"We've hit":** *Newsweek*, 9/13/01, Bamford, *Pretext*, 54, notes of Stephen Cambone, 9/11/01, released under FOIA to Thad Anderson, www.outragedmoderates .com; **"Although in our":** Tenet, 167; **"beyond a doubt":** Tenet, xix.

156   **"We could then":** *60 Minutes*, CBS News, 9/11/02. The flight manifests were not released by any government source at the time. The airlines involved, however, quickly released lists of those they described as "victims" or passengers whose next of kin had been identified—but did not include the names of those believed to have been hijackers. That omission, especially, led to speculation that there had not really been any Arabs on the flights, that some hijackers might have used stolen identities, or that some of those being named in the press as hijackers might still be alive. The authors have analyzed the available material—including passenger lists for the four flights as released by the FBI to author Terry McDermott, lists submitted as exhibits during the trial of Zacarias Moussaoui, and lists for Flights 175 and 93 that appear in released 9/11 Commission files. The names on the above match the list of those believed to have been hijackers released by the FBI on September 14, 2001. The names, moreover, occur consistently in the documented evidence of the hijackers' activity in the months and weeks before 9/11. Finally, photographs—apparently mostly from visa forms—were "verified by fam-

ily members of thirteen of the hijackers—including presumed hijacking pilots Marwan al-Shehhi (175) and Hani Hanjour (77). That Ziad Jarrah had been aboard United 93 was established by comparison of DNA material from the home of his girlfriend Aysel Sengün in Germany and from one of four sets of unidentified human remains recovered at the crash site of Flight 93 ("victims"/next of kin: United Airlines press release, 9/12/01, American Airlines press release, 9/12/01; questions: e.g., see "Hijack 'Suspects' Alive and Well," www.bbc.co.uk, 9/23/01, *Telegraph* [U.K.], 9/23/01, *Newsday*, 10/22/01, "Passenger Lists," www.911research.wtc7.net, Gerard Holmgren, "Media Published Fake Passenger Lists for AA Flight 11," 5/14/04, www.archive.indymedia.be; manifests: McDermott, manifests reproduced in photo section, "Flight 93 Manifest," & "Flight 175 Misc. Manifest," B17, T7, CF, corr. Kristen Wilhelm, 2010, *U.S. v. Zacarias Moussaoui*, Exhibits P200018; FBI list: "FBI Announces List of 19 Hijackers," 9/14/01, www.fbi .gov—Flight 175 hijacker Fayez Ahmed Banihammad is identified on the FBI list only as Fayez Ahmed—the portion of his name that appears on the manifest, and misspells Flight 93 hijacker Ziad Jarrah's last name—correctly rendered on the available manifest—as "Jarrahi"; documented evidence: e.g., "Hijacker's True Name Usage," *U.S. v. Zacarias Moussaoui*, Exhibit OG00013, Dulles Airport Command Post, Intelligence Log, FBI 265D-NY-280350, "Aliases & Id," B62, T5, CF, & see Jeremy Hammond, "9/11 Hijackers Not on Manifests," www.foreignpolicyjournal.com, 4/5/10, "No Hijacker Names on Passenger Manifests," www.911myths.com, "Panoply of the Absurd," www.spiegel .de, 9/8/03; photographs: Legat Riyadh to Counterterrorism, 11/20/01, "Aliases & Ids," B62, T5, CF; Jarrah DNA: PENTTBOM, Misc. Req. 42, "Aliases & Ids," B62, T5, CF).

156–58   **flight attendants/Suqami/Shehris/Atta:** FBI 302 of int. Kip Hamilton, 9/11/01 & re Lead Control Numbers DL267 and CE66, 9/13/01, "DOJ Documents Requests #35-13," B13, T7, CF, *New York Observer*, 2/15/04, entry for 10:59 A.M., Chicago to Director, 9/12/01, INTELWIRE, entries for 10:51 A.M. & 11:26 A.M., TSA Incident Log, 9/11/01, "DOJ Documents Request," B20, T7, CF, MFR 03007067, 9/11/03; **Graney/"clenched":** FBI 302 of int. Diane Graney, 9/22/01, "FBI 302s—Ground Security Coordinator," B1, T7, CF, MFR 04020036, 4/15/04, MFR 04020016, 5/27/04; **camera recorded/calls:** "Chronology of Events for Hijackers, 8/16/01," *U.S. v. Zacarias Moussaoui*, Exhibits OG00020.2, FO07011, FO07021, FO07022, FO07023, FO07024, "265D-NY-280350, TWINBOM-PENTTBOM, Biographical Report," 11/26/01, National Drug Intelligence Center for the FBI, authors' collection, FBI press release, 10/14/01, entries for 9/10/01 & 9/11/01, "Hijackers Timeline [redacted]," 11/14/03, INTELWIRE, FBI 302 of [name redacted], 10/15/01, "FBI 302s of Interest," B17, T7, CF, FBI Timeline of 9-11 Hijacker Activity & Movements, "Timelines 9-11, 2 of 2," B20, T7, CF; **Nissan:** ibid., *WP*, 10/6/01; **Hyundai/Banihammad/Milner/ticket:** MFR 04020636, 2/2/04, "American Airlines Flight 11, PENTTBOM, 265A-NY-280350," 4/19/02; **Mitsubishi found:** "American Airlines Flight 11, PENTTBOM, 265A-NY-280350," 4/19/02, Staff Report, "The Four Flights & Civil Aviation Security," CF, exhibits list, "Breeder Documents," B8, T5, CF, MFR 04020636, 2/2/04, MFR 03007050, 8/15/03; **Park Inn:** "American Airlines Flight 11, PENTTBOM, 265A-NY-280350," 4/19/02; **Ghamdis/Charles Hotel/taxi:** MFR 04020636, 2/2/04; **draped towels:** *WP*, 9/16/01; **novels/***Penthouse*/ **condoms:** Warrant Issued on Vehicle ID JT2AE92E9J3137546, 9/13/01, "FBI 302s of Interest," B17, T7, CF, "Ziad Jarrah," FBI summary, 4/19/02, www.scribd.com; **prostitutes:** *BG*, 10/10/01, MFR 04020636, 2/2/04; **phone records:** MFR 04020636, 2/2/04.

158   **money trail:** ibid., Evidence Inspected at FBI HQ 5/14/04, "Breeder Documents," B8, T5, CF, Staff Report, "Monograph on Terrorist Financing, CO, *Newsweek*, 11/11/01. The two key financial facilitators in the UAE were Ali Abdul Aziz Ali and Mustafa al-Hawsawi. Both men, arrested in Pakistan in 2003, became part of the group known as "High-Value Detainees" held at Guantánamo Bay. As of spring 2011, they were still

there (Staff Report, "Monograph on Terrorist Financing," CO, *NYT,* 6/30/10, "The Guantánamo Docket," www.nyt.com); **"A maid":** Counterterrorism to All Field Offices, 9/22/01, FBI 265A-NY-280350, released under FOIA to Mike Williams, www.911myths .com, "Hijackers Timeline [redacted]," 11/4/03, INTELWIRE.

158   **ominous indications/"sleepers":** Of these three leads, the authors found no indica-tion that the first—relating to the man who answered the door at the Park Inn—was ever resolved. The two names were found at Dulles Airport in a car registered to Nawaf al-Hazmi, one of the Flight 77 hijackers. One was that of Osama Awadallah, a Yemeni living in San Diego who turned out to have known two of the hijackers and had material about bin Laden. Though suspected of having had prior knowledge of the attacks, he was not charged in that connection. The name written in highlighter related to Mohamed Abdi, a naturalized U.S. citizen working as a Burns security guard. Like Awadallah, he was not charged with any terrorism offense (Awadallah: MFR 04017544, 11/18/03, CR, 220, 250, 532n175, *San Diego Union-Tribune,* 9/14/02, *NYT,* 11/18/06; Abdi: *U.S. v. Mohamed Abdi,* Case No. 01–1053-M, U.S. District Court for the Eastern District of Virginia, www.findlaw.com, MFR 04016253, 10/16/03, *WP,* 9/27/01, 1/12/02, *Human Events,* 10/15/01).

159   **Dulles/Security camera/pass:** The available evidence, however, is less than consis-tent. An FBI document states that the video evidence "indicates that two of the hijack-ers . . . passed through the security checkpoints and baggage claim areas" on September 10. This appears to have occurred at 4:51 P.M. on the eve of the attacks. Checkpoint supervisor Eric Safraz Gill, however, spoke of having challenged an "Arab-looking" man equipped with a swipe pass, and two with apparently adequate identification at about 8:15 P.M. They had attempted to get two other men—who had no such ID—through a secure door. All the men left, following an altercation with Gill ("indicates": Counterter-rorism to Field Offices, 9/22/01, FBI 265A-NY-280350, & see entry for 9/10/01, "Hi-jackers Timeline [redacted]," 11/14/03, INTELWIRE, MFR 04020030, 4/6/04, MFR 04016235, 2/10/04; Gill: Susan B. Trento & Joseph J. Trento, *Unsafe at Any Altitude,* Hanover, NH: Steerforth, 2007, 1–, 43–).

159   **Corolla/personal belongings/investigative treasure/involvement in aviation:** "Nawaf al-Hazmi," FBI summary, 4/19/02, www.scribd.com, Warrant Issued on Vehicle IDJT2AE92E9J3137546, 9/13/01, "FBI 302s of Interest," B17, T7, CF, Criminal Com-plaint, *U.S. v. Mohamed Abdi,* Case No. 01–1053-M, U.S. District Court for the Eastern District of Virginia, 9/23/01, MFR 04016253, 10/16/03, San Diego to Ottawa et al., 4/11/02, Leads from Hijackers' Cars, INTELWIRE, "Ali Ahmad Mesdaq," 1/28/02, FBI Document re PENTTBOM, INTELWIRE. Also recovered, at Newark Airport, was a red Mitsubishi Galant rented by Ziad Jarrah. Jarrah, a Lebanese citizen, is be-lieved to have led the hijack team on United Flight 93. Though the car contained far less evidence than did Hazmi's, agents did recover a speeding ticket Jarrah had incurred in the early hours of September 10. In a trash can at Newark's Days Inn, meanwhile, the FBI found the used Spirit Airlines ticketing that had brought Jarrah and Saudis Saeed al-Ghamdi, Ahmed al-Nami, and Ahmad al-Haznawi from Fort Lauderdale to Newark on September 7. Other evidence aside, the joint travel before 9/11 indicated that the four men shared a common purpose (Ziad Jarrah summary, Prepared by UA93 Investigative Team, FBI, 4/19/02, www.scribd.com, Evidence Inspected at FBI HQ 5/14/04, "Breeder Documents," B8, T7, CF, Longman, 101).

159–60   **duffel bags:** MFR 04017509, 11/5/03, "Hijackers Timeline [redacted]," 11/14/03, INTELWIRE, *San Diego Union-Tribune,* 9/3/02; **Portland car:** Evidence Inspected at FBI HQ, 5/14/04, "Breeder Documents," B8, T5, CF; **manuals:** "Ziad Jarrah," FBI summary, www.scribd.com; **"Everybody was gathered":** int. Mark Mikarts; **"It was the** sort"/"**His bearing**": *Birmingham Post* (U.K.), 9/25/01, Jane Corbin, *The Base*, London: Pocket, 2003, 162; **Dekkers:** transcript of interview of Rudi Dekkers, ibid., *News-Press* (Fort Myers, Fl.), 9/13/01.

160   **Atta luggage:** Review of Investigation Conducted by the FBI of Atta's Suitcases at Boston, 2/10/04, "Detainee Reports," B53, T5, CF, FBI 302 of [redacted] DePasquale, 9/17/01, "Atta Luggage," B18, T7, CF, Recovered Identification Documents, "Breeder Documents," B8, T5, CF. Also in Atta's bag were a folding knife and some First Defense pepper spray. Omari's bag contained an Arabic-to-English dictionary, English grammar books, his Saudi passport, and a bank checkbook (Recovered Identification Documents, "Breeder Docs.—Entire Contents," B8, T5, CF, MFR of Review of Investigation by the FBI of Atta's suitcases at Boston, 2/10/04, "Detainee Reports," B53, T5, CF).

161   **document in luggage/at Dulles/at 93 site:** "Synopsis of Captioned Investigation as of 11/4/01," PENTTBOM, Major Case 182, 11/5/01, authors' collection. The document has been variously referred to as having five, four, and three pages. The first report, by Bob Woodward in *The Washington Post*, had it as five. A 2006 study, by Professor Hans Kippenberg and Professor Tilman Seidensticker, suggests that a fifth page was recovered but not published. CBS News, which reported on a copy of the Dulles Airport document, said it was "similar but not identical to the document found in Atta's luggage, and parts of a document found in the Pennsylvania wreckage" (Woodward: *WP*, 9/28/01; four: eds. Hans Kippenberg & Tilman Seidensticker, *The 9/11 Handbook*, London: Equinox, 2006, 1–, *Observer* [London], 9/30/01; three: "PENTTBOM, Major case 182, Summary of Captioned Investigation as of 11/4/01," FBI document, 11/5/01; CBS News: "Translated Text: Hijackers' How-To," www.cbsnews.com, 10/1/01).

161   **Commission not mention:** Congress's Joint Inquiry report on the attacks did cite a statement by FBI director Mueller including the fact that a "three-page letter handwritten in Arabic" had been found, and stating that it contained "instructions on how to prepare for a mission applicable, but not specific, to the September 11 operation" (JI, Report, 142–, Statement of Robert Mueller, 9/25/02, www.fas.org).

161   **"Spiritual Manual"/"Handbook"/"mutual pledge":** all from the translation in eds. Kippenberg & Seidensticker, 11–. There have been several translations and commentaries of the document the FBI released. The authors of this book have relied primarily on the 2006 book *The 9/11 Handbook*, by Hans Kippenberg, professor of Comparative Religious Studies at Jacobs University in Bremen, Germany, and Tilman Seidensticker, professor of Arab and Islamic Studies at the Friedrich Schiller University in Jena. There have been other commentaries of note—by Professor Kanan Makiya of Brandeis University and Hassan Mneimneh, a senior fellow at the Hudson Institute, Professor Juan Cole of the University of Michigan, and David Cook, an associate professor at Rice University. In their book *Masterminds of Terror*, Al Jazeera's Yosri Fouda and *The Sunday Times*'s Nick Fielding reported Fouda's 2002 interview of self-confessed 9/11 conspirator Ramzi Binalshibh—which offered confirmation that the "Spiritual Manual" is authentic. All the sources mentioned treat the document as having been written for the 9/11 hijackers. The translators of the version used by CBS News in 2001, however, stated in a note that the document did "not in any way sound like instructions to a hijacker or a terrorist." In the context of its content and circumstances of discovery, however, the document can only be pertinent to 9/11 (Kanan Makiya & Hassan Mneimneh, "Manual for a Raid," *NY Review of Books*, 1/17/02, Yosri Fouda & Nick Fielding, *Masterminds of Terror*, Edinburgh: Mainstream, 2003, 141–, Juan Cole, "Al Qaeda's Doomsday Document and Psychological Manipulation," 4/9/03, www.juancole.com, David Cook, *Understanding Jihad*, Berkeley: Univ. of Calif. Press, 2005, 195–, "Translated Text: Hijackers How-To," 10/1/01, www.cbsnews.com).

161–64   **manual:** FBI press release, 9/28/01, www.fbi.gov; **re *"q"/Qiblah*:** Fouda & Fielding, 147; **"To those who":** corr. Hans Kippenberg, 2010. Some, pointing to anomalies in the document, have raised the possibility that the hijackers' manual might be a forgery. Professor Kippenberg, however, who has conducted the most in-depth analysis, cites a skein of persuasive evidence to the contrary (anomalies: e.g., Robert Fisk, *The Great War for Civilization*, London: Fourth Estate, 2005, 1039–; **evidence:** Kippenberg, 4–).

164–65   **"We believe":** *Telegraph* (U.K.), 9/13/01, int. of Jamal Ismael for Palladin InVision, 2006, supplied to author, *WP*, 12/9/01, Peter L. Bergen, *The Osama bin Laden I Know*, New York: Free Press, 2006, 312; **"I would like"/Taliban accepted:** CNN, 9/17/01; **"As a Muslim":** *Daily Ummat* (Karachi), 9/28/01, www.justresponse.net; **"Whenever we kill"/"As concerns":** ed. Bruce Lawrence, *Messages to the World*, London: Verso, 2005, 106–.

165–66   **On the eve:** The night before the attacks, according to a CBS News report citing Pakistani intelligence sources, bin Laden entered a military hospital in Rawalpindi, Pakistan, for kidney dialysis. This report appears to have been unfounded. There was an oft-repeated story that he required dialysis, but the best evidence is that he did not. Al Qaeda operatives' accounts, moreover, place bin Laden at a camp in Afghanistan the following morning, September 11 (CBS news, 1/28/02, and see notes for Ch. 30, pp. 548–49); **call to mother/"In two days"/"I would never":** *NYT*, 10/2/01, MSNBC, 10/1/01, *Mail on Sunday* (U.K.), 12/23/01.

166   **"I asked Osama":** Mir quoted in Georgie Anne Geyer, "Reporting on Terrorist Can Be Deadly," http://sentinelsource.com, 6/28/09, but see Bergen, *OBL I Know*, 319, corr. Peter Bergen, 2010. The only other post-9/11 interview bin Laden gave was for television, with Taysir Alluni of Al Jazeera. Alluni was later arrested in his home country, Spain, on charges of supporting al Qaeda, and not released until 2005.

Only in 2007, on an audiotape that a U.S. official judged authentic at the time would bin Laden clearly admit responsibility for 9/11. The voice believed to be his on the tape said, "The events of Manhattan were retaliation against the American-Israeli alliance's aggression against our people in Palestine and Lebanon, and I am the only one responsible for it. The Afghan people and government knew nothing about it. America knows that" (Alluni: ed. Lawrence, 106–, 139–; 2007 tape: msnbc.com, 11/29/07).

CHAPTER 15

This is a transitional chapter, and the majority of episodes described in it will be more fully covered and sourced in later chapters. For that reason, there is reference in the sources below only to points that will not be covered elsewhere.

167   **"Without conspiracy"/"Official answers":** *Nation*, 5/31/02, 7/12/02.

168   **"No one has taken":** Richard Falkenrath, "The 9/11 Commission Report: a Review Essay," *International Security*, Vol. 29, No. 3, Winter 04/05, Shenon, 392, 438n, & see *CounterPunch*, 2/23/08, *WP*, 7/13/08. The rather larger death toll figure of 2,973, used by the authors in the Prologue, was the official figure as of 2011.

168–69   **"Why did":** int. of Patrick Leahy by Amy Goodman, www.democracynow.org, 9/29/06; **"As each day":** *NYT*, 10/26/03; **"officials from FAA":** Statement of Bogdan Dzakovic, 5/22/03, CO; **half summaries/"encouraged"/no drive:** Farmer, 98–, Staff Statement 3, CO; **"bad feeling":** *Chicago*, 3/11; **"I've been with":** *New York Observer*, 6/20/04.

169   **"September the 11th":** ABC News, 12/19/02. The fellow agent was John Vincent, the assistant U.S. attorney Mark Flessner. The 9/11 Commission did not interview any of the three.

169–71   **"more than":** Phoenix, Squad 16 to Counterterrorism, 7/10/01, www.justice.gov; **"well-managed":** *WP*, 8/21/07; **"no examination":** Executive Summary, "Report on

CIA Accountability with Respect to the 9/11 Attacks," Office of the Inspector General, Central Intelligence Agency, 6/05; **"points"/"Both the CIA":** Graham with Nussbaum, xv; **irritated:** Tenet, 169.

172   **Mossad:** The Mossad—more formally the Institute for Intelligence and Special Operations—can and does operate all over the world, emboldened by the knowledge that the United States is Israel's staunch ally and protector. Mossad's audacity was exemplified as recently as 2010, when its operatives were caught using the forged passports of several other nations in the course of a hit on a Hamas leader in Dubai.

The full extent of Israeli and U.S. liaison on intelligence, however, is a foggy area. Days after 9/11, the *Telegraph* newspaper in the U.K., citing a "senior Israeli security official," reported that "two senior experts" with Mossad had been sent to Washington in August to warn that a large terrorist cell was "preparing a big operation." The *Los Angeles Times* picked up the story, only to amend it within days and publish a CIA denial that there had been such a warning.

The authors looked at specific episodes that have been taken to suggest Israeli intelligence activity within the United States at the time. One occurred on the morning of 9/11, when a woman in a New Jersey apartment across the river from Manhattan telephoned the police. She had seen below her a group of men, on the roof of a van, shooting video footage of the burning Trade Center and—she thought—celebrating. Film taken from the men's camera, sources said later, did appear to show them "smiling and clowning around." The onlooker who called the police reported the van's registration number, noting that it was marked "Urban Moving Systems."

Arrested that afternoon, the men with the van turned out to be five young Israelis. They were held for more than two months, questioned repeatedly, and eventually deported back to Israel. Their boss, Dominic Suter, also an Israeli, abruptly left the United States soon after the attacks. Two of the men, it was later reported, had been Mossad operatives and one—Paul Kurtzberg—said he had previously worked for Israeli intelligence in another country.

Former CIA counterterrorism chief Vincent Cannistraro told ABC News that—though the men "probably" did not have advance knowledge of 9/11—there was speculation in U.S. intelligence that Urban Moving was a front for spying on "radical Islamics in the area." Available information indicates that the Israelis had been living and working in New Jersey within a few miles of locations where Hazmi, Mihdhar, and four other members of the hijacking team had spent from spring to midsummer.

A study by lawyer Gerald Shea, submitted to the 9/11 Commission and the Senate and House Intelligence Committees, drew attention to the odd activities in 2000 and 2001 of more than a hundred Israelis—working in groups of eight to ten across the United States, who had represented themselves as art students peddling artwork. Because the "students" were repeatedly noticed at Drug Enforcement Administration offices, DEA Security investigated—and came to suspect the "students" might be involved in organized crime.

Lawyer Shea, though, noted that those identified had primarily operated in Florida—close to the main southern staging area for the hijackers. He suggested in his study that the Israelis' purpose had included "keeping Arab groups in our country under surveillance, including the future hijackers." There is good reason to doubt Shea's theory, however, for the Israeli students also operated in states where the hijackers had not been located.

The puzzling incident of the New Jersey Israelis, however, did deserve serious public examination. Yet the possible role of Israeli intelligence in the 9/11 case—at any level—has been investigated by no official body (Dubai: *NYT,* 2/18/10; "senior Israeli": *Telegraph* [U.K.], 9/16/01, *LAT,* 9/20/01, 9/21/01; men on van: *20/20,* ABC News, 6/21/02—transcript available at www.911myths.com, *Forward*, 2/3/03, *CounterPunch*, 3/07/07; "art students": Gerald Shea, "Israeli Surveillance of the Future Hijackers and FBI Suspects in the Sept. 11 Attacks," Memorandum to the National Commission on Terrorist Attacks Upon the United States et al., 9/15/04. Also, see Justin Raimondo, *The Terror Enigma*, NY: iUniverse, 2003).

172   **"hostile service":** James Risen, *State of War*, NY: Free Press, 2006, 181.

CHAPTER 16

173–75   **"BUSH CALLS"/memorial service, etc./"After all":** int. Ari Fleischer by Scott Pelley, 8/6/02, & by Terry Moran, 8/9/02, "EOP Press Interviews," B1, T3, CF, *NYT*, 9/15/01, "With the President: A Reporter's Story of 9/11," www.rochester.edu; **"hunt down":** CNN, 9/12/01; **"We're gonna":** Sammon, 113; **McWilliams/flag:** "Raising the Flag at the WTC," www.famouspictures.org, "About the Photo," www.groundzerospirit .org, DiMarco, 181fn; **memorial service/"Battle Hymn":** ABC News video at www .youtube.com, int. Condoleezza Rice by Bob Woodward, 10/24/01, "Farmer Misc.," B9, NYC files, CF; **"monumental":** "Remarks by the President," 9/12/01, www.avalon.law .yale.edu. See Note re death toll in sourcing for Preface. Accounts differ on the authorship of the President's speech and the way it developed. Gerson aside, aides involved Bush's counselor Karen Hughes, and speechwriters Matthew Scully and David Frum (*WP*, 1/27/02, "Present at the Creation," *Atlantic*, 9/07, "The President's Story," 9/11/02, www.cbsnews.com, *Nation*, 2/13/03, David Frum, *The Right Man*, NY: Random House, 2003, 142, Michael Gerson, *Heroic Conservatism*, NY: HarperOne, 2007, 69); **war council:** CR, 330; **Muttawakil:** "Defending Bin Laden," www.newsweek.com, 9/11/01; **Taliban propose:** *Foreign Policy Journal*, 8/12/09; **"We're not only":** int. Ari Fleischer by Scott Pelley; **never considered:** int. Condoleezza Rice by Bob Woodward; **ultimatum:** "Bush Delivers Ultimatum," www.unwire.org, 9/21/01; **rejected:** *LAT*, 9/22/01.

175   **Musharraf:** Pervez Musharraf, *In the Line of Fire*, NY: Free Press, 2006, 201–. According to the 9/11 Commission Report, and the 2006 biography of Colin Powell, Musharraf complied with all the U.S. demands. In a memoir the same year, Musharraf said he balked at permitting the U.S. military "blanket overflight and landing rights" and "use of Pakistan's naval ports, air bases and strategic locations on borders." Instead, he wrote, he offered "only a narrow flight corridor" and "only two bases . . . for logistics and aircraft recovery." Deputy Secretary of State Richard Armitage, who delivered the American demands, for his part denied that he had threatened to bomb Pakistan. There was clearly massive pressure, however. In the words of CIA director Tenet, Armitage "dropped the hammer on them" (CR, 331–, Karen DeYoung, *Soldier*, NY: Alfred A. Knopf, 2006, 349, Tenet, 179).

175   **"Need to move":** Notes of Stephen Cambone, 9/11/01, released under FOIA to Thad Anderson, www.outragedmoderates.com; **"I know":** DOD press conference, 9/18/01, www.defenselink.mil; **"urged the President":** CR, 330, 558n34; **OBL/hijackers Saudis:** Staff Report, "Monograph on Terrorist Travel," CO.

175–76   **"do Iraq":** CR, 335, Bob Woodward, *Plan of Attack*, NY: Simon & Schuster, 2004, 26. The need to "do Iraq" is referred to in Ch. 9, p. 87. As noted there, it is not clear whether Rumsfeld spoke of "doing" Iraq on the night of 9/11 or at a meeting the following day. **"Look":** Richard Clarke, 32–, CR, 334 & see Ben-Veniste, 302; **Pressure to act:** CR, 334–, MFR of int. Colin Powell, 1/21/04, CF; **formal order:** Woodward, *Plan of Attack*, 26; **contingency plan:** CR, 335, Testimony of Condoleezza Rice, 4/8/04, CO, & see MFR 04021460, 4/9/04. The most vocal proponent of hitting Iraq was Deputy Defense Secretary Wolfowitz. To Secretary of State Powell, it seemed that "some of his colleagues were trying to use the events of 9/11 to promote their own policy obsessions and settle old scores" (MFR of Colin Powell, 1/21/04, CF, DeYoung, 348–, CR, 335–).

176–77   **Camp David/prayer:** DeYoung, 350–; **"patience":** DOD press conference, 1/9/02, www.defenselink.mil; **Black briefed:** Tenet, 177; **Shelton:** DeYoung, 351–; **"When we're through":** Ron Suskind, *The Price of Loyalty*, NY: Simon & Schuster, 2004, 185; **"comfort food"/"Amazing Grace"/O'Neill:** ibid., 189–; **CIA proposing/Memorandum:** *New Yorker*, 8/17/07, 8/4/03, *NYT*, 9/10/06, 12/15/02, Joseph Margulies, *Guantánamo and the Abuse of Presidential Power*, NY: Simon & Schuster, 2006, 189, CR, 333, "Who Authorized the Torture of Abu Zubaydah," www.huffingtonpost.com, 4/28/09; **"war on terrorism":** *NY Daily News*, 9/17/01, BBC News, 9/16/01; **"war on terror":** Bush address, CNN, 9/20/01.

177–78   **joint session:** The joint session was on September 30. On the 14th, the Congress had passed a resolution authorizing the use of "all necessary and appropriate force against those nations, organizations, or persons he [the President] determines planned, authorized, committed, or aided" the 9/11 attacks "or harbored such organizations or persons." The resolution passed in the Senate by 98 votes to 0, in the House by 420 votes to 1 (Richard Grimmett, "Authorization for Use of Military Force in Response to the 9/11 Attacks," Congressional Research Service); **"I want":** CNN, 9/17/01, int. Dan Bartlett by Scott Pelley, 8/12/02, "Press Interviews of Staff," B1, T3, CF; **"platter":** *Meet the Press*, www.cbsnews.com, 9/16/01; **"Gentlemen":** Gary C. Schroen, *First In*, NY: Ballantine, 2005, 40; **"The mission":** Ron Suskind, *The One Percent Doctrine*, NY: Simon & Schuster, 2006, 21.

178   **British commandos:** The British contingent was from the Special Boat Service, or SBS, similar to the better known SAS—Special Air Service—but drawn largely from the ranks of the Royal Marines. Though specializing in amphibious operations, the unit also operates overland. British and American special units have long collaborated. As for the overall number of operatives initially sent into Afghanistan, the authors have used the figure given by the commander of the Delta Force unit on the ground. Perhaps referring to a total at a somewhat later stage of the operation, Bob Woodward referred in his book *Bush at War* to a larger figure: "about 110 CIA officers and 316 Special Forces personnel" (SBS: "The Special Boat Service," www.hmforces.co.uk, "British Special Forces Member Killed in Afghanistan," *Guardian* [U.K.], 7/2/10, Alastair Finlan, "The [Arrested] Development of UK Special Forces and the Global War on Terror," *Review of International Studies*, Vol. 35, 2009; overall number: Dalton Fury, *Kill bin Laden*, NY: St. Martin's, 2008, xix, Woodward, *Bush at War*, 314).

178   **"This is why":** Schroen, 33; **"Tell them":** Gary Berntsen & Ralph Pezzullo, *Jawbreaker*, NY: Three Rivers, 2005, 289.

178–82   **Dalton Fury:** "Dalton Fury" is the pen name the major used as author of a 2008 book on the operation against bin Laden. While protecting his identity, the media have accepted his authenticity (Fury, 200; major media: e.g., *60 Minutes*, CBS, 10/5/08); **"A cloudy":** Fury, xx; **$100 bills/"Money":** Schroen, 29,38, 88, 93–; **duffel bags:** Fury, 105; **defeat:** Tommy Franks with Malcolm McConnell, *American Soldier*, NY: Regan, 2004, 322; **"God has":** ed. Lawrence, 104; **"great, long-term":** Bergen, *OBL I Know*, 316; **"safe and sound":** ibid., 322; **poor intelligence:** Berntsen & Pezzullo, 156, 108; **Atef:** Hamid Mir, "How Osama Has Survived," www.rediff.com, 9/11/07, bin Ladens & Sasson, 271; **OBL Jalalabad:** *Christian Science Monitor*, 3/4/02, Berntsen & Pezzullo, 239, *Sunday Times* (London), 1/15/09, John Miller & Michael Stone with Chris Mitchell, *The Cell*, NY: Hyperion, 2002, 319, Corbin, 262–; **"Black Widow":** *Newsweek*, 12/10/01, BBC News, 9/27/08; **Towr Ghar:** Fury, 107, "The Caves & Graves of Tora Bora," www .legionmagazine.com, 9/1/03; **"purpose-built":** *The Independent* (U.K.), 11/27/01 & see "The Lair of Bin Laden," www.edwardjepstein.com; **no electricity/water:** bin Ladens & Sasson, 185–; **schoolhouse:** Berntsen & Pezzullo, 253, Fury, 108; **Afghan generals:** e.g., Berntsen & Pezzullo, 272, 275, 280–, Fury, 114–, 124, 129–, 257; **negotiating:**

Berntsen & Pezzullo, 289–, *NYT,* 9/11/05, Fury, 216–, 234, 244; **OBL largesse/sons:** Fury, 209, 108; **"flawed":** Fury, 99, Berntsen & Pezzullo, 213–; **reluctance:** Berntsen & Pezzullo, 277–, 290, 295, 305–, 309, 314, "In the Footsteps of Bin Laden," CNN, 8/23/06; **airpower:** e.g., Berntsen & Pezzullo, 270, 274–, Fury, 170–, 192; **Marine:** Berntsen & Pezzullo, 34–, 283–; **"tall":** ibid., 291; **6´4˝:** "Most Wanted Terrorists," www.fbi .gov; **BLU-82:** description at www.globalsecurity.org, Berntsen & Pezzullo, 291, Fury, 127; **Used on plains:** Berntsen & Pezzullo, 137–; **delivered:** ibid., 295–, Fury, 149–; **BLU-82:** described at www.fas.org, Michael O'Hanlon, "A Flawed Masterpiece," *Foreign Affairs,* 3/02; **"too hot"/"hideous":** "Tora Bora Revisited: How We Failed to Get Bin Laden and Why It Matters Today," Report, U.S. Senate Committee on Foreign Relations, Washington, D.C.: U.S. Government Printing Office, 2009, 7; **movement orders:** Fury, 230.

182   **"victory or death"/"Father":** According to Delta Force leader Fury, bin Laden was overheard saying in desperation, "arm your women and children against the infidel!" His lead bodyguard Abu Jandal has recalled that "all bin Laden's wives knew how to handle weapons. They had taken a military course while al Qaeda was in the Sudan." It seems unlikely, though, that the terrorist leader would have expected young children to take part in the battle (Fury, 233, Nasser al-Bahri [Abu Jandal] with Georges Malbrunot, *Dans l'Ombre de Ben Laden,* Neuilly-sur-Seine, France: Michel Lafon, 2010, 199).

182   **Dec. 13/listened to a voice:** The CIA's Gary Berntsen dated this last intercept as having occurred not on December 13 but the 15th. Fury suggested that bin Laden was overheard once more, a day or so later. What he said, Fury wrote, came over as "more of a sermon than issuing orders" (Fury, 233–, 236–, Berntsen & Pezzullo, 307).

182–83   **devastation:** Fury, 270, 272, Berntsen & Pezzullo, 296; **not a trace/"punched"/ rubble/Exhumations:** Fury, 286, 282, *Newsweek,* 10/31/08; **"real war":** Fury, 293; **"We need":** Berntsen & Pezzullo, 290; **Dailey:** Berntsen & Pezzullo, e.g., 307, 276; **"We have not said":** DOD press conference, 11/8/01, www.defense.gov, & see Franks with McConnell, 388; **skirted discussion:** ibid.

183   **As recently as 2009:** In testimony to the Senate Armed Services Committee, and on the PBS program *Frontline,* Franks suggested that the drive to "get into Tora Bora" came from the Afghan commanders. A decision was made, he said, to support the Afghan operation and to "work with the Pakistanis along the Pakistani border." He declared himself "satisfied with the decision process." CIA's Gary Berntsen has responded by writing that Franks was "either badly misinformed or blinded by the fog of war." Berntsen had made it clear in his reports, he said, that the Afghans were less than keen to attack Tora Bora. General Franks, meanwhile, has also said he had concerns as to the amount of time it would have taken to get U.S. troops into the mountains. He has pointed out, too, most recently in 2009, that relying principally on Afghan ground forces in the field had worked in overthrowing the Taliban ("get into"/"work with": int. Tommy Franks for *Frontline,* www.pbs.org; "satisfied": Testimony of Tommy Franks, U.S. Senate Armed Services Committee, 7/31/02, www.access.gpo.gov; Berntsen: Berntsen & Pezzullo, 290–; concerns: *New Republic,* 12/22/09).

183   **"conflicting":** *New Republic,* 12/22/09 & see *NYT,* 10/19/04, MFR 04021460, 4/9/04. General Michael DeLong, who had been Franks's deputy at CentCom, wrote in his September 2004 memoir that bin Laden "was definitely there when we hit the caves." Then, after Franks had expressed doubt in an October 19 article, he abruptly reversed himself. "Most people fail to realize," DeLong wrote in a November 1 article in *The Wall Street Journal,* "that it is quite possible that bin Laden was never in Tora Bora to begin with." There was a report the same month—citing what Taliban sources had purportedly said at the time—that bin Laden had been "nowhere near Tora Bora" but had sent a decoy there to deceive U.S. intelligence. If the Taliban did make such a claim, there is no good

reason to credit it. If bin Laden was indeed at Tora Bora, the claim was as likely disinformation designed to take pressure off. (For what it is worth, bin Laden himself in a 2003 audiotape spoke of the Tora Bora battle as though he was present.) The intelligence cited by Berntsen and Fury as to bin Laden having been at Tora Bora, on the other hand—information from human sources coupled with voice recognition of intercepted radio conversations—remains persuasive ("was definitely": U.S. Senate, *Tora Bora Revisited*, 8; "Most people": *WSJ*, 11/1/04 & see MFR 04021460 4/9/04, CF; "nowhere near": *CounterPunch*, 11/1/04—citing Kabir Mohabbat; bin Laden: ed. Lawrence, 18–).

183   **"The generals"**: Fury, xxiii–.

183   **"never took"**: *NYT*, 10/19/04. During his 2004 campaign against Bush for the presidency, Senator John Kerry claimed the President "took his eye off the ball, off of Osama bin Laden" (second Bush-Kerry debate, 4/10/08, cbsnews.com); **"get" bin Laden**: Woodward, *Bush at War*, 254, 224, 311, *The Times* (London), 10/14/01; **"going to lose"**: Suskind, *One Percent*, 58–; **"asking"**: Fury, 148; **"obsessed"**: Suskind, *One Percent*, 96, Woodward, *Bush at War*, 338; **"Terror's bigger"**: Bush press conference, http://archives.cnn.com, 3/13/02.

184   **taken Rumsfeld**: Woodward, *Plan of Attack*, 1–; **"Goddamn!"**: ibid., 8 & see Franks, 315; **general pestered**: Woodward, *Plan of Attack*, 31, 36–, 42– & see Michael Gordon & Bernard Trainor, *Cobra II*, NY: Pantheon, 2006, 25–.

184–85   **"a natural"**: *al-Wafd* (Egypt), 12/26/01, citing Pakistan *Observer*, www.opednews.com, Fox News, 12/26/01; **escape/wound**: *Newsweek*, 10/31/08, Fury, 286, *New Republic*, 10/22/07, *NYT*, 9/23/02, Bergen, *OBL I Know*, 334–, U.S. Senate, *Tora Bora Revisited*, 2; **2011 reports/tribes**: *Guardian* (U.K.), 4/26/11, Michael Scheuer, *Osama bin Laden*, NY: Oxford University Press, 2011, 131.

185   **Good evidence/02/03/04**: Not included here as an indication of bin Laden's survival is a videotaped statement shown by Al Jazeera on December 26, 2001. Though that transmission postdated the Tora Bora battle, all one knows for sure—because of a reference in the statement to the bombing "some days ago" of a mosque at Khost—is that it was recorded shortly after November 16. Thus not necessarily after the Tora Bora conflict ended—on December 17 (ed. Lawrence, 151–, U.S. Senate, *Tora Bora Revisited*, 14).

185   **"We agreed"**: Though not all the hijacked flights took off on time on 9/11, they had been scheduled to take off within the same twenty-five-minute period. The authors have in these paragraphs cited letters and tapes attributed to bin Laden, edited by Professor Bruce Lawrence, humanities professor of religion at Duke University, translated by James Howarth, and published in book form.

"Although the question of authenticity inevitably arises whenever a message is released in bin Laden's name," Howarth wrote, the statements in the book had all "been accepted as genuine by a majority of the experts and officials who have examined them." Lawrence and others have cast doubt on the authenticity of other taped statements attributed to bin Laden, allowing for the possibility of forgery for propaganda purposes.

It is not a ridiculous notion, for the CIA is on record as having fabricated film footage. In the late 1950s it arranged for the making of a film purportedly showing President Sukarno of Indonesia in bed with a woman in the Soviet Union. As late as 2003, before the invasion of Iraq, there was discussion about making a video showing Saddam Hussein having sex with a teenage boy. According to a *Washington Post* report, the CIA actually did make a video "purporting to show Osama bin Laden and his cronies sitting around a campfire swigging bottles of liquor and savoring their conquests with boys."

Doubts have been expressed about a videotape released in December 2001, supposedly following its seizure by U.S. troops in Afghanistan. It purports to show bin Laden in conversation the previous month with a visiting sheikh, openly acknowledging his foreknowledge of the 9/11 attack. While there may be other good reasons to doubt the tape's authenticity, the authors suggest that a couple of points made in support of the forgery theory have no validity.

Skeptics noted that the bin Laden figure wears a ring in the video—supposedly out of character for him, perhaps even contrary to religious law. As noted in another chapter, his wife Najwa had given him a ring as a token of her affection just before leaving Afghanistan on the eve of 9/11. He is, moreover, shown wearing a ring in another video accepted as authentic. Bin Laden's son Omar, meanwhile, has scotched the argument that a shot of his father writing with his right hand is a giveaway—as the real Osama was supposedly left-handed. "My father," Omar wrote in 2009, "is right-handed."

That is not to say that the "confession" videotape is necessarily authentic. Professor Lawrence did not use the transcript of it in his published collection on bin Laden, and has reportedly expressed the view that the tape is indeed a fake. No quotations from it have been used in this book (scheduled: CR, 10; ed. Lawrence, 158–244 & see BBC News, 4/15/04, "The Osama bin Laden Tapes," Special Report, undated, www.guardian .co.uk; Sukarno: Interim Report, "Alleged Assassination Plots Involving Foreign Leaders," U.S. Senate Select Committee to Study Govt. Ops with Respect to Intelligence Activities, 94th Cong., 1st Sess., Washington, D.C.: U.S. Govt. Printing Office, 11/20/55, 74n4, Anthony Summers, *Goddess*, NY: Macmillan, 1985, 182; Hussein sex/"purporting": *WP*, 5/25/10; video 12/01: transcript by Defense Dept. cited www.defenselink.mil, *NYT*, 12/14/01; not ring: e.g., Griffin, *The New Pearl Harbor Revisited*, 209, "Farce: Control of the Village Through Terror," 2/6/07, www.opednews.com; had ring: bin Ladens & Sasson, 282 & see "Confession Video," www.911myths.com; left-handed: David Ray Griffin, *Osama bin Laden*, Gloucestershire, U.K.: Arris, 2009, 30, Bergen, *OBL I Know*, 335; "right-handed": bin Ladens & Sasson, 159–; reportedly expressed: Griffin, *OBL*, 36).

185   **"I knew":** Fury, 286; **"This was where":** *National Geographic*, 12/04.

Part IV: **PLOTTERS**

CHAPTER 17

189   **phenomenon:** Staff Statement 13, CO, Lawrence Wright, *The Looming Tower*, NY: Alfred A. Knopf, 2006, 176–, CR, 278; **target:** James F. Pastor, *Security Law & Methods*, NY: Butterworth-Heinemann, 2006, 522, 539, Barrett & Collins, 107.

189   **OBL visit to U.S.:** bin Ladens & Sasson, 25–, 302, & see (1981 visit) *New Yorker*, 12/14/08. Though the best, firsthand source, Najwa is not the first to refer to an early bin Laden visit to America. Kahled Batarfi, a boyhood friend, has spoken of the episode, offering details that to some extent conform with Najwa's account. Bin Laden's sometime supervisor at the family construction firm, Walid al-Khatib, said bin Laden made "trips" to America. Allowing for confusion over the date, Khatib's and Najwa's recollections may be corroborated by the account of wealthy Saudi businessman Yassin Kadi. Kadi said he met bin Laden in Chicago in 1981, when the future terrorist leader was recruiting engineers for the family business. Khaled Bahaziq, a boyhood friend of bin Laden who knew Azzam, has recalled that Azzam was "lecturing in America in the 1970s." He certainly visited repeatedly in the 1980s (Batarfi: Bergen, *OBL I Know*, 22, Coll, *Bin Ladens* 209–; Khatib: Coll, *Bin Ladens*, 209–, but see *New Yorker*, 6/30/09, citing Khatib as referring to visiting "once"; Kadi: *NYT*, 12/13/08, Bahaziq: Robert Lacey, *Inside the Kingdom*, London: Hutchinson, 2009, 114–).

190–91   **lectured/led prayers:** Andrew McGregor, "Jihad and the Rifle Alone," *Journal of Conflict Studies* (Univ. of New Brunswick), Fall 2003, Gilles Kepel, *Jihad*, Cambridge, MA: Belknap, 2002, 314, Abdel Bari Atwan, *The Secret History of Al Qaeda*, Berkeley:

Univ. of Calif. Press, 2006, 42, Wright, 95; **third-year:** bin Ladens & Sasson, 25; **"cleric":** Gerald Posner, *Secrets of the Kingdom*, NY: Random House, 2005, 36, Bergen, *OBL I Know*, 92; **"scholar":** e.g., Bergen, *OBL I Know*, int. Jamal Ismael, courtesy Paladin InVision, 2006, "Jihad and the Rifle"; **village overrun:** bin Ladens & Sasson, 29, Bamford, *Pretext*, 98; **"Emir":** e.g., Anouar Boukhars, "At the Crossroads, Saudi Arabia's Dilemma," *Journal of Conflict Studies* (Univ. of New Brunswick), Summer 2006; **jihad:** John Esposito, *Islam*, NY: Oxford Univ. Press, 1998, 20–; **liberate:** Atwan, 73–; **imposing/speaker:** Wright, 95; **Sadat:** Gerald Posner, *Why America Slept*, NY: Ballantine, 2003, 30; **Mohammed/Sayid Qutb:** "Jihad & the Rifle"; Jason Burke, *Al Qaeda*, London: Penguin, 2004, 47, Kepel, 314, ed. Lawrence, xii, Ian Hamel, *L'Énigme Oussama Ben Laden*, Paris: Payot, 2009, 64; **Qutb re Jews:** Sayyid Qutb, *In the Shade of the Qu'ran*, Falls Church, VA: WAMY International, 1995, *WP*, 8/10/10; **read Qutb:** Bergen, *OBL I Know*, 19; **OBL at lectures:** Hamel, 64, Wright, 79–; **Azzam travel:** Lacey, *Inside the Kingdom*, 115, Rohan Gunaratna, *Inside Al Qaeda*, NY: Columbia Univ. Press, 2002, 101, Terry McDermott, *Perfect Soldiers*, NY: HarperCollins, 2005, 96–; **Azzam useful:** corr. Barnett Rubin, 2010, 9/10. *New Yorker*, 3/27/95; McDermott, 96–, eds. *Der Spiegel*, 169, Samuel Katz, *Relentless Pursuit*, NY: Forge, 2002, 38–. Pulitzer Prize–winning author Steve Coll wrote in 2004 that Prince Turki al-Faisal and the GID "became important supporters" of Azzam. In a letter to Coll the following year, however, Turki would claim that "Azzam was never supported by me or the GID." Support for the mujahideen, Turki wrote, was "measured by the ISI [Pakistani intelligence] and then evaluated by both the CIA and G.I.D." ("became": Coll, *Ghost Wars*, 156; "Azzam was": Coll, *Bin Ladens*, 295, 612n21).

191   **GID/CIA liaison:** int. Prince Turki al-Faisal in *Arab News*, 9/18/02, Anthony Cordesman, "Saudi Security & the War on Terror," paper for Center for Strategic & International Studies, 4/22/02, Posner, *Secrets*, 80–, int. Joseph Trento, Joseph Trento, *Prelude to Terror*, NY: Carroll & Graf, 2005, xiii, 100–, Coll, *Ghost Wars*, 79–, press briefing, U.S. Dept. of State, 11/2/07; **Azzam & OBL:** *Arab News*, 11/7/01; **Encyclopedia:** *Time*, 10/21/01, Burke, 3; **"To our much":** Burke, 294n5.

191   **"a man worth":** The authors have here used the translation provided by the Arab satellite TV channel Al Jazeera, but "worthy of a nation" might be more apt. The Arabic word bin Laden used was *"umma"*—which Professor Bruce Lawrence interprets as meaning "the global Islamic community, or Islamic supernation" (Transcript, "Usamah Bin-Ladin, the Destruction of the Base," Al Jazeera, 6/10/99 & see ed. Lawrence, 4fn4, 77).

191   **found al Qaeda:** Wright, 129–; **economics:** bin Ladens & Sasson, 29.

191   **"God Almighty":** transcript, "Usamah bin-Ladin, The Destruction of the Base," Al Jazeera, 6/10/99.

191   **1377 hegira:** Year 1 hegira relates to the year the Prophet Mohammed moved from Mecca to the city of Medina in—Western style—A.D. 622. The February 15 birth date is taken from the 2009 book by bin Laden's first wife, Najwa, and her son Omar. Bin Laden himself said he thought he was born in the Islamic month that corresponds to January 1958. Other birth dates offered have included March 10, June 30, and July 30, 1957. The author who studied the family in greatest depth, Steve Coll, notes that most Saudis did not note birth dates. The Saudi government was not keeping records at the time bin Laden was born (hegira: ed. Lawrence, x; Feb. 15: bin Ladens & Sasson, 301; himself: Coll, *Bin Ladens*, 74; other birth dates: AP, 3/11/07, Jean-Charles Brisard & Guillaume Dasquié, *Forbidden Truth*, NY: Thunder's Mouth, 2002, 226, German Nachrichtendienst note seen by authors).

191–2   **full name/al-Qatani:** bin Ladens & Sasson, 301; **"Lion":** e.g. entry, Muslim Internet Dictionary.

192   **"I was named":** transcript, int. of OBL, ABC News, 1/2/99, & see "Usama's Expedi-

tion," www.al-islam.org. According to Bin Laden's son Omar, "Ossama Binladen" is the more correct rendering. U.S. officialese, meanwhile, frequently renders the first name as "Usama." The authors use "Osama bin Laden" because that is the version most commonly used in Western publications. Variations arise as a result of transliteration from the Arabic (bin Ladens & Sasson, 291 & re "Usama" e.g., "Most Wanted List," www.fbi .gov).

192   **"My father"**: transcript, "Usmah bin-Laden, Destruction of the Base." The exact year of Mohamed bin Laden's birth remains unknown, but he was apparently born in the first decade of the twentieth century. Family biographer Steve Coll writes that he was fourteen or fifteen when he arrived in Saudi Arabia, while author Lawrence Wright reckoned he was twenty-three (Coll, *Bin Ladens*, 26, 583n11, Wright, 62, & see bin Ladens & Sasson, 292).

192   **Mohamed legend/rise, etc.**: For the historical background of the bin Ladens' early lives, the authors have, except where indicated, drawn on Steve Coll's definitive study, *The Bin Ladens*, and on Lawrence Wright's authoritative *The Looming Tower.*

192–93   **memory**: Wright, 65; **Mohamed/Saudi royals/loan**: Wright, Simon Reeve, *The New Jackals*, London: André Deutsch, 1999, 158–, Atwan, 40–; **"Religion"**: Coll, *Bin Ladens*, 201; **Religion/royalty/banning/Wahhabism**: Stephen Schwartz, *The Two Faces of Islam*, NY: Doubleday, 2002, 69–, 261, Posner, *Secrets*, 18–, Lacey, *Inside the Kingdom*, 10–, Yaroslav Trofimov, *The Siege of Mecca*, NY: Doubleday, 2007, 13–, 16, Wright, 63; **"fascism"**: Schwartz, 105; **beheading/crucifixion**: Amnesty International, "Reported Death Sentences and Executions 2009," 3/10, John R. Bradley, *Saudi Arabia Exposed*, NY: Palgrave Macmillan, 2006, 144, Reuters, 2/22/09, Mark Hollingsworth with Sandy Mitchell, *Saudi Babylon*, Edinburgh: Mainstream, 2006, 62, 228, UPI, 11/4/09, Amnesty International, "Man Beheaded & Crucified," 6/1/09, AP, 8/19/10; **Human rights**: *Economist*, 7/25/09, AFP, 7/23/09; **Women**: Lacey, *Inside the Kingdom*, 277, Qanta A. Ahmed, *In the Land of Invisible Women*, Naperville, IL: Source Books, 2008, refs.; **Mohamed devout/"Your highness"**: transcript, int. OBL by Hamid Mir, 3/19/97, translated by FBIS, bin Ladens & Sasson, 17, Craig Unger, *House of Bush, House of Saud*, London: Gibson Square, 2007, 91.

193   **Osama product:** Osama told an interviewer he was one of twenty-five sons fathered by Mohamed bin Laden. Author Coll refers to twenty-five sons and twenty-nine daughters. Osama's son Omar believes Osama was the eighteenth of twenty-two sons. The total number of Mohamed's offspring must remain approximate (int. of OBL by Hamid Mir, 3/18/97, translation by FBIS, Coll, *Bin Ladens*, 126–, bin Ladens & Sasson, 292).

193–95   **short marriage/Allia:** bin Ladens & Sasson, 291–, Atwan, 41–, Wright, 72; **"a shocking"**: bin Ladens & Sasson, 169; **remarried/loved "more"**: Wright, 73, Atwan, 41, bin Ladens & Sasson, 166; **"In my whole"/"when he met"**: bin Ladens & Sasson, 190, 168–, 40, Bergen, *OBL I Know*, 17; **"Most of us"**: *Evening Standard* (U.K.), 5/26/06; **"very anti-Israel"**: Bergen, *OBL I Know*, 7–, Unger, *House of Bush, House of Saud*, 91, *Der Spiegel*, 6/6/05; **bellicose noises/tanks**: John Ciorciari, "Saudi-US Alignment After the Six-Day War," *Middle East Review of International Affairs*, Vol. 9, No. 2, 6/05, David Holden & Richard Johns, *The House of Saud*, NY: Holt, Rinehart & Winston, 1981, 251–. This according to the Pakistani editor Hamid Mir, citing one of his interviews with Osama bin Laden (Bergen, *OBL I Know*, 7–); **father/10,000**: Coll, *Bin Ladens*, 128, Gunaratna, 17; **"right arm"**: transcript, int. OBL by Hamid Mir, 3/19/97; **$1 billion**: as calculated at www.measuringworth.com; **present/cars**: bin Ladens & Sasson, 20, 169–; **"shy . . . aloof," etc.**: Atwan, 41, Coll, *Bin Ladens*, 138–, Bergen, *OBL I Know*, 8, *In the Footsteps of Bin Laden*, CNN, 8/23/06; **Quaker school Beirut/Saudi school**: Coll, *Bin Ladens*, 140–, Wright, 75. Published reports have suggested that later, as a teenager, bin Laden indulged in Beirut's fabled nightlife. That seems out of character, and family biographer Coll concludes that such stories are mere rumor. They may reflect confusion with one of Osama's siblings (reports: e.g., see Rex Hudson, *The Sociology & Psychology of Terrorism*, Washington: Federal Research Division, Library of Congress, 1999, 117, Reeve, 159–, rumor: Coll, *Bin Ladens*, 141); **"extraordinarily"/"not very"/mediocre:** Bergen, *OBL I Know*, 8–; **"normal":** Wright, 75; **"No calculator":** bin Ladens & Sasson, 42; **"top fifty":** Bergen, *OBL I Know*, 8; **taller:** Bergen, *OBL I Know*, 8, 214, Wright, 83; **soccer/movies/bully:** *In the Footsteps of Bin Laden*, CNN, 8/23/06. Coll, *Bin Ladens*, 141, Lacey, *Inside the Kingdom*, 57, Bergen, *OBL I Know*, 13–.

195–97 **Syria/camping/"soft-spoken"/"unanticipated"/wedding/"so conservative"/married life/11 children:** bin Ladens & Sasson, 8–, 12–, 17, 19–, 22, 25, 270, Bergen, *OBL I Know*, 17; **arduous work:** Scheuer, *Osama bin Laden*, 35; **shaking hands, etc./rules:** Bergen, *OBL I Know*, 20–, 14–, bin Ladens & Sasson, 19–, 41, Carmen bin Ladin, *The Veiled Kingdom*, London: Virago, 2004, 76, 91, *Le Monde*, 10/13/02, Wright, 75–; **"Around 18 or 19":** "Dateline," NBC, 7/10/04; **"His family":** Carmen bin Ladin, 77; **"following the example":** Bergen, *OBL I Know*, 22; **economics:** transcript, int. OBL by Hamid Mir, 3/18/97, Bergen, *OBL I Know*, 16, bin Ladens & Sasson, 29; **"I was almost":** Bergen, *OBL I Know*, 16; **Osama no longer:** ibid., 16, 21, Wright, 77, bin Ladens & Sasson, 187; **"impassioned":** bin Ladens & Sasson, 22; **Syrian teacher/Muslim Brotherhood/ Qur'an:** Coll, *Bin Ladens*, 144–, Lacey, *Inside the Kingdom*, 59–, Wright, 78; **wept re Palestine:** Wright, 75–; **"religious chants":** Bergen, *OBL I Know*, 15; **'73 war/embargo:** Hollingsworth with Mitchell, 93–, 98, Dore Gold, *Hatred's Kingdom*, Washington, D.C.: Regnery, 2003, 84–; **new century:** Peter L. Bergen, *Holy War Inc.*, NY: Free Press, 2001, 48.

198 **toppling monarchy Iran:** Iran, of course, ascribes overwhelmingly not to the Sunni but the Shia branch of Islam. The former predominates in Saudi Arabia; **"For forty years":** int. OBL by Hamid Mir, 3/18/97.

198 **Mahdi/Grand Mosque seizure:** Trofimov, refs. & see esp. 46–, 66–, 69–, 160–. During the siege, according to Jamal Khashoggi, Osama and his half-brother Mahrouz were arrested on suspicion of involvement, but released. Osama's friend Batarfi said Osama had thought it crazy to "seize the holiest place in Islam, then bring in weapons and kill people." An Afghan journalist, on the other hand, has quoted him as saying that the men who seized the mosque were "innocent of any crime . . . true Muslims" (arrested: Trofimov, 247, Wright, 94; Batarfi: Lacey, *Inside the Kingdom*, 59; Afghan journalist: Burke, *Al-Qaeda*, 57, 41).

198 **40,000/100,000:** "The 1978 Revolution & the Soviet Invasion," www.globalsecurity .org; **terrible conflict:** Coll, *Ghost Wars*, 49–.

199 **"My father":** Bergen, *Holy War Inc.*, 52; **"I was put":** bin Ladens & Sasson, 176; **"the nightmare":** *Mail on Sunday* (U.K.), 12/23/01.

CHAPTER 18

201 **Badeeb:** Coll, *Bin Ladens*, 248–; **"decent":** ibid., 249, citing Badeeb int. Orbit TV, 2001; **Turki:** profile at www.saudiembassy.net; **GID/CIA liaise:** Coll, *Ghost Wars*, 79–, Wright, 99; **shuttling/ISI/worked together:** ibid., 82–.

201 **"When the invasion":** *The Independent* (U.K.), 12/6/03, Scheuer, *Osama Bin Laden*, 49. Some historians doubt that bin Laden involved himself in the Afghan episode as promptly as he claimed, but there is no special reason to question his account. One can speculate that his early visit or visits, to Pakistan rather than Afghanistan itself, were made at bin Laden's initiative—and triggered GID's decision to use him.

202 **"To confront":** *France-Soir*, 8/27/98, citing int. of 1995; **Turki admitted:** *Arab News*, 11/7/01, & see int. Turki al-Faisal, "Inside the Kingdom," www.pbs.org; **"had a strong":** Coll, *Bin Ladens*, 295–, citing Badeeb int. Orbit, TV, 2001; **"He was our":** Coll, *Ghost*

Wars, 87; **"to provide"**: Ahmed Rashid, *Taliban*, New Haven: Yale Univ. Press, 2000, 131, int. of Robert Fisk, 3/5/07, www.democracynow.org; **spread/cultivate:** Coll, *Bin Ladens*, 250–; **"will not end"**: Bergen, *Holy War*, 53; **Saudi support/Azzam's request:** Coll, *Bin Ladens*, 254, 282, bin Ladens & Sasson, 51.

203   **Beit al-Ansar:** Rashid, *Taliban*, 13, Bergen, *OBL I Know*, 29, Wright, 103–, Coll, *Bin Ladens*, 256. While the building in Pakistan was "Beit" [Place of] al-Ansar, the apartment used in Germany by Mohamed Atta and his comrades was known by them as "Dar" [House of] al-Ansar. Translations vary—e.g. House of the Supporters v. House of the Followers (CR, 164, 495n82, Fouda & Fielding, 108).

203   **Azzam toured:** Bergen, *OBL I Know*, 33, John Cooley, *Unholy Wars*, London: Pluto, 2002, 69–; **Azzam "enlisted":** corr. Barnett Rubin, 2010, *New York*, 3/27/95.

203   **CIA ratcheted/deniability/Pakistan control/ISI:** Cooley, xvii, 41–, 64–, 69, 87–, Bergen, *Holy War*, 63–, 54, Rashid, *Taliban*, 129–, 184, 248. Veteran intelligence officer Vincent Cannistraro, who was involved in Afghan policy at the time, has said that only half a dozen CIA officers—"administrators"—served in Pakistan at any one time. Milton Bearden, who was station chief in the Pakistani capital, said the agency "did not recruit Arabs." More obliquely, Bearden has said he "stayed pretty much away from the crowd of Gulf Arabs who were doing the fund-raising. . . . They were not a major part of the war." He also said, "We knew who bin Laden was back then." (Cannistraro: Bergen, *Holy War Inc.*, 65; Bearden: Coll, *Ghost Wars*, 155, *BG*, 9/23/01).

203   **officers trained/Special Forces:** Cooley, 13, 21, 64, 67–, 70, 75–. *Jane's Defence Weekly* reported that Pakistani ISI operatives received instruction from "Green Beret commandos and Navy Seals in various U.S. training establishments." (*Jane's Defence Weekly*, 9/14/01; **cash went/collaborate OBL:** Bergen, *Holy War Inc.*, 68–, Cooley, 47, Rashid, *Taliban*, 132–; **Springmann:** transcript of int. Michael Springmann, 7/3/02, www.bt internet.com, "Newsnight," 11/6/01, http://news.bbc.co.uk, Michael Springmann, "The Hand that Rules the Visa Machine Rocks the World," *Covert Action Quarterly*, Winter 01.

203–4   **"former CIA"/"U.S. emissaries":** Reeve, 167, 176n33. Another allegation linking bin Laden to the CIA, however, is certainly unreliable. The author Jim Marrs reported a claim that bin Laden, under the name "Tim Osman," was brought to America in 1986 to meet government agents. According to Marrs, the meeting was "confirmed" by one of those present, a former FBI agent named Ted Gunderson. Gunderson, however, has made other entirely bizarre assertions (Marrs, 103,415n103, www.tedgunderson.net); **OBL "was a product":** *Guardian* (U.K.), 7/8/05; **"I created":** *France-Soir*, 8/27/98, citing int. of 1995; **"Personally":** *The Independent* (U.K.), 12/6/96.

204–7   **"The Saudi government":** transcript of int. OBL of 10/21/01, CNN, 2/5/02; **Najwa overheard/helicopter/"stop thinking":** bin Ladens & Sasson, 32–; **Jaji/running:** Bergen, *OBL I Know*, 55, *In the Footsteps of Bin Laden*, CNN, 8/23/06; **Lion's Den:** Scheuer, *Osama bin Laden*, 61; **bravery:** int. Huthaifa Azzam, 2006, courtesy Paladin InVision; **crying:** Bergen, *Holy War Inc.*, 12; **"thirst":** Wright, 106; **"martyrdom":** ibid., *The Independent* (U.K.), 12/6/93; **"requires":** Coll, *Bin Ladens*, 255–; **"As Muslims":** *The Independent* (U.K.), 12/6/93; **Russian pullout/new phase:** Wright, 137, Coll, *Bin Ladens*, 334, Coll, *Ghost Wars*, 184–; **Jalalabad/"took charge":** Bergen, *OBL I Know*, 87–, Coll, *Bin Ladens*, 340; **disagreements:** Bergen, *OBL I Know*, 62–, 68, Coll, *Bin Ladens*, 304, Wright, 112; **Azzam death:** bin Ladens & Sasson, 78, Bergen, *OBL I Know*, 92–; **hero/ Abdullah/feted/talks:** Posner, *Why America Slept*, 44, Lacey, *Inside the Kingdom*, 123, Posner, *Why America Slept*, 45, bin Ladens & Sasson, 73; **back to work:** "The Sociology & Psychology of Terrorism," Federal Research Division, Library of Congress, 9/99, 117–, Rashid, *Taliban*, 133; **wives/"his aim":** bin Ladens & Sasson, 49–; **jokes:** Bergen, *OBL I Know*, 47, *Telegraph* (U.K.), 7/23/07; **"I have":** ibid.; **children/divorce/ annulment, etc.:** bin Ladens & Sasson, 301–; **"I never":** Bergen, *OBL I Know*, 26; **"a good"/"corrupted"/forbade/milk/"We were"/"live just"/asthma/"From the time": bin Ladens & Sasson, 42–, 54, 60–; **"how to be":** Bergen, *OBL I Know*, 26; **Abdullah war zone:** bin Ladens & Sasson, 77, 305; **"like a":** Coll, *Ghost Wars*, 153 & see Miller & Stone, 185, int. of Fouad Ajami, 2006, courtesy of Paladin InVision; **"still, silent":** *Canada Free Press*, 9/14/06, www.mail-archive.com.

207   **CIA thought:** Coll, *Ghost Wars*, 182–.

207   **"tactical alliance"/"In our struggle":** *France-Soir*, 8/27/98, citing int. of 1995. During the anti-Soviet conflict, bin Laden appeared grateful for the American contribution—in private. "In the mid-eighties," Saudi Arabia's Prince Bandar, who was his country's ambassador to the United States, told CNN's Larry King, "he came to thank me for my efforts to bring the Americans, our friends, to help us against the atheists" (*Larry King Live*, CNN, 10/1/01).

207   **"Every Muslim":** ed. Lawrence, 87.

208   **Rohrabacher:** speech, 5/5/04, *USA Today*, 9/18/01. Rohrabacher, a Republican who was elected to Congress in 1989, is a controversial figure. Given the corroborative accounts that follow, however, this story about bin Laden is credible (controversial: e.g., "Rogue Statesman," www.ocweekly.com, 9/5/02, *Telegraph* (U.K.), 9/13/08); **Girardet:** *National Geographic*, 12/1/01, *In the Footsteps of Bin Laden*, CNN, 8/23/06; **Simpson:** John Simpson, *Simpson's World*, NY: Miramax, 2003, 82–, *Telegraph* (U.K.), 9/16/01, Bergen, *Holy War Inc.*, 65.

209   **"vanguard"/"al qaeda":** Bergen, *OBL I Know*, 75, Gunaratna, 3–; **discussed plans:** "TAREEKHOSAMA/50/Tareekh Osama," minutes of meeting 8/11/88, INTELWIRE, Coll, *Bin Ladens*, 336–, Bergen, *OBL I Know*, 74–, Wright, 131–, Burke, 1–, ed. Lawrence, 108.

209–10   **never heard/first used:** Flagg Miller, *"Al-Qaeda* as a 'Pragmatic Base,' " *Language & Communications*, Vol. 28, 2008, "On 'The Summit of the Hindu Kush': Osama bin Laden's 1996 Declaration of War Reconsidered," speech by Flagg Miller, supplied to authors, int. Huthaifa Azzam, 2006, courtesy Paladin InVision. Only in 1996 did a CIA report refer to "al-Qaeda." The word was first used by the State Department in 1998 (ed. Lawrence, 108fn); **"He rang":** Lacey, *Inside the Kingdom*, 148; **"playing":** Rashid, *Taliban*, 129; **"I mentioned":** Benazir Bhutto, *Daughter of the East*, London: Simon & Schuster, 2008, 410. Bhutto said she first heard of bin Laden in 1989, when told he had bribed members of parliament to vote against her in a no-confidence motion. In 2008, after Bhutto's assassination, a newspaper editor in Pakistan claimed to have been present when bin Laden tried to bribe then–Pakistan Muslim League party leader—later prime minister—Nawaz Sharif to see that the no-confidence motion was tabled. The newspaper editor had reportedly himself been prosecuted on a separate matter, and the authors have seen no corroboration of this allegation (Bhutto, 405–, Bergen, *Holy War Inc.*, 61, Coll, *Ghost Wars*, 212, *Daily Frontier Post* [Pakistan], 7/1/01, & see Reeve, 171, 179).

210–11   **Zawahiri:** Wright, 128, 139–, Bergen, *OBL I Know*, 203, 319–, int. Huthaifa Azzam, 2006, courtesy PaladinInVision; **Rahman:** bin Ladens & Sasson, 130–, Wright 138, Bergen, *OBL I Know*, 68; **Mohammed:** McDermott, 121, *Financial Times*, 2/15/03, Bergen, *OBL I Know*, 300; **Yousef:** Reeve, 120, Miller & Stone, 78, *Newsday*, 4/16/95, Bergen, *Holy War Inc.*, 138; **Atta:** McDermott, 15–, CR, 160; **Hanjour/Jarrah/Shehhi:** eds. *Der Spiegel*, 253–, McDermott, 50, *The Independent* (U.K.), 9/16/01; **"concerned, sad":** Wright, 75–.

211   **"to reclaim":** Bergen, Scheuer, *OBL I Know*, 15, *Osama bin Laden*, 77. Suggestions that Palestine was not an issue for bin Laden do not appear well founded. It appears true, however, that he neither directed terrorist attacks on Israeli targets nor supplied funds to Palestinian groups. The Palestinian author and journalist Abdel Bari Atwan, who interviewed him in 1996, said Palestine "wasn't actually No. 1 on his agenda . . . he wasn't really that

informed about Palestine. He didn't like Yasser Arafat . . . maybe because he was involved with the Soviets . . . used to be considered an unbeliever." For obvious reasons, organizations like Hamas and Islamic Jihad have been careful not to associate their groups with bin Laden (not a genuine: e.g., Gold, 10; Atwan: int., 2007; Hamas, etc.: Burke, 12).

211   **boycott:** bin Ladens & Sasson, 61, 110, ed. Lawrence, 115; **not drink:** bin Ladens & Sasson, 60, Bergen, *OBL I Know*, 39.

211   **"The Americans":** ed. Lawrence, 115. Recalling this speech in an interview after 9/11, bin Laden said it occurred in 1986. Author Lawrence Wright, in his book *The Looming Tower*, cites a speech with almost identical wording that he made in 1990. That speech did not mention Palestine (ed. Lawrence, 115, Wright, 151, 405n); **time and again:** e.g., ed. Lawrence, 9, 36, McDermott, 253–, CBS News, 5/16/08.

211   **"America allowed"/"The idea":** Lawrence, 239. Then–U.S. secretary of state Alexander Haig was to insist that the United States was not a party to the Israeli invasion. Others, including the military correspondent for Israel's *Ha'aretz* newspaper, have said Washington gave Israel "the green light" (Haig: *Business Week*, 2/20/10; others: *Foreign Policy*, Spring 1983, Fisk, *The Great War*, 1037); **"The events":** MSNBC, 11/29/07.

CHAPTER 19

212–15   **stocked up/despised Saddam/"will attack":** bin Ladens & Sasson, 79–, Coll, *Bin Ladens*, 373, Bergen, *OBL I Know*, 179; **"The defense":** David Ottoway, "The U.S. and Saudi Arabia Since the 1930s," *Foreign Policy Research Institute*, 8/09; **"If you ask":** William Simpson, *The Prince*, NY: Regan, 2006, 205; **delegation:** ibid., 209–, Richard Clarke, 57–; **"flooding":** H. Norman Schwarzkopf with Peter Petre, *It Doesn't Take a Hero*, NY: Bantam, 1992, 353; **"This is something":** int. Prince Amr ibn Mohammad al-Faisal, *Frontline:* "House of Saud," www.pbs.org; **religious study/"the last":** excerpts, *Frontline:* "Saudi Time Bomb," www.pbs.org; **Committee raids:** Felice Gaer et al., "Report on Saudi Arabia," U.S. Commission on International Religious Freedom, Washington, D.C., 5/2/03; **Censors:** bin Ladin, 63; **hall/phone recordings:** *New Yorker*, 1/5/05; **Bible:** *WSJ*, 5/20/05; **"The unbelievers":** ed. Nina Shea, "Saudi Publications on Hate Ideology Invade American Mosques," Center for Religious Freedom, Washington, D.C., 1/28/05; **debate/Abdullah urged:** Rachel Bronson, *Thicker than Oil*, NY: Oxford Univ. Press, 2006, 194, Posner, *Secrets*, 135–; **"Okay":** William Simpson, 209; **female soldiers/entertainers/carols/Sabbath/Bibles/Ramadan:** Schwarzkopf, 386–, 430, 461–, William Simpson, 225–; **"Pollution":** bin Ladens & Sasson, 84; **OBL meetings/Sultan/"kept asking":** MFR 04019365, 2/24/04, Snell et al. to Zelikow, "Summary of Interviews Conducted in Saudi Arabia," 2/25/04, CF, *Arab News*, 11/7/01, bin Ladens & Sasson, 82–, ed. Lawrence, 257; Prince Sultan is the father of long-time Saudi ambassador to the U.S. Prince Bandar (William Simpson, 12); **"didn't care":** MFR 04019365, 2/24/04; **"Don't call":** transcript, *Frontline:* "House of Saud," 11/23/04, www.pbs.org; **OBL outraged/ "colony":** bin Ladens & Sasson, 83–; **5,000 remained/bases:** Alfred Prados, "Saudi Arabia, Current Issues and U.S. Relations," Foreign Affairs, Defense & Trade Division, Congressional Research Service, Washington, D.C., 9/15/03, "Desert Stronghold," *Air Force Magazine*, 2/99, BBC News, 4/29/03.

215   **groundswell:** *NYT*, 3/7/04, Gold, 161, **Yemen:** int. of Abdul Bari Atwan for Paladin-InVision, 2006, Miller & Stone, 158–, Lacey, *Inside the Kingdom*, 155; **passport/movements:** Lacey, *Inside the Kingdom*, Atwan, 161; **cleared:** CR, 57; **"One day"/business:** bin Ladens & Sasson, 85; **conference:** Coll, *Ghost Wars*, 231–; **"We didn't say":** int. Prince Bandar bin Sultan, *Frontline:* "Looking for Answers," www.pbs.org.

216   **"the U.S. government":** Coll, *Ghost Wars*, 231. Bin Laden himself would reportedly claim that, far from the Saudis having asked to protect him, the regime asked the intel-

ligence services in Pakistan—his first stop on leaving his homeland—to kill him. (*NYT*, 1/14/01); **"using the"**: Scheuer, *Osama bin Laden*, 83, 218n27.

216 **"pledge"**: Wright, 161. The PBS *Frontline* program, meanwhile, obtained a document stating that an unnamed bin Laden brother persuaded Naif's younger brother, Deputy Interior Minister Prince Ahmed bin Abdul Aziz, to lift the travel ban while Naif was out of the country (Prince Ahmed: Documents supplied to *Frontline* by an associate of OBL, "Hunting bin Laden," www.pbs.org).

216 **"with help"**: CR, 57. On the purported help from a "dissident" royal family member, the sources the Commission cited were self-confessed 9/11 planner Khalid Sheikh Mohammed and fellow terrorist Tawfiq bin Attash—under interrogation after their capture— and bin Laden associate Jamal al-Fadl, who defected in 1996. (CR, 57, 467n33).

216–18 **"Go to Sudan"**: Reeve, 172; **property**: Bergen, *Holy War Inc.*, 78; **wives/motorcade/ guest**: bin Ladens & Sasson, 94, Burke, 143–; **Khartoum houses/no pictures/auster- ity**: bin Ladens & Sasson, 94–, 107–, 111–, Bergen, *OBL I Know*, 123; **"You know"**: int. Jamal Khashoggi for Paladin InVision, 2006; **no air conditioning**: bin Ladens & Sasson, 115, *Los Angeles Times*, 12/19/09; **no education for girls**: bin Ladens & Sasson, 109–; **more time**: ibid., 96; **"wooden cane"**: ibid., 116; **apoplectic/"Why do"**: ibid., 164; **"My husband"**: bin Ladens & Sasson, 97; **"agriculturalist"**: *The Independent* (U.K.), 12/6/93; **training/plotting**: MFR 04013804, 12/4/04, Staff Statement 15, CO; **"Jihad"**: Burke, 73–; **"every place"**: ed. Lawrence, 49.

219 **Yousef Philippines**: Fouda & Fielding, 94, Maria N. Ressa, *Seeds of Terror*, NY: Free Press, 2003, 26; **Yousef names**: statement by Michael McCurry, U.S. Dept. of State, 7/23/93, Reeve, 112.

219 **"emissary"**: Zachary Abuzza, "Belik Terrorism: The Return of the Abu Sayyaf," Strate- gic Studies Institute, U.S. Army War College, 9/05. The source of the "emissary from bin Laden" quote was Edwin Angeles, a Philippines government agent who penetrated the separatist group. Angeles is variously described as having been an "undercover agent for the Defense Intelligence Group in the Philippines' Defense Department"—pen- etrating the Abu Sayyaf group—or a defector. The Abu Sayyaf group launched some seventy attacks between 1991 and 1995, killed about 136 people and injured hundreds ("Balik-Terrorism. The Return of the Abu Sayyaf," *WT*, 6/5/95, Marites Dañguilan Vitug & Glenda M. Gloria, *Under the Crescent Moon*, Quezon City, Philippines: Ateneo Center for Social Policy, 2000, 198–, 205).

219 **on behalf of Rahman**: *WP*, 6/5/95; **OBL would claim**: ed. Lawrence, 53.

CHAPTER 20

220–21 **twenties/lean/degrees/"hard-working"**: Lance, *1000 Years*, 9, 460n19, *The Times* (London), 10/18/97; **"poised"/languages**: Statement of Thomas Pickard, 4/13/04, CO; **political/"Palestinian"/"the right"**: *The Times* (London), 10/18/97, Reeve, 125, 127, Bergen, *OBL I Know*, 145; **explosives/"Chemist"**: Bergen, *OBL I Know*, Abuzza, "Belik Terrorism"; **phone call**: *U.S. v. Omar Ahmad Ali Abdel Rahman et al.*

221 **"Boom!"**: McDermott, 130. The friend, Abdul Murad, was later to become deeply in- volved in Yousef's plotting and later—once captured—talked at length. The "chocolate" story is from the record of an FBI interview (FBI 302 of int. Abdul Hakim Ali Murad, 5/11/95, "Various Interrogation Reports," B24, T1, CF).

221 **"break"/"exploding"**: *U.S. v. Omar Ahmad Ali Abdel Rahman et al.*, U.S. Court of Ap- peals for the 2nd District, 189 F.3d 88, 8/16/99, "The Muslim Interfaith Charade," 5/6/08, www.militantislammonitor.org, Daniel Benjamin & Steven Simon, *The Age of Sacred Terror*, NY: Random House, 2003, 6–. Heavy with implication as they are, one cannot read too much into the Blind Sheikh's remarks. In captivity, Yousef would insist

that the 1993 World Trade Center bombing was his idea and his alone. His contact Abdul Murad, for his part, would reportedly claim he proposed the bombing—after Yousef asked him to suggest a suitable "Jewish" target (McDermott, 130, Lance, *1000 Years*, 199, Peter Lance, *Triple Cross*, NY: Regan, 2006, 121); **"targeting"**: *Village Voice*, 3/30/93.

221   **flew NY/passports/suspicions/asylum:** Staff Report, "Monograph on Terrorist Travel, CO, *The Times* (London), 10/18/97, MFR 04020564, 3/22/04. The accomplice was Ahmad Ajaj. He would remain incarcerated until Yousef's attempt to bring down the Twin Towers in February 1993, was later tried as an accomplice, and is serving a life sentence (Staff Report, "Monograph on Terrorist Travel," CO).

221   **Al Khifa contact:** The contact at the Al Khifa center was Mahmoud Abouhalima, an Egyptian-born veteran Yousef had reportedly known in Afghanistan. Yousef's principal accomplices in the weeks that followed were Mohammad Salameh, a Palestinian whose grandfather and uncle had served time in Israeli prisons, Nidal Ayyad, a chemical engineer—like Yousef born in Kuwait—and a Jordanian named Eyad Ismoil. There was no hard evidence to implicate Blind Sheikh Omar Abdel Rahman, but he was charged in the summer of 1993 with conspiring with others to commit bombings of other New York landmarks (Reeve, 143, 114, 62, *Village Voice*, 3/30/93, *U.S. v. Omar Ahmad Ali Abdel Rahman et al.*, S5 93 Cr. 181, 1/17/96).

221–23   **Yousef acquired/loaded/rented/escape:** Reeve, 6–, 24–, 36–, Burke, 101; **"largest":** Reeve, 154; **earthquake/"like Christmas tree"/devastation/elevators/dead:** ibid., 10–, 13–, 15; **"Achilles' heel":** *New Yorker*, 3/30/93; **bring down Tower:** *NYT*, 6/9/02, Wright, 178; **"Liberation"/"The American"/"Our calculations"/phoned in:** Lance, *Triple Cross*, 116, Burke, 111, *WP*, 9/13/01.

223   **tracked down/identified:** Reeve, 39–, 42–, 56, *U.S. v. Ramzi Ahmed Yousef et al.*, U.S. Court of Appeals for the 2nd Circuit, 8/01, CR, 72–.

223   **plot new mayhem:** In July 1993, five months after attacking the World Trade Center, Yousef tried to bomb the home of Pakistan's Benazir Bhutto, then a candidate for prime minister. He suffered a serious eye injury when the detonator exploded, and spent months recovering. By early 1994 he was in Thailand and again preparing a bomb attack—on the Israeli embassy. That attack also failed at the last moment, when an accomplice crashed the van carrying the bomb to the target. Yousef mulled attacking President Bill Clinton, either with explosives or a rocket, when he visited Manila in November 1994. The following month, with Pope John Paul due to arrive in the city, he prepared a number of pipe bombs. He and accomplice Abdul Murad had already purchased priest's clothing, Bibles, and crucifixes—as cover for those carrying the bombs to the target—when police raided their bomb factory (see text) (Bhutto: Reeve, 50–, 69, Vitug & Gloria, 231; Thailand: Reeve, 63–; Clinton: Reeve, 76–, CNN, 8/25/98; John Paul: Ressa, 31–, Reeve, 78, 85–).

223   **Pope/"Just some"/"Saeed" arrest:** *WP*, 12/30/01.

224   **tortured/"Agents hit":** Vitug & Gloria, 223, McDermott, 153. The reporters were Marites Dañguilan Vitug, who has reported for *Newsweek* and *The Christian Science Monitor*, and Glenda Gloria, who holds a master's degree in political sociology from the London School of Economics. The reporting cited here is from the award-winning book on the Muslim rebellion in Mindanao, in the eastern Philippines. (Vitug & Gloria, 222–).

224–26   **transcript:** Murad Interrogation, 1/7/95, posted at www.thesmokinggun.com, & see *NY Daily News*, 7/24/96, Ressa, 39–; **Murad/"to blow up"/summoned/disguises/watches:** FBI 302 of int. Abdul Hakim Ali Murad, 5/11/95, "Various Interrogation Reports," B24, T1, CF, Lance, *1000 Years*, 259; **device in theater:** Reeve, 77, Benjamin & Simon, 493, Lance, *1000 Years*, 236–; **Italian/bomb:** Lance, *1000 Years*, 237–, Reeve, 78–; **Murad bomb/Parker pen/"cause":** FBI 302 of int. Abdul Hakim Ali Murad;

United Flight 2: Philippine National Police (PNP) "After Debriefing Report," 1/17/95; **11 airliners/terrorists:** Reeve, 90–, 94–; **"TIMER":** WP, 12/20/01; **airlines alerted/grounded:** Richard Clarke, 93–, MFR 04017178, 11/21/03, Lance, *Triple Cross*, 441; **4,000 could have died:** Reeve, 90.

226   **"BOJINKA":** Khalid Sheikh Mohammed reportedly told CIA interrogators after 9/11 that *bojinka* was not a Serbo-Croatian word for "big bang," as reported—just "a nonsense word he adopted after hearing it on the front lines in Afghanistan." The authors have been unable to pin down a meaning for the word in Serbo-Croat, but there is a Croatian word *bočnica*, meaning "boom" (explosion: *Time*, 1/1/95; loud bang: WP, 5/19/02; big bang: www.FrontPageMagazine.com, 5/20/02; boom: www.eudict.com; "a nonsense": CR, 488n7).

226   **Yousef arrested:** Katz, 162–, 186–, Reeve, 101; **cooperative Bhutto:** John Esposito, *Political Islam*, Boulder: Lynne Rienner, 1997, 150; **face trial:** Reeve, 237; **Found guilty/ "I am":** ibid., 242, CNN, 9/5/96, 11/12/97; **240 years:** NYT, 4/5/03.

226   **helicopter/"See":** Coll, *Ghost Wars*, 272. This exchange has been described several times, with varying details. They are summarized by author Peter Lance in his book *1000 Years for Revenge*, 298, 482n13; **prostrate:** Lance, *1000 Years*, 9–; **mastermind:** Coll, *Ghost Wars*, 273, NYT, 4/12/95—citing *Al Hayat*; **leaders inspired:** Coll, *Ghost Wars*, 272.

226–27   **"substantial":** Staff Statement 15, CO, Peter Lance, *Cover-Up*, NY: Regan, 2004, 209—the staff member was Douglas MacEachin; **camp:** Corbin, 46–, Reeve, 120, Benjamin & Simon, 8, 503n14, *Los Angeles Times*, 9/11/02 & see Evan Kohlmann, "Expert Report I: U.S. v. Oussama Kassir," 3/09; **"emissary":** Abuza, "Balik Terrorism"; **separatist:** *Time*, 6/17/02, Reeve, 136, 156–; **manual:** NYT, 1/14/01, 6/9/02, Lance, *1000 Years*, 110; **calls:** Reeve, 47–, Lance, *1000 Years*, 234; **Beit Ashuhada:** "Summary of Captioned Investigation as of 11/4/01," PENTTBOM, 11/5/01, authors' collection, Cooley, 102, "State Dept. Fact Sheet on Bin Laden," 8/14/96 reprinted in Brisard & Dasquié, 169.

227   **"good friend"/"trenches":** transcript int. of OBL for ABC News, *Frontline*: "Hunting bin Laden," www.pbs.org, Miller & Stone, 138–, 189. The separatist leader with whom Yousef had early contact in the Philippines was Abdurajak Janjalani, the founder of the extremist Abu Sayyaf group. As identified in a previous note, the companion refused admission was Ahmad Ajaj. The Yousef accomplice who had fought with bin Laden was Wali Kahn Amin Shah (Reeve, 136, 156–, CR, 59).

227–28   **Shaikha/"Imagine":** CNN, 11/24/04, 9/24/06, Bergen, *OBL I Know*, 46–, Wright, 97–; **"missionary":** "Mohammad Khalifa's Network in the Philippines," in ed. J. M. Berger, *Mohammed Jamal Khalifa*, Vol. 1, INTELWIRE, 2007; **"philanthropist":** *The Inquirer* (Philippines), 1/22/07, Vitug & Gloria, 208, 213, 235–; **OBL Philippines:** Ressa, 16; **spreading money:** ibid., 27, 73, 107, 227n22, *Christian Science Monitor*, 2/1/02; **introduced Yousef:** Ressa, 108; **left country/police report:** Ressa, 10–, 16; **arrested:** "Memorandum of Points and Authorities in Support for Motion re Return of Property," *Mohammad Jamal Khalifa v. U.S.*, U.S. District Court for the Northern District of California, Cr 95–, in ed. Berger; **phone book:** *U.S. v. Benevolence International Foundation, Inc. et al.*, U.S. District Court for the Northern District of Illinois, 02 CR 0414, 4/29/02, in ed. Berger; **bomb factory:** J. M. Berger, "Mohammad Jamal Khalifa: Life and Death Secrets," 1/31/07, INTELWIRE; **explosives/weaponry:** "In the Matter of Mohammad J. Khalifah, Respondent," U.S. Dept. of Justice, Immigration and Naturalization Service, A29–457–661, 3/10/95, in ed. Berger; *Khalifa*, **entry for OBL:** *U.S. v. Benevolence International Foundation, Inc., et al.*; **card in suitcase/Khalifa alias:** *U.S. v. Benevolence International Foundation Inc., et al.*; **co-conspirator:** ed. Berger, *Khalifa*, iii.

228   **"alleged financier":** JI, Report, 128. The "alleged financier" reference also appears in a post-9/11 FBI report. A CIA investigation, the BBC was reportedly told by an agency

interviewee in 1998, indicated that bin Laden was "Yousef's principal financial backer." The overall story of the way Khalifa was handled by U.S. authorities in 1995 remains complex and unsatisfactorily explained. His U.S. visa had been withdrawn on the ground that he had "engaged in terrorist activity," not in the United States but in Jordan, where he had been convicted in absentia in connection with a bombing campaign. Khalifa was subsequently deported to Jordan, retried, and acquitted—though he admitted that he had known the bombers and sent them funds. Khalifa was then allowed to leave for Saudi Arabia. He claimed in interviews after 9/11, in the face of all evidence to the contrary, that he and bin Laden had been estranged since the war against the Soviets in Afghanistan. Khalifa was killed by unknown assailants in Madagascar in 2007—days after Interpol had forwarded a bulletin on him to U.S. agencies. Relevant Interpol documents are heavily redacted. ("alleged financier": "Summary of Captioned Investigation as of 11/4/01," PENTTBOM, 11/5/01, authors' collection; "Yousef's principal": Vitug & Gloria, 234; "engaged": *Mohammad Jamal Khalifah v. U.S.*, Memorandum of Points and Authorities in Support of Motion for Return of Property, U.S. District Court for the Northern District of California, CR 95–, 3/6/95; in absentia/retried/acquitted: ed. Berger, *Khalifa*, ii–; admitted: *John Doe v. Al Baraka Investment & Development Corporation et al.*, Complaint, U.S. District Court for the District of Columbia; estranged: e.g. CNN, 9/2/07, Wright, 113; killed/Interpol: J. M. Berger, "U.S., Interpol Tracking Khalifa in Days Before Madagascar Murder," 2/16/07, INTELWIRE).

228   **never charged:** ed. Berger, i.

228   **clues/"Zahid":** Miller & Stone, 137, McDermott, 162.

228   **Zahid uncle:** Reeve, 48. Khalid Sheikh Mohammed has long been described as Ramzi Yousef's uncle. The most informative account, by journalist Terry McDermott and colleagues at the *Los Angeles Times*, concludes that he is the brother of Yousef's mother, Hameda. Author Steve Coll writes that the CIA concluded that Mohammed is not only Yousef's uncle, but that the two men's wives are sisters. Absent documentation, the exact nature of their relationship remains elusive—Arabs sometimes use the word "uncle" loosely. Both men were apparently born in Kuwait to immigrant families from the Baluchistan region of southwest Pakistan. "I am Palestinian on my mother's side," Yousef told an Arab newspaper in 1995. "My grandmother is Palestinian" (uncle: e.g. Corbin, 47, Reeve, 91, *Time*, 6/17/02; informative: McDermott, 107–, 128, & see Fouda & Fielding, 88–; wives: Coll, *Ghost Wars*, 326; "I am Palestinian": int. Yousef by Raghida Dergham, *Al Hayat*, 4/12/95 & see *NYT*, 4/12/95).

228   **photos of OBL:** *Financial Times*, 2/15/03.

228   **no sign of either brother:** KSM's brother Zahid spent much of the 1990s in the United Arab Emirates, until being deported in 1998 for involvement with the Muslim Brotherhood. He was working as a business executive in Bahrain as of 2010 (*New Yorker*, 9/13/10).

228–29   **Yousef many calls:** Miller & Stone, 137, NBC News, 10/18/00; **call to KSM:** CR, 147, 488n6; **Tiffany Mansions:** McDermott, 144; **bar girls/phone:** Ressa, 18–; **"Abdul Majid"/met in Pakistan/electronics business/"must have":** FBI 302 of int. Abdul Hakim Ali Murad, 5/11/95, "Various Interrogation Reports," B24, T1, CF, CR, 147; **"I was":** "Verbatim Transcript ISN 10024"; **"idea":** "Substitution for the Testimony of Khalid Sheikh Mohammed," *U.S. v. Zacarias Moussaoui*; **target CIA/WTC:** CR, 153, 491n33.

229   **"plan":** Philippines National Police, "After Debriefing Report," 1/20/95. A 1995 FBI memo refers to Murad's statement about attacking CIA HQ, but cites him as saying he would fly a plane filled with explosives into the building" (*WP*, 6/6/02, Coll, *Ghost Wars*, 278–, Lance, *Triple Cross*, 188, Appendix XI).

230   **Mendoza:** CNN, 9/18/01. Former CIA official and deputy director of the State Department's Office of Counterterrorism, Larry Johnson, has characterized Mendoza's asser-

tions as "bullshit." Contemporary Philippines police reports on the Murad interrogation, Johnson asserted in 2006—publishing copies of some of them—do not reflect questioning of Murad by Mendoza. Nor, he said, do they contain any reference to talk of flying airliners into buildings other than the CIA. Johnson wrote that author Peter Lance, who gave credence to Mendoza's account in his books on 9/11, had been "sold a bill of goods." Johnson, however, is himself a controversial character, said to have been instrumental in spreading a smear story about President Obama's wife, Michelle. He has been mocked for having written a *New York Times* piece stating that "terrorism is not the biggest security challenge confronting the United States"—two months before 9/11 (Larry Johnson, "Peter Lance's Flawed *Triple Cross*,"12/6/06, www.huffingtonpost.com, David Weigel, "Larry Johnson's Strange Trip," 6/24/08, www.prospect.org, Larry Johnson, "Whitey Tapes," 10/21/08, www.noquarterusa.net, *Time*, 6/12/08).

230   **"The targets"**: "Investigating Terror," CNN, 10/20/01, Ressa, 32—citing 9/16/01 int. of Tiglao.

230   **Garcia/"selected targets"**: *Village Voice*, 9/25/01, Rafael Garcia, "Decoding Bojinka," *Newsbreak* (Philippines), 11/15/01, Fouda & Fielding, 99, Lance, *Triple Cross*, 185 & see "Authorities Told of Hijack Risks," AP, 3/5/02. In other versions of his account, Garcia recalled that the computer file also named the Pentagon as a proposed target. "Murad," Garcia wrote, "was to fly the plane that would be crashed into the CIA headquarters." The subject of the computer, and other evidence on it, came up at Yousef's trial in 1996. Defense attorneys sought unsuccessfully to challenge the evidence on the computer, alleging tampering ("Murad": Rafael Garcia, "Decoding Bojinka," *Newsbreak* [Philippines], 11/15/01, *Village Voice*, 9/25/01, Fouda & Fielding, 99; tampering?: *NYT*, 7/18/96, *WP*, 12/6/01).

230–31   **"claims"**: CR, 491n33; **FBI "effectively"**: JI, Report, 9, 101–, 210; **"We shared"/"I believe"**: *Portsmouth Herald*, 3/5/02, CNN, 3/14/02; **Mendoza insisted:** Lance, *1000 Years*, 282; **"We told"/"I still"**: *WP*, 12/30/01.

231–32   **Defense Dept. panel/"Coming"/"It was"**: *WP*, 10/2/01 & see re not in published version "Terror 2000," www.dod.gov.

CHAPTER 21

233–34   **"You need"**: *NYT*, 11/14/09—agent was Daniel Byman; **"manager"**: "Khalid Shaykh Muhammad: Preeminent Source on Al Qa'ida," CIA, 7/13/04, released 2009; **"Khalid"/born Kuwait**: JI, Report, 30, *New Yorker*, 9/13/10; **imam/washed bodies**: Fox News, 3/14/07; **Palestinians**: McDermott, 109; **"so smart"/theater**: *Financial Times*, 2/15/03, *New Yorker*, 9/13/10. KSM studied first at Chowan College, in Murfreesboro, then at North Carolina Agricultural and Technical State University in Greensboro. Also attending the latter college was Ramzi Yousef's brother (New York to Counterterrorism, Charlotte, 6/10/02, FBI 265A-NY-252802, INTELWIRE, CR, 146); **Palestine/prayers/reproach**: New York to Counterterrorism, Charlotte, 6/10/02, FBI 265A-NY-252802, INTELWIRE, CR, 146, McDermott, 115–; **"racist"**: KSM, "Preeminent Source," McDermott, 114–; **1987/Afghan conflict**: CR, 146. During the war, KSM became aide to Abdul Rasool Sayyaf, a former Kabul theology professor and an adherent to a form of Islam similar to the creed practiced in Saudi Arabia. Sayyaf, who lived for some time in Saudi Arabia, had links to bin Laden (Fouda & Fielding, 91); **one brother/two killed**: CR, 488n5, *Financial Times*, 2/15/03; **KSM relatives**: e.g. "KSM: Preeminent Source," Staff Report, "9/11 and Terrorist Travel," CO, *Time*, 5/1/03, Reuters, 2/1/08, *WP*, 4/13/07, **across world/Bosnia**: CR, 488n5, Fouda & Fielding, 97, Al Jazeera, 5/5/03, McDermott, 175; **short/balding**: Fouda & Fielding, 88, *Los Angeles Times*, 9/1/02, "Khaled Shaikh Mohammad," information sheet for Rewards for Justice program, Bureau of Diplomatic Security, U.S. Dept. of State; **employment**: NY to National Security, Bangkok et al., FBI 265A-NY-252802, 7/8/99, INTELWIRE; **Thani:** CR, 147–, 488n5; **indictment:** ibid., 73.

234   **tipped off/assisted flying out:** The circumstances in which KSM was allowed to escape have been told in some detail by former CIA case officer Robert Baer, drawing on information given him in 1997 by former police chief Sheikh Hamad bin Jassem bin Hamad al-Thani, then in exile in Syria. The Qatari fiasco has also been described by Richard Clarke, and—more circumspectly—by former FBI director Louis Freeh (Baer: Robert Baer, *Sleeping with the Devil*, NY: Three Rivers, 2003, 18, 190–, Robert Baer, *See No Evil*, NY: Three Rivers, 2002, 270; Freeh: Statement & Testimony of Louis Freeh, 4/13/04, CO & see CR, 147, 488n5, Staff Statement 5, CO, Bamford, *Pretext*, 164, Coll, *Ghost Wars*, 326–, 631n35).

234–35   **anger:** Richard Clarke, 152–; **$5 million/"Armed"/lookout:** "Mohammad," information sheet, FBI, INS Lookout Notice, 2/13/96, "KSM, FBI-INS Misc. Info.," B11, T5, CF.

235   **"al-Balushi":** CR, 276–. e.g., KSM's nephew Ammar al-Baluchi (also of Baluchi nationality and otherwise known as Ali Abdul Aziz Ali) was allegedly involved in transferring al Qaeda funds to the 9/11 hijackers; another example is senior al Qaeda military commander Abu Faraj al-Libi (the Libyan Mustafa al-'Uzayti). Both were among the group of U.S. captives known as High Value Detainees ("Detainee Biographies," www.defense. gov); **visa/alias:** Staff Report, "Monograph on Terrorist Travel," CO; **"recruiting":** CR, 255; **"Based on":** Statement of Eleanor Hill, 9/18/02, JI.

235   **"failure":** Executive Summary, "CIA Accountability with Respect to the 9/11 Attacks," Office of the Inspector General, CIA, 6/05. Though a summary was made public after congressional pressure, the full inspector general's 2005 "Report on CIA Accountability with Respect to the 9/11 Attacks" has not been released. ("Executive Summary," Central Intelligence Agency, Office of the Inspector General, 06/05, www.cia.gov, *NYT*, 10/5/05, AP, 5/18/07).

235–36   **KSM capture:** Fouda & Fielding, 181–, Tenet, 251–. Questions were raised as to the circumstances and timing of the arrest. The family of one of the men detained with KSM denied that the fugitive had been in the house. Some reports suggested he had been captured by Pakistani forces acting alone, others that it had been a joint U.S.-Pakistani operation. There were differing claims, too, as to who had custody of the suspect in the immediate aftermath. Red Cross staff and KSM's own defense team, however, who interviewed the prisoner, have not apparently raised questions as to the timing and circumstances of the arrest (questions: e.g. *Sunday Times* [London], 3/9/03, *NYT*, 3/3/03, *The Guardian* [U.K.], 3/3/03, ABC News, 3/11/03, Fouda & Fielding, 181– & see Paul Thompson, "Is There More to the Capture of Khalid Shaikh Mohammed than Meets the Eye?," 3/4/03, www.historycommons.org; Red Cross/defense team: Red Cross Report, 5, 20, 33–, "Verbatim Transcript of Combatant Status Review Tribunal Hearing for ISN 10024," www.defense.gov); **"Nothing like":** Tenet, 252; **leads/$25 million:** *LAT*, 3/2/03, Suskind, *One Percent*, 204–, *Guardian* (U.K.), 3/11/03, Tenet, 253; **"wonderful"/"hard":** *LAT*, 3/2/03; **"This is equal":** Fox News, 3/3/03; **"No person":** Tenet, 250; **"disorient"/"break":** *LAT*, 3/2/03; **"crouched":** *Der Spiegel*, 10/27/03, *New Yorker*, 8/13/07; **Commission Report/211:** authors' analysis based on Robert Windrem, "Cheney's Role Deepens," 5/13/09, www.thedailybeast.com; **"enhanced":** Special Review, "Counterterrorism Detention and Interrogation Activities," Office of Inspector General, CIA, 5/7/04, www.cia.gov; **"dark side":** transcript, int. of Richard Cheney, *Meet the Press*, NBC, 9/16/01; **"certain acts":** "Memorandum for Alberto Gonzales from Asst. A.G. Jay Bybee," 8/1/02.

236   **Red Cross monitors/asked in vain/"torture"/leaked/"suffocation," etc.:** FAQ, www .icrc.org, Mark Danner, "The Red Cross Torture Report: What It Means," *NY Review of*

Books, 4/30/09, "Report on the Treatment of Fourteen 'High Value' Detainees," International Committee of the Red Cross, 2/07, www.nyrb.com. Measures defined as "torture" or "cruel, inhuman or degrading treatment" of prisoners of war are illegal under the Third Geneva Convention (1949) and the U.N. Convention Against Torture (1984). To circumvent the treaties, and after advice from the Justice Department, President Bush formally determined in early 2002 that the 1949 Geneva Convention did not apply to the conflict with al Qaeda, and that the group's detainees therefore did not qualify as "prisoners of war."

The Red Cross determined that—in addition to KSM—thirteen other prisoners, suspected of having been in al Qaeda's "inner circle," suffered mistreatment constituting torture. The authors here confine themselves to U.S. treatment of prisoners relevant to the 9/11 story, but the mistreatment extended to captives elsewhere—as at Abu Ghraib prison after the invasion of Iraq. As well as pertinent documents referred to below, there has been groundbreaking reporting by Seymour Hersh, Jane Mayer, and Mark Danner ("inner circle": Summary of High Value Detainee Program, Office of the Director of National Intelligence, 9/06, www.c-span.org; torture: Red Cross Report; pertinent documents: e.g. as excerpted in eds. John Ehrenberg et al., *The Iraq Papers*, NY: Oxford Univ. Press, 2010, 403–. In addition to the previously cited Red Cross Report, see also "The Treatment by the Coalition Forces of Prisoners of War and Other Protected Persons by the Geneva Conventions in Iraq During Arrest, Internment & Interrogation," Report, International Committee of the Red Cross, 2/04).

238   **"complain"**: "Lesson 18," al Qaeda Manual, www.justice.gov. The "manual" was among items confiscated in May 2000 from the home of a suspected al Qaeda member, Anas al-Liby, following a search by the Manchester (U.K.) police. The document was supplied to the United States, translated, and used by the prosecution in the 2001 embassy bombings trial (transcript, *U.S. v. Usama bin Laden et al.*, U.S. District Court for the Southern District of NY, S [7] 98-CR-1023, 3/26/01, "Inquiry into the Treatment of Detainees in U.S. Custody," Committee on Armed Services, U.S. Senate, 110th Cong, 2nd Sess., Washington, D.C., U.S. Govt. Printing Office, 11/20/08, Executive Summary, xii).

238   **review acknowledged**: Special Review, "Counterterrorism," & see "Memorandum for John Rizzo, CIA from Asst. A.G. Jay Bybee, 8/1/02, & see *LAI*, 12/22/02, *Telegraph* (U.K.), 3/9/03 ; **"my eyes"**: Red Cross Report.

239   **"If anything"**: Special Review, "Counterterrorism." The reference to a threat to kill KSM's children appears in the CIA's 2004 "Special Review" of counterterrorism detention and interrogation activities. According to the 2007 statement of another detainee's father, KSM's children were at one point "denied food and water," at another "mentally tortured by having ants or other creatures put on their legs to scare them and get them to say where their father was hiding." A Justice Department memo released in 2009 shows that approval was given to use insects to frighten an adult detainee into talking, while another document reports that the CIA never used the technique. According to a cousin, one of KSM's sons is mentally disabled and the other epileptic. As of this writing both boys were reportedly with their mother in Iran (threat: Special Review, Office of the Inspector General, CIA, 5/7/04, www.cia.gov; statement: "Verbatim Transcript of Combatant Status Review Tribunal Hearing for ISN 10020," www.defense.gov—the statement was made by Ali Kahn, father of Majid Kahn; memos: Memorandum for John Rizzo, CIA from Jay Bybee, Asst. A.G., 8/1/02, Memorandum for John Rizzo, CIA from Stephen Bradbury, Principal Asst. Deputy A.G., 5/10/05, www.aclu.org; disabled/epileptic: *New Yorker*, 9/13/10; with mother: ibid., *WP*, 11/14/09).

239   **Poland/"verge"/"I would"**: Red Cross Report; **14 seconds/2½ minutes**: ABC News, 11/18/05; **183 times**: Special Review, "Counterterrorism."

239–41   **long history**: "Waterboarding: A Tortured History," NPR, 11/3/07, *NYT*, 3/9/08,

WP, 11/5/06, Margulies, 73–; **"in violation"**: ibid., 74; **executed Japanese:** "History Supports McCain's Stance on Waterboarding," 11/29/07, www.politifact.com; **"The United States"/"alternative"/"separate program"/"I thought"/"take potential":** "President Bush Discusses Creation of Military Commissions to Try Suspect Terrorists," 9/6/06, http://georgewbush-whitehouse.archives.gov, George Bush, *Decision Points*, London: Virgin, 2010, 169; **"a great many":** *NY Review of Books*, 4/30/09; **"would not":** *New Yorker*, 1/21/08; **"provable":** *Toronto Star*, 11/20/10; **agents:** *NYT*, 6/22/08, 4/23/09; **"intensely disputed":** *NY Review of Books*, 4/30/09; **Obama banned:** ibid.; **"The use":** Mark Danner, "US Torture: Voices from the Black Sites," *NY Review of Books*, 4/9/09.

241   **"Any piece":** *NY Review of Books*, 4/30/09.

241   **spewed information:** KSM's most recent known admissions, to the military tribunal in Guantánamo, included the "A to Z" of 9/11, the 1993 attack on the Trade Center, the beheading of *Wall Street Journal* reporter Daniel Pearl, the failed attack on a plane by shoe bomber Richard Reid, and the murder of U.S. soldiers in Kuwait. He said he planned more than twenty other crimes, including a "Second Wave" of attacks on American landmarks to follow 9/11, attacks on nuclear power plants, on London's Heathrow Airport, on Gibraltar, on the Panama Canal, on NATO headquarters in Brussels, on four Israeli targets, and on targets in Thailand and South Korea. Whatever the truth about most of this string of claims, there may now be less doubt than previously as to his claim to have killed reporter Pearl. A 2011 study by Georgetown University and the International Consortium of Investigative Journalists, however, indicated that KSM had—as he claimed—been the killer. A man named Ahmed Omar Saeed Sheikh was sentenced to death in connection with Pearl's murder in 2002 and is currently imprisoned in Karachi awaiting an appeal ("Verbatim Transcript of Combatant Status Review Tribunal Hearing for ISN 10024," www.defense.gov, AP, 3/18/07, *New Yorker*, 1/21/08, *Irish Times*, 1/21/11, JTA, 1/20/11, *Times of Oman*, 3/28/11, Musharraf, 228).

241–43   **"Detainee has":** *New Yorker*, 8/13/07; **"I gave":** Red Cross Report; **"some level":** *Times-Dispatch* (Richmond, VA), 7/6/08; **"We were not":** "Cheney's Role Deepens," 5/13/09, www.thedailybeast.com; **"Never, ever":** Richard Ben-Veniste, *The Emperor's New Clothes*, NY: Thomas Dunne, 2009, 248; **Commission not told/turned down/ blocked:** MFR of int. George Tenet, 12/23/03, Kean & Hamilton, 119–; **"incomplete":** Shenon, 391; **"We never":** *New Republic*, 5/23/05; **"reliance":** Farmer, 362; **"Assessing":** CR, 146. Of 1,744 footnotes in the report, it has been estimated that more than a quarter refer to information extracted from captives during questioning that employed the interrogation techniques authorized after 9/11 (*Newsweek*, 3/14/09).

243–44   **Fouda scoop:** Fouda & Fielding, 23–, 38, 105, 114–, 148–, 156–, & see int. Yosri Fouda for Paladin InVision, 2006, conv. Nick Fielding, corr. Yosri Fouda, 2011. Fouda's book on the case, written with Nick Fielding of the *Sunday Times* (London), was published as *Masterminds of Terror* in 2003; **Binalshibh:** Ramzi Binalshibh, a Yemeni, was an associate of the three 9/11 hijackers based in Germany until 2000, when they left for the United States. He had himself wished to take part in the operation but, unable to obtain a U.S. visa, functioned as go-between. Like KSM, Binalshibh was by 2002 a fugitive (Staff Report, "9/11 and Terrorist Travel," CO, 5, 11–, 36); **footnote:** CR, 492n40; **evidence:** "Summary of Evidence for Combatant Status Review Tribunal," 2/8/07, http://projects .nytimes.com & see int. Udo Jacob—Motassadeq attorney; **Suskind:** Suskind, *One Percent*, 102–, 133–, 156; **Bergen:** Bergen, *OBL I Know*, 301–.

244   **authentic:** Others, notably Paul Thompson and Chaim Kupferberg, have raised doubts about Fouda's account. Both noted that Fouda did not tell the truth about the date of the interview with KSM and Binalshibh, raising the possibility that his overall reporting of the interviews may be inaccurate. It is true that the reported date of the interview changed after the story broke in September 2002. While Fouda initially claimed the

interviews were conducted in Karachi in June of that year, he later revealed that the interviews had taken place two months earlier, in the third week of April. Questioned about the discrepancy in late 2002, Fouda said, "I lied because I needed to lie . . . if something went wrong and I needed to get in touch with them . . . they [KSM and Binalshibh] would be the only ones who would know that I had met them one month earlier than I had let on, and so I'd know I was talking to the right people" (doubts: Paul Thompson, "Is There More to the Capture of Khalid Shaikh Mohammed Than Meets the Eye?," 3/03, www.historycommons.org, Chaim Kupferberg, "Khalid Sheikh Mohammed: The Official Legend of 9/11 Is a Fabricated Setup," 3/15/07, www.globalresearch.ca; changed dates: *Sunday Times* (London), 9/8/02, *Guardian* (U.K.), 3/4/03, Fouda & Fielding, 23, 29, 148; "I lied": int. Fouda by Abdallah Schleifer, Fall/Winter 2002, www.tbsjournal .com.

245   **"a close":** Fouda & Fielding, 113; **chairman:** ibid., 117.

CHAPTER 22

246–47   **first meeting:** CR, 488n1; **"very calm":** *In the Footsteps of Bin Laden*, CNN, 8/23/06; **projects:** MFR 04013804, 12/4/03, Wright, 168–; **all manner:** Bergen, *OBL I Know*, 133; **rich and poor:** bin Ladens & Sasson, 111, 115; **financial support S.A.:** *Time*, 9/15/03, Peter Dale Scott, *The Road to 9/11*, Berkeley: Univ. of Calif. Press, 2007, 149–; **veterans:** Bergen, *Holy War Inc.*, 86, Richard Clarke, 137; **OBL to Bosnia/citizenship:** *Ottawa Citizen*, 12/15/01, *WSJ*, 11/1/01; **Flottau:** John Schindler, *Unholy Terror*, Minneapolis: Zenith, 2007, 123– & see "British Journalist Eye-Witnessed Osama Bin Laden Entering Alija Izetbegovic's Office," 2/3/06. www.slobodan-milosevic.org, *The Times* (London), 9/28/07; **KSM twice:** CR, 147, 488n5; **funds Chechnya:** Benjamin & Simon, 113, Loretta Napoleoni, *Terror Incorporated*, NY: Seven Stories, 2005, 95; **holdouts:** *Newsweek*, 8/19/02.

247–48   **Two hijackers:** JI, Report, 131, Testimony of George Tenet, 6/18/02, JI. The future 9/11 hijackers who fought in Bosnia were Khalid al-Mihdhar and Nawaf al-Hazmi. Zacarias Moussaoui, who was arrested before 9/11, reportedly served as a recruiter for the Chechen mujahideen (Mihdhar/Hazmi: Staff Statement 16, CO; Moussaoui: Legat, Paris to Minneapolis, FBI 199M-MP-60130, 8/22/01, Defense Exhibit 346, *U.S. v. Zacarias Moussaoui*, Tenet, 202); **Zawahiri in Sudan/directed/Mubarak:** Wright, 185–, 213, 215–, bin Ladens & Sasson, 129–; **Zubaydah/manager:** CR, 59, 169, 175, Thomas Jocelyn, "The Zubaydah Dossier," 8/17/09, www.weeklystandard.com; **"The snake":** Testimony of Jamal al-Fadl, *U.S. v. Usama Bin Laden et al.*, U.S. District Court for the Southern District of NY, S(7) 98-CR-1023, 2/6/01, CR, 59; **Yemen attacks:** Staff Statement 15, CO, Atwan, 166. There were no American fatalities in the bombings, but an Australian tourist was killed (Staff Statement 15, CO); **Somalia/Black Hawks:** transcript int. of OBL by Hamid Mir, 3/18/97, www.fas.org, Staff Statement 15, CO, int. Abdel Bari Atwan, Atwan, 36; **Riyadh attack:** CR, 60, Staff Statement 15, CO, Wright, 211–, Burke, 154–; **"paved":** ed. Lawrence, 36–; **"adopt":** int. OBL by Hamid Mir; **Dhahran:** Staff Statement 15, CO, CR, 60, Bamford, *Pretext*, 163, Benjamin & Simon, 224, William Simpson, 275; **Iran responsible?:** CR, 60; **traveled Qatar/purchase:** Christopher Blanchard, "Qatar: Background & U.S. Relations," Congressional Research Service, Washington, D.C., 1/24/08, Stephen Hayes, "Case Closed," 11/24/03, www.weekly standard.com, Gareth Porter, "Investigating the Khobar Tower Bombing," 6/24/09, *CounterPunch*.

248–49   **"heroes":** ed. Lawrence, 52. The debate over responsibility for the Dhahran attack was prolonged and bitter. Vital reading on the subject includes the relevant part of a memoir by the FBI director of the day, Louis Freeh, and—for a very different view—a series of 2009 articles by reporter Gareth Porter (Louis Freeh, *My FBI*, NY: St. Martin's, 2005, 1–, Gareth Porter, *CounterPunch*, 6/24/09); **interview:** int. Abdel bari Atwan, Atwan, 36; **"They called":** *France-Soir*, 8/27/98, citing int. of 1995 & see bin Ladens & Sasson, 127; **royals persuaded/"They beseeched":** bin Ladens & Sasson, 104, Corbin, 57, MFR 04013955, 12/3/03, AP, 6/15/08, Bergen, *OBL I Know*, 150; **"behavior":** "State Dept. Issues Fact Sheet on Bin Laden," 8/14/96 cited at Brisard & Dasquié, 169; **share sold off:** Staff Report, "Monograph on Terrorist Financing, CO, Lacey, *Inside the Kingdom*, 177–, AP, 6/15/08.

249   **formal cutoff/future:** Bergen, *Holy War Inc.*, 102, CR, 62, bin Ladens & Sasson, 128. Men who worked for bin Laden in Sudan have recalled him saying that money was short. One man, Jamal al-Fadl, defected following a clash over funding and became a useful informant for the United States. Bin Laden's son Omar remembered a time in the Sudan when funds were limited after his father "lost access to his huge bank accounts in the Kingdom" (money short/Fadl: Testimony of L'Hossaine Kerchtou, 2/22/01, & Jamal al-Fadl, 2/7/01, *U.S. v. Usama bin Laden et al.*, U.S. District Court for the Southern District of NY, S[7]98-CR-1023, CR, 62; **"lost":** bin Ladens & Sasson, 12).

249   **"Blood is":** int. of Rahimullah Yusufzai for Paladin InVision, 2006, Bergen, *OBL I Know*, 203 but see FBI 302s of int. bin Laden family members, "Saudi Flights," B70, T5, CF; **"OBL has kept":** Note de Synthèse, 7/24/00 in "Oussama Bin Laden," leaked DGSE report, 9/13/01, seen by authors; **Yeslam:** Scheuer, *Osama bin Laden*, 28; **"Some female":** Statement of Vincent Cannistraro, Hearings, Committee on International Realations, U.S. House of Reps, 107th Cong., 1st Sess., 10/3/01.

250   **funding cut off:** Whether or not bin Laden was really "disowned" by his family, there were over the years many suggestions that he had a personal fortune of some $300 million—from which he funded operations. According to the 9/11 Commission, this is merely "urban legend." A commission analysis suggests he received approximately $1 million a year from the family coffers between 1970 and 1993—the year in which his share of the family business was sold and OBL's portion "frozen." The author Peter Bergen, writing in 2001, cited a source close to the family as saying bin Laden's inheritance from his father was $35 million. In his 2008 biography of the bin Laden clan, Steve Coll stated that the value placed on OBL's share of the family business at the time he was reportedly stripped of it was a surprisingly low $9.9 million. Even taken together, these sums total far less than the rumored $300 million figure.

The approximately $30 million consumed annually by al Qaeda operations prior to 9/11 apparently came from a core of "financial facilitators" and "fundraisers" in the Gulf—particularly in Saudi Arabia. The 9/11 operation itself cost only $400,000–$500,000. Khalid Sheikh Mohammed told his interrogators that bin Laden provided 85–90 percent of that. Investigators believe, however, that this money came not from personal funds, but rather from monies he controlled (official estimates: MFR 03010990, 11/4/03, CF, FBI memo, "Ali Ahmad Mesdaq, International Terrorism, Usama bin Laden," 1/28/02, INTELWIRE, *WP*, 8/28/98; popular reports: e.g. *WP*, 8/28/98, "Tracing bin Laden's Money," 9/21/01, www.ict.org; **"myth"/$1 million:** Staff Report, "Monograph on Terrorist Financing," CO; **$35 million:** Bergen, *Holy War Inc.*, 101–; **$9.9 million:** Coll, *Bin Ladens*, 405–, 485–; **$30 million/"fundraisers"/KSM:** Staff Report, "Monograph on Terrorist Financing," CO).

250   **$4.5 million:** Note de Synthèse; **"$3,000,000"/"wealthy Saudis"/"siphoning":** Statement of Vincent Cannistraro, *Boston Herald*, 10/14/01; **considerable:** Chouet int. for *Le Monde*, 3/29/07, http://alain.chouet.free.fr, *Politique Étrangère*, March/April 03, int. Alain Chouet; **$30 million/donations/"wealthy":** Staff Report, "Monograph on Terrorist Financing," CO; **"subterfuge"/manipulate:** Chouet int. for *Le Monde*, 3/29/07, http:// alain.chouet.free.fr, int. Alain Chouet.

251   **"sponsorship"/OBL funding:** MFR 04013804, 12/4/03, MFR 04013803, 12/30/03, *WP*, 10/3/01; **"We couldn't"/"We asked"/"hot potato":** *USA Today*, 11/12/01, Bill Clinton, *My Life*, NY: Alfred A. Knopf, 2004, 797–; **"My calculation":** *WP*, 10/3/01; **"probably the biggest":** *Sunday Times* (London), 1/5/02; **"perhaps"/"probably the best":** *Frontline:* "Hunting bin Laden," www.pbs.org, *New Yorker*, 1/24/00.

251–53   **"whisked"/refueled:** bin Ladens & Sasson, 139–, 142, 309. Other accounts have suggested that the plane was allowed to refuel in Qatar. The authors have deferred to what Omar bin Laden—who was there—said. According to him, the plane stopped to refuel at Shiraz, in Iran (Coll, *Ghost Wars*, 325); **"Our plane":** bin Ladens & Sasson, 180–, *Asia Times*, 11/28/01; **Jalalabad:** bin Ladens & Sasson, 149–, CR, 65; **desolate/"new home"/"I was put":** bin Ladens & Sasson, 150–, 156, 161, 174–, 176–; **cabin:** Atwan, 28, Bergen, *Holy War Inc.*, 93; **Kalashnikov:** bin Ladens & Sasson, 165; **tapes/fax:** int. Dr. Flagg Miller, Univ. of Calif.; **satellite phone:** Bamford, *Shadow Factory*, 8, Gunaratna, 141; **dictating:** bin Ladens & Sasson, 165; **fax transmission:** int. Abdel Bari Atwan, Atwan, 53; **"summit"/hundreds of thousands:** Flagg Miller, "On 'The Summit of the Hindu Kush': Osama bin Laden's 1996 Declaration of War Reconsidered," unpub. ms. courtesy of Miller.

253   **"Declaration":** full text, "Ladenese Epistle: Declaration of War," Pts. I, II, III, www .washingtonpost.com [web only], 9/21/01. Though often described as a fatwa, the declaration seems not to fit the usual meaning of that word—"a ruling on a point of Islamic law given by a recognized authority" (worldnetweb.princeton.edu/perl/webwn); **KSM-Atef meeting:** CR, 148.

253–54   **traveled together:** The authors suggest that the travel together may have been to Bosnia, because—as noted earlier in this chapter—bin Laden and KSM are both known to have made visits there during that period (JI, Report, 313).

254   **KSM proposal/"theater"/"Why do you":** KSM SUBST, CR, 148–, 153–, 489n11–14, Tenet, 251. The source of this second version of the proposal, citing bin Laden's supposed retort, was reportedly Abu Zubaydah—another senior aide to bin Laden (CR 491n35, JI, Report, 130); **"would not focus":** KSM SUBST; **OBL priority:** Tenet, 248.

255   **"not convinced":** KSM SUBST. Bin Laden did, however, invite KSM to join al Qaeda, he told the CIA. He demurred, he said, because he wanted to retain the ability to approach other terrorist groups (CR 154).

255   **video of Twin Towers, etc.:** "The Fifth Estate: War Without Borders," www.cbc.ca, AP, 7/17/02, CR, 530n145, AP, 7/17/02. The filming in the United States was done in 1997 by a Syrian living in Spain named Ghasoub al-Abrash Ghalyoun, who was arrested after 9/11. According to the Spanish Interior Ministry, "the style and duration of the recordings far exceed tourist curiosity." Spanish investigators believed that an al Qaeda courier delivered copies of the tapes to Afghanistan (AP, 7/17/02, CR, 530n145, "The Fifth Estate: War Without Borders," www.cbc.ca).

255   **"to study":** KSM SUBST.

255   **"individuals":** Statement of Eleanor Hill, 2/17/02, JI. The 9/11 Commission noted that there had been significant radical Islamic activity in Arizona prior to 9/11. The Islamic Center of Tucson was a branch of the Office of Services, long since established by bin Laden and Abdullah Azzam in Pakistan. It had begun distributing its journal throughout the United States as early as 1986. Two former FBI informants claimed after 9/11 that they had alerted the FBI to the presence of suspicious Arabs at Arizona flight schools in 1996 (Commission: CR, 226–, 520–; Center: Steven Emerson, *American Jihad*, NY: Free Press, 2002, 129–, *Frontline:* "The Man Who Knew," www.pbs.org, *NYT*, 6/7/02; claim: *WP*, 9/23/01, 5/24/02, *NYT*, 5/24/02, FBI IG, Aukai Collins, *My Jihad*, Guilford, CT: Lyons, 2002, 213–).

255–56   **"different person"/beard, etc.:** "Hijackers Timeline [redacted]," FBI, 2/1/07, INTELWIRE, Report, JI, 135, Testimony of George Tenet, 6/18/02, JI, Graham with Nussbaum, 40–; **Atta/27:** Staff Statement 16, *WSJ*, 10/16/01, McDermott, 2–, 31 but see re Mecca twice 57; **"colony"/"Resistance":** Fisk, *The Great War*, 21–.

Part V: PERPETRATORS

CHAPTER 23

259–63   **Wiley:** MFR 04017164, 11/25/03; **"independent":** JI, Report, Appendix, 5; **"flake":** Benjamin & Simon, 243; **"terrorist financier":** Richard Clarke, 96, Tenet, xi; **"Ford Foundation":** Benjamin & Simon, 242; **not named:** Executive Order 12947, 1/23/95, *Federal Register*, Vol. 60, No. 16, Staff Report, "Monograph on Terrorist Financing," CO; **9 speeches:** Richard Clarke, 129–, e.g., "American Security in a Changing World," speech, 8/5/96, U.S. Department of State, Dispatch, Vol. 7, No. 32, & see "Presidential Speech Archive," www.millercenter.org; **PDD-39/rendition/coordinated:** "Memorandum for the Vice President et al. from William J. Clinton," 6/21/95 [PDD-39], www .fas.org, Benjamin & Simon, 230, CR, 101; **badgered:** Richard Clarke, 135; **"foaming":** Benjamin & Simon, 243; **"It just seemed":** Clarke, 135; **"asleep":** Hollingsworth with Mitchell, 101; **approval of Lake:** Bamford, *Pretext*, 205, int. Michael Scheuer for Paladin InVision; **dozen/40:** CR, 479n2; **FBI liaison/"buzz saw":** Statement of George Tenet, 10/17/02, JI, FBI IG; **focus/women/shopping complex/committed/zealot:** Shenon, 188–, MFR 04020389, 6/21/04, CR, 109; **CTC-TFL:** Staff Report, "Monograph on Terrorist Financing," CO; **more operational:** MFR 04017164, 11/25/03; **changed name:** Tenet, 100; **"My God"/"truly dangerous":** Shenon, 189; **"civilians and military":** int. of OBL for ABC News, transcript available at *Frontline:* "Hunting bin Laden," www.pbs.org; **"They chose":** int. of OBL for CNN, 3/97, www.cnn.com; **"If they":** Bergen, *OBL I Know*, 242; **"snatch":** Richard Clarke, 149; **surveillance/human intelligence:** Farmer, 29; **eavesdropping/phone:** Bamford, *Pretext*, 162–, Gunaratna, 12, *WP*, 4/24/01; **training camp:** CR, 111; **CIA plan/"half-assed"/"perfect":** Tenet, 112–, Wright, 265–, Michael Scheuer, *Marching Toward Hell*, New York: Free Press, 2008, 272n3, CR, 111–, Richard Clarke, 149; **memo:** Scheuer, *Marching*, 271; **"They could not":** Shenon, 190; **Nairobi bomb/casualties:** Report of Accountability Review Boards, Bombings of the US Embassies in Nairobi, Kenya and Dar es Salaam, Tanzania on Aug. 7, 1998, U.S. Dept. of State, www.fas.org, Wright, 270, Corbin, 73; **Dar es Salaam:** Report of Accountability Review Boards, *The Independent* (U.K.), 8/8/98; **worst:** Unger, *House of Bush, House of Saud*, 183, Robert Johnston, "Worst Terrorist Attacks— Woldwide," www.johnstonarchive.net; **bomber/met OBL/for OBL:** Testimony of Stephen Gaudin, *U.S. v. Usama Bin Laden et al.*, U.S. District Court for the Southern District of NY, S(7) 98-CR-1023, 1/8/01, Bergen, *Holy War Inc.*, 107, Corbin, 71, Criminal Complaint Against Mohamed Rashed Al-'Owhali, U.S. Federal Court for the Southern District of NY, 8/26/98, http://avalon.law.yale.edu, Reeve, 198–; **bomber/OBL calls:** Gaudin testimony, JI, Report, 129–, Wright, 276–.

263   **"I did"/Odeh/"my leader":** Bergen, *Holy War Inc.*, 53, 113, Reeve, 201. The four men convicted for their roles in the Kenya and Tanzania bombings were Mohamed al-'Owhali, Mohamed Odeh—the two terrorists referred to in the text—Khalfan Mohamed, and bin Laden's former secretary Wadih al-Hage. They were convicted in May 2001. A fifth man, Ahmed Ghailani, who had been charged on a total of 285 counts, was in 2010 acquitted of multiple murder and attempted murder charges. Though found guilty only of con-

spiracy to damage U.S. property, he was handed a life sentence (4 men: AP, 11/24/08; Ghailani: BBC, 1/25/2011).

263–64   **"excited and happy":** bin Ladens & Sasson, 237; **"juice":** int. of Abdulrahman Khadr, *Frontline:* "Son of al Qaeda," www.pbs.org, "Al Qaeda Family: The Black Sheep," 3/3/04, www.cbc.ca; **"Only God"/"real men"/"Our job":** int. of OBL for ABC News, 12/23/98 available at http://pws.prserv.net, *Time,* 1/11/99; **"the greatest":** int. of OBL for Al Jazeera, 12/98, http://wasarch.ucr.edu; **"respond":** MFR 04021459, 1/29/04; **opportunity/attack:** Tenet, 115–, Miller & Stone, 210–, Clinton, 803–, Burke, 52; **Security tight:** MFR 04021469, 12/19/03, Richard Clarke, 187; **told Pakistan/Ralston:** Clinton, 799, Richard Clarke, 186–; **"Our target":** text of President Clinton's address, CBS News, 8/20/98.

264   **circumlocution:** CR, 113–, 126–, 484n101, Executive Order 12333, United States Intelligence Activities, 12/4/81. National Security Adviser Sandy Berger, who had succeeded Lake, would tell the 9/11 Commission that the intention of the missile strikes had been "to be bouncing bin Laden into the rubble." Under Secretary for Political Affairs Thomas Pickering told commission staff the primary objective had been "to kill bin Laden and other senior leaders he was meeting with" (Berger: testimony of Sandy Berger, 3/34/04, CO; Pickering: MFR 04013744, 12/22/03, CF).

264   **"intently focused":** Clinton, 798.

264–65   **some fatalities:** CR, 117, bin Ladens & Sasson, 240–, Bergen, *Holy War Inc.,* 121–, int. of OBL for ABC News, 12/23/98. National Security Adviser Berger told the 9/11 Commission that "20–30 people in the camps" were killed. Interviewed in late 1998, bin Laden acknowledged that seven "brothers" were killed and "20-something Afghans." In addition, according to Bruce Lawrence, editor of bin Laden's public statements, seven Pakistanis also died (CR, 117, 482n46, int. of OBL by Rahimullah Yusufzai, 12/23/98, ABC News online, www.cryptome.org, ed. Lawrence, 83fn); **factory destroyed/intelligence shaky:** Reeve, 202, Tenet, 117, CR, 118, Stephen Hayes, "The Connection," 6/7/04, www.weeklystandard.com; **$750,000:** Bamford, *Pretext,* 209; **$10,000:** CR, 498n127; **propaganda victory/T-shirts:** Hamel, 216, *WP,* 10/3/01; **"a highly":** bin Ladens & Sasson, 238.

265   **"He had been":** MFR 03013620, 12/12/03, CR, 117. Bin Laden himself appeared to confirm as much a month later when he told Al Jazeera: "I was hundreds of kilometers away from there. As for the information that was supposed to have reached us, we found a sympathetic and generous people in Pakistan who exceeded all our expectations, and we received information from our beloved ones and helpers of jihad for the sake of God against the Americans." Omar bin Laden's recent account seems more worthy of credence than the story told by one of his father's former bodyguards, Abu Jandal. According to Jandal, only a whimsical change of mind led bin Laden to change his plans and head for Kabul instead of the targeted camp ("I was hundreds": ed. Lawrence, 7; whimsical: Nasser al-Bahri with Georges Malbrunot, *Dans l'ombre de Ben Laden,* Neuilly-sur-Seine, France: Michel Lafon, 2010, 149–, transcript, *CNN Presents: In the Footsteps of bin Laden,* 8/23/06).

265   **"In 1996":** JI, Report, 217; **"conspiracy":** ibid., 129, Statement of Mary Jo White, 10/2/02, JI, Report; **200-page/$5 million:** Indictment, *U.S. v. Usama bin Laden et al.,* U.S. District Court for the Southern District of NY, 98 CR, 11/4/1998, *WP,* 11/5/98; **$25 million/double:** Kenneth Katzman, "Terrorism: Near Eastern Groups and State Sponsors, 2002," Congressional Research Service, Washington, D.C., 2/13/02, BBC News, 7/13/07 **"Tier 0":** JI, Report, 40; **"We are":** CR, 357, JI, Report, 124.

265   **"lethal force":** CR, 131–, 485n123, Shenon, 357. Clinton, Berger, and others told the 9/11 Commission that the president's intent was clear—he wanted bin Laden dead. Ac-

cording to Tenet, however: "Almost all the 'authorities' [presidential authorizations] provided to us with regard to bin Laden were predicated on the planning of a capture operation." Other senior officials agreed with this interpretation. Attorney General Janet Reno, Tenet wrote later, "made it clear . . . that she would view an attempt simply to kill bin Laden as illegal" (intent: CR, 133; Tenet: Tenet, 111–, "Director's Statement on the Release of the 9/11 IG Report Executive Summary," 8/21/07, www.cia.gov; Reno: CR, 132–).

265   **operations against:** Executive Summary, "Report on CIA Accountability with Respect to the 9/11 Attacks," 6/05, CR, 132–, 142; **"Policy makers":** Tenet, 123.

265   **"two chances":** Scheuer, *Marching Toward Hell*, 61. The Scheuer reference relates to the period between May 1998 and May 1999. A 9/11 Commission staff report noted only three occasions in that time frame on which strikes were considered. In December 1998, when there was intelligence indicating that bin Laden was at a location near Kandahar, an operation was called off—according to Tenet—because of doubt as to whether the information was good and the risk of killing people in a nearby mosque. In February 1999, bin Laden was firmly believed to be at a location in the desert in Helmand province. U.S. officials vacillated, however, because members of the government of the United Arab Emirates were hunting nearby. The opportunity passed. Another strike was considered in May 1999, but scrubbed because some doubted the reliability of the source. In July that year, President Clinton authorized the CIA to work with Pakistani and Uzbek operatives to capture bin Laden. It is not clear what stage that project reached (Staff Statement 6, CO, CR, 130–, 485n116–488n194, & see Scheuer, *Marching Toward Hell*, 284n8, 285n15).

266   **"Tenet consistently":** *WP*, 4/29/07.

266   **"cared little"/"moral cowardice":** Scheuer, *Marching Toward Hell*, 48, 75, 82, 84, 85, 290. Scheuer was closely informed on everything to do with the pursuit of bin Laden until some point in 1999. Sometime after the aborted strike in February 1999 (see previous note), however, he was removed as head of Alec Station—after a clash with an FBI manager assigned to the unit. Much of Scheuer's 2008 book comes over as a furious venting of his feelings (Wright, 291–, Shenon, 188, Scheuer, *Marching Toward Hell*, refs.).

266–67   **"pathetically":** Clarke, 204; **"authorized":** int. of Bill Clinton by Fox News, 9/24/06; **"kill authority":** Shenon, 357–; **"attacks":** CR, 120; **"My father":** bin Ladens & Sasson, 239; **went to ground:** ibid.; **stopped using phone:** *Mail on Sunday* (U.K.), 12/23/01, Kessler, 84–, Corbin, 88, JI, Report, 69; **"wished to send":** Atwan, 55–.

267   **"But things":** Gaudin testimony. The bomber arrested after running away was Mohamed al-'Owhali (see above). The accomplice he named was Abdullah Ahmed Abdullah (aka Saleh), who is still at large. FBI agent Stephen Gaudin, who questioned him in Nairobi, cited the passage quoted in federal court (Testimony of Stephen Gaudin, *U.S. v. Usama Bin Laden et al.*, U.S. District Court for the Southern District of NY, S[7] 98-CR-1023, 1/8/01).

267   **summoned/"could work":** KSM SUBST. KSM provided "inconsistent information" as to whether bin Laden approved the operation in late 1998 or in early 1999, according to CIA accounts of his various interrogation sessions (CR, 492n38); **Kenya/alias:** JI, Report, 313.

267   **decoy:** *Financial Times*, 2/14/03. Another report, however, has it that—as of that same month—KSM was working as an "escort" for his longtime mentor Sheikh Abdul Sayyaf, leader of Ittehad-e-Islami, the Islamic Union Party (NY to Bangkok et al., FBI265A-NY-253802, 7/8/09, INTELWIRE, CR, 146–); **persuaded:** CR, 149, 490n16.

267   **"full support"/Atef:** KSM SUBST, CR, 154. Al Qaeda suspects questioned in Jordan were to allege that Atef seized on the concept following the 1999 EgyptAir crash off the

coast of Massachusetts, which was never satisfactorily explained. The NTSB found that the crash probably occurred "as a result of the relief first officer's flight control inputs. The reason for the relief first officer's actions was not determined." The first officer's exclamation was initially interpreted as "I place my fate in the hands of God," and later revised to "I rely on God." EgyptAir and Egypt's Civil Aviation Authority advised that the statement was "very often used by the Egyptian layman in day to day activities to ask God's assistance for the task at hand." The officer uttered the exclamation nine times while alone, twice more after the captain returned to the cockpit. Two hundred and seventeen people died in the crash (Aircraft Accident Brief, EgyptAir 990, NTSB, 3/13/02, www.ntsb.gov).

267   **influenced:** *WP,* 9/11/02.

267–68   **targeting/operatives:** KSM SUBST, CR, 154. The plan was adjusted according to the number of suitable operatives available. It would turn out early on that only two of four men originally selected to be pilot hijackers were able to obtain U.S. visas. The two who had no visas, it was then hoped, would explode planes in midair over Asia at the same time their accomplices were hitting targets in the United States. Thinking it too difficult to synchronize the operation, bin Laden would later cancel the Asia part of the operation (KSM SUBST); **"military committee":** Fouda & Fielding, 158; **two years:** KSM SUBST; **"planes operation":** CR, 154; **Omar disillusioned:** bin Ladens & Sasson, 201, 212–, 218–, 248–; **"I have heard":** ibid., 254; **"gigantic":** ibid., 277.

268   **Noonan/"History":** *Forbes,* 11/30/98.

CHAPTER 24

269–71   **"The mighty"/curbed:** bin Ladens & Sasson, 244, Bergen, *OBL I Know,* 321, 455n20; **candidates/two parts/too complicated:** KSM SUBST; **Yemenis' visas/in vain:** Staff Report, "9/11 and Terrorist Travel," CO, 13–. The Yemenis were Walid bin Attash— also known as Khallad—who had lost a leg on the Afghan battlefield, and Abu Bara al-Tai'zi, on whom there appears to be scant information. Bin Laden had known Attash in Saudi Arabia. He was to play a role at later points in the story (KSM SUBST, CR 155–) **two Saudis/aged 24/23:** National Drug Intelligence Center for the FBI, "265D-NY-280350, TWINBOM-PENTTBOM, Biographical Report," 11/26/01, authors' collection, Blair Oakley to Janice Kephart, 3/23/04, "Hijacker Primary Documents—AA77," B50, T5, CF; **friends:** Testimony of George Tenet, 6/18/02, JI, Bamford, *Shadow Factory,* 9; **well-to-do/married Yemeni/veterans:** ibid., 9, Staff Statement 16, CO, Report, JI, 131, Wright, 309–. Mihdhar's relations by marriage were the Hada family in Yemen's capital, Sana'a—their connection to terrorism will be reported later. The future 9/11 conspirator to whom Mihdhar was linked by marriage was Ramzi Binalshibh, one of the Germany-based accomplices (marriage: Bamford, *Shadow Factory,* 7–, McDermott, 183 & see AP, 12/23/07; Binalshibh: *WP,* 9/11/02); **"Jihad Ali"/Inspired:** KSM SUBST, Testimony of Stephen Gaudin, *U.S. v. Usama Bin Laden et al.;* **Saudi visas easy:** Staff Report, "9/11 and Terrorist Travel," CO, 14–, 116–; **had sworn:** JI, Report, 131–, Testimony of George Tenet, JI, 6/18/02; **"I swear"/"hijrah":** KSM SUBST. In its literal sense, the word *hijrah* or *hegira* refers to the Prophet's move from Mecca to what is now Medina in A.D. 622—the first year of the Muslim era. It has thus come to be synonymous with migration. In the context used here it appears to denote a spiritual "migration" or transformation of the self (corr. Hans Kippenberg, 2010); **"the joys"/"My father":** bin Ladens & Sasson, 262–; **candidates in Gulf:** KSM SUBST; **Italy:** McDermott, 209, 299n65. The source cited on the reported KSM visit to Italy is a senior Italian investigator; **Germany:** Leading U.S. news sources have cited "intelligence reports" indicating that KSM visited Hamburg in 1999. "We have indications from various sources," Walter

Wellinghausen, a senior official of the Hamburg Interior Ministry, told *The New York Times*, "that [KSM] was in Hamburg for a period, but we have not been able to definitively verify this" (*Newsweek*, 9/9/02, *NYT*, 11/4/02, *WP*, 9/11/02).

271   **Atta:** Texas Service Center, 911 Terrorist Review, "Hijacker Primary Documents—AA11," B51, T5, CF, McDermott, 10; **friends:** int. Mounir Motassadeq; **1992/architecture/Cairo:** McDermott, 18–; **father divorced:** Timeline Pertaining to Hijackers in Florida, "Timelines 9/11, 2 of 2," B20, T7, CF; **"never stopped":** *NYT*, 10/10/01; **mother's lap:** *Sunday Times* (London), 1/6/02; **"child feelings":** *Frontline:* "Inside the Terror Network," 1/17/02, www.pbs.org; **insect/"brainless":** *Time*, 9/30/01; **cardiologist/professor:** McDermott, 14; **did all right/arranged meeting:** ibid., 19.

271   **flew to Germany:** Atta had done a course in German at Cairo's Goethe Institute. In Germany, he was at some stage sponsored by the Carl Duisberg Gesellschaft, which assists young professionals from many foreign countries (Goethe: Uwe Michaels statement to Bundeskriminalamt, Hamburg, 10/2/01, authors' collection; Duisberg: *Tagespiel* [Germany], 10/16/01).

272–75   **"exceedingly":** Uwe Michaels Statement to Bundeskriminalamt, Hamburg, 10/2/01, authors' collection; **own meals/pots/video/risqué:** *Chicago Tribune*, 3/7/03; **blouse:** *Sunday Times* (London), 1/26/02, *LAT*, 1/27/02; **"that person":** int. of Michaels Jr. by Hannah Cleaver; **"words":** *Chicago Tribune*, 1/27/02; **clashes:** McDermott, 25–; **"a dear human":** *Newsweek*, 10/1/01 **applied self/trips:** transcript, int. Dittmar Machule, 10/18/01, *Four Corners: A Mission to Die For*, 10/18/01, www.abc.net.au; **Omar arrive/ phony/returned:** MFR 04016498, 1/13/04, *LAT*, 9/1/02, CR, 161; **aspired:** CR, 161, Fouda & Fielding, 74; **"in love":** McDermott, 48; **"very funny":** int. Mounir Motassadeq; **"disgusting"/read Qur'an:** eds. *Der Spiegel*, 197; **newcomer/father muezzin:** McDermott, 55; **prayer tape:** Corbin, 134; **"regular guy":** CR, 162; **"happy":** int. Mounir Motassadeq; **jokes:** Miller & Stone, 263; **"dreamy":** McDermott, 54; **military:** CR, 162; **marine engineering:** McDermott, 53–; **$4,000:** Corbin, 136; **"explode":** *Sun Sentinel* (Fort Lauderdale), 9/23/01; **never spoke:** McDermott, 54; **recite/ imagined:** ibid., 54, 87; **"What is":** ibid., 48; **Jarrah flew in/grew up:** Corbin, 137, *LAT*, 10/23/01, CR, 163, "The Fifth Estate: The Story of Ziad Jarrah," www.cbc.ca, 10/10/01; **civil servant/teacher:** Fisk, *The Great War*, 1052, Aysel Sengün statement to Bundeskriminalamt, 9/15/01, authors' collection; **great-uncle:** *Der Spiegel*, 9/17/08, conv. Gunther Latsch, Fouda & Fielding, 85; **cousin:** *NYT*, 2/19/09; **Sunni/Christian schools/skipped prayers:** Aysel Sengün statement to Bundeskriminalamt, 9/15/01, authors' collection, Fisk, *The Great War*, 1051–; **alcohol/"Once":** Corbin, 137, eds. *Der Spiegel*, 190; **nightclubs:** *The Independent* (U.K.), 9/16/01, *LAT*, 10/23/01; **girls:** eds. *Der Spiegel*, 246; **Sengün:** Aysel Sengün statement to Bundeskriminalamt, 9/15/01, authors' collection, Corbin, 137, McDermott, 51, 80; **got religion:** McDermott, 51; CR, 163, *Newsday*, 8/15/07; **imam/"terrorist":** Tenet identified the imam as Abdulrahman al-Makhadi (Testimony of George Tenet, JI, 6/18/02, & see National Drug Intelligence Center for the FBI, "265D-NY-280350, TWINBOM-PENTTBOM, Biographical Report," 11/26/01, authors' collection); **"criticized":** Aysel Sengün statement to Bundeskriminalamt, 9/15/01, authors' collection; **dentistry/switched:** CR, 163; **"Someone explained"/pregnant:** *LAT*, 1/27/03; **Shehhi moved/emulating:** CR, 162–; **Atta/"leader":** transcript, int. Dittmar Machule; **talked angrily:** *MSNBC Investigates: The Making of the Death Pilots*, MSNBC, 4/7/02 & see *Chicago Tribune*, 9/11/04.

275   **"always"/"the war":** *Four Corners: A Mission to Die For*, 10/18/01, www.abc.net.au. The student was Ralph Bodenstein. One account of Bodenstein's recollections states that Atta was angered by Israel's treatment of Palestinians but that—as an Egyptian—he was "most vehement about matters in his own country." He often raised the Palestine issue at religious classes he gave to younger Muslims. In his youth, Atta may have been influenced

on the Palestine issue by his father. Australian reporter Liz Jackson has recalled that after 9/11, when she approached Atta Sr. for an interview, he "said he'd only talk if we paid US $25,000 to the Palestinian intifada. Without that, if we continued filming, he'd break the camera" (one account: Miller & Stone, 251; raised: *Chicago Tribune*, 9/11/04, McDermott, 36; Atta Sr.: *Four Corners: A Mission to Die For*, 10/18/01, www.abc.net.au).

275 **Brotherhood abjures violence:** see "History of the Muslim Brotherhood," www.ikhan web.com; **exceptions:** Benjamin & Simon, 86; **recruiting grounds/engineering club:** *WP,* 9/22/01; **men from Allepo:** transcript, int. Dittmar Machule, McDermott, 29.

275 **Zammar/Darkazanli:** CR, 164, 167, McDermott, 72–. Zammar has languished in a jail in Syria since his arrest the month after 9/11. A Syrian court convicted him of membership of the Muslim Brotherhood, which is banned in Syria. Because he was allegedly tortured in prison, Amnesty International has issued an appeal on his behalf. Darkazanli has not been accused of any crime in Germany. Spanish prosecutors sought his extradition, however, in 2004, citing alleged contacts with al Qaeda operatives there. Darkazanli was in Spain in summer 2001 at approximately the same time as Atta and Binalshibh (Zammar: "Unfair Trial & Sentencing of Muhammad Haydar Zammar," Appeal Case, 3rd Update, 3/22/07, www.amnestyusa.org, *Der Spiegel*, 11/21/05; Darkazanli: "Germany's Imam Mamoun Darkazanli," www.jamestown.org, 8/27/10, JI, Report, 183–).

276 **"coincidence":** *Chicago Tribune*, 11/16/02, Derek Flood, "Germany's Imam Mamoun Darkazanli," Vol. 1, No. 8, www.jamestown.org.

276 **boxes/books/"I will pay":** *WP,* 9/11/02; **Atta vanished/"Don't ask":** CR, 168, Fouda & Fielding, 123, transcript, int. Dittmar Machule, *LAT*, 9/1/02, but see Corbin, 139— which suggests he disappeared for more than a year. Tenet so speculated, even though KSM apparently denied to interrogators that Atta went to Afghanistan prior to late 1999 (Testimony of George Tenet, JI, 6/18/02, KSM SUBST).

276–79 **passport lost/new one:** Testimony of George Tenet, JI, 6/18/02, McDermott, 57; **speculation:** ibid., Testimony of George Tenet, MFR 04019351, 12/10/03; **"serve the interests":** ed. Lawrence, 60–; **"This was sensitive":** Kean & Hamilton, 284–; **bring attack forward:** KSM SUBST; **KSM concern:** McDermott, 117–; **"the atrocities":** KSM SUBST; **KSM claims:** "Verbatim Transcription of Combatant Status Review Tribunal hearing for ISN 10024," 3/10/07, www.defense.gov; **"entitled":** int. Yousef by Raghida Dergham, *Al Hayat*, 4/12/95; **"If you ask":** McDermott, 13; **"world Jewish conspiracy":** CR, 161; **"great-grandparents":** *LAT*, 10/17/04; **"How can you":** CR, 162; **"He enlightened":** McDermott, 80; **"With God's":** ed. Lawrence, 61; **"The problem":** McDermott, 82; **met/prayed, etc.:** ibid., 58–; **apartment:** "Hamburger Mietvertrag für Wohnraum," Marienstrasse 54, 10/31/98, authors' collection; **Dar al-Ansar:** McDermott, 63, CR, 164, 495n82. See Notes for Ch. 18, p. 501; **"the highest":** McDermott, 62; **"dissatisfied":** ibid., 51–, 275n15; **dying for faith:** ibid., 49; **"love death":** "Ladenese Epistle: Declaration of War," pts. I, II, III, www.washingtonpost .com.

279–80 **"The morning"/"the smell":** McDermott, 88, 280n43. Jarrah's notes, found with his Hamburg college papers, are in German police files. The 1996 bin Laden declaration—reported in Ch. 22, p. 253—not only includes the "death as you love life" reference but also multiple references to Paradise. Bin Laden was to use almost exactly the same phrase in a letter in Arabic posted on the Internet in October 2002 (notes: McDermott, 89, 280n43; OBL letter: ed. Lawrence, 172); **"Paradise":** McDermott, 85; **"Muslims are":** *WP,* 9/11/02, CR, 496n88. *Washington Post* reporter Peter Finn dated the Atta Nickels exchange as having occurred in November 1999. The commission dates it merely to the year 1999 (*WP,* 9/11/02, CR, 496n88).

280 **traveled Afghanistan:** "Hijackers Timeline [redacted], FBI, 2/1/07, INTELWIRE, Report, JI, 134–, MFR 04019351, 12/10/03. Binalshibh, the sole survivor of the group from

Germany, would tell interrogators that they had initially planned to fight in Chechnya. The decision to go instead to Afghanistan, he claimed, was the outcome of an encounter with a man he and two others of the Hamburg group met by chance on a train. This claim may or may not be true. According to Binalshibh, the man on the train—whom he identified as Khalid al-Masri—advised them to talk with a second man named Mohamed Slahi. Slahi, when they went to see him, allegedly said it was difficult to get to Chechnya and suggested they travel instead to Afghanistan via Pakistan. Khalid al-Masri, if he ever existed, has yet to be identified. (He is not the man of the same name who after 9/11 was seized in Macedonia by a U.S. "snatch team," reportedly tortured, and—when CIA officials concluded he had been wrongfully detained—released by being dumped at the roadside in Albania. Slahi was arrested soon after 9/11 and eventually transferred to Guantánamo. A Senate inquiry found that he was subjected to serious ill treatment. Though Slahi admitted having met Binalshibh and his two comrades, he denied having suggested they go to Afghanistan. At the time of writing he remains in Guantánamo but has not been charged. A federal judge ruled in March 2010 that a prosecution of Slahi was impossible because his file was "so tainted by coercion and mistreatment." In November 2010, a U.S. appeals court ordered the judge to review the case. Mohammed Zammar, meanwhile—who had also reportedly been tortured, not in U.S. custody but in a Syrian jail—told visiting German investigators that he "helped" Binalshibh and the others get to Afghanistan (encounter/Masri/advised: CR, 165, 496n90, German translation of interrogation of Binalshibh provided to prosecution in Motassadeq case, *Vereinigte Staaten Von Amerika gegen Zacarias Moussaoui*, 4/28/05, authors' collection; snatched/dumped Albania: *WP*, 12/4/05, *The Independent* [U.K.], 5/1907; Slahi: Report, "Inquiry into the Treatment of Detainees in U.S. Custody," U.S. Senate, Committee on Armed Services, 110th Cong. 2nd Sess., 11/20/08, http://armed-services.senate.gov, 138–, *Miami Herald*, 11/5/10, *WP*, 3/24/10; Zammar: *Der Spiegel*, 11/21/05).

280   **bodyguard recalled:** The bodyguard was Nasser al-Bahri. Fahd al-Quso, a Yemeni interrogated after 9/11, said he, too, had seen Shehhi in Kandahar, when he became sick (Bahri: *Newsweek*, 9/3/07, Wright, 366 & see *Sunday Times* [London], 10/1/06; Quso: *New Yorker*. 7/10 & 17/06); **Another jihadi:** Bergen, *OBL I Know*, 262; **handwritten note:** FBI translation,12/21/01, "Misc. Requests for Documents, FBI-03013592, Packet 2," CF.

280   **videotape/"will":** The footage was described in a story by Yosri Fouda in the London *Sunday Times* on October 1, 2006. The same day, NBC News showed still photos from the videotape. According to the *Times* article, the videotape was "obtained through a previously tested channel." The article also said that sources from both al Qaeda and the United States had confirmed the authenticity of the tape, "on condition of anonymity." Date marks on the footage show that bin Laden was filmed on January 8 and the future hijackers on January 18, 2000. Atta, Jarrah, and Binalshibh apparently were in Afghanistan on both those days. The different date marks seem to indicate that bin Laden was not present when Atta and Jarrah recorded their martyrdom statements. NBC's story reported, however, that "U.S. government analysis . . . identifies hijackers Atta and Jarrah in the large crowd at bin Laden's feet" (*Sunday Times* [London] & NBC News, 10/1/06).

281–82   **KSM/Binalshibh described:** KSM SUBST, CR, 166–, Fouda & Fielding, 123–, 126, Staff Statement 16, CO; **Shehhi left/ailment:** ibid., CR, 166, *New Yorker*, 7/10/06, "PENTTBOM, Summary of Captioned Investigation," 11/5/01, authors' collection; **"middling":** KSM SUBST; **oath:** Staff Statement 16, CO, CR, 166–. Shehhi had apparently taken the oath before leaving (CR 166–); **OBL considered/select targets:** KSM SUBST; **Jarrah endured:** Fouda & Fielding, 128; **tricks of trade:** KSM SUBST; **airline schedules:** Staff Statement 16, CO **"learning"/"be normal":** KSM SUBST; **phone**

code: *New Yorker,* 9/13/10; **"PlayStation":** *Daily Mail* (U.K.), 4/17/10; **"worked hard"/ Hazmi deputy:** KSM SUBST; ***kunyahs*:** These *kunyahs,* and all the honorifics assigned to what became a nineteen-man hijack team, appear in *Masterminds of Terror,* by Yosri Fouda and Nick Fielding, 110, 121n15.

283–84 **"wonderful evening":** Clinton, 881; **Jordan/Zubaydah:** *NYT,* 1/15/01, Tenet, 125; **Ressam caught/plan:** Counterterrorism to All Field Stations, FBI 265A-SE-83340, etc., 12/29/1999, INTELWIRE, CR, 176–, Staff Statement 15, CO, Richard Clarke, 211, Bergen, *Holy War Inc.,* 140–, *NYT,* 12/15/01, Burke, 198–, 208–; **"aware":** Burke, 209, Report, JI, Appendix, 44, CR, 261; **Clinton rang:** Coll, *Ghost Wars,* 487; **Berger met:** Shenon, 234, 261; **wiretap orders:** Farmer, 39; **"Foreign":** CR, 179; **Berger/Clarke Christmas:** Richard Clarke, 213, MFR 04021455, 2/13/04; **thousands on duty/vigil:** Richard Clarke, Testimony of Louis Freeh, 4/13/04, CO; **O'Neill:** Miller & Stone, 222–.

284 **"I think"/"popped":** Richard Clarke, 214. U.S. intelligence worried not only about December 31 as the date of a possible attack, but also about January 3 and 6. The 3rd is considered a night of destiny in Islam, while January 6, 2000, coincided with the end of Ramadan. As discovered later, an attack was indeed planned for the 3rd—a bombing of the U.S. destroyer *Sullivans,* which was visiting the Yemeni port of Aden. The explosives-loaded boat, however, sank in the surf before the operation could be carried out. This botched effort preceded by nine months the successful attack on the USS *Cole,* also in Aden, which is covered in Ch. 25. Walid bin Attash, one of the Yemenis bin Laden initially selected for the 9/11 operation, reportedly played a role in planning both bombings (Jan. 3/6: FBI IG; *Sullivans*/Attash: Staff Statement 2, CO).

284 **"They said":** Benjamin & Simon, 313.

284–85 **"All Islamic":** Staff Report, "Monograph on the Four Flights and Civil Aviation Security," 8/26/04, CF; **1998 exercise:** Kean & Hamilton, 109, CR, 345; **"bin Laden and his":** CR, 128; **"unconventional":** *Sunday Times* (London), 6/9/02; **"America":** "New World Coming: American Security in the 21st Century," Commission on National Security, 9/15/99, www.fas.org. The commission was chaired by former U.S. senators Gary Hart and Warren Rudman; **Library of Congress report:** Rex Hudson, "The Sociology & Psychology of Terrorism: Who Becomes a Terrorist and Why?," Federal Research Division, Library of Congress, Washington, D.C., 9/99, 7, *NYT,* 5/18/02.

285 **America West/"walked into"/door locked/alerted/handcuffs/interrogation:** Judgment, *Muhammad Al-Qudhai'een et al. v. America West Airlines et al.,* Case No. C-2-00-1380, US District Court for the Southern District of Ohio, Eastern Division, 4/30/03 Manager, Chicago Civil Aviation Security Office to Director, undated FAA Memo, "Other Flights 9/11, FAA Memo re America West 90," B7, T7, CF, Report, JI, 6; **"casing":** MFR 04017521, 1/7/04, MFR 04019354, 7/22/03; **"tied":** MFR 04019354, 7/22/03; **poster:** Statement of Eleanor Hill, 9/24/02 (as supplemented 10/17/02), JI; **"explosive":** ibid.

285 **arrested with Zubaydah:** CR, 521n60. The man who tried the cockpit door was Muhammad al-Qudhai'een and his companion Hamdan al-Shalawi. Both insisted that Qudhai'een had merely wished to find the airplane lavatory. They subsequently sued America West, alleging racial stereotyping, but the suit was dismissed. Qudhai'een, interviewed in Saudi Arabia by 9/11 Commission staff, said he thought the perpetrators of 9/11 were "ignorant" people. In his interview, Shalawi said he recalled having encountered future pilot hijacker Hani Hanjour before the incident on the airplane. He acknowledged having done "charity work" in Afghanistan back in 1987, but denied ever having been there since. Three officers of the Mabahith, Saudi Arabia's internal security service, were present during the commission's interviews of both Shalawi and Qudhai'een. The associate with a bin Laden poster on his wall was Zacaria Soubra, then a student at Embry-Riddle Aeronautical University in Prescott, Arizona (Qudhai'een,

Shalawi sued: Judgment, *Muhammad Al-Qudhai'een et al. v. America West Airlines et al.*, No. C-2-00–1380, US District Court for the Southern District of Ohio, 4/30/03; "ignorant"/"charity work"/Mabahith: MFR int. Muhammad al-Qudhai'een, 10/26/03 & MFR int. Hamdan bin al-Shalawi, 10/23/03, "Staff Delegation International Trip," T1A, CF; Soubra: Statement of Eleanor Hill, 9/24/02 [as supplemented 10/17/02], JI, FBI IG).

286   **exploratory trips:** Fouda & Fielding, 158, Bergen, *OBL I Know*, 302; **1999 reports:** Report, JI, 334, Statements of Eleanor Hill, 9/18/02, 9/24/02 (as supplemented 10/17/02), JI, FBI IG; **"The purpose"/found no indication/INS:** ibid., Statement of Eleanor Hill, 9/24/02, (as supplemented 10/17/02), JI; **"very frustrating";** MFR 04018415, 12/16/03, CF.

CHAPTER 25

287–88   **training camp/combat/magazines/games/movies:** CR, 157, 493n50, 54; **phone directories/English/two Yemenis:** KSM SUBST, CR, 157–.

288   **Mihdhar left early:** Detainees' accounts varied as to whether Mihdhar completed the physical training course. KSM said Mihdhar was not present for the familiarization-with-U.S.-life sessions that Hazmi attended—he had supposedly had similar instruction earlier (CR, 493n50 & 53); **on choosing optimal:** ibid., 158, 493n54; **Attash dry run/ no visas/he learned:** ibid., 158–, KSM SUBST; **box cutter/knife:** CR, 159, "Charge Sheet, Khalid Sheikh Mohammed," 4/15/08, www.findlaw.com; **toothpaste/art supplies:** CR, 493n59; **ploy worked:** ibid., 159.

288   **condominium in K.L.:** ibid. It remains unclear who exactly may have been with the trio at the condominium, which belonged to a former Malaysian army captain named Yazid Sufaat. Their comrade from the training period, Abu Bara al Tai'zi (see notes for Ch. 24), was there. So, too, reportedly, was Riduan Isamuddin, an Indonesian terrorist leader known as "Hambali." In his insightful book *The Looming Tower*, Lawrence Wright wrote that a dozen terrorist associates came and went from the condominium. There have also been unconfirmed reports that KSM and Ramzi Binalshibh joined the group. The claim that KSM was present is unsupported by any available evidence. A senior German police official has referred to evidence, apparently credit card receipts, indicating that Binalshibh was there (Tai'zi/Sufaat: CR, 156–; Isamuddin: *New Straits Times* [Malaysia] 2/10/02, *Time Asia*, 4/1/02 CR, 158; dozen: Wright, 311; KSM: e.g. *Newsweek*, 7/9/03; Binalshibh: *LAT*, 9/1/02, *NYT*, 8/24/020).

288   **boarded UA flight/"tourists":** Staff Report, 9/11 and Terrorist Travel," CO, 13–, Timeline, "Hijackers Primary Docs, AA77, 2 of 2," & FBI 302 of Special Agent [redacted], 9/12/01, "Hijackers Primary Docs, AA77, 1 of 2," B50, T5, CF. After 9/11 it would emerge that U.S. intelligence had been aware, even before it began, that suspected terrorists were to meet in Kuala Lumpur. The men were surveilled while they were there and an attempt was made to follow them afterward, when they left for Thailand. Most stunning of all, the CIA knew even before Mihdhar reached Kuala Lumpur that he had a current visa to enter the United States. Within months, moreover, it learned the equally alarming fact that Hazmi had entered the United States. Agency spokesmen have claimed that, even so, the CIA took no action until just before 9/11. Why not? The issue is of enormous significance and will be covered in Ch. 31 (e.g., Staff Statement 2, CO, CR, 353–, FBI IG).

288–89   **no "facilitator":** KSM SUBST; **Commission not believe:** CR, 215; **no trace:** CR, 514n8, Staff Statement 16, CO, MFR 040204580, 6/23–24/04, CF.

289   **chauffeur/"two Saudis"/"an apartment"/tour:** int. of Qualid Benomrane, FBI 302, 265A-LA-228901, 4/6/02, INTELWIRE. The statements of the driver, a Tunisian named Qualid Benomrane, contain unresolved issues. He did not, for example, have an official taxi driver's license until several months after Hazmi and Mihdhar's arrival. Ben-

NOTES AND SOURCES 527

omrane said it was Fahad al-Thumairy, an imam at the King Fahd mosque, who asked him to drive the two Saudis around—at the request, in turn, of someone at the Saudi consulate. At one point, however, he said the "two Saudis" were sons of a sick father seeking treatment in Los Angeles—which would not fit Hamzi and Mihdhar. Thumairy, for his part, denied knowing Benomrane but said he did know a "son and sick father." Commission staff who interviewed Thumairy in Saudi Arabia, however, judged him "deceptive."

9/11 Commission senior counsel Dieter Snell asserted in a 2004 memo that Benomrane's information appeared to be of "uniquely significant value" to understanding the facts behind the 9/11 attacks. Benomrane had by then been deported from the United States, however, and the Commission never did interview him. Journalist Judith Miller reported in 2007 that Los Angeles Police Department detectives were convinced that "Benomrane and al-Thumairy were militants in the al Qaeda support network and that Benomrane's passengers were, in fact, the two hijackers" (license: e.g. MFR 04018787, 4/19/04, MFR 04018782, 4/21/04; Thumairy: CR, 515n14, Line of Inquiry: Qualid Moncef Benomrane, B36, T1A, CF; sons of sick father: int. Qualid Benomrane, FBI 302, 265A-LA-228901, 4/6/02; Thumairy denied: MFR 04019362, 2/23/04; "deceptive": Dieter Snell et al. to Philip Zelikow, 2/25/04, Summary of Interview Conducted in Saudi Arabia, ARC Identifier no. 2610841, CF; "uniquely": Dieter Snell to Pat O'Brien, 1/16/04, "Benomrane Folder," B37, T1A, CF; deported/never interviewed: CR, 515n14; LAPD convinced: Judith Miller, "On the Front Line in the War on Terrorism," Summer 07, www.city-journal.org).

289–91   photographs: CR, 515n14; "barely"/"instructed": KSM SUBST; address in CA: CR, 150, 514n4, Guardian (U.K.), 11/12/06, Telegraph (U.K.), 11/7/06; CIA concluded: CR, 514n4; "possibly" Long Beach: CR, 157, 514n7; language schools LA: CR, 216; San Diego directories: KSM SUBST; "idea": ibid.; Bayoumi 42: DHS Document Request 3, "Doc Requests, Entire Contents," T5, B9, CF; rental application: San Diego Union-Tribune, 10/25/01; Bayoumi employee/mosque, etc.: ibid., FBI IG; "ghost": CR, 515n18, Don/trip to LA/consulate/restaurant: MFR of int. Omar al Bayoumi, 10/16–17/003, "Staff Delegation International Trip, Tab 1," T1A, MFR 04017552, 9/29/03, & MFR 04019254, 4/20/04, CF, FBI 302 of int. Caysan bin Don, 10/8/01, INTELWIRE, CR, 217-, 515n15, 17. Bin Don has also used the name Isamu Dyson. His birth name was Clayton Morgan (CR, 435); newspaper: McDermott, 189; "description"/sought out/apartment: MFR of int. Bayoumi, MFR 04016481, 1/12/04, National Drug Enforcement Center for the FBI, "265D-NY-280350, TWINBOM-PENTTBOM, Biographical Report,"11/26/01, authors' collection; pure chance: MFR 04019254, 4/20/04, MFR 04016231, 11/18/03, CF; "to pick up": Report, JI, 173; contacts imam: Dieter Snell, et al., to Philip Zelikow, "Summary of Interviews in Saudi Arabia," 2/25/04, MFR, CF; cell phone: MFR, 040175541A, 11/17/03, CF, CR, 516n26; jihad material/salary: Report, JI, 174; distinguishing mark: CR, 516n19; "We do not": CR 218; "very suspicious": int. Eleanor Hill.

291   "We firmly": Newsweek, 8/3/03. As noted earlier in this chapter, KSM has denied that there were helpers in place in the U.S. He also specifically denied that he had ever heard of Bayoumi (CR, 516n19, CBS News, 8/3/03); Aulaqi 29/imam: FBI Memo, "Ansar Nasser Aulaqi, IT-UBL," 9/26/01, INTELWIRE; four calls: MFR 04017541A, 11/17/03 & MFR 04017531, 11/17/03, CF, "Hijackers Timeline [redacted]," 11/14/03, INTELWIRE, CR, 221, 517n33; attended mosque: CR, 517n33, MFR 04017542, 11/18/03, CF; "closed-door": Report, JI, 178, NYT, 5/8/10, Jamie Reno, "Public Enemy #1," www.sandiegomagazine.com; Hazmi respected/spoke: MFR of [name redacted], 4/23/04, CF—since reported to have been Abdussattar Shaikh; "very calm": FBI Memo, "Ansar Nasser Aulaqi, IT-UBL," 9/26/01, INTELWIRE; "spiritual advisor": Report, JI, 27.

291   **Aulaqi relocated/no contact:** The record seems contradictory on this. The Commission Report quoted Aulaqi as denying having had contact in Virginia with Hazmi or his companion at that point, future fellow hijacker Hani Hanjour. A May 2004 Commission memo, however, states that Aulaqi "admits contact with the hijackers" at both the Virginia and San Diego mosques. (CR, 229–, MFR 04019202, 5/6/04).

291–92   **had investigated/"procurement":** CR, 517n33; **"potentially":** CR, 221; **prison:** *WP,* 2/27/08; **terrorist attacks:** (Fort Hood shooting/bomb on Detroit-bound plane/ Times Square car bomb) *Christian Science Monitor,* 5/19/10, Fox News, 10/20/10, CNN, 1/7/10, *Guardian* (U.K.), 10/31/10, MSNBC, 11/1/10; **Harman:** *Christian Science Monitor,* 5/19/10;

292   **KSM suggested:** KSM SUBST; **passes Zoo/SeaWorld:** *LAT,* 9/1/02; **bank accounts/ car/ID:** FBI IG, Staff Report, Monograph on Terrorist Financing," CO, MFR.

292–93   **driver's licenses/phone directory:** CR, 539n85, Lance, *Triple Cross,* 349. The two terrorists moved in May 2000 to the home of a man named Abdussattar Shaikh, and— though Mihdhar left that summer—Hazmi stayed until December. Shaikh, the subject of controversy not least because he was an FBI informant, will be covered in the notes for Ch. 33 (CR, 220, 516n28, MFR of [name redacted], 4/23/04, CF, www.scribd.com, Nawaf al-Hazmi timeline, "Hijacker Primary Documents," B50, T5, CF, Graham with Nussbaum, Shaikh refs., Shenon, 53–); **sociable/"brooding":** Corbin, 174–, *Newsweek,* 6/10/02; **soccer/"psychotic":** CR 220, MFR 04017531, 11/17/03, CF; **"You'll know":** *Newsweek,* 6/10/02; **phone calls/computer/Yahoo:** "Hijackers Timeline [redacted]," 11/14/03, INTELWIRE, Bamford, *Shadow Factory,* 25; **KSM told:** KSM SUBST; **Hazmi enrolled/Mihdhar not start:** ibid., Staff Statement 16, CO, CR, 221, 517n30, 36, FBI 302 of int. Omer Bakarbashat, 9/17/01, INTELWIRE; **flight school/few lessons:** CR, 221–, 517n36; **praying:** Corbin, 174; **"They just"/"Dumb":** *Newsweek,* 6/10/02; **flying not for them:** *WP,* 9/30/01.

293   **dropped out/flew back:** KSM SUBST, CR, 220. Though Mihdhar supposedly went home to rejoin his family, he also went on to travel to Malaysia, Afghanistan, and Saudi Arabia. FBI director Mueller suggested to Congress's Joint Inquiry that his role may have included helping to organize the so-called muscle hijackers. (CR, 222, Statement of Robert Mueller, JI, 9/26/02).

293   **overruled/progressive:** KSM SUBST.

293   **shed clothing/beards:** CR, 167, FBI report, "The 11 September Hijacker Cell Model," 2/03, INTELWIRE.

293–94   **31 emails/"We are"/"lost"/new passports:** Testimony of George Tenet, 6/18/02, JI, CR, 168, 497n108, Transcript of Jury Trial, *U.S. v. Zacarias Moussaoui,* 3/7/06. Atta had entered a lottery for a U.S. visa as early as October the previous year, perhaps a further indication that he knew something of the bin Laden plan before heading to Afghanistan in November. He applied for and got a visa in the regular way, however, only in May 2000 (MFR 04019351, 12/10–11/03, Staff Report, "9/11 and Terrorist Travel," CO, 15–).

294   **Binalshibh:** Staff Report, 9/11 and Terrorist Travel, CO, 17–, CR, 225, 519n52. Binalshibh applied for a visa three times in the year 2000, each time unsuccessfully; **Shehhi/Atta to NY:** Staff Report, 9/11 and Terrorist Travel, CO, 15; **Bronx/Brooklyn:** Staff Statement 16, CO, Report, JI, 136; **calling card:** "Hijackers Timeline [redacted]," 11/14/03, INTELWIRE, Bamford, *Shadow Factory,* 53; **Jarrah arrives:** Staff Report, 9/11 and Terrorist Travel, CO, 17; **flight school:** MFR 04019350, 3/18/04, CF, *Herald-Tribune* (Sarasota), 9/10/06; **"He was":** Corbin, 160, & see MFR 04018408, 4/12/04, CF; **"occasional":** Fouda & Fielding, 131; **Private Pilot License/aviation mechanics:** CR, 224, biographical note "Ziad Jarrah," FBI 03212, JICI 4/19/02, www.scribd.com, "Airman Records for Jarrah," B45, T5, CF; **"He wanted":** Corbin, 161; **Oklahoma**

school/FBI regional office: Statement of Eleanor Hill re "The FBI's Handling of the Phoenix Electronic Communication and Investigation of Zacarias Moussaoui Prior to Sept. 11, 2001," 9/24/02 (as updated 10/17/02), JI.

294 **toured school:** Title: PENTTBOM, "Summary of Captioned Investigation as of 11/4/01," 11/5/01, authors' collection, CR, 224. The two hijackers' visit was to Airman Flight School, where bin Laden pilot Ihab Ali had trained several years earlier. Zacarias Moussaoui, who was part of KSM's wider operation and would be arrested shortly before 9/11, would also train at Airman, in early 2001 (Ali: CR, 224, "Paving the Road to 9/11," www.intelwire.com; Moussaoui: "Paving the Road to 9/11," www.intelwire.com, CR, 246, 273–).

294 **Huffman:** CR, 224. Daniel Hopsicker, an author who has concentrated on the hijackers' Venice stay, has written extensively about Venice Airport and those who operated flight schools there in 2000. In a 2009 article, he reported having discovered "covert CIA and military operations dating back to at least 1959" involving the airport. Hopsicker has focused on information indicating that the airport has a history of narcotics trafficking. He refers, too, to the seizure in July 2000—the month Atta and Shehhi began flight training—of a Learjet co-owned by Wallace Hilliard, the financier behind Huffman Aviation, with a large shipment of heroin on board. Hilliard maintained that he was the "innocent owner" of the plane. Huffman's Rudi Dekkers, for his part, had what the *St. Petersburg Times* termed "a checkered history" of bankruptcies, business problems, and visa issues (he is a Dutch national). According to the *Times*, he was cited by the FAA in 1999 for several violations, and his pilot's license was suspended. In interviews with a law enforcement official and an aviation executive, the authors got the impression that Venice Airport has indeed seen much illegal activity over the years. A Commission staff memo suggests that Atta and Shehhi were accepted as students of Huffman without strict adherence to INS regulations—sloppy procedure that had the effect of legitimizing their continued stay in the United States. It may conceivably be of significance that Yeslam bin Laden, one of Osama's half-brothers, had paid for an acquaintance's flight instruction at the school—a bizarre fact that may be no more than a coincidence (Hopsicker: Daniel Hopsicker, *Welcome to Terrorland*, Eugene, OR: MadCow, 2004/2007; CIA: "Big Safari, the Kennedy Assassination, & the War for Control of the Venice Airport," 9/9/09, "The Deep History of the Venice Municipal Airport," 9/21 & 9/24/09, "Venice Was a Quiet Mena, Arkansas," 4/16/10, www.madcowprod.com, Hopsicker, 128–; Hilliard: *Orlando Sentinel*, 8/2/00; Aircraft Bill of Sale, N351WB, U.S. Dept. of Transportation (FAA), World Jet, Inc., to Plane I Leasing—Wallace J. Hilliard, President, filed 11/15/99, Hearing on Motion of Forfeiture Proceedings, *U.S. v. Edgar Javier Valles-Diaz, et al.*, U.S. District Court for the Middle District of FL, 11/3/00; Dekkers: *St. Petersburg Times*, 7/25/04; Commission/legitimizing: Kephart-Robert to Ginsberg, 2/26/04, "Hijacker Pilot Training," B21, T7, CF; interviews: ints. Coy Jacobs & FBI Joint Terrorism Task Force agent; Yeslam: *New Yorker*, 11/12/01).

294–97 **No reliable source:** McDermott, 195; **"had an attitude"/"likeable":** transcript int. Rudi Dekkers, *Four Corners: A Mission to Die For*, 10/18/01, www.abc.net.au; **"When you"/immaculate/"Generally":** int. Mark Mikarts; **no better/another school/failed/argued:** FBI 302 of int. Ivan Chirivella, 9/16/01, INTELWIRE, Corbin, 10–, "Hijackers Timeline [redacted]," 11/14/03, INTELWIRE, CR, 224, *WSJ*, 10/16/01; **"a gesture"/Saudi/cushion:** transcript of int. Ann Greaves, *Four Corners: A Mission to Die For*, 10/18/01, www.abc.net.au; **"I don't want":** "Mohammed Atta's Last Will & Testament, *Frontline*: "Inside the Terror Network," www.pbs.org, *NYT*, 10/4/01; **"We had female":** int. Mark Mikarts; **"very rude":** FBI 302 of Ivan Chirivella, 9/16/01, INTELWIRE; **Outlook bar:** int. Lizsa Lehman. Allegations that several members of the terrorist team—Atta included—indulged in heavy drinking at bars in Florida in the days prior to the attack are covered in Ch. 28, on page 348. Reports of Atta's heavy drinking are probably apocryphal. Lizsa Lehman's firsthand recollection of Atta and Shehhi drinking beer in moderation at the Outlook, however, seems credible.

298   **Jarrah License:** MFR 04021445, 1/13 & 1/25/04, CF, Staff Statement 16, CO; **fall trip/ Paris/photographed:** Aysel Sengün statement to Bundeskriminalamt, 9/15/01, authors' collection, Hijackers Timeline [redacted], 11/14/03, INTELWIRE, Staff Report, 9/11 and Terrorist Travel, CO, 21–, [Name Redacted] to [Name Redacted], INS, 9/19/01, re Saeed A.A. Al Ghamdi, & attachments, "Inspector Interviews, UA 93, Notes & Memos," B49, T5, CF; **"I love you":** McDermott, 198; **Mitsubishi:** Jarrah timeline, "03009470, Packet 6, Ziad Jarrah chronology," www.scribd.com; **Bahamas:** Report of Investigation, U.S. Customs Service, Case no. TA09FR01TA003, & Letter re plane piloted by Jarrah, N833OU, "Hijacker Primary Docs, UA 93," B51, T5, CF; **Atta/Shehhi licenses:** MFR 04021445, 1/13 & 1/25/04, CF, Staff Statement 16, CO; **Christmas trip:** Aysel Sengün statement to Bundeskriminalamt, 9/15/01, authors' collection, Hijackers Timeline [redacted], 11/14/03, INTELWIRE, Staff Report, 9/11 and Terrorist Travel, CO, 21–; **abandoned plane:** MFR 04021445, 1/13 & 1/25/04, CF, Testimony of Rudi Dekkers, Subcommittee on Immigration & Claims, Committee on the Judiciary, U.S. House of Reps., 107th Cong., 2nd Sess., 3/19/02; **videos:** Indictment, *U.S. v. Zacarias Moussaoui*, 12/01; **727 simulator/"They just":** *Daily Record* (Glasgow, Scotland), 9/15/01, *NYT*, 9/14/01, Hijackers Timeline [redacted], 11/14/03, INTELWIRE.

298   **Some have argued:** Skeptics have questioned whether Hani Hanjour had the piloting skill to fly American 77 into the Pentagon at almost ground level. While some flying instructors commented on his inadequacies, however, others recalled having found him competent. One, who flew with Hanjour in August 2001, went so far as to describe him as a "good" pilot. (Skeptics: e.g., Griffin, *New Pearl Harbor*, 78–; inadequacies/competent: e.g., CBS News, 5/10/02, *Newsday*, 9/23/01; "good": MFR 0401840, 4/9/04—citing Eddie G. Shalev. Contrary to an assertion by skeptic Griffin, who questioned the existence of instructor Shalev, 9/11 Commission files contain the record of an interview of him by a commission staffer and an accompanying FBI agent. Shalev, moreover, is listed in various public records. Griffin, *New Pearl Harbor*, 286n99, & see, e.g., www.intelius .com.)

298   **767 simulator:** ibid., Statement of Robert Mueller, JI, 9/26/02, Transcript of Jury Trial, *U.S. v. Zacarias Moussaoui*, Vol. II-A, 3/7/06. Jarrah and Hani Hanjour, the other 9/11 hijack pilots, also trained on simulators (CR, 226–, Testimony of James Fitzgerald, *U.S. v. Zacarias Moussaoui*, 3/7/06).

299   **OBL impatient 2000:** CR, 251. The authors here cite the date used in the Commission Report, which in turn refers to KSM interrogations of 2003 and 2004. The longer account of KSM's statements, the one generally used in this book, states that bin Laden tried in spring 2000 to bring the attacks forward—surely unlikely, as he well knew the hijack pilots had at that time barely embarked on their training (CR 250, 532n177, KSM SUBST).

299–300   **KSM resisted/new candidate:** KSM SUBST, MFR 04019351, 12/10–11/03, CF; **well-to-do:** *BG*, 3/3/02, *WP*, 9/10/02; **back and forth:** Statement of Robert Mueller, JI, 9/26/02, Staff Report, 9/11 and Terrorist Travel, 12, *WP*, 9/10/02; **Hanjour license:** MFR 04021445, 1/13 & 1/25/04, CF, copies of license documents, "Airman Records— Hanjour," B45, T5, CF; **pretending:** *WP*, 9/10/02, *BG*, 3/3/02; **"frail":** FBI 302 of [name redacted], 9/18/01, "FBI 302s of Interest," B17, T7, CF; **"quiet":** MFR 04017517, 1/7/04, CF; **"mouse":** McDermott, 204; **drink/pray:** MFR 04017518, 1/5/04, CF; **in tears:** CR, 520n55; **Afghanistan at 17:** Report, JI, 135, Staff Statement 16, CO; **Atef sent KSM/KSM dispatched/thought:** KSM SUBST; **Hanjour to U.S./Hazmi/flight school:** Staff Report, 9/11 and Terrorist Travel, CO, 19–, Statement of Robert Mueller,

JI, 9/26/02, CR, 226; **school owner/"No":** *WP*, 10/21/01, 9/10/02, *Newsday*, 9/23/01; **"content"/"warrior":** *The Times* (London), 9/20/01; **"'Orwah":** Fouda & Fielding, 111.

300–301   **computer/"I went":** transcript of int. Ann Greaves, *Four Corners: A Mission to Die For*, 10/18/01, www.abc.net.au, ints. Mark Mikart; **Cole:** Katz, 269–, Miller & Stone, 226–, Wright, 319–, Graham with Nussbaum, 59–, Fox News, 1/13/09; **OBL deny/ praise:** ABC News, 3/1/00; **A destroyer:** *Time*, 9/24/01, Unger, *House of Bush, House of Saud*, 229, Wright, 333; **"With small":** *Newsweek*, 9/24/01.

301–2   **"To those":** Clinton address, 10/18/00, http://usinfo.org; **"Let's hope":** *NYT*, 10/13/01; **"What's it gonna":** Richard Clarke, 224; **"major":** State of the Union address in *WP*, 1/27/00; **"not satisfactory":** CR, 187, Report, JI, 301. National Security Adviser Berger dated this memo as February 2000. Without giving a clear source, the 9/11 Commission dated it as early March (Report, JI, 301, CR 187, 505n99); **Predator:** Staff Statement 7, CO, CR, 506n118, 513n238; **negotiations:** *CounterPunch*, 1/16/08, 9/9/09, 11/1/04, Reuters, 6/4/04; **U.N. resolution:** Resolution 1333, 12/19/00, http://avalon.law.yale.edu; **Tenet warned:** Tenet, 128.

302   **Pakistani told FBI:** Statement of Eleanor Hill, 9/18/02, JI, NBC News, 7/26/04, *Sunday Times* (London), 2/13/05. The Pakistani was Niaz Kahn, a former waiter from Oldham, near Manchester in the U.K., who apparently became involved in terrorism not because of his ideals but because he needed money. Two men he met in the U.K., he said, encouraged him to go to a camp in Pakistan, where he was given instruction in "conventional" hijackings, not suicide operations. He was eventually flown by a roundabout route to New York, but evaded the contact waiting for him and went to the FBI. Kahn's story was first reported publicly in late 2004 (NBC News, 7/26/04, *Vanity Fair*, 11/04, transcript, int. Niaz Khan, 5/18/04, in collection of Jean-Charles Brisard).

303   **Italian police/"studying":** int. Bruno Megale, Bergen, *OBL I Know*, 281, Miller & Stone, 274–. A U.S. Justice Department official was quoted after 9/11 as saying that a "small cadre of U.S. intelligence experts might have been privy to the Italian surveillance material." On the other hand, other press reporting suggests that the surveillance of the two Yemenis was "not translated by Italian police" until May 2002 (*LAT*, 5/29/02, *Chicago Tribune*, 10/8/02).

303   **Olympics:** *Sydney Morning Herald*, 9/20/01. In October, the Defense Department held a tabletop exercise simulating the crash of an airliner into the courtyard of the Pentagon. Critics have cited this as an indication that the Pentagon received early intelligence of terrorist plans to target the building with an airplane. On the evidence, however, the exercise may simply have been designed to ensure readiness for any possible sort of plane crash into the Pentagon—which is close to Reagan National Airport ("Contingency Planning Pentagon MASCAL Exercise," 11/3/00, www.dcmilitary.com, UPI, 4/22/04).

303   **FBI/FAA downplayed:** In April 2000, an FAA advisory issued to airlines and airports had stated that U.S. airliners could be targeted but that hijacking was "more probable outside the United States." The advisory would not have been replaced as of September 11, 2001 (Staff Report, "The Four Flights and Civil Aviation Security," 8/26/04, CF, 59); **"do not suggest":** Statement of Eleanor Hill, 9/18/02, JI, Report, JI, 104–; **"imprudent":** Report, JI, 334.

303–4   **"Americans would":** CR, 198; **Clinton authorized:** Tenet, 135; **Cheney/Powell/Rice:** Testimony of Sandy Berger, 3/24/04, CO, *Time*, 8/12/02, DeYoung, 344; **"As I briefed":** Richard Clarke, 229; **"sitting"/"cognizant":** Rice int., www.whitehouse.gov, 3/24/04, Testimony, 4/8/04, CO; **did not know:** Richard Clarke, 31; **"not an amateur":** ibid., 328; **Commission/"on American":** Phase III Report, *Road Map for National Security: Imperative for Change*, U.S. Commission on National Security, 2/15/01, viii, 6, Tenet, 16, *Columbia Journalism Review*, Nov/Dec 2001; **pressed to see:** Hurley to Gorelick, 4/5/04, "Commissioner Prep for Rice," B7, T3, CF; **"did not remember":** CR, 199, Ben-Veniste, 302–; **OBL biggest/"listened":** Clinton, 935–.

CHAPTER 26

305–6 **"We are not"**: George W. Bush, Inaugural Address, 1/20/01, www.bartleby.com, *Time*, 1/20/01; **"empty rhetoric"**: *WP*, 1/20/02; **"They ridiculed"**: int. of Clinton for Fox News, 9/24/06; **"What we did"**: "Report: Rice Challenges Clinton on Osama," http://wcbstv.com, 9/26/06; **"I'm tired"**: CR, 202 & see Testimony of Condoleezza Rice, 4/8/04, CO, CR, 510n185, int. of Stephen Hadley, *60 Minutes*, CBS, 3/21/04; **"just solve"**: "Transcript: Clarke Praised Bush Team in 02," Fox News, 3/24/04.

306   **nothing effective done:** As Rice recalled it, it was in May that the President told her he was tired of swatting at flies. Clarke said Bush's directive came to him in March. Bush did write to President Musharraf in February 2001, emphasizing that bin Laden was a threat to the United States that "must be addressed." Though he urged Musharraf to use his influence with the Taliban over bin Laden, the approach proved unproductive. So were further Bush administration contacts with the Pakistanis later in the year (Rice/Clarke: CR, 510n185; Musharraf: CR, 207).

306   **memo/"not some narrow"/"multiple":** Clarke to Rice & attachments, 1/25/01, www2.gwu.edu. The memorandum and the December 2000 "Strategy" document have been released, with some redactions. The September 1998 "Political-Military Plan DELENDA" [a reference to the vow to destroy Carthage, in the days of ancient Rome] has not been released (Clarke to Rice, 1/25/01, & Tab A, released to National Security Archive, www2.gwu.edu, CR, 120, Richard Clarke, 197–).

306–8 *Cole* **linked al Qaeda:** FBI IG; **"No al Qaeda plan"**: *WP*, 3/22/04; **no recommendations:** Testimony of Condoleezza Rice, 4/8/04, CO; **"Having served"**: int. Eleanor Hill; **no longer member/instead report:** CR, 200, 509n169, Clarke, 230; **no retaliation for** *Cole*: CR, 201–; **"tit-for-tat"**: Testimony of Condoleezza Rice, 4/8/04, CO & see Ben-Veniste, 304–; **"ancient history"**: MFR 04018415, 12/16/03, CF; **deputies not meet/April:** CR, 203, Richard Clarke, 231; **Wolfowitz/tetchy:** Richard Clarke, 231; **"We are going"**: Benjamin & Simon, 336.

308   **"to be paying"**: "Big Media Networks Ignore Gorelick Role, Highlight Bremer Rebuke of Bush Team," 4/30/04, citing Bremer int. for CBS News, 2/26/01, www.freerepublic .com, *LAT*, 4/30/04. Three years later, by which time he had become U.S. administrator in occupied Iraq, Bremer would attempt to backtrack and say his 2001 comment had been "unfair" to Bush, that his speech had reflected frustration that none of the National Commission's recommendations had been implemented by either the Clinton or the new Bush administration. (AP, 5/2/04); **"The highest"**: DCI's Worldwide Threat Briefing, 2/7/01, www.cia.gov; *Le Monde* **scoop:** "11 Septembre 2001: Les Français en savaient long," *Le Monde*, 4/16/07.

309   **passed on to CIA:** The DGSE document, one of more than three hundred pages leaked, is dated January 5, 2001, and numbered 00007/CT. Its heading reads: "Note de Synthèse—Projet de Détournement d'Avion par des Islamistes Radicaux," and it draws on information passed on by the intelligence service of Uzbekistan. The overall dossier leaked is entitled "Oussama bin Laden" and dated 9/13/01. The authors have seen the entire dossier. The celebrated French fortnightly, *Le Canard Enchaîné*, reporting on the material as early as October 2001, stated that "most" of the reports on bin Laden had been shared with the CIA and the FBI. *Le Monde*, in its major story of April 19, 2007, reported as a fact that the January 5 report was passed to the CIA. *Le Monde* quoted former senior DGSE official Pierre-Antoine Lorenzi as saying that such information would have been passed to the Agency as a matter of routine. Alain Chouet, former head of the Security Intelligence department, took the same view when interviewed by the authors (attachment, James to Zelikow, 4/14/04, "Motley Submission," B10, T2, CF).

309–10   **FAA 50 summaries/no action:** Staff Report, "The Four Flights and Civil Aviation Security," CO, Farmer, 96–, *New York Observer*, 6/20/04; **met Tenet almost daily:** Tenet, 137; **40 PDBs:** CR, 254.

309 **Atta January trip:** Staff Statement 16, CO. Atta flew to and back from Europe via Madrid, leaving on January 4 and returning on January 10. There is evidence suggesting he was in Berlin during that period, and the Commission Report states that his purpose in going was to see Binalshibh in Germany. It has been suggested that Madrid was more than a stopover en route to Germany, that at one point in the round-trip from the States Atta paused to meet a contact in Spain. An al Qaeda cell was active in Spain at the time. An allegation that Atta made another trip to Europe in April, during which he met with an Iraqi official in Prague, will be covered in Ch. 34 and related notes (trip: Staff Report, 9/11 & Terrorist Travel, CO, 23–, "Hijackers Timeline [redacted], 11/14/03, INTELWIRE; Binalshibh: CR, 227, 243 Staff Statement 16, CO; contact/cell: *Der Spiegel*, 10/27/03, CR, 530n145; Prague: CR,228).

309 **Shehhi Morocco:** Staff Report, 9/11 and Terrorist Travel, CO, 26–, 215n95; **Jarrah reentered/Aysel to U.S./Key West/tourist:** Aysel Sengün statement to Bundeskriminalamt, 9/15/01, authors' collection, Hijackers Timeline [redacted], 11/14/03, INTELWIRE, Staff Report, 9/11 and Terrorist Travel, CO, 21–.

309–10 **Atta hurdle/Shehhi referred/"I thought":** Staff Report, 9/11 and Terrorist Travel, CO, 22–, FBI int. [name redacted], Primary Inspector for Atta on 1/10/01, 11/27/01, "Inspector Interviews, AA11" B49, T5, CF & see "The Immigration & Naturalization Service's Contacts with Two September 11 Terrorists," Office of the Inspector General, U.S. Dept. of Justice, 5/20/02. In early May, Atta and two companions—one of whom was probably Jarrah—would go to the Miami Immigration Office to try to get the visa of one of the trio extended to eight months. The inspector not only declined that request but shortened Atta's own permitted stay to six months. Atta left without making a fuss. The second of his companions, the inspector came to suspect after 9/11, had been Adnan Shukrijumah. Shukrijumah, believed to have been an al Qaeda operative reporting to bin Laden, had as of this writing long been on the FBI's Most Wanted List. Though born in Saudi Arabia, he was entitled to live in the United States—his family had moved to Florida in the mid-1990s, but left the country shortly before 9/11. Shukrijumah's late father, an imam, had once served at the al-Farooq mosque in Brooklyn, the hub for jihadi recruiting during the anti-Soviet war (INS visit: [name redacted] Immigration Inspector to Mr. Garofano, 10/23/01, appointment list for May 2, 2001, follow-up interviews, Miami District Office, INS, 4/16/02, & MFR of [name redacted] Customs & Border Protection, 3/25/04, "Inspector Interviews," B49, T5, CF, Staff Report, 9/11 & Terrorist Travel, CO, 30–; Shukrijumah: Staff Report, 9/11 & Terrorist Travel, CO, 216n114, 256n138, CNN, 8/6/10, *NY Daily News*, 8/6/10, "Father Knows Terrorism Best," 10/27/03, www.frontpagemag.com, *Newsweek*, 4/7/04, *NYT*, 9/3/06).

310 **Atta/Shehhi turned up/rented/asked:** Hijackers Timeline [redacted], 11/14/03, INTELWIRE, Counterterrrorism to All Field Offices, 9/15/01, FBI 265A-NY-280350, Serial 2268, released under FOIA to Mike Williams of www.911myths.com, FBI memorandum, PENTTBOM, Summary of captioned investigation as of 11/4/01, 11/5/01, authors' collection, AP, 10/19/01, *WP*, 12/16/01.

310 **optional targets:** KSM SUBST. Separately, there was to be much reference to a claim by Johnelle Bryant, a loan officer for the Department of Agriculture in Homestead, Florida, that Atta came to her office to inquire about a loan to buy a plane for conversion into a crop duster. When told he did not qualify, she said, he made threats, spoke of the destruction of U.S. monuments, and praised bin Laden. Bryant dated the incident as having occurred between late April and mid-May 2000. So far as is known, however, Atta did not arrive in the United States until June 3, 2000 (Timeline Pertaining to Hijackers

in Florida, "Timelines 9/11, 2 of 2," B20, T7, CF, ABC News, 6/6/02, Edward Epstein, "The Terror Crop Dusters," www.edwardjayepstein.com, but see Miller & Stone, 268–).

310   **Hanjour certificate:** Hani Hanjour, AA Flight 77, FBI summary 03096, 4/19/02, www.scribd.com, Counterterrrorism to All Field Offices, 9/15/01, FBI 265A-NY-280350, Serial 2268, released under FOIA to Mike Williams of www.911myths.com, FBI 302 of int. FNU Milton, 4/12/02, INTELWIRE, CR, 226–; **Sporty's video:** Hijackers' Timeline [redacted], 11/14/03, INTELWIRE; **Grand Canyon:** Nawaf al-Hazmi, AA Flight 77, FBI summary 03177, 4/19/02, www.scribd.com; **greet muscle:** Bamford, *Shadow Factory*, 50, Staff Report, 9/11 & Terrorist Travel, CO, 29–.

310   **new arrivals/"The Hour":** CR, 231, *BG*, 3/3/02, 3/4/02. The thirteen were: Satam al-Suqami, Wail al-Shehri, Waleed al-Shehri, Abdul Aziz al-Omari, Ahmed al-Ghamdi, Hamza al-Ghamdi, Mohand al-Shehri, Majed Moqed, Salem al-Hazmi, Saeed al-Ghamdi, Ahmad al-Haznawi, and Ahmed al-Nami—all Saudis—and Fayez Banihammad, from the UAE. Also in the muscle group on 9/11 would be Hamzi and Mihdhar (the latter having arrived back in the United States as of early July). The group included two pairs of brothers, Nawaf and Salem al-Hazmi and Wail and Waleed al-Shehri—though Mohand al-Shehri was unrelated. The three Ghamdis appear to have been not close relatives but merely members of the large Ghamdi tribe. Saudi press reports noted that in Saudi Arabia "the names al Ghamdi and al Shehri are as common as the name Smith in the United States" (CR, 231, 237, *Arab News*, 9/18/01, 9/20/01, 9/22/01, *BG*, 3/3/02).

311   **OBL picked:** CR, 235; **5'7":** ibid., 231; **martyr:** ibid., 234; **visa easy/Express:** Staff Report, 9/11 & Terrorist Travel, CO, 32–, 111–, CR, 235, **"teater"/"Wasantwn":** Non-immigrant Visa Application of Wail al-Shehri, Joel Mowbray, "Visas for Terrorists," *National Review*, archived at www.webcitation.org; **"did not think":** Staff Report, 9/11 & Terrorist Travel, CO, 125, MFR 04016462, 12/5/03, CF; **sky marshals:** CR, 236; **butcher/"to muddy"/told Dubai:** KSM SUBST.

311–12   **travel pairs/"businessman"/tourists/unsatisfactory:** Staff Report, 9/11 & Terrorist Travel, CO, 29–, Janice Kephart, "The Complete Immigration Story of 9/11 Hijacker Satam al Suqami," 9/10, www.cis.org. The authors refer here to documentation that was inadequate on its face, but passed muster at Immigration or Customs control. Four of the muscle hijackers, meanwhile, had markers in their passports later understood to have been signs of tampering associated with al Qaeda (Staff Report, 9/11 Terrorist Travel, 29, 33, 34).

312   **prior arrangement:** KSM SUBST; **flew DC/NY:** Staff Report, 9/11 & Terrorist Travel, CO, 29–; **Atta/Hazmi/money:** CR, 237; **videos/"We left":** *Guardian* (U.K.), 4/16/02, Bruce Hoffman, *Inside Terrorism*, NY: Columbia Univ. Press, 2006, 133, CR 235, 525n104. The first hijacker videotape was released in April 2002 (*Guardian* [U.K.], 4/16/02).

312–14   **Massoud/"If President Bush":** Roy Gutman, *How We Missed the Story*, Washington, D.C.: U.S. Institute of Peace Press, 2008, 246–; Steve Coll, "Ahmad Shah Massoud Links with CIA," 2/23/04, www.rawa.org, *WP*, 1/19 & 20/02; **"gained limited":** Defense Intelligence Agency, cable, "IIR [redacted]/The Assassination of Massoud Related to 11 September 2001 Attack," 11/21/01, as released to the National Security Archive, www.gwu.edu, Schroen, 95–; **"was sending":** Tenet, 156; **Cairo/"We knew":** *NYT*, 6/4/02; **"something big was coming":** MFR 03009296, 11/3/03, MFR 04017179, 10/3/03; **Freeh/Ashcroft/denied:** *Newsweek*, 5/27/02; **briefing documents/"public profile":** Staff Statement 10, CO, Shenon, 151–. The exception is the PDB of August 6, which is covered later in this chapter; **triumphalist speeches:** Bergen, *OBL I Know*, 293–, *Orange County Weekly*, 9/7/02; **"They send":** *The Australian*, 12/21/07, *The Age* (Melbourne),

12/21/07; **"All the people"**: *Guardian* (U.K.), 11/28/02; **Mihdhar/"I will make"**: Bamford, *Shadow Factory*, 64; **"the success"**: CR, 251; **"It's time"**: Fouda & Fielding, 166.

314 **Taliban asked:** CR, 251. The Taliban appear to have been concerned not only about U.S. reprisals, but also as to what bin Laden should target. Taliban leader Mullah Omar reportedly favored attacking Jews—not necessarily the United States. Emails found later on the terrorist computer obtained by *Wall Street Journal* reporter Cullison show there was also dissension amongst the terrorists as to whether to give bin Laden full support at this time. "Going on," one writer complained, "is like fighting ghosts and windmills" (CR, 250–, *WSJ*, 7/2/02).

314 **MBC reporter/"some news"/"coffin"**: *In the Footsteps of Bin Laden*, 8/23/06, www.cnn .com, Bergen, *OBL I Know*, 284–. According to CIA reporting of KSM's interrogations, KSM and Atef "were concerned about this lack of discretion and urged bin Laden not to make additional comments about the plot." It seems odd then that Atef, normally described as having been professional, should have taken part in the MBC interview. He may have hoped at least to blur the truth by referring to the coming attacks as targeting "American and Israeli interests"—thus avoiding giving away the fact that the attack would be on U.S. territory. If that was his intention, the deception was successful—many in the U.S. had the impression that the attack would take place overseas ("were concerned": KSM SUBST, Atef: CR, refs.; successful: e.g. CR, 256–).

314–15 **impatient/Cole**: KSM SUBST, e.g. Mehnaz Sahibzada, "The Symbolism of the Number 7 in Islamic Culture and Rituals," www.wadsworth.com; **dreams:** e.g., Fouda & Fielding, 109, Lacey, *Inside the Kingdom*, 21, *WP*, 9/11/02; **OBL bombarded/Sharon visit/Arafat not invited:** KSM SUBST, *NYT*, 6/20/01; **"big gift"**: Bergen, *OBL I Know*, 284–.

315–16 **"like Captain Ahab"**: Richard Clarke, 234; **"Clarke was driving"**: Conclusions from Review of NSC papers, "Misc. 9/11 Commission Staff Notes About Drafting Final Report," 16095055, CF; **"When these attacks"**: CR, 256; **rated a seven:** Tenet, 145–; **was "recruiting"/high alert:** CR, 256–; **"very, very"/Clarke duly:** CR, 257, Bamford, *Shadow Factory*, 55; **July 10 assessment/"There will"/"put his elbows"**: Tenet, 150–.

316 **"felt"/"The decision"/"Adults"**: Bob Woodward, *State of Denial*, NY: Simon & Schuster, 2006, 49–. It seems clear from this passage—in his 2006 book, *State of Denial*—that he interviewed Cofer Black. Also, perhaps, former CIA director Tenet. While Woodward reported that Tenet left the meeting "feeling frustrated," Tenet stated in his memoir the following year that Black and the head of the Agency's bin Laden unit departed feeling that "at last . . . we had gotten the full attention of the administration." Within two days, a congressional report shows, Tenet went to the Capitol to give a similar briefing to U.S. senators. Only a handful turned up. It was a mystery to him, Tenet wrote, why the 9/11 Commission Report failed to mention the July 10 meeting with Rice—he had told the commissioners about the encounter in closed testimony. It was established that Tenet had indeed told the Commission of the meeting. As others have noted, the Commission's executive director, Philip Zelikow, was closer to Rice and other Bush appointees than was healthy for a man heading a supposedly even-handed investigation—he had even coauthored a book with Rice. According to 9/11 Commissioner Richard Ben-Veniste, Tenet thought Rice "understood the level of urgency he was communicating."

"It is shocking," Peter Rundlet, a former Commission counsel, has written, "that the administration failed to heed such an overwhelming alert from the two officials in the best position to know. Many, many questions need to be asked and answered about this revelation" (meeting: Woodward, *State of Denial*, 50–, Tenet, 151–; congressional report: Report, "Tora Bora Revisited: How We Failed to Get Bin Laden and Why It Matters Today," Committee on Foreign Relations, U.S. Senate, 111th Cong., 1st Sess.,

U.S. Govt. Printing Office, Washington, D.C., 11/30/09, 4; indeed given: *WP,* 10/3/06; Zelikow: e.g., Shenon, 40–, 65–, 106–, Woodward, *State of Denial,* 52; understood: McClatchy Newspapers, 10/2/06; Rundlet: Peter Rundlet, "Bush Officials May Have Covered Up Rice-Tenet Meeting from 9/11 Commission," http://thinkprogress.org).

316–17   **Black/Scheuer/UBL unit head resignations:** MFR 03009296, 9/3/03, Shenon, 395, CR, 259–; **"The purpose"/Williams concerns/Zubaydah/connected/Hanjour/Williams recommended:** Phoenix, Squad 16 to Counterterrorism, 7/10/01, www .justice.gov, FBI IG, Statement of Eleanor Hill re "The FBI's Handling of the Phoenix Electronic Communication and Investigation of Zacarias Moussaoui Prior to Sept. 11, 2001," 9/24/02 [as updated 10/17/02]. The suspicious activity on the America West flight, which may have been reconnaissance for the 9/11 operation, is described in Ch. 24; **minimal circulation:** *NYT,* 6/10/05, Amy B. Zegart, *Spying Blind,* Princeton: Princeton University Press, 2007, 261n55; **"racial profiling":** Report, JI, 5; **"exercise":** NLETS Message (All Regions), from Counterterrorism, 7/2/01, INTELWIRE; **"I had asked":** Richard Clarke, 236–.

318   **"I don't want":** The Justice Department told the Commission that Ashcroft, his former deputy, and his chief of staff denied that he had made such a comment to Pickard. Ashcroft himself also denied it in his April 2004 Commission testimony. Pickard, for his part, reiterated his allegation in testimony, in Commission interviews, in a letter to the commission—and in a later long interview with reporter Philip Shenon. The commission was unable to resolve the contradictory accounts. It found, though, that—whatever the truth about the Ashcroft/Pickard relationship, "The domestic agencies never mobilized in response to the threat. They did not have direction, and did not have a plan" (Justice Dept./Ashcroft denials: Hearing transcript & Testimony of Ashcroft, 4/13/04, CO; Pickard: CR, 265, 536n52, Shenon, 246, 432n, Ch. 35).

318   **"Fishing rod"/"Frankly":** CBS News, 7/26/01. Ashcroft and senior FBI officials had received recent briefings on the increased terrorist threat level. It is conceivable, however, that the decision that Ashcroft not fly commercial was taken because of threats of a different nature. From early on, reportedly, there had been threats to Ashcroft's personal safety—sparked by his opposition to abortion and gun control (briefings: CR, 258, MFR 04019823, 6/3/04, e.g. Briefing Material, Weekly with Attorney General, 7/12/01, "Ashcroft," B1, Dan Marcus files, CF; threats: Shenon, 243–).

318   **G8 summit:** CR, 258, Shenon, 243–; **slept ships/Pope/airspace:** BBC News, 6/21/01, CNN, 7/17/01, *WP,* 1/19/02, *NYT,* 9/26/01.

318   **Mubarak:** Benjamin & Simon, 342, *Daily Record* (Glasgow), 9/27/01. Warnings of a possible bin Laden attack at Genoa, specifically targeting Bush, also reportedly came from German and Russian intelligence. There were also concerns that violent protest might disturb public order during the summit (BBC News, 6/27/01, CNN, 7/17/01).

CHAPTER 27

319   **Dubai/passport copied:** *New Yorker,* 7/10/06, Wright, 311, Report, JI, 144, but see Bamford, *Shadow Factory,* 18–.

319   **CIA had not placed:** In spite of the discovery of an internal CIA cable alleging that the visa information had been shared with the FBI, complex investigation did nothing to substantiate the assertion. Other documents, the 9/11 Commission reported, "contradict" the claim that the visa information was shared with the Bureau. The Commission flatly states that "no one alerted the INS or the FBI" to look for Mihdhar or his traveling companion, Nawaf al-Hazmi (CR, 502n44, 354, & see Tenet, 195).

320   **Mihdhar/visas/July 4:** Staff Report, 9/11 & Terrorist Travel, 33–, 37; **two groups/NJ/Fort Lauderdale:** CR, 230, 240, 248, 253, *WP,* 9/30/01, Hijackers Timeline [redacted], 11/14/03, INTELWIRE; **Mihdhar/crammed:** ibid., CR, 240–, McDermott,

221; **Hazmi bride:** CR, 222, **marriage obligatory:** Fouda & Fielding, 81, & see, e.g., "The Importance of Marriage in Islam," www.sunniforum.com.

320   **Atta:** *Chicago Tribune*, 9/11/04, *Newsweek*, 10/1/01, Bernstein, 105, MFR 04017500, 12/4/03. In a 2004 book, author Daniel Hopsicker gave an account of a supposed relationship, covering periods in 2000 and 2001, between Atta and a young woman named Amanda Keller. Widely circulated on the Internet, the account presents a picture of a deeply unpleasant character who—were the account to prove accurate—frequented sleazy nightspots, beat his girlfriend, and—in one savage incident—killed and dismembered one of her cats and an entire litter of kittens. After lengthy analysis of a tangled scenario, however, the authors concluded that this has been a matter of mistaken identity. A young woman who—according to the Hopsicker account—accompanied Atta and Keller on a trip to the Florida Keys did not recognize pictures of the authentic Atta as the "Mohamed" who made the trip. Keller's mother and sister are reported as having said that her Mohamed was "tall," "lanky," while Atta was only five foot seven. She said early on her boyfriend was French Canadian, and that he told her he had fathered a child in France. That could of course have been a lie—except for another element. According to Keller, the name her Mohamed used at one point to sign a document was "Mohamed Arajaki"—and an official list of men of interest to law enforcement after 9/11 includes a reference to an "Arakj, Mohamad" with a French address.

    In the transcript of a long interview with Hopsicker, Keller refers to her sometime boyfriend only as Mohamed, not as Atta or as definitely having been Atta. Press reports of interviews with Keller, moreover, have twice thrown doubt on the notion that her boyfriend was future hijacker Atta. Phone checks, said a counterterrorism agent cited in the second report—in 2006—indicated that the real Atta and Keller never called each other. Keller herself was quoted in that report as saying her Mohamed had been "another flight student not connected to 9/11." If she had given the impression that he was the real Atta, she reportedly said, that had been "my bad for lying. . . . I really didn't think about it until after I did it." The authors did not succeed in reaching Keller for interview. (Hopsicker account: Hopsicker, refs., Keller videotape seen by authors, transcript provided by Hopsicker; trip to Keys: ints. & corr. Linda Lopez; "tall"/"lanky": *Sarasota Herald-Tribune*, 9/24/01; 5'7": Temporary Airman Certificate, "Airman Records," B45, T5, CF; "Arajaki": Hopsicker, 76; list: AP, 10/12/01, list inadvertently released first in Finland, later in Italy, in authors' collection; press reports: *Sarasota Herald-Tribune*, 9/23/01, 9/10/06; in addition, relevant authors' interviews included Elaine Emrich, Stephanie Frederickson, Vicky Keyser, Earle Kimel, Tony & Vonnie LaConca, and Neil Patton).

320–21   **injections:** *NYT,* 4/25/11; **KSM stipend:** CR, 518n40.

321   **muslimmarriage.com:** MFR of int. [name redacted], 2/23/04, CF. Two of the hijack pilots had married or gone through a form of marriage. As early as 1999, Jarrah and his girlfriend, Aysel, took part in a wedding ceremony at a Hamburg mosque, and—though she would later say she did not consider it binding (the marriage was not registered with the state)—Aysel referred to herself in a letter as Jarrah's "yearning wife." Under pressure from his family, Shehhi had married during a trip back to the United Arab Emirates in early 2000—only to decline to go through with the relationship afterward. Mohamed Atta's father, meanwhile, was to say he found his son a prospective wife who was "nice and delicate, the daughter of a former ambassador." By one account, Atta agreed to get engaged to the woman in 1999—but any prospect of the union becoming a reality vanished with his extended stay in Germany and growing commitment to jihad. One account holds that Atta spoke of marrying a Turk rather than an Egyptian, because he thought Turkish women "more obedient." Binalshibh, for his part, picked up a young woman—believed to have been a Japanese Roman Catholic!—in 2000, and proposed within twenty-four hours. She would have to dress and behave in the way required of a

Muslim wife, he told her, and that their children would have to be brought up to hate Jews. Though they never met again after the initial five-day interlude, Binalshibh later wrote her emails signed: "Your King, Ramzi." Records, meanwhile, indicate that two of the muscle hijackers, Banihammad and Omari, were married (Jarrah: McDermott, 78–; Shehhi: ibid., 54, Corbin, 224, Berlin to Counterterrorism, 12/5/03, FBI 315N-WF-227135, INTELWIRE; Atta: *Newsweek*, 10/1/01, Bernstein, 105, MFR 04017500, 12/4/03, CF; Binalshibh: McDermott, 199–; Banihammad: Riyadh to Counterterrorism, 10/15/01, FBI 265A-NY-280350, Misc. Request 54, "Aliases and Ids," B62, T5, CF; Omari: Visa Application, 6/8/01, www.oldnationalreview.com).

321   **fishing:** Hijackers Timeline [redacted], 11/14/03, INTELWIRE; **Wacko's:** ibid., "Exclusive: 9/11 Hijacker Stayed at Jacksonville Hotel," www.firstcoastnews.com.

321   **lap dancing/movies/sex toys:** "Agents of Terror Leave Mark on Sin City," 10/4/01, www.sfgate.com, Hijackers Timeline [redacted], 11/14/03, INTELWIRE, FBI report, "The 11 September Hijacker Cell Model," 2/03, released under FOIA to INTELWIRE. Shehhi's reported visit to a lap dancing club occurred during a trip to Las Vegas, reported later in this chapter. Earlier, in California in 2000, Hazmi and Mihdhar had also reportedly visited strip clubs. The hijacker who visited the Adult Lingerie Center was Majed Moqed (Shehhi: *San Francisco Chronicle*, 10/4/01; Hazmi/Mihdhar: *LAT*, 9/11/02, *Newsweek*, 6/10/02, 10/15/01; Moqed: *Newsday*, 9/23/01, *Newsweek*, 10/15/01, *WP*, 9/30/01, summary re Majed Moqed, JICI, 4/19/02, FBI03135, www.scribd.com).

321–22   **Jarrah to Germany:** Hijackers Timeline [redacted], 11/14/03, INTELWIRE; **Rodriguez/"very humble":** Jeffrey Steinberg, "Cheney's 'Spoon-Benders' Pushing Nuclear Armegeddon," 8/26/05, *Executive Intelligence Review*, eds. *Der Spiegel*, 104–; **fitness classes:** Hijackers Timeline [redacted], 11/14/03, INTELWIRE, "Hijackers' True Name Usage," *U.S. v. Zacarias Moussaoui*, Exhibit 0G0013; **knives:** "Hijacker Knife Purchases," B18, T7, CF; **Hortman:** MFR 04018712, 4/27/04, & MFR 04018407, 4/12/04, CF, Staff Statement 16, CO; **Hanjour Hudson/practice flight DC:** Hijackers Timeline [redacted], 11/14/03, INTELWIRE, Staff Statement 16, CO.

322   **familiarize routine/Vegas, etc.:** "Hijackers' True Name Usage," *U.S. v. Zacarias Moussaoui*, Exhibit 0G0013, Report, JI, 139, MFR, 04016230 [Las Vegas Investigative Summary, undated], MFR 04018564, 1/5/04, MFR 04016240, 1/5/04, & MFR 04016244, 1/5/04, CF. Jarrah was accompanied in Las Vegas by an older fellow Arab. The unidentified Arab resembled the "uncle" who had accompanied him days earlier when he rented a small plane at a Philadelphia airport (MFR 04016240, 1/5/04, MFR 04016239, 1/5/04, CF).

322   **74 times:** McDermott, 222, MFR 04019351, 12/10–11/03, CF; **knives:** MFR 04019351, 12/10–11/03, CF.

322   **needed talk/rendezvous Europe/Spain:** CR, 243–, 530n145. The Commission Report suggests that the pair talked at a hotel not far from Cambrils, near Barcelona, and that Atta rented accommodations in the area until July 19. The experienced author Edward Epstein, who had interviewed prominent Spanish investigating magistrate Baltasar Garzón, wrote in a 2007 article that Atta and Binalshibh "dropped from sight leaving no hotel records, cellphone logs or credit-card receipts" from July 9 to July 16. Judge Garzón reasoned that they spent that time at a prearranged safe house organized by a Spanish-based Algerian accomplice and al Qaeda activists in Spain. Phone intercepts showed that Binalshibh was in touch with the Algerian a few weeks later. Other intercepts indicated that the Germany-based Syrian suspect Marmoun Darkazanli (see Ch. 24) was in Spain at approximately the same time. Binalshibh would claim under interrogation that he met no one but Atta in Spain (Cambrils: CR, 244, 530n145; "dropped"/Algerian accomplice: Edward J. Epstein, "The Spanish Connection," 2/22/07, www.opinionjournal.com, *LAT*, 1/14/03, CNN, 10/31/01; Darkazanli: *LAT*, 1/14/03; Binalshibh: CR, 244).

322–23   **OBL wanted/security/"symbols"/"preferred":** Staff Report, "9/11 & Terrorist Travel," CO, 207, 244; **WH too tough/streets:** CR, 244; **"in the hands":** KSM SUBST; **necklaces/phones:** CR, 245.

323   **Atta admitted:** Staff Report, "9/11 & Terrorist Travel," CO, 38. If the identifications made by witnesses at the Pelican Alley restaurant in Venice, Florida, are accurate, then Atta and Shehhi may have been back in Venice in late July—with a dark-complexioned companion—engaged in what appeared to be a heated argument (ints. Tom & Renee Adorna, Jeff Pritko).

323–24   **drop out?/called Aysel/ticket/"emotional":** CR, 246–, Staff Statement 16, CO, MFR 04019350, 3/18/04, CR, Hijackers Timeline [redacted], 11/14/03, INTELWIRE.

323   **Binalshibh told KSM:** How we come to know about this exchange, which was conducted on the phone, will be discussed in Ch. 30. If meant literally, the reference to cost in the conversation is odd (and perhaps merely code) unless, as the Commission was to surmise, KSM was referring to the cost and trouble of organizing a replacement hijacking pilot. The notional replacement, the commission thought, was likely Zacarias Moussaoui, the French-born terrorist who had been sent to the United States for pilot training early in 2001. During his conversation with Binalshibh, KSM authorized the sending of "skirts" to "Sally," an instruction believed to mean that Binalshibh was to send Moussaoui $14,000. Binalshibh did so in early August. According to KSM, however, he at no stage contemplated using Moussaoui as a pilot on the 9/11 operation, but rather in a later "second wave" of attacks. As will emerge later in this chapter, Moussaoui would be detained in August because of his suspect behavior at a flight school in Minnesota (CR, 246–, Indictment, 12/01 & Superceding Indictment, 7/02, *U.S. v. Zacarias Moussaoui*, Staff Statement 16, CO).

324–25   **"We spent":** Aysel Sengün statement to Bundeskriminalamt, 9/15/01, authors' collection; **apartment:** Jarrah timeline, "03009470, Packet 6, Ziad Jarrah chronology," www.scribd.com; **"This House":** *Newsweek*, 9/24/01; **"big planes":** int. Rosmarie Canel by Hannah Cleaver; **GPS:** Jarrah timeline; **Atta/Hazmi stopped by police:** Hijackers Timeline [redacted], 11/14/03, INTELWIRE, Mohamed Mohamed Elamir Awad Elsayed Atta, Enforcement Operations Division, Texas Service Center, Intelligence Division, INS, "Hijacker Primary Documents—AA11," B51, T5, CF, & see Graham with Nussbaum, 36–; **"Every cop":** MFR of George Tenet, 12/23/03, CF; **"five or six weeks":** Staff Statement 16, CO, CR, 243; **"Salaam":** McDermott, 225.

325   **warnings:** Chicago attorney David Schippers said soon after 9/11 that he had received information on a coming terror attack on Manhattan and that—"a month before the bombing"—he had tried to get a warning to Attorney General Ashcroft. He said he was never able to reach Ashcroft and was brushed off by Justice Department officials. Schippers's sources, he said, included FBI agents and policemen. In the summer of 2001, Schippers was attorney for Chicago FBI counterterrorism agent Robert Wright, whose book—a "blueprint on how the events of September 11 were inevitable"—was to be suppressed by the FBI. Schippers had also become a vocal advocate for Jayna Davis, an Oklahoma journalist whose research on the bombing of the Alfred P. Murrah building posits a Middle East connection to that attack (see Ch. 22). The warnings Schippers said he attempted to pass on were not just of a coming attack on New York City but also covered Davis's research and information on the infiltration of the United States by the Palestinian group Hamas. The totality of his information, Schippers later concluded, was to lead people to think he was "crazy." Schippers had earlier served as chief investigative counsel to the House Judiciary Committee during the impeachment probe of President Clinton (int. David Schippers, *The Alex Jones Show*, 10/10/01, www.infowars.com, *Indianapolis Star*, 5/18/02, *Chicago* magazine, 10/02, Jayna Davis, *The Third Terrorist*, Nashville: WND, 2004, Foreword).

325   **DGSE:** "Motley Submissions—French Intelligence Passed to the U.S.—Moussaoui—Planes as Weapons Widely Known," B10, T2, CF, "Oussama Bin Laden," leaked DGSE report, 9/13/01, seen by authors.

325   **Russian FSB;** AFP, 9/16/01'; **"20 al Qaeda":** *60 Minutes II: The Plot*, CBS, 10/9/02.

325   **Muttawakil:** Muttawakil's information was given him, according to the emissary, by the head of the Islamic Movement of Uzbekistan, Tahir Yildash. The detail is relevant, for the earliest French intelligence information on bin Laden's hijacking plans came from Uzbek contacts (see pp. 308–9). Following the U.S. rout of the Taliban regime that he had predicted, former Taliban minister Muttawakil surrendered in early 2002, was for some time held in American custody, then freed. His emissary, who told his story on condition of anonymity, stayed on in Kabul—apparently at liberty. U.S. diplomat David Katz declined to discuss the episode when contacted in 2002. The story was reported by the BBC and the British newspaper *The Independent*, based on an interview of the emissary by the journalist Kate Clark (BBC News, *The Independent* [U.K.], 9/7/02).

326–28   **plans postponed:** CR, 259, 534n28; **"will still happen":** ibid., 260, 534n32; **Miller/"very spun-up":** FBI IG; **slow progress/"But the Principals' ":** Testimony of Richard Clarke, 4/8/04, CO; **Bush vacation/"I'm sure":** ABC News, 8/3/01, AP, 8/6/01, *USA Today*, 8/3/01; **Cheney:** *Jackson Hole News & Guide* (Wyoming), 8/15/01; **poll/"too much":** *USA Today*, 8/6/01, "Public Critical of Bush's Vacation Plans," 8/7/01, www.gallup.com, *WP*, 8/7/01. As things turned out, the president was to return to Washington a few days earlier than planned, on August 30 (Public Papers of the Presidents, George W. Bush, 2001, www.gpoaccess.gov, 1569); **CBS re PDB/"bin Laden's":** "What Bush Knew Before September 11," 5/17/02, www.cbsnews.com; **Fleischer/"very generalized":** press briefing, 5/16/02, http://georgewbush-whitehouse.gov; **Fleischer follow-up:** press briefing, 5/17/02, http://georgewbush-whitehouse.gov; **Rice/"not a warning"/"an analytic"/"hijacking"/"could have":** press briefing, 5/16/02, http://georgewbush-whitehouse.archives.gov; **"historical":** ibid., Testimony of Condoleezza Rice, 4/8/04, CO; **struggle:** e.g. Report, JI, 1, Kean & Hamilton, 89–; **"the most highly":** press briefing by Ari Fleischer, 5/21/02, http://georgewbush-whitehouse.gov; **CIA refused:** Report, JI, 1; **several released:** Thomas Blanton, "The President's Daily Brief," National Security Archive, 4/12/04, www.gwu.edu; **leather binder:** Tenet, 31; **"top-secret":** Graham, with Nussbaum, 80; **"news digest":** Blanton, "The President's Daily Brief"; **truly secret/dull:** ibid., Shenon, 220; **Joint Inquiry pressed:** Report, JI, 1; **Commission/"What did":** Kean & Hamilton, 89–, Zelikow to Kean & Hamilton, Proposal for Breaking PDB Impasse, 9/25/03, "Letters & Memos, Negotiations over Access to PDBs," B6, Dan Marcus files, CF; **"blowtorch":** Ben-Veniste, 239; **heading had not read:** *The Washington Post* had reported the correct headline as early as May 19, 2002, two days after Fleischer misstated it. The significance of the press secretary's omission of the word "in," however, got lost in the fog of the subsequent White House effort to minimize the PDB's overall importance ("Press Briefing by Ari Fleischer," 5/17/02, www.gwu.edu, *WP*, 5/19/02, *Nation*, 4/12/04).

328   **Aug. 6 PDB:** released 4/10/04, "Withdrawal Notice re 4–12–04 memo re Aug. 6 PDB, Withdrawal Notice re 5–16–01 Daily UBL Threat," B6, Dan Marcus files, CF. The PDB also referred to the fact that, as indicated by the attacks on the American embassies in Africa in 1998, bin Laden prepared operations "years in advance and is not deterred by setbacks." The PDB also stated that the FBI was currently "conducting approximately 70 full field investigations throughout the U.S." that it considered bin Laden–related. This last assertion turned out to be a CIA misunderstanding of a liaison call to the FBI. Some seventy *individuals* were apparently being investigated by the FBI (Testimony of Thomas Pickard, 4/13/04, CO, Zegart, 109).

328–29   **redacted:** Fact Sheet on Aug. 6, 2001, PDB, Office of the Press Secretary, 4/10/04, www.gwu.gov; **"said nothing"/at own request:** remarks by the President to the Travel Pool [Fort Hood, TX], 4/11/04, www.whitehouse.gov; **Bush/Commission meeting/ Ben-Veniste account:** Ben-Veniste, 293– & see Shenon, 291–, 340–, CR, 260–, Kean & Hamilton, 206–; **Clarke "in writing":** see CR, 255, 263, 535n5; **"I really don't":** Testimony of Condoleezza Rice, 4/8/04, CO.

329   **nobody could have foreseen:** Rice acknowledged in her 2004 Commission testimony that she had misspoken in her comment to the press in 2002 that "no one" could have predicted hijackers using planes as missiles. Given the Genoa situation, she said—and given that others had indeed foreseen the possibility—Rice said she ought to have said only that *she* could not have imagined an attack using planes in that way. By contrast, Louis Freeh—FBI director until June 2001—told the Commission that the possible use of planes in suicide missions had in his experience been part of the planning for potential terrorist events (misspoken/*she* could not: Testimony of Condoleezza Rice, 4/8/04, CO, Ben-Veniste, 251, Press Briefing by Condoleezza Rice, 5/16/02, http://georgewbush-whitehouse.archives.gov; Freeh: Testimony of Louis Freeh, 4/13/04, CO).

331   **follow up/discussed with Ashcroft?:** The job of making contact with domestic agencies, Bush told Commissioner Jamie Gorelick, was not Rice's but that of White House chief of staff Andy Card. This assertion was impossible to check because the commission was bound by yet another condition, not to raise questions arising from the Rice or Bush-Cheney interviews with other White House officials. (Ben-Veniste, 303).

331   **Rice in Texas?:** A contemporary *Washington Post* report of the President's activity on August 6 stated that he "held a 45-minute meeting with four senior officials here and talked *by telephone* with National Security Advisor Condoleezza Rice about Macedonia." (authors' italics) (*WP,* 8/7/01, *USA Today*, 8/6/01, 10:24 P.M. update); **doubt/"asked for it":** Ben-Veniste, 300, remarks by the President to the Travel Pool, [Fort Hood, TX], 4/11/04, www.whitehouse.gov; **"All right":** Suskind, *One Percent Doctrine*, 1–, Ben-Veniste, 300, additional information gathered by authors, not for attribution; **"no formal":** Tenet to Kean & Hamilton, 3/26/04, "PDB—letter from Tenet re Aug. 6 PDB," B6, Dan Marcus files, CF; **"none":** Ben-Veniste, 391.

331   **"current"/"pay more":** Shenon, 379, 437n. This account of the August 6 PDB episode is intended by the authors to be not an assessment of the document's quality but a summary of its content—in the context of the way President Bush, National Security Adviser Rice, and press secretary Fleischer described its contents. Author Amy Zegart severely criticized the quality of the PDB in her book *Spying Blind*, on the CIA and the FBI and their role prior to 9/11. She judged it a "tragically shoddy piece of intelligence." Former CIA counterterrorism chief Cofer Black, however, characterized it as a "place-marker" or "reminder" that bin Laden's ultimate objective was "to strike hard against the United States" (Zegart, 108, Testimony of Cofer Black, 4/13/04, CO).

331   **"had written":** Ben-Veniste, 301–.

332–33   **manager alerted/Moussaoui/"goal"/"I am sure"/$6,800:** Stipulation, 3/1/06, *U.S. v. Zacarias Moussaoui*, 3/1/06; **"joy ride":** "Moussaoui, Zacarias, IT—Other," 8/19/01, *U.S. v. Zacarias Moussaoui*, Exhibit 692; **string of questions/detained/"martyrs"/ "unambiguous"/"convinced"/:** CR, 273–, FBI IG, MFR 04019350, 3/18/04, CF, Report, JI, 22–; **KSM would tell/"problematic personality":** KSM SUBST, CR, 247, 531n162; **met Binalshibh/$14,000/telephone number:** Staff Report, "Monograph on Terrorist Financing," CO, MFR, 04019350, 3/18/04, Indictment & Exhibits MN00601, MN00601.1, MN00601.2, *U.S. v. Zacarias Moussaoui*, CR, 225, 520n54.

333   **agents knew nothing:** Had agents been cleared to examine Moussaoui's possessions, they would have discovered letters purporting to show that Moussaoui was acting as consultant in the States for a company called "InFocus Tech." The signature on the letters was that of Yazid Sufaat, the owner of the Kuala Lumpur condominium in which the

terrorist meeting—attended by Mihdhar and Hazmi—had been held in January 2000. The FBI had been aware of that meeting at the time, so—had the Bureau's system been adequately coordinated—discovery of the letters in timely fashion would immediately have linked Moussaoui to al Qaeda. (Report, JI, 26, Exhibit OK01043, *U.S. v. Zacarias Moussaoui*).

333   **appeals/70 messages:** Statement of Eleanor Hill re "The FBI's Handling of the Phoenix Electronic Communication and Investigation of Zacarias Moussaoui Prior to Sept. 11, 2001," 9/24/02 [as updated 10/17/02], JI, *USA Today*, 3/2/06, *Newsday*, 3/21/06, *LAT*, 3/21/06; **"spun up"/"take control":** FBI IG.

333   **"That's not":** Statement of Eleanor Hill. The headquarters failure to respond positively on Moussaoui was to lead to protracted outrage and regret. The wrangle had centered on the complex matter of how legally to get access to Moussaoui's possessions. The options available were either a criminal search warrant or a Foreign Intelligence Surveillance (FISA) warrant—permitted, in this context, if it can be shown that the subject is an agent of an international terrorist group and is engaged in terrorism on behalf of that group. The case agent in Minneapolis, concerned that there was insufficient probable cause for a criminal warrant, favored the FISA option—only to be confronted by legalistic hurdles thrown up by headquarters. The go-ahead was given only on September 11, after the two strikes on the World Trade Center. Evidence and detainee statements were eventually to link Moussaoui to KSM and Binalshibh, and he is now serving a life sentence for conspiracy to commit acts of terror and air piracy. As of this writing, the only other person convicted—of being an accessory to the murder of the people aboard the planes on 9/11— is Mounir Motassadeq, who is serving fifteen years in Germany. Motassadeq, an associate of the Hamburg-based hijackers, was accused of helping the hijackers prepare for the 9/11 operation. In a lengthy prison interview, Motassadeq told the authors that—while he had certainly been an associate and friend of the future hijackers in Hamburg—he had had no knowledge whatsoever of what they were plotting. The authors came away from the interview doubting that he was guilty as charged (warrant options: e.g., Graham with Nussbaum, 51; go-ahead: FBI IG; evidence/sentence: Indictment, *U.S. v. Zacarias Moussaoui*, 12/01, AP, 5/4/06, CNN, 4/23/05; Motassadeq: *NYT*, 1/9/07, *Der Spiegel*, 1/12/07, *Economist*, 9/3/02, CBS News, 10/22/02, ints. Motassadeq, Udo Jacob, 2009).

333–34   **second development/New information/Wilshire reconsidered/"Something bad":** CR, 266–,FBI IG. In the 9/11 Commission Report, and in a 2004 review of the FBI's handling of pre-9/11 intelligence information issued by the Justice Department's inspector general, relevant CIA and FBI personnel are referred to by pseudonyms. True names of many of the individuals were revealed in evidence prepared in 2006 for Moussaoui's trial. Others have been asserted by independent writers, notably Lawrence Wright and Kevin Fenton, and the authors have used these identifications in the text. The CIA officer named here as Tom Wilshire is "John" in the official reports. The FBI analyst Margarette Gillespie is "Mary" in reports, while the FBI analyst Dina Corsi appears to be identical with "Jane" in the Commission Report and with "Donna" in the inspector general's review. Steve Bongardt is "Steve B." in the Commission Report and "Scott" in the review. Robert Fuller is "Robert F." in the Commission Report and "Richard" in the review (CR 267–, & 537n63 et seq., FBI IG, McNulty to Troccoli 3/1/06, *U.S. v Zacarias Moussaoui*, Exhibit 952.B, Wright, 311, 340–, 352–, 425n, Kevin Fenton, "Aliases of 9/11 Figures Revealed," 7/15/08, http://hcgroups.wordpress.com).

334–35   **Wilshire suggested to Gillespie:** Lawrence Wright's *The Looming Tower* reads as if it was not Wilshire but CIA supervisor Clark Shannon who assigned Gillespie to this task. Wright's *New Yorker* articles, however, also in 2006, say Wilshire assigned the work. So do other relevant sources (Wright, 340–. CR, 269–, *New Yorker*, 7/10/06, Substitution for the Testimony of "Mary," *U.S. v. Zacarias Moussaoui*, Exhibit 940); **"It all** clicked"/"watchlist": CR, 266–, FBI IG; **not in U.S./FAA not informed:** Report, JI, 15, Staff Report, "9/11 & Terrorist Travel," CO, 42, Staff Statement 2, CO; **Corsi sent email/red tape/misinterpretation:** FBI IG; **"Disneyland":** Wright, 353–; **"Someday"/Fuller:** FBI IG; **"assigned no":** CR, 538n77.

335–36 **Tenet fishing:** Breitweiser, 193; **Tenet directed:** Tenet, 159; **Tenet briefed/Aug. 23:** ibid., CR, 275; **seriously/"If this guy":** Tenet, 202–; **"brow furrowed"/"no one ever":** Ben-Veniste, 301; **"I didn't see"/lied:** Testimony of George Tenet, 4/14/04, CO, Shenon, 361–.

336 **Harlow re Aug. 17 & 31:** *Salt Lake Tribune, WP*, 4/15/04. Probably because of an informal exchange Bush had with reporters the following day, it has been suggested that Tenet also met with the President on August 24. The wording of one of his answers could be taken to indicate to the press that there had been a Tenet visit on the 24th. The sense Bush intended, however, is not entirely clear and could equally refer to the visit of August 17 (exchange: *Public Papers of the Presidents, George W. Bush, 2001,* www.gpoaccess.gov, 1037; suggested: e.g. Robert Schopmeyer, *Prior Knowledge of 9/11,* Palo Alto, CA: Palo Alto Publishing, 2007, 512, corr. Robert Schopmeyer, 2011).

336 **"to make sure":** Tenet, 159; **"not recall":** CR, 262.

336–37 **"The question":** *Newsweek,* 5/25/02; **"I do not believe":** Testimony of Condoleezza Rice, 4/8/04, CO; **"an appalling":** *Vanity Fair,* 2/09; **"There was no":** Ben-Veniste, 307– & see 265.

CHAPTER 28

338 **Hello Jenny:** With a few minor changes to ensure verbatim translation from the German, the "Dear Jenny" message is as reported by Al Jazeera reporter Yosri Fouda, drawing on his encounter with Binalshibh in Karachi in 2002 (see pp. 243–45). Binalshibh dated the message as having been sent on or about August 21, 2001. According to Fouda, Binalshibh produced the message "on a floppy disk" and showed it to him "on screen." The 9/11 Commission Report does not reproduce the "Dear Jenny" message, but refers to coded August "communications" between Atta and Binalshibh that were recovered when KSM was captured. These messages included a discussion of targets dated as having occurred on August 3. In a related note, the Commission quotes Binalshibh as claiming that the words "law" and "politics" were both used to refer only to the Capitol—though the reference was surely in fact to two separate targets (Fouda & Fielding, 138–, *The Australian,* 9/9/02, *Sunday Times* [London], 9/802, CR 248–, 531n 165/166).

339 **August 29 call/Atta riddle:** Reporter Fouda, who learned of the puzzle in 2002 from Binalshibh, rendered it as reproduced in the text. The Commission Report referred to it as "two branches, a slash, and a lollipop." A factor in choosing the date September 11, according to a note found on KSM's computer following his capture, was that the U.S. Congress would be in session in the Capitol by that time (Fouda & Fielding, 140, CR, 249, Staff Statement 16, CO).

340 **Binalshibh passed on:** The Commission Report, drawing on reports of the interrogations of KSM and Binalshibh, states that KSM was informed of the date by Zacaria Essabar, an associate Binalshibh used to carry the message from Germany to KSM in Pakistan. KSM said Essabar brought him the date in a letter, while Binalshibh has said he entrusted Essabar only with a verbal message. Binalshibh has also claimed that he called KSM on the subject. The fact that information was extracted from the prisoners under torture may account for the seeming contradictions. As of this writing, Essabar's whereabouts are unknown (CR249, 531n173, KSM SUBST, Wanted Notice, Bundeskriminalamt Wiesbaden, 2008).

340 **inspector doubts/Kahtani/"He started":** MFR 04016447, 11/12/03, CF, CR, 12, 248, 564n33; **"round out":** KSM SUBST; **"like a soldier":** MFR 04016447, 11/12/02, CF.

340   **five rather than four:** Kahtani, who was captured in Afghanistan after 9/11, was one of the prisoners "tortured"—in the words of the retired judge appointed to decide on prosecutions at Guantánamo. The record indicates that he strongly resisted interrogation. He remains a Guantánamo detainee as of this writing. Commission staff identified nine other recruits who were at some point considered for assignment to the 9/11 operation (captured/"tortured": *WP*, 1/14/09; resisted: Interrogation Log, Detainee 063, www .ccrjustice.org, "The Guantánamo Docket," *NYT* website, as of 1/12/11; nine other: Staff Statement 16, CO, CR, 235).

341–42   **Atta at airport:** Staff Statement 16, CO, Mohammed al-Kahtani, "RFBI 03013592, Documents Relating to PENTTBOM Briefing of Dec. 10, 2003, Packet 2, CF; **Atta free/rental cars/flying/hijackers everyday activities:** "Hijackers Timeline [redacted]," 11/14/03, INTELWIRE; **moved out Paterson/flight manuals:** MFR 04016237, 11/6/03, CF, *NYT*, 10/28/01; **Valencia/"thought they were gay":** *Die Zeit* (Germany), 10/2/02; **men tugging/retrieve towel:** *St. Petersburg Times*, 9/1/02. Simpson believed the men who tried her door were Ahmad al-Haznawi and Ahmed al-Nami; **Surma:** ibid.; **Warrick:** ibid., *Observer* [U.K.], 9/16/01, int. Brad Warrick.

342   **Longshore/Dragomir:** *WP*, 10/5/01, *Chicago Tribune*, 9/18/01. Though this incident was reported in major newspapers, it is not certain that the men Dragomir remembered were Jarrah and a companion—or indeed that the companion was Atta, as the manager thought he might have been. The date of the incident is also not entirely clear—it was reported both as having occurred on August 30 and in "late August." That said, Jarrah was in the area on August 30, having just returned from Baltimore. He moved out of the accommodations he had been renting for some time on August 31, took another condominium close by—and was apparently using the Internet at a Kinko's in Hollywood—where the reported Longshore Motel incident occurred—on September 3, at a time Atta was also there ("Hijackers Timeline [redacted]," 11/14/03, INTELWIRE, Profile, Ziad Samir Jarrah, ACS Download Documents, Pkt. 6, 03009470, CF).

342   **Hazmi phoned:** CR, 223, 249; **Abdullah had known/helped:** CR, 216, 220, 516n20, Los Angeles to Counterterrorism, 1/8/02 , FBI 302 re canvas of hotels, 1/15/02, & FBI 302 re int. instructors Sorbi Flight School, 4/11/02 INTELWIRE, *San Diego Union-Tribune*, 5/26/04, *LAT*, 7/24/04, MSNBC, 9/8/06; **activist/another man/"planes falling":** San Diego to Ottawa, 4/11/02, San Diego, Squad 15, to San Diego, 2/4/03, INTELWIRE, CR, 218–.

342   **"acting"/"nervous":** MFR 04017535, 11/18/03, MFR 04017543, 11/18/03, CF. In detention after 9/11, first as a material witness and then on immigration charges, Abdullah would refuse a 9/11 Commission request to interview him. While in prison, it was alleged, he told other inmates that he had known that Hazmi and Mihdhar were involved in plans for a terrorist attack. According to one inmate, he said he had known the plan was for a 9/11-style attack and that he "found out" three weeks before the attacks occurred. Abdullah, who had arrived in the United States via Canada using a Yemeni passport identifying him as "al Mihdhar Zaid" but then changed his name, was charged with an immigration offense and deported in 2003. 9/11 Commission executive director Philip Zelikow has described the report's findings on Abdullah as "ominous." In a 2004 interview with *The Washington Post*, however, Abdullah denied having had any foreknowledge of the 9/11 attacks. Reports suggest the possibility that the hijacking references in the notebook found among his possessions may have been written by someone else (refuse: CR, 517n31; involved: ibid., 218–; "Zaid": "Inside I.C.E. [Immigration and Customs Enforcement]," Dept. of Homeland Security, Vol. 4, 5/25–6/7/04, www.ice.gov; "ominous": Zelikow to Shenon, 2/12/07, www.philipshenon.com; denied: *WP*, 8/10/04; notebook: ibid., 516n21, 218).

343   **obtained IDs:** Staff Report, "9/11 & Terrorist Travel," 39, FBI 302 of int. Victor Lopez-

Flores, 9/23/01, 9/25/01, 10/06/01, 11/8/01, 11/13/01, "Lopez-Flores," B11, T5, CF, Graham, with Nussbaum, 76; **airline reservations/tickets:** "Hijackers Timeline [redacted]," 11/14/03, INTELWIRE; **frequent flier:** ibid., Staff Report, "Monograph on the Four Flights & Civil Aviation Security," CF, *MH*, 9/18/01; **changed assignments:** "Hijackers Timeline [redacted]," 11/14/03, INTELWIRE; **Muslim meals:** *Time*, 9/24/01; **beyond destinations:** "Hijackers Timeline [redacted]," 11/14/03, INTELWIRE; **transcontinental/fuel/explosive:** ibid., eds. *Der Spiegel*, 32.

343   **Atta thought:** CR, 531n171. As things were to turn out, and as noted in Ch. 2 on p. 20, many Trade Center workers did not reach their place of work before the attacks began. They were delayed by voting in local elections and traffic jams.

343   **shopped knives/Stanley two-piece/Leatherman/Dollar House/folding knife:** Staff Report, "Monograph on the Four Flights & Civil Aviation Security," CF, "Hijackers Timeline [redacted]," 11/14/03, INTELWIRE, witness list, "Hijacker Knife Purchases," B18, T7, CF. The folding knife would be found later in Atta's shipped baggage, which failed to make the transfer to American 11, the plane he hijacked on 9/11 (witness list, "Hijacker Knife Purchases," B18, T7, CF).

344–45   **Principals convened/draft NSPD:** CR, 213–, Farmer, 65–, Richard Clarke, 26; **State had told:** *WP*, 1/20/02; **debate re Predator/dueled:** ibid., Benjamin & Simon, 345–, CR, 214, Tenet, 160, corr. Miles Kara; **"I just couldn't":** *Vanity Fair*, 2/09; **reconnaissance:** CR, 214; **"I didn't really":** Testimony of Richard Clarke, 3/24/04, CO; **"grasp the enormity":** MFR 04018415, 12/16/03, CF; **"It sounds":** *New Yorker*, 8/4/03; **strongly worded note:** Staff Statement 8, CO, CR 212–, 343–, 513n247–; **Directive approved:** CR, 213–.

345   **money left over/returned:** Staff Report, Monograph on Terrorist Financing," CO, PENTTBOM, Summary of Captioned Investigation," 11/5/01, authors' collection, Staff Statement 16, CO, Stipulation, *U.S. v. Zacarias Moussaoui*, 3/1/06. The return of funds notwithstanding, it has been alleged that Atta received $100,000 as late as August 2001. A story emerged in the Indian press soon after 9/11, supposedly citing sources in the FBI and Indian intelligence, claiming that the director of the Pakistani ISI, Lieutenant General Mahmoud Ahmed, ordered the supposed wire transfer of the money in either the summer of 2001 or 2000. The FBI told 9/11 Commission staff that there was no evidence Atta received a payment from the Pakistani ISI. Nor, indeed, were there "any unexplained funds at all." One would wonder—if such a payment was made in August 2001— why it was required so late in the operation. Given the long-running enmity between Pakistan and India, the allegation may merely have been Indian propaganda. That said, Pakistani intelligence has had a long involvement with the Taliban, and allegedly with bin Laden. The U.S. government, meanwhile, has never determined the original source of *any* of the money used in the attack, though the mechanics of how it reached the hijackers is known ($100,000: e.g., *Times of India*, 10/9/01, Press Trust of India, 10/8/01, 10/15/01, *WSJ*, 10/10/01; ISI/al Qaeda: e.g., AP, 2/21/02, Fox News, 10/8/01, *Asia Times*, 1/5/02; no evidence: MFR 04019767, CF, Staff Report, "Monograph on Terrorist Financing," CO).

345–46   **"brothers":** Fouda & Fielding, 141; **Binalshibh flew/marathon/"The message":** ibid., MFR 04019351, 12/10–11/03, CF, *Der Spiegel*, 10/27/03, McDermott, 230.

346   **"referred":** *Sunday Times* (London), 10/7/01; **"information about":** *NYT*, 6/4/02; **Gary Hart/"preparedness"/Rice "said":** *Salon*, 9/12/01, *Columbia Journalism Review*, Nov./Dec. 2001, Statement by the President, 5/8/01, http://usgovinfo.about.com, *WP*, 1/20/02, CR, 204; **Bush met Tenet:** *Salt Lake Tribune*, 4/15/04.

346–47   **agent getting started/"security"/tentative feelers/ChoicePoint:** CR, 270–, FBI IG, Kevin Fenton, *Disconnecting the Dots*, Walterville, OR: TrineDay, forthcoming, 345–. Another New York FBI agent, who ran an Internet search on September 11 after the attacks, found Mihdhar's San Diego address "within hours." (JI, 43); **traffic policeman/ Hazmi featured, etc.:** "Hijackers Timeline [redacted]," 11/14/03, INTELWIRE. The previous occasions Hamzi had come to the notice of the police are reported on p. 324.

348   **Shuckums:** *Time,* 9/24/01, Hopsicker, 81–, *Newsweek,* 9/24/01, *St. Petersburg Times,* 9/1/02. FBI agents who looked into the Shuckums story evidently thought it occurred on September 6. Atta could not have been there on the 7th, as some press reports had it, as he flew from Fort Lauderdale to Baltimore that day ("Hijackers Timeline [redacted]," 11/14/03, INTELWIRE).

348   **Atta/Jarrah sold cars/headed north:** ibid., Stipulation, 3/1/06 & Exhibit OG0020.2, *U.S. v. Zacarias Moussaoui,* Chronology of Events for Hijackers, Ziad Jarrah chronology, 3/20/02, "03009470 ACS Download Documents, Packet 6," CF, Staff Statement 16, CO. A story would emerge that Atta and Shehhi were at the Holiday Inn at Longboat Key that day, in west Florida and not far from where President Bush would arrive on the eve of 9/11. The authors interviewed Darlene Sievers and Mark Bean, hotel workers who thought they saw them there, but the record indicates that they were mistaken (*Longboat Observer,* 11/21/01, ints. Darlene Sievers, Mark Bean).

348–49   **Sweet Temptations:** MFR 04020636, 2/2/04, "Hijackers Timeline [redacted]," 11/14/03, INTELWIRE; **"the most"/twice:** *Boston Herald,* 10/10/01, 10/11/01; **$100 apiece:** *BG,* 10/10/01, *The Independent* (U.K.), 10/11/01; **porn video:** "Hijackers Timeline [redacted]," 11/14/03, INTELWIRE, *WSJ,* 10/16/01; **paid dancer:** *NYT,* 9/27/01, 10/28/01; **Panther Motel/found:** "Hijackers Timeline [redacted]," 11/14/03, INTEL-WIRE, *St. Petersburg Times,* 9/1/02; **Jarrah ticket:** *NY Daily News,* 1/9/02, Ziad Jarrah chronology, 3/20/02, "03009470 ACS Download Documents, Packet 6," CF; **Jarrah called:** Ziad Jarrah chronology, 3/20/02; **$2,000:** Fisk, *The Great War,* 1051; **sister's wedding/suit:** *LAT,* 10/23/01.

349   **Jarrah package:** Stipulation, *U.S. v. Zacarias Moussaoui,* letter reproduced at http:// en.wikepedia.org—Arabic & Turkish translated for the authors by Hans Kippenberg & Tilman Seidensticker, "The Fifth Estate: The Story of Ziad Jarrah," 10/10/01, www.cbc .ca. Jarrah's mind was evidently on his girlfriend, Aysel, a great deal during his last days alive. He called more than usual, she would remember, four times between the Thursday of the week before 9/11 and the morning of the strikes. He appears to have made the final call when he was already at Newark Airport preparing to board United Flight 93. As fate would have it, according to Sengün, she had to cut the call short because it was a busy moment in the hospital where she was working. There had been nothing out of the ordinary about the call, she would remember—Jarrah had said he loved her. Sengün has not given interviews and it is thought German authorities placed her under some form of witness protection (Sengün sworn statement to police in Germany, 9/15/01, in authors' collection).

351   **told later/she would hope:** *LAT,* 1/27/03.

351–52   **Mihdhar packet:** Stipulation, *U.S. v. Zacarias Moussaoui,* 3/1/06, Bamford, *Shadow Factory,* 81. One FBI document suggests Mihdhar's letter to his wife was in fact sent not by Mihdhar but by Hazmi. This is clearly in error, not least because—unlike Mihdhar—Hazmi had no wife. As reported earlier, he had been attempting and failing to find himself a wife; **Atta had told/called father:** CR, 249; **KSM to Pakistan:** Khalid Sheikh Mohammed, Charge Sheet," 4/15/08, www.findlaw.com; **told disperse/alert:** Bergen, *OBL I Know,* 307–, Fouda & Fielding, 141; **"big plan"/"far"/"My mother":** bin Ladens & Sasson, 279–; **Najwa asked/condition/ring:** ibid., 281–, 312. The children allowed to leave were two-year-old Nour, a boy, four-year-old Rukhaiya, a girl, and Abdul Rahman, a son born in 1978. In the spring of 2002, the Saudi-owned journal was to publish an interview supposedly given by one of bin Laden's wives, identified only as "A.S." Before 9/11, according to her purported interview, bin Laden "came to the house, gave me a telephone, and told me to call my family and tell them we were going somewhere else and that there would be no news of me for a long time." There is much accompanying detail, including a reference to the interviewee's "sons." The authenticity of the interview is dubious. Though the initials match those of Amal al-Sadah, a seventeen-year-old Yemeni bin Laden married in late 2000 or early 2001, she has reportedly borne him only a daughter. She could hardly have given birth to sons by early 2002 (Nour et al.: bin Ladens & Sasson, 282; "A.S.": BBC, AP, 3/13/02); **"soft-spoken":** bin Ladens & Sasson, 8; **Najwa prayed:** ibid., 282.

Part VI: TWENTY-FOUR HOURS

CHAPTER 29

355–56   **Fuller search/"Sheraton":** FBI IG, CR, 271–, 539n84–85, Fenton, 312; **tracks all over:** *Newsweek*, 6/10/06, Lance, *Triple Cross*, 349–, CR, 539n85; **Moussaoui detention/ agents begged/blocked/Samit shared/Harry/Permission:** FBI IG, Kiser to Samit, 9/10/01, Exhibit 334, *U.S. v. Zacarias Moussaoui*, ABC News, 3/20/06; **Ashcroft turned down/not increased:** Staff Statement 9, CO, *Newsweek*, 5/27/02, Benjamin & Simon, 348; **"very docile":** *NYT*, 6/2/02.

357   **"The Big Wedding"/"aircraft":** John Cooley, a renowned Middle East specialist, reported in 2002 that the "Big Wedding" warning came in "late summer," and referred to an attack within the United States involving airplanes. CNN, reporting earlier, referred to a Jordanian warning "a few days" before 9/11—but suggested that it related to a coming attack not in the United States but on resort hotels in Jordan. According to CIA director Tenet, "a source we were jointly running with a Middle Eastern country" went to his foreign handler on September 10 to say "something big" was about to happen. He was ignored ("Wedding": Cooley, 229, *International Herald Tribune*, 5/21/02, CNN, 11/19/01; "something big": Tenet, 160).

357   **France passed:** *Le Figaro*, 11/1/01; **Feinstein/"One of"/"Despite":** *Late Edition*, CNN, 7/1/01, Statement of Dianne Feinstein, 5/17/01, http://feinstein.senate.gov, *Newsweek*, 5/27/02, MSNBC, 9/28/06.

357–58   **Massoud assassinated/"journalists'":** CR, 214, *Time*, 8/12/02, Burke, *Al-Qaeda*, 197. After 9/11, when U.S. strikes on Afghanistan had routed Taliban and al Qaeda forces, *Wall Street Journal* reporter Alan Cullison made remarkable discoveries on a computer that had belonged to the terrorists. The hard drive contained a letter, apparently crafted by Ayman al-Zawahiri, purporting to be the "journalists' " request for the Massoud interview (*WSJ*, 12/31/01); **widow:** Bergen, *OBL I Know*, 297–; **O'Neill had warned/ frustrated/resigned/"We're due":** Murray Weiss, *The Man Who Warned America*, NY: Regan, 2003, 180–, 320–, 362, 370–, *Frontline:* "The Man Who Knew," PBS, 10/3/02.

358–59   **Putin:** int. of Putin for *Iran & the West: Nuclear Confrontation*, BBC, 2/7/09. While Putin was to say clearly that he spoke with Bush the day before the attack, the former President referred in his 2010 memoir only to a conversation afterward (Bush, 369–); **Massoud assassination/analyzed implications:** Coll, *Holy War Inc.*, 582–, Tenet, 174; **memoir not refer:** e.g. see Bush, 187, 196; **Deputies tinkered/eliminate OBL:** CR, 206, Farmer, 68; **"literally headed":** CBS News, 9/11/02; **"eerie":** int. Rice by Bob Woodward, "Farmer Misc.," B9, NYC files, CF; **PM of Australia:** Sept. 10 entries, *Public Papers of the Presidents, 2001*, www.gpoaccess.gov; **helicopter:** Goldberg et al., Ch. 4; **Bush at Colony:** int. Katie Moulton, *Sarasota Magazine*, 11/01, *Sarasota Herald-Tribune*, 9/10/02; **"soft event":** *WP*, 1/27/02; **"Tomorrow"/"The match":** Report, JI, 32, 205, 375, Graham with Nussbaum, 138–, CBS News, 6/20/02, Bamford, *Shadow Factory*, 92.

359   **Arabs gathered/"finally":** MFR 04017535, 11/18/03, MFR 04017537, 11/18/03, CR 249–; **Dulles/Boston/Newark hotels:** "Hijackers Timeline [redacted]," 11/14/03, INTELWIRE, Stipulation, *U.S. v. Zacarias Moussaoui,* 3/1/06.

359   **drove Portland/Comfort Inn/ATM/Walmart/Pizza Hut/phone calls:** What Atta bought at the Walmart, though, according to an FBI document, was a "6-volt battery converter"—a puzzling purchase for a would-be hijacker expecting to go to his death in the morning. "Chronology of Events for Hijackers, 8/16/01," *U.S. v. Zacarias Moussaoui,* Exhibits OG00020.2, FO07011, FO07021, FO07022, FO07023, FO07024, "265D-NY-280350, TWINBOM-PENTTBOM, Biographical Report," 11/26/01, National Drug Intelligence Center for the FBI, authors' collection, FBI press release, 10/14/01, entries for 9/10/01 & 9/11/01, "Hijackers Timeline [redacted]," 11/14/03, INTELWIRE, FBI 302 of [name redacted], 10/15/01, "FBI 302s of Interest," B17, T7, CF, FBI Timeline of 9–11 Hijacker Activity & Movements, "Timelines 9–11, 2 of 2," B20, T7, CF.

360   **Kara:** "Chaos and Ghosts," www.oredigger61.org, corr. Miles Kara, 2010.

360   **Rolince:** "Staff Notes of Int. Michael Rolince, 6/9/04," B70, T5, CF. The authors note that by an FBI account Caysan bin Don, the American Muslim who featured in an episode in January 2000—he was Bayoumi's companion the day he and Bayoumi had their supposedly chance meeting with newly arrived Mihdhar and Hazmi—was in Portland on September 11. It is hard to imagine, though, why Atta could conceivably have needed to meet with bin Don just before 9/11. Other hypotheses to try to explain the Portland expedition include the suggestion (not dissimilar to Miles Kara's) that Atta was worried lest the sight of as many as ten Arabs checking in at Boston for the two targeted flights to Los Angeles attract undue attention. The bottom line is that the trip remains unexplained. As the 9/11 Commission Report noted, "no physical, documentary, or analytical evidence" explains the Portland trip (location of bin Don: MFR 04018561, 11/20/03, MFR 04019254, 4/20/04, & see *National Enquirer,* 11/6/01; met bin Don: "Staff Notes of Int. Michael Rolince, 6/9/04," B70, T5, CF; other hypotheses: AP, 10/4/01, *NYT,* 9/11/02; Commission: CR, 451n1).

360–61   **ritual/"spiritual manual":** FBI report, "The 11 September Hijacker Cell Model," Feb. 03, INTELWIRE. The "spiritual manual" and the ritual it called for is described at length on pp. 161–64; **"noticed large amounts":** MFR 04020636, 2/2/04, CF, "Hijackers Timeline [redacted]," 11/14/03, INTELWIRE. Similar evidence had been found at locations used by the terrorists involved in the bombings of the U.S. embassy in Kenya in 1998 and of the USS *Cole* in 2000 (*New Yorker,* 7/10 & 7/17/06); **"the mutual pledge":** see sources for Ch. 14; **"God willing":** Fouda & Fielding, 109, translation of Binalshibh audiotape by Naouar Bioud, authors' collection; **green:** e.g. *Slate,* 6/9/09, "The Prophet's Mosque," www.sacred-destinations.com.

362   **When the news started:** translation of Binalshibh audiotape by Naouar Bioud, in authors' collection. The tape was obtained by reporter Yosri Fouda, and the material is used with his permission.

Part VII: UNANSWERED QUESTIONS

CHAPTER 30

365–66   *Le Figaro* **story/picked up by press/According to report:** *Le Figaro,* 10/21/01, Reuters, 11/14/01, *NYT,* 11/1/01, *Guardian* (U.K.), 11/1/01 int. Alexandra Richard.

366   **medical tests:** Rumors long circulated that bin Laden suffered from serious kidney disease requiring dialysis. His son Omar refuted that allegation in the 2009 memoir written with his mother, Najwa—both of whom had intimate contact with bin Laden until well into 2001. Omar conceded, however, that his father—along with others in the

extended family—"had a tendency to suffer from kidney stones. Those stones caused immense pain until they had passed out of his body, but his kidneys were strong otherwise." Interviewed by the Pakistani journalist Hamid Mir on November 8, 2001—the only post-9/11 newspaper interview—bin Laden himself said, "My kidneys are all right" (rumors: e.g. Gunaratna, 48, *Eye Spy* magazine, no. 57, 2008; Omar: bin Ladens & Sasson, 172; "all right": ed. Lawrence, 144); **Callaway declined:** *Le Figaro*, 10/21/01; **Koval denied:** *NYT*, 11/1/01; **Mitchell told:** int. Alexandra Richard & authors' int. with Dubai source; **possible OBL did visit Dubai:** In the November 2001 interview cited above, bin Laden said, "I did not go to Dubai last year." The meeting with the CIA, of course, is not alleged to have happened the previous year—2000—but in July 2001 (ed. Lawrence, 144).

366–68   **Chouet:** int. & corr. Alain Chouet, 2009 & 2011, Chouet int. for *Le Monde*, 3/29/07, http://alain.chouet.free.fr. In the furor after initial publication of the story, a *New York Times* article suggested that the allegation of the Dubai meeting was planted by French intelligence "to suggest a continuing covert linkage between the CIA and bin Laden." In her description of how the story developed, however, reporter Alexandra Richard made clear that she first learned of it from a private source she had long trusted—in Dubai. As described in the text, moreover, she firmed it up with further research. Another French journalist, Richard Labévière, meanwhile, told the authors he received corroboration of the Dubai meeting from three other sources. (*NYT*, 11/1/01, *Guardian* [U.K.], 11/1/01, ints. Richard Labévière); **contacts with Taliban/improved cooperation/assistance/ threats:** *Guardian* (U.K.), 9/22/01, *Le Monde Diplomatique*, 1/02, *Nation*, 7/12/02, BBC News, 9/18/01; **Simons pressed:** *Guardian* (U.K.), 9/22/01, *Le Monde Diplomatique*, 1/02, *Nation*, 7/12/02, BBC News, 9/18/01; **Rice "whether any":** CR, 204.

368–69   **major stories re Atta:** e.g. *Chicago Tribune*, 9/16/01; **"had been trailing":** corr. Kate Connolly, 2009; **German intelligence interest/CIA/Joint Inquiry aired:** Report, JI, 29–, 183–; **Commission Report ignored:** CR, 495n81; **sequence of events/Zammar/ Darkazanli/card/phone tapped:** ibid., CR, 164, 495n81, McDermott, 71–, *Chicago Tribune*, 10/5/03, "Germany's Imam Mamoun Darkazanli," Vol. 1, No. 8, www.jamestown .org. See earlier references to Zammar and Darkazanli in Chs. 24 and 27 and their related notes; **incoming call/"Marwan"/second/third calls:** "Memorandum, Investigative Proceedings Against Mohmammcd Haydar Zammar," 11/19/01, Bundeskriminalamt ST 23–067–256/01, authors' collection, Report, JI, 185–, *Der Spiegel*, 11/23/06, *Frankfurter Allgemeine Sonntagzeitung*, 2/2/03, CR, 495n81; **"particularly valuable"/CIA "didn't sit"/"uncertain":** *NYT*, 22/24/04, 2/25/04, Testimony of George Tenet, Hearings, U.S. Senate Select Committee on Intelligence, 2/24/04, www.intelligence.senate.gov, Report, JI, 185–, Staff Statement 11, CO, Graham with Nussbaum, 61; **Volz:** McDermott, 71–, 75–, 278n11, *Stern* (Germany), 8/3/03, & see *Chicago Tribune*, 11/16/02.

369   **Landesamt:** Landesamt für Verfassungsschutz translates in English as the State Office for the Protection of the Constitution. Each of Germany's sixteen states has such an office, which in turn answer to the Bundesamt für Verfassungsschutz, the federal body. Together, they function as Germany's domestic intelligence service.

369–70   **"had knowledge"/"turned"/tried approaching:** *Chicago Tribune*, 11/16/02. In an extraordinary episode right after 9/11, German police raided Mamoun Darkazanli's apartment only to find it empty of documents. The raid was followed, however, by the mysterious delivery to the authorities of a bag of Darkazanli's papers—by a man claiming to be a burglar who had stolen them from the suspect. The "burglar's" account, however, appeared to be bogus. In light of the earlier CIA insistence on trying to persuade Darkazanli to become an informant, one German investigator remembered, "We all thought, 'CIA.' " As of this writing, Darkazanli was reportedly still in Hamburg and at liberty (*Chicago Tribune*, 11/16/02).

370   **Jarrah stopped Dubai/"It was":** Corbin, 179–; **"because his name":** McDermott, 294n3; **learn fly/spread Islam:** Corbin, 180, McDermott, 186; **"What happened":** McDermott, 187.

370–71   **item redacted:** Ziad Jarrah chronology, "03009470—ACS Download Documents, Packet 6," CF. The FBI's "Hijackers' Timeline [redacted]" has also been heavily censored at that point. Because the episode was first reported as having occurred in January *2001*—not, as was in fact the case, in 2000—U.S. sources were initially able to deny that Jarrah had been questioned at Dubai in response to a CIA request. They also denied ever having been told about it. *Vanity Fair* reported in 2004 that the CIA had merely asked foreign border agencies to "question *anyone* [authors' italics] who may have been returning from a training camp in Afghanistan." While acknowledging that U.S. officials said it was untrue that Jarrah had been stopped specifically because his name was on a U.S.-supplied watchlist, investigative reporter Terry McDermott noted in 2005 that Washington had abandoned its initial denial it had been advised of about the Jarrah stop. "The United States," McDermott wrote, "has acknowledged in internal documents and in communications with German investigators that the Emiratis did contact them. . . . They decline to say what they told the Emiratis" (Timeline: "Hijackers Timeline [redacted]," 11/14/03, INTELWIRE; reported as 2001: CNN, 8/1/02, McDermott, 294n3, Corbin, 179–; deny: CNN, 8/1/02, Statement of Eleanor Hill, 9/20/02, JI; McDermott: McDermott, 186, 294n3).

371   **DIA/disquieting claim/four on radar:** Statement of Mark Zaid, U.S. Senate Judiciary Committee, 9/21/05, MFR 04021341, 7/13/04, CF, MFR [names & number redacted], Defense HUMINT Service Officers, Bagram Base, 10/21/03, CF; *WSJ*, 11/17/05, *NYT*, 8/9/05, 8/11/05, Fox News, 8/28/05, Lance, *Triple Cross*, 330–; **"data mining"/"use of high-powered"/visa records:** Anthony Shaffer, *Operation Dark Heart*, NY: Thomas Dunne, 2010, 17–,164–, 245–, 272–, *Bergen Record* (N.J.), 8/14/05.

371   **evidence destroyed:** Though the Able Danger claim had not yet emerged when Congress's Joint Inquiry was at work, its staff did question Major Keith Alexander of the U.S. Army Intelligence and Security Command, and twice visited the unit from which much of the Able Danger material reportedly originated. On both occasions, asked whether they knew of any evidence that the government had prior knowledge or should have had prior knowledge of the attack, military personnel said they knew of none.
    A Defense Department report, and a Senate Intelligence Committee review, were to conclude in 2006 that the Able Danger claims were unsupported by the evidence. It is clear from both documents that witnesses' memories were confused, as one might expect so long after the fact. Relevant documentary material that existed in 2003 now does not. Some was inadvertently destroyed during an office move. Some duplicate documentation Shaffer kept at his office, his attorney told the Committee on the Judiciary, was "apparently destroyed—for reasons unknown—by DIA in spring 2004." The DOD report says no such documentation was found at Shaffer's office (Joint Inquiry: corr. Miles Kara, 2011; claims unsupported: Defense report: "Alleged Misconduct by Senior DOD Officials Concerning the Able Danger Program & Lt. Col. Anthony Shaffer," U.S. Dept of Defense, Office of the Inspector General, 9/18/06; Senate review: Roberts & Rockefeller to colleagues, 12/22/06, www.intelligence.senate.gov; had Commission followed/destroyed?: Statement of Mark Zaid, Judiciary Committee, U.S. Senate, 9/21/05, Shaffer, 164–, 246–, Kean & Hamilton, 114, 294–, MFR 04021341, 7/13/04, CF).

371   **Grenzfahndung:** The two known to have been under border watch were Said Bahaji and Mounir Motassadeq (ints. Mounir el-Motassadeq, Motassadeq's lawyer Udo Jacob, Dr. Manfred Murck, Dr. Herbert Müller, McDermott, 73–, 297n23, *Stern* [Germany], 8/13/03, *Frankfurter Allgemeine Sonntagszeitung*, 2/2/03).

372   **officials unhelpful:** The two other organizations that declined interview requests were

the Generalbundesanwalt, or Public Prosecutor's Office—which has responsibility for terrorist cases—and the Bundeskriminalamt, the Federal Criminal Police Agency. The latter was the source of most German-related information in the 9/11 Commission Report.

372–73   **Müller "Atta was":** Dr. Müller serves with the Landesamt für Verfassungsschutz Baden-Württemberg—Stuttgart is the state capital of Baden-Württemberg; **"Some countries":** Staff Statement 11, CO; **intermittent friction:** Executive Summary, "Report on CIA Accountability with Respect to the 9/11 Attacks," Office of the Inspector General, 06/05, Report, JI, 186–, 274–; **Polt:** MFR 04016468, 10/9/03; **"They lied":** int. Dirk Laabs.

373   **coded conversation:** MFR 04019350, 3/18/04 (re Moussaoui team briefing), CF, corr. Kristen Wilhelm, 2011, CR, 245–530n151–152, Staff Statement 16, CO. The exchange was referred to earlier on pp. 323–24.

373   **intercept by Germans?:** At one stage, in 2000, the Germans had repeatedly discussed applying for clearance to wiretap the Marienstrasse apartment, but at that point decided there was insufficient evidence to justify the request. The 9/11 Commission Report states: "Only after 9/11 would it be discovered that [KSM] had communicated with a phone that was used by Binalshibh ... the links to Binalshibh might not have been an easy trail to find and would have required substantial cooperation from the German government" (discussed: *Vanity Fair*, 11/04, *NYT*, 6/20/02; "Only after": CR, 277, & see 245).

374   **Berlin visit:** The German officials known to have spoken with the U.S. congressional delegation were Ronald Schill, minister of the interior for Hamburg, Deputy Minister Walter Wellinghausen, Reinhard Wagner, chief of the Landesamt für Verfassungsschutz Hamburg, his deputy Manfred Murck, and Bruno Franz of the Hamburg police. (Contemporary information provided to the authors)

CHAPTER 31

375   **Soon after 1:00 P.M./"Oh, Jesus":** Suskind, *One Percent Doctrine*, 3–, & see Tenet, 167. Tenet's aide Michael Morell, the president's CIA briefer, remembered of the videoconference on the afternoon of 9/11, "They had done name traces on the flight manifests. And when we got to Omaha, and we got to the briefing area, George Tenet briefed the President on the fact that we already knew three of these guys were al Qaeda." Tenet has recalled that, when he told Bush the CIA had been aware of information about Mihdhar and Hazmi he "shot Mike Morell one of those, 'I thought I was supposed to be the first to know' looks." The reference to three, as distinct from two, of the men on the planes being associated with al Qaeda presumably includes Nawaf al-Hazmi's brother Salem (Suskind, 9; Tenet, 169).

375–76   **manifest:** Exhibit P200054, *U.S. v. Zacarias Moussaoui*,; **Tenet claimed/"CIA had multiple":** Tenet, 195–, 205; **Tenet on oath/"like a grand":** Shenon, 256–; **"We just didn't believe"/outraged:** *New Yorker*, 11/8/04.

377   **NSA identified/Hada/"hub":** Bamford, *Shadow Factory*, 7–, FBI report, "PENTTBOM, Summary of Captioned Investigation," 11/5/01, authors' collection, transcript, *Nova: The Spy Factory*, 2/3/09, www.pbs.org, Wright, 275–; **NSA did not share:** Report, JI, 145, *Atlantic*, 12/04, Bamford, *Shadow Factory*, 16, 26–, & see Scheuer, *Marching Toward Hell*, 91–.

377   **Hada phone/FBI/1998 attack/OBL phone/link:** Report, JI, 129, 145, Wright, 277–, 343, Testimony of [unnamed] CIA Officer [accepted as Wilshire], 9/20/02, JI. Bin Laden stopped using his satellite phone in September 1998, apparently because he knew or guessed it was being intercepted (*WP*, 12/22/05, Report, JI, 69).

378   **1999 intercept/"Khalid"/"Nawaf"/Malaysia:** The intercepted conversation also in-

cluded a reference to "Salem" as making the trip, too—evidently Hazmi's brother Salem, who was also to be one of the hijackers. Although the NSA had access to information indicating that the three first names were all linked to the surnames Hazmi and Mihdhar, they did not pass those names to the CIA and FBI—thus making the CIA's task more difficult than it need have been (CR, 181, JI Report, 145–, 155–, Staff Statement 2, CO, Bamford, *Shadow Factory*, 16–).

378   **"something more":** CR, 181; **"operational"/"operatives":** ibid., Report, JI, 144; **passport photographed:** The Dubai stopover and the copying of Mihdhar's passport was briefly mentioned earlier in Ch. 27, p. 319. **"This is as good":** Mayer, 18; **Mihdhar tracked/photographed/pay phones/computers:** CR, 181–, Staff Statement 2, CO, *Die Zeit*, 10/2/02, FBI IG; **directors/Berger/Clarke:** Staff Statement 2, CO, CR, 181.

379   **Bangkok:** Staff Statement 2, CO. It would later be established that two suspects who had already, on January 6, made short trips out of Malaysia—for only a matter of hours—had also been Attash and Hazmi (Staff Statement 2, CO, CR, 159).

379–81   **according CIA trail lost/Thai authorities responded/Jan. 15 to LA/cables:** CR, 181–, FBI IG, Staff Statement 2, CO, Tenet, 196–. The two terrorists flew in aboard UA 002, arriving at 1:27 P.M. Bin Laden aide Attash had reportedly headed back to Afghanistan via Karachi to report to bin Laden (UA 002: "Hijackers Timeline [redacted]," 11/14/03, INTELWIRE; Attash: CR, 159); **"OBL associates":** Executive Summary, Report on CIA Accountability with Respect to the 9/11 Attacks, Office of the Inspector General, CIA, 6/05; **"Action Required":** Report, JI, 147; **"The threat":** CR, 176, 501n17; **"It is important":** ibid., CTC Watchlisting Guidance, cited at Report, JI, 1; **CIA did not alert State/FBI:** Report, JI, 40–, 144–, Executive Summary, Report on CIA Accountability with Respect to the 9/11 Attacks, Office of the Inspector General, CIA, 6/05, FBI IG, Graham with Nussbaum, 7–, CR, 355; **"promised to let":** Staff Statement 2, CO; **"Michelle"/"to the FBI":** FBI IG, & see Executive Summary, Report on CIA Accountability with Respect to the 9/11 Attacks, Office of the Inspector General, CIA, 6/05; **"James"/"as soon as"/"in the event":** Statement of Eleanor Hill, 9/20/02, JI, Report, JI, 81, FBI IG; **refused interview:** FBI IG; **"Michelle" prevaricated:** FBI IG; **Wilshire/"did not know":** ibid. In the transcript of a hearing before a U.S. Senate subcommittee, the former deputy chief's name is rendered not as "Wilshire" but as "Wilshere." The authors have used "Wilshire," the spelling most commonly used. ("The Global Reach of al Qaeda," Hearings, Subcommittee on International Operations & Terrorism, Committee on Foreign Relations, U.S. Senate, 107th Cong., 1st Sess., 12/18/01, 7–); **Wilshire deliberately/draft cable/Miller CIR/"pls hold":** FBI IG, & see Executive Summary, Report on CIA Accountability with Respect to the 9/11 Attacks, Office of the Inspector General, CIA, 6/05.

381   **"Doug came"/"Is this a no go":** Bamford, *Shadow Factory*, 18–. In a detailed note for his book *Disconnecting the Dots*, due for publication in 2011, author Kevin Fenton would note that Rossini was to resign from the FBI in 2008 after breaching regulations. He had, according to an FBI press release, used Bureau computers to find out information for personal purposes. Fenton argues cogently, however, that the lapse does not detract from Rossini's credibility on the matter of the blocked CIR. The fact of its blocking, and that the agent saw relevant cables in 2000, is well documented (Fenton, proof copy kindly shared with the authors, 2011, 44n26).

381   **"unable to locate":** FBI IG; **Wilshire int. redacted:** corr. Kristen Wilhelm, 2011.

381   **Wilshire proposed:** FBI IG. Wilshire's actions in July 2001 were reportedly spurred by his review of the CIA cable and email traffic recording Mihdhar's movements in January the previous year—including the information that Mihdhar had a valid U.S. multiple-entry visa. For reasons unknown, but perhaps because he feared discovery of the fact that he had been in the United States the previous year, Mihdhar had meanwhile obtained a

new passport and a new visa in June 2001. He used this new visa when he reentered the United States on July 4. There is no evidence that Wilshire or anyone else at CIA was aware of the new passport and visa at the time the search for Mihdhar was renewed in July 2001 (Wilshire spurred: CR, 267–, FBI IG; new passport/visa: Staff Report, 9/11 & Terrorist Travel, CO, 33–.)

381 **Following a series:** FBI IG, CR, 267–, & re discovered/search see Chs. 27, 28, & 29. Aside from the events described here, the CIA and the FBI disputed each other's versions of events about the identification of Tawfiq bin Attash (referred to in the Commission Report as "Khallad") in the Malaysia surveillance photos. The identification was made by a source the FBI and the CIA shared—a circumstance that led to a prolonged tussle between the agencies. This barely penetrable story is detailed in the Justice Department's inspector general's report. The bottom line is that FBI agents working the *Cole* investigation, who knew of Attash's connection to that attack, would have been far more concerned—and pressed to know all the CIA knew about the Malaysia meeting—had they been told that Attash had been present. As it was, they would learn nothing of Attash's link to Mihdhar and Hazmi until after 9/11. The CIA's performance on this matter notwithstanding, it is evident that once the information on Mihdhar's and Hazmi's likely presence in the United States was passed to the Bureau in August 2001, the FBI fumbled badly. As described in Chapter 27 of this book, the agent at Bureau headquarters who processed the information misinterpreted regulations, with the result that the assignment of looking for Mihdhar and Hazmi was given to an inexperienced intelligence agent, rather than to the experienced criminal agents working the *Cole* investigation (FBI IG, Wright, 340–, *New Yorker*, 7/10 & 17/06).

382 **"The weight":** Staff Statment 2, CO; **"that Mihdhar":** FBI IG; **CIA summary/acknowledged/accountability board:** Executive Summary, Report on CIA Accountability with Respect to the 9/11 Attacks, Office of the Inspector General, CIA, 6/05; **Goss declined/"amongst the finest":** Director's Statement on Office of Inspector General's Report, "CIA Accountability with Respect to the 9/11 Attacks," 10/6/05, www.cia.gov.

382 **"excessive workload":** Executive Summary, Report on CIA Accountability with Respect to the 9/11 Attacks, Office of the Inspector General, CIA, 6/05; **"nobody read":** *NYT*, 10/17/02; **"All the processes":** Report, JI, 151.

382 **"It is clear":** Fenton, 311, 104. Fenton goes on to suggest that CIA officers may have been aware of the 9/11 plot and "desired the outcome we saw on our television screens." Fenton has done an intriguing analysis, but the authors do not accept that there is sufficient evidence or rationale to accept such a heinous possibility (e.g., Fenton, 95, 239, 281, 241–, 327).

382–84 **"good operational":** Executive Summary, Report on CIA Accountability with Respect to the 9/11 Attacks, Office of the Inspector General, CIA, 6/05; **Maxwell:** *New Yorker*, 7/10 & 17/06; **"They purposely":** Bamford, *Pretext*, 224.

384 **run operations in U.S.:** For evidence of the CIA having engaged in operations within the United States, readers could consult, for example, the report of the Senate committee that investigated intelligence agency abuses in the wake of the Watergate scandal. That report, published in 1976, details a number of such operations, including four mail-opening programs spanning a twenty-year period, and CHAOS, launched in 1967 to gather information that might reveal foreign government influence on antiwar and civil rights protesters (Final Report, *Supplementary Detailed Staff Reports on Intelligence Activities and the Rights of Americans*, U.S. Senate Select Committee to Study Government Operations with Respect to Intelligence Activities, 94th Cong., 2nd Sess., Washington, D.C.: U.S. Govt. Printing Office, 1976, 559–, 679–).

384–86 **Yousef/"wanted to continue"/"fought":** *New York*, 3/27/95; **some Bureau agents:** Wright, 312; **"Without penetrations"/select group:** Report, JI, 388–. This was the Small Group, which typically included Secretary of State Madeleine Albright, Secretary of Defense William Cohen, Attorney General Janet Reno, National Security Adviser Sandy Berger, CIA director Tenet, and Chairman of the Joint Chiefs General Hugh Shelton, and counterterrorism coordinator Richard Clarke (CR, 119–, 199, Shenon, 255); **Berger episode:** unless otherwise indicated—Biography of Samuel Berger, http://clinton4.nara .gov, Investigative Summary & Exhibits, "Report of Investigation: Samuel R. Berger," Office of the Inspector General, National Archives & Records Administration, www.fas .org, Kean & Hamilton, 183–, 297, Shenon, 1–249–, Fox News, 1/23/07; **MAAR/recommendations:** Clarke, 215–, 219–, CR, 182, 504n78, Farmer, 41; **handwritten notes?:** Farmer, 41; **"desperate":** ibid., 289; **"What information?":** www.usnewswire.com, 7/20/04.

386–87   **"Michelle" "we need":** Staff Statement 2, CO; **"to determine":** Report, JI, 147; **"believed they were":** KSM SUBST. Ramzi Binalshibh was to tell reporter Yosri Fouda after 9/11, before his arrest, that "Brothers Marwan [Shehhi] and Ziad [Jarrah] were tailed by security officers throughout their reconnaissance flight from New York to California . . . But Allah was with them" (Fouda & Fielding, 135); **Cambone note:** Notes of Stephen Cambone, 9/11/01, released under FOIA to Thad Anderson, www.outraged moderates.org.

CHAPTER 32

389   **"Had the hijackers":** Kean & Hamilton, 234; **"The terrorists"/"a sensitive":** press briefing, 9/18/01, www.defenselink.mil.

390   **Iran not know re 9/11:** CR, 241. Iranian contacts with al Qaeda went back at least as far as bin Laden's time in Sudan. Up to ten of the future muscle hijackers traveled through Iran, as did Binalshibh—who said they did so because Iran did not stamp Saudi passports. Numerous al Qaeda operatives fled to Iran following the U.S. invasion of Afghanistan after 9/11, and members of the bin Laden family were given sanctuary there. In 2010, in what was surely a crude exercise in political mischief making, Iran's president, Mahmoud Ahmadinejad, claimed that 9/11 had been merely a "big fabrication" to justify U.S. actions abroad (CR, 240, trial transcript, *U.S. v. Ali Mohamed*, U.S. District Court for the Southern District of NY, 10/20/00, Shenon, 372, int. Thomas Joscelyn, *FrontPage Magazine*, 9/28/07, ABC News, 2/11/10, *Newsweek*, 8/19/02, Tenet, 244, *The Independent* [U.K.], 3/7/10); **"convincing evidence":** www.thedailybeast.com, 5/20/11, *Daily Mail* (U.K.), 5/20/11, www.newsmax.com, 5/19/11.

390   **no evidence Iraq:** CR, 66, Staff Statement 15, CO; **last-minute changes/Snell/Jacobson/De:** Shenon, 398–.

390–92   **Bandar delight/posted:** press statement, 7/22/04, www.saudiembassy.net. Prince Bandar's own name and that of his wife, Princess Haifa—whose name featured in an intriguing part of the investigators' work, described later, in the Notes to Ch. 33—made fleeting appearances in the Report's endnotes, but not in the text (CR, 482n66, 498n123, 557n27, 563n19); **"no evidence"/"problematic"/"a commitment":** CR, 171, 371–; **Khilewi/"A Saudi citizen":** *Middle East Quarterly*, 9/98, & see *WP*, 8/25/94, *New Yorker*, 10/22/01; **Khalifa:** see Ch. 20 and related Notes, "In re search of luggage and personal belongings, *Khalifa v. U.S*," 3/6/95 cited in ed. Berger, *Khalifa*, "Top al Qaeda Fundraiser Dead," www.counterterrorismblog.org.

392   **limousine/"high-ranking"/Prince Sultan:** Anonymous, *Through Our Enemies' Eyes*, Washington, D.C.: Brassey's, 2002 [author was in fact Michael Scheuer], 138–, Lance, *Triple Cross*, 166, "Mohammed Jamal Khalifa: Life & Death Secrets," INTELWIRE. *Philippine Daily Inquirer*, 8/11/00. The authors are unaware of any response by or on behalf of Prince Sultan to the report that he welcomed Khalifa home. Nor have they been able to establish that Khalifa did carry a diplomatic passport.

392–94   **"Since 1994"/" '96 is the key":** *New Yorker*, 10/16/01; **Paris meeting/protection money:** Complaint, *Thomas Burnett et al. v. al Baraka Investment & Development et al.*,

U.S. District Court for the District of Columbia, pt. 1080, Trento, 306–, Greg Palast, *The Best Democracy Money Can Buy*, NY: Plume, 2004, 99–; **Kerrey:** *LAT*, 6/20/04; **"It's a lovely":** transcript, *Frontline:* "Saudi Time Bomb," www.pbs.org; **Turki recalled:** *Time*, 8/31/03, int. Turki, *OnLine NewsHour: Inside the Kingdom*, 1/21/02, www.pbs.org, Lacey, *Inside the Kingdom*, 208–, 364, Wright, 266–, 288–, Anthony Cordesman, "Saudi Security & the War on Terrorism," Center for Strategic & International Studies, 4/22/02, Bergen, 240; **Others say two trips:** Rashid, 48 & see *LAT*, 6/20/04; **Khaksar/deal:** *Guardian*, 3/2/03, *NYT*, 3/24/09 & see *WP*, 1/15/06; **Turki deny:** MSNBC, 9/5/03; **met with OBL:** Reeve, 194—citing interview with U.S. intelligence source; **"at least two"/"The deal was":** *U.S. News & World Report*, 1/6/02; **named the two:** Henderson, formally a journalist with the BBC and the *Financial Times*, later named Naif and Sultan in this connection in articles in *The Wall Street Journal* and in a paper published by the Washington Institute for Near East Policy. The authors are not aware that Prince Naif or Prince Sultan has commented on the allegation (*WSJ*, 8/3/05, "After King Abdullah: Succession in Saudi Arabia," *Policy Focus 96*, 8/09);**"hundreds"/"Saudi official":** int. & corr. Simon Henderson, *WSJ*, 8/12/02.

394–95 **7,000:** *WSJ*, 2/15/11; **"They would go out":** MSNBC, 9/5/03 & see *WP*, 7/19/07; **"We've got":** *U.S. News & World Report*, 10/11/98; **"an interminable"/"Your Royal Highness":** Tenet, 106–; **Gore/"The United":** CR, 122.

395–96 **"never lifted"/clerics:** Baer, *See No Evil*, 33. The two clerics were Salman al-Awadah and Safar al-Hawali (*National Review*, 3/11/03, Erik Stakelback, "The Saudi Hate Machine," 12/17/03, www.investigativeproject.org); **"the Saudi government":** Report, JI, 110; **"As one of"/"foreign enemy":** Scheuer, *Marching Toward Hell*, 72, 15; **"You've got to be":** Wright, 238.

396 **"All the answers":** Brisard & Dasquié, xxix. The O'Neill conversation was with Jean-Charles Brisard, who began investigating terrorist finances for French intelligence in 1997. After 9/11, he became a lead investigator for the legal firm Motley Rice in connection with the civil action brought by 9/11 victims' families against a list of Saudi-based Islamic charities, a number of financial institutions, and several members of the Saudi royal family. He provided written testimony to the U.S. Committee on Banking, Housing and Urban Affairs in 2003 (inrs. Jean-Charles Brisard, Written Testimony, Committee on Banking, Housing & Urban Affairs, U.S. Senate, 10/22/03, www.banking.senate. gov, Brisard & Dasquié, xxvii–, xxi).

396 **longtime head:** Prince Turki had resigned as GID chief, after a quarter of a century, just ten days before 9/11. The reason for the resignation remains unclear. Turki's departure was the more striking, reportedly, because he had been confirmed in his post as recently as the end of May (Simon Henderson, "A Prince's Mysterious Disappearance," NPR, 10/22/10, Hamel, 237).

396–97 **"At the instruction":** *Arab News*, 9/18/02. On another occasion, in a 2010 CNN interview, Prince Turki said much the same. "From my previous experience, there is a continuous exchange of information between the CIA and the Saudi security agencies" (CNN, 11/17/10); **GID/U.S. understanding:** e.g., Cordesman, "Saudi Security"; **specifically/"What we told":** *USA Today*, 10/16/03, *Salon*, 10/18/03; **Bandar hinted:** transcript of int. Bandar, *Frontline:* "Looking for Answers," www.pbs.org; **Abdullah now king:** Abdullah had succeeded to the throne in 2005, on the death of his long-ailing and incapacitated half-brother King Fahd; **"Saudi security":** ABC News, 11/2/07, CNN, 11/2/07; **"We have sent"/British deny:** John Simpson int. of King Abdullah, BBC News, 10/29/07, CNN, 10/29/07; **denial:** Wright, 448; **silence:** Scheuer, *Marching Toward Hell*, 72–; **"There is not":** *USA Today*, 10/16/03.

397 **Turki stood by/Badeeb:** Wright, 448, 310. A Saudi security consultant, Nawaf Obaid, also told author Lawrence Wright that the terrorists' names were passed to the CIA sta-

tion chief in Riyadh. Wright believed Turki's 2003 account, and indicated in a *New Yorker* article that the CIA had consulted the Saudi authorities—after learning from an intercept on the Yemen phone "hub" that Mihdhar was headed to Kuala Lumpur (Wright, 310, 376n, 448, *New Yorker*, 7/10 & 16/06).

397–98   **Scheuer/"fabrication":** Scheuer, *Marching Toward Hell*, 72–; **Bandar/Commission:** MFR of int. Prince Bandar, Access Restricted, Item (3 pages) withdrawn, 10/14/08, CF.

398   **Turki/"I can":** corr. Kristen Wilhelm. This reply to the authors' inquiry is known as a "Glomar Response" to a request under the Freedom of Information Act—so called after the first occasion on which it was used, when the CIA sought to prevent publication of a *Los Angeles Times* story on the agency's operation to raise a sunken Soviet submarine. The U.S. ship that had been intended for use in the operation to raise the sub was called the *Glomar Explorer*. The Glomar Response has been used in cases involving both national security and privacy issues ("The Glomar Response," http://nsarchive.wordpress.com).

398   **"penetrated al Qaeda":** *Seattle Times*, 10/29/01; **returned to Saudi/disclosed:** Report, JI, 131–.

399   **"presented with":** Staff Report, "9/11 & Terrorist Travel," 12, 15, 37. Before 9/11, according to the Commission's staff report on terrorist travel, neither State Department personnel processing visa applications nor immigration inspectors were aware of such indicators. Even two years after the attacks, the information had "yet to be unclassified and disseminated to the field."

399   **Commission footnote:** The Commission footnote appears to distinguish the cases of Mihdhar, the Hazmi brothers, and two other hijackers from those of the other ten Saudi hijackers. This may reflect the possibility that only the passports of Mihdhar and his named comrades were marked by the Saudi authorities. Absent fuller and clearer information, it is impossible to know (CR, 563n32).

399   **"contained a secret":** Bamford, *Shadow Factory*, 58; **Trento account/"We had been":** Joe Trento, "The Real Intelligence Cover-up," 8/6/03 & Joseph Trento & Susan Trento, "The No Fly List," 1/11/10, http://dcbureau.org, & Trento & Trento, refs., conv. Joseph Trento.

399   **Kuala Lumpur "to spy":** Trento & Trento, 7–. The administrator of the Islamic Center of San Diego, whom Mihdhar and Hazmi asked for assistance following their arrival in early 2000, said after 9/11 that he had "suspected that Mihdhar might have been an intelligence agent of the Saudi government" (CR, 517n29, 220).

399   **Mihdhar multiple-entry visa:** Trento & Trento, 8. According to the Trentos, citing Michael Springmann, who had years earlier served as head of the visa department in the Jeddah consulate, the CIA would have known this fact even sooner—because a CIA officer in the Jeddah consulate "routinely approved visas for Saudi intelligence operatives as a courtesy" (Trento & Trento, 8—see Michael Springmann, "A Sin Concealed—the Visas for Terrorists Program," 12/13/07, http://visasforterrorists.blogspot.com).

399–400   **"were perceived":** Trento & Trento, 9; **"Many terrorists":** ibid, 187; **"because they were":** Joe Trento, "The Real Intelligence Cover-up," 8/6/03, http://dcbureau.org; **"In fact":** Trento & Trento, 9.

400   **account bumps facts?:** The Trento account, for example, asserts that the "complacency" of the Bush administration in summer 2001 is explained by CIA assurances that it had high-level penetration of al Qaeda via the GID. In fact, as documented in this book, the CIA leadership was far from complacent that summer, desperately worried and telling the White House—notably Condoleezza Rice—as much (Trento & Trento, 193; see—re far from complacent—pp. 315–16).

400   **"[name redacted]":** Executive Summary, Report on CIA Accountability with Respect to the 9/11 Attacks, 6/05, www.cia.gov; **"hostile service"/passed to al Qaeda:** Risen,

State of War, 181–; **"On some occasions":** Report, JI, 274; **Rahman defense:** *New York,* 3/27/95.

401   **screen saver:** The intelligence counterparts who told the CIA about bin Laden's picture being used as a screen saver were those of Jordan—apparently in the late 1990s (Risen, 182); **"80% sympathetic":** *The Times* (London), 7/5/04.

CHAPTER 33

402–3 **tens of thousands:** Reuters, 9/11/01; **honked horns:** transcript, *Frontline:* "Saudi Time Bomb," www.pbs.org; **killed camels:** int. of Saad al-Fagih for *Frontline:* "Looking for Answers," www.pbs.org; **screen savers/"somebody":** int. of person in Saudi Arabia who asked to remain anonymous; **Ahmed/"muted"/"So, they lost":** Qanta Ahmed, 395.

403   **survey/Prince Nawwaf:** The survey was conducted by the Saudi GID, the intelligence service, and leaked to *The New York Times* a year later by a U.S. administration official. Prince Nawwaf had become GID chief following the resignation of Prince Turki. In a 2004 interview, Prince Bandar was to claim the situation was very different, that a Zogby poll "showed 91 percent of Saudis said they like America." What the poll actually said was that 91 percent of Saudis said they had "no quarrel with the people of the United States, yet their overall impression of the American people is 70% unfavorable, 24% favorable" (leaked survey: *NYT,* 1/27/02, *Middle East Economic Digest,* 9/14/01; Bandar: int. Bandar, *Meet the Press,* NBC, 4/25/04).

403   **"Almost unanimously":** Kean & Hamilton, 113.

404–5 **Bandar/"not Arabs"/"My God":** *New Yorker,* 3/24/03; **Palestinians celebrating:** There were numerous reports of Palestinians celebrating the attacks. It has been suggested, though, that some news footage of Palestinians supposedly celebrating 9/11 was a distortion—that it in fact showed celebration of something else. For more on the reaction to 9/11 across the Middle East, see Ch. 14, p. 154 (ed. Woods, 12); **"condemned":** statement, 9/11/01 cied in Cordesman, "Saudi Official Statements on Terrorism, After the Sept. 11 Attacks," Center for Strategic & International Studies, 11/01; **Abdullah fumed/declined/snapped/"I reject"/Bush responded:** *WP,* 2/10/02, *New Yorker,* 3/24/03, Unger, *House of Bush, House of Saud,* 241–, *Online NewsHour: Inside the Kingdom,* www.pbs.org.

405   **Abdullah pulled:** *Atlantic Monthly,* 5/03, Lacey, *Inside the Kingdom,* 232, *WP,* 2/12/02. Though Saudi Arabia at the time produced only some 18 percent of the crude oil consumed by the United States, it has what other oil-producing countries do not have—the world's only surplus production capacity. It means that world oil prices are controlled by Saudi Arabia, according to its decisions as to how much oil to make available at any given time. It had used the oil weapon in 1973, after the Yom Kippur War, by joining with other countries in cutting off the oil supply and in 1990–1991—in reverse—by increasing supply when Iraqi oil was cut off during the Gulf War (*Atlantic,* 2/21/08, *Statistical Abstract of the U.S., 2007,* Washington, D.C.: U.S. Govt. Printing Office, 2007, 821).

405–6   **15 were Saudi:** *Newsweek,* 11/19/01, *New Yorker,* 3/24/03; **"That was a":** transcript, *Frontline:* "House of Saud," www.pbs.org; **75 royals/Caesars Palace:** Las Vegas to Counterterrorism, 9/25/01, FBI documents obtained under FOIA by Judicial Watch; **One of OBL's brothers:** Unger, 7; **more than 20:** e.g., re International Flight 441 from Boston, 9/17/03, "Ryan Air folder," B70, T5, CF; **Prince Ahmed/yearling:** Jason Levin, *From the Desert to the Derby,* NY: Daily Racing Form Press, 2002, 1, 15, Unger, 7, 255–; **unable to charter/flight on 13th:** MFR of Dan Grossi, "Dan Grossi, Tampa-Lexington Flight," B70, T5, CF, **"his father or his uncle":** ibid., Unger, 9; **Bandar statement:** press release, 9/12/01, www.saudiembassy.net; **Bush appointment/welcomed/cigars:**

Unger, 7, William Simpson, 315, *New Yorker*, 3/24/03; **assistant rang/Watson/Clarke:** int. of Bandar, *Meet the Press*, 4/24/04, Staff Report, 9/11 & Terrorist Travel, 171–, MFR 04019823, 6/3/04, CR, 557, Shenon, 287; **photo published:** Woodward, *State of Denial*, facing p. 274; **"not inclined":** corr. Jodie Steck, George W. Bush Presidential Library, 2011.

407 **Florida/Kentucky flight:** e.g., Unger, 7–. The confusion about the Tampa charter persisted in part because the FBI accepted, even after having been challenged by journalists, a secondhand report that Prince Ahmed's son and his friends had driven rather than flown to Lexington, and because the Bureau's own reports reflected confusion as to when U.S. airspace reopened to charter flights (Final Draft of response to October 2003 *Vanity Fair* article, "Saudi Flights," B68, T5, CF, The Saudi Flights—A Summary, "Saudi Flights," B6, Dan Marcus Files, CF, CTD to Counterterrorism, 9/24/03, FBI 265A-NY-280350, serial 1234567890, *Vanity Fair*, 10/03).

407 **after airspace open:** FAA Notices to Airmen [NOTAM], 1/9817, 1/9832, 1/9853, www.aopa.org, corr. Laura Brown, FAA. The records show that U.S. airspace was open to almost all aircraft—including charter flights—as of 11:00 A.M. EDT on September 13. The exception was for "general aviation" flights—which, contrary to previous reporting, did not include charters such as the Tampa flight. In any event, the Tampa-to-Lexington flight took off at approximately 4:30 P.M.

407 **on their way home:** Staff Report, 9/11 & Terrorist Travel, 171–, 270n49/50; **charter:** Judicial Watch press release, 6/20/07, Counterterrorism to Boston, 9/21/01, FBI 265A-NY-280350, serial 1652; **watchlist:** CR, 558, n31; **most not interviewed:** CR, 557n28. It has been reported that one of those interviewed was Prince Ahmed, but there is no evidence of such an interview in FBI files thus far released (The Saudi Flights—A Summary, "Saudi Flights," B6, Dan Marcus Files, CF).

407 **agents interviewed family/Omar:** FBI 302s of ints. Bin Laden family members 9/13–24/01 (inc. Omar Awadh), all in "Ryan Air folder," B70, T5, CF.

407 **Omar shared/briefly investigated:** Coll, *The Bin Ladens*, 483–, 526–, Brisard & Dasquie, 176–, *WP*, 10/2/03. The group, of which Abdullah bin Laden was listed as president, was the World Assembly of Muslim Youth, or WAMY. The U.S. branch was operated by Abdullah, according to *The Washington Post*, until 9/11. Though it has been reported that Abdullah was on a flight with Saudis on board that departed on September 20—Ryan International 441—his name is not on the passenger list supplied by the charter company (Coll, 483–, *WP*, 10/2/03, passenger list in "Saudi Flights, FBI Docs., 3 of 4," B70, T5, CF, Staff Report, 9/11 & Terrorist Travel, 272n94).

407–8 **"Although":** *NYT*, 3/27/05; **"there is the existence":** CNN, 9/4/03. The reference is to the brother of Adel al Jubeir, mentioned earlier in this chapter (*Washington Report on Middle East Affairs*, 11/07).

408 **public relations firms/Another firm:** The firms initially hired were Burson Marsteller and Qorvis Communications. Patton Boggs was used for the contacts with Congress. On one infamous occasion, Saudi PR maneuvers misfired. New York mayor Giuliani handed back a $10 million donation made to the Twin Towers Fund by Prince Alwaleed bin Talal in light of the press release the prince's staff distributed following the presentation. It read: "We must address some of the issues that led to such a criminal attack. I believe the government of the United States of America should re-examine its policies in the Middle East and adopt a more balanced stance toward the Palestinian cause. . . . Our Palestinian brethren continue to be slaughtered at the hands of the Israelis while the world turns the other cheek." This caused outrage in the United States. Prince Alwaleed, however, has also said: "You have to ask the simple question. Why fifteen Saudis? You can't just say it happened by coincidence. Clearly, there's something wrong with the way of thinking here [in Saudi Arabia], with the way people are raised" (PR firms: *New Internationalist*, 3/1/02, "Terrorism

to End Terrorism," fall 2001, www.prwatch.org, *WP,* 3/21/02, *Washington Times,* 12/9/04, Gold, 193; Alwaleed: *Arab News,* 10/14/01; *Irish Times,* 8/3/09, Giuliani, 374–).

408   **"We feel what":** transcript, *Larry King,* CNN, 10/1/01; **Abdullah to ranch/"Yes, I":** Lacey, *Inside the Kingdom,* 284–, Suskind, *One Percent Doctrine,* 104–, Remarks by the President After Meeting with Crown Prince Abdullah, 4/25/02, posted at www.global security.org, Fox News, 4/26/02.

409   **"probably" stolen:** *BG,* 9/15/01. The spokesman, Gaafar Allagany, was to say on September 19 that two men with the same names as those of two hijackers, a Salem al-Hazmi and an Abdulaziz al-Omari, had indeed had their passports stolen over the past few years. The two cases cited by Allagany turned out to be cases of mistaken identity—there is no evidence the passports of hijackers Hazmi or Omari had been stolen. On the issue of hijackers' identity, see also Ch. 14 and its related Notes (*WP,* 9/20/01, 10/7/01, *Telegraph* [U.K.], 9/23/01).

409-10   **"most people":** int. of Hatoon al Fassi for *Frontline:* "House of Saud," www.pbs .org; **"There is no proof":** Gold, 185, citing *Al Hayat,* 10/23/01; **"another power":** *NYT,* 10/23/01; **Naif/"The names":** *USA Today,* 2/6/02; **"It is enough":** Lacey, *Inside the Kingdom,* 231; **"Zionists"/"we put big":** AP, 12/5/02 citing int. Naif by *Al Siyasa* (Kuwait), *'Ain al Yaqeen,* 11/29/02 citing same int.; **"We're getting":** *LAT,* 10/13/01; **"They knew":** *New Yorker,* 10/16/01; **not allowed access:** *Philadelphia Inquirer,* 7/30/03; **"dribble out":** *NYT,* 12/27/01.

410   **blocked attempts:** *U.S. News & World Report,* 1/6/02, Suskind, *One Percent Doctrine,* 109. A State Department spokesman, Richard Boucher, had said in November that Saudi Arabia had been "prominent among the countries acting against the accounts of terrorist organizations . . . in compliance with UN Security Council Resolution 1333." The following month, however, following a visit to Saudi Arabia by Treasury Department assets control chief Richard Newcombe, it was reported that the Saudis "had balked at freezing bank accounts Washington said were linked to terrorists." Working with the Saudis had apparently been "like pulling teeth" (Boucher: State Department briefing, 11/27/01, http://usinfo.org; Newcombe: *U.S. News & World Report,* 1/6/02).

410-11   **"It doesn't look":** *BG,* 3/3/02; **few fluent Arabic:** Report, JI, 59, 245, 255, 336, 358; **men believed to have helped:** For information not particularly cited here, see Ch. 25 and its related Notes; **Thumairy diplomat:** Kean & Hamilton, 308; **"in a Western":** MFR 04019254, 4/20/04; **"uncertain":** MFR of int. Omar al-Bayoumi, 10/18/03, CF; **Bayoumi's income:** Graham with Nussbaum, 167, int. Bob Graham; **three-page section:** Report, JI, 175–; **Graham re payments:** Graham with Nussbaum, 24–, 167–, 224–, int. Bob Graham.

411   **payments originated embassy?:** The 9/11 Commission was to report that it found no evidence that Mihdhar and Hazmi received money from Basnan—or Bayoumi. The public furor around the Basnan money centered on reports that it came to the Basnans in cashier's checks in the name of Saudi ambassador Prince Bandar's wife, Princess Haifa. The royal couple were predictably outraged by the notion that there could have been a link between the princess and terrorists. Such payments would have been in line, a Saudi embassy spokesman said, with her normal contributions to the needy. 9/11 Commissioner John Lehman surmised that the princess simply signed checks put in front of her by radicals working in the embassy's Islamic Affairs office. *Newsweek* has reported that Saudi wire transfers amounting to $20,000 were made to an individual who was featured in another terrorist case, also in connection with medical treatment for the individual's wife. *Newsweek* made no mention of Princess Haifa in that regard (Commission: CR, 516n24; furor: e.g., *Newsweek,* 11/22/02, 12/9/02, *Washington Times,* 11/26/02; outraged: Fox News, 11/27/02, *LAT,* 11/24/02, *CounterPunch,* 12/3/02, Lehman: Shenon, 185; $20,000: *Newsweek,* 4/7/04, *Daily Times* [Pakistan], 8/8/08).

411–12   **Thumairy "might be":** CR, 217; **Bayoumi attracted/"connections"/left country:** FBI IG, Report, JI, 173; **Basnan came up:** Report, JI, 176; **party:** ibid., 177; **did more for Islam:** MFR 04017541A, 11/17/03, CF; **"wonderful":** *Newsweek*, 11/22/02; **contact with Binalshibh:** MFR 04017541A, 11/17/03, CF.

412   **agent or spy:** Graham with Nussbaum, 11, 24–, 168–, 224–. At least five people told the FBI they considered Bayoumi to be some sort of government agent. According to Dr. Abdussattar Shaikh, in whose San Diego home future hijackers Hazmi and Mihdhar eventually rented accommodations, one of those who expressed that view was none other than Hazmi himself. In an early interview with *The New York Times* after 9/11, Shaikh said Hazmi and Midhar had been his friends, that their identification as hijackers was perhaps a case of stolen identities. Congressional investigators would later be startled to discover something Sheikh had certainly not revealed to the *Times*—and that the FBI initially sought to conceal from the investigators. Shaikh had long been an FBI informant, and had regularly shared information with a Bureau agent named Steven Butler. Butler had on occasion talked with Shaikh at home while Hazmi and Mihdhar were in a room nearby. According to the agent, Shaikh had mentioned the pair by their first names, saying that they were Saudis. That rang no alarm bells for him, Butler recalled, because "Saudi Arabia was considered an ally." The FBI, backed up by Bush officials, refused to allow Joint Committee staff to interview Shaikh. A 9/11 Commission memorandum, identifying Shaikh only as Dr. Xxxxxxxxxx Xxxxx, makes it clear that 9/11 Commission staff did talk to Shaikh. The memorandum does not say whether Shaikh shared with Agent Butler his belief that Bayoumi, the man who had introduced the hijackers to San Diego, was a Saudi agent. Nor is there evidence that Commission staff queried Shaikh about inconsistencies in his story of how he first met the two future hijackers. Shaikh's simultaneous relationship with both the two terrorists and the FBI just might have led to their being unmasked—an even more glaring might-have-been when one recalls that the CIA had early on identified both men as terrorist suspects, *and* known they had visas for travel to the United States—yet failed to inform the FBI (see pp. 379–80). Much remains to be explained. The former chair of Congress's joint probe, former senator Bob Graham, accepts that the FBI may at first have tried to conceal its relationship with Shaikh simply because it was a "big embarrassment." Graham also raised the possibility, though, that what the FBI tried to hide was that Shaikh knew something that "would be even more damaging were it revealed." What, too, of the report in the press that Agent Butler's interview with congressional investigators had been "explosive," that he "had been monitoring a flow of Saudi Arabian money that wound up in the hands of the two hijackers"? Butler, an official was quoted as having said, "saw a pattern, a trail, and he told his supervisors, but it ended there." As of 2009, Shaikh was still living in San Diego.

Because of agencies' iron rules about the protection of informants—whatever the full story of Shaikh's relationship with the hijackers or with the FBI—there is little likelihood of learning more about him anytime soon. He is virtually invisible in the Commission Report, not even named in the index.

Much the same applies to the Report's handling of Ali Mohamed, a truly significant figure in the sorry story of U.S. agencies' understanding—or lack of it—of al Qaeda. "No single agent of al Qaeda," the author Peter Lance has written, "was more successful in compromising the U.S. intelligence community than a former Egyptian army captain turned CIA operative, Special Forces advisor, and FBI informant" than former Egyptian army major Mohamed. "Mohamed succeeded in penetrating the John F. Kennedy Special Warfare Center at Fort Bragg, while simultaneously training the cell that blew up the World Trade Center in 1993. He went on to train Osama bin Laden's personal bodyguard, and photographed the U.S. embassy in Kenya—taking the surveillance pictures bin Laden himself used to target the [1998] suicide truck bomb."

Though beyond the scope of this book, there is much more to this labyrinthine tale. While the August 6, 2001, CIA brief delivered to President Bush did not mention Mohamed by name, it was shot through with references to him. He was that summer due to be sentenced for his crimes, having pled guilty to multiple terrorist offenses, including his role in the embassy bombings. FBI agent Jack Cloonan, who interviewed Mohamed in prison after 9/11, had the eerie sense that he "knew every detail" of the attacks, in spite of having been in custody for years. As of 2006, though reportedly still a prisoner at an unknown location, Mohamed had yet to be sentenced. There is just one reference to him in the 9/11 Commission Report—and no mention of his relationship with U.S. intelligence agencies (Hazmi view: MFR [unnumbered], 4/23/04, CF; *Times* interview: *NYT*, 10/24/01; investigators startled: Graham with Nussbaum, 159–, ints. Bob Graham, Eleanor Hill; informant/Butler talked: FBI IG, Report, JI, 162, "Conspiracy Theories: The Intelligence Breakdown," www.cbc.ca; "ally": Report, JI, 162; FBI refused: Joint Inquiry, Report, 3, Graham with Nussbaum, 162; Bush officials: "Bush Should Cry Uncle and Release Saudi Info," 6/28/03, www. opednews.com, Report, JI, 3; Commission memorandum: MFR [unnumbered], 4/23/04, CF; inconsistencies: CR, 517n28; might-have-been: Report, JI, 19–; "big embarrassment"/"did know": Graham with Nussbaum, 166; "explosive"/"monitoring": *U.S. News & World* Report, 11/29/02; Shaikh 2009: Miriam Raftery, "Abdussattar Shaikh, Co-Founder of San Diego's Islamic Center, Honored for 50 Years of Service Promoting Religious Tolerance," 10/8/09, www.eastcountymagazine .org; "No single": "A Conversation with Peter Lance," 12/06, www.internetwriting journal.com & see Wright, 179–, Bergen, *OBL I Know*, 142–; Aug. 6 brief: J. M. Berger, "What the Commission Missed," 10/4/06, www.intelwire.com; "knew every": ibid.; pled guilty: J. M Berger, ed., *Ali Mohamed Sourcebook*, INTELWIRE, 2006, 311; unknown location/yet to be sentenced: Bergen, *OBL I Know*, 433, Scott, 348n28, 157, 159; one reference: CR, 68 & see Staff Report, "9/11 & Terrorist Travel, CO, 57).

412   **"incontrovertible":** Report, JI, 395. The document, which Graham dated as August 2, 2002, is partially cited in Congress's Joint Inquiry Report in a passage about a CIA memo that cited "incontrovertible evidence that there is support for these terrorists [words redacted]." The Report goes on to state that "it is also possible that further investigation of these allegations could reveal legitimate, and innocent, explanations for these associations." Senator Graham cast doubt on an FBI finding that Bayoumi and Basnan were neither agents nor accomplices in the 9/11 plot. Former Saudi ambassador Bandar, for his part, described reports that Bayoumi was a Saudi agent as "baseless" (Graham with Nussbaum, 169, 224–, 11n, Bandar press release, "Bayoumi is not a government agent," 7/23/03, www.saudiembassy.net).

412–13   **Commission interviews:** e.g., MFR 04019365, 2/24/04; **Thumairy "deceptive"/ denied/prompted/second interview/"say bad"/"implausible":** Snell, De, & Jacobson to Zelikow, 2/25/04, MFR 04019362, 2/23/04, CF; **Bayoumi favorable/stuck to story:** Shenon, 309–, MFR of int. Omar al-Bayoumi, 10/18/03, CF; **Zelikow think not agent:** Zelikow to Shenon, 10/18/07, www.philipshenon.com; **distinguishing mark:** CR, 516n19; **salary approved/picture found:** Report, JI, 174 & see Staff Statement 16, DOCEX 199-HQ-1361032, "Hijacker Primary Docs, PENTTBOM Memo re CD found," B50, T5, CF; **"cleansed"/"deceptive":** MFR 04019367, 2/24/04, Snell, De, & Jacobson to Zelikow, 2/25/04, CF; **"the witness' utter":** MFR int. of Osama Basnan, 10/22/03, CF.

414   **Hussayen/Mosques/in States:** *WSJ*, 2/10/03. In October 2001 the FBI began an investigation of Hussayen's nephew Sami. He eventually became the first person to be charged under the broadened "material support" for terrorism provisions of the then new USA Patriot Act. The government sought to prove that Hussayen used his expertise as an Internet "webmaster" to further the cause of terrorists and promote violent jihad.

The hard drive of a computer he had used, according to an agent's testimony, contained "thousands" of photographs, of the World Trade Center, of the Pentagon, and of planes hitting buildings. Sami Hussayen was eventually found not guilty and returned to Saudi Arabia (Second Superceding Indictment, *U.S. v. Sami Omar al Hussayen,* U.S. District Court for the District of Idaho, AP, 3/12/03, Dept. of Justice press release, "Indictments Allege Illegal Financial Transfers to Iraq; Visa Fraud Involving Assistance to Groups that Advocate Violence," 2/26/03, www.usdoj.gov, *Seattle Times,* 11/22/04).

414–15   **Marriott Sept. 10/"muttering"/Paramedics/"faking"/kitchenette/"I don't":** MFR 04017480, 10/9/03, MFR 04017486, 10/9/03, MFR 04017482, 10/9/03, MFR 04019354, CF, *WSJ,* 2/10/03, *Telegraph* (U.K.), 10/2/03, *WP,* 10/2/03, 3/12/03; **Aulaqi contact/move:** See pp. 291–92; **son of minister:** *Dallas Morning News,* 12/25/09; **preached Capitol:** *NYT,* 5/8/10, Fox News, 11/11/10; **lunched Pentagon:** *NY Daily News,* 10/21/10; **remained U.S.:** *WSJ,* 2/10/03, ABC News, 11/30/09; **phone number/Binalshibh:** Report, JI, 178; **Fort Hood/Detroit bomb/Times Square/cargo planes:** *Christian Science Monitor,* 5/19/10, Fox News, 10/20/10, CNN, 1/7/10, *Guardian* (U.K.), 10/31/10, MSNBC, 11/1/10; **capture or kill:** *Christian Science Monitor,* 5/19/10, *NYT,* 4/6/10; **"loose end":** McClatchy News, 11/21/09.

416   **"that the Saudis":** int. Bob Graham.

416   **"persuasive evidence"/"did not find":** Zelikow to Shenon, 10/18/07, www.philip shenon.com. The Commission, according to its Report, believed that al Qaeda likely did have "agents" in California, "one or more individuals informed in advance" of Mihdhar and Hazmi's arrival. During their research, the authors also saw information suggesting that hijacker leader Mohamed Atta had contact in Florida with one or more wealthy Saudis. A senior law enforcement officer in Florida told the authors—on condition that he not be identified—that he was personally involved after 9/11 in investigating the activities of "a man married into one of the Saudi ruling families." Until his sudden departure on August 30, 2001, the man had lived not far from Venice, where Atta, Shehhi, and Jarrah had trained to fly. The information gathered convinced the authors' source that the three future hijackers visited the man's house, where alcohol and women were made available. The authors have also seen a lengthy taped interview with a former Venice Yellow Cab driver named Bob Simpson. Simpson described having picked up a "wealthy Saudi businessman" at Orlando Executive Airport and later that day having taken him to an apartment building where he had previously picked up Mohamed Atta. After 9/11, Simpson said, the FBI questioned him about the Saudi. Simpson did work for Yellow Cab in 2001, but the authors' efforts to trace him were unsuccessful ("agents": CR, 215; Simpson: videotape & transcript in the collection of Daniel Hopsicker).

416–18   **page 395:** Report, JI, 395–; **CIA not obstruct:** corr. office of Bob Graham, 2009; **Bush himself:** ibid., Graham with Nussbaum, 228, 215–, 231, *NYT,* 6/24/09, *Salon,* 9/8/04; **Pelosi:** CNN, 7/30/03; **"I went back":** *Nation,* 7/29/03.

418   **should be made public:** Prince Bandar, then ambassador to Washington, said in 2003 that there was nothing to hide, and Foreign Minister Prince Saud al-Faisal said it was an "outrage to any sense of fairness that 28 blank pages are now considered substantial evidence to proclaim the guilt of a country." The Saudis, it was suggested, saw publication of the classified material as "a chance to clear their Kingdom's name." Senator Graham did not buy it. "It seemed to me," he has written, "that George W. Bush and Prince Bandar were performing a sort of good cop–bad cop routine, in which Prince Bandar got to claim innocence of behalf of Saudi Arabia, while George W. Bush protected him by being the bad cop who wouldn't release troubling information" (Bandar: "Saudi Ambassador Responds to Reports of Saudi Involvement in 9/11," 7/24/03, www.saudiembassy.net; "outrage": AP, 7/29/03; "a chance": AP, 7/30/03; "It seemed": Graham with Nussbaum, 228–).

418–19   **"I can't tell you"**: int. Eleanor Hill; **leaks/details/"central figure"/"very direct"/**
"cannot be"/Graham/"apparent": *Newsweek*, 2/3/03, *LAT*, 8/2/03, Shenon, 50–, 308–,
AP, 7/27/03, *NYT*, 8/1/03; **Zubaydah waterboarded June/July:** int. of CIA OIG John
Helgerson, *Der Spiegel*, 8/31/09, "Yoo's Legal Memos Gave Bush Retroactive Cover for
Torture," 2/23/09, http://pubrecord.org, BBC News, 7/13/09.

419   **Kiriakou/Zubaydah:** As reported, what Kuriakou learned about Zubaydah's references
to the princes came to him not firsthand but from those reading the cable traffic. For
that reason and because of the passage of time, he told the authors, he is today unsure
whether the Zubaydah/princes element first surfaced during interrogation or because he
was questioned about something found in the journal Zubaydah had kept.

Refuting suggestions that Zubaydah may not have given good information, or that he
may even have been mentally unstable, Kiriakou said he thought the contrary was true,
that he did give reliable information and was "not crazy" but "bright, well-read, a good
conversationalist."

The Kiriakou interview for this book is first corroboration of the core elements of an
account written by author Gerald Posner in 2003, with different detail and citing only
anonymous sources. The Posner account, according to Kiriakou, got important detail
and chronology skewed. The relevant interrogation of Zubaydah that produced the lead
about the Saudi prince did not occur—as Posner wrote—within days of his capture but
only months later, after he had been waterboarded. (This would fit with the account of
FBI investigator Ali Soufan, who took part in interrogations of Zubaydah until June.
During that early period, the link to the Saudi princes did not come up.)

As reported by Posner, Zubaydah was tricked into believing that he had been moved
from U.S. to Saudi custody—in hopes that fear of the truly gruesome torture practiced in
Saudi Arabia would lead him to start talking. Instead, by the Posner account, he seemed
relieved and promptly urged his "Saudi" interrogators to telephone Prince Ahmed bin
Salman—even providing the prince's phone numbers from memory. Prince Ahmed, he
said, "will tell you what to do." Later, according to Posner's account, he added the names
and numbers of the two other princes. Bin Laden, Zubaydah reportedly said, had made a
point of letting the Saudi royals know in advance, without sharing details, that there was
going to be an attack on the United States on September 11.

Again according to Posner, the CIA decided to share what Zubaydah had said with
Saudi intelligence, with a request that it probe further. *New York Times* journalist and
author James Risen added a new detail in 2006. When Zubaydah was captured, sources
told Risen, he had on his person two bank cards, one from a Saudi bank and another from
an institution in Kuwait. American investigators worked through a Muslim financier to
check on the accounts, only to be frustrated. There no longer was a way to trace the
money that had gone into the accounts, the financier reported, because "Saudi intelligence officials had seized all the records relating to the card from the Saudi financial
institution in question; the records then disappeared."

Not only Posner and Risen but also a third writer, Tom Joscelyn, have probed the
Zubaydah story. Joscelyn told the authors that one of his interviewees said he had seen
the Zubaydah interrogation logs and that they corroborate the Zubaydah/princes scenario. Kiriakou's interview with the authors now becomes the first on-the-record corroboration from a former CIA officer.

Absent the logs, proof positive that Zubaydah did make the claims attributed to him
is unobtainable—for the worst of reasons. Though the 2002 interrogations of Zubaydah
were videotaped, the Agency has admitted that it has since destroyed the tapes. While the
destruction was deplorable, it may have been done to obscure evidence of brutal interrogation rather than of what Zubaydah said. The waterboarding of the prisoner occurred
weeks before the CIA received formal authority to use that violent measure (Kiriakou:

int. John Kiriakou; Soufan: Testimony of Ali Soufan, 5/13/09, http://judiciary.senate.gov,
corr. Daniel Freedman, the Soufan Group; 2011 Posner account: Posner, *Why America
Slept*, 202–; gruesome torture: e.g., Hollingsworth & Mitchell, 11–, 21–, 56, 62; princes
died: AP, 9/2/03, "Prince Ahmed Cited in New Book on Sept. 11 Attacks," 9/4/03, www
.bloodhorse.com; Risen: Risen, 173–, 187; Joscelyn: conv. Thomas Joscelyn; destroyed
tapes: *WP*, 12/12/07, *NYT*, 3/3/09).

419–20   **"wrongdoing":** *LAT*, 8/1/03; **credible:** int. Bob Graham; **"assistance":** *Financial
Times* (U.K.), 7/25/03; **40 clamored:** CNN, 7/30/03; **"engaged"/"to protect"/"He
has":** Graham with Nussbaum, xv, 231; **"being kept"/"It was":** ibid., 215–; **"If the 28":**
New Republic, 8/3/04.

CHAPTER 34

421   **Bush seeded/Cheney said:** In his address to the nation of October 7, 2002, for example,
Bush said: "We know that Iraq and al Qaeda have had high-level contacts that go back a
decade. . . . After September 11, Saddam Hussein's regime gleefully celebrated the terrorist attacks on America." The President mentioned 9/11 eight times at his press conference
just before the invasion of Iraq. "The White House played endless semantic games on the
issue," *The New York Times*'s Philip Shenon has written. "When pressed, Bush was careful not to allege that Iraq had any role in the 9/11 attacks, at least no direct role. But he
insisted that if Saddam Hussein had remained in power, he . . . would have been tempted
to hand over [weapons of mass destruction] to his supposed ally Osama bin Laden. Vice
President Cheney went further . . . suggesting repeatedly, almost obsessively, that Iraq
may in fact have been involved in the September 11 plot." The Vice President liked to
cite the Czech intelligence report suggesting that hijack leader Atta had met with an Iraqi
agent in Prague. See note below—evidence was developed strongly suggesting that the
report was unreliable (10/7/02 address: "Address to the Nation on Iraq," www.presidency
.ucsb.edu; mentioned 9/11: *Christian Science Monitor*, 3/14/03; "White House played":
Shenon, 126–, 381–, & see Report, "Whether Public Statements Regarding Iraq by U.S.
Government Offcials Were Substantiated by Intelligence Information," U.S. Senate Intelligence Committee, 110th Cong., http://intelligence.senate.gov).

421   **polls:** The references are to a Pew Research poll of February 2003, a Knight-Ridder poll
in January that year, and a *Washington Post* poll in September 2003. (*Editor & Publisher*,
3/26/03, *USA Today*, 9/6/03).

422   **Atta/Prague/Iraqi intelligence:** An informant reported to Czech intelligence after 9/11
that photographs of Mohamed Atta resembled a man he had seen meeting with an Iraqi
diplomat and suspected spy named Ahmad Khalil Ibrahim Samir al-Ani in Prague at
11 A.M. on April 9, 2001. Investigation indicated that neither Atta nor Ani had been in
Prague at the time alleged. Atta was recorded on closed-circuit TV footage in Florida
on April 4, and his cell phone was used in the state on the 6th, 9th, 10th, and 11th. Atta
and Shehhi, moreover, apparently signed a lease on an apartment on the 11th. This information, while not certain proof, strongly suggests that Atta was in the United States
on April 9. CIA analysts characterized the alleged Prague sighting as being "highly unlikely." Nevertheless, the report crept into prewar intelligence briefings as having been a
"known contact" between al Qaeda and Iraq.

In addition to the alleged Atta meeting, rumors have long circulated that two other
hijackers, Mihdhar and Hazmi, had contact with an Iraqi agent. This was alleged to have
been Ahmad Hikmat Shakir, who acted as a greeter for Arab visitors in Kuala Lumpur
at the time of the terrorist summit there in 2000. Shakir was captured in 2002. The CIA
later received information that "Shakir was not affiliated with al Qaeda and had no connections with IIS [Iraqi intelligence]."

(Atta/Prague: CR, 228–, Report, "U.S. Intelligence Community's Prewar Intelligence Assessments on Iraq," U.S. Senate, Select Committee on Intelligence, 108th Cong., 2nd Sess., Washington, D.C.: U.S. Govt. Printing Office, 2004, 340–, "Review of the Pre-Iraqi War Activities of the Office of the Under Secretary of Defense for Policy," Office of the Inspector General, U.S. Dept. of Defense, 2/9/07, 5–, but see Edward Jay Epstein, "Atta in Prague," *NYT*, 11/22/05; Shakir: Report, "Postwar Findings About Iraq's WMD Programs and Links to Terrorism and How They Compare with Prewar Assessments," U.S. Senate Select Committee on Intelligence, 109th Cong., 2nd Sess., Washington, D.C.: U.S. Govt. Printing Office, 9/8/06, 111.)

422   **Mylroie propagated:** e.g. *National Interest*, Winter 95/96, *New Republic*, 9/24/01, CR, 336, 559n73, Laurie Mylroie, *The War Against America*, NY: Regan, 2001, *WSJ*, 4/2/04, "The Saddam-9/11 Link Confirmed," 5/11/04, www.frontpagemagazine.com; **Investigation:** Michael Isikoff and David Corn, *Hubris*, NY: Three Rivers Press, 2007, 72–, and refs., Clarke, 94–, 232; **multiple/"My view":** *Washington Monthly*, 12/03.

422   **"We went back":** int. of Michael Scheuer for *Frontline:* "The Dark Side," www.pbs.org. As described earlier in this book, bin Laden had an antipathy for Saddam Hussein and had sought Saudi government backing to use his fighters to oust Iraqi forces from Kuwait (see p. 212). Though there are reports that bin Laden and Iraqi representatives did meet to discuss possible cooperation as early as 1992, there is no evidence that anything came of the encounters. Reporting in 2004, the Senate Intelligence Committee concluded that prior to the invasion of Iraq, the CIA had "reasonably assessed that there were likely several instances of contacts between Iraq and al Qaeda throughout the 1990s, but that these contacts did not add up to an established formal relationship . . . no evidence proving Iraqi complicity or assistance in an al Qaeda attack" (e.g. Wright, 295–, Report, "U.S. Intelligence Community's Prewar Intelligence Assessments on Iraq," 346–).

422   **CIA Report 2003/"no credible"/pressure/"questions":** Report, "U.S. Intelligence Community's Prewar Intelligence Assessments on Iraq," 314, 322, 353, 363, 449–.

423   **Duelfer/senior intelligence officials:** The detainee to whom Duelfer referred was Muhammed Khudayr al-Dulaymi, who had headed the M-14 section of the Mukhabarat, the principal Iraqi intelligence agency. Duelfer noted the episode in a 2009 book and in an interview. The story was reported by Robert Windrem, senior research fellow at New York University's Center on Law and Security and a longtime producer for NBC (Charles Duelfer, *Hide and Seek*, NY: PublicAffairs, 2009, 416, Robert Windrem, "Cheney's Role Deepens," 5/13/09, www.dailybeast.com).

423   **"There were two"/"We were not":** McClatchy News, 4/21/09, Report, "Inquiry into the Treatment of Detainees in U.S. Custody, U.S. Senate Committee on Armed Services," 110th Cong., 2nd Sess. 11/20/08, 72.

423–24   **Suskind/forgery/brief storm/denials:** Following Ronald Suskind's account of the forgery's origins in his 2008 book, *The Way of the World*, House Judiciary Committee chairman John Conyers wrote letters saying he intended to follow up. As this book went to print, however, there was no sign that he did. The Suskind book suggests that the forgery was handwritten by former Iraqi intelligence chief Tahir Habbush, who began cooperating with the CIA even before the Iraq invasion and was eventually paid off and "resettled." The purported memo was slipped to a British reporter, billed as authentic, by an aide in the Interim Governing Council in Iraq, and published in late 2003 in Britain's *Sunday Telegraph* (Ronald Suskind, *The Way of the World*, NY: Harper, 2008, 361–, CIA statement, 8/22/08, www.cia.gov, "Statement from Rob Richer," http://suskinsresponse .googlepages.com, "A Note to Readers," www.ronsuskind.com, Letters from Rep. Conyers to Rob Richer, John Maguire, A. B. "Buzzy" Krongard, & John Hannah, 8/20/08, www.judiciary.house.gov).

424   **Giraldi:** Philip Giraldi, "Suskind Revisited," 8/7/08, www.amconmag.com; **"manufac-tured":** int. Paul Pillar for *Frontline:* "The Dark Side," www.pbs.org; **"Unfortunately"/ It's my belief:** press release, 6/5/08, http://intelligence.senate.gov, Report, cited above.

424   **reputable estimates re deaths:** www.iraqbodycount.org, http://icasualties.org. In addi-tion to the American military casualties, more than three hundred non-U.S. troops had died as of early 2011 (Iraq Coalition Casualty Count, www.icasualties.org).

CHAPTER 35

426–27   **"led and financed":** Richard Falkenrath, "The 9/11 Commission Report," *In-ternational Security*, Vol. 29, Winter 04; **only three nations:** CR, 122; **"Pakistani military"/"held the key":** CR, 63–.

427   **financial transactions:** Known 9/11-related money transfers were handled out of Dubai in the UAE. In anticipation of pursuit in the wake of the attacks, the al Qaeda agents involved headed for Pakistan.

427–28   **Rawalpindi, headquarters:** Fouda & Fielding, 181; **Defense Society:** ibid., 15; **Zubaydah caught:** ibid., 20, int. John Kiriakou; **"Pakistani people":** Scheuer, *Osama bin Laden*, 121; **"We found":** ed. Lawrence, 71; **"As for Pakistan":** Rashid, 138; **called on the faithful:** Scheuer, *Osama bin Laden*, 121.

428   **"the most complicated":** *Sunday Times* (U.K.), 8/1/10; **Kashmir:** CR, 58, 63–, Coll, *Ghost Wars*, 292. China also controls part of Kashmir. The region is a tinderbox.

429–31   **Hamid Gul:** Rashid, 129; **trained in camps:** CR, 67, Clinton, 799, Rashid, 137, Coll, *Ghost Wars*, 341; **"Whatever":** Scheuer, *Osama bin Laden*, 121; **security system:** Coll, *Ghost Wars*, 341; **"shoehorned":** *Time*, 8/19/08; **"always" support:** *Foreign Policy Journal*, 9/20/10; **"actually were":** MFR 03012967, 10/8/03; **additional cash:** Coll, *Ghost Wars*, 296; **"the most influential":** *Sunday Times* (U.K.), 8/1/10, *Salon*, 10/18/03, Napoleoni, 82; **"shadow government":** Coll, *Ghost Wars*, 296, *NYT*, 5/12/11; **"help-lessness"/tensions:** MFR 04021470, 12/12/03; **commando operation:** *WP*, 12/19/01; **Clinton visit/"the moon":** *WP*, 12/20/01, CR, 183, 503n64; **"people who"/"not per-suasive":** *WP*, 12/19/01; **Sheehan:** Benjamin & Simon, 515; **"influential":** Clarke to Rice, 1/25/01; **"loss of urgency":** Tenet, 139; **"Full Monty":** *NYT*, 5/12/11.

431   **foreknowledge:** The authors have seen no evidence of Pakistani involvement in 9/11. Soon after publication of the 9/11 Commission Report, however, the distinguished re-porter Arnaud de Borchgrave reported that—according to an "unimpeachable source"—former Pakistani intelligence officers knew beforehand all about the September 11 attacks." This information, de Borchgrave wrote, had reached the Commission only as its report was being printed. UPI, 8/3/04.

431   **"Stone Age":** Musharraf, 201.

431   **demands:** There are differences between the language of Washington's demands as ren-dered in Musharraf's memoir—seemingly verbatim—and the version reproduced in the 9/11 Commission Report. Musharraf found a demand to help "destroy" bin Laden il-logical, he remembered. How could the United States be so sure that bin Laden and al Qaeda were behind 9/11, he wondered, if it was still searching for evidence? Musharraf, 205, CR 331, 558n37.

431   **reservations/cooperated:** CR, 331, Musharraf, 206; **"We have done":** Musharraf, 223; **3,021:** *Sunday Times* (U.K.), 8/1/10; **some 700/369 handed over/bounty:** Musharraf, 237, 369; **Grenier:** *NYT*, 5/12/11; **best-known:** Musharraf, 237–, 220, 240–.

432   **"destroy"/"We have done":** Musharraf, 205, 220.

432–34   **"still visiting":** MFR 03012967, 10/8/03; **McFarland:** Fox News, 1/7/11; **"I'm con-vinced":** "Whatever Happened to bin Laden?," http://afghanistan.blogs.cnn.com; **"You** in the West"/poll: *Sunday Times* (U.K.), 8/1/10; **S Section:** *NYT*, 5/12/11; **"They were very":** *Sunday Times* (U.K.), 3/8/08; **Better to do/officials:** *Sunday Times* (U.K.), 8/1/10, Fox News, 1/7/11; **"We will kill":** transcript, 2nd presidential debate, 10/7/08; **no statements:** *NYT*, 10/2/10; **"I think":** transcript, *Meet the Press*, NBC News, 8/15/10; **audio messages/still shaped:** *NYT*, 10/2/10; **"senior NATO":** CNN, 10/18/10; **"sightings"/"years":** New York *Daily News*, 10/18/10.

434   **intelligence:** In late November 2010, Saudi Arabia's Prince Turki said in an interview that he thought bin Laden was moving to and fro across the Pakistani/Afghan border, communicating by messenger, and still giving orders. "I think they should find him," Turki said, "I think the United States should call the countries that are of interest, like Saudi Arabia, Pakistan, Afghanistan, Russia, China, and set a plan in motion to capture or—or eliminate him." Transcript, int. of Turki, *Situation Room*, CNN, 11/17/10.

434–37   **"launched":** *Courrier International* (France), 5/5/11; **bulletin/Post:** breaking news alerts, *WP*, 5/1/11; **Tonight/Jubilant:** text of Obama address, *Telegraph* (U.K.), 5/2/11, *WP*, 5/2/11; **shield/unfounded/"Resistance"/nightclothes:** e.g., *Telegraph* (U.K.), 5/3/11, 5/4/11, 5/5/11, Reuters, 5/4/11; **"full authority":** *Irish Times*, 5/4/11; **"before the Pakistanis":** *Independent* (U.K.), 5/8/11; **"captured alive":** *Al-Arabiya*, 5/4/11, *Guardian* (U.K.), 5/5/11; **Abbottabad:** Musharraf, 39–, *Independent* (U.K.), 5/4/11, *Weekly Standard*, 5/2/11, AP, 5/2/11; **"involved"/"inconceivable"/"whether there":** *Financial Times*, 5/4/11, *Spectator*, 5/7/11, *LAT*, 5/8/11; **"was not anywhere":** *Independent* (U.K.), 5/4/11; **"a bit amazing":** AP, 5/2/11; **couriers:** *WSJ*, 5/4/11, *Telegraph* (U.K.), 5/4/11, 5/5/11, *Independent* (U.K.), 5/4/11; **Musharraf on al-Libi:** Musharraf, 258–, 221; **"It was decided":** *Irish Times*, 5/5/11; **"a few minutes":** AP, 5/2/11; **under surveillance?:** *Telegraph* (U.K.), 5/4/11.

437–38   **Bush/Musharraf deal reported, et seq.:** *Guardian* (U.K.), 5/9/11. As this book went to press, the authors were unaware of any response by either the U.S. administration or Prime Minister Gilani to the report that there had been a deal in place. The All Pakistan Muslim League, however, posted a legal notice denying the reported deal by Musharraf (http://www.facebook.com/note.php?note_id=10150198113099339).

438   **Musharraf denial:** *Indian Express*, 5/10/11; **disposed of at sea:** *WP*, 5/2/11; **"trophies"/ Congress/DNA:** *Telegraph* (U.K.), 5/5/11, *Irish Times*, 5/13/11, *Sunday Times* (U.K.), 5/8/11; **al Qaeda acknowledged:** *Telegraph* (U.K.), 5/7/11, *Irish Times*, 5/7/11.

AFTERWORD

439–43   **"We are sure":** Miller & Stone with Mitchell, 187; **"the noblest":** AP, 9/23/09; **"Palestine":** ed. Lawrence, 9; **"Crusaders' ":** ibid., 17; **"theft"/"paltry":** ibid., 163; **"have surrendered":** ibid., 163, 171, and Scheuer, *Osama bin Laden*, 155; **$144:** AP, 9/28/01, *NYT*, 10/14/01; **$100:** ed. Lawrence, 272; **$146:** BBC News, 7/3/08; **$124:** AFP, 4/8/11; **permitted:** Lacey, *Inside the Kingdom*, 291, *Guardian* (U.K.), 4/30/03; **a constant:** see ed. Lawrence, 4, & refs., Scheuer, *Osama bin Laden*, 99, 153, & refs.; **motivation:** see pp. 233, 276–77, and 279–80. **"We wanted":** Bergen, *OBL I Know*, 225; **bled:** ibid., 316, bin Ladens & Sasson, 177, CR, 191: **"I am rejoicing":** ed. Lawrence, 208; **second only:** *NYT*, 7/24/10, CNN, 7/20/10; **Pew:** "Muslim Publics Divided on Hamas and Hezbollah," 12/2/10, http://pewglobal.org; **"Brand":** "Bin Laden Is a Dying Brand," 1/7/10, www.businessinsider.com; **Leiter:** Fox News, 2/9/11, citing testimony to House Homeland Security Committee; **Aulaqi target:** *Sunday Times* (London), 5/8/11; **pastor/Qur'an:** *NYT*, 4/1, 4/2/11, New York *Daily News*, 4/2/11, *Irish Times*, 4/2, 4/4, 4/6/11; **mosque:** *Washington Times*, 8/18/10, *WSJ*, 8/15/10, *NYT*, 7/13/10, 8/21/10, 4/1/11, press release, 5/24/10, www.911familiesforamerica.org, "Proposed Muslim

Community Center Near Ground Zero," 5/21/10, www.huffingtonpost.com; **Museum/ remains/disagreements:** press release, 12/11/09, National Sept. 11 Memorial Museum, AP, 8/10/10, *NYT,* 4/1/11, 5/12/11, AP, 4/3/11; **Phoenix:** *Arizona Daily Star,* 4/2/11, *Yuma Sun,* 3/29/11; ***Aeneid:*** *NYT,* 4/1, 4/6, 4/8/11.

SELECTED BIBLIOGRAPHY

This list includes some two hundred books that are cited in the Notes and Sources. It does not include the many other books used for general reference and background only. Nor does it include newspaper and magazine articles or official documents, which are cited in full in the Notes and Sources.

Aaronovitch, David. *Voodoo Histories: The Role of the Conspiracy Theory in Shaping Modern History*. London: Jonathan Cape, 2009.

Ahmed, Nafeez Mosaddeq. *The War on Freedom*. Brighton, U.K.: Media Messenger, 2002.

———. *The War on Truth*. Northampton, MA: Interlink, 2005.

Ahmed, Qanta A. *In the Land of Invisible Women*. Naperville, IL: Source Books, 2008.

Anonymous. *Through Our Enemies' Eyes: Osama bin Laden, Radical Islam, and the Future of America*. Washington, D.C.: Brassey's, 2002.

Ashcroft, John. *Never Again: Securing America and Restoring Justice*. NY: Center Street, 2006.

Atwan, Abdel Bari. *The Secret History of al Qaeda*. Berkeley: University of California Press, 2006.

Aust, Stephan, and Codt Schnibben, and the Staff of *Der Spiegel*, eds. *Inside 9–11: What Really Happened*. NY: St. Martin's, 2002.

Baer, Robert. *See No Evil*. NY: Three Rivers, 2002.

———. *Sleeping with the Devil: How Washington Sold Our Soul for Saudi Crude*. NY: Three Rivers, 2003.

al-Bahri, Nasser, with Georges Malbrunot. *Dans l'Ombre de Ben Laden*. Neuilly-sur-Seine, France: Michel Lafon, 2010.

Ball, Howard; *Bush, The Detainees and the Constitution*. Lawrence, KS: University Press of Kansas, 2007.

Bamford, James. *Body of Secrets*. NY: Doubleday, 2001.

———. *A Pretext for War: 9/11, Iraq, and the Abuse of America's Intelligence Agencies*. NY: Doubleday, 2004.

———. *The Shadow Factory*. NY: Doubleday, 2008.

Barrett, Wayne, and Dan Collins. *Grand Illusion: The Untold Story of Rudy Giuliani and 9/11*. NY: Harper, 2006.

Bawer, Bruce. *While Europe Slept: How Radical Islam Is Destroying the West from Within*. NY: Doubleday, 2006.

Begg, Moazzam. *Enemy Combatant: My Imprisonment at Guantánamo, Bagram and Kandahar*. NY: New Press, 2006.

Benjamin, Daniel, and Steven Simon. *The Age of Sacred Terror*. NY: Random House, 2003.

Ben-Veniste, Richard. *The Emperor's New Clothes*. NY: Thomas Dunne, 2009.

Bergen, Peter L. *Holy War Inc*. NY: Free Press, 2001.

———. *The Osama bin Laden I Know: An Oral History of al Qaeda's Leader*. NY: Free Press, 2006.

Berger, J. M., ed. *Ali Mohamed Sourcebook*. Intelwire, 2006.

———. *Mohammed Jamal Khalifa Sourcebook*. Intelwire, 2007.

Bernstein, Richard. *Out of the Blue*. NY: Times Books, 2002.

Berntsen, Gary, and Ralph Pezzullo. *Jawbreaker: The Attack on Bin Laden and Al-Qaeda*. NY: Three Rivers, 2005.

Bhutto, Benazir. *Daughter of the East*. London: Simon & Schuster, 2008.

bin Laden, Najwa, Omar bin Laden, and Jean Sasson. *Growing Up bin Laden*. NY: St. Martin's, 2009.

bin Ladin, Carmen. *The Veiled Kingdom*. London: Virago, 2004.

Bodansky, Yossef. *Bin Laden: The Man Who Declared War on America*. Roseville, CA: Forum, 1999.

———. *Target America*. NY: SPI, 1993.

———. *Terror: The Inside Story of the Terrorist Conspiracy in America*. NY: SPI, 1994.

Boyd, James. *After September 11*. Saddle River, NJ: Prentice Hall, 2003.

Bradley, John. *Saudi Arabia Exposed*. NY: Palgrave Macmillan, 2006.

Breitweiser, Kristin. *Wake-up Call: The Political Education of a 9/11 Widow*. NY: Warner, 2006.

Brisard, Jean-Charles, and Guillaume Dasquié. *Forbidden Truth: U.S.-Taliban Secret Oil Diplomacy and the Failed Hunt for Bin Laden*. NY: Thunder's Mouth, 2002.

Broeckers, Mathias. *Conspiracies, Conspiracy Theories and the Secrets of 9/11*. Joshua Tree, CA: Progressive, 2006.

Bronson, Rachel. *Thicker than Oil*. NY: Oxford University Press, 2006.

Bugliosi, Vincent. *The Prosecution of George W. Bush for Murder*. Cambridge, MA: Vanguard, 2008.

Burke, Jason. *Al-Qaeda: The True Story of Radical Islam*. London: Penguin, 2004.

———. *On the Road to Kandahar*. London: Allen Lane, 2006.

Bush, George W. *Decision Points*. London: Virgin, 2010.

Carrington, Patricia, Julia Collins, Claudia Gerbasi, and Ann Haynes. *Love You, Mean It*. NY: Hyperion, 2006.

Chomsky, Noam. *Imperial Ambitions: Conversations with Noam Chomsky on the Post-9/11 World*. London: Hamish Hamilton, 2005.

Clarke, Richard. *Against All Enemies*. NY: Free Press, 2004.

Clarke, Torie. *Lipstick on a Pig*. NY: Free Press, 2006.

Clinton, Bill. *My Life*. NY: Alfred A. Knopf, 2004.

Cockburn, Andrew. *Rumsfeld*. NY: Scribner, 2007.

Coll, Steve. *The Bin Ladens*. London: Allen Lane, 2008.

———. *Ghost Wars: The Secret History of the CIA, Afghanistan, and bin Laden, from the Soviet Invasion to September 11, 2001*. NY: Penguin, 2004.

Collins, Aukai. *My Jihad*. Guilford, CT: Lyons, 2002.

Cook, David. *Understanding Jihad*. Berkeley: University of California Press, 2005.

Cooley, John. *Unholy Wars: Afghanistan, America and International Terrorism*. London: Pluto, 2002.

Corbin, Jane. *The Base*. London: Pocket, 2003.

Davis, Jayna. *The Third Terrorist*. Nashville: WND, 2004.

Dean, John W. *Worse than Watergate*. NY: Warner, 2004.

DeYoung, Karen. *Soldier: The Life of Colin Powell*. NY: Alfred A. Knopf, 2006.

DiMarco, Damon. *Tower Stories: The Autobiography of September 11, 2001*. NY: Revolution, 2004.

Duelfer, Charles. *Hide and Seek: The Search for Truth in Iraq*. NY: PublicAffairs, 2009.

Dunbar, David, and Brad Reagan, eds. *Debunking 9/11 Myths: Why Conspiracy Theories Can't Stand Up to the Facts*. NY: Hearst, 2006.

Dwyer, Jim, and Kevin Flynn. *102 Minutes: The Untold Story of the Fight to Survive Inside the Twin Towers*. NY: Times Books, 2005.

Ehrenberg, John, et al., eds. *The Iraq Papers*. NY: Oxford University Press, 2010.

Ehrenfeld, Rachel. *Funding Evil*, Chicago: Bonus, 2003.

Emerson, Steven. *The American House of Saud*. NY: Franklin Watts, 1985.

———. *American Jihad: The Terrorists Living Among Us*. NY: Free Press, 2002.

———. *Jihad Incorporated: A Guide to Militant Islam in the U.S.* NY: Prometheus, 2006.

Esposito, John. *Islam: The Straight Path*. New York: Oxford University Press, 1998.

———. *Political Islam*. Boulder: Lynne Rienner, 1997.

Faludi, Susan. *The Terror Dream*. NY: Metropolitan, 1985.

Fandy, Mamoun. *Saudi Arabia and the Politics of Dissent*. London: Palgrave, 1999.

Farmer, John. *The Ground Truth*. NY: Riverhead, 2009.

Feith, Douglas. *War and Decision*. NY: Harper, 2008.

Fenton, Kevin. *Disconnecting the Dots*. Walterville, OR: TrineDay, forthcoming.

Fisk, Robert. *The Great War for Civilization: The Conquest of the Middle East*. London: Fourth Estate, 2005.

———. *Pity the Nation*. NY: Thunder's Mouth/Nation Books, 2002.

Fleischer, Ari. *Taking Heat: The President, the Press, and My Years in the White House*. New York: William Morrow, 2005.

Fouda, Yosri, and Nick Fielding. *Masterminds of Terror*. Edinburgh: Mainstream, 2003.

Franks, Tommy, with Malcolm McConnell. *American Soldier*. NY: Regan, 2004.

Freeh, Louis. *My FBI*. NY: St. Martin's, 2006.

Freni, Pamela S. *Ground Stop*. NY: iUniverse, 2003.

Friend, David. *Watching the World Change: Stories Behind the Images of 9/11*. NY: Farrar, Straus & Giroux, 2006.

Frum, David. *The Right Man*. NY: Random House, 2003.

Fury, Dalton. *Kill bin Laden*. NY: St. Martin's, 2008.

Gellman, Barton. *Angler: The Shadow Vice Presidency of Dick Cheney*. London: Allen Lane, 2008.

Gerson, Michael. *Heroic Conservatism*. NY: HarperOne, 2007.

Gertz, Bill. *Betrayal: How the Clinton Administration Undermines American Security*. Washington, D.C.: Regnery, 1999.

———. *Breakdown: The Failure of American Intelligence to Defeat Global Terror*. NY: Plume, 2003.

Gilbert, Martin. *Israel*. London: Black Swan, 1999.

Giuliani, Rudolph W., with Ken Kurson. *Leadership*. NY: Hyperion, 2002.

Gold, Dore. *Hatred's Kingdom*. Washington, D.C.: Regnery, 2003.

Goldberg, Alfred, et al. *Pentagon 9/11*. Washington, D.C.: Office of the Secretary of Defense, 2007.

Gordon, Michael, and Bernard Trainor. *Cobra II*. NY: Pantheon, 2006.

Graham, Bob, with Jeff Nussbaum. *Intelligence Matters*. NY: Random House, 2004.

Graham, Bob, and Jim Talent, eds. *World at Risk*. NY: Vintage, 2008.

Griffin, David Ray. *Debunking 9/11 Debunking*. Northampton, MA: Olive Branch, 2007.

———. *The Mysterious Collapse of World Trade Center 7*. Northhampton, MA: Olive Branch, 2009.

———. *The New Pearl Harbor: Disturbing Questions About the Bush Administration and 9/11*. Gloucestershire, U.K.: Arris, 2005.

———. *The New Pearl Harbor Revisited: 9/11, the Cover-up and the Exposé*. Northampton, MA: Olive Branch, 2008.

———. *The 9/11 Commission Report: Omissions and Distortions*. Gloucestershire, U.K.: Arris, 2005.

———. *9/11 Contradictions*. Northampton, MA: Olive Branch, 2008.

———. *Osama bin Laden: Dead or Alive?* Gloucestershire, U.K.: Arris, 2009.

Griffin, David Ray, and Peter Dale Scott, eds. *9/11 and American Empire: Intellectuals Speak Out*. Northampton, MA: Interlink, 2007.

Gunratna, Rohan. *Inside al Qaeda, Global Network of Terror.* NY: Columbia University Press, 2002.

Gutman, Roy. *How We Missed the Story.* Washington, D.C.: U.S. Institute of Peace Press, 2008.

Halberstam, David. *Firehouse.* NY: Hyperion, 2002.

Hamel, Ian. *L'Énigme Oussama Ben Laden.* Paris: Payot, 2008.

Harris, Sam. *The End of Faith.* London: Free Press, 2004.

Hayes, Stephen. *Cheney.* NY: HarperCollins, 2007.

———. *The Connection.* NY: HarperCollins, 2004.

Henshall, Ian, and Rowland Morgan. *9/11 Revealed: Challenging the Facts Behind the War on Terror.* London: Robinson, 2005.

Hersh, Seymour M. *Chain of Command: The Road from 9/11 to Abu Ghraib.* NY: HarperPerennial, 2004.

Hicks, Sander. *The Big Wedding: 9/11, the Whistle-Blowers, and the Cover-up.* NY: VoxPop, 2005.

Hilton, Christopher. *The Women's War.* Stroud, U.K.: History Press, 2003.

Hoffman, Bruce. *Inside Terrorism.* New York: Columbia University Press, 2006.

Holden, David, and Richard Johns. *The House of Saud.* NY: Holt, Rinehart & Winston, 1981.

Hollingsworth, Mark, with Sandy Mitchell. *Saudi Babylon.* Edinburgh: Mainstream, 2006.

Hopsicker, Daniel. *Welcome to Terrorland: Mohamed Atta and the 9/11 Cover-up in Florida.* Eugene, OR: MadCow, 2004/2007.

Hufschmid, Eric. *Painful Questions.* Goleta, CA: Self-published, 2002.

Hussain, Ed. *The Islamist.* London: Penguin, 2007.

Hussain, Zahid. *Frontline Pakistan: The Struggle with Militant Islam.* NY: Columbia University Press, 2007.

Isikoff, Michael, and David Corn. *Hubris: The Inside Story of Spin, Scandal, and the Selling of the Iraq War.* NY: Three Rivers, 2006.

Jacquard, Roland. *In the Name of Osama bin Laden.* Durham: Duke University Press, 2002.

Jefferson, Lisa D., and Felicia Middlebrooks. *Called: "Hello, My Name Is Mrs. Jefferson, I Understand Your Plane Is Being Hijacked?"* Chicago: Northfield, 2006.

Katz, Samuel M. *Relentless Pursuit: The DSS and the Manhunt for the al-Qaeda Terrorists.* NY: Forge, 2002.

Kean, Thomas, and Lee Hamilton. *Without Precedent: The Inside Story of the 9/11 Commission.* NY: Alfred A. Knopf, 2006.

Keegan, William, with Bart David. *Closure: The Untold Story of the Ground Zero Recovery Mission.* NY: Touchstone, 2006.

Kepel, Gilles. *Jihad.* Cambridge, MA: Belknap, 2002.

Kessler, Ronald. *The Terrorist Watch.* NY: Crown, 2007.

Kippenberg, Hans, and Tilman Seidensticker, eds. *The 9/11 Handbook.* London: Equinox, 2006.

Labévière, Richard. Trans. Martin DeMers. *Dollars for Terror: The United States and Islam,* NY: Algora, 2000.

Labévière, Richard. *Les Coulisses de la Terreur.* Paris: Bernard Grosset, 2003.

Lacey, Robert. *Inside the Kingdom.* London: Hutchinson, 2009.

———. *The Kingdom.* NY: Avon, 1981.

Lance, Peter. *Cover-up: What the Government Is Still Hiding About the War on Terror.* NY: Regan, 2004.

———, *1000 Years for Revenge: International Terrorism and the FBI.* NY: Regan, 2004.

———. *Triple Cross: How Bin-Laden's Master Spy Pentrated the CIA, the Green Berets, and the FBI—and Why Patrick Fitzgerald Failed to Stop Him.* NY: Regan, 2006.

Landis, Paul. *A Real 9/11 Commission.* Self-published, 2005.

Langewiesche, William. *American Ground: Unbuilding the World Trade Center.* NY: North Point, 2002.

Laurent, Eric. *La Face Cachée du 11 Septembre.* Paris: Plon, 2004.

Lawrence, Bruce, ed. *Messages to the World: The Statements of Osama bin Laden.* London: Verso, 2005.

Levin, Jason. *From the Desert to the Derby.* NY: Daily Racing Form Press, 2002.

Levy, Bernard-Henri. *Who Killed Daniel Pearl?* Hoboken, NJ: Melville House, 2003.

Longman, Jere. *Among the Heroes.* NY: HarperPerennial, 2003.

Margulies, Joseph. *Guantánamo and the Abuse of Presidential Power.* NY: Simon & Schuster, 2006.

Marrs, Jim. *The Terror Conspiracy: Deception, 9/11 and the Loss of Liberty.* NY: Disinformation, 2006.

Mayer, Jane. *The Dark Side: The Inside Story of How the War on Terror Turned into a War on American Ideals.* NY: Doubleday, 2008.

McDermott, Terry. *Perfect Soldiers.* NY: HarperCollins, 2005.

Mearsheimer, John, and Stephen Walt. *The Israel Lobby and U.S. Foreign Policy.* NY: Farrar, Straus & Giroux, 2007.

Meyssan, Thierry. *9/11: The Big Lie.* London: Carnot, 2002.

Miles, Hugh. *Al Jazeera.* London: Abacus, 2005.

Miller, John, and Michael Stone, with Chris Mitchell. *The Cell: Inside the 9/11 Plot, and Why the FBI and CIA Failed to Stop It.* NY: Hyperion, 2002.

Miniter, Richard. *Losing Bin Laden.* Washington, D.C.: Regnery, 2003.

Murphy, Tom. *Reclaiming the Sky.* NY: Amacom, 2007.

Musharraf, Pervez. *In the Line of Fire: A Memoir.* NY: Free Press, 2006.

Mylroie, Laurie. *The War Against America:* NY: Regan, 2002.

Napoleoni, Loretta. *Terror Incorporated.* NY: Seven Stories, 2005.

Nasiri, Omar. *Inside the Jihad: My Life with Al-Qaeda.* NY: Basic Books, 2006.

National Commission on Terrorist Attacks Upon the United States. *9/11 and Terrorist Travel.* Franklin, TN: Hillboro, 2004.

———. *The 9/11 Commission Report.* NY: W. W. Norton, 2004.

O'Clery, Conor. *May You Live in Interesting Times.* Dublin: Poolbeg, 2009.

Ottaway, David. *The King's Messenger.* NY: Walker, 2008.

Picciotto, Richard, with Daniel Paisner. *Last Man Down.* NY: Berkley, 2002.

Palast, Greg. *The Best Democracy Money Can Buy.* NY: Plume, 2004.

Pape, Robert. *Dying to Win.* NY: Random House, 2006.

Pearl, Marianne. *A Mighty Heart.* NY: Scribner, 2003.

Posner, Gerald. *Secrets of the Kingdom.* NY: Random House, 2005.

———. *Why America Slept: The Failure to Prevent 9/11.* NY: Ballantine, 2003.

Posner, Richard. *Not a Suicide Pact: The Constitution in a Time of National Emergency.* NY: Oxford, 2006.

Pyszcynski, Tom, Sheldon Solomon, and Jeff Greenberg. *In the Wake of 911: The Psychology of Terror.* Washington, D.C.: American Psychological Association, 2003.

Qutb, Sayyid. *Milestones.* New Delhi: Millat Book Centre, undated.

Raimondo, Justin. *The Terror Enigma.* NY: iUniverse, 2003.

Rashid, Ahmed. *Descent into Chaos.* NY: Viking, 2008.

———. *Taliban.* New Haven: Yale University Press, 2001.

Rees, Phil. *Dining with Terrorists: Meetings with the World's Most Wanted Militants.* London: Pan, 2006.

Reeve, Simon. *The New Jackals: Osama bin Laden and the Future of Terrorism.* London: André Deutsch, 1999.

Ressa, Maria. *Seeds of Terror.* NY: Free Press, 2003.

Rich, Frank. *The Greatest Story Ever Sold: The Decline and Fall of Truth from 9/11 to Katrina.* NY: Penguin, 2006.

Ridgeway, James. *The Five Unanswered Questions About 9/11.* NY: Seven Stories, 2005.

Risen, James. *State of War.* NY: Free Press, 2006.

Rove, Karl. *Courage and Consequence: My Life as a Conservative in the Fight.* NY: Threshold, 2010.

Rubinfien, Leo. *Wounded Cities.* Göttingen, Germany: Steidl, 2008.

Rumsfeld, Donald. *Known and Unknown.* NY: Sentinel, 2011.

Ruppert, Michael C. *Crossing the Rubicon: The Decline of the American Empire at the End of the Age of Oil.* Gabriola Island, B.C.: New Society, 2004.

Ruthven, Malise. *A Fury for God.* London: Granta, 2002.

Sageman, Marc. *Leaderless Jihad.* Philadelphia: University of Pennsylvania Press, 2008.

Editors, Salon.com. *Afterwords: Stories and Reports from 9/11 and Beyond.* NY: Washington Square, 2002.

Sammon, Bill. *Fighting Back.* Washington, D.C.: Regnery, 2002.

Scheuer, Michael. *Imperial Hubris: Why the West Is Losing the War on Terror.* Washington, D.C.: Potomac, 2004.

———. *Marching Toward Hell.* NY: Free Press, 2008.

———. *Osama bin Laden.* NY: Oxford University Press, 2011.

Schindler, John. *Unholy Terror.* Minneapolis: Zenith, 2007.

Schopmeyer, Robert. *Prior Knowledge of 9/11*. Palo Alto, CA: Palo Alto Publishing, 2008.

Schroen, Gary C. *First In: An Insider's Account of How the CIA Spearheaded the War on Terror in Afghanistan*. NY: Ballantine, 2005.

Schultheis, Rob. *Hunting bin Laden*. NY: Skyhorse, 2008.

Schwartz, Stephen. *The Two Faces of Islam*. NY: Doubleday, 2002.

Schwarzkopf, General H. Norman, with Peter Petre. *It Doesn't Take a Hero*. NY: Bantam, 1992.

Scott, Peter Dale. *The Road to 9/11*. Berkeley: University of California Press, 2007.

Shaffer, Anthony. *Operation Dark Heart*. NY: Thomas Dunne, 2010.

Shaler, Robert C. *Who They Were*. NY: Free Press, 2005.

Sheehy, Gail. *Middletown, America*. NY: Random House, 2003.

Shenon, Philip. *The Commission*. NY: Twelve: 2008.

Sifaoui, Mohamed. *Inside Al-Qaeda: How I Infiltrated the World's Deadliest Terrorist Organization*. NY: Thunder's Mouth, 2003.

Simpson, John. *Simpson's World: Dispatches from the Front*. NY: Miramax, 2003.

Simpson, William. *The Prince*. NY: Regan, 2006.

Smith, Dennis. *Report from Ground Zero*. New York: Viking, 2002.

Smucker, Philip. *Al Qaeda's Great Escape: The Military and the Media on Terror's Tail*. Washington, D.C.: Brassey's, 2004.

Spencer, Lynn. *Touching History*. NY: Free Press, 2008.

Strasser, Steven, ed. *The 9/11 Investigations*. NY: PublicAffairs, 2004.

Suskind, Ron. *The One Percent Doctrine: Deep Inside America's Pursuit of Its Enemies Since 9/11*. NY: Simon & Schuster, 2006.

———. *The Price of Loyalty*. NY: Simon & Schuster, 2004.

———. *The Way of the World*. NY: Harper, 2008.

Swanson, Gail. *Behind the Scenes at Ground Zero*. NY: TRAC Team, 2003.

Sylvester, Judyth, and Suzanne Hoffman. *Women Journalists at Ground Zero*. Lanham, MD: Rowman & Littlefield, 2002.

Taheri, Amir. *Holy Terror: The Inside Story of Islamic Terrorism*. London: Sphere, 1987.

Taibbi, Matt. *The Great Derangement*. NY: Spiegel & Grau, 2009.

Tarpley, Webster Griffin. *9/11: Synthetic Terror: Made in USA*. Joshua Tree, CA: Progressive, 2006.

Taylor, John B. *Global Financial Warriors*. NY: W. W. Norton, 2007.

Tenet, George, with Bill Harlow. *At the Center of the Storm: My Years at the CIA*. NY: HarperCollins, 2007.

Thompson, Paul. *The Terror Timeline*. NY: Regan, 2004.

Thorn, Victor. *9/11 on Trial: The World Trade Center Collapse*. State College, PA: Sisyphus, 2006.

Trento, Joseph. *Prelude to Terror: Edwin P. Wilson and the Legacy of America's Private Intelligence Network*. NY: Carroll & Graf, 2005.

Trento, Susan B., and Joseph J. Trento. *Unsafe at Any Altitude*. Hanover, NH: Steerforth, 2007.

Trofimov, Yaroslav. *The Siege of Mecca*. NY: Doubleday, 2007.

Trost, Cathy, and Alicia Shepard. *Running Toward Danger: Stories Behind the Breaking News of 9/11*. Lanham, MD: Rowman & Littlefield, 2002.

Unger, Craig. *The Fall of the House of Bush*. NY: Scribner, 2007.

———. *House of Bush, House of Saud*. London: Gibson Square, 2007.

Ventura, Jesse, with Dick Russell. *American Conspiracies*. NY: Skyhorse, 2010.

Vitug, Marites Dañquilan, and Glenda M. Gloria. *Under the Crescent Moon*. Quezon City, Philippines: Ateneo Center for Social Policy, 2000.

Warde, Ibrahim. *The Price of Fear*. Berkeley: University of California Press, 2007.

Weiner, Tim. *Legacy of Ashes: The History of the CIA*. NY: Doubleday, 2007.

Weiss, Murray. *The Man Who Warned America*. NY: Regan, 2003.

Weldon, Curt. *Countdown to Terror*. Washington, D.C.: Regnery, 2005.

Williams, Eric D. *9/11 101: 101 Points that Everyone Should Know and Consider That Prove 9/11 Was an Inside Job*. Williamsquire, 2006.

———. *The Puzzle of 9/11*. Booksurge, 2006.

Williams, Paul L. *Al Qaeda: Brotherhood of Terror*. Alpha, 2002.

———. *The Day of Islam*. Amherst, NY: Prometheus, 2007.

———. *Osama's Revenge: The Next 9/11*. Amherst, NY: Prometheus, 2004.

Woods, Ian., ed. *9/11: The Greatest Crime of All Time*, Vol. 2. Ontario: Global Outlook, 2006.

Woodward, Bob. *Bush at War*. NY: Simon & Schuster, 2002.

———. *Plan of Attack*. NY: Simon & Schuster, 2004.

———. *State of Denial, Bush at War, Part III*. NY: Simon & Schuster, 2006.

Wright, Lawrence. *The Looming Tower, Al-Qaeda and the Road to 9/11*. NY: Alfred A. Knopf, 2006.

Yoo, John. *War by Any Other Means: An Inside Account of the War on Terror*. NY: Atlantic Monthly Press, 2006.

al-Zayyat, Montasser. *The Road to Al-Qaeda: The Story of Bin Laden's Right-Hand Man*. London: Pluto, 2004.

Zegart, Amy B. *Spying Blind*. Princeton: Princeton University Press, 2007.

Zwicker, Barrie. *Towers of Deception: The Media Cover-up of 9/11*. Gabriola Island, B.C.: New Society, 2006.

PHOTO CREDITS

FIRST SECTION

Second plane approaches Trade Center: Carmen Taylor/AP/Press Association Images. Daniel Lewin: courtesy of Marco Greenberg; Hansons: courtesy of Hanson family; trapped office workers: Jeff Christensen/Reuters; workers make way to safety: Shannon Stapleton/Reuters; Pentagon memorial: Mariana Perez; CeeCee Lyles' ID card: Moussaoui trial exhibit; Barbara Olson: Reuters.

New Yorkers ran: Paul Hawthorne/AP/Press Association Images; Bush is told: Paul J. Richards, AFP/Getty Images; Operations Center: Presidential Materials, U.S. National Archives; firefighters retrieve bodies: Getty Images.

Pentagon façade: U.S. Dept. of Defense; After, in New York: AFP/Getty Images; Wreckage/Voice Recorder: Moussaoui trial exhibits; Investigators search: Tim Shaffer/ Reuters.

Last girder removed: Peter Morgan/Reuters.

SECOND SECTION

Bin Laden acclaimed: (upper) AFP/Getty Images; (lower) Ruth Fremson/*New York Times*/Redux Pictures. Binalshibh: Flashpoint Partners; Zubaydah wounded: authors' collection; nineteen hijackers: Getty Images; poster: used in Birmingham, UK; Young Atta: Getty Images; bearded Atta & Jarrah: AP Photo/*Sunday Times*; "Reward" poster:courtesy of Diplomatic Security Service, Dept. of State. Al-Shehhi & Hanjour: Moussaoui trial exhibits; Jarrah in cockpit & with Sengün: Terry McDermott; al-Mihdhar & al-Hazmi: Moussaoui trial exhibits; Abdullah: Earnie Grafton/Zuma Press; bin Don: Steven Hirsch/Splash News; al-Bayoumi: government of Saudi Arabia; Aulaqi: *Washington Post*/Getty Images; al-Hussayen: government of Saudi Arabia.

Turki: government of Saudi Arabia; Tenet: Getty images; Naif: AP; Graham/Shelby 2003: *Washington Post*/Getty Images; Commission members watch video: AP; some of the bereaved: Brendan Smialowski/AFP/Getty Images; Bush & Abdullah 2005: Getty Images; Bush & Abdullah seven months after: AFP/Getty Images; Bandar at White House: White House photo.

Bin Laden in hiding: AP; Americans celebrated: (upper) Reuters/Eric Thayer (second) AP.

INDEX

Page numbers in *italics* refer to illustrations.

Jonas, Jay, 78
Jones, Steven, 99, 105–6, 471*n*,
    473*n*–74*n*
Jones, Terry, 441–42
Jones-Pinkney, Natalia, 36
Jordan, 283, 392, 510*n*, 520*n*, 547*n*
    9/11 warnings from, 356–57
Joscelyn, Tom, 563*n*
Journal of 9/11 Studies, 106
Jubeir, Adel al-, 405, 408, 419, 558*n*
Judge, Mychal, 71
Julian Studley company, 19
Jullian, Timothy, 107
Justice Department, U.S., 41, 42, 152,
    236, 284, 313, 317, 318, 380, 382,
    489*n*, 513*n*, 536*n*, 539*n*, 542*n*, 553*n*

Ka'bah, 192
Kadi, Yassin, 500*n*
Kahn, Niaz, 531*n*
Kahtani, Mohamed el-, 340–41
Kallstrom, Robert, 410
Kane, Howard, 22
Kara, Miles, 125, 133, 143, 360, 456*n*,
    479*n*, 483*n*, 548*n*
Katz, David, 325–26, 540*n*
Kean, Thomas, 6, 120, 276, 389, 402
Keller, Amanda, 537*n*
Kennedy, John F., 91
Kerrey, Bob, 6
Kerrick, Donald, 308
Kerry, John, 420
Khadr, Abdurahman, 263
Khaksar, Mohammed, 393
Khalifa, Jamal, 197, 206–7, 226–27,
    392, 510*n*
Khalil-Khalil, Professor, 214
Khashoggi, Jamal, 209, 217, 503*n*
Khatib, Walid al-, 500*n*
Khilewi, Mohammed al-, 391–92
Khmer Rouge, 240
Kimmons, John, 241
King, Amy, 26
King, Larry, 505*n*
King Abdul Aziz University, 190
Kippenberg, Hans, 164, 493*n*–94*n*
Kiriakou, John, 419, 432, 563*n*–64*n*
Kiser, Catherine, 356
Knight-Jadczyk, Laura, 113–14
Knight-Ridder poll, 421–22
Kolstad, Ralph, 472*n*

Korea, Democratic People's Republic of
    (North Korea), 239
Korea, Republic of (South Korea), 514*n*
Koval, Bernard, 366
Kraus, Mary Ellen, 481*n*
Krepinevich, Andrew, 477*n*
Kruithof, Arne, 294
Kupferberg, Chaim, 514*n*
Kurtila, Heikki, 472*n*
Kurtz, Louise, 46
Kurtz, Paul, 141, 286, 345
Kurtzberg, Paul, 495*n*
Kuwait, 212, 215, 233, 326
Kwiatkowski, Karen, 101

Laabs, Dirk, 373
Labévière, Richard, 549*n*
Labor Department, U.S., 100
Laborie, Kathryn, 26
Lake, Anthony, 260, 265, 519*n*
Lamb, Christina, 433
Lamont-Doherty Earth Observatory,
    455*n*, 465*n*
Lance, Peter, 511*n*, 560*n*
Landesamt für Verfassungsschutz
    (German intelligence service),
    369, 549*n*
Langewiesche, William, 74–75
Langley Air Force Base, 122, 127, 146
Larry King Live, 408
Latas, Jeff, 101
Lava Trading, 19
Lawrence, Bruce, 499*n*, 501*n*, 519*n*
Leahy, Patrick, 168
Lebanon, 154, 218, 261, 273, 274, 298
    Israeli invasion of, 210
Lee, Stuart, 22
Lee, William, 113
Lehman, John, 559*n*
Lehman, Lizsa, 297–98, 530*n*
Leiter, Michael, 441
Lewin, Daniel, 12–13, 15, 454*n*, 464*n*
Lewis, Jennifer, 113
Lewis, Kenneth, 113
Libby, Lewis "Scooter," 114, 141–42,
    357, 485*n*, 486*n*
Libi, Abu Faraj al- (Mustafa al-'Uzayti),
    437, 512*n*
Library of Congress, 285
Libya, 175, 273
Lieberman, Joe, 420

Anthony Summers is the award-winning author of seven bestselling non-fiction books. Originally a journalist, he covered events in the United States and the conflicts in Vietnam and the Middle East for the BBC's flagship current affairs programme *Panorama*. **Robbyn Swan**, his co-author and wife, has partnered Summers on two previous books – biographies of Richard Nixon and Frank Sinatra. They have been consultants on documentaries for the BBC, the History Channel and CNN.